D0745668

Health / Fitness Instructor's Handbook

Edward T. Howley, PhD
University of Tennessee

B. Don Franks, PhD
University of Tennessee

Human Kinetics Publishers, Inc.
Champaign, Illinois

Library of Congress Cataloging-in-Publication Data

Howley, Edward T., 1943-
Health/fitness instructor's handbook.

Bibliography: p.
Includes index.
1. Physical fitness. 2. Physical fitness—Testing.
3. Exercise. I. Franks, B. Don. II. Title.
GV481.H734 1986 613.7'1 86-10250
ISBN 0-87322-064-1

Developmental Editor: Sue Wilmoth, PhD
Production Director: Ernie Noa
Copy Editor: Kristen Gallup
Proofreader: Lise Rodgers
Typesetter: Yvonne Winsor
Text Design: Julie Szamocki
Text Layout: Janet Little
Printed By: Braun-Brumfield, Inc.
Cover photo courtesy of Leo De Wys, Inc.

ISBN: 0-87322-064-1

Printed in the United States of America

10 9 8 7 6 5 4 3

Human Kinetics Publishers, Inc.
Box 5076, Champaign, IL 61820
1-800-DIAL-HKP
1-800-334-3665 (in Illinois)

Dedication
to
Ann & Liz

Contents

Preface ix
Acknowledgment xi
Author Biographies xiii

Part I **Fitness and Positive Health** **1**

Chapter 1 Fitness, Lifestyle, and Health 3

The Multidimensional Nature of Fitness 4
Role of the Health/Fitness Instructor 5
General ACSM Objectives for Health/Fitness Instructors 5
Risk Factors and Achieving Health 6
Summary 7
Suggested Reading 8

Chapter 2 Evaluation of Health Status 9

Screening 16
Guidelines for Referrals 17
Supervised Fitness Program 17
All Fitness Activities 18
Educating Participants 19
Summary 19
Suggested Reading 19

Part II **Basic Exercise Science** **21**

Chapter 3 Exercise Physiology 23

Relationship of Energy and Work 24
Metabolic, Cardiovascular, and Respiratory Responses to Exercise 25
Cardiovascular Responses to Exercise for Males and Females 34
Cardiovascular Responses to Weight-Training Activities 34
Summary 35
Suggested Reading 35

Chapter 4 Anatomy and Kinesiology 37

Functional Anatomy 38
Muscle Group Involvement in Selected Activities 43
Basic Mechanical Concepts Related to Human Movement 46
Summary 47
Suggested Reading 48

Part III **Physical Fitness** **49**

Chapter 5 Relative Leanness 51

Body Composition 52
Evaluating Body Fatness 52
Caloric Balances and Weight Control 59
Interaction of Diet and Exercise 61
Basic Foods and Functions 62
Dietary Goals and Evaluation of Dietary Intake 66
Fads and Gimmicks Related to Weight Control 72
Exercise and Weight Control 75
Diet, Exercise, and Lipids 76
Summary 78
Suggested Reading 79

Chapter 6 Cardiorespiratory Fitness 81

Sequence of Testing 82
Field Tests 84
Graded Exercise Tests 85
Calibrating Equipment 86
Commonly Measured Variables 86
Graded Exercise Testing 88
Summary 97
Suggested Reading 97

Chapter 7 Strength, Endurance, and Flexibility 99

Muscular Strength and Endurance 100
Flexibility 105
Low-Back Problems 108
Summary 113
Suggested Reading 113

Chapter 8 Relaxation and Arousal 115

Personality and Physical Activity 116
Stress Continuums 119
Physical Activity and Stress 120
Stress and Health 121
Recommendations 122
Summary 123
Suggested Reading 124

Part IV **Activity Recommendations** **125**

Chapter 9 Exercise Programming for Aerobic Activity 127

General Basis for Physiological Changes 128
Exercise Recommendations for the Untested Masses 128
Exercise Programming for the Fit Population 133
Exercise Recommendations With Knowledge of Functional Capacity and Cardiovascular Responses to Exercise 134
Case Studies 136
Special Considerations in Making Exercise Recommendations 145
Program Selection 147
Updating the Exercise Program 148
Environmental Concerns 148
Summary 152
Suggested Reading 152

Chapter 10 Energy Costs of Activity 153

Ways to Measure Energy Expenditure 154
Ways to Express Energy Expenditure 155
Formulas for Estimating the Energy Cost of Activities 155
Energy Requirements of Common Activities 156
Caloric Cost of Walking and Running 1 Mile 159
Caloric Costs of Other Activities 163
Estimation of the Energy Expenditure Without Formulas 166
Environmental Concerns 166
Summary 166
Suggested Reading 167

Chapter 11 Exercise Programs 169

Phases of Activities 170
Exercise Leadership 170
Walk/Jog/Run Programs 172
Cycling 177
Games 178
Aquatic Activities 179
Exercise to Music 181
Summary 184
Suggested Reading 184

Chapter 12 ECG and Medications 185

Coronary Arteries 186
Oxygen Use of the Heart 187
Electrophysiology of the Heart 187
The Conduction System of the Heart 187
Electrocardiogram 188
Cardiovascular Medications 195
Summary 197
Suggested Reading 198

Chapter 13 Behavior Modification 199

General Points to Consider in Modifying Behavior 200
Exercise Adherence 201
Smoking Behaviors 202
Alcoholic Drinking Habits 203
Weight Reduction 204
Reducing Stress 205
Summary 206
Suggested Reading 206

Part V **Special Concerns** **209**

Chapter 14 Injury Prevention and Treatment 211

Minimizing Injury Risk 212
Treatment of Common Injuries 213
Heat Illness 217
Prevention of Heat Injury 218
Common Orthopedic Problems 222
Exercise Modification 228
CPR and Emergency Procedures 229
Summary 231
Suggested Reading 232

Chapter 15 Administrative Concerns 233

Responsibilities 234
Issues 246
Summary 248
Suggested Reading 249

Appendix A ACSM Preventive Tract: Core Behavioral Objectives 251
Appendix B Health Status Questionnaire—Long Form 257
Appendix C Percent Fat Estimates for Men and Women 281
Appendix D Nutritive Value of Commonly Used Foods 285
Appendix E Calculation of Oxygen Uptake and Carbon Dioxide Production 323
Definitions 329
References 357
Index 371

Coordinated Texts for Health/Fitness Instructors, Leaders, and Participants

Written by fitness experts Don Franks and Edward Howley, the three handbooks in this set provide health/fitness program administrators with a coordinated set of resources to enhance fitness instruction.

- *Health/Fitness Instructor's Handbook* (Edward T. Howley & B. Don Franks) is for advanced fitness instructors and supervisors.
- *Fitness Leader's Handbook* (B. Don Franks and Edward T. Howley) is for the exercise leader with little previous formal training who is responsible for leading safe and effective fitness classes.
- *Fitness Facts: The Healthy Living Handbook* (B. Don Franks and Edward T. Howley) is for the participants in these fitness classes.

These coordinated resources are especially helpful in providing consistently high quality instruction and information in programs where many fitness leaders are coordinated by a fitness supervisor. This series of handbooks complements the American College of Sports Medicine fitness certification program. *Health/Fitness Instructor's Handbook* includes all the competencies for the ACSM health/fitness instructor certification, and has been widely used to prepare for this examination.

Fitness Leader's Handbook emphasizes more of the ''how to'' and less of the ''why'' to provide leaders with the practical competencies needed for effective instruction. This book contains all of the *practical* competencies for the ACSM exercise leader/aerobics certification.

Fitness Facts is an especially useful handbook for students because it concisely and accurately expresses the information in the instructor and leader texts.

Each handbook can certainly be used alone for its specific purpose, but supervisors of fitness programs in commercial fitness centers, the workplace, YMCAs, and universities will find the greatest value in using these books as a coordinated set. Instructors preparing for any fitness instructor certification will discover these handbooks to be indispensable as will instructors or leaders looking for review materials.

Preface

The terms *fitness* and *physical fitness* have been used and misused to refer to almost everything from archery to coronary arteries, bowling to blubber, and calisthenics to karate. "Fitness tests" have measured how fast, far, high, and with what load a person can run, jump, throw, and lift. Recommendations have included taking pills, wearing or carrying special devices, sitting or lying on machines of all sorts, working out a few seconds a day, and running many miles per week. The result of these varied definitions, activities, and tests for "fitness" has led to widespread confusion about fitness.

This book is aimed at three fitness needs:

1. The rationale for and the components of fitness
2. The basis for fitness programs
3. The practical application of fitness tests and activities to diverse populations

The lack of clarity concerning fitness has been found not only in the public, but also in health, physical education, and related professions. Some encouraging trends do, however, provide the basis for less ambiguity about fitness in two of our professional organizations. The American Alliance for Health, Physical Education, Recreation, and Dance (AAHPERD) has provided the basis for reducing confusion by separating fitness related to positive health from performance of specific tasks. The positive health (fitness) concept is expanded in Part I to further clarify the relationship of physical fitness to total fitness and to differentiate fitness from performance. Part II reviews the disciplinary knowledge base that is essential for fitness professionals. The components of physical fitness and strategies for their improvement are amplified in Parts III and IV. Part V suggests ways that programs can be safely and efficiently administered.

Another progressive step in the fitness arena has been the American College of Sports Medicine's (ACSM) certifications for postcardiac rehabilitation programs and (more recently) fitness leadership for the average person. These certification examinations have emphasized both theoretical knowledge and clinical abilities. This book includes the knowledge base related to all of the competencies required for the ACSM Health/Fitness Instructor (HFI). We have gone beyond the minimum competencies to provide additional suggestions that are useful in dealing with fitness for people of all ages in a variety of fitness conditions.

Fitness programs are found in many settings, including public and private, profit and nonprofit, and educational, medical, and industrial institutions. People who lead exercise in these programs usually have some formal education in health and physical education, as well as inservice education provided by the fitness program. This handbook supplements the education of fitness professionals working with apparently healthy populations by providing a review of the current information related to fitness, including definitions of relevant terms. In addition, the handbook is a source of ideas for day-to-day fitness testing and activities. What steps are recommended? What form, test, and instrument can be used to screen, measure, and evaluate? This book provides usable tools needed by all people involved with physical fitness. Keep in mind that while specific recommendations made in the book can be justified, some alternatives are also valid. We deliberately selected one recommendation from among many options because the HFI needs tools that can be used immediately in a variety of professional settings.

Keeping abreast of the latest findings in all aspects of physical fitness is impossible. Our purpose is to provide theory and practice based on the best current evidence for all aspects of physical fitness. This book would not have been possible without the insights of the contributing authors. They have provided the substance for much of the fitness framework provided by AAHPERD and ACSM.

Finally, the theory and practice in this field is evolving based on the ever-expanding, research-based body of knowledge and the higher levels of education and amount of experience of fitness professionals. We do not think this is the "final word"; rather it is our attempt to present information at the current state of the field that will need revision in the future. We welcome reactions, suggestions, and questions concerning both our theoretical bases and the practical implications and applications we have presented.

Ed Howley
Don Franks

Acknowledgment

We want to thank our contributing authors, whose knowledge of theory and practice in many areas has made it possible to provide a comprehensive book for the HFI. Brenda Copeland assisted with the Exercise to Music section (chapter 11). Thanks to Barbara Porter for the art work.

The folks at Human Kinetics—Rainer Martens, Julie Simon, and our Developmental Editor, Sue Wilmoth—provided encouragement and assisted us in numerous ways. Russ Pate and Neil Sol made helpful suggestions from an early draft. Other authors and publishers were kind enough to allow us to use materials from their articles and books.

In a more general way, we are indebted to our students and professional colleagues in AAHPERD and ACSM, too numerous to list, who have educated us over the past 20 years. A special thanks to Bruno Balke and T.K. Cureton, Jr. whose influence in our lives continues to this day. It would be difficult to name any two people who have had more of an impact on physical fitness in this country. Their vision, research supervision, and teaching have had far-reaching effects, and their ideas have more often than not been validated in the research studies in our field. They must smile when they read about "new" concepts of fitness—many of which they have advocated for the past 4 decades.

Author Biographies

About the Authors

Edward T. Howley received his BS degree in physical education at Manhattan College in New York City and his MS and PhD degrees in physical education at The University of Wisconsin, Madison. His research interests include the measurement of the metabolic costs of physical activities and the evaluation of hormonal responses to exercise and other stressors. He is a professor at the University of Tennessee, where he has received the Outstanding Teacher Award for the School of Health, Physical Education, and Recreation. He has been active in the American College of Sports Medicine both as a Fellow and as President of the Southeast Chapter. He has also served on the ACSM Preventive and Rehabilitative Committee that developed the college's various certification programs. He enjoys soccer and paddleball and is on the rising portion of the learning curve in golf.

B. Don Franks grew up in Arkansas and received his BS and MEd degrees in physical education at the University of Arkansas, Fayetteville. He received his PhD in physical education from the University of Illinois at Urbana-Champaign in 1967 and served on the faculty there until 1970. He has also served on the faculty of Paine College in Augusta, Georgia, and Temple University in Philadelphia. He is currently a professor of physical education and Director of the Center of Physical Activity and Health at the University of Tennessee, Knoxville. His research interest is in the area of physical activity and stress, especially the cardiovascular response to exercise and psychological stressors. He is a Fellow of the American College of Sports Medicine and the Research Consortium of the American Alliance for Health, Physical Education, Recreation, and Dance. He has been President of the AAHPERD Physical Fitness Council and of the Research Consortium, where he has advocated the ''health-related'' approach to physical fitness. He enjoys and participates in many forms of physical activity, including all sorts of fitness games as well as fishing and golf.

About the Contributing Authors

Wendy J. Bubb received her MS degree in physical education with an emphasis in exercise physiology from the University of Tennessee, Knoxville (UTK). She is currently completing her doctoral studies in physiology at UTK, where her research interests focus on understanding the etiology of obesity. As a graduate student, she was twice the recipient of an Alumni Association Scholarship for outstanding scholastic achievement and academic excellence. She was also named a UTK Woman of Achievement for outstanding scholarship. Bubb is presently working at the UTK College of Veterinary Medicine, where she conducts research and clinical work in muscle fiber typing and assists in the Electrodiagnostics and Urodynamics Laboratory. She has served in the Dominican Republic with the Christian Medical Society and is involved in a prison ministry.

Sue Carver received her MS degree in physical education with a specialization in athletic training from Indiana University in 1978. She obtained her N.A.T.A. Certification the same year. She served as the Women's Athletic Trainer at the University of Tennessee from 1978-1982 before accepting a position in the Sports Treatment and Rehabilitation (STAR) Center at Fort Sanders Regional Medical Center in Knoxville. Carver has helped STAR to become a model diagnostic center not only for young athletes but also for middle-aged fitness participants. She has worked at the Olympic Training Center in Colorado Springs and was selected to work at the 1985 National Sports Festival in Baton Rouge. She was certified as a Fitness Instructor by the American College of Sports Medicine in 1985.

Mark A. Hector received a doctorate in counseling from Michigan State University in 1973. Since then he has been a professor in the Educational and Counseling Psychology Department at the University of Tennessee. His main teaching responsibilities are in the areas of counseling practice and research methods of problem solving. Dr. Hector is also interested in cross-cultural issues and has spent four years teaching in West Africa. For recreation, he plays paddleball and squash several times a week.

Jean Lewis received her doctorate in education (Physical Education with an emphasis in Exercise Physiology) from the University of Tennessee, Knoxville, where she now teaches. She was involved in the establishment of undergraduate major concentrations in physical fitness and exercise physiology and has also developed courses in applied anatomy, applied kinesiology, and weight control, fitness, and exercise. Dr. Lewis is known for her innovative teaching methods, which help physical education majors understand how to apply kinesiological concepts. She has experience in playing and coaching several team sports. Hiking in the Smoky Mountains and bicycling are her current favorite recreational activities.

Wendell Liemohn is a professor of physical education at the University of Tennessee. His extensive research in the area of motor skill for special populations has gained national prominence, and he has also published in the areas of strength development and muscle injuries. His interest in low back pain originated at the University of Iowa, where his doctoral assistantship included working with low-back pain patients.

Daniel Martin earned his BS degree in physical therapy from the University of Tennessee Center for Health Science and his PhD in education from the University of Tennessee. He worked for several years with Dr. Joe Acker in the Cardiac Rehabilitation Program at Fort Sanders Regional Medical Center, Knoxville. Dr. Martin is currently an assistant professor of physical therapy at the University of Florida. His research interests are in exercise testing and methods of training cardiac and pulmonary patients, and he has presented papers on these topics at national meetings. He is a member of the American College of Sports Medicine and the American Physical Therapy Association. A former All-American javelin thrower at Tennessee, he now enjoys distance running and hiking.

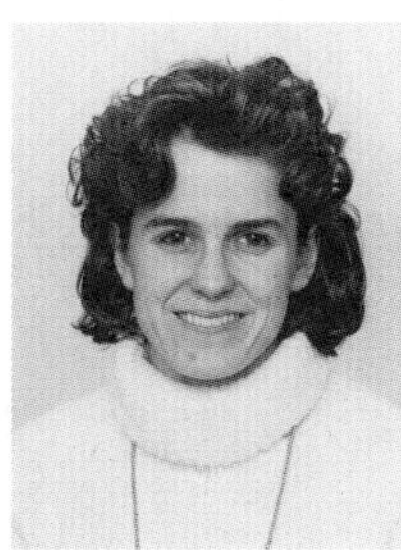

Gina L. Sharpe received her master's degree in physical education from Indiana University, Bloomington, in 1983. She is presently pursuing a doctoral degree with a concentration in kinesiology at the University of Tennessee, Knoxville. As a graduate teaching assistant, Sharpe has taught a variety of fitness courses. Her recreational activities include swimming, hiking, and camping.

Part I

Fitness and Positive Health

- Definitions
- How health status is evaluated

The *Health/Fitness Instructor's Handbook* appropriately should begin with concepts of fitness, health, and performance. The role of the Health/Fitness Instructor (HFI) in fitness programs, as well as the basic qualifications needed by the HFI as outlined by the American College of Sports Medicine (ACSM), is also included in chapter 1. The first chapter concludes with a description of the primary and secondary risks to a healthy life. Chapter 2 provides procedures to determine an individual's health status and suggests criteria to screen potential fitness participants.

Chapter 1

Fitness, Lifestyle, and Health

- Physical fitness and performance
- The role of the HFI
- Primary and secondary risks to health
- Risks that can be altered with an active lifestyle

Fitness is the capacity to achieve the optimal quality of life. This dynamic, multidimensional state has a positive health-base and includes individual performance goals. Table 1.1 illustrates the quality of life continuum which includes various stages from death, known illness, apparent health, to life. Because fitness is related to positive health, a change in a fitness characteristic affects health and thus causes movement along the death/life scale.

The Multidimensional Nature of Fitness

Imagining the highest quality of life would be difficult without including intellectual, social, spiritual, and physical components. Mental alertness and curiosity, emotional feelings, meaningful relations with other humans, awareness and involvement in societal strivings and problems, and the physical capacity to accomplish personal goals with vigor and without undue fatigue appear to be essential elements of life. These aspects of fitness are interrelated; a high level of fitness in one of the areas enhances the other areas, and conversely; thus a low fitness level in any area restricts the accomplishments possible in other areas.

Inherited Limits

Each person can achieve fitness goals up to his or her genetic potential. An inherited aspect, however, exists for both health and performance. But exactly determining the relative portion of a person's health or performance that is determined by heredity and development is not possible. Most people can lead healthy or unhealthy lives regardless of their inheritances. Thus a person's genetic background neither dooms him or her to a low fitness level nor guarantees a high fitness level.

Environmental Factors

Certain aspects of our environment can be controlled—many of the mental and physical exercises we do are a matter of choice. However, we are all limited in various ways by our past and current environment. For example, some children have inadequate food as a part of their environment and obviously cannot think about other aspects of fitness until that basic need is fulfilled.

Dynamic

An optimal quality of life requires a person to strive, grow, and develop; but an optimal quality of life may never be achieved in the fullest sense. The fit person continually approaches the highest quality of life possible.

Table 1.1 Fitness Continuum

Continuum	Disease	Function & Activity	Domain
DEATH	—	—	Undertaker
Death	Severe	Very little	Medical
death	Known	Limited	Medical
life	High risks but no diagnosed disease	Limited	HPERD[1] & related fields
Life	None	Normal	HPERD
LIFE	Positive health	Unlimited	HPERD

[1]HPERD (Health, Physical Education, Recreation, and Dance).

General Health Base

Mental, emotional, and physical health provide a base for everyone's fitness. One of the major purposes of the family, public education, and other institutions is to provide experiences that promote a healthy life.

Individual Goals

Fitness also includes unique aspects for each individual, dependent on that person's interests and aims in life. Various body positions and postures for extended periods of time, as well as varying levels and types of physical activity, may be part of a person's vocation. The things people enjoy doing during leisure time also may have many different physical characteristics and requirements.

Role of the Health/ Fitness Instructor

The HFI needs to be aware of the broad perspective included in total fitness. However, the focus of this book and most of the HFI's activity is directed to the general *physical* health base for fitness. This physical fitness foundation is included in an atmosphere that is conducive to mental, emotional, and social fitness relationships. This atmosphere helps the individual strive for inherited potential in a dynamic and wholesome environment. The general physical health base allows the participant to develop and achieve personal performance goals.

General ACSM Objectives for Health/Fitness Instructors

The following general competencies are required for the ACSM Certification for the HFI (ACSM, 1986). Specific objectives for the certification are found in Appendix A. The chapter(s) dealing with the different objectives are indicated in parentheses.

ACSM Preventive Tract: Core Behavioral Objectives

Exercise Physiology. The candidate will demonstrate a knowledge of basic exercise physiology (chapter 3).

The candidate will demonstrate an understanding of the basic principles involved in muscular strength, endurance, and flexibility training (chapter 7).

Nutrition and Weight Management. The candidate will demonstrate an understanding of basic nutrition and weight management (chapter 5).

Exercise Programming. The candidate will understand the role of exercise for persons with stable disease or no disease and demonstrate competence in designing and implementing individualized and group exercise programs (chapters 9, 11).

Emergency Procedures. The candidate will demonstrate competence in basic life support and implementation of first aid procedures, which may be necessary during or after exercise (chapter 14).

Health Appraisal and Fitness Evaluation Techniques. The candidate will demonstrate or identify appropriate techniques for health appraisal and use of fitness evaluations (chapters 2, 6).

Exercise Leadership. The candidate will demonstrate an understanding of principles and practices of leading physical activity (chapter 11).

The candidate will be competent in exercise leadership (chapter 11).

Human Behavior/Psychology. The candidate will demonstrate an understanding of basic behavioral psychology, group dynamics, and learning techniques (chapter 13).

Human Development/Aging. The candidate will demonstrate an understanding of the special problems of human development and aging (chapters 3, 8, 9).

Functional Anatomy and Kinesiology. The candidate will demonstrate a knowledge of human functional anatomy and kinesiology (chapter 4).

The candidate will demonstrate a knowledge of concepts in the prevention, recognition, and management of injury associated with physical activity participation (chapter 14).

Risk Factor Identification. The candidate will identify risk factors that may require consultation with medical or allied health professionals prior to participation in physical activity or prior to major increases in physical activity intensities and habits (chapters 1, 2).

Health/Fitness Instructor: Behavioral Objectives

Exercise Physiology. The fitness instructor will demonstrate an understanding of exercise physiology (chapter 3).

Emergency Procedures. The Health/Fitness Instructor will demonstrate competence in the use, maintenance, and updating of appropriate emergency equipment, supplies, and patient transport plans (chapter 15).

Exercise Leadership. The fitness instructor will demonstrate competence in the administrative concerns of effective exercise leadership (chapter 15).

Functional Anatomy and Kinesiology. The fitness instructor will demonstrate an understanding of general anatomy and kinesiology (chapter 4).

Risk Factors and Achieving Health

The HFI should be able to identify characteristics and behaviors that cause a person to have greater risks of incurring health problems. Most of the research studies concerning risk factors for health problems have dealt with some aspect of cardiovascular disease. That will be the focus of this chapter, although factors related to low back problems will also be included.

The risks determined from epidemiological studies of large populations are normally divided into primary and secondary risk factors. *Primary* risk factors are those characteristics that are highly associated with a particular health problem (e.g., heart disease) independent of all other variables. For example, someone who smokes (primary risk factor) has a high risk of heart disease even if she is young, white, active, lean, has no family history of heart disease, copes well with stress, and has normal levels of blood pressure and cholesterol. *Secondary* risk factors, on the other hand, have a high relationship with the health problem only when other factors are present. For example, if a person's parent died at an early age with heart disease (secondary risk factor), that person would not be at high risk if no other risk factors were present. However, family history of heart disease does increase the risk when other risk factors are present. Another way to classify risk factors is to distinguish inherited risk factors that cannot be altered from lifestyle behaviors that can be modified.

Unavoidable Risks

Some of the risk factors are easily identified but unfortunately cannot be altered. People with the following characteristics have greater risks of heart disease, especially if they adopt unhealthy behaviors:

- Family history of heart disease
- Older age
- Male
- Black

These coronary heart disease (CHD) risk factors are secondary risk factors. They only cause a person to be at high risk when they are added to some other risk factor(s). In addition, part of the risk associated with family history and age are behaviors that can be changed. Part of the family history risks are an unhealthy diet, smoking, and stress behaviors that tend to be transmitted from parents to children. These are the types of behaviors that can be corrected with proper attention throughout life, especially in early childhood. In terms of aging, many fitness characteristics (e.g., maximum cardiovascular function and amount of fat) get worse with age, that is, if people from 20-80 years old were tested and the results were plotted, a steady deterioration (i.e., decreased cardiovascular function, increased fat) would occur with each decade. This decline, starting in the middle 20s, has been called the *aging curve*. However, a portion of the deterioration seen in aging curves is caused by less activity in older individuals—not aging itself. People who maintain active lifestyles slow down the fitness decline seen in typical aging curves.

Risks That Can Be Altered

Many of the risks for heart disease and back problems can be modified.

Primary. Some characteristics and behaviors cause a higher risk for CHD even in the absence of other risk factors. The independent, primary risk factors are the following:

- Smoking
- High-fat diet
- High serum concentrations of low-density lipoprotein cholesterol (LDL-C)
- Low serum concentrations of high-density lipoprotein cholesterol (HDL-C)
- High blood pressure

Secondary. Some characteristics and behaviors cause an increased risk of CHD only when other risk factors are present. In addition to the factors that cannot be altered (i.e., age, family history, gender, and race), other secondary risk factors exist:

- Physical inactivity[1]
- Obesity[1]
- Inability to cope with stress
- Coronary-prone personality
- High triglyceride levels

[1]Most reviewers have classified this as a secondary risk factor, but increasing evidence suggests that it is a primary risk factor.

Pulmonary and metabolic problems. Many of the previously mentioned risk factors are related to pulmonary (e.g., chronic obstructive pulmonary disease) and metabolic (e.g., diabetes; see chapter 9) health problems.

Low-back factors. Clinical evidence indicates that several risk factors are associated with low-back problems (see chapter 7):

- Lack of abdominal muscle endurance
- Lack of flexibility in the midtrunk and hamstrings
- Poor posture—lying, sitting, standing, and moving
- Poor lifting habits
- Inability to cope with stress

Personal Control of Health Status

One of the frustrating and exciting aspects of current health problems is that individuals can modify their health statuses and control major health risks. The frustrating aspect is that many people have difficulties trying to change unhealthy lifestyles. But the exciting aspect is that they can gain control of their health. The HFI is at the cutting edge of health, in much the same way that the scientist discovering vaccines for major health problems was at the turn of the 20th century. This opportunity to provide assistance to people who wish to alter their unhealthy lifestyles carries the responsibility to make recommendations based on the best evidence available. The HFI can help people gain control of their lives through an evaluation of their risk factors and behaviors related to health. Chapter 2 deals with these types of health appraisal.

Summary

Physical fitness is defined as the aspects of an ultimate quality of life that are related to positive physical health. Physical fitness is a necessary ingredient of fitness, but fitness includes much more than the physical aspects. Thus a person cannot achieve total fitness without a good physical health base. On the other hand, a person with a high level of physical fitness without the other aspects of fitness would live a sterile existence. The general competencies, identified by the ACSM, and the role of the HFI in promoting those aspects of physical fitness that can be improved through appropriate physical activity are included. Primary and secondary risk factors, which can and cannot be altered, are associated with heart disease. Recognizing the characteristics and behaviors associated with health problems is a first step in gaining personal control over the factors contributing to poor health.

Suggested Reading for Chapter 1

American Alliance for Health, Physical Education, Recreation, and Dance (1980)

American College of Sports Medicine (1986)

American Medical Association and American Alliance for Health, Physical Education, Recreation and Dance (1964)

Blackburn (1974)

Blair, Jacobs, and Powell (1985)

Cureton (1965)

Fox (1983)

Franks (1984c)

Fuchs, Price, Richards, and Marcotte (1985)

Getchell (1983)

Heyward (1984)

Huelster (1982)

Kraus and Raab (1961)

Morris, Pollard, Everitt, and Chave (1980, December 6)

Nieman (1985)

Pate (1983)

Pooley (1984)

Powell and Paffenbarger (1985)

Ross et al. (1985)

Thomas, Lee, Franks, and Paffenbarger (1981)

U.S. Department of Health and Human Services (1980)

Wilmore (1982a)

See reference list at the end of the book for a complete source listing.

Chapter 2

Evaluation of Health Status

- Health status
  - Individual characteristics
  - Fitness test results
- Criteria for assignment
  - Medical referral
  - HFI-supervised program
  - Unsupervised program

The first responsibility of the HFI to potential fitness participants is to determine their current health statuses. Health status includes five major categories. The first four categories are the following:

1. Diagnosed medical problems
2. Characteristics that increase the risk of health problems
3. Signs or symptoms indicative of health problems
4. Lifestyle behaviors related to positive/negative health

The following Health Status Questionnaire is an example of a health status form that focuses on illness, characteristics, symptoms, and behaviors that are related to health problems. (A more detailed questionnaire is included in Appendix B.) Part 1 of the questionnaire provides personal and emergency information about the individual. Part 2 includes a medical history of the participant and his or her family. Part 3 deals with behaviors known to be related to safety and health. Part 4 includes some of the psychological aspects of fitness and personal attitudes that are associated with a healthy life. Individual questions and parts of questions are coded to help the HFI utilize the information.

A fitness program probably would not use all of the items on this form—the HFI or Program Director should decide what items are relevant for a specific fitness program. The information provided on such a health evaluation form is used for the following purposes:

1. To screen people into appropriate programs or to refer them to a physician
2. To provide the HFI with information concerning specific illnesses, risk factors, behaviors, and attitudes of the fitness participants
3. To help determine what educational information, workshops, or professional help is needed for particular people

Health Status Questionnaire—Short Form

The following code will assist you in using the information on this form.

EI = Emergency Information—must be readily available

MS = Medical Supervision needed (*SEP* assumed)

MC = Medical Clearance needed (*SEP* assumed)

SEP = Special Emergency Procedures needed (may also need *SLA*)

PRF = Primary Risk Factor for CHD (*ED* also needed)

SRF = Secondary Risk Factor for CHD (*ED* needed)

SLA = Special or Limited Activities may be needed

ED = Provide Educational Material and/or Workshop in this area

OTHER (not marked) = Personal information that may be helpful for files or research

Instructions

Complete each question accurately. All information provided is confidential. In most cases, please CIRCLE the correct answers. Fill in the spaces provided.

Part 1. Information About the Individual

1. ________ - ______ - ____________ ____________
   Social Sec. No. Date

2. ______________________________ ____________
   Legal Name Nickname

3. ______________________________ ____________
   Mailing Address Home Phone

   ______________________________ ____________
   Bus. Phone

4. *EI* ______________________________ ____________
   Personal Physician Phone

   ____
   Address

5. *EI* ______________________________ ____________
   Person to contact in emergency Phone

6. *SRF* Gender (circle one): Female Male (*SRF*)

7. *SRF* Date of Birth: ________ Month ____ Day ____ Year

8. Number of hours worked per week:

   Less than 20 20-40 41-60 Over 60

9. *SLA* More than 25% of time spent on job (circle all that apply)

   Sitting at desk Lifting or carrying loads Standing Walking Driving

Part 2. Medical History

10. *SRF* Circle any who died of heart attack before age 60:

    Father Mother Brother Sister Grandparent

11. Date of

    Last medical physical exam: ________ Year

    Last physical fitness test: ________ Year

12. Circle operations you have had:

Back *SLA*	Heart *MS*	Kidney *SLA*	Other ________
Ears *SLA*	Hernia *SLA*	Lung *SLA*	
Eyes *SLA*	Joint *SLA*	Neck *SLA*	

13. Please circle any of the following for which you have been diagnosed or treated by a physician or health professional:

Alcoholism *SEP*	Diabetes *SEP*	Kidney problem *MC*
Anemia, sickle cell *SEP*	Emphysema *SEP*	Mental illness *SEP*
Anemia, other *SEP*	Epilepsy *SEP*	Neck strain *SLA*
Asthma *SEP*	Eye problems *SLA*	Obesity *PRF*
Back strain *SLA*	Gout *SLA*	Phlebitis *MC*

Bleeding trait *SEP*	Hearing loss *SLA*	Rheumatoid arthritis *SLA*
Bronchitis, chronic *SEP*	Heart problem *MC*	Stroke *MC*
Cancer *SEP*	High blood pressure *PRF*	Thyroid problem *SEP*
Cirrhosis, liver *MC*	Hypoglycemia *SEP*	Ulcer *SEP*
Concussion *MC*	Hyperlipidemia *PRF*	Other ______________
Congenital defect *SEP*	Infectious mononucleosis *MC*	

14. *ED* for all. Circle all medicine taken in last six months:

Blood thinner *MC*	Epilepsy medication *SEP*	Nitroglycerin *MS*
Diabetic pill *SEP*	Heart rhythm medication *MC*	Other _________
Digitalis *MS*	High blood pressure medication *MC*	
Diuretic *MC*	Insulin *MC*	

15. (Any of these health symptoms that occur frequently is the basis for medical attention.) Circle the number indicating how often you have each of the following:

5 = VERY OFTEN
4 = Fairly Often
3 = Sometimes
2 = Infrequently
1 = PRACTICALLY NEVER

a. Cough up blood *MC*

1 2 3 4 5

b. Abdominal pain *MC*

1 2 3 4 5

c. Low back pain *SLA*

1 2 3 4 5

f. Chest pain *PRF MC*

1 2 3 4 5

g. Swollen joints *MC*

1 2 3 4 5

h. Feel faint *MC*

1 2 3 4 5

d. Leg pain *PRF MC*

1 2 3 4 5

e. Arm or shoulder pain *PRF MC*

1 2 3 4 5

i. Dizziness *PRF MC*

1 2 3 4 5

j. Breathless with slight exertion *PRF MC*

1 2 3 4 5

Part 3. Health-Related Behavior

16. *PRF* Do you now smoke? Yes No

17. If you are a smoker, indicate number smoked PER DAY:

 Cigarettes: 40 or more 20-39 10-19 1-9

 Cigars or pipes ONLY: 5 or more or any inhaled Less than 5, none inhaled

18. *PRF* Do you exercise regularly? Yes No

19. How many days per week do you normally spend at least 20 minutes in moderate to strenuous exercise?

 0 1 2 3 4 5 6 7 days per week

20. Can you walk 4 miles briskly without fatigue? Yes No

21. Can you jog 3 miles continuously at a moderate pace without discomfort? Yes No

22. Weight now: ______ lbs. One year ago: ______ lbs. Age 21: ______ lbs.

Part 4. Health-Related Attitudes

23. *ED* Circle the degree of satisfaction (1-6). Circle YES if you plan to change, and NO if you do not plan to change:

 6 = COMPLETELY SATISFIED
 5 = Largely satisfied
 4 = Somewhat satisfied
 3 = Somewhat dissatisfied
 2 = Largely dissatisfied
 1 = COMPLETELY DISSATISFIED

							Plan to Change	
My weight	1	2	3	4	5	6	Yes	No
My use of alcohol	1	2	3	4	5	6	Yes	No
My use of over-the-counter drugs	1	2	3	4	5	6	Yes	No
My level of exercise	1	2	3	4	5	6	Yes	No
My pattern of sleeping	1	2	3	4	5	6	Yes	No
My pattern of eating	1	2	3	4	5	6	Yes	No
My use of cigarettes	1	2	3	4	5	6	Yes	No
My blood pressure	1	2	3	4	5	6	Yes	No
My overall physical fitness	1	2	3	4	5	6	Yes	No
My handling of tension/stress	1	2	3	4	5	6	Yes	No
My use of seat belts	1	2	3	4	5	6	Yes	No

24. *SRF* (These are traits that have been associated with coronary-prone behavior.) Circle the number that corresponds to how you feel:

    6 = STRONGLY AGREE
    5 = Moderately agree
    4 = Slightly agree
    3 = Slightly disagree
    2 = Moderately disagree
    1 = STRONGLY DISAGREE

    I am an impatient, time-conscious, hard-driving individual

    1 2 3 4 5 6

25. List everything not already included on this questionnaire that might cause you problems in a fitness test or fitness program:

ening

Portions of Parts 2-4 of the Health Status Questionnaire determine whether to refer the person to a physician, request medical clearance before the person can enter the program, or begin the fitness testing procedures. Table 2.1 lists the items included in the fitness testing. The results of the physical fitness tests provide the fifth category of health status. Chapters 5, 6, and 7 include detailed recommendations for fitness testing.

Pulmonary Measurements

Pulmonary function is frequently evaluated as a part of the screening aspect of a fitness program. Although many of these variables change little during a typical fitness program, the HFI can provide a service to participants by suggesting that people with low values participate in additional testing.

Vital capacity (VC). VC is the maximal volume of air expelled after a maximal inspiration. A person whose VC is less than 75% of the value predicted for his or her age, gender, and height should be referred to a physician for further testing.

Forced expiratory volume in 1 sec (FEV1). FEV1 is the ratio of the volume of air expelled in 1 sec compared to the total VC. A person who can expel less than 75% of his or her VC in 1 sec should be referred to a physician.

Maximum ventilation. VC and FEV1 are recommended for screening tests. Maximal voluntary ventilation (MVV) is the maximum volume of air that can be moved in and out of the lungs for 1 min. MVV is normally tested for a short period of time (6, 10, or 15 sec). Ventilation is, of course, also included as part of the $\dot{V}O_2$max test.

Table 2.1 Physical Fitness Test

Minimum Battery		Additional Variables
	REST	
HR (b/min)		12 lead ECG[a]
BP (mmHg)		Blood profile[b]
% Fat		Muscular endurance—upper body
Sit and reach (cm)		Overall flexibility
Sit-ups (#/min)		VC, FEV_1, MVV
	SUBMAXIMAL	
HR		ECG
BP		
RPE (#, 0-10)		
	MAXIMAL	
BP		VO_2
RPE		
Time to max (min)		ECG
Functional capacity (METS)		

[a]ECG abnormalities are medically evaluated to determine appropriate referral/placement of the person.
[b]This includes total cholesterol, HDL, triglycerides, and glucose.

Decisions Based on Health Status

The HFI may take one of the following actions after reviewing a person's health status form and fitness test:

1. Deny the person's request for entry to a fitness program and/or immediately refer that person for medical attention
2. Admit the person to one of the following fitness programs:
   - Medically supervised
   - Carefully prescribed and supervised by the HFI
   - Any fitness activity offered by a fitness center

This chapter outlines procedures whereby the HFI can make a decision concerning the appropriate placement/referral for an individual based on his or her health status.

Guidelines for Referrals

The values listed for medical referral and for supervised programs are guidelines to be used along with other information by the fitness program director. Other factors might cause a person with the characteristics listed under *supervised programs* to be medically referred (e.g., multiple risk factors close to the referral value). Or the medical consultant may recommend that someone in the *refer* category be in the supervised program based on a recent medical examination or conversation with the personal physician. Programs with excellent and accessible medical and emergency personnel may want to use higher values for referral than the program that is isolated from medical and emergency facilities. Each program, in consultation with its medical advisors, should have its own standards.

Medical Referral

All people who indicate illness, characteristics, or symptoms coded MS (Medical Supervision) or MC (Medical Clearance) should be referred to appropriate medical personnel. With the permission of the appropriate physician, the individual can be placed in an MS or MC (HFI-supervised) fitness program. Table 2.2 lists the items that fall into those categories and the test scores from the fitness tests that would be the basis for medical referral.

Borderline Readings

Some of the variables may be influenced by pretest activities and reaction to the testing situation itself (especially in people who are not used to being tested), so borderline scores, especially at rest and during light work, should be replicated before medical referral. For example, if a person has a high resting HR or BP, the HFI might check to see if the person had eaten, smoked, taken medicine, or participated in physical exercise just prior to the test. Does the person seem anxious about taking the test itself? Did unusual conditions exist during the test (lots of people, noise, etc.)? The HFI may have the person rest for a few minutes, reassure him or her about the purpose and safety of the test, and retest. Or a test session might be scheduled for another day. If the questionable test result is repeated, then the person is referred to a physician.

Supervised Fitness Program

A person indicating items coded SEP (Special Emergency Procedure) or PRF (Primary Risk Factor for CHD) can be placed in a carefully supervised fitness program with the necessary emergency procedures. The following items indicate a need for special emergency procedures (the numbers in parentheses indicate the items on the Health Status Questionnaire):

- Recently diagnosed or treated alcoholism, anemia, asthma, bleeding trait, bronchitis, cancer, hypoglycemia, mental illness, colitis, congenital defect, peptic ulcer, diabetes, emphysema, epilepsy, attempted suicide, or thyroid problem (13)
- Someone who has had current allergy shots or taken medicine for pain or any of the above (14)

Table 2.2 Basis for Medical Referral[a]

Conditions	Test Scores[b]
Heart Operation, Disease, or or Problem[c] (12, 13)	Rest HR > 100 Rest SBP > 160
Cirrhosis (13)	Rest DBP > 100
Concussion (13)	% Fat > 40, female; > 30, men
Phlebitis (13)	Cholesterol > 260
Stroke (13)	Chol/HDL > 5
Current medication for heart, blood pressure, or diabetes (14)	Triglycerides > 200 Glucose > 120
Cough up blood (15)	Vital capacity < 75% predicted
Pain in the abdomen, leg, arm, shoulder, or chest (15)	FEV(1) < 75%
Swollen joints (15)	
Faintness or dizziness (15)	
Breathless with slight exertion (15)	

[a]Any condition or test value that causes the person or the HFI to be concerned for the person's health and/or safety is the basis for medical referral.
[b]Any of these individual scores would be the basis for referral. A person might also be referred if more than one test score approached these values.
[c]Numbers in parentheses refer to the question number(s) on the health status questionnaire.

- Pregnant women with records of regular fitness activities—without problems—prior to pregnancy

The following PRFs are indicated either in the Health Status Form or from the Fitness Test (those with higher values are referred for medical attention):

- Hypertension (140-155/90-95 mm Hg); hyperlipidemia (cholesterol 240-255 mg/dl, or when divided by HDL, 4.5-4.8); or obesity (30-38% for women, or 23-28% for men) (13)
- Smoking, > 20 cigarettes/day (17)
- Exercise, < 1-1/2 hr/week at or above moderate intensity (19)

All Fitness Activities

People who do not have any of the above codes (MS, MC, SEP, or PRF) can be admitted to any of the fitness activities. However, numerous problems might call for special or limited activities:

- Sitting, standing, lifting, or driving for a long period of time (9)
- Past operations on the back, joint, lung, neck, eyes, or for hernia (12)
- Hearing loss, hernia, neck strain, eye problems, arthritis, or gout (13)
- Low back pain (15)

From the Fitness Test, the following would be cause for concern:

- Values of risk factors close to the ones listed above
- Any of the reasons for stopping a *maximal* test (see chapter 6) that occur at *light* to *moderate* work

- Max RPE < 5
- Max METS < 8 for males, < 6 for females
- Max $\dot{V}O_2$ < 30 for males, < 20 for females

Educating Participants

The Health Status Form also provides the HFI with information concerning needed education and workshops. All people with PRF or SRF should receive information about their increased risks. No quantification of risk has been provided—limited basis exists for assigning a specific risk number. However, sufficient evidence allows the HFI to indicate areas of potential health problems, assist individuals to become aware of the risk characteristics that cannot be changed, and help people with health-related behaviors that can be modified. Chapter 8 will assist the HFI in understanding and dealing with some of the personality characteristics that may be revealed in Part V of the Health Status Form. Chapter 13 will assist the HFI in helping to modify behavior for desired behavior changes as indicated in Part III. In addition, a number of questions indicate a need for education in exercise, nutrition, alcohol, smoking, and stress management. This information is useful for the program director and HFI in deciding what workshops and educational materials should be offered to the participants.

Summary

The first responsibility of the HFI is to evaluate the current health status of a potential fitness participant. This information can be used to refer the person to an appropriate exercise program or for additional tests and/or place the individual in appropriate risk factor modification programs. The Health Status Form and suggested fitness test items identify characteristics that need medical referral, and distinguish among those conditions and risk factors suggesting a supervised, versus an unsupervised, exercise program.

Suggested Reading for Chapter 2

Blair, Jacobs, and Powell (1985)

Chisholm et al. (1975)

Chusid (1983)

Cooper (1977)

Gibbins, Cooper, Meyer, and Ellison (1980)

Goldman and Cook (1984)

Haskell (1984)

Hayes, Feinleib, and Kannel (1980)

Holmes and Rahe (1967)

Hubert, Feinleib, McNamara, and Castelli (1983)

Kammermann, Doyle, Valois, and Statford (1983)

Laporte, Adams, Savage, Brenos, Dearwater, and Cook (1984)

Montoye (1975)

Paffenbarger and Hyde (1984)

Paffenbarger, Wing, Hyde, and Jung (1983)

Pate and Blair (1978)

Pollock, Wilmore, and Fox (1984)

Siscovick, Laporte, and Newman (1985)

Sonstroem (1978)

U.S. Department Health and Human Services (1981)

U.S. Department Health and Human Services, Public Health Service, Office on Smoking and Health (1983)

WHO Expert Committee (1982)

See reference list at the end of the book for a complete source listing.

Part II

Basic Exercise Science

- What should the HFI know about the structure and functions of the human body?

The first section of this book dealt with the definition and evaluation of health-related physical fitness. This section deals with the foundation for exercise science—the structure and functions of the human body. Future advances in fitness will result as an increased understanding of anatomy, exercise physiology, and biomechanics leads us to better ways of testing and improving fitness components. The reasons for including or excluding particular exercises (for special people or in order to achieve specific goals) are often based on the information in these fields. These two chapters cannot, of course, substitute for detailed textbooks or courses. However, chapters 3 and 4 will help the HFI review aspects of exercise science that deal directly with human movement, especially physical activities that enhance fitness.

Chapter 3
Exercise Physiology

- Cardiorespiratory structure and function
- Response to exercise type and intensity
- Effects of:
  - Age, gender, and fitness level
  - Environmental conditions

Several kinds of energy exist in biological systems: electrical energy in nerves and muscles; chemical energy in the synthesis of molecules; mechanical energy in the contraction of a muscle to move an object; and thermal energy, derived from all of these processes, that helps to maintain body temperature. The ultimate source of the energy for biological systems is the sun. The radiant energy from the sun is captured by plants and is used to convert simple atoms and molecules into carbohydrates, fats, and proteins. The sun's energy is trapped within the chemical bonds of these food molecules.

Relationship of Energy and Work

For the cells to use this energy, the foodstuffs must be broken down in a manner that conserves most of the energy contained in the bonds of the carbohydrates, fats, and proteins. In addition, the final product must be in a form that can be used by the cell. Cells use adenosine triphosphate (ATP) as the primary energy source for biological work, whether electrical, mechanical, or chemical. ATP is a molecule that has three phosphates linked together by high energy bonds. When the bond between the phosphates is broken, energy is released and may be used by the cell. At this point the ATP has been reduced to a lower energy state: adenosine diphosphate (ADP) and inorganic phosphate (Pi).

When a muscle is doing work, the ATP is constantly being broken down to ADP and Pi. The ATP must be replaced as fast as it is being used if the cell is to continue to work. The muscle cell has a great capacity to replace ATP under a wide variety of circumstances, from a short quick dash to a 26-mi, 385-yd marathon. Edington and Edgerton (1976) devised a logical approach to this topic of supplying energy for muscle contraction. They divided the energy sources into *Immediate, Short-Term,* and *Long-Term* sources of ATP.

Immediate Sources of Energy

The very limited amount of ATP stored in a muscle might meet the energy demands of a maximal effort lasting about 1 sec. Creatine phosphate (CP), another high-energy phosphate molecule, is the most important immediate source of energy. CP can donate its phosphate (and the energy therein) to ADP and make ATP, allowing the muscle to continue working. This reaction takes place as fast as the muscle forms ADP. Unfortunately, the CP store in muscle lasts only 3-5 sec when the muscle is working maximally. This process does not require oxygen and is one of the anaerobic (without oxygen) mechanisms of producing ATP. CP would be the primary source of ATP during a shot put, vertical jump, or during the first seconds of a sprint.

Short-Term Sources of Energy

As the muscle store of CP decreases, the cell begins to break down muscle glycogen (the muscle glucose store) to produce ATP at a very high rate. This process is called *glycolysis* and it does not require oxygen (anaerobic). Glycolysis allows the muscle to continue doing intense work, but the process has its limits. An end product of this process is lactic acid; as exercise continues, the acid accumulates in the muscle cell and the blood. This accumulation of acid in the muscle slows down the rate at which the glycogen can be broken down and may actually interfere with the mechanism involved in muscle contraction. While supplying ATP via glycolysis has its obvious shortcomings, it does allow a person to run at high rates of speed for short distances. This short-term source of energy is of primary importance in events involving maximal work lasting 2 min or less.

Long-Term Sources of Energy

The long-term source of energy involves the production of ATP from a variety of fuels, but this method requires the utilization of oxygen (aerobic). The primary fuels include muscle glycogen, blood glucose, plasma-free fatty acids, and intramuscular fats. These food molecules are broken down so they can transfer the energy contained in their chemical bonds to a site in the cell where ATP is synthesized. Most of these reactions occur in the mitochondria of the cell where the oxygen is used. ATP production by this method is slower than that obtained from the immediate and short-term sources of energy, and it may be 2-3 min before the ATP-needs of the cell are completely met by this aerobic process during submaximal work. One reason for this lag is the time it takes for the heart to increase the delivery of oxygen-enriched blood to the muscles at the rate needed to meet the ATP demands of the muscle.

Muscles vary in their abilities to produce ATP by the mechanisms described. Some muscle fibers have an innate capacity to produce great amounts of force when stimulated, but they fatigue quickly. These muscle fibers produce most of their ATP by using CP and relying on high-glycolytic activity. Other muscle fibers produce only a small amount of force when stimulated, but they have a great resistance to fatigue. These fibers produce most of their ATP with oxygen and are called *oxidative fibers*. They have many mitochondria and a relatively large number of capillaries helping to deliver oxygen to the mitochondria. Lastly, an intermediate muscle fiber can produce a great force when stimulated, and it possesses a resistance to fatigue. These three fiber types are called Fast Glycolytic, Slow Oxidative, and Fast Oxidative Glycolytic, respectively, to describe the speed of contraction of the fibers and the means by which the ATP is supplied. Endurance training programs not only increase or maintain cardiorespiratory function, but they also increase the oxidative (endurance) capacity of the muscle fibers involved.

The proportion of energy coming from the anaerobic sources (immediate and short-term) is very much influenced by the muscle-fiber type involved and the intensity/duration of the activity. During an all-out activity lasting less than 1 min (e.g., 400 m dash), the muscles obtain the majority of the ATP from anaerobic sources. In a 2-min maximal effort, approximately 50% of the energy comes from anaerobic sources and 50% comes from aerobic sources; in a 10-min maximal effort, the anaerobic component drops to 15%. Thus the anaerobic component would be considerably less than 15% in a 10-min submaximal training session.

Metabolic, Cardiovascular, and Respiratory Responses to Exercise

A primary task of the HFI is to recommend physical activities that increase or maintain cardiorespiratory function. Activities that demand the production of energy (ATP) by aerobic mechanisms automatically cause the circulatory and respiratory systems to deliver the oxygen to the muscle to meet the demand. The selected aerobic activities must be strenuous enough to challenge the cardiorespiratory systems to cause the systems to improve. This crucial link between aerobic activities and cardiorespiratory function provides the basis for much of exercise programming. The following sections present a summary of selected metabolic, cardiovascular, and respiratory responses to submaximal work and to a graded exercise test taken to maximum.

Submaximal Steady-State Exercise

How does oxygen get to the mitochondria? Oxygen enters the lung when a person inhales and some oxygen moves (diffuses) from the lung into the blood. The oxygen is bound to hemoglobin in the red blood cell, and the heart delivers the oxygen-enriched blood to the muscles. The oxygen then diffuses into the muscle cell to the mitochondria where it is used (consumed) in the production of ATP.

How is oxygen consumption measured during exercise? Oxygen consumption ($\dot{V}O_2$) is measured by subtracting the volume of oxygen exhaled from the volume of oxygen inhaled. Oxygen consumption $= O_2$ inhaled $- O_2$ exhaled. In general, the subject breathes through a special valve containing "flaps" that allow room air (containing 20.93% O_2 and 0.03% CO_2) to be inhaled into the lungs while directing exhaled air to a collection bag (meteorological balloon or Douglas bag; see Figure 3.1). A volume meter measures the liters of air inhaled per minute, which is called the *pulmonary ventilation*. The exhaled air contained in the collection bag is analyzed for its oxygen and carbon dioxide content, and the oxygen consumption (uptake) is calculated by simply multiplying the volume of air breathed by the percent of oxygen extracted. *Oxygen extraction* is the percent of oxygen extracted from the inhaled air, the difference between the 20.93% O_2 in room air, and the percent of O_2 in the collection bag.

The following example indicates the general steps used to calculate $\dot{V}O_2$—the exact procedure is in Appendix E.

$\dot{V}O_2$ = ventilation (liters/min) × O_2 extraction (%)

If ventilation = 60 liters/min, and exhaled O_2 = 16.93%; then

$\dot{V}O_2$ = 60 liters/min × (20.93% O_2 − 16.93% O_2) = 60 liters/min × 4.0% = 2.4 liters/min

During light exercise, the cardiovascular/respiratory systems can supply a sufficient amount of oxygen to the muscles to produce most, if not all, of the ATP aerobically. At these low intensities, the muscle uses fat in preference to carbohydrate. The fat store is larger and this, in effect, spares the carbohydrate store of the muscle or liver for other uses. As the intensity of the work increases, the muscle uses more carbohydrate. This has an adaptive advantage—the muscle obtains about 6% more energy from each liter of oxygen

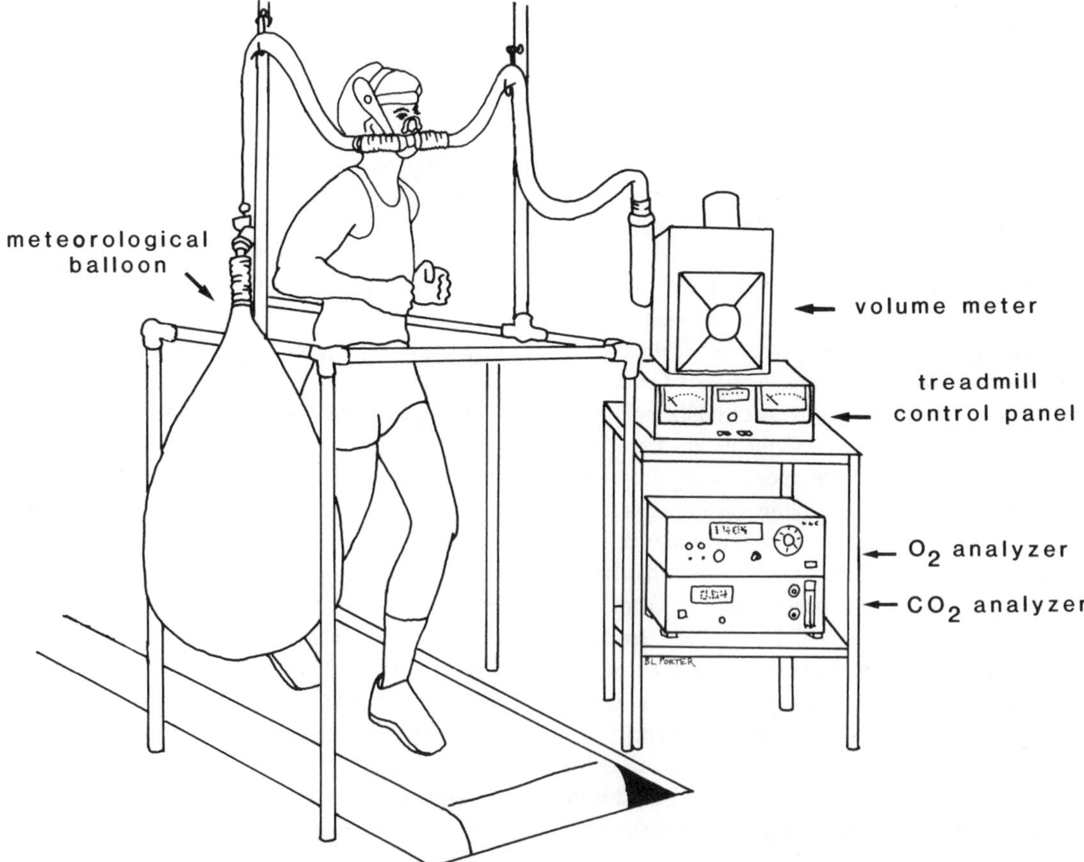

Figure 3.1 Conventional equipment involved in the measurement of oxygen uptake.

when using carbohydrate (5 kcal/liter O_2) compared to fat (4.7 kcal/liter O_2). At high intensities of work, this "shift" to carbohydrate allows a person to get the most ATP per unit of oxygen.

Some people might mistakenly assume from the discussion of the immediate, short- and long-term sources of energy that these various sources of ATP are used in distinct activities and do not work together to allow a person to make the transition from rest to exercise. If an individual were to step onto a treadmill with the belt moving at a velocity of 200 m/min, the ATP requirement would increase from the low level needed to stand alongside the treadmill to the new level of ATP required by the muscles to run at 200 m/min. This change in the ATP supply to the muscle must take place in the first step onto the treadmill. Failure to do so results in the individual going off the back of the treadmill. What sources supply the ATP during the first minutes of work?

The cardiovascular/respiratory systems cannot instantaneously increase the delivery of oxygen to the muscles to completely meet the ATP demand by aerobic processes. In the interval between the time when a person steps onto the treadmill and the time that his or her cardiovascular/respiratory systems deliver the correct amount of oxygen, the immediate and short-term sources of energy supply the needed ATP. The term *oxygen deficit* is used to describe the volume of oxygen that is "missing" in the first few minutes of work (Figure 3.2). CP produces some of the needed ATP, and the breakdown of glycogen to lactic acid provides the rest until the oxidative mechanisms come into play. When the oxygen uptake levels-off during submaximal work, the value is said to represent the "steady state" oxygen requirement for the activity. At this point the ATP-need of the cell is being met by the production of ATP with oxygen on a "pay-as-you-go" basis.

When the individual stops running and steps off the treadmill, the ATP-need of the muscles that were involved in the activity drops suddenly back toward the resting value. The oxygen uptake decreases quickly at first and then more gradually approaches the resting value. This elevated oxygen uptake in recovery from exercise is called the oxygen repayment or *oxygen debt* (Figure 3.2).

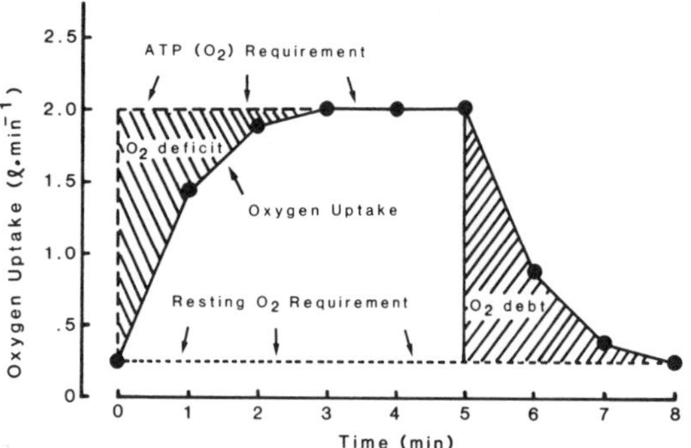

Figure 3.2 Oxygen deficit and oxygen debt (repayment) for a submaximal work bout of 850 kgm/min.

In part, the extra oxygen is being used to make additional ATP to bring the CP store back to normal (remember that it was depleted somewhat at the onset of work). The remainder of the "extra" oxygen taken in during recovery from exercise is used to pay the ATP requirement for the higher heart rate and breathing during recovery (compared to rest). A small part of the oxygen repayment (20%) is used to convert a portion of the lactic acid produced at the onset of work to glucose (in the liver).

If an individual reaches the steady state oxygen requirement faster during the first minutes of work, then the person incurs a smaller oxygen deficit. This results in less CP depletion and the production of less lactic acid. Endurance training speeds up the kinetics of oxygen transport, that is, it decreases the time it takes to reach a steady state of oxygen uptake. People in poor condition, as well as people with cardiovascular or pulmonary disease, take longer to reach the steady state oxygen requirement. As a result, they incur a larger oxygen deficit and must produce more ATP by the immediate and short-term sources of energy at the onset of work.

This link between the cardiorespiratory responses to work and the time it takes to reach the steady state oxygen requirement should be no surprise. Figure 3.3 shows the typical heart rate and pulmonary ventilation responses to a *submaximal* work test. The shape of the curve in each case resembles the curve for oxygen uptake described earlier.

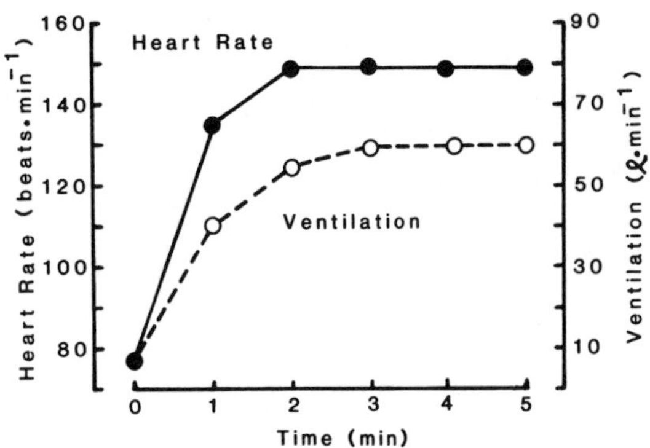

Figure 3.3 Heart rate and pulmonary ventilation responses to a submaximal work bout of 850 kgm/min, carried out for 5 min.

Additionally, the muscle has something to do with the lag in the oxygen uptake response at the onset of work. An untrained muscle has relatively few mitochondria available to produce ATP aerobically and also has relatively few capillaries per muscle fiber to bring the oxygen-enriched arterial blood to those mitochondria. Following an endurance training program, both of these factors increase so the muscle can produce more ATP aerobically at the onset of work. The result is a reduction in lactic acid production and a lowering of the blood lactic acid concentration for a fixed submaximal work-rate following an endurance training program.

Graded Exercise Test

A clear link exists between oxygen consumption and cardiorespiratory fitness because oxygen delivery to tissue is dependent on lung and heart function. One of the most common tests used to evaluate cardiorespiratory function is a Graded Exercise Test (GXT) in which the subject exercises at progressively increasing work rates until the maximum work tolerance is reached. During the test the subject may be monitored for cardiovascular variables (ECG, heart rate, blood pressure), respiratory variables (pulmonary ventilation, respiratory frequency), and metabolic variables (oxygen uptake, blood lactic acid level). The manner in which an individual responds to each stage of the GXT gives important information about cardiorespiratory function.

Oxygen uptake and maximal aerobic power. Oxygen uptake, measured as described earlier, is expressed per kilogram of body weight to facilitate comparisons between people and for the same person over time. The $\dot{V}O_2$ value in liters/min is simply multiplied by 1,000 to convert the $\dot{V}O_2$ to ml/min; that value is divided by the subject's body weight. Figure 3.4 shows a GXT conducted on

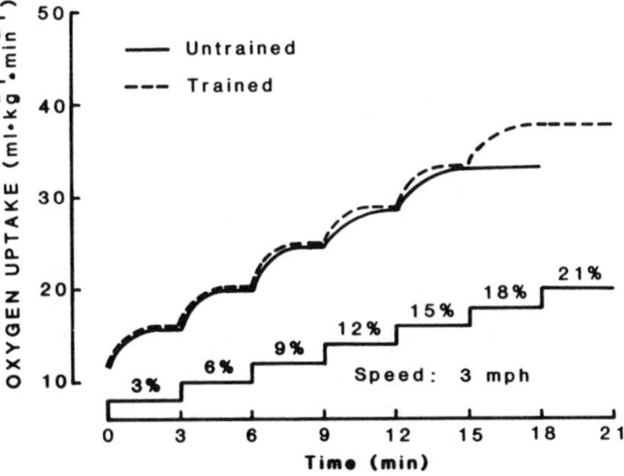

Figure 3.4 Oxygen uptake responses to a graded exercise test. Data adapted from *Nutrition Weight Control, and Exercise* (p. 52) by F.I. Katch and W.D. McArdle, 1977, Boston: Houghton Mifflin.

a treadmill where the speed is constant (3 mph) and the grade changes 3% every 3 min. With each stage of a GXT the oxygen uptake increases to meet the ATP demand of the work rate. At each stage of the GXT the subject incurs a small oxygen deficit as the cardiovascular system tries to adjust to the new demand placed on it by the increased work rate.

Nagle, Balke, Baptista, Alleyia, and Howley (1971) and Montoye (1975) have shown that apparently healthy individuals reach the new steady state requirement by 1.5 min or so of each stage of the test up to moderately heavy work. Those who have low cardiorespiratory fitness or who possess cardiovascular and pulmonary diseases may not be able to reach the expected value in the same amount of time and might incur a larger oxygen deficit with each stage of the test. The oxygen uptake that would be measured at various stages of the test on these latter subjects would be lower than expected because they could not reach the expected steady state demands of the test at each stage (see chapter 10—Energy Cost of Activity).

Toward the end of a GXT a point is reached at which the work rate changes (i.e., an increased grade on the treadmill) but the oxygen uptake does not. In effect the limits of the cardiovascular system to transport oxygen to the muscle have been reached. This point is called *maximal aerobic power* or maximal oxygen uptake ($\dot{V}O_2$max). This leveling-off in the oxygen consumption is not seen in all cases because it requires the subject to work one stage past the actual point at which $\dot{V}O_2$max is reached. This requires the subjects to be highly motivated. The effect of an endurance training program is shown with the dashed line in Figure 3.4.

Maximal aerobic power describes the greatest rate at which the human body (primarily muscle) can produce ATP aerobically. The term also describes the upper limit that the cardiovascular system can deliver the oxygen-enriched blood to those muscles. Thus maximal aerobic power is not only a good index of cardiorespiratory fitness, but it is also a good predictor of performance capability in aerobic events such as distance running, cycling, cross-country skiing, and swimming.

In the apparently healthy person, maximal aerobic power is usually understood as the quantitative limit at which the cardiovascular system can deliver oxygen to tissues. This usual interpretation must be tempered by the mode of exercise (test type) used to impose the workrate on the subject. For the average person, the highest value for maximal aerobic power is measured when the subject completes a GXT involving uphill running. A GXT conducted at a walking speed usually results in a $\dot{V}O_2$max value 4-6% below the graded running value, and a test on a cycle ergometer may yield a value 10-12% lower than the graded running value. Lastly, if a subject works to exhaustion on a GXT on an arm ergometer, then the highest oxygen uptake value is less than 70% of that measured with the legs. Knowledge about these variations in maximal aerobic power has great meaning when the HFI makes recommendations about the intensity of different exercises needed to reach target heart rate (THR). At any given work rate, most physiological responses (heart rate, blood pressure, and blood lactic acid) are higher for arm work than for leg work.

Maximal aerobic power is influenced by a variety of factors: endurance training, heredity, gender, age, altitude, and cardiovascular and pulmonary disease. Typically, endurance training programs increase $\dot{V}O_2$max 5-25% with the magnitude of the change dependent primarily on the initial level of fitness. A person with a low $\dot{V}O_2$max makes the largest percent change. Eventually a point is reached where further training does not increase the $\dot{V}O_2$max. It has been convincingly demonstrated that the extremely high values of maximal aerobic power (expressed in ml per kg per min) found in elite cross-country skiers and distance runners are related to a genetic predisposition for having a superior cardiovascular system. Because endurance training programs may increase $\dot{V}O_2$max by only 20% or so, it is unrealistic to expect a person with a $\dot{V}O_2$max of 40 $ml(kg \cdot min)^{-1}$ to increase the value to 80 $ml(kg \cdot min)^{-1}$, a value measured in some elite cross-country skiers and distance runners.

Women have $\dot{V}O_2$max values that are about 15% lower than men's; that difference exists across ages 20-60 years. The 15% difference between men and women is an average difference; a considerable overlap in $\dot{V}O_2$max values exists in these populations. The aging effect indicates a gradual but systematic reduction in $\dot{V}O_2$max over time. Given that the average person becomes more sedentary and heavier with age, the decrease in $\dot{V}O_2$max may be as much a reflection of these changes as a specific aging effect.

Maximal aerobic power decreases with increasing altitude. At 7,400 ft (2,300 m) $\dot{V}O_2$max is only 88% of the sea level value. This decrease in $\dot{V}O_2$max is due primarily to the reduction in the arterial oxygen content that occurs as the oxygen pressure decreases with increasing altitude.

Pulmonary and cardiovascular diseases decrease $\dot{V}O_2$max by diminishing the delivery of oxygen from the air to the blood and reducing the capacity of the heart to deliver blood to the muscles. These patients have some of the lowest $\dot{V}O_2$max (functional capacity) values measured, but they also make the largest percent changes in $\dot{V}O_2$max while participating in endurance training pro-

Table 3.1 Maximal Aerobic Power Measured in Healthy and Diseased Populations

Population	Males Max $\dot{V}O_2$	Females Max $\dot{V}O_2$
Cross-country	82	66
Distance runners	79	62
College students	45	38
Middle-aged adults	35	30
Postmyocardial infarction patients	22	18
Severe pulmonary-diseased patients	13	13

Note. Data compiled from Åstrand and Rodahl, Fox and Mathews, and the Fort Sanders Cardiac Rehabilitation Program.

grams. Table 3.1 shows common values for VO_2max in a variety of populations.

Blood lactic acid. Lactic acid produced by a muscle is released into the blood. Figure 3.5 shows that during a GXT blood lactate concentration changes little or not at all at the lower work rates. As the stages of the GXT continue to increase, a point is reached at which the lactate concentration suddenly increases. The work rate at which the lactate concentration equals a certain value (i.e., 4 millimoles per liter—4 times the resting value) is called the *lactate threshold*. It should not be called the *anaerobic threshold* because several conditions other than an oxygen lack (hypoxia) at the muscle cell can result in lactate production and release into the blood. An endurance training program will cause the lactate threshold to occur at a later stage in the GXT, as shown by the dashed line (Figure 3.5).

Heart rate. Figure 3.6 shows that once the heart rate reaches about 110 beat/min it increases linearly with each work rate in a GXT until the maximal heart rate is reached. Estimates of maximal heart rate are usually obtained by the formula

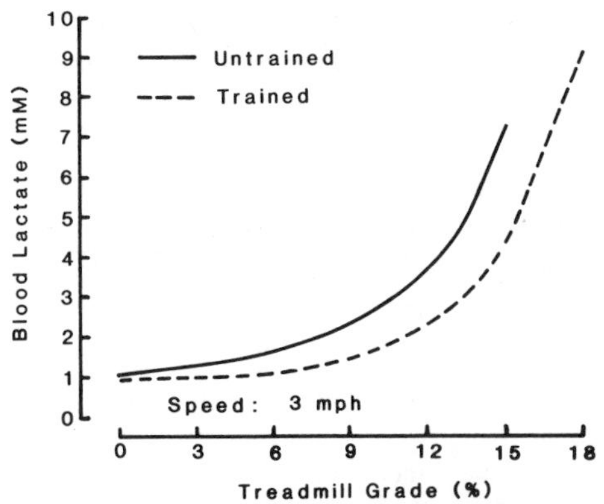

Figure 3.5 Changes in the blood lactic acid (lactate) concentration during a graded exercise test. Data adapted from "Effect of Training on Circulatory Response to Exercise" by B. Ekblom, P.O. Åstrand, B. Saltin, J. Stenberg, and B. Wallstrom, 1968, *Journal of Applied Physiology*, 24. Reprinted with permission.

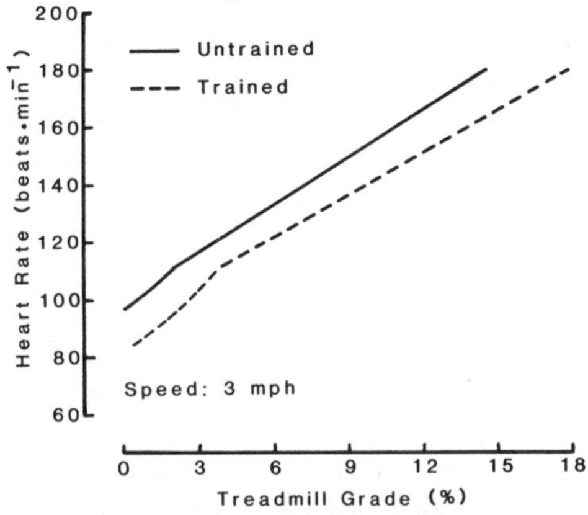

Figure 3.6 The heart rate response to a graded exercise test. Data adapted from *The Physiological Basis of Physical Education and Athletics* (p. 231) by E.L. Fox and D.K. Mathews, 1981, Philadelphia: Saunders College Publ. Reprinted with permission.

220 minus age, recognizing that the maximal heart rate decreases with increased age. When using this formula, however, it must be remembered that maximal heart rate varies considerably at any age. While the maximal heart rate at the age of 30 might be calculated to be 190 beat/min, the range (expressed as plus or minus 3 standard deviations) is from 160 to 220. The dashed line on the graph shows the influence of a training program on the subject's heart rate response at the same work rates. The lower heart rate at submaximal work rates is a beneficial effect because it decreases the oxygen needed by the heart muscle. The maximal heart rate decreases only slightly as a result of an endurance training program.

Stroke volume. The volume of blood pumped by the heart per beat is called the stroke volume. Figure 3.7 shows the stroke volume response to a GXT. Stroke volume increases in the early stages of the GXT until about 40% $\dot{V}O_2$max, and then levels off. Consequently, the heart rate is the sole factor responsible for the increased flow of blood from the heart to the working muscles after a work rate equal to 40% maximal aerobic power is reached. That observation is what makes the heart rate a good indicator of the metabolic rate during exercise. One of the primary effects of an endurance training program is an increase in stroke volume at rest and during work. This allows the heart to pump the same volume of blood per minute at a lower heart rate. The effect of an endurance training program is shown by the dashed line on Figure 3.7.

Cardiac output. Cardiac output (liters/min) is the volume of blood pumped by the heart per minute and is calculated by multiplying the heart rate (beat/min) by the stroke volume (ml/beat). Figure 3.8 shows the cardiac output as it increases linearly with each work rate. Generally, the cardiac output response to light and moderate work is not affected by an endurance training program. What is changed is the manner in which the cardiac output is achieved, with a lower heart rate and a higher stroke volume. The maximal cardiac output (highest value reached in a GXT) is the most important cardiovascular variable determining maximal aerobic power because the oxygen-enriched blood (carrying about 0.2 ℓ O_2 per liter of blood) must be delivered to the muscle for the mitochondria to use. If a person's maximal cardiac output is 10 ℓ/min, only 2 ℓ of oxygen would leave the heart per minute for the tissues (i.e., 0.2 ℓ O_2 per liter of blood times a cardiac output of 10 ℓ/min, thus $10 \times 0.2 = 2$). A person with a maximal cardiac output of 30 ℓ/min would deliver 6 ℓ of oxygen per minute to the tissues. One of

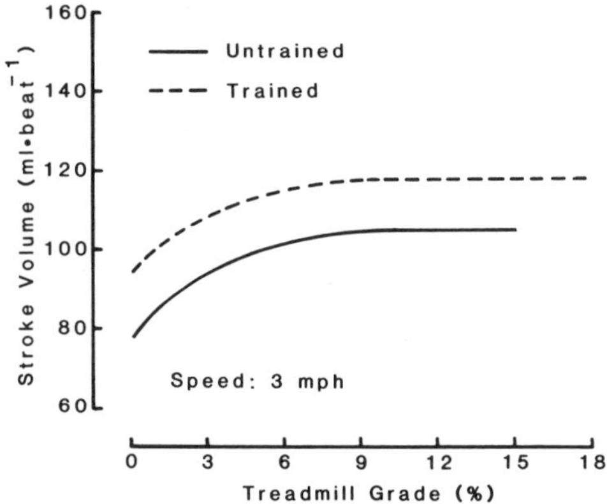

Figure 3.7 The stroke volume response to a graded exercise test. Data adapted from *The Physiological Basis of Physical Education and Athletics* (p. 231) by E.L. Fox and D.K. Mathews, 1981, Philadelphia: Saunders College Pub.

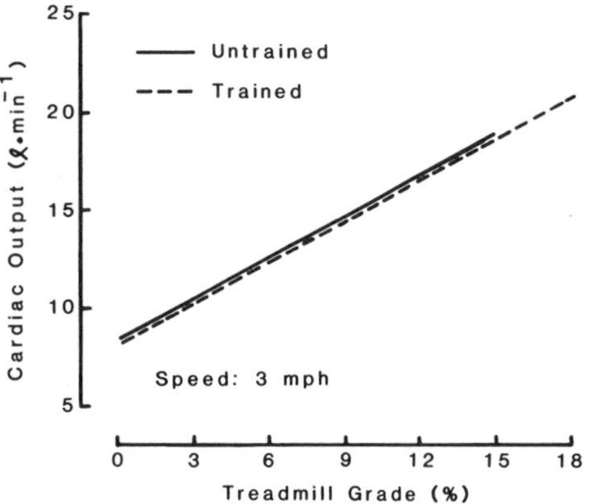

Figure 3.8 The cardiac output response to a graded exercise test. Data adapted from *The Physiological Basis of Physical Education and Athletics* (p. 231) by E.L. Fox and D.K. Mathews, 1981, Philadelphia: Saunders College Pub.

the effects of an endurance training program is an increase in the maximal cardiac output and thus the delivery of oxygen to muscles. This increase in maximal cardiac output explains 50% of the increase in maximal oxygen uptake that occurs in previously sedentary subjects who engage in endurance training programs.

In the normal population the major variable influencing the maximal cardiac output is the stroke volume. Differences in maximal cardiac output and maximal aerobic power that exist between males and females, between trained and untrained individuals, and between the world class endurance athlete and the average person can be explained to a large degree on the basis of differences in maximal stroke volume. This is shown clearly on Table 3.2 where $\dot{V}O_2$max varies by a factor of 3 among 3 distinct groups, while maximal heart rate is almost the same for all 3 groups.

Oxygen extraction. Two factors determine the oxygen uptake at any time: the volume of blood delivered to the tissues per minute (cardiac output) and the volume of oxygen extracted from each liter of blood. Oxygen extraction is calculated by subtracting the oxygen content of venous blood (as it returns to the heart) from the oxygen content of the arterial blood. This is called the arterio-venous oxygen difference or the a-vO_2 difference. The a-vO_2 difference is a measure of the ability of the muscle tissues to extract oxygen, and it increases with exercise intensity as shown in Figure 3.9. The ability of a tissue to extract oxygen is a function of the capillary to muscle fiber ratio, the number of mitochondria in the muscle fiber, and the activity of the oxidative enzymes in the mitochondria. Endurance training programs increase all of these factors, which leads to an increase in the maximal capacity to extract oxygen in the last stage of the GXT. This increase in the a-vO_2 difference can explain 50% of the increase in $\dot{V}O_2$max that occurs with endurance training programs in previously sedentary subjects.

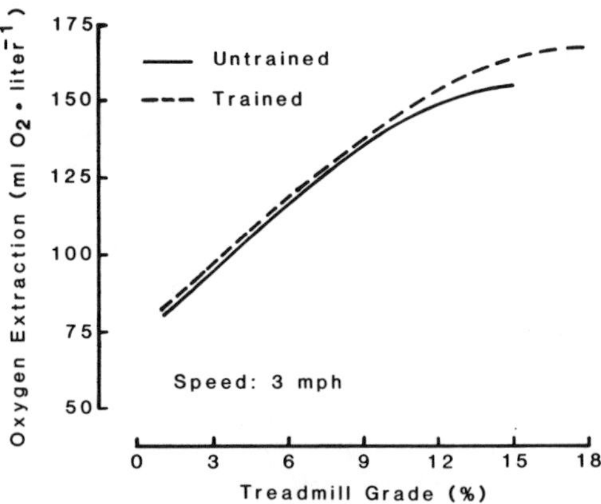

Figure 3.9 The changes in oxygen extraction (difference between the oxygen content of arterial blood and the mixed venous blood in the right heart) during a graded exercise test. From *The Physiological Basis of Physical Education and Athletics* (p. 216) by E.L. Fox and D.K. Mathews, 1981, Philadelphia: Saunders College Pub.

Table 3.2 Maximal Values of $\dot{V}O_2$ Heart Rate, Stroke Volume, and a-v Oxygen Difference in 3 Groups Having Very Low, Normal, and High Maximal $\dot{V}O_2$ (2, 19)

Group	Max $\dot{V}O_2$ L/min	=	Heart Rate beats/min	×	Stroke Volume ml	×	a-v Oxygen Difference ml/100 ml
Mitral stenosis	1.6	=	190	×	50	×	17
Sedentary	3.2	=	200	×	100	×	16
Athlete	5.2	=	190	×	160	×	17

Note. From "Circulation" by L. Rowell, 1969, *Medicine and Science in Sport,* **1**, 15-22.
(2, 19) signify two references in Rowell's paper: (2) Åstrand, P.-O. New records in human power. *Nature* **179**:922-923, 1955. (19) Granath, A., B. Jonsson, and T. Strandell. Circulation in healthy old men, studied by right heart catheterization at rest and during exercise in supine and sitting position. *Acta. Med. Scand.* **176**:425-446, 1964.

Blood pressure. Blood pressure is monitored at each stage of a GXT. Figure 3.10 shows the changes in systolic and diastolic pressures with increasing work rates. The systolic pressure increases with each stage until maximum work tolerance is reached. At that point the systolic pressure might decrease. A fall in systolic pressure with an increase in work rate is used as one of the indicators of maximal cardiovascular function and can aid in determining the end point for a test.

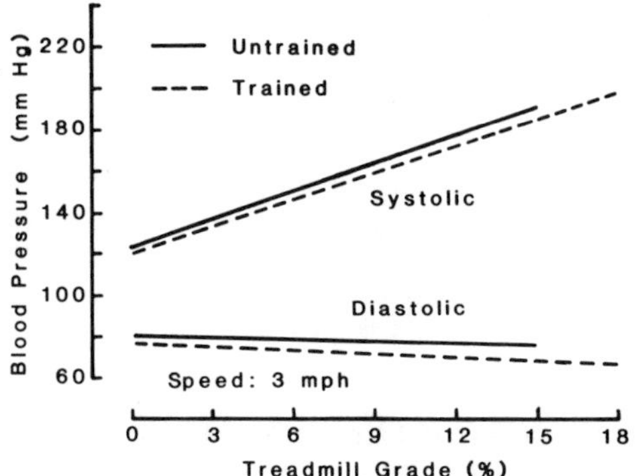

Figure 3.10 The systolic and diastolic blood pressure responses to a graded exercise test.

Diastolic blood pressure tends to remain the same or decrease during a GXT. An increase in diastolic blood pressure toward the end of the test is an indicator that a person's functional capacity has been reached. Endurance training programs result in a reduction in the blood pressure responses at fixed submaximal work rates.

Two factors that determine the oxygen demand (work) of the heart during aerobic exercise are the heart rate and the systolic blood pressure. The product of these two variables is called the *rate pressure product* or the *double product*, and is proportional to the myocardial oxygen demand (i.e., the volume of oxygen needed by the heart muscle per minute to function properly). Factors that decrease the heart rate and blood pressure responses to work increase the chance that the coronary blood supply to the heart muscle will adequately meet the oxygen needs of the heart. Endurance exercise decreases the heart rate and blood pressure responses to fixed submaximal work tasks and is seen as "protective" against any diminished blood supply (ischemia) in the myocardium. Drugs are also used to reduce the heart rate and blood pressure responses to try to reduce the work of the heart (see chapter 12).

Pulmonary ventilation. Pulmonary ventilation is the volume of air inhaled or exhaled per minute and is calculated by multiplying the frequency of breathing by the tidal volume (the volume of air moved in one breath). The pulmonary ventilation increases linearly with each grade of the GXT until 50-80% of $\dot{V}O_2$max, at which point the ventilation increases at a faster rate (Figure 3.11). The inflection point in the pulmonary ventilation response is called the *ventilatory threshold*. The increase in pulmonary ventilation is mediated by changes in the frequency of breathing (from about 10-12 breaths/min at rest to 40-50 breaths/min during maximal work) and the tidal volume (from 0.5 ℓ/min breath at rest to 2−2.5 ℓ/breath in maximal work). Endurance training programs result in a lower pulmonary ventilation during submaximal work; the ventilatory threshold occurs later into the GXT. The maximal value for pulmonary ventilation tends to change in the direction of $\dot{V}O_2$max.

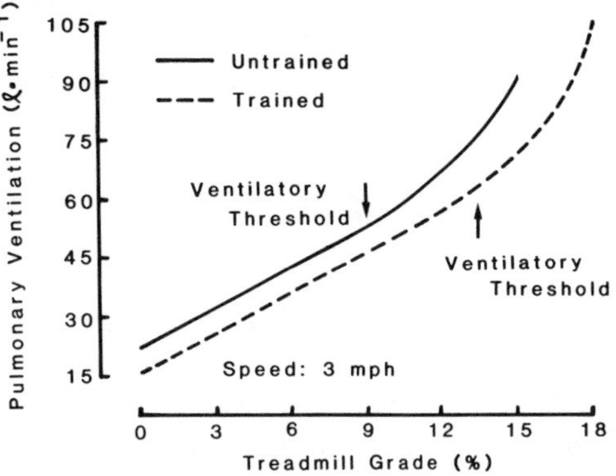

Figure 3.11 The pulmonary ventilation response to a graded exercise test. (The ventilatory threshold is shown with an arrow.) Data adapted from *The Physiological Basis of Physical Education and Athletics* (p. 185) by E.L. Fox and D.K. Mathews, 1981, Philadelphia: Saunders College Pub.

Cardiovascular Responses to Exercise for Males and Females

Generally, little or no difference exists between boys and girls in $\dot{V}O_2$max or in their cardiovascular responses to submaximal exercise. During puberty, differences between boys and girls appear and are related to the female's higher percent body fat, lower hemoglobin, and smaller heart size relative to body weight. These latter factors also affect a woman's cardiovascular responses to submaximal work. For example, if an 80-kg male were walking on a 10% grade on a treadmill at 3 mph, the $\dot{V}O_2$ would be 2.07 ℓ/min or 25.9 ml(kg•min)$^{-1}$. The heart rate might be 140 b/min for this person. If he had to now carry a backpack weighing 15 kg, the $\dot{V}O_2$ expressed per kg would not change [25.9 ml(kg•min)$^{-1}$], but the total oxygen requirement would increase 389 ml/min [15 kg × 25.9 ml(kg•min)$^{-1}$] in order to carry the load. His heart rate would obviously be higher with this load than without, even though the $\dot{V}O_2$ expressed per kg body weight is the same.

When a postpubescent female walks on a treadmill at a given grade and speed, her heart rate is higher than a comparable male's heart rate because of the additional fat weight that is carried. In addition, the lower hemoglobin and smaller relative heart size cause the heart rate to be higher at the same oxygen uptake expressed per unit body weight.

The differences between males and females in the cardiovascular response to submaximal work becomes more exaggerated when work is done on a cycle ergometer where a given work rate demands the same $\dot{V}O_2$ in liters/min, independent of size, gender, or training. The average woman has less hemoglobin and a smaller heart volume compared to the average male. In order to deliver the same volume of oxygen to the muscles, the woman has to have a higher heart rate to compensate for the smaller stroke volume and must have a slightly higher cardiac output to compensate for the lower hemoglobin concentration. These differences between men and women in the cardiovascular responses to cycle ergometry are shown in Figure 3.12.

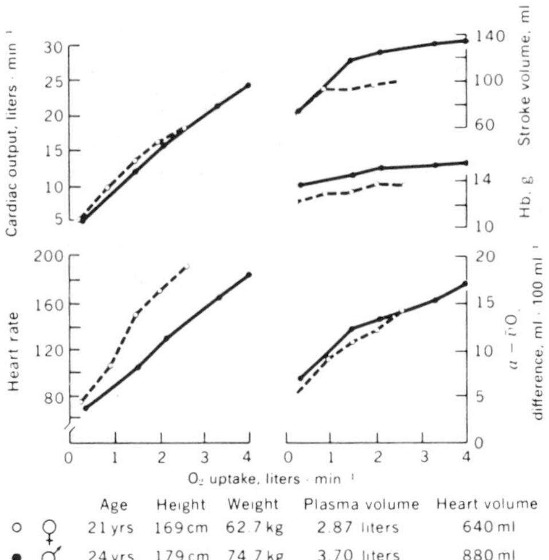

Figure 3.12 The cardiovascular responses of well-trained men and women to cycle ergometry exercise. From *Textbook of Work Physiology* (p. 198) by P.O. Åstrand and K. Rodahl, 1977, New York: McGraw-Hill.

Cardiovascular Responses to Weight-Training Activities

Most endurance exercise programs use dynamic activities involving a large muscle mass, placing a load on the cardiorespiratory system. The previous summary indicates the rather proportional nature of the cardiovascular load to the exercise intensity. But this is not necessarily the case for activities that fall into the "strength training" category, in which a person can have a disproportionately high cardiovascular load relative to the exercise intensity.

In the previous discussion of cardiovascular responses to a GXT, there was a progressive rise in the heart rate and systolic blood pressure response with each stage of the test. Figure 3.13 shows the heart rate and blood pressure response to an isometric exercise test (sustained handgrip) at only 30% maximal voluntary contraction strength. The most impressive change is in blood pressure; the systolic and diastolic pressures increase over time, and the magnitude of the systolic pressure exceeds 220 mmHg. This kind of exercise places an additional load on the heart and is not recommended for strength-training programs for older adults or people with heart disease.

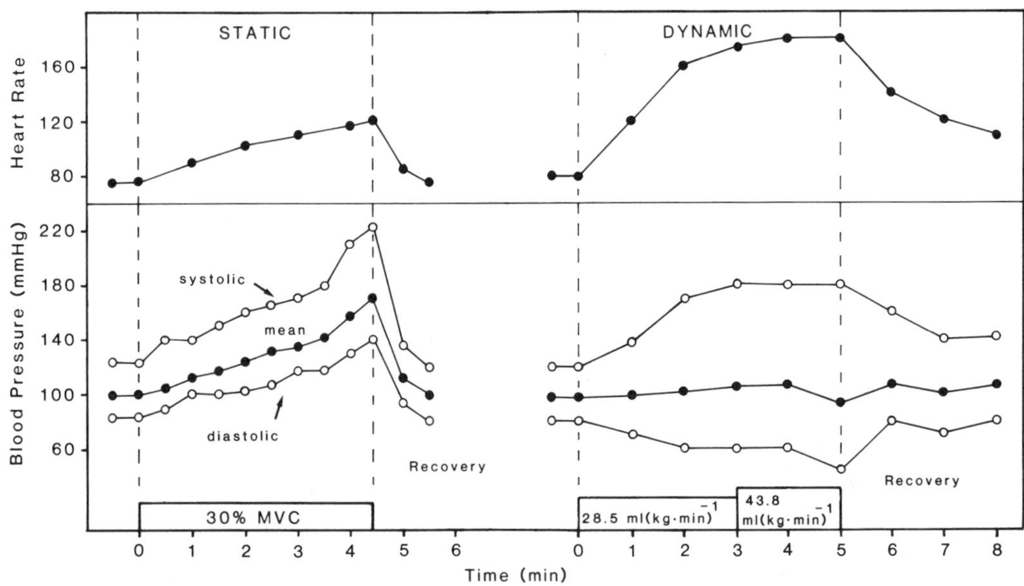

Figure 3.13 Comparison of the heart rate and blood pressure responses to a fatiguing, sustained hand-grip contraction at 30% of maximal voluntary contraction strength (30% MVC) and an exhausting treadmill test. Redrawn from "Muscular Factors Which Determine the Cardiovascular Responses to Sustained and Rhythmic Exercise" by A.R. Lind and G.W. McNicol, 1967, *Canadian Medical Association Journal*, 96. Reprinted with permission.

Summary

Muscles use ATP to develop tension, and ATP must be supplied as fast as it is used; otherwise, fatigue will occur. Muscles can supply ATP from stored energy sources (CP), anaerobic metabolism of carbohydrates (glycolysis), and through the oxidation of various substrates (oxidative phosphorylation). The lag in the circulatory and ventilatory responses at the onset of submaximal exercise necessitates the use of anaerobic sources of ATP. In 2-3 min, the oxygen uptake meets the ATP demand of the muscles. During a GXT the oxygen uptake increases with each grade until the functional capacity of the cardiovascular system to deliver oxygen has been reached. This increased oxygen delivery is directly related to increases in heart rate, cardiac output, pulmonary ventilation, and an increased extraction of oxygen from the arterial blood. The influences of endurance training and of gender on these responses were also presented.

See reference list at the end of the book for a complete source listing.

Suggested Reading for Chapter 3

ACSM (1986)

Åstrand and Rodahl (1977)

Blomquist (1978)

deVries (1980)

Edington and Edgerton (1976)

Ekblom, Åstrand, Saltin, Stenberg, and Wallstrom (1968)

Fox and Mathews (1981)

Holmgren (1967)

Lind and McNicol (1967)

Montoye (1975)

Nagle, Balke, Baptista, Alleyia, and Howley (1971)

Rowell (1969)

Sharkey (1984)

Wilmore (1982b)

Chapter 4

Anatomy and Kinesiology

Jean L. Lewis

- Bones, muscles, and joints:
  - Properties and functions
  - Role in physical activity
- Mechanics of movement

Knowledge and understanding of anatomical and mechanical concepts as they relate to human movement is essential for anyone who is working with exercising individuals. Applying this information results in better planning by the leader and more successful participation of the exercisers.

Functional Anatomy

Functional anatomy encompasses the study of bones of the skeletal system, joints, and muscles that are involved in human movement.

Skeletal Framework

Most of the 200 distinct bones in the human skeleton are involved in human movement. Their high mineral content makes them rigid and the protein content makes them resistant to tension. The two types of bone tissue are (a) *compact*, which is the hard outer layer of bone, and (b) *spongy* or *cancellous*, which has a lattice-like structure to allow greater structural strength along the lines of stress at a reduced weight. Bones are often divided into four classifications—long, short, flat, and irregular.

Long bones. The long bones, found in the limbs and digits, serve primarily as levers for movement. Each long bone consists of the diaphysis or shaft, which is compact bone around the hollow medullary cavity; the epiphysis at each end, composed of spongy bone with a thin outer layer of compact bone; the articular cartilage, a thin layer of hyaline cartilage over the articulating surfaces (the surfaces of a bone that meet another bone to form a joint); and the periosteum, a fibrous membrane covering the entire bone except where the hyaline cartilage is present. (See Figure 4.1.)

Short bones. The tarsals and carpals are the short bones. Their cubic shapes and compositions (spongy bone with a thin outside layer of compact bone) give greater strength but decrease movement potential.

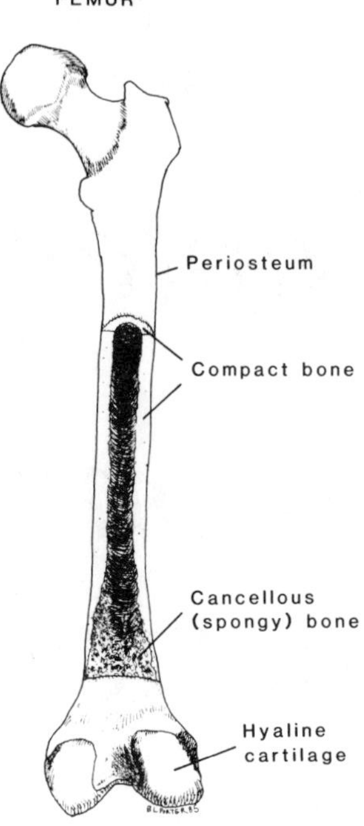

Figure 4.1 The Femur, an example of a long bone.

Flat bones. The flat bones, such as the ribs, ilium, and scapula, serve primarily as broad sites for muscle attachments and, in the case of the ribs and ilium, as protection of cavities. These bones also are spongy and are covered with a thin layer of compact bone.

Irregular bones. The ischium, pubis, and vertebrae are irregular bones that serve special purposes such as protecting internal parts and supporting the body movement.

Figures 4.2 and 4.3 show the anterior and posterior views of the skeleton. The skeleton begins as a cartilaginous structure that is gradually replaced by bone (*ossification*). This process begins at the center of ossification in the diaphysis of long bones and spreads towards the epiphyses. Other centers of ossification develop in the epiphyses and some bony protuberances, such as the tibial tuberosity. The epiphyseal plates between the diaphyses and epiphyses are the growth areas where the cartilage is replaced by bone; growth continues until the epiphyseal plates are ossified. Dates of closure vary. Although some epiphyseal

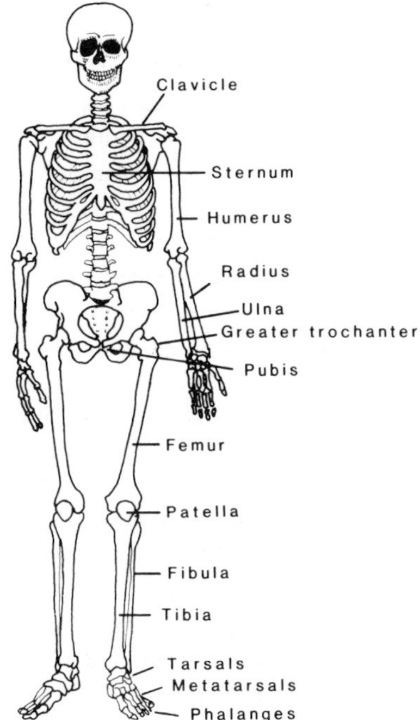

Figure 4.2 Front view of the human skeleton.

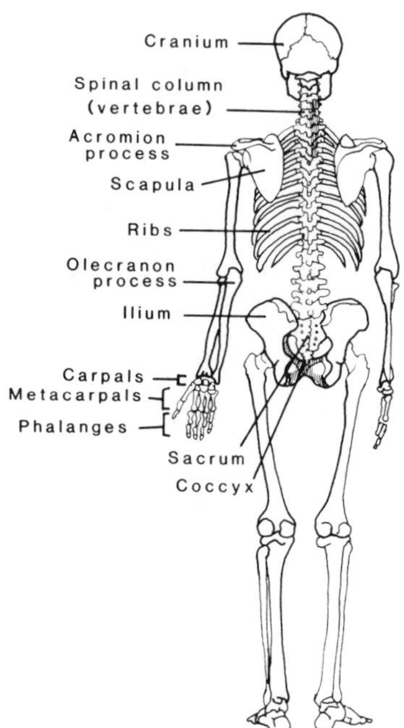

Figure 4.3 Back view of the human skeleton.

plates are closed by the age of 6, most of the closures of the plates of the long bones do not occur until the late teens. Premature closing, which results in a shorter bone length, can be caused by trauma and abnormal stresses.

Types of Joints

Joints, those places where bones meet or articulate, are often classified according to the amount of movement that can take place at those sites.

Synarthrodial joints. The synarthrodial or fibrous joints are the immovable joints. The bones merge into each other and are bound together by fibrous tissue which is continuous with the periosteum. The sutures, or the lines of junction, of the cranial bones of the skull are prime examples of this type of joint.

Amphiarthrodial joints. The amphiarthrodial or cartilaginous joints allow only slight movement in all directions. Usually a fibrocartilage disk separates the bones, and movement can only occur by the deformation of the disk. Examples of these joints are found in the pubic symphysis and between the bodies of the vertebrae. Ligaments, which are tough fibrous bands of connective tissue, connect the bones to each other.

Diarthrodial joints. Diarthrodial or synovial joints are freely movable joints that allow a variety of movement direction and range; therefore, most of the joint movements during physical activity occur at diarthrodial joints. Strong and fairly inelastic ligaments and the muscle tendons that cross the joint are responsible for maintaining the integrity of the joint. To reduce frictional rubbing, tendons are often surrounded by tendinous sheaths—cylindrical sacs lined with synovial membrane. Bursae, or sacs of synovial fluid that lie between muscles, tendons, and/or bones, also reduce friction between the tissues and act as shock absorbers.

The articulating surfaces of all bones are covered by the articular cartilage, a type of hyaline cartilage that reduces friction and acts somewhat as a shock absorber. Each joint is enclosed by a capsular ligament which may be fairly thin in spots or thick enough to be considered as a separate ligament. The synovial membrane, which secretes synovial fluid to bathe the joint, lines the inner surface of the capsule. Normally, the joint cavity is very small and therefore contains little synovial fluid, but an injury to the joint can result in an increased secretion of synovial fluid and swelling. Some diarthrodial joints, such as the sternoclavicular, distal radioulnar, and knee joints, also have a partial or complete fibrocartilage disk between the bones to aid in the absorption of shock and, in the case of the knee, to give greater stability to the joint. (See Figure 4.4.)

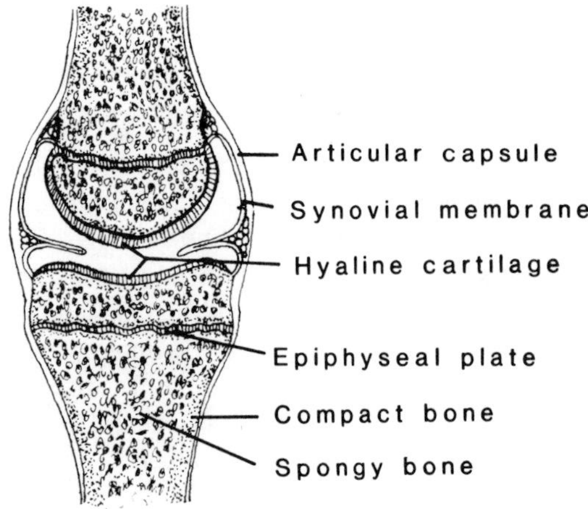

Figure 4.4 A synovial joint.

Factors That Determine Range of Motion

The structure of the bones at and near their articulating ends largely determines both the range of motion and the direction of movement. Ball and socket joints, which are found at the hip and shoulder, allow a wide range of movement in all directions; but a hinge joint, such as the elbow joint, restricts movement because bone impinges on bone. The length of the ligaments and, to a lesser extent, the extent of their elasticity are also factors. For example, the iliofemoral ligament at the anterior hip joint is a strong but short ligament that prohibits much hip hyperextension. A third factor is the elasticity of tendinous tissue. This elasticity is determined by the amount and type of physical activity in which an individual engages.

Voluntary (Skeletal) Muscle

A muscle consists of thousands of muscle fibers (e.g., the brachioradialis has approximately 130,000 fibers; the gastrocnemius has over 1,000,000) and its connective tissue attachments. Each fiber is enclosed by the connective tissue endomysium. The fasciluli, or bundles of fibers grouped together, are surrounded by perimysium, and the entire muscle is enclosed by epimysium. Each muscle is attached to the bone itself, to the periosteum of the bone, or to deep thick fascia by tendons and the perimysium and epimysium connective tissues. The size and shape of the tendons vary and depend upon their functions. Some tendons (e.g., the hamstrings and Achilles) are obvious significant parts of the entire muscle length, but other muscles, for example, the supraspinatus and infraspinatus, seem to lie directly on the bone with no observable tendon. Broad and flat tendons are called *aponeuroses*. Refer to Figures 4.5 and 4.6 for anterior and posterior views of surface muscles.

Classifying muscle fibers into two or more types, depending upon their speed of contraction

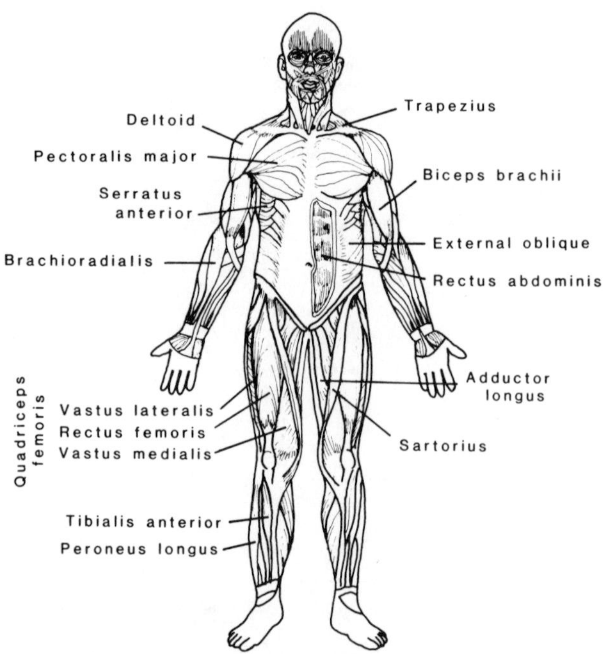

Figure 4.5 Muscles of the human body: front view.

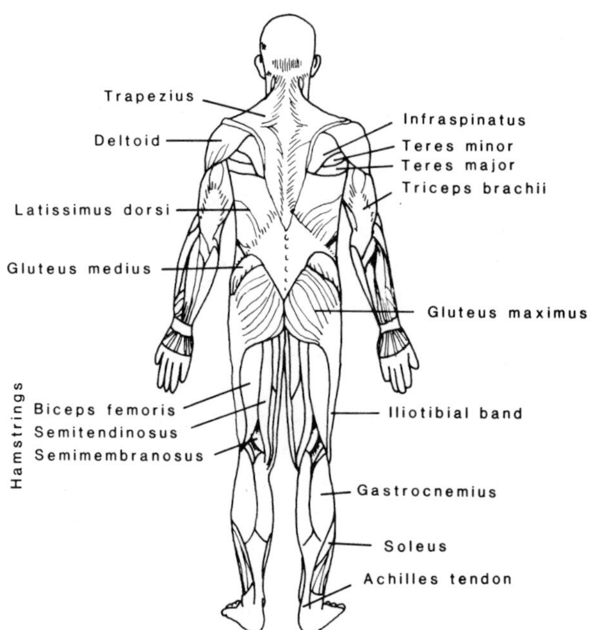

Figure 4.6 Muscles of the human body: back view.

when responding to a stimulus, is common. Fast-twitch (white) fibers are suited for speed work. They are basically anaerobic and therefore fatigue quickly; slow-twitch (red) fibers can sustain activity longer but are dependent on the oxygen supply. All muscles have both fiber types, but some have a predominance of one type. Success in athletic activity depends in part on the fiber-type composition of the working muscles. The leg muscles of long-distance runners tend to have fewer fast-twitch fibers and more slow-twitch fibers than a sprinter. The oxidative (aerobic) potential of white muscle fibers can increase to that of red muscle fibers as a result of intensive endurance training without losing their speed of contraction. No gender difference is apparent in muscle composition.

Muscle Contraction

Many muscle fibers are stimulated by the same branch of a motor neuron. This functional organization is called the *motor unit*. With a sufficiently strong stimulus, each muscle fiber within that motor unit contracts maximally; muscular tension increases with the stimulation of more motor units. A muscle that has the primary purpose of a strength or power movement rather than delicate movement has a large number of muscle fibers and also has many fibers per motor unit.

When a muscle contracts, it tends to shorten toward the center of the muscle, pulling on all of its bony attachments. Whether or not movement occurs depends upon the force of contraction and the resistance to that contraction.

Concentric contraction. A concentric contraction is when the muscle exerts a force that results in a muscular torque that is greater than a resistance torque. The muscle shortens and pulls its bones of attachment closer to each other, causing movement at the joint. For example, gravity is an external force that pulls objects toward earth, and in order to lift a weight from the floor or jump into the air, the muscular force must be greater than the gravitational pull. Resistance training with free weights uses the gravitational pull as the resistive force; the use of wall or ceiling pulleys changes the direction of the gravitational pull, offering resistance to movement in other directions.

Other forces can also resist movement. Slight internal tissue friction is always present but is not usually noticed except perhaps during unaided stretching activities when additional muscular force is necessary to overcome the joint resistance. Some weight-training equipment uses internal hydraulics or air pressure as the resistive force to be overcome. Although gravity is not a factor in water, the water itself resists movement in all directions.

A concentric contraction is also necessary when an external force causes the desired movement without any muscular contraction, but too slowly. An example of this is seen in the arm movements during the second count of a jumping jack. Gravity lowers the arms to the side of the body, but concentrically contracting muscles cause the movement to occur much more quickly.

Eccentric contraction. An eccentric contraction is when the muscle exerts a force that results in a muscular torque that is less than a resistance torque. This other force causes the movement, but muscles contracting eccentrically control the speed of that movement. For example, the pull of gravity returns an elevated arm down to the side of the body with no muscular help. Muscles can contract eccentrically and act as a brake, causing the arm movement to occur more slowly than what would result from the gravitational pull only. The muscles are exerting force, but their lengths are increasing. The same muscles that initially contracted concentrically to elevate the arm against the force of gravity now contract eccentrically to control the speed of the downward movement caused by gravity. Eccentric contraction may also occur when a muscle's maximum effort still is not great enough to overcome the opposing force; movement will be caused by that force in spite of the maximally contracting muscle.

A ballistic or fast movement in which resistance is insignificant, such as throwing, requires a burst of concentric contractions to begin the movement. Once movement has begun, the muscles that contracted to cause that movement basically shut down; any further contraction slows the movement. Other muscles are active in guiding the movement in the appropriate directions. Eccentric contractions of muscles that are antagonistic or opposite to the muscles that initiated the movement decelerate and eventually stop the movement.

Isometric or static contraction. During an isometric or static contraction, the muscle exerts a force that results in a muscular torque that is the same as a resistance torque. The muscle length does not change so no movement occurs, and that joint position is maintained. The contractive part of the muscle shortens, but the elastic connective tissue lengthens proportionately; no overall change in the entire muscle length occurs. Holding the arm out to the side requires static contraction—just enough muscle force to counteract the pull of gravity, resulting in no movement. The effort in trying to push a wall over is another example of isometric contractions. Although the amount of muscular force can be maximal, no joint movement will occur. The rehabilitation exercise "quad sets," in which the knee extensor muscles are contracted with the knee already in the extended position, is another example of a static contraction.

Roles of Muscles

Muscles have several functions and can act in one or several ways according to Rasch and Burke (1978).

Prime mover. A muscle that is very effective in causing a certain joint movement is a *prime mover* or *agonist*. *Assistant movers* are muscles that are not as effective for the same movement.

Antagonist. An *antagonist muscle* (sometimes called a *contralateral muscle*) is one that, when it concentrically contracts, causes a movement directly opposite the movement caused by another muscle. For example, a knee flexor muscle such as the semitendinosus is an antagonist to the vastus medialis, a knee extensor.

Fixator or stabilizer. A muscle may also act as a fixator or stabilizer and contract isometrically to prevent movement of a bone. Another muscle that is concentrically contracting will pull on all of the bones to which it is attached. Usually only one of the bones moves; a fixator muscle prevents movement of the other bone. A fixator muscle can also prevent undesirable movement caused by an external force. For example, a push-up exercise should be done without sagging or hyperextension of the trunk and hips, which the pull of gravity tends to cause. Isometric contraction of the abdominal muscles prevents this sagging—these muscles stabilize the trunk in its proper position.

Neutralizer or synergist. Another role of a muscle is to counteract an undesirable action caused by the concentric contraction of another muscle. The concentric contraction of most muscles causes more than one movement. If only one of those movements is intended, a neutralizing muscle contracts to prevent the undesirable movement. If the muscle also assists with the desired movement, the muscle is a helping synergist. For example, a concentric contraction by the biceps brachii muscle pulls on the radius (other muscles are stabilizing its other bony attachment, the scapula) and causes both flexion at the elbow joint and supination at the radioulnar joint. If only flexion is intended, a neutralizing muscle must contract to counteract the supination. In this example a concentric contraction by the pronator teres, which causes both elbow flexion and radioulnar pronation, would aid the flexion but neutralize the supination.

Muscle Groups

A muscle group includes all of the muscles that cause the same movement at the same joint. The group is named for the joint where the movement takes place and the common movement that is caused by the concentric contraction of those muscles in the group. The term *elbow flexors* denotes a muscle group composed of the specific muscles that are responsible for flexion at the elbow joint when the muscles contract concentrically. Table 4.1 lists the muscles that are prime movers of the muscle groups. Understand that a movement being observed at a joint does not necessarily involve the muscle group for the movement that is occurring—the muscle group responsible for the opposite action may be contracting eccentrically to control the movement. For example, the elbow flexor muscle group exerts force to flex the elbow joint during the elbow curl exercise. To return to the starting position, the pull of gravity extends the joint to the original position, but the elbow flexors are still exerting force to control the speed of that movement with eccentric contractions. To maintain the elbow in a flexed position requires an isometric contraction by those same elbow flexors.

Muscle Group Involvement in Selected Activities

Human movement is caused and controlled by muscle forces. The following briefly analyzes the involvement of muscle groups in some common physical activities.

Walking, Jogging, Running

The different phases and the muscle group involvement in walking, jogging, and running are similar, but the force of the muscle contractions increases as the speed increases. The three basic phases are the push-off, the recovery of the push-off leg, and the landing.

Push-off. The push-off is accomplished by the concentric contraction of the hip extensors, the talocrural plantar flexors, and, to a lesser extent, the metatarsalphalangeal flexors; some work is done by the knee extensors. The gluteus maximus muscle assumes a greater role in hip extension as speed increases. Medial rotation takes place at the hip joint, but because the foot is fixed on the ground, this movement is seen at the pelvis.

Recovery. At the beginning of the recovery phase, the hip flexors contract concentrically to begin the forward leg swing. This is basically a ballistic movement, so the momentum initiated by the hip flexors continues the motion. The rotation at the pelvis is aided by the lateral hip rotators.

Table 4.1 Muscles That Are Prime Movers (and Assistant Movers)

Joint	Prime (and Assistant) Movers
Intertarsal joint	Invertors—tibialis anterior, tibialis posterior; (extensor hallucis longus, flexor digitorum longus, flexor hallucis longus)
	Evertors—extensor digitorum longus, peroneus bevis, peroneus longus, peroneus tertius
Talocrural joint	Dorsiflexors—tibialis anterior, extensor digitorum longus, peroneus tertius; (extensor hallucis longus)

(Cont.)

Table 4.1 Cont.

	Plantar flexors—gastrocnemius, soleus; (peroneus longus, peroneus brevis, flexor digitorum longus, flexor hallucis longus, tibialis posterior)
Knee joint	Flexors—biceps femoris, semitendinosus, semimembranosus; (sartorius, gracilis, gastrocnemius, plantaris)
	Extensors—rectus femoris, vastus lateralis, vastus medialis, vastus intermedius
Hip joint	Flexors—psoas, iliacus, pectineus, rectus femoris; (sartorius, tensor fascia latae, gracilis, adductor longus, adductor brevis)
	Extensors—gluteus maximus, biceps femoris, semitendinosus, semimembranosus
	Abductors—gluteus medias; (gluteus minimus, tensor fascia latae, psoas, iliacus, sartorius)
	Adductors—adductor brevis, adductor longus, adductor magnus, gracilis, pectineus
	Lateral rotators—gluteus maximus, six deep lateral rotators; (psoas, iliacus, sartorius)
	Medial rotators—gluteus minimus; (tensor fascia latae, pectineus)
Spinal column (thoracic and lumbar areas)	Flexors—rectus abdominis, external oblique, internal oblique
	Extensors—erector spinae group
	Rotators—internal oblique, external oblique, erector spinae group
	Lateral flexors—internal oblique, external oblique, quadratus lumborum multifidus, rotatores; (erector spinae group)
Shoulder girdle	Abductors—pectoralis minor, serratus anterior
	Adductors—middle fibers of trapezius, rhomboids; (upper and lower fibers of trapezius)
	Upward rotators—upper and lower fibers of trapezius, serratus anterior
	Downward rotators—rhomboids, pectoralis minor
	Elevators—levator scapulae, upper fibers of trapezius, rhomboids
	Depressors—lower fibers of trapezius, pectoralis minor
Shoulder joint	Flexors—anterior deltoid, clavicular portion of pectoralis major; (short head of biceps brachii)
	Extensors—sternal portion of pectoralis major, latissimus dorsi, teres major; (posterior deltoid, long head of triceps brachii)
	Abductors—middle deltoid, supraspinatus; (anterior deltoid, long head of biceps brachii)
	Adductors—latissimus dorsi, teres major, sternal portion of pectoralis major; (short head or biceps brachii, long head of triceps brachii)
	Lateral rotators—infraspinatus, teres minor; (posterior deltoid)
	Medial rotators—latissimus dorsi, teres major, pectoralis major, subscapularis; (anterior deltoid)
Elbow joint	Flexors—biceps brachii, brachialis, brachioradialis; (pronator teres, flexor carpi ulnaris and radialis)
	Extensors—triceps brachii; (anconeus, extensor carpi ulnaris and radialis)

(Cont.)

Table 4.1 Cont.

Radio-ulnar joint	Pronators—Pronator teres, pronator quadratus, brachioradialis
	Supinators—supinator, biceps brachii, brachioradialis
Wrist joint	Flexors—flexor carpi ulnaris, flexor carpi radialis; (flexor digitorum superficialis and profundus)
	Extensors—extensor carpi ulnaris, extensor carpi radialis longus and brevis; (extensor digitorum)
	Abductors—flexor carpi radialis, extensor carpi radialis longus and brevis; (extensor pollicis)
	Adductors—flexor carpi ulnaris, extensor carpi ulnaris

The knee flexors bend the knee initially and then work eccentrically to control the knee extension at the end of the recovery phase. The talocrural joint is dorsiflexed to clear the foot from the ground and prepare for the landing.

Landing. Just prior to landing, the hip extensors contract eccentrically to decelerate the forward leg swing. On contact, the knee extensors contract eccentrically to cushion the impact. During the landing phase in walking, the talocrural dorsiflexors contract eccentrically to control the speed of movement of the ball of the foot to the ground.

Walking or running up an incline elicits a greater force of contraction from the gluteus maximus muscle at the hip and from the knee extensors. The talocrural dorsiflexors are more active immediately before the landing, and because the talocrural joint is in a greater dorsiflexed position, the plantar flexors begin contracting during the push-off from a more stretched position. There is also more eccentric contraction by the knee extensors during the landing in downhill than uphill running. As a result, these muscle groups are more apt to become fatigued and be sore afterwards.

Cycling

The main force in cycling comes from the hip and knee extensor muscles during the downward push. The gluteus maximus is more involved in cycling than in walking because the extension begins from a flexed position at the hip. When toe clips are used, the hip and knee flexors aid in returning the pedal to the up position.

Jumping

The hip and knee extensors, followed by the talocrural plantar flexors, forcibly contract to propel the body upward. The trunk extends and the arms flex from a hyperextended position just prior to the leg action. If the reach height is important, the scapula elevates. During the landing, the hip and knee extensors and the talocrural plantar flexors contract eccentrically.

Overarm Throwing

In preparation for throwing, there is a weight shift to the back foot, a medial rotation of the back leg (because the leg is fixed to the ground, the pelvis is the moving bone), trunk rotation and lateral flexion, a horizontal extension of the throwing arm accompanied by the adduction of the scapula, a flexion of that elbow, and hyperextension of the wrist.

The weight shift forward is the initial movement in the throwing pattern. This is accomplished by the hip abductors, the talocrural plantar flexors, and the intertarsal evertors of the back leg. The forward hip medially rotates; the back hip rotates laterally. The trunk then laterally flexes and rotates, beginning at the lumbar area and continuing through the thoracic vertebrae. There is a forcible lateral and then medial rotation of the throwing arm. Although there is also some horizontal flexion, most of the force of the arm in an overhand throw comes from this medial rotation. The elbow extends and the wrist flexes. Depending upon the desired spin on the ball, the radioulnar supinators and the wrist adductors also may be involved. Because the actions involved in throwing, especially those at the shoulder and elbow joints, are ballistic movements, the shoulder horizontal extensors and elbow flexors contract eccentrically to decelerate the movements.

Swimming

Swimming is a unique activity because the water medium offers resistance to movements in all directions. Exercises or movements performed in water demand concentric contractions.

Lifting and Carrying Objects

The weight to be lifted should be located close to the lifter's spread feet, and the spine should be kept erect. The actual lifting should be accomplished by leg rather than spine or arm action. The knee extensors, along with the hip extensors, are the primary muscle groups responsible for correct lifting. The weight should be carried close to the body with the trunk assuming a position that allows the line of gravity to fall well within the area of the base. The trunk lateral flexors are more active when the weight is carried on one side; the extensors are more active when the weight is in front of the body; and when the weight is carried across the top of the back, as in backpacking, the abdominals are more active, especially during a hill descent.

Basic Mechanical Concepts Related to Human Movement

Knowledge of the laws and principles of mechanics is also important to the understanding of human movement, and provide a sound basis for analyzation of movement. Some of these basic but important concepts are described below.

Stability

For an individual to maintain balance, the line of gravity must fall within the area of the base. The degree of stability is directly proportional to the weight of the body and to the distance from the line of gravity to the outer limits of the base; the degree of stability is inversely proportional to the height of the body's center of gravity above the base. Stability can be increased by moving the feet apart to widen the base and flexing the knees and hips to lower the center of gravity. To help maintain stability against a potentially upsetting force, the weight should be shifted toward that force. When locomotion is going to occur, a position close to instability is attained by shifting the weight closer to the outer limits of the base in the direction of the intended movement. During locomotion, as the line of gravity moves outside the limits of the base (which is the area of the push-off foot), a new base is established when the other foot lands, and stability is maintained.

Rotational Inertia

Rotational inertia (also referred to as *the moment of inertia*), or the reluctance of a body segment or segments to rotate around an axis or joint, is dependent upon its mass and the distribution of that mass around the joint. A leg, for example, possesses a greater degree of rotational inertia than an arm, not only because of its heavier mass but also because its mass is concentrated a greater distance away from its axis. The amount of muscular force necessary to cause movement at a joint is proportional to the rotational inertia of the limb to be moved. During jogging, for example, the knee of the recovery leg is flexed to reduce the leg's rotational inertia around the hip joint. Less muscular force is needed to swing the recovery leg forward, thus the possibility of local fatigue of the hip flexor muscles is reduced. In sprinting, the quicker the recovery leg is brought forward, the faster the running speed will be. More powerful contractions of the hip flexors and a greater knee flexion than is found in jogging accomplishes this increased speed.

Torque

The effect produced when a force causes rotation is called the *torque* (T) or the moment of the force. Torque is the product of the magnitude of the force itself (F), and the shortest or perpendicular distance from the axis to the point of application of the force (MA, or moment arm). Algebraically, torque can be expressed as $T = F \times MA$. The MA of a muscle, often referred to as the force arm, is the distance between the joint axis and the muscle attachment on the bone. An individual whose muscle attachments are located closer to the axis than another individual's must apply more muscular force to achieve the same torque. Other forces, such as the pull of gravity or a pushing or pulling by another person on a body part, result in opposing torques which resist limb movements, therefore they are often referred to as resistance forces. The force produced by gravity is the mass of the object; the moment or resistance arm is the distance from the center of gravity of that mass to the joint. The resistance arm of a force applied by someone pushing or pulling on a limb is the distance from the point of application of that resistance to the joint. For muscular contraction to cause movement of a bone, the muscular torque must be greater than the opposing or resistance torque. When the muscular torque equals the resistance torque, no movement occurs, and the muscle is contracting isometrically. If, however, the muscular torque is greater, either because of an increased force of muscular contraction or a reduction of the resistance torque (less resistance and/or a shorter resistance arm), movement occurs and the muscular contraction is concentric. A greater resistance torque results in movement being caused by that torque, and the muscle contracts eccentrically. This principle can be applied to individualized exercises. The amount of muscular contraction necessary during exercise can be modified by altering the amount of the resistance and/or the resistance arm. For example, the resistance torque can be increased with the use of external weights which would therefore require stronger muscle contractions. The resistance can also be changed by altering the positions of the body parts. In the execution of side lateral trunk bends, for example, the arms may be held at the sides of the body to bring the upper body mass closer to the axis of rotation. This position requires less muscular force by the trunk muscles than a position with the arms held overhead.

Angular Momentum

Angular momentum, or the quantity of angular motion, is expressed as the product of the rotational inertia and the angular velocity.

Transfer of momentum. Angular momentum can be transferred from one body segment to another by stabilizing the initial moving body part at a joint, which will result in angular movement of another body part. For example, in performing a curl-up exercise for the abdominal muscles, a flinging forward of the arms from an overhead position results in a transfer of their momentum to the trunk, which decreases the amount of muscular contraction needed by the trunk flexors.

Conservation of angular momentum. The angular momentum of a rotating body or segment remains the same, or is conserved, until an opposing torque is applied. This principle is best applied to skills in which an individual is rotating in the air, on ice, or on other highly frictionless surface. If the rotational inertia changes during the rotation, a proportional change of the angular velocity occurs in the opposite direction. For example, a diver rotating in air possesses a certain amount of angular momentum which must be conserved while he or she is free of support. If the limbs are moved closer to the axis of rotation, as in a tuck position, the rotational inertia decreases, resulting in an increase in the angular velocity. Before entering the water, the diver assumes a straight position which increases the rotational inertia, thus reducing the velocity.

Summary

Knowledge of the structure and function of muscles, bones, and joints is essential to understand human movement. The length and shape of the bones, the amount of movement possible at a joint, the length and elasticity of the ligaments and tendons at the joint, and the type of muscle initiating the movement all influence the rate and range of possible motion. Muscles are classified as fast and slow, in terms of speed of contractions, and can shorten (concentric) or lengthen (eccentric) while developing tension. If a muscle is a prime mover of a joint, it is called an agonist. An antagonist is a muscle that opposes this action. Muscles can also act to stabilize other joints during a movement or prevent an inappropriate movement. Finally, the basic mechanical concepts of stability, torque, rotational inertia, and angular momentum, as applied to human movement, are summarized.

Suggested Reading for Chapter 4

Barham (1978)

Basmajian (1980)

Basmajian and MacConaill (1977)

Broer and Zernicke (1979)

Cooper and Glassow (1982)

Gray (1966)

Hay and Reid (1982)

Hinson (1981)

Jensen, Schultz, and Bangerter (1983)

Kreighbaum and Barthels (1985)

Logan and McKinney (1982)

Luttgens and Wells (1982)

Northrip, Logan, and McKinney (1979)

Rasch and Burke (1978)

Thompson (1981)

See reference list at the end of the book for a complete source listing.

Part III

Physical Fitness

- Components that meet the criteria for physical fitness

Part I defined physical fitness and described general health status. Part II provided a review of the basic exercise sciences. Part III deals with specific aspects of fitness. The components of physical fitness that appear to be related to positive health and that can be improved with appropriate activity are the following:

1. Relative leanness
2. Cardiovascular-respiratory function
3. Flexibility, muscular strength, and muscular endurance
4. Arousal/relaxation balance

Sufficient evidence exists to show that improvement in these fitness components increases a person's potential for the highest quality of life, while conversely, a decrement in any of these areas increases a person's risk of developing serious health problems. The four chapters in this section further define the selected component, explain how it can be evaluated, and suggest ways to improve it. This list of fitness components should not be viewed as the final word. Further research may indicate that some of these areas are not as important as we now think, or (more likely) that additional characteristics meet the fitness criteria and should be included. Currently, however, we believe that the aforementioned physical fitness components are appropriately included.

Chapter 5
Relative Leanness

Wendy J. Bubb

- Body composition
  - Components
  - Desired levels
  - How to test and improve
  - Relation to exercise and diet

- Nutrition
  - Basic ingredients
  - Recommended health diet

Obesity is either a cause of or is correlated with a variety of hazards to health. Particularly noteworthy are diabetes, coronary artery disease, and hypertension. Many agree that reducing the incidence of obesity would advance public health.

Our society is tremendously preoccupied with obesity. Physicians and their afflicted patients engage in frustrating efforts to correct it. In recent years, weight reduction has become a multimillion-dollar industry; reducing clubs and health spas are spreading rapidly. Nevertheless, obesity persists in our society.

Body Composition

Body weight consists of many components, the relative proportions of which vary among individuals. Total body weight includes bone, muscle, fat, blood, and viscera. Total body weight is conveniently divided into the lean body mass and fat mass. *Lean body mass* refers to the weight of all body tissue except fat. *Total body fat* is stored in various organs of the body such as the heart, liver, lungs, and brain. In addition, body fat is retained in adipose tissue, including the fat surrounding various internal organs as well as the subcutaneous layer of fat just beneath the skin. Some body fat is essential as an energy store, for protection of internal organs, and as insulation against heat loss. Essential body fat is about 3% and 12% of the total body weight for adult males and females, respectively. These values represent the lower limits of body fat necessary to maintain good health.

The amount and sites of fat deposition vary among individuals and between sexes. The larger quantity of fat in the female presumably relates to her child-bearing function. Fat deposition occurs in areas that are genetically unique to each individual. The hormone estrogen dictates fat deposition in the thighs, buttocks, and breasts in women. Men have minimal fat in these areas because they have lower levels of estrogen. A man is more likely to have fat in his back, lower abdomen and at the top of his iliac crest.

The difference between being overweight and being overfat is an important distinction. Overweightness is frequently defined as 10% in excess of the normal body weight range. Unfortunately, this does not consider the amount of body fat. Regarding relative leanness for positive health, the percentage of a person's body weight that is body fat is far more meaningful. Men and women are overfat if they possess greater than 23% and 30% body fat, respectively. Body fatness is addressed more fully in the next section.

Research has shown that the number and size of fat cells in the body are also important criteria in the degree of fatness. In adults, fat loss or gain occurs because of a decrease or increase, respectively, in the size of fat cells, with no change in the number of fat cells. For children, however, obesity occurs when an increase occurs in the number of fat cells and the size of fat cells. This is also believed to be related to the difficulty that an obese child has in being cured of obesity. Some studies suggest that an overabundance of fat cells may cause regulatory or metabolic dysfunctions which make it difficult for a person with a large number of fat cells to lose and maintain weight loss. Presumably, the appetite centers of the brain signal the body to increase appetite in an attempt to satisfy, to a certain extent, the large number of fat cells.

Evaluating Body Fatness

An evaluation of body composition is essential prior to making specific recommendations about a person's need to lose body weight or body fat. Frequently, recommendations for weight loss have been made on the basis of the standard weight for height charts published by insurance companies. It has generally been suggested that a person whose body weight is 10% above the average weight for height according to insurance company statistics is overweight. Unfortunately, definition of body frame size often becomes an arbitrary judgment. In addition, these tables fail to consider the relative amounts of muscle and fat tissue. When these standards are applied to physically fit athletes, they frequently weigh more than an average or desirable body weight. By evaluating body composition, however, it may be determined that they actually have a relatively low percentage of body fat and often do not need to reduce weight. Likewise, some thin individuals may be considered underweight according to height/weight standards, but they have a high percentage of body fat. In the "average" population, excess weight is generally fat weight. Thus overweight and overfat are essentially equal. Height/weight standards are not as precise as some of the others to be discussed; therefore, people with small or large amounts of muscle may be misevaluated. Recognizing what information is provided by scale weighing, what factors affect scale weight, and how to properly interpret the information obtained should lead to the proper utilization of scale weights.

When body weight is measured on a scale, consistency is rare. Several factors influence scale weight independent of adipose tissue loss. Scale weight can vary during the day as a result of eating, urinary and fecal elimination, and loss of sweat. Certain factors can cause temporary loss or retention of water. A low carbohydrate diet, for example, may cause an immediate weight loss due to water being released by the body. This apparent weight loss is temporary and the body will return to its original weight when water balance is restored. Diarrhea can result in temporary weight loss for the same reason. On the other hand, a high carbohydrate diet or menstruation may lead to water retention and temporary weight gain. This does not reflect changes in adipose tissue.

When using weighing scales, the following guidelines are recommended:

1. Beam scales with nondetachable weights should be used. They should be calibrated to zero and permit reading to the nearest 1/4 pound.
2. Weighing should be done prior to breakfast, after the bladder has been emptied.
3. Clothing should be light, without shoes.
4. Measurements should be accurately noted and recorded and compared with previous weight measurements to determine possible weight loss.

The most accurate methods to determine body composition are by chemical analysis of human cadavers; however, this is of no use to the health and fitness instructor. Several indirect methods that are widely used by exercise specialists have been validated by the information obtained from these direct measurements. These include hydrostatic (underwater) weighing, measurement of skinfold thickness, and circumference measurements.

Underwater Weighing

With the application of Archimedes principle, percentage of body fat can be calculated from body density using underwater or hydrostatic weighing. Since body density is equal to the ratio of body weight to body volume (weight/volume), the use of hydrostatic weighing requires determination of body volume. If an object's loss of weight in water is equal to the weight of the volume of water that it displaces, then body volume can be calculated as the difference between body weight in air and body weight measured during water submersion (i.e., body volume = weight in air − weight in water). Therefore,

$$\text{Body density (g/cc)} = \frac{\text{Body weight in air}}{\text{Wt. in air} - \text{Wt. in water}}$$

Hydrostatic weighing has its greatest disadvantage in the time and equipment necessary to perform it. The essential equipment includes a special chair suspended from a balance scale that measures to the nearest 10 g, a weight belt, and a tank into which the subject is submerged. A swimming pool with the scale and chair suspended from a support at the side of the pool is a suitable alternative to the tank. In addition, for accurate measurements a closed-circuit oxygen dilution system is necessary to measure residual volume.

Body weight is determined in air with a balance scale; the subject is dressed in a lightweight swimming suit. The person being weighed is seated in the chair suspended from the scale and is submerged beneath the water. A weight belt fitted around the waist prevents the subject from floating toward the surface. Prior to submersion, as much air as possible is expired from the lungs. This forced expiration is maintained for 5-10 s while the underwater weight is recorded. The underwater weight of the belt and the chair is determined beforehand and subtracted from the total underwater weight of the subject. With repeated weighings, subjects apparently learn to expel more air from the lungs. It is therefore suggested that 10-12 weighing trials be taken. Because errors in measurement are more likely to result from the subject not exhaling completely, the highest score should be selected. The scale pointer will tend to fluctuate during the measurement; therefore, weight should be recorded as the midpoint of the fluctuation.

Following a maximal expiration, some air, defined as the *residual volume*, remains in the lungs. Because this volume contributes to buoyancy, the total volume must be corrected for the residual lung volume prior to the actual calculation of body density. An error in determining the relatively large residual volume (1,000-1,500 ml) could seriously affect the accuracy and usefulness of the underwater weighing technique. Without measuring residual volume directly, an assumed average value for all subjects or an estimated value based on height and weight can be used. In addition, residual volume can be estimated as the vital capacity × 0.24 for males and vital capacity × 0.28 for females, although the relationship between these parameters is relatively low. Because the accuracy of the residual volume measurement can seriously affect the validity of subsequent calculations of body density and thus body fat, the practice of using either an assumed average value for all subjects or predicting the residual volume from other parameters is questionable. Note that when assuming a constant value or using a percentage of vital capacity, the potential error in the calculated values for percentage body fat is as great as when circumference and skinfold measures are used. For this reason, it is questionable whether the extra time and cost are justified for hydrostatic weighing if measurement of residual volume using standard oxygen dilution techniques is not possible. The temperature of the water is recorded and the volume is corrected for the density of water at the recorded temperature. With these corrections, the body density equation becomes

$$\text{Body density (g/cc)} = \frac{\text{Weight in air}}{\dfrac{\text{Wt. in air} - \text{Wt. in } H_2O}{\text{Temp. corr.}} - \text{Residual volume}}$$

The following example illustrates the use of these measurements in calculating body density:

Body weight	100 kg
Underwater weight	4.0 kg
Residual volume	1.0 ℓ
Water temperature correction	0.9965

$$\text{Body density} = \frac{100 \text{ kg}}{\dfrac{100 \text{ kg} - 4 \text{ kg}}{0.9965} - 1.0\ \ell}$$

$$= 1.0489 \text{ kg}/\ell \text{ or g/cc}$$

The equations by Siri (1956) and Brozek, Grande, Anderson, and Keys (1963) discussed later are used to calculate percentage of body fat.

Skinfold Method

Determination of body composition by measuring the thickness of skinfolds has had the widest use, compared to the other techniques. The basis of measuring body fat in this way is that approximately 50% of the total fat content of the body is located subcutaneously, or just beneath the skin. Measuring the thickness of a skinfold involves grasping a fold of skin and fat away from the underlying muscle. A skinfold caliper is used to measure the skinfold thickness to the nearest 1/2 mm.

Harpenden[1] and Lange[2] calipers are recommended, but other less expensive calipers are suitable alternatives[3], except for research studies requiring greater precision.

The success of the measurement of skinfolds depends on meticulous attention to detail in the techniques. Practice of the techniques should be extensive, and anatomical locations should be correct to establish test/retest reliability prior to performing the technique on a group of subjects. Although some suggest taking three consecutive measurements at a single site and using the middle score, a more objective technique is to measure different sites in succession, repeating the succession two to three times without looking at the previous value. Average 2-3 measurements to determine the skinfold thickness. If consecutive measurements are made at a given site before moving to another, the technique of measurement should be repeated completely, including locating the site and regrasping the skinfold. For test/retest reliability, where possible, the same test administrator should be used on subsequent testing periods. If more than one person is to be used for skinfold measurements, each person should be checked for objectivity against a standard (i.e., an experienced tester).

The most frequently measured skinfold sites are the triceps, subscapular, suprailiac, thigh, abdomen, and chest. The specific anatomical locations are

Triceps: parallel muscle to the longitudinal axis of the upper arm measured at the midline halfway between the olecranon and acromion processes with the arm hanging freely at the side.

Subscapular: an oblique fold measured just below the inferior angle of the scapula.

Suprailiac: a slightly oblique fold that is lifted to follow the natural contour of the skinfold just above the iliac crest at the anterior axillary line.

Thigh: a vertical fold in the anterior midline of the thigh, taken midway between the patella and the hip.

Abdomen: a vertical fold measured 2 cm (1 inch) to the right of the umbilicus.

Chest: a diagonal fold located one-half of the distance between the anterior axillary line and the nipple for men and one-third of the distance for women.

These sites are illustrated in Figure 5.1. The skinfold, which is grasped between the thumb and

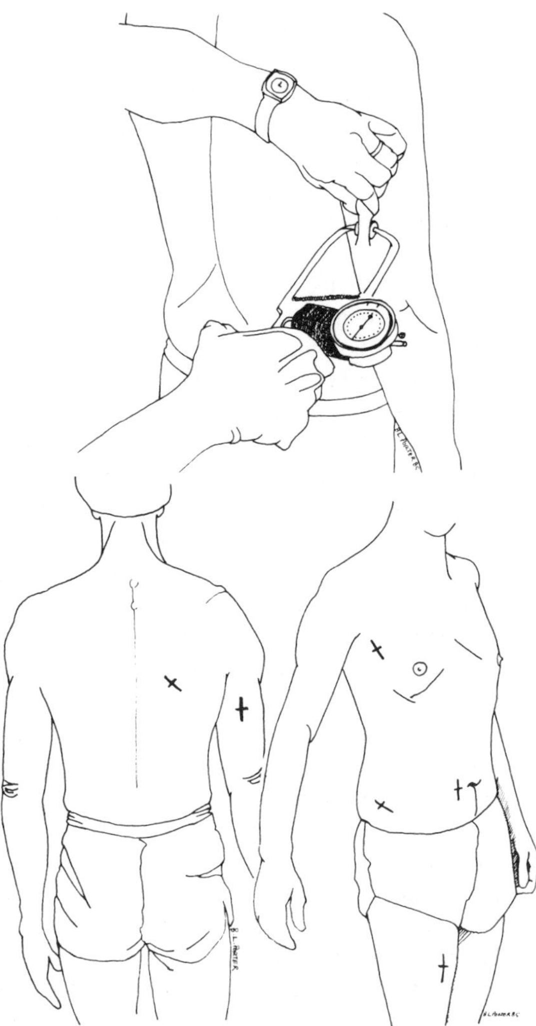

Figure 5.1 Skinfold sites used in the evaluation of body fatness.

[1]Quinton Instrument Co., Seattle, WA.

[2]Cambridge Scientific Industries, Cambridge, MD.

[3]For example, the Fat-O-Meter by Health Education Services Corp., Bensenville, IL.

forefinger, includes two thicknesses of skin and subcutaneous fat, but no muscle. The caliper is placed 1/2 inch above or below the finger, midway between the crest and the base of the skinfold. All measurements are conventionally made on the right side of the standing subject's body.

The values obtained from skinfold measurements can be used in several ways. Values from several sites can be totaled to arrive at the *sum of skinfolds*. The sum of skinfolds can be used to rank-order individuals within a given group. This indicates a person's relative fatness compared to others in the group. The sum of skinfolds can also be used to evaluate body fatness changes following dietary restriction and/or exercise conditioning programs. The use of sum of skinfolds can be recommended as a guide toward achieving the goal of decreasing the total amount of body fat, independent of a fixed body fat percentage. Using this approach, a person's sum of skinfolds is compared over time to assess relative changes in body fatness.

Another way the sum of skinfolds can be used is to determine percentile scores as in the AAHPERD health-related physical fitness test. Using the norms or percentile scores, the criterion for the desired degree of fatness is above the 50th percentile. Individuals below the 25th percentile need special programs to help them reach between the 25th and 50th percentile. Likewise, individuals between the 25th and 50th percentile can be encouraged to move above the 50th, and those people between the 50th and 75th percentile can move above the 75th percentile; individuals above the 75th percentile should be encouraged to maintain their low skinfold levels.

Skinfold measurements can also be used with mathematical equations to predict percentage of body fat. A word of caution is warranted regarding the more than 100 prediction equations available. These equations have been unequivocally proven to be more specific than general. That is, equations derived from one segment of the population do a poor job of predicting percentage of body fat when used on other populations. The equations are applicable only to groups similar in age and activity level to those from which the equations were derived. As might be expected, the equations are also gender specific. Most of the equations that exist were formulated with data from average college-age men and women and, therefore, are best applied to these populations. The equation specificity points out the need for discriminate use of some of these equations for very fat or very thin individuals, athletic men and women, or individuals involved in strenuous weight-training programs.

The regression equations combine such variables as skinfold, girth, height, and weight to most commonly predict body density and less often predict percentage body fat or lean body weight. Where body density is predicted, such as in underwater weighing, percent body fat is computed with formulas such as the following:

$$\text{Percent fat} = \frac{495}{\text{density}} - 450 \text{ (Siri, 1956)}$$

$$\text{Percent fat} = \frac{4.570}{\text{density}} - 4.12 \times 100 \text{ (Brozek et al., 1963)}$$

These equations provide similar values for percentage of body fat for a given body density value.

Discussion of the various regression equations that have been derived for various populations is beyond the scope of this chapter. For the HFI, a convenient method to determine body density, especially with large numbers of subjects, is to use one of the recently developed generalized equations. These equations can be used with samples that vary greatly in age and body fatness. The obvious advantage of generalized equations is that one equation replaces several, without compromising accuracy. The following generalized regression equations are recommended for the HFI. Separate equations are provided for men and women to account for sex differences:

Men:

$$\text{Body density} = 1.1125025 - 0.0013125(X_1) + 0.0000055(X_1)^2 - 0.0002440(X_2)$$

X_1 = sum of chest, triceps, and subscapular skinfolds

X_2 = age in years (Jackson & Pollock, 1985)

Women:

Body density = 1.089733 − 0.0009245(X_1) + 0.0000025$(X_1)^2$ − 0.0000979(X_2)

X_1 = sum of triceps, suprailiac, and abdominal skinfolds

X_2 = age in years (Jackson & Pollock, 1985)

Appendix C is provided to expedite the calculation of percent body fat from these equations. Because these equations were developed on men and women 18-61 years of age, their use is not recommended for subjects outside this age range. Furthermore, larger than normal prediction errors can be expected with extremely obese individuals. Therefore, these equations should be used cautiously with obese individuals.

The sum of skinfolds and percent body fat can also be used to broadly classify individuals as *lean, normal,* or *obese* (Tables 5.1 and 5.2). Because of the many factors that influence body weight and body fatness, making specific individual recommendations is difficult. Desirable body weight likely varies from individual to individual. Several key points need to be emphasized. First, as implied by Table 5.2, different standards are applied for different purposes. An athlete, for example, should expect to maintain a lower fat percentage than an individual desiring fitness for positive health. Second, desirable body fat percentages are presented as ranges in order to deal with the lack of precision in all of the methods used to arrive at these percentages. Finally, health problems seem to be associated with percent body fat in excess of 30% and 23% for females and males, respectively. Therefore, men and women should maintain body fat percentages of 14-17% and 21-24% or less, respectively. For people who have very high percentages of body fat, values higher than those recommended are more appropriate as initial goals. Table 5.3 includes typical percent body fat values for various segments of the population.

Table 5.1 Body Fat Norms Based on the Sum of Six Skinfolds[1]

Classification	Women (mm)	Men (mm)
Lean	<80-95	<75
Average	95-120	75-100
Above-normal fat	120-160	100-140
Obese	>160	>140

[1]The skinfold sites are the following: triceps, subscapular, chest, suprailiac, abdomen, thigh

Table 5.2 Body Fat Norms Based on Percent of Body Weight That is Fat

Classification	Women (% fat)	Men (% fat)
Essential fat	10.0-12.0%	2.0- 4.0%
Endurance athlete	14.0-16.0%	6.0- 8.0%
Athletes	17.0-20.0%	10.0-13.0%
Fitness	21.0-24.0%	14.0-17.0%
Borderline problem	25.0-29.0%	18.0-22.0%
Obese	30.0 and higher	23.0 and higher

Table 5.3 Typical Percent Body Fat Values for Various Population Groups

Population	Females	Males
World-class runners	14-18%	6.0-8.0%
College students	20-27%	12-17%
Active middle-aged	20-25%	15-20%
Sedentary middle-aged	25-35%	20-25%

Having determined the percentage of a person's body weight that is fat, simple calculations are used to arrive at a desirable body weight based on the present lean body weight.

1. Fat weight = current weight × $\frac{\% \text{ fat}}{100}$
2. Lean body weight (LBW) =

   current weight − fat weight
3. Desirable weight = $\frac{\text{LBW}}{1.00 - \% \text{ fat desired}}$
4. Desirable fat loss = Present weight − Desirable body weight

For example, assume a man weighs 190 lb and his skinfold measures or hydrostatic weighing indicate a body fat of 22%. Fifteen percent is in the desirable body fat range for men.

1. Fat weight = 190 lb x $\frac{22}{100}$ = 41.8 lb
2. LBW = 190 − 41.8 lb = 148.2 lb
3. Desirable weight =

   $\frac{148.2}{1 - (15\%/100)}$ = 174.4 lb
4. Desirable fat loss = 190 − 174.4 lb = 15.6 lb

A range of desirable weights should be used to account for the measurement error associated with estimating body fatness. Furthermore, individuals should be re-evaluated on these variables when they have reached the half-way points of their original goals.

Circumference Method

When other techniques are unavailable or cost-prohibitive, measuring the circumference of various body parts is a viable alternative. This technique is easy to learn, and, with practice, very consistent and accurate measurements can be obtained. Close attention should be paid to specific anatomical locations for these measurements. Tighten a standard measuring tape snugly but not so tightly as to cause skin indentation or pinching. A minimum of two measurements should be taken at each site, and the average value should be used as the circumference score. When the difference between the first two differs by more than 1%, a third measurement should be taken. Measurements should be accurately recorded in centimeters. The measurements obtained can be recorded and compared to previous or subsequent measurements to determine possible change.

The body sites most frequently recommended and the average circumference values given for various populations are listed in Table 5.4, followed by an anatomical description of these sites. By convention, measurements are generally made on the right side of the body.

Abdomen: 1/2 inch above the umbilicus.

Buttocks: the maximum protrusion with heels together.

Right thigh: the upper thigh, just below the buttocks.

Right upper arm: the midpoint between the shoulder and elbow with the straight arm extended in front of the body, palm up.

Table 5.4 Recommended Body Sites and Average Circumference Values for Various Populations

Recommended body sites			
Young women (17-26 years)	*Older women* (27-55 years)	*Young men* (17-26 years)	*Older men* (27-55 years)
1. Abdomen	Abdomen	Right upper arm	Buttocks
2. Right thigh	Right thigh	Abdomen	Abdomen
3. Right forearm	Right calf	Right forearm	Right forearm

Average values for circumferences, cm				
Sites	*Young women*	*Older women*	*Young men*	*Older men*
Midabdomen	72.3	82.7	78.8	91.1
Right forearm	22.6	24.4	26.0	29.2
Right thigh	55.5	57.6	55.4	59.0
Right calf	34.7	34.4	37.1	36.9
Right upper arm	25.2	28.6	27.7	34.0

Note. From *Nutrition, Weight Control, and Exercise* (p. 120 & 133) by F.I. Katch and W.D. McArdle, 1977, Boston: Houghton Mifflin Co. Copyright 1977 by Houghton Mifflin Co. Reprinted with permission.

Right forearm: the point of maximum circumference with arm extended in front, palm up.

Right calf: the area of maximum circumference, halfway between the knee and the ankle.

Caloric Balances and Weight Control

Caloric balance expresses the relationship between caloric intake and caloric expenditure (i.e., the number of calories taken in from food and drink compared to those expended by basal metabolism and voluntary activity). The energy balance equation expresses this relationship mathematically as

Caloric intake = Caloric expenditure.

A *calorie* is a unit of energy defined as the amount of heat necessary to raise the temperature of 1 g of water 1° C. In nutrition and exercise circles the term *calorie* is frequently used for what is actually a kilocalorie. A *kilocalorie* is the amount of heat needed to increase the temperature of 1 kg of water 1° C. One kcal equals 1,000 cal.

Several terms have evolved to refer to the various situations that can exist between these two variables. *Isocaloric Balance* defines a condition in which caloric intake and caloric expenditure are equal. For example, if a person consumes an average of 2,500 kcal per day and expends 2,500 kcal per day, the energy equation is in balance; tissue mass neither increases nor decreases.

When caloric intake exceeds caloric expenditure, a person is in *Positive Caloric Balance*. For example, a caloric intake of 2,800 kcal per day while expending only 2,500 kcal per day leads to a positive 300-kcal balance per day. These 300 kcal that are not expended by the body are stored as adipose tissue, resulting in weight gain.

If energy expenditure exceeds caloric intake, a person is in *Negative Caloric Balance*, or a caloric deficit exists. An example would be a person who consumes 2,500 kcal per day while expending 3,000 kcal. The 500-kcal caloric deficit leads to weight loss as the body primarily uses stored adipose tissue to meet its daily energy needs.

People in physical activity and weight-reduction programs need to know that a balance must be achieved between the number of calories taken in and the number expended in order to stay at the same weight. If more calories are consumed than expended, fat is stored in adipose tissue. One pound of adipose tissue equals 3,500 kcal. Thus if 3,500 more kcal are eaten than expended, 1 lb of adipose tissue is gained. Conversely, to lose 1 lb of body fat, a 3,500 kcal deficit must occur. A deficit of 500 kcal per day, therefore, leads to the loss of approximately 1 lb of adipose tissue in 1 week.

Negative caloric balance can be attained by decreasing caloric intake, increasing energy expenditure through exercise, or combining a decrease in caloric intake and participation in regular physical activity. As discussed in a subsequent section, a combination of restricted caloric intake and exercise is recommended. In any case, daily caloric deficit should not exceed 1,000-1,200 kcal per day. This results in a fat loss of approximately 2 lb per week.

Total caloric intake comes from the consumption of foods and drinks. The carbohydrates, fat, and proteins in these foods contain energy which can be expressed as heat energy or in terms of kilocalories. The number of kilocalories in a particular food can be determined in a bomb calorimeter. In this procedure, foods are combusted in a water-insulated chamber. The amount of heat absorbed by the water as the food is burned is used to determine how many calories the food contains.

Many factors affect a person's caloric intake at any particular time. Included among these are cultural and family influences. Some people react to various emotional states such as stress or depression by over- or undereating. Various physiological mechanisms may influence food intake. Hormonal or central nervous regulatory mechanisms may be impaired, leading to overconsumption of food.

Total caloric expenditure, or the number of calories used by the body, is determined by basal metabolism and voluntary metabolism. Basal metabolism is the energy expended when the body is at rest. Basal metabolic rate (BMR) is usually measured at least 12 hr after the last meal (i.e., postabsorptive state) and at least 12 hr after muscular activity. The BMR can be directly measured using calorimeters constructed for this purpose. However, because of practical considerations, BMR is usually determined by indirect calorimetry. In this procedure, the amount of oxygen consumed and carbon dioxide produced is measured, with the person supine in a quiet, comfortable room. Oxygen consumption can be related to the number of calories expended in the basal state because approximately 5 kcal are produced per liter of oxygen consumed. Since BMRs are difficult and time-consuming measurements, a person's daily basal metabolism can be conveniently estimated by multiplying the body weight in pounds by 12 kcal per pound. For example, a 200-lb male expends approximately 2,400 kcal per day for the body's basal activities.

Basal metabolic rate (BMR) is influenced by several factors; the primary determinant is body size. Specifically, BMR is in direct proportion to body surface area, which is related to height and weight. BMR decreases with age and is highest in a growing child. The decrease with advancing age may be because of muscle tissue loss. Even when corrections are made for body size, women have lower BMRs than men. Extremely muscular individuals frequently have higher BMRs than their inactive counterparts, presumably because of increased muscular tone.

Voluntary metabolism is the energy required for muscle contraction and represents all of the energy expended by the body above the BMR. The number of calories expended by voluntary activity depends primarily on body weight and the amount of physical activity in which a person engages. Caloric expenditure is directly related to an individual's body weight. If two people, one weighing 100 lb and the other weighing 130 lb, jog 1 mi together, the heavier person will expend more energy. In addition, caloric expenditure is directly proportional to the amount of physical activity involved. Thus the caloric cost of running or jogging is greater than for walking.

Basal metabolic rate can be measured directly or indirectly, as already described. The limited size of calorimeters constructed to accommodate humans presents practical difficulty in determining the caloric cost of various physical activities. Therefore, the caloric expenditure of various physical activities is determined almost exclusively by indirect calorimetry. In this procedure, the oxygen consumed during various activities is measured. Like the BMR, oxygen consumption can be related to caloric expenditure because approximately 5 kcal are expended for each liter of oxygen consumed. The caloric cost of various activities is discussed in chapter 10.

Several convenient methods can be used to estimate a person's daily total caloric expenditure. Because the caloric costs of many activities have been determined, daily energy expenditure can be approximated by keeping a minute-by-minute daily activity record and finding the caloric cost of the activities. Adding together the cost of all activities provides an estimation of the total daily expenditure. This method of estimation is cumbersome, and precisely recording all activities in an entire day is difficult. Furthermore, as previously mentioned, caloric costs of activities depend on the amount of physical activity involved. For example, many of the available caloric cost tables fail to indicate whether the reported cost of a given activity was determined at a leisurely or a fast pace.

Several techniques exist to estimate energy expenditure based on body weight and estimate how physically active a person is during the day. Two of these methods are outlined:

Method One

1. Estimate your level of physical activity according to the following table.
2. To get an estimation of daily caloric expenditure, multiply the number that represents the number of calories expended per pound of body weight by body weight in pounds.

Example:

A 120-lb woman has a somewhat active lifestyle.

15 kcal/lb × 120 lb = 1,800 kcal/day

Method Two

1. Multiply a person's body weight in pounds by 11 kcal/lb.
2. Add 400-800 kcal, depending on whether the person is sedentary or very active.

Example:

A 165-lb man is somewhat active.

165 lb × 11 kcal/lb = 1,815 kcal

1,815 kcal + 600 kcal = 2,415 kcal/day

Interaction of Diet and Exercise

One way the energy equation can be unbalanced to achieve weight reduction is to reduce caloric intake. For example, a woman may consume an average of 2,650 kcal each day. If she reduces her caloric intake by 500 kcal per day to 2,150 kcal

Men	(kcal/lb)	Women	(kcal/lb)
Sedentary	15 or 16	Sedentary	13 or 14
Somewhat active	17 or 18	Somewhat active	15 or 16
Active	19	Active	17

and maintains the same level of physical activity, she will lose approximately 1 lb of body fat per week. By maintaining this reduced intake she will lose approximately 4 lb per month, or 48 lb per year. However, a serious drawback to weight reduction by caloric restriction alone is apparent. Research has shown that 35-45% of the weight loss is lean body tissue with this method of weight control.

Exercise can also be used to produce a caloric deficit. To achieve the same daily 500-kcal deficit as above using exercise alone would require that a person do the equivalent of a 5-mi run or jog each day. Such a commitment is overwhelming for almost anybody. Regarding body composition changes, it has been shown that regular exercise generally leads to the loss of body weight accompanied by a decrease in the percentage of body fat. Lean body mass may increase or not change.

A more reasonable way to create a caloric deficit is through a combination of caloric restriction and exercise. For example, caloric intake can be decreased by 300 kcal per day and caloric expenditure can be increased by 200 kcal per day (equivalent to a 2-mi run/jog). This leads to the same loss of approximately 1 lb of fat per week. However, more fat loss occurs with this method than with caloric restriction alone, and less than one half of the lean muscle mass loss occurs. Additional advantages are increased muscle tone and improved cardiovascular fitness.

Also, consider the consequences of weight gain resulting from a positive caloric balance. If caloric intake exceeds caloric expenditure and a person is engaging in a strenuous exercise program, weight gain is primarily in the form of muscle gain. Because of the hormone testosterone, muscle weight gain is more true of men than women. On the other hand, if a person is engaging in moderate or no exercise and caloric intake exceeds expenditure, then the weight gain is in the form of fat. If caloric consumption and expenditure are in balance and a person engages in regular exercise, body weight remains about the same. However, lean muscle mass increases and fat tissue correspondingly decreases. Conversely, if a person is in caloric balance and decreases the physical activity level, lean muscle mass is lost and fat tissue increases.

Basic Foods and Functions

Clear evidence shows that diet and nutrition are of considerable importance to positive health. Daily dietary habits can influence the risk of developing heart disease, stroke, high blood pressure, and, one of America's leading health problems, obesity, which is often linked to an increase in the incidence of diabetes.

A healthy diet depends not on any single nutrient or group of nutrients; rather, the overall structure of the diet is important. Individual foods are not nutritionally complete. A basic nutritional principle is to consume a wide variety of foods containing complementary patterns of nutrients. This is the premise behind structuring the diet according to the Basic Four Food Groups discussed in a later section. Foods are placed in a particular group because the foods in that group tend to contain the same nutrients. Thus, by choosing foods from all four of the basic groups, the nutritional needs of the body are easily met.

More than 50 known nutrients are needed by the body. The nutrients are divided into carbohydrates, fats, proteins, vitamins, minerals, and water. This section discusses each of these basic foods, including their functions and food sources. Where appropriate, their roles as energy sources during exercise are addressed.

Carbohydrates

Carbohydrates are commonly referred to as sugars or starches. Sugars are monosaccharides such as glucose, galactose, and fructose. Vegetables, fruits, grains, and refined sugar are sources of glucose. Fruits and sugars also provide fructose, while galactose is primarily supplied by milk products. Three or more molecules of monosaccharides form a polysaccharide or starch. Vegetable foods such as potatoes, beans, corn, and peas contain polysaccharides, as do various grains used in breads, cereals, pastries, and spaghetti. Currently 40-50% of the caloric intake in the average American diet comes from carbohydrates. The recommendation is to increase this to 55-60% while deriving less from refined sugar and more from complex carbohydrates including vegetables, fruits, cereals, and breads.

Carbohydrates are a primary source for the production of ATP. This includes blood glucose which is used by all tissues in the body and is the exclusive energy source for the central nervous system. In addition, liver and muscle tissues store excess carbohydrates in the form of many glucose molecules linked together to form large glycogen molecules.

Fats

Fats found in the body are classified as simple fats, compound fats, and derived fats. These are also referred to, respectively, as triglycerides, phospholipids, and cholesterol. Triglycerides, consisting of a glycerol and three fatty acid molecules, represent more than 90% of the fat stored in the body. Fatty acids differ in the number of carbon atoms they contain and the degree of saturation of the carbon atoms in the fatty acid chain with hydrogen. Free fatty acids are *saturated* when the carbon atoms are saturated with hydrogen atoms or *unsaturated* when the carbon atoms are not saturated with hydrogen atoms. Fats with large amounts of saturated fats are solid at room temperature and come primarily from animal sources. Beef, pork, lamb, shellfish, and dairy products contain high levels of saturated fats. Unsaturated fats, which are liquid at room temperature, are vegetable oils such as corn oil, cottonseed oil, peanut oil, and soybean oil. The compound fats, particularly lipoproteins, and derived fats such as cholesterol are discussed in the section dealing with diet, exercise, and lipids.

Because of the large quantities stored in adipose tissue and muscle tissue throughout the body, triglycerides represent a large potential energy store. In addition, they are a concentrated source of energy; 1 g of fat contains 9 kcal, more than twice the energy provided by carbohydrates or proteins. Besides their energy supplying functions, fats protect vital organs against trauma and insulate during cold exposure. Dietary fats also transport the fat-soluble vitamins A, D, E, and K throughout the body.

Proteins

Protein is constructed from separate subunits called amino acids, arranged in various chemical and physical configurations. Of the 22 different amino acids required by the body, eight are considered *indispensable* because of the body's inability to synthesize them. They must, therefore, be provided in the dietary intake. Dietary proteins vary in amino acid composition and in their provision of the indispensable amino acids for protein synthesis. Animal proteins such as meat, fish, poultry, milk, and eggs are high-quality proteins because they contain all eight indispensable amino acids. Because certain amino acids are missing, plant sources are lower in quality. The protein requirement can be met on a vegetarian diet, but combinations of foods must be carefully planned because indispensable amino acids must be consumed together to be synthesized together into proteins.

The daily protein requirement is 0.8–0.9 g of protein per kilogram of body weight. For children, this value increases to approximately 3 g per kilogram of body weight. Contrary to popular belief, protein is the least important nutrient as an energy source at rest or during exercise. Its key value is to furnish the chemical building blocks for bodily structures. Under resting conditions, protein metabolism equals 3.1 g/hr and supplies approximately 17% of the body's energy needs. During exercise, the rate of protein metabolism as measured by nitrogen excretion remains at 3.1 g/hr. Because the metabolic rate is elevated by a factor of 10 or more above the resting level during exercise, protein constitutes less than 2% of the energy for muscular work. Thus carbohydrates and fats are the primary fuels of concern during exercise.

Research has demonstrated that protein requirements do not increase with activity, either for energy needs or for increased muscle mass. Like excess calories from any nutrient, additional protein calories are converted to and stored as fat, primarily in adipose tissue. A commonly held myth is that athletes involved in strength programs and growing athletes have special requirements for supplemental protein. The excess calories typically consumed by these individuals should meet any additional protein needs. An intake of 1 g of protein per kilogram body weight provides a sufficient margin of safety for any increase in body mass that occurs in adult athletes.

The chemical composition of carbohydrates, fats, and proteins dictates that different amounts of oxygen are required for their oxidation. Likewise, the caloric value of 1 ℓ of oxygen depends on the nutrient being metabolized. A useful calculation in determining the nutrient being utilized and its caloric equivalent is the respiratory quotient (RQ), which is defined as the ratio of carbon dioxide produced to oxygen consumed during the same period of time. The same measurement made at the lung level is referred to as the respiratory exchange ratio (R). Under conditions of steady state, without hyperventilation or appreciable amounts of lactic acid being produced, the respiratory exchange ratio is assumed to represent metabolic activity at the cellular level. This calculation is useful during exercise as an indicator of the relative utilization of the various nutrients for energy. Because protein constitutes less than 2% of the energy for muscular work, the use of a nonprotein RQ during exercise is legitimate. RQ, therefore, indicates the relative usage of carbohydrates and fats.

During the oxidation of carbohydrates, all oxygen consumed is used to oxidize the carbon from the carbohydrate molecule to carbon dioxide. Therefore, an RQ of 1.0 would be expected for a pure carbohydrate:

$$C_6H_{12}O_6 + 6\ O_2 \rightarrow 6\ CO_2 + 6\ H_2O$$

$$RQ = \frac{\dot{V}CO_2}{\dot{V}O_2} = \frac{6\ CO_2}{6\ O_2} = 1.0$$

When fats are utilized for fuel, more oxygen is required for oxidation to carbon dioxide and water. For example, for palmitic acid, 23 oxygen molecules are consumed to produce 16 carbon dioxide molecules:

$$C_{16}H_{32}O_2 + 23\ O_2 \rightarrow 16\ CO_2 + 16\ H_2O$$

$$RQ = \frac{16\ CO_2}{23\ O_2} = 0.696$$

The RQ for the oxidation of 100% fat is considered to be 0.70. Obviously, pure carbohydrates or pure fats are rarely oxidized, but instead are a mixture of these nutrients. An R of 0.85 would represent the metabolism of a mixture of 50% carbohydrate and 50% fat.

At rest, carbohydrates, fats, and protein contribute to energy needs. During light exercise protein's contribution to energy expenditure is reduced, and carbohydrate and fat contribute equally to energy expenditure. Thereafter, R clearly increases as the intensity of exercise increases, indicating a predominant shift to carbohydrate metabolism. During moderate-intensity exercise, however, R progressively decreases with increasing duration as fat becomes the fuel of choice.

Vitamins

Vitamins as a group of nutrients have attracted considerable attention. The importance of these organic substances has long been known. Contrary to popular opinion, however, they provide no calories and therefore cannot increase a person's level of energy. Because the body generally cannot manufacture vitamins, they are required in the diet in very small amounts (i.e., milligram or microgram quantities).

The 14 known vitamins are classified as water soluble or fat soluble. Daily intake of the four fat-soluble vitamins, A, D, E, and K, is not necessary because they can be stored in the fat tissues of the body. The water-soluble vitamins include 8 B-complex vitamins and vitamin C. Because water-soluble vitamins are not stored in the body, adequate daily consumption is essential. Excess water-soluble vitamins are eventually eliminated via the urine or sweat.

Marginal nutrient intakes exist in some segments of the population; vitamin supplementation in these instances is justified. Likewise, vitamins are correctly prescribed for pregnant women and infants. While in the normal population a daily multivitamin is no reason for alarm, such supplementation is not a suitable remedy for poor dietary habits. The potentially dangerous megadosing of vitamins is strongly discouraged. Taking too many vitamins is economically unjustified and may pose serious health hazards. Because of their storage capabilities, megadoses of fat-soluble vitamins can lead to conditions of hypervitaminosis with potentially severe consequences. Furthermore, recent studies indicate that water-soluble vitamins, once thought to be safe, also pose dangers when ingested in excessive amounts.

Vitamins have various functions; most of them are involved in regulating the metabolic reactions whereby energy is released from carbohydrates, fats, and proteins. Generally, they serve as coenzymes by assisting enzymes in carrying out their functions. Table 5.5 summarizes the primary functions of each of the vitamins.

Minerals

Minerals are inorganic compounds that are found in minuscule quantities in the body and that carry out a wide range of functions. Major minerals, or macrominerals, are present in comparatively large quantities and include calcium, potassium, magnesium, sulfur, sodium, and chloride. Iron, iodine, copper, zinc, fluorine, selenium, manganese, molybdenum, and chromium compose the trace minerals, or microminerals. The key function of minerals is as enzyme components in cellular metabolism.

The daily requirement of essential minerals can usually be met through the foods a person eats; supplementation is generally not necessary. Exceptions to this may include calcium among the macrominerals and iron and zinc from the microminerals. Iron-deficiency anemia is the nation's most common nutritional deficiency. American women of child-bearing age, infants, young children, and adolescents are most likely to suffer. Since only a small percentage of iron consumed is absorbed, dietary intake must exceed the actual

Table 5.5 Vitamins and Their Functions

Vitamin	Function	Sources
Thiamin (B-1)	Functions as part of a coenzyme to aid utilization of energy	Whole grains, nuts, lean pork
Riboflavin (B-2)	Involved in energy metabolism as part of a coenzyme	Milk, yogurt, cheese
Niacin	Facilitates energy production in cells	Lean meat, fish, poultry, grains
Vitamin B-6	Absorbs and metabolizes protein; aids in red blood cell formation	Lean meat, vegetables, whole grains
Pantothenic acid	Aids in metabolism of carbohydrate, fat, and protein	Whole grain cereals, bread, dark green vegetables
Folic acid	Functions as coenzyme in synthesis of nucleic acids and protein synthesis	Green vegetables, beans, whole wheat products
Vitamin B-12	Involved in synthesis of nucleic acids, red blood cell formation	Only in animal foods, not plant foods
Biotin	Coenzyme in synthesis of fatty acids and glycogen formation	Egg yolk, dark green vegetables
Choline	Precursor of neurotransmitter acetylcholine	Egg yolks, grains
C	Intracellular maintenance of bone, capillaries, and teeth	Citrus fruits, green peppers, tomatoes
A	Functions in visual processes; formation and maintenance of skin and mucous membranes	Carrots, sweet potatoes, margarine, butter, liver
D	Aids in growth and formation of bones and teeth; promotes calcium absorption	Eggs, tuna, liver, fortified milk
E	Forms red blood cells and muscles; prevents cell membrane damage	Vegetable oils, whole grain cereal and bread, green leafy vegetables
K	Important in blood-clotting	Green leafy vegetables, peas, potatoes

need. Rich sources of iron are organ meats, such as kidney, heart, and liver, and beans, peas, and green vegetables.

Water

Although it contains no calories and does not contribute any nutrients to the diet, water is necessary for life. It serves as a transport mechanism for nutrients, gases and waste products. It is also involved in heat-regulating functions of the body.

Dietary Goals and Evaluation of Dietary Intake

Beginning in the 1970s, Americans became increasingly interested in nutrition, partly as a result of scientific research linking America's leading ills to poor nutritional habits. An evaluation by the Senate Select Committee on Nutrition and Human Needs indicated that the typical American diet contains too much fat (particularly saturated fat), too much refined sugar, and too many calories. One third of the fat is saturated fat and most of the dietary protein comes from animal sources and is rich in fat and cholesterol. Based on this evaluation, the Committee made some general recommendations to ease nutrition-related diseases, including heart disease, stroke, and obesity. Accepting the initiative from the Senate Committee, other agencies such as the U.S. Departments of Agriculture and Health, Education, and Welfare have made similar recommendations. Figure 5.2 presents a comparison of current eating trends and the recommended guidelines. To meet these guidelines, more fruits, vegetables, and whole grains should be consumed, accompanying a decrease in refined sugars and flours, egg yolks, and other foods high in fat and cholesterol. In addition, eating meats, fish, and poultry that contain less fat and cholesterol is encouraged. A further recommendation is to reduce salt intake to less than 5 g per day and cholesterol to 300 mg per day. The values for these two nutrients are less than one half of that currently contained in the American diet.

These guidelines are clearly beginning to shape America's nutritional behavior. Remember that the overall structure of the diet is important, rather

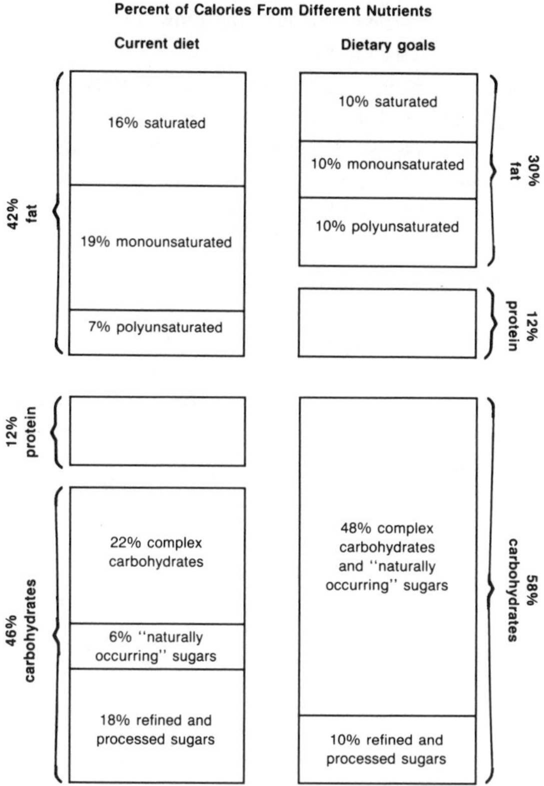

Figure 5.2 Dietary goals for the United States. From Senate Select Committee on Nutrition and Human Needs. Used with permission.

than an underemphasis or overemphasis on certain food items. This means that variety in selection should be emphasized as the easiest and most realistic way to achieve the dietary recommendations. Likewise, a gradual change in a person's eating habits is preferred over immediate drastic changes that may lead to resentment and poor adherence.

The Recommended Dietary Allowances, or RDAs (see Table 5.6), established by the National Research Council of the National Academy of Sciences, are the levels of intake of essential nutrients considered to be adequate to meet the needs of almost all healthy people. The RDAs are to be applied to population groups and should not be confused with requirements for a specific individual. They are designed to meet the needs of 98% of the population. They represent acceptable nutrient intake for nearly all healthy people and are generous levels for most people. The RDAs are established by estimating average population requirements and variability for each nutrient. This number is then increased to meet the needs of 90% of the population, followed by an additional increase in the allowance to counter inefficient nutrient utilization such as poor absorption or inadequate conversion of a precursor to an active form. Therefore, in order to meet the needs of those individuals with the highest requirements, the RDAs exceed what most people require. For ease of application, the RDAs are recommended as daily allowances. There is no cause for alarm, though, if a person's diet is below one day and above the next day, because mechanisms exist to compensate for previous deficiencies. Averaging intakes over a period of several days to a week is acceptable.

In addition to those nutrients for which the RDA has been established, some nutrients are listed as estimated safe and adequate daily dietary intakes. The levels for these nutrients, which are listed in

Table 5.6 **Recommended Daily Dietary Allowances,[a] Revised 1980**
Designed for the maintenance of good nutrition of practically all healthy people in the U.S.A.

							Fat-Soluble Vitamins				Water-Soluble Vitamins						Minerals					
	Age (years)	Weight (kg)	(lbs)	Height (cm)	(in)	Protein (g)	Vitamin A (μg R.E.)[b]	Vitamin D (μg)[c]	Vitamin E (mg α T.E.)[d]	Vitamin C (mg)	Thiamin (mg)	Riboflavin (mg)	Niacin (mg N.E.)[e]	Vitamin B_6 (mg)	Folacin[f] (μg)	Vitamin B_{12} (μg)	Calcium (mg)	Phosphorus (mg)	Magnesium (mg)	Iron (mg)	Zinc (mg)	Iodine (μg)
Infants	0.0-0.5	6	13	60	24	kg × 2.2	420	10	3	35	0.3	0.4	6	0.3	30	0.5[g]	360	240	50	10	3	40
	0.5-1.0	9	20	71	28	kg × 2.0	400	10	4	35	0.5	0.6	8	0.6	45	1.5	540	360	70	15	5	50
Children	1- 3	13	29	90	35	23	400	10	5	45	0.7	0.8	9	0.9	100	2.0	800	800	150	15	10	70
	4- 6	20	44	112	44	30	500	10	6	45	0.9	1.0	11	1.3	200	2.5	800	800	200	10	10	90
	7-10	28	62	132	52	34	700	10	7	45	1.2	1.4	16	1.6	300	3.0	800	800	250	10	10	120
Males	11-14	45	99	157	62	45	1000	10	8	50	1.4	1.6	18	1.8	400	3.0	1200	1200	350	18	15	150
	15-18	66	145	176	69	56	1000	10	10	60	1.4	1.7	18	2.0	400	3.0	1200	1200	400	18	15	150
	19-22	70	154	177	70	56	1000	7.5	10	60	1.5	1.7	19	2.2	400	3.0	800	800	350	10	15	150
	23-50	70	154	178	70	56	1000	5	10	60	1.4	1.6	18	2.2	400	3.0	800	800	350	10	15	150
	51 +	70	154	178	70	56	1000	5	10	60	1.2	1.4	16	2.2	400	3.0	800	800	350	10	15	150
Females	11-14	46	101	157	62	46	800	10	8	50	1.1	1.3	15	1.8	400	3.0	1200	1200	300	18	15	150
	15-18	55	120	163	64	46	800	10	8	60	1.1	1.3	14	2.0	400	3.0	1200	1200	300	18	15	150
	19-22	55	120	163	64	44	800	7.5	8	60	1.1	1.3	14	2.0	400	3.0	800	800	300	18	15	150
	23-50	55	120	163	54	44	800	5	8	60	1.0	1.2	13	2.0	400	3.0	800	800	300	18	15	150
	51 +	55	120	163	54	44	800	5	8	60	1.0	1.2	13	2.0	400	3.0	800	800	300	10	15	150
Pregnant						+30	+200	+5	+2	+20	0.4	+0.3	+2	+0.6	+400	+1.0	+400	+400	+150	h	+5	+25
Lactating						+20	+400	+5	+3	+40	+0.5	+0.5	+5	+0.5	+100	+1.0	+400	+400	+150	h	+10	+50

[a]The allowances are intended to provide for individual variations among most normal persons as they live in the United States under usual environmental stresses. Diets should be based on a variety of common foods in order to provide other nutrients for which human requirements have been less well defined. See Table 12.2 for heights, weights and recommended intake.

[b]Retinol equivalents. 1 Retinol equivalent = 1 φg retinol or 6 φg β carotene.

[c]As cholecalciferol. 10 φg cholecalciferol = 400 I.U. vitamin D.

[d]α-tocopherol equivalents. 1 mg d-α-tocopherol = 1 α T.E.

[e]1 N.E. (niacin equivalent) is equal to 1 mg of niacin or 60 mg of dietary tryptophan.

Note. From "Recommended Dietary Allowance," Revised 1980, by the Food and Nutrition Board, National Academy of Sciences, National Research Council. As appears in *Dairy Council Digest*, **51**:2 March-April. Reprinted with permission of the National Dairy Council.

[f]The folacin allowances refer to dietary sources as determined by *Lactobacillus casei assay* after treatment with enzymes ("conjugases") to make polyglutamyl forms of the vitamin available to the test organism.

[g]The RDA for vitamin B_{12} in infants is based on average concentration of the vitamin in human milk. The allowances after weaning are based on energy intake (as recommended by the American Academy of Pediatrics) and consideration of other factors such as intestinal absorption.

[h]The increased requirement during pregnancy cannot be met by the iron content of habitual American diets nor by the existing iron stores of many women; therefore the use of 30-60 mg of supplemental iron is recommended. Iron needs during lactation are not substantially different from those of nonpregnant women, but continued supplementation of the mother for 2-3 months after parturition is advisable in order to replenish stores depleted by pregnancy.

Table 5.7, are based on less complete data than the RDA and are presented as ranges. They serve as useful guides and represent the best available knowledge.

Of the approximately 50 known nutrients, the RDAs have been determined for some, and estimated safe and adequate intake ranges have been identified for others. Some nutrients, however, are known to be required but have no established allowances. It is, therefore, assumed that attempts to achieve the recommended dietary allowances are based on a wide variety of food selections. A varied diet that meets the requirements of known nutrients also likely satisfies the requirements of those nutrients for which no allowance has been established.

The USRDAs were developed by the Food and Drug Administration to be used for nutritional labeling. The 26 age and gender categories of the RDA have been condensed into four groups: infants, children under 4 years of age, males and females over 4 years old, and pregnant and lactating women. For several reasons, the USRDA on food labels exceeds the requirements of most people. In addition to the added amounts included in the RDA, the USRDAs for males and females over 4 years of age are based on the highest RDA (i.e., those for teenage boys).

The nutritional guidelines discussed are designed to serve as useful guides in food selection. Nevertheless, meal planning should not become a mathematical frustration. Variety with enjoyable foods is the most important factor in meal planning, because unappealing foods that are not eaten have no nutritional value. Several methods are available to aid the nutritionally conscious person in meeting the suggested dietary standards. Perhaps the best known of these is the Basic Four Food Groups, which is a convenient grouping of foods based on similar nutrient content. Foods are placed into one of the four groups:

1. Meat, Fish, and Poultry,
2. Milk and Milk Products,
3. Bread and Cereal, and
4. Fruit and Vegetables.

Adequate nutrition is based on combining specified numbers of servings of foods chosen from

Table 5.7 Estimated Safe and Adequate Daily Dietary Intakes of Selected Vitamins and Minerals[a]

		Vitamins			Trace Elements[b]						Electrolytes		
	Age (years)	Vitamin K (µg)	Biotin (µg)	Pantothenic Acid (mg)	Copper (mg)	Manganese (mg)	Fluoride (mg)	Chromium (mg)	Selenium (mg)	Molybdenum (mg)	Sodium (mg)	Potassium (mg)	Chloride (mg)
Infants	0-0.5	12	35	2	0.5-0.7	0.5-0.7	0.1-0.5	0.01-0.04	0.01-0.04	0.03-0.06	115- 350	350- 925	275- 700
	0.5-1	10-20	50	3	0.7-1.0	0.7-1.0	0.2-1.0	0.02-0.06	0.02-0.06	0.04-0.08	250- 750	425-1275	400-1200
Children	1-3	15-30	65	3	1.0-1.5	1.0-1.5	0.5-1.5	0.02-0.08	0.02-0.08	0.05-0.1	325- 975	550-1650	500-1500
and	4-6	20-40	85	3-4	1.5-2.0	1.5-2.0	1.0-2.5	0.03-0.12	0.03-0.12	0.06-0.15	450-1350	775-2325	700-2100
Adolescents	7-10	30-60	120	4-5	2.0-2.5	2.0-3.0	1.5-2.5	0.05-0.2	0.05-0.2	0.1 -0.3	600-1800	1000-3000	925-2775
	11 +	50-100	100-200	4-7	2.0-3.0	2.5-5.0	1.5-2.5	0.05-0.2	0.05-0.2	0.15-0.5	900-2700	1525-4575	1400-4200
Adults		70-140	100-200	4-7	2.0-3.0	2.5-5.0	1.5-4.0	0.05-0.2	0.05-0.2	0.15-0.5	1100-3300	1875-5625	1700-5100

As appears in *Dairy Council Digest*, Vol. 51, No. 2, March-April 1980.

[a]Because there is less information on which to base allowances, these figures are not given in the main table of the RDA and are provided here in the form of ranges of recommended intakes.

[b]Since the toxic levels for many trace elements may be only several times usual intakes, the upper levels for the trace elements given in this table should not be habitually exceeded.

Note. From "Recommended Dietary Allowances," Revised, 1980, by the Food and Nutrition Board, National Academy of Sciences, National Research Council. As appears in Dairy Council Digest, 51:2 March-April. Reprinted with permission of the National Dairy Council.

each group to receive all of the required nutrients (Table 5.8). Even diets that meet the requirements of the Basic Four Food Groups are frequently deficient in Vitamins E and B-6, magnesium, zinc, and iron. The following modifications of the Basic Four are recommended to compensate for these common deficiencies. The meat group should be met using low-fat meats and protein from vegetable sources. Foods high in saturated fat, salt, and refined sugar should be strongly discouraged. Likewise, cooking methods that limit excess fat, salt, and sugar should be used. People should be encouraged to meet the dairy requirement by using products containing less than 2% fat. Selections from the bread and cereal group should include whole-grain products. Finally, the fruits and vegetables group should include daily servings of a dark green vegetable and a food rich in Vitamin C.

Dietary Exchange Lists are another popular dietary management system. Although they were first developed for diabetics, their use has been extended to others who require a more structured dietary regimen, particularly for weight management, through the combined efforts of the American Diabetes Association and the American Dietetic Association. The exchange list consists of six groups of foods that are placed together in a particular group because of similar nutrient and caloric values. Therefore, foods within a group may be "exchanged" for one another.

Another new concept in nutrition education is *nutrient density*. The nutrient density of a food measures the amount of proteins, carbohydrates,

Table 5.8 The Basic Four Food Groups

Food Group	Daily Servings			Main Nutrients
	Child	Teen	Adult	
Milk[a]	3	4	2	Vitamin D Calcium Riboflavin Protein
Meat[b]	2	2	2	Protein Calcium Iron Thiamin Riboflavin
Fruit/vegetable[c]	4	4	4	Vitamin A Vitamin C Carbohydrate
Bread/cereal[d]	4	4	4	Carbohydrate Thiamin Iron Niacin

The following equal one serving:

[a]1 cup of milk or yogurt *or* calcium equivalent:
1-1/2 oz. cheese
1 cup pudding
2 cups cottage cheese

[b]2-3 oz. lean cooked meat, fish, poultry, *or* protein equivalent:
2 eggs
2 oz. cheese
1 cup beans, peas
1/2 cup cottage cheese

[c]Include one good source of Vitamin C
1 cup raw
1/2 cup juice

[d]1 slice bread
1 cup cereal

fats, vitamins, and minerals per 100 kcal of the food. Low-nutrient-density foods, foods rich in calories containing a low level of essential nutrients, should be discouraged, particularly for those people on caloric-restrictive diets. As calories are restricted, the nutrient density of foods should be higher to assure that the person will receive all of the required nutrients.

Success in changing a person's dietary habits depends on determining what, how, and how much is eaten. A simple dietary history should be taken before making specific recommendations. In addition to a diet history, people should complete a daily record of foods eaten or dietary recall. Answers to questions similar to those in Table 5.9 provide insight into how a person's lifestyle affects his or her dietary choices.

The caloric content of each food is found from available tables, and the total daily caloric intake is determined. Inexpensive calorie counting guides that list most food items are available; many guides list foods according to commercial brand names (see Appendix D). The emphasis is to maintain an accurate record for at least 7 days and meticulously record everything that is eaten. Because eating patterns are significantly different on Saturdays and Sundays than on other days of the week, the food record must include a weekend sequence. Assistance should be given in analyzing the food diary to discover poor eating habits with suggestions made for eliminating poor habits and developing new, more appropriate habits.

Studies show that many factors besides food influence eating behavior. Included among these are certain places, life events, and emotions. Recording the time of eating, mood, degree of hunger, associated activity, and place of eating with the types and quantity of foods eaten provides additional information that may be valuable in restructuring a person's eating habits. Table 5.10 presents

Table 5.9 Suggested Questions for a Dietary History

1. How often do you eat?
2. Do you enjoy eating?
3. Do you eat only when you are hungry or do you eat according to a time schedule?
4. What time do you eat meals? Snacks?
5. What foods do you eat most often?
6. What are your favorite snacks?
7. What are some of your least favorite foods?
8. How long does it take you to eat a meal?
9. Would you estimate that you eat more or less than most other people?
10. Do you or have you recently followed any special diet plan? If so, describe it.
11. Do you take vitamin supplements?
12. Describe your use of fats and oils.
13. Do you add salt to foods during cooking? At the table?
14. What kinds of meat and dairy products do you normally eat?
15. How are most of your foods prepared?
16. How long has your weight been about what it is now?
17. Who usually cooks the food if you eat at home?
18. How often do you eat out? For what meals?

Note. Adapted from "Choosing Foods for Health" by G.A. Leveille and A. Dean, 1979. In D.T. Mason and H. Guthrie (Eds.), *The Medicine Called Nutrition* (pg. 25), Englewood Cliffs, NJ: Best Foods. Reprinted by permission of Mazola Nutrition/Health Information Service.

Table 5.10 Suggested Dietary Recall Format

	Time	Food	Amount	Calories	Where are you?	Who is with you?	What are you doing?	How do you feel?
Day 1 Breakfast								
Lunch								
Dinner								
Day 2 Breakfast								
Lunch								
Dinner								
Day 3 Breakfast								
Lunch								
Dinner								

Note. Adapted from *Nutrition, Weight Control, and Exercise* (p. 164) by F.I. Katch and W.D. McArdle, 1977, Boston: Houghton Mifflin Co. And from *Slim Chance in a Fat World: Behavioral Control of Obesity* by R.B. Stuart and B. Davies, 1971, Champaign, IL: Research Press. Copyright 1977 by Houghton Mifflin Company and copyright 1971 by Research Press. Adapted by permission.

a suggested daily dietary recall form. Chapter 13 deals more specifically with behavioral modification of dietary habits.

In addition to total caloric intake, the information gathered from daily food records can be used to assess the general overall nutritional value of a person's diet. The foods eaten each day can be evaluated on the basis of meeting the recommended number of servings from each of the Basic Four Food Groups. A suggested format for this purpose is shown in Table 5.11.

A relatively recent innovation in dietary evaluation and counseling is a computer-assisted analysis of food intake. A person's daily caloric intake can be evaluated based on the RDAs for essential vitamins, minerals, carbohydrates, fats, and proteins. Total daily cholesterol and sodium intake are also frequently assessed. In addition to the quantitative information supplied, some marketed programs assess the input relative to recommended levels of nutrients for age, gender, and activity level and offer specific individual recommendations to increase or decrease levels of certain nutrients and/or calories.

Table 5.11 Three-Day Record for Four Food Groups

Instructions:

1. By referring to your record of food intake, determine for each day the actual number of servings you had in each food group and record this in the appropriate box below. If you ate no servings in a food group, record a zero.
2. The Vegetable and Fruit Group is divided into three categories. Treat each of these separately. If you ate more than one serving in the Vitamin A or C subgroups, record just one serving for that Vitamin and count the servings above one in the additional group.
3. Total the number of servings in each food group for the three days and record this in the appropriate box.
4. Divide this by the number given which represents the recommended minimum servings of that group for 3 days.
5. Multiply the above results by 100 to find the percentage, and record it in the appropriate box.

Food Groups	Rec. Min. Daily Servings	1st Day	2nd Day	3rd Day	Total	Divide by	Average Daily Percentage
1. Meat Group	2					6	
2. Vegetable and Fruit Group	A-1					3	
	C-1					3	
	addt-2					6	
3. Milk Group	2					6	
4. Bread and Cereal Group	4					12	

With increasing numbers of dietary analysis programs available, identifying and evaluating programs may be time-consuming and frustrating. Some software programs are effective, but some may be more of a hindrance than a help. A review of a wide variety of nutritional software programs is available (Byrd-Bredbenner & Pelican, 1984). This can be used by HFIs to select software programs that are most appropriate to the intended use and their particular needs.

Fads and Gimmicks Related to Weight Control

Millions of people are involved in weight reduction programs. In the United States, over 100 million dollars are spent annually on weight reduction. In spite of this, there has been no nationwide decrease in obesity. As many as 90% of all individuals who lose weight regain it within 1 year. As the number of undesirable weight control programs continues to increase, an obvious need exists for guidelines to properly control weight.

In its Position Statement on Proper and Improper Weight Loss Programs, the American College of Sports Medicine (1983) made specific recommendations for a desirable weight loss program. In order to ensure adequate nutrition, daily caloric intake should be at least 1,200 kcal, providing a 500-1,000-kcal deficit per day. This results in gradual weight loss not to exceed 2 lb per week. A weight loss program should also include an endurance exercise program. This results in weight loss primarily in the form of fat. For long-term weight control, behavior modification techniques, aimed at identifying and eliminating

Weight-Loss Diet Evaluation Checklist

The following checklist can be used to evaluate weight loss diets. A *No* answer to any of the questions indicates an inadequate weight reduction plan. Does it

		Yes	No
1.	Aim for a weight loss of 1-2 lb per week?	☐	☐
2.	Provide at least 1,200 kcal per day?	☐	☐
3.	Recommend a regular endurance exercise program?	☐	☐
4.	Provide a balance of foods from all four food groups?	☐	☐
5.	Provide for variety to prevent boredom?	☐	☐
6.	Establish eating and exercise habits that can be maintained the rest of your life?	☐	☐
7.	Conform to your personal lifestyle?	☐	☐
8.	Work without pills, drugs, or other gadgets?	☐	☐

poor nutritional habits, are recommended (see chapter 13). A tool similar to the Weight-Loss Diet Evaluation Checklist can be used to evaluate weight reduction diets.

Many individuals successfully lose weight by decreasing caloric intake and/or increasing energy expenditure through exercise. Unfortunately, in a vast majority of cases, having achieved a desired weight-loss goal, most of the weight is regained. This is because most weight-control programs do not result in permanent lifestyle changes.

Caloric deficits can be created by decreasing food intake, increasing energy expenditure, or preferably combining these two. Two points should be emphasized in counseling individuals for weight control. First, no single method of weight control can be recommended for all people. The necessity of structuring the program to the individual cannot be overemphasized. Second, one of the most important goals should be to reeducate a person's dietary and exercise habits, resulting in lifestyle patterns that can be continued indefinitely.

Commercial and Fad Diets

The public is bombarded with a barrage of commercial and fad diets, dietetic foods, appetite suppressants, and exercise devices aimed at quick and easy weight loss. Unfortunately, much of this is medically unsound, potentially dangerous, ineffective, and expensive. An attempt to discuss every type of fad and crash diet available would prove futile. Nevertheless, these tend to have certain characteristics in common. The person searching for a proper weight reduction plan can also be alerted to claims and gimmicks that seem to characterize many improper weight-loss programs. The series of claims presented in the Unsafe Claims checklist can be used to identify ineffective or potentially dangerous weight-loss diets. Following is a brief description of broad types of fad diets, including their proposed mechanisms of action and possible harmful effects. All of these dietary regimens have the disadvantage of not being long-lasting plans. No provision is made for long-term maintenance of weight loss.

Unsafe Claims Checklist

Improper weight-control programs frequently make the following claims. A *yes* answer to any question indicates a questionable practice. Does it

		Yes	No
1.	Claim that calories do not count?	☐	☐
2.	Guarantee spot reduction and sudden weight loss?	☐	☐
3.	Promise cure for disease through diet and say that most disease is because of faulty diet?	☐	☐
4.	Recommend drastic changes in a person's eating habits?	☐	☐
5.	Not recommend an exercise program?	☐	☐
6.	Guarantee quick, easy weight loss and success for everyone?	☐	☐
7.	Recommend extreme amounts of certain nutrients or the elimination of certain nutrients?	☐	☐
8.	Use spectacular advertising claims including testimonials to back up its claims?	☐	☐
9.	Recommend that everyone take vitamins or health foods and claim that natural vitamins are better than synthetic ones?	☐	☐

High-protein diets require almost exclusive consumption of protein and large amounts of water. They are based on the theory that because protein is a complex molecule, its digestion expends extra calories. It has been claimed that as much as 20-30% of the food energy from protein is expended for its digestion. This value is probably not that high, but even if it were, weight loss would likely be no greater than one-half pound per week. This small potential weight loss must be weighed against the increased risk of ketone bodies in the blood and urine and the accompanying health hazards of this condition, including kidney stones, calcium loss, and danger to an unborn child. Furthermore, because most high-protein foods are also high in saturated fat and cholesterol, blood cholesterol levels may become elevated.

Low carbohydrate diets drastically reduce, without completely eliminating, carbohydrates from the diet. Many of these diets are not nutritionally sound and recommend that carbohydrates in the form of complex sugars be eliminated. This leads to a decreased caloric intake and weight loss. Much of the weight loss is likely to be water, especially initially, as the body's carbohydrate stores are diminished.

High-fat diets aim at eating foods high in fat while consuming little or no carbohydrates. Their promoters claim that this leads to the mobilization and utilization of fat as fuel. In addition, the promoters claim that the elimination of ketone bodies, a potential energy source, permits consumption of large numbers of calories while still losing weight. The dangers associated with ketosis and diets high in saturated fats have already been discussed. Diarrhea, fatigue, dehydration, and hypotension are frequently associated with these diets. The diets can be further criticized because no evidence exists to suggest, as is claimed, that weight loss can occur without a caloric deficit.

Besides being nutritionally unbalanced, diets consisting of one or two foods such as grapefruit, eggs, or bananas have their greatest disadvantage by failing to bring about a permanent change in a person's eating habits. They can be initially effective for weight loss, but monotony soon dictates a return to previous eating patterns, and weight is frequently regained.

Diet Medications and Appliances

A variety of diet medications are available both as over-the-counter drugs and by prescription. Many of these preparations serve as appetite suppressants and are effective for only 1-6 weeks for most individuals. These may lead to physical or psychological dependence, nervousness, irritability, and depression.

- Diuretics cause temporary weight loss by eliminating water. Side effects include dehydration, nausea, and weakness.
- Laxatives speed the passage of food through the intestinal tract to decrease nutrient absorption of foods before they are eliminated as waste products. The loss of calories by this method is minimal and any potential weight loss is far outweighed by possible health hazards from long-term laxative use.
- Rubber or plastic suits worn during exercise are effective for losing water weight but they serve no useful purpose in fat reduction. During exercise the body must continually release heat from metabolism. The evaporation of sweat from the body is important in removing heat from the body. Rubber or plastic suits prevent sweat from reaching the air to be evaporated and are therefore very dangerous, particularly when the temperature and relative humidity are high.
- Elastic or inflatable belts are advertised as increasing the temperature around the waistline and "melting" away fat. The falsity of this claim is obvious because no caloric deficit is created. In some cases, the belts may result in a temporary decrease in waist size. This, however, is caused by compression of tissues and abdominal strengthening exercises that are included in the instructions.
- Sauna baths result in temporary weight loss that is only water loss. When liquids are consumed, water is replenished and the weight loss is regained.
- Vibrators and massagers are frequently promoted as effective weight-loss mechanisms. While these may be effective muscle relaxants, their claim to "break-up" fat is unfounded because only energy expended by the body, not by machines, can contribute to caloric deficits.

Exercise and Weight Control

Many weight-control programs attend almost exclusively to reducing caloric intake, and they leave energy expenditure virtually unexplored. In a review of weight-reduction studies, 40% of the studies attempted to change eating behavior, while 50% utilized a drug treatment. Only 6% of the studies reviewed incorporated exercise into the weight management program (Wing & Jeffrey, 1979). Exercise provides a way to increase energy output relative to energy input, which may cause weight loss in itself or accelerate the effects of a reduction in caloric intake by dieting. If energy intake remains constant over time, then an increase in energy expenditure can produce a negative energy balance and weight loss, regardless of the cause of excess accumulation of adipose tissue.

A common misconception is that exercise cannot create an effective caloric deficit because of its stimulatory effects on appetite. Actually, food intake is regulated by physical activity for nonsedentary individuals. Thus when activity increases, intake increases slightly. However, no change in body weight or in body fat occurs. But very high levels of physical activity have a definite appetite-stimulating effect. For example, lumberjacks and marathon runners may consume more than 6,000 kcal per day. However, this increased caloric intake is required just to meet the body's daily energy output. This is evident by the fact that individuals who are engaged in physical labor and intense athletic training are characteristically quite lean, in spite of large caloric intakes. On the other hand, when physical activity is at the sedentary level, the regulation of caloric intake is disrupted, and intake paradoxically increases. Sedentary individuals eat more, rather than less, and are heavier.

Regarding the acute effects of exercise on appetite, Epstein, Masek, and Marshall (1978) found that decreased food intake followed prelunch exercise in previously sedentary obese children. The amount of exercise was inversely related to the decrease in caloric intake. The greatest decrease in intake was observed in children with the greatest increase in energy expenditure. One frequently overlooked benefit of a regular program of physical activity is its diversionary effects on caloric intake. In other words, while exercising, a person cannot be eating or snacking. The longer and more frequent the exercise, the greater the potential caloric deficit by decreasing eating.

Another frequently advanced argument against exercise as an effective weight management tool is that relatively little energy is expended. For example, in jogging 1 mi, a 150-lb man expends only 100 kcal. At a cost of 3,500 kcal per pound of fat, if caloric intake remains constant, he must jog 35 mi to create a deficit equal to a 1-lb fat loss. On a long-term basis, however, the situation is not as discouraging. If he jogs 2 mi per day, 5 days per week, he will lose approximately 1 lb of fat every 3-1/2 weeks. This is equivalent to 16 lb per year if caloric intake is not changed. With a concomitant slight decrease in intake, weight loss can be substantially accelerated. Remember that a caloric deficit of 3,500 kcal results in a 1-lb fat loss, whether it occurs all at once or over a long period of time.

Individuals involved in weight-management programs should be encouraged to make exercise a regular part of their daily routines at home, work, or school by substituting physical work for patterns of inactivity. Chapter 13 deals with specific suggestions for increasing energy expenditure as a part of the regular daily routine. In addition, increased energy expenditure should be promoted during leisure time by using exercise programs. The major criterion for choice of an exercise for weight loss is total caloric expenditure. This choice, however, must be balanced against behavioral and physiological requirements. While long-duration exercise increases caloric expenditure, it may also cause decreased adherence. For most people, social activities promote adherence more than solitary ones, and the activity chosen should not promote injuries that would limit further participation. A model exercise for weight control would, therefore, be aerobic in nature leading to a large total energy expenditure (compared to calisthenics, for example). Exercise should be done with others, require minimal equipment, should not have a high injury rate, and many people should be able to experience success in its participation. Walking, jogging, aerobic dance, swimming, and bicycling best meet these criteria.

Many people think that exercises that involve a certain area of the body actually reduce the amount of fat over that area. Unfortunately, *spot-reducing* is not based on fact. Genetic and hormonal factors control to a large extent fat deposition. Even with considerable energy expenditure, nothing guarantees that fat will be lost in the area exercised. This is not to imply that calisthenics and resistance exercises are of no value. They can increase strength and muscle tone, giving a slimming effect. In general, fat loss occurs first from the area of the body where it was last deposited.

Diet, Exercise, and Lipids

Increasing numbers of cross-sectional studies indicate a strong relationship between the risk of heart disease and dietary levels of triglycerides and cholesterol. While the mechanism of this relationship remains unclear, the communication of its existence to the public has led to significant dietary changes. The American public today consumes less saturated fat and cholesterol and more unsaturated fats than 25 years ago. *Atherosclerosis*, the accumulation of cholesterol deposits in arteries, accounts for nearly 50% of the deaths in this country.

Cholesterol is present throughout the body and serves many important functions; it is a component of cell membranes and nerve fibers and is required for the production of steroid hormones, bile acids, and vitamin D. In addition to that which is ingested (mostly in egg yolks, organ meats, and milk products), the body synthesizes approximately 1,000 mg of cholesterol each day. In fact, on the average, 65-70% of the cholesterol in the body is produced by the body itself. While the biosynthesis of cholesterol occurs in nearly all cell types, the liver and small intestine mucosa are the primary organs that produce cholesterol.

Triglycerides and cholesterol do not circulate freely in the plasma. They are carried in the bloodstream, bound to a protein, forming a lipoprotein. The partitioning of cholesterol into its lipoprotein fractions is of great importance. Until recent years, only the total cholesterol level was considered in a CHD risk factor profile. The total cholesterol level, however, represents the cholesterol contained in different lipoproteins, namely, very low-density lipoproteins (VLDL), low-density lipoproteins (LDL), and high-density lipoproteins (HDL). Recent evidence suggests that the distribution of cholesterol among these various lipoproteins may be a more powerful predictor of heart disease than simply the total blood cholesterol level. The plasma total cholesterol is only weakly related to coronary artery disease risk, and the ratio of HDL to LDL or HDL to total cholesterol may thus be the best lipid index (Table 5.12). The total cholesterol/HDL ratio is getting increased diagnostic use. For example, two individuals may have blood cholesterol levels of 240 mg/dl. If one individual has an HDL level of 80 mg/dl, the total cholesterol/HDL ratio is 3.00, which is lower than that of the average American. On the other hand, in a person with the same total blood cholesterol of 240 mg/dl, with an HDL level of 25 mg/dl, the total cholesterol/HDL index is 10.4. This value is more than two times the average. LDL and VLDL encourage cholesterol to remain in the circulation network by transporting it throughout the body to the cells, including the smooth muscle layers of the arterial walls, which frequently leads to narrowing of the artery. The portion of total cholesterol in LDL is the primary atherogenic component of total blood cholesterol. HDL apparently serves as cholesterol scavengers by removing cholesterol from the periphery, including arterial walls, and returning it to the liver where it can be excreted as bile. HDL may also interfere with the binding of LDL to the cell membrane. The contrasting roles of these types of lipoproteins have led to frequent reference to HDL as the "good" kind of cholesterol.

Table 5.12 Predicting Coronary Heart Disease Risk Based on LDL/HDL Ratio or Total Cholesterol/HDL Ratio

Risk	LDL/HDL	Total Cholesterol/HDL
Women:		
Below average	1.47	3.27
Average	3.22	4.44
2 × average	5.03	7.05
3 × average	6.14	11.04
Men:		
Below average	1.00	3.43
Average	3.55	4.97
2 × average	6.25	9.55
3 × average	7.99	23.39

Note. From "Nutrition and Atherosclerosis" by W.B. Kannel, 1979. In D.T. Mason and H. Guthrie (Eds.), *The Medicine Called Nutrition* (p. 37), Englewood Cliffs, NJ: Best Foods. Copyright 1979 by Best Foods. Printed with permission of Mazola Nutrition/Health Information Service.

Epidemiologic data and longitudinal studies indicate that the risk of coronary artery disease (CAD) is positively correlated with LDL levels and inversely related to the plasma HDL concentration. In fact, an inverse HDL-CHD relationship persists even after adjusting for the major CHD risk factors. The low incidence of CHD among people with high levels of HDL has led to the suggestion that HDL is an independent risk-lowering factor.

Understandably, there has been considerable interest in factors that appear to enhance HDL levels. Although not in complete agreement, results of studies relating HDL concentrations to physical patterns and dietary factors show a somewhat consistent pattern. Regular physical activity is associated with decreased plasma triglycerides, VLDL and LDL, and increased levels of HDL. Also, total blood cholesterol sometimes, but not always, falls. In addition, high HDL levels are strongly related to lower plasma triglyceride levels, decreased smoking, and loss of body weight.

Dietary manipulation can significantly influence the body's rate of cholesterol synthesis. With very little dietary cholesterol consumption, enough cholesterol is manufactured to maintain body functions. If the amount of cholesterol from food increases, then the body will respond with compensatory mechanisms, including reduced cholesterol synthesis and increased cholesterol excretion. The efficacy of these compensatory mechanisms varies among individuals. They are not effective in some individuals and instead lead to elevations in blood cholesterol levels. In people prone to tissue deposition of cholesterol, the risk of atherosclerosis may be enhanced.

The extent to which diet affects the total/HDL cholesterol ratio remains unclear. Studies comparing runners, joggers, and sedentary people indicate that HDL differences are associated more with the total distance run than with dietary factors. Other studies, however, have measured higher HDL levels among individuals who adhere to fat-controlled diets designed to lower total plasma cholesterol concentrations. The results of research studies have served as a reassurance that measures to prevent CHD do not adversely affect the blood cholesterol profile. If anything, conventional preventive measures are related to increased levels of HDL cholesterol. Until further investigations differentiate and clarify the causality of these factors, increased physical activity, weight reduction, smoking reduction, and a fat-controlled diet can be recommended to positively influence HDL levels and presumably decrease a person's risk of heart disease.

Summary

Excess body fat is a risk factor for heart disease and diabetes. The HFI must be able to estimate body fatness and predict an ideal weight consistent with optimum health. Underwater weighing, skinfold measurement, and circumference techniques can be used for this purpose. To maintain body weight, caloric intake must equal caloric expenditure. Caloric intake can be estimated by dietary recall, and caloric expenditure can be predicted on the basis of body size, gender, and estimated activity level. A deficit of 3,500 kcal is needed to lose 1 lb of fat. A balanced program of exercise and dietary reduction, compared to diet alone, is recommended for weight loss.

Proper nutrition is important in reducing the risks associated with hypertension, stroke, obesity, and diabetes. Basic nutrients include proteins, carbohydrates, fats, vitamins, minerals, and water. New dietary goals recommend that the total caloric intake be divided among fat (30%), protein (12%), and carbohydrate (58%). While vitamins are essential for good health, an excess will not increase health. In fact, large quantities of fat-soluble vitamins can be harmful. The use of extreme diets, drugs, and appliances to lose body fat is usually successful only in causing a temporary reduction in water weight. Body fat appears to be lost first from the last place the fat was added, so spot reduction does not appear to be a reality. Diet and exercise interact to favorably influence the blood lipid profile by lowering total cholesterol and raising the HDL cholesterol.

Suggested Reading for Chapter 5

American College of Sports Medicine (1983)

American Heart Association (1978)

Brozek, Grande, Anderson, and Keys (1963)

Byrd-Bredbenner and Pelican (1984)

Epstein, Masek, and Marshall (1978)

Jackson and Pollock (1985)

Kannel (1979)

Katch and McArdle (1977)

King, Cohenour, Corruccini, and Schenneman (1978)

Siri (1956)

Stuart and Davies (1971)

U.S. Senate Select Committee on Nutrition and Human Needs (1977)

Williams (1983b)

Wilmore (1983)

Wing and Jeffrey (1979)

See reference list at end of book for complete source listing.

Chapter 6

Cardiorespiratory Fitness

- The relation of CRF to health
- Testing CRF
  - Testing modalities
  - Rest, submax, max

The usual introduction to a chapter dealing with cardiorespiratory function (CRF) delineates heart disease as the major cause of death and proceeds to describe the role of exercise in prevention and rehabilitation programs. But a greater need is to focus attention on a high level of CRF as a normal, lifelong goal that is needed to enjoy life. That alone merits the inclusion of CRF in any discussion about positive health. The terms *cardiorespiratory* or *cardiovascular* are used to include the heart (cardiac), lungs (respiratory), and blood vessels (vascular). It might be technically more correct to use *cardiorespiratoryvascular*, but why use a word that can't be said in less than 10 sec?

Historically, measurements of heart rate (HR), blood pressure (BP), and the electrocardiogram (ECG) taken at rest were used to evaluate CRF. Some static pulmonary function tests (e.g., vital capacity) were used to characterize respiratory function. However, it became clear that measurements made at rest told a doctor little about the way a person's cardiorespiratory systems respond during work. We are now familiar with the use of a GXT to evaluate the HR, ECG, BP, ventilation, and oxygen-uptake responses during work.

The results from these tests are used to write exercise recommendations and allow the HFI or physician to evaluate positive or negative changes in CRF as a result of physical conditioning, aging, illness, or inactivity. Given the statistics about the increase in obesity and inactivity in children, good reason exists to include an evaluation of CRF throughout life, from early childhood to old age. This information can serve as a marker of where the individual stands relative to others, and more importantly, it will alert the individual to subtle changes in lifestyle that may compromise positive health. The nature of the tests and the level of monitoring should vary across the ages to reflect the type of information that is needed.

One point typically made about exercise tests or activities is the risk involved. The tendency is to deal with this question of risk by identifying various classes of individuals for whom a certain type of medical examination (test) is recommended before initiating an exercise program (see chapter 2). However, Per Olaf Åstrand, a well-known Swedish physiologist, has offered another view. He states that consulting a physician is advisable if there are any doubts about health; however, "there is less risk in activity than in continuous inactivity." Further, he states, "It is more advisable to pass a careful medical examination if one intends to be sedentary in order to establish whether one's state of health is good enough to stand the inactivity!" (Åstrand & Rodahl, 1970, p. 608).

Chapter 9 deals with the recommendation of activities for improvement of CRF. This chapter emphasizes the evaluation of CRF. CRF testing depends on the purpose(s) of the test, the type of person, and the work tasks available.[1] Reasons for testing include the following: (a) determining CRF response to rest, submaximal, and/or maximal work; (b) providing a basis for exercise programming; (c) screening for CHD; and (d) determining ability to perform a specific work task.

The choice of an appropriate test depends on several factors. People differ in age, fitness levels, known health problems, and risks of CHD. Also, financial considerations determine the amount of time that can be devoted to each individual and the type of work tasks available.

Sequence of Testing

A logical sequence for fitness testing (and activities) exists when people come to the same fitness center over a period of time:

1. Screening
2. Informed consent
3. Background information
4. Resting CRF, body composition, and psychological tests
5. Submaximal CRF

[1]Much of the material in this section is adapted from Franks (1979).

(Begin light activity program here)

6. Maximal CRF

(Revise activity program, include games and sports here)

7. Periodic retest (and activity revision)

In those cases when people come in for fitness testing and do not have continuing involvement with the fitness center, the submaximal and maximal tests are usually a part of the same testing protocol.

Screening

The first decision is to determine whether or not the person needs medical permission to be in a fitness program. Although the standards in this area are evolving, the following recommendations represent the current thinking. People with CHD or other known major health problems MUST HAVE medical supervision or clearance prior to any fitness testing or program. People with any primary risk factor for CHD or other health problems that would cause some exercises to be a high risk should be in a carefully supervised program.

Apparently healthy people who have no known major health problems or symptoms can be tested or begin the type of fitness program recommended in this book with minimal risk. In a sense, it is a waste of time, energy, and money to insist that people without known health problems, characteristics, signs, or symptoms of health problems go through a complete medical examination with a stress test prior to easing into regular exercise. Chapter 2 identifies the people who need medical supervision, medical clearance, a carefully supervised program, and educational information about health problems and behaviors.

Informed Consent

The person to be tested needs to understand clearly all of the procedures, potential risks, and benefits and understand that the data will be confidential and that any test can be terminated at any time by the individual participant. A sample consent form is included in chapter 15.

Health History

Chapter 2 deals with procedures for determining current health status. This information can be used to determine appropriate testing protocol and activity recommendations. In addition, follow-up testing should be advised for people with symptoms of health problems. Referrals to other professionals might be warranted based on the person's history.

Resting CRF

Typical resting tests include a 12-lead ECG, BP, and blood chemistry profile. Evaluation of the ECG by a physician determines if any abnormalities require further medical attention. Those people with extreme BP or blood chemistry values should also be referred to their personal physicians.

Submaximal CRF

If the resting tests reflect normal values, then a submaximal test is administered. The submaximal test provides the HR and BP response to different intensities of work from light up to a predetermined point (usually 70-85% of predicted maximum HR). This test can use a bench, cycle ergometer, or treadmill. Once again, if unusual responses to the submaximal test appear, then the person is referred for further medical tests. If the results appear normal, then an activity program is begun at intensities less than those reached on the test (e.g., a person goes to 85% of max HR on the test and starts the fitness program at 70%). After the person has become accustomed to regular exercise and appears to be adjusting to fitness activities, then a maximal test can be administered.

Maximal Tests

If no problems occur up to this point, then a maximal test is administered. Two basic types of maximal tests are used to indicate CRF—laboratory tests involving the measurement of physiological responses (e.g., oxygen consumption) to increasing levels of work and unmonitored endurance performance tests (e.g., time to exhaustion on a treadmill, or time in a 2-mi run). The results of the maximal test can be used to revise the activity program. After achieving a minimum level of fitness, then a wider variety of activities (e.g., games and sports) can be included in the fitness program. Finally, all of the tests should be retaken periodically to determine the progress being made and to revise the program in areas where the gains are not as great as desired.

Field Tests

Endurance runs of a set distance for time (at least 9 min) or a set time for distance (at least 1 mi) provide information about a person's cardiorespiratory endurance. The advantages include its moderately high correlation to maximum oxygen uptake, participation in a natural activity, and the large numbers that can be tested in a short period of time. The disadvantages of endurance running tests are the difficulty of monitoring physiological responses, the possibility that other factors affect the outcome (e.g., motivation), and the fact that it cannot be used for graded or submaximal testing.

The most popular field test used to estimate functional capacity is the 12-min run, made popular by Kenneth Cooper. The aim is to find the average velocity that can be maintained for 12 min (distance in meters/12 min). This test is based on original work by Balke (1963) who showed that running tests of 10-20 min duration could be used to estimate the subject's $\dot{V}O_2$max. He found the optimal duration to be 15 min. The test is based on the relationship between the velocity of running and the oxygen uptake required to run at that velocity (Figure 6.1). The greater the running speed, the greater the oxygen uptake required. The reason for the duration of 12-15 min is that the running test has to be long enough to diminish the contribution that the anaerobic sources of energy (immediate and short-term) make to the average velocity. In essence, the average velocity that can be maintained in a 5- or 6-min run overestimates the $\dot{V}O_2$max. If the run is too long, the person is not able to run close to 100% of $\dot{V}O_2$max, and the estimate is too low (Figure 6.2).

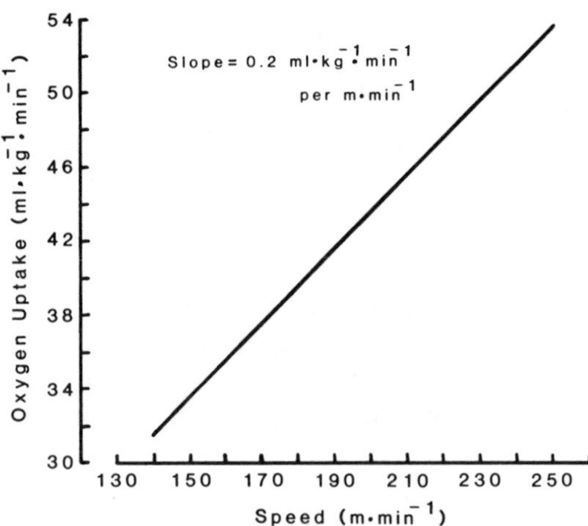

Figure 6.1 The relationship between the steady state oxygen uptake and the speed of running. Adapted from Bransford, D. and Howley, E.T. (1977). *Medicine and Science in Sports,* 9:41-44.

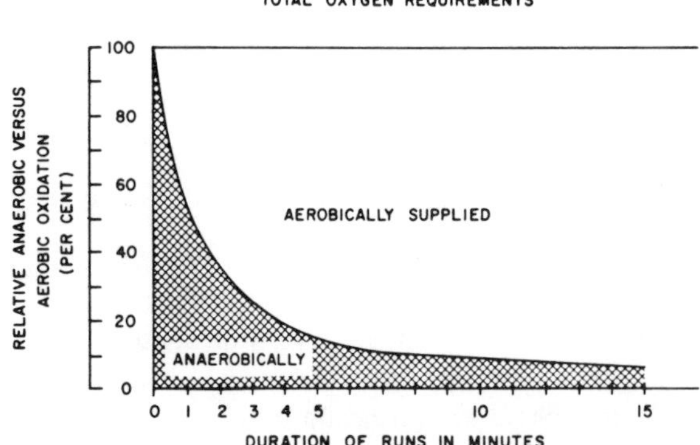

Figure 6.2 The relative role of aerobic and anaerobic energy sources in best-effort runs of various durations. From Balke, B. (1963). Federal Aviation Agency Report 63.6. Used with permission.

Using the formula in chapter 10 for estimating the oxygen cost of running, calculating the $\dot{V}O_2$ associated with a specific running speed is possible. These estimates are reasonable for adults who jog/run the whole 12 min. The formulas underestimate the $\dot{V}O_2$max of children, because of the higher O_2 cost of running for children, and overestimate the $\dot{V}O_2$max of those people who walk through the 12 min test, because the cost of walking at moderate speeds is less than that of running.

Norms for endurance runs and maximal oxygen uptake are found in Table 6.1.

The advantage of the 12-min run is that it can be used on a regular basis to evaluate current CRF without expensive equipment. It is easily adapted to cyclists and swimmers, who can evaluate their progress by determining how far they can ride or swim in 12 min. While no equations exist that can relate cyclists' and swimmers' respective performances to $\dot{V}O_2max$, each participant is able to make a personal judgment about the current state of CRF and improvements resulting from training.

As Cooper (1977) and others agree, an endurance run should *not* be used at the beginning of an exercise program. A person should begin an exercise program at low intensities (e.g., a walking program) to make some fitness improvements prior to using an endurance-run test.

Graded Exercise Tests

Many fitness programs use a GXT to evaluate CRF. These multilevel tests can be administered using a bench, cycle ergometer, or treadmill.

Table 6.1 Standards for Maximal Oxygen Uptake and Endurance Runs[a]

Age[b]	$\dot{V}O_2max$ ml•(kg•min)$^{-1}$		1.5-Mi Run (min:sec)		12-Min Run (mi)	
	Female	Male[c]	Female	Male	Female	Male
			Good			
15-30	>40[d]	>45	<12	<10	>1.5	>1.7
35-50	>35	>40	<13:30	<11:30	>1.4	>1.5
55-70	>30	>35	<16	<14	>1.2	>1.3
			Adequate for Most Activities			
15-30	35	40	13:30	11:50	1.4	1.5
35-50	30	35	15	13	1.3	1.4
55-70	25	30	17:30	15:30	1.1	1.3
			Borderline			
15-30	30	35	15	13	1.3	1.4
35-50	25	30	16:30	14:30	1.2	1.3
55-70	20	25	19	17	1.0	1.2
			Needs Extra Work on CRF			
15-30	<25	<30	>17	>15	<1.2	<1.3
35-50	<20	<25	>18:30	>16:30	<1.1	<1.2
55-70	<15	<20	>21	>19	<0.9	<1.0

[a]These standards are for fitness programs. People wanting to do well in endurance performance need higher levels. For those at the *Good* level, the emphasis is on maintaining this level the rest of their lives. For those in the lower levels, emphasis is on setting and reaching realistic goals.
[b]CRF declines with age.
[c]Women have lower standards because they have a larger amount of essential fat.
[d]> = more than; < = less than.

Bench Step

Bench stepping is very economical. It can be used for both submaximal and maximal testing. The disadvantages include the number of stages that can be feasibly included for any one bench height and individual fitness level, the difficulty of taking certain measurements during the test (e.g., BP), and the relatively poorer reproducibility of work done compared with the cycle ergometer or treadmill.

Cycle Ergometer

The cycle ergometer is less expensive than a treadmill. Additional measurements can be easily obtained because the upper body is essentially stationary. One difference between the cycle ergometer and the other task forms normally used is that the body weight is supported by the seat (this may be viewed as either an advantage or disadvantage, depending on the purpose of the test). One of the major disadvantages of using the cycle ergometer for maximal tests with noncycling populations is that local muscle fatigue is often a limiting factor. Remember that when a small person does the same work rate as a large person, the smaller individual is operating at a higher MET level.

Treadmill

A particular testing protocol on the treadmill is very reproducible because a person must keep up with the set pace (whereas a person may go too slow or too fast on either the bench or cycle). Its major disadvantage is that it is the most expensive of the work tasks.

Calibrating Equipment

All equipment must be checked with known standards. The speed and grade of the treadmill, resistance scale on the cycle ergometer, timing devices, gas analyzers, and other equipment should all be calibrated at specific intervals. Manuals for the equipment normally include detailed instructions for calibration. No dial setting or meter can be assumed to be accurate. In addition, the work rates (grade/speed on a treadmill, load/rpm on a cycle, or stepping rate on a bench) must be carefully monitored and adjusted throughout a test. Only in those rare cases in which the level of work, the ability to compare the response to work, or the ability to later replicate the work are unimportant can calibration be disregarded.

Commonly Measured Variables

The variables that are commonly used for resting and submaximal tests include HR, BP, and Rating of Perceived Exertion (RPE). For maximal testing, $\dot{V}O_2max$, time to exhaustion on a GXT, or time to cover a set distance (or distance run in a set time) is often used.

Heart Rate

HR is often used as a fitness indicator at rest and during a standard submaximal work task. When an ECG is being recorded, the HR can be taken from the ECG strip (see chapter 12). When no ECG is being recorded, HR can be taken by auscultation with a stethoscope or manual palpation of an artery at the wrist or neck. People should use their fingers (not thumb) to take a HR and preferably take it at the wrist. If a person takes it at the neck, caution should be used not to apply too much pressure because it could trigger a reflex that causes the HR to slow down. Maximal HR is useful for determining the target heart rate (THR) for fitness workouts, but it is not a good fitness indicator because it changes very little with training. The HR at rest or during a steady-state exercise should be taken for 30 sec for higher reliability. However, when taking HR after exercise, it should be taken at exactly the same time after work (e.g., 10 sec) and taken for 10 or 15 sec because the rate changes so rapidly. The 10-sec or 15-sec rate is multiplied by 6 or 4, respectively, to calculate beats per minute (see Table 6.2).

Blood Pressure

Systolic blood pressure (SBP) and diastolic blood pressure (DBP) are often determined at rest, during work, and after work. The proper sized

Table 6.2 Heart-Rate Conversion From Beats Per Minute to Beats in 10, 15, or 30 Sec

	Heart Rate . . . Number of Beats Per		
Min	10 Sec	15 Sec	30 Sec
40	7	10	20
45	8	11	23
50	8	13	25
55	9	14	28
60	10	15	30
65	11	16	32
70	12	18	35
75	13	19	38
80	13	20	40
85	14	21	43
90	15	23	45
95	16	24	48
100	17	25	50
105	18	26	53
110	18	28	55
115	19	29	58
120	20	30	60
125	21	31	63
130	22	33	65
135	23	34	68
140	23	35	70
145	24	36	73
150	25	38	75
155	26	39	78
160	27	40	80
165	28	41	83
170	28	43	85
175	29	44	88
180	30	45	90
185	31	46	93
190	32	48	95
195	33	49	98
200	33	50	100
205	34	51	103
210	35	53	105
215	36	54	108
220	37	55	110
225	38	56	113
230	38	58	115

cuff and a sensitive stethoscope are required to get accurate values at rest and during work. At rest, the person should have both feet flat on the floor and be in a relaxed position with the arm supported. The cuff should be wrapped securely around the arm, usually with the tube on the inside of the arm. The stethoscope should be below (not under) the cuff—the placement will depend on where the sound can be most easily heard, often toward the inside of the arm. The first and fourth Korotkoff sounds (first sound heard and when sound changes tone or becomes muffled) should be used for SBP and DBP, respectively. During exercise, if SBP fails to increase, or the DBP increases rapidly with increased work, then the work should be stopped.

Rating of Perceived Exertion

Borg (1982) introduced the Rating of Perceived Exertion (RPE), based on a scale from 6 to 20 (roughly based on resting to maximal HR, i.e., 60-200). Table 6.3 contains this scale as well as his revised 10-point RPE scale (Borg, 1982). Either can be used with a GXT to provide useful information during the test as the person approaches exhaustion and to be a reference point for exercise prescription.

Table 6.3 Rating of Perceived Exertion

Original Rating	Description
6	
7	Very, very light
8	
9	Very light
10	
11	Fairly light
12	
13	Somewhat hard
14	
15	Hard
16	
17	Very hard
18	
19	Very, very hard
20	

(Cont.)

Table 6.3 Cont.

Revised Rating	Description
0	Nothing
0.5	Very, very light (just noticeable)
1.0	Very light
2	Light (weak)
3	Moderate
4	Somewhat hard
5	Heavy (strong)
6	
7	Very heavy
8	
9	
10	Very, very heavy (almost max)

Note. From "Psychological bases of physical exertion" by G.A.V. Borg, 1982, *Medicine and Science in Sport and Exercise,* **14**(5). Reprinted with permission.

Graded Exercise Testing

Because the resting and submaximal HR, BP, and RPE responses to work are influenced by a variety of factors, care must be taken to minimize these, or at least to minimize the variation in each from one testing period to the next. These factors include, but are not limited to, temperature and relative humidity of the room, number of hours of sleep, emotional state, hydration state, medication, time of day, time since last meal, cigarette smoking, caffeine intake, and exercise. Attention to these factors increases the likelihood that changes in HR, BP, or RPE from one test to the next are caused by changes in physical activity habits.

Estimation Versus Measurement of Functional Capacity

Functional capacity is defined as the highest work rate (oxygen uptake) reached in a GXT during which time HR, BP, and ECG responses are within the normal range for heavy work. For cardiac patients, the highest work rate does *not* normally reflect a measure of the maximal capacity of the CR systems because the GXT might be stopped for ECG changes, angina, claudication pain, and so on. For the apparently healthy person, functional capacity can be called maximal aerobic power or maximal oxygen uptake ($\dot{V}O_2$max). (See chapter 3 for procedures to be used in measurement of oxygen uptake.)

The oxygen uptake increases with each stage of the GXT until the upper limit of the CRF is reached. At that point, $\dot{V}O_2$ does not increase further when the test moves to the next stage. The person's $\dot{V}O_2$max has been reached. Given the complexity and cost of these procedures, $\dot{V}O_2$max is usually estimated with equations relating the stage of the GXT to a specific oxygen uptake.

As discussed in chapter 10, a variety of formulas may be used to estimate oxygen uptake on the basis of the stage reached in a GXT. In general, these formulas give reasonable estimates of the $\dot{V}O_2$ achieved in a GXT if the test has been suited to the individual (Montoye, 1975). However, if the increments in the stages of the GXT are too large relative to the person's CRF, or if the time for each stage is too short, then the person might not be able to reach the steady state oxygen requirement associated with that stage. Failure to achieve the oxygen requirement for a GXT stage results in an overestimation of the $\dot{V}O_2$ at each stage of the test with the overestimation growing larger with each stage. Inability to reach the oxygen requirement is a common problem with low-fit individuals (e.g., cardiac patients). This inability suggests that more conservative (i.e., smaller increments between stages) GXT protocols should be used to allow the less-fit individual to reach the oxygen demand at each stage. A more complete explanation of this problem is found in chapter 3.

Shorter stages and larger increments between stages in a GXT can be used if the purpose of the test is to screen for ECG abnormalities (rather than to estimate $\dot{V}O_2$max). In addition, changes in CRF over time can be determined by periodically using the same GXT on an individual.

Termination of the GXT

A series of *end points* should be used to stop a GXT. The following are taken from the ACSM guidelines (1980). While some of these guidelines refer specifically to maximal testing, many can be applied to submaximal testing.

A. $\dot{V}O_2max$ is reached, the *normal* end point for the apparently healthy individual.

B. Abnormal signs and symptoms
   1. Dizziness, mental confusion, staggering, or unsteadiness
   2. Angina, claudication, or other pain
   3. Nausea
   4. Marked dyspnea
   5. Cyanosis or pallor
   6. Severe fatigue, facial distress

C. ECG changes (see chapter 12)
   1. ST-segment displacement above or below the baseline
   2. Ventricular arrhythmia
      a. ventricular tachycardia
      b. Ectopic ventricular complexes occurring every second or third beat
      c. frequent ventricular complexes
   3. Atrioventricular or ventricular conduction disturbances
      a. AV block
      b. bundle branch block

D. Abnormal blood pressure response
   1. Fall in systolic pressure of 10 mmHg with a stage increase in the GXT, or a systolic pressure of 250 mmHg
   2. A rise of 20 mmHg in the diastolic pressure, or a diastolic pressure of 110 mmHg

E. Heart-rate response
   1. Age-adjusted estimated max heart rate can alert the tester that the subject is nearing maximum.
   2. A percent of maximal heart rate (e.g., 70% or 85%) can be used to stop submaximal tests.
   3. Should *not* be used as the end point for a max test

F. Respiratory response
   1. Marked dyspnea

G. Malfunctioning equipment
   1. Stop the test and reschedule for later time.

Submaximal and Maximal Tests

GXTs have been used to evaluate CRF in fitness programs for healthy populations and in the clinical assessment of ischemic heart disease. In this condition, an inadequate blood flow to the heart muscle can cause changes in the ECG. Exercise is used to place a load on the heart to determine the cardiovascular response and/or to see if changes occur in the ECG. Some controversy has arisen concerning whether to use submaximal or maximal tests. On the basis of thousands of exercise stress tests conducted over the past 2 decades, a *maximal* exercise test is generally recommended to be used to determine the presence of ischemic heart disease. While *submaximal* exercise tests are not as effective in identifying disease conditions, they represent an appropriate means of evaluating cardiorespiratory fitness prior to and following exercise programs.

In those cases where the same fitness center is responsible for both the testing and the program, the sequence of testing/activity recommended earlier provides for the advantages of each, while minimizing the disadvantages. The main objection to maximal tests is the stress that they put on a person who has been inactive. Although the risk of a maximal GXT is very small with adequate screening and qualified testing personnel, the discomfort of a person going to his or her maximum without prior conditioning may discourage participation in a fitness program. Objections to the submaximal test include finding fewer abnormal responses to exercise and inaccurately estimating someone's maximal level from submaximal data. In a fitness program for apparently healthy people, the objections for both maximal and submaximal tests alone are overcome by administering the submaximal test early in the fitness program and waiting until the participant has been involved in a regular exercise program to administer the maximal test. Any of the GXT protocols can be used for submaximal or maximal testing—the only difference is the criterion for stopping the test. Either test is stopped with abnormal responses listed above. In the absence of abnormal responses, the submaximal test is usually terminated when the person reaches a certain HR (often 70% or 85% of max HR), while the maximal test continues to voluntary exhaustion.

Maximal Testing Protocols

Figure 6.3 includes various popular testing protocols for submaximal and maximal tests. No one protocol is appropriate for all types of people. The time, starting points, and increments between stages should vary with the type of person. Young active, normal sedentary, and people with questionable health status should start at 6, 4, and 2 METs, respectively. The same three groups should increase 2-3, 1-2, and 0.5-1 METs, respectively, for stages of the test. If using the test to compare CRF at different times, then 1-2 min per stage can be used. However, if trying to predict $\dot{V}O_2max$, the time per stage should be 2-3 min. Table 6.4

FUNCTIONAL CLASS	CLINICAL STATUS	O_2 REQUIREMENTS ml O_2/kg/min	STEP TEST	TREADMILL TESTS						BICYCLE ERGOMETER**
			NAGLE, BALKE, NAUGHTON*	BRUCE†		KATTUS‡		BALKE**	BALKE**	
			2 min stages 30 steps/min	3-min stages		3-min stages		% grade at 3.4 mph	% grade at 3 mph	For 70 kg body weight
			(Step height increased 4 cm q 2 min)	mph	%gr	mph	%gr			kgm/min
NORMAL AND I	PHYSICALLY ACTIVE SUBJECTS	56.0						26		
		52.5						24		
		49.0				4	22	22		1500
		45.5	Height (cm)	4.2	16			20		
		42.0	40			4	18	18	22.5	1350
		38.5	36					16	20.0	1200
	SEDENTARY HEALTHY	35.0	32			4	14	14	17.5	1050
		31.5	28	3.4	14			12	15.0	900
		28.0	24			4	10	10	12.5	
	DISEASED, RECOVERED	24.5	20	2.5	12	3	10	8	10.0	750
II	SYMPTOMATIC PATIENTS	21.0	16					6	7.5	600
		17.5	12	1.7	10	2	10	4	5.0	450
		14.0	8					2	2.5	300
III		10.5	4						0.0	150
		7.0								
IV		3.5								

Figure 6.3 Various popular testing protocols for submaximal and maximal tests. Reproduced with permission, American Heart Association. (1972). *Exercise Testing and Training of Apparently Healthy Individuals: A Handbook for Physicians*. American Heart Association.

Table 6.4 Testing Protocol for Different Groups

Stage	METs	Bench HT (cm)	Bench Steps/ (min)	Cycle Work Rate (Kpm/min)	Cycle RPM	Treadmill Speed (km/hr)	Treadmill Grade (%)
				Individuals With Questionable Health			
1	2	0	24	0	50	3.2	0
2	3	16	12	150	50	4.8	0
3	4	16	18	300	50	4.8	2.5
4	5	16	24	450	50	4.8	5.0
5	6	16	30	600	50	4.8	7.5
				"Normal" Inactive Individuals			
1	4	16	18	300	60	4.8	2.5
2	6	16	30	600	60	4.8	7.5
3	7-8	36	18-24	750-900	60	4.8-5.5	10.0
4	9	36	27	1050	60	5.5	12.0
5	10-11	36	30-33	1200-1350	60	9.7	0-1.75
				Young Active Individuals			
1	6	16	30	600	70	4.8	7.5
2	9	36	27	1050	70	5.5	12.0
3	12	36	36	1500	70	9.7	3.5
4	15	50	33	1950	70	11.3	7.0
5	17	50	39	2250	70	11.3	11.0

Note. Adapted from "Methodology of the Exercise ECG test: Technical Aspects" by B.D. Franks, 1979. In E.K. Chung (Ed.), *Exercise Electrocardiography: Practical Approach* (p. 56), Baltimore: Williams and Wilkins.

illustrates how those criteria might be used for a bench, cycle, or treadmill test.

The following testing protocols are examples of tests that could be used for different populations. The National Exercise and Heart Disease Project protocol (see Table 6.5) could be used with deconditioned subjects by starting at a very low MET level, walking slowly, and increasing 1 MET per stage. The Balke Standard protocol (see Table 6.6) could be used for *typical* inactive adults by progressing at 1 MET per stage and starting at a higher MET level. More active, or younger, people could be tested on the Bruce protocol (see Table 6.7), which starts at a moderate MET level and goes up 2-3 MET per stage. Unfortunately, some testing centers attempt to use the same testing protocol for all people, resulting in an initial stage that is too high or too low and use increments in work for each stage that are either too little or too much for the individual being tested.

Table 6.5 Treadmill Protocol for Deconditioned People

Stage	METs	Speed (mph)	Grade (%)	Time (min)
1	2.5	2	0	3
2	3.5	2	3.5	3
3	4.5	2	7	3
4	5.4	2	10.5	3
5	6.4	2	14	3
6	7.3	2	17.5	3
7	8.5	3	12.5	3
8	9.5	3	15	3
9	10.5	3	17.5	3

Note. From "Methods of Exercise Testing" by J.P. Naughton and R. Haider, 1973. In *Exercise testing and exercise training in coronary heart disease*, by J.P. Naughton, H.R. Hellerstein, and L.C. Mohler (Eds.), New York: Academic Press.

Table 6.6 Balke Standard Treadmill Protocol for Normal Inactive People

Stage	METs	Speed (mph)	Grade (%)	Time (min)
1	4.3	3	2.5	2
2	5.4	3	5	2
3	6.4	3	7.5	2
4	7.4	3	10	2
5	8.5	3	12.5	2
6	9.5	3	15	2
7	10.5	3	17.5	2
8	11.6	3	20	2
9	12.6	3	22.5	2
10	13.6	3	25	2

Note. From "Advanced Exercise Procedures for Evaluation of the Cardiovascular System," *Monograph*, by B. Balke, 1970, Milton, Wisconsin: The Burdick Corporation.

Table 6.7 Treadmill Protocol for Young Active People

Stage	METs	Speed (mph)	Grade (%)	Time (min)
1	5	1.7	10	3
2	7	2.5	12	3
3	9.5	3.4	14	3
4	13	4.2	16	3
5	16	5.0	18	3

Note. From "Multi-stage treadmill test of maximal and submaximal exercise" by R.A. Bruce, 1972. In American Heart Association, *Exercise testing and training of apparently healthy individuals: A handbook for physicians* (pp. 32-34), New York: American Heart Association.

Submaximal Exercise Test Protocols

Any GXT protocol can be used for submaximal or maximal testing. The HFI typically uses a submaximal GXT to estimate a person's $\dot{V}O_2$max or to simply show before to after changes in selected variables because of an exercise program. Changes in HR, BP, and RPE as a result of an exercise conditioning program make a submaximal test a good mechanism for showing improvements in cardiorespiratory function.

Submaximal GXT treadmill protocol. The initial stage and rate of progression of the GXT should be selected on the basis of the criteria mentioned earlier. In the following example, a Balke Standard Protocol (3 mph, 2.5% grade increase each 2 min) was used; HR was monitored in the last 30 sec of each stage. The test was terminated at 85% of age-adjusted maximal HR. Maximal aerobic power was estimated by extrapolating the HR response to the person's estimated maximal HR. Figure 6.4 presents the results of this test with a graph showing the HR response at each work rate. Note that the HR response is rather flat between the 0 and 5% grade. This is not an uncommon finding (see later discussion on YMCA test) and may be because the subject is too excited, or the stroke volume changes are accounting for the changes in cardiac output at these low work rates. The HR response is normally quite linear between 110 b/min and the subject's 85% of max HR cutoff.

To estimate $\dot{V}O_2$max, a line is drawn through the HR points from 7.5% grade to the final work rate. The line is extended (extrapolated) to the person's estimated maximal HR (183 b/min). A vertical line is dropped from the last point to the base line to estimate the subject's maximal aerobic power, which is 11.8 MET or 41.3 ml(kg•min)$^{-1}$. Remember that the estimated maximal HR may be inaccurate and that the estimate of maximal oxygen uptake will be influenced by this possible inaccuracy. The subject presented in this figure was later found to have a measured maximal HR of 195 b/min and was able to finish the 2-min stage equal to 12.8 METs.

Cycle ergometer submaximal GXT protocol. The submaximal cycle ergometer protocol is taken from *The Y's Way to Physical Fitness*. This protocol relies on the observation that a linear relationship exists between HR and work rate ($\dot{V}O_2$)

once an HR of approximately 110 b/min is reached. The test simply requires the person to complete one more stage past the one causing a HR of 110 b/min. The intent of the test is to extrapolate the line describing the HR work-rate relationship out to the person's age-adjusted maximal HR (as was done for the treadmill protocol) to estimate the person's $\dot{V}O_2$max. Each stage of the test lasts 3 min unless a person's HR has not yet reached a "steady state" (> 5 b/min-difference between 2nd- and 3rd-min heart rate). In that case, an extra minute is added to that stage. The pedal rate is maintained at 50 rpm so that, on a Monark cycle ergometer, a 0.5 kg increase in load is equal to 150 kgm/min (25 watts). Seat height is adjusted so that the knee is slightly bent when the pedal is at the bottom of the swing through on revolution. The seat height is recorded for future reference. HR is monitored during the later half of the 2nd and 3rd min of each stage.

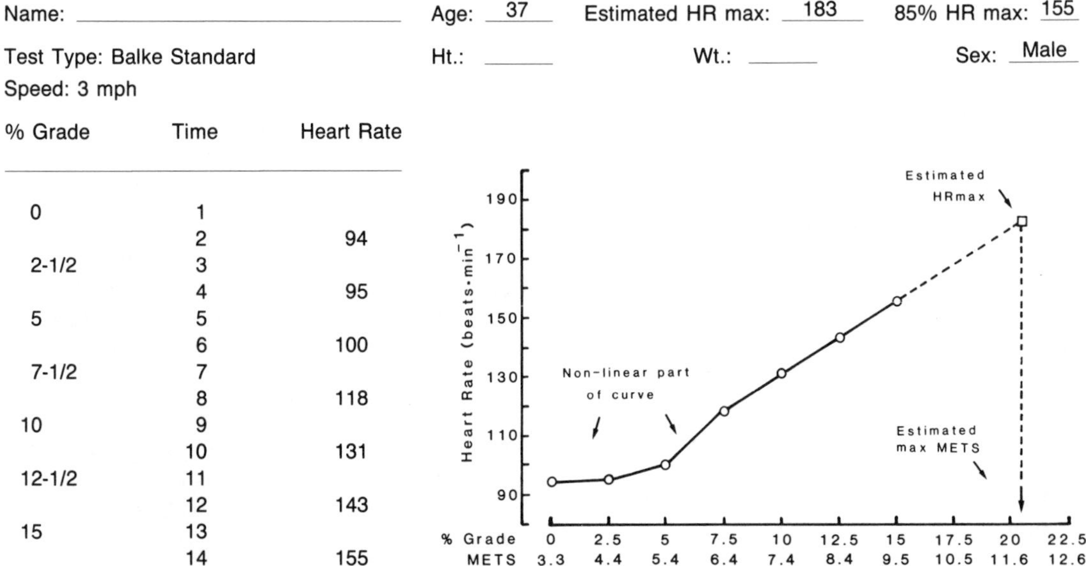

Figure 6.4 Maximal aerobic power estimated by measuring the heart rate response to a submaximal graded exercise test on a treadmill.

Table 6.8 Selection Criteria for Cycle Ergometer Protocol[a]

Body Weight Kg (lb)	Past 3-Month Activity Level Vigorous, >15 min, 3 days/week? No	Yes
	Test Protocol	
<73 (160)	A	A
74-90 (161 – 199)	A	B
>91 (200+)	B	C

Test Protocol	Test Stages (Min) I (1-2)	II (3-4)	III (5-6)	IV (7-8)
A	150[b]	300	450	600
B	150	300	600	900
C	300	600	900	1200

[a]Modified from ACSM (1986).
[b]Workrate is kpm/min.

Proper selection of the initial work rate and the rate of progression of the work rate on the cycle ergometer should take into consideration the person's weight, sex, age, and level of fitness. The ACSM deals with this problem by recommending three cycle ergometer protocols depending on body weight and recent pattern of physical activity. Table 6.8 outlines this information. People less than 73 kg (160 lb) would use Protocol A independent of activity status; thus Protocol A would be suitable for most women in our society.

The YMCA procedure does not consider the weight of the subject, but it does consider the activity status. Figure 6.5 shows that gender is the

a **GUIDE TO SETTING WORKLOADS FOR MALES ON THE BICYCLE ERGOMETER**

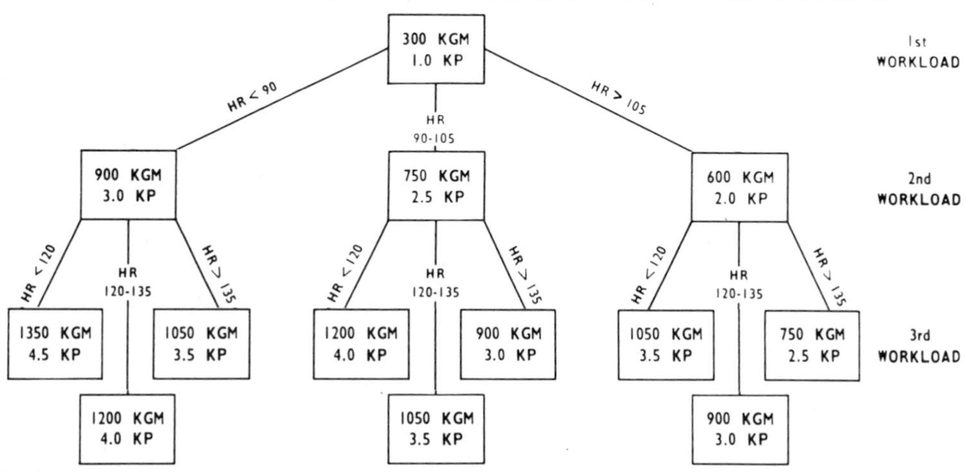

DIRECTIONS

1. **Set the 1st workload at 300 kgm/min (1.0 KP)**
2. **If HR in 3rd min is: Less than (<) 90, set 2nd load at 900 kgm (3 KP)**
   Between 90 and 105, set 2nd load at 750 kgm (2.5 KP)
   Greater than (>) 105, set 2nd load at 600 kgm (2.0 KP)
3. **Follow the same pattern for setting 3rd and final load.**
4. **NOTE: If the 1st workload elicits a HR of 110 or more, it is used on the graph, and only ONE more workload will be necessary.**

b **GUIDE TO SETTING WORKLOADS FOR FEMALES ON THE BICYCLE ERGOMETER**

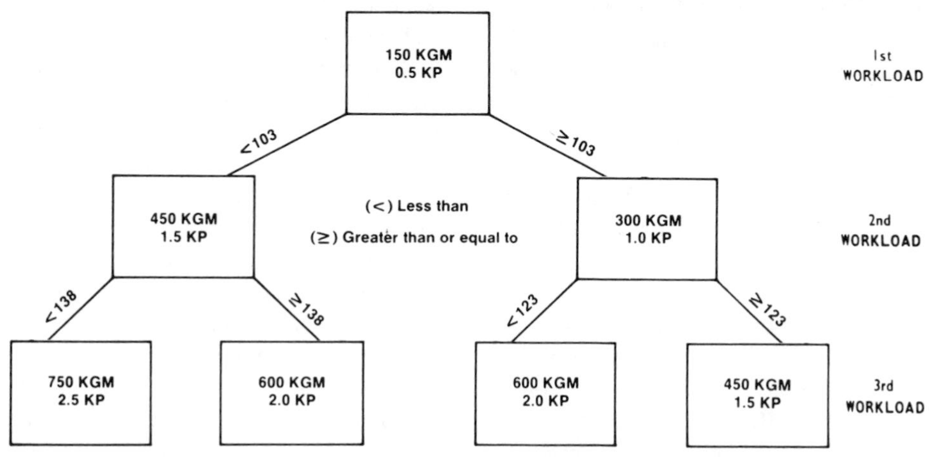

DIRECTIONS

1. **Set the first workload to 150 kgm/min (.5 KP).**
2. **If steady-state heart rate is < 103, set 2nd load at 450 kgm/min (1.5 KP).**
   If steady-state heart rate is ⩾ 103, set 2nd load at 300 kgm/min (1.0 KP).
3. **Follow this same pattern for setting the third and final load.**
4. **NOTE: If the 1st workload elicits a HR of 110 or more, it is used on the graph, and only ONE more workload will be necessary.**

Figure 6.5 **YMCA guidelines for setting the work rate on cycle ergometer graded exercise tests: standards for men and women. *The Y's Way to Physical Fitness*. (1982). Reprinted with permission.**

Form for YMCA Protocol

Name: ______________ Estimated HR max: 170 Ht.: ___ in Wt.: ___ lbs

Sex: Female Age: 50 85% HR max: 145 ___ cm ___ kg

Work Rate kgm/min	Heart Rate 2nd min	Heart Rate 3rd min
150	100	101
300		
450	138	140
600	153	156

1. Plot 3rd min HR for each work rate
2. Draw line through points starting at HR > 110
3. Extrapolate line to subject's estimated HR max
4. Drop vertical line from HR max to base line
5. Record estimated $\dot{V}O_2$ max in liters/min

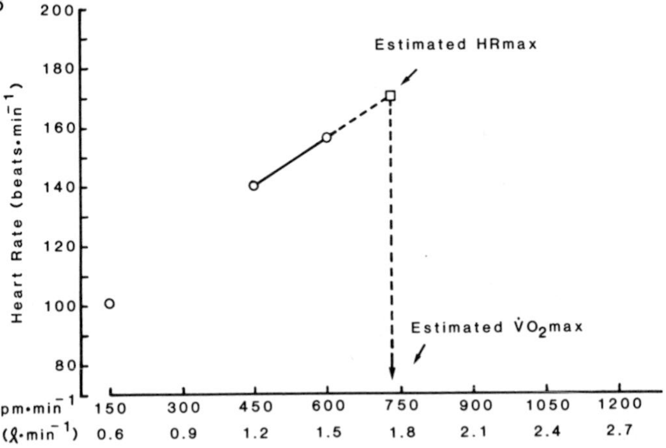

Figure 6.6 Maximal aerobic power estimated by measuring the heart rate response to a submaximal graded exercise test on a cycle ergometer, using the Y's Way of Fitness protocol. Adapted from *The Y's Way to Physical Fitness.* (1982). Used with permission.

primary variable for protocol selection. The stages are modified depending on the HR response to the specified work task. Emphasis is placed on a conservative choice of the initial work rate and the progression. A person does not need to have more than one additional HR measure past the work rate demanding a HR of 110 b/min.

The HR values for the 2nd and 3rd min of each work rate are recorded and directions are followed to estimate $\dot{V}O_2$max in liters/minute. These directions and an example are presented in Figure 6.6 for a 50-year-old woman. The stages followed the pattern dictated by the HR response to the initial work rate of 150 kpm/min. A line was drawn through the last two HR values and extrapolated to the estimated maximal HR. The $\dot{V}O_2$max was estimated to be 1.77 l/min. This value was multiplied by 1,000 to give 1,770 ml/min and divided by the 59-kg body weight to give an estimated $\dot{V}O_2$max of 30 ml(kg•min)$^{-1}$.

Step test submaximal GXT protocol. A multistage step test can be used to estimate $\dot{V}O_2$max and to show changes in cardiorespiratory function with training or detraining. As always, attention must be given to the initial stage and rate of progression of the stages so that the test is suited to the individual. Just as treadmill protocols vary, step test protocols vary. Table 6.4 presents three examples of step test protocols. The subject must be instructed to follow the metronome (4 counts per cycle, i.e., up-up-down-down) and step all the way up and all the way down. Each stage should last at least 2 min, with HR monitored in the last 30 sec of each 2 min period. HR is more difficult to monitor during a step test protocol if the palpation technique is used. An alternative is to put a BP cuff on the subject's arm and, when a HR measure is needed, to pump the cuff up to just above diastolic pressure (around 100 mmHg). Using the stethoscope, the pulse rate can be counted for 10

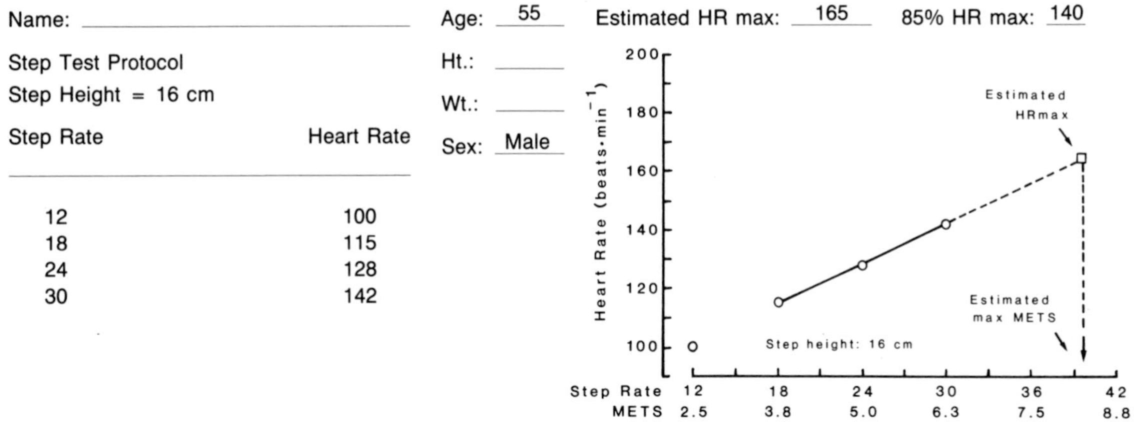

Figure 6.7 **Maximal aerobic power estimated by measuring the heart rate response to a submaximal graded exercise step test.**

or 15 sec. Release the pressure after each measurement.

As in the treadmill test protocol, the HR is plotted against the $\dot{V}O_2$ for each stage and the line drawn through the points to the age-adjusted maximal HR. A line is drawn to the baseline to obtain an estimate of $\dot{V}O_2$max. Figure 6.7 shows the results of a step test for a sedentary 55-year-old man prior to a training program. His estimated $\dot{V}O_2$max was about 29 ml(kg•min)$^{-1}$, or 8.3 METs.

Summary

The evaluation of CRF includes the screening of participants not suitable for CRF testing. Before any testing takes place, the individual signs a consent form that outlines the procedures, benefits, and risks. Test data are obtained at rest, during submaximal work, and, if appropriate, during maximal work. CRF evaluation might be in the form of a field test, such as the 1.5-m run, which is easy to administer. However, many tests of CRF use a GXT protocol on a treadmill, cycle ergometer, or step. An advantage of a GXT test over a field test is the ability to monitor physiological variables (such as BP, HR, and oxygen uptake) at different levels of work. A variety of maximal and submaximal protocols for a treadmill, cycle, or bench are presented for low-, moderate-, and high-fit individuals. Methods for estimation of maximal oxygen uptake are included. Procedures allowing the HFI to safely obtain accurate data are emphasized.

Suggested Reading for Chapter 6

AAHPERD (1980)

ACSM (1980)

ACSM (1986)

Åstrand and Rodahl (1970)

Balke (1963)

Balke (1970)

Borg (1982)

Bransford and Howley (1977)

Bruce (1972)

Cooper (1977)

Ellastad (1980)

Franks (1979)

Golding, Myers, and Sinning (1982)

Kasch, Phillips, Ross, Carter, and Boyer (1966)

Leblanc, Bouchard, Godbout, and Mondor (1981)

Margaria, Cerretelli, Aghemo, and Sassi (1963)

McArdle, Katch, and Pechar (1973)

McArdle and Magel (1970)

Montoye (1975)

Nagle, Balke, Baptista, Alleyia, and Howley (1971)

Naughton and Haider (1973)

Pollock, Schmidt, and Jackson (1980)

Pollock, Wilmore, and Fox (1984)

U.S. Department Health and Human Services (1981)

Willerson and Dehmer (1981)

See reference list at the end of the book for a complete source listing.

Chapter 7

Strength, Endurance, and Flexibility

Gina S. Sharpe and Wendell P. Liemohn

- Components
- Relation to health
- Relation to low-back pain
- Testing
- Recommendations for improvement

In addition to cardiorespiratory endurance activities, each exercise session should ideally include activities aimed at developing and maintaining desired levels of muscular strength, muscular endurance, and joint flexibility. This chapter defines each of these additional fitness/performance components and discusses their roles in enhancing an individual's ability to perform daily tasks. *Joint flexibility*, or particularly maintenance of range of motion (ROM), is an important consideration in exercise programming for the elderly. Also of special concern for this population is the condition of *osteoporosis*, typically a concomitant of aging and/or disuse wherein the density of bone decreases and becomes more susceptible to fracture. Exercise programs that develop and/or maintain strength can also play a role in allaying osteoporosis. This chapter focuses on (a) methods for improving muscular strength, endurance, and flexibility, (b) factors that may influence muscular development, (c) tools that can be used to assess these components, and (d) low-back functioning as it relates to these variables.

Muscular Strength and Endurance

Muscular strength refers to the maximum amount of force that can be exerted by a muscle. *Muscular endurance* refers to the ability of a muscle to exert a force repeatedly over a period of time. Muscular strength and endurance are related; an increase in one of these components usually results in some degree of improvement in the other. A reasonable amount of strength and endurance may help an individual be more efficient in performing daily tasks. Furthermore, the strength of the abdominal musculature can be a factor in helping to prevent low-back pain.

Improving Strength and Endurance

The amount of strength desired, beyond that needed to support the weight of the body and perform daily activities, is a personal choice. To improve strength, a muscle or group of muscles must exert a force against a resistance that is greater than what is normally encountered. The term *overload principle* is often used to convey this concept; strength development programs should focus on the progressive overloading of a muscle. The concept of overload dates back into Greek mythology and the story of Milo of Crotona who wanted to become the strongest man in Greece. When he was a youth he began lifting a young bull every day; he thereby developed enough strength to lift the bull when it was fully grown. A term used today, *progressive resistance exercise* (PRE), aptly describes Milo's experience. Progressive resistance exercise is a generic term that can apply to any physical training program. In strength training, PRE implies overload; once an individual can easily exert a force against a set resistance, the amount of resistance must be increased to produce further strength gains. Achieving overload is also possible by reducing the total time in which the exercise is performed.

Training programs that emphasize exertion of forces against a high resistance for a small number of repetitions enhance gains in strength, muscle size, and, to a lesser extent, endurance. Many believe that programs that emphasize a relatively low resistance and a high number of repetitions enhance muscular endurance and, to a smaller degree, strength. These examples exemplify the concept of *specificity of training*; the type of gain relates to the type of regimen followed in the workout. Most individuals who participate in a fitness program can achieve and maintain a desired amount of strength and endurance using the low-resistance, high-repetition approach.

Regular participation in a high-resistance, low-repetition program usually results in an increase in muscle girth. This increase, referred to as *hypertrophy*, typically corresponds to an increase in the diameter of the muscle fibers within a muscle. The degree of hypertrophy and the corresponding improvements in strength vary between individuals; however, a linear relationship does exist between strength and a muscle's cross-sectional area. Regular participation in a low-resistance, high-repetition program usually results in an increase in muscle endurance. The latter may be because of an increase in muscle (a) myoglobin concentration (b) mitochondrial enzymes, and/or (c) mitochondrial size and number.

Women are often concerned that PRE programs may make their muscles bulky and larger than they desire. Studies have shown, however, that women tend to increase their strength without undesirable increases in muscle bulk (Wilmore, 1982). An important factor in this is the relative amounts of testosterone present in males and females. Because endogenous testosterone levels become higher in males than females after puberty, postpubertal males have a much greater capacity to increase muscle bulk than females. Therefore, women can enjoy the benefits of weight-training with the confidence that typical weight-training programs are not likely to give enough definition to their muscles to make them look bulky. Both sexes appear to reach their asymptotes with respect to their abilities to gain strength during the late teens and twenties. Although the trainability difference between sexes is at its maximum at this time, endogenous testosterone levels appear to decrease at a faster rate in males than in females with aging; however, testosterone levels always tend to remain higher in males.

Strength Training Programs

Three basic types of strength development programs exist; they utilize isometric, isotonic (with and without varying resistance), and/or isokinetic protocols. The first type of program to be discussed is isometric training; it involves a static muscle contraction wherein the overall length of the muscle does not change during the application of a force against a fixed resistance. An example of an isometric exercise is attempting to move an immovable object. In physics, work is force multiplied by distance ($W = Fd$); because the distance the resistance is moved is zero in a static contraction; ''work'' per se is not accomplished.

Isometric exercises were very popular in the 1950s and early 1960s; however, because of their inherent limitations and certain contraindications, their usage is now minimal. One of the major criticisms of isometric training is that, because it does not require limb movement, strength gains are specific to the angle at which exercise takes place and do not occur equally throughout the entire range of motion. Another drawback to isometric exercises is that they can be potentially dangerous for individuals with cardiovascular symptomatology. Here a problem can occur because a person tends to hold his or her breath during isometric exercises; if this is done with a closed glotis, the increased pressures in the thoracic and abdominal areas can inhibit the return of blood to the heart and cause an increase in the blood pressure. This is called the *Valsalva maneuver*.

The second type of PRE program to be discussed is *isotonic training*; in this program, exercises are typically done with (a) free weights (e.g., dumbbells or barbells) or (b) machines in which the resistance is ''steered'' along a fixed path (e.g., a configuration that includes a lever, a cable or chain, and/or a pulley). Isotonic exercises involve concentric as well as eccentric contraction of muscle. In concentric contraction the muscle shortens as the weight is moved against the force of gravity; therefore positive work is accomplished. In an eccentric contraction the muscle lengthens as the weight is moved in the direction of the force of gravity; under these circumstances, gravity, rather than muscle contraction, is the force responsible for the movement. The effect of the lengthening (eccentric) contraction is to slow down the movement. In executing an arm curl with a dumbbell, a concentric contraction occurs as the weight is lifted; an eccentric contraction occurs as the weight is lowered.

Isotonic PREs can include the exertion of a force against a constant or variable resistance. The previously cited arm curl exercise with a set weight is an example of an isotonic exercise with a constant resistance; the dumbbell's weight is constant although the lifter's leverage varies during the exercise and he or she can notice some points in the range of motion that seem to be easier as well as some that seem to be harder. At the easier points the muscles are not required to contract to their maximum, in part, because of the lifter's leverage or mechanical advantage. Accommodating (variable) resistance-type training equipment was designed in an attempt to require the lifter to exert maximum effort throughout the range of movement. This type of equipment theoretically provides a greater resistance at the joint angles at which the lifter is stronger, and a lower resistance at his or her weaker positions; in other words it accommodates the lifter's leverage or strength. In some equipment (e.g., Nautilus), pulleys, which change the direction of a force, are replaced by cams, which vary the resistance while changing the force's direction. Other equipment (e.g., Universal Gym) achieves accommodating resistance features by altering the lifter's leverage; this is accomplished by varying the length of the moment arm of resistance. *Dynamic variable resistance* (DVR) is the label used to describe this feature.

Isokinetic equipment has both accommodating or variable resistance and speed-governing features. The performer can choose a speed at which he or she wants to exercise; maximal effort is required when the performer's rate of movement matches the preset speed. Isokinetic equipment typically utilizes a hydraulic form of resistance that is controlled by a speed governor. Because isokinetic equipment controls the rate of muscle contraction, it can potentially train the different muscle-fiber types (e.g., fast-twitch with fast contractions, slow-twitch with slow contractions). This type of equipment is employed in strength-training regimens (e.g., Mini Gym Corporation's *Leaper* and *Charger*); isokinetic equipment is also seen extensively in clinical and/or rehabilitation settings (e.g., Lumex Corporation's Cybex II and Orthotron).

The cost of accommodating resistance equipment may preclude its usage in many programs. Free weights and conventional types of strength-training equipment (i.e., machines that do not provide variable or accommodating resistance) are perhaps most often used. Moreover, despite some of the aforementioned inherent limitations of free-weight PRE regimens, free weights are very popular in strength-training programs designed to improve the performance of athletes. Free weights are favored because the lifts often (a) closely resemble the strength employment seen in athletics, (b) require the development of more skill because the movement is not steered, (c) involve complete muscle groups rather than isolated muscles and/or muscle groups, and (d) permit ballistic-type movements that are integral to many sport

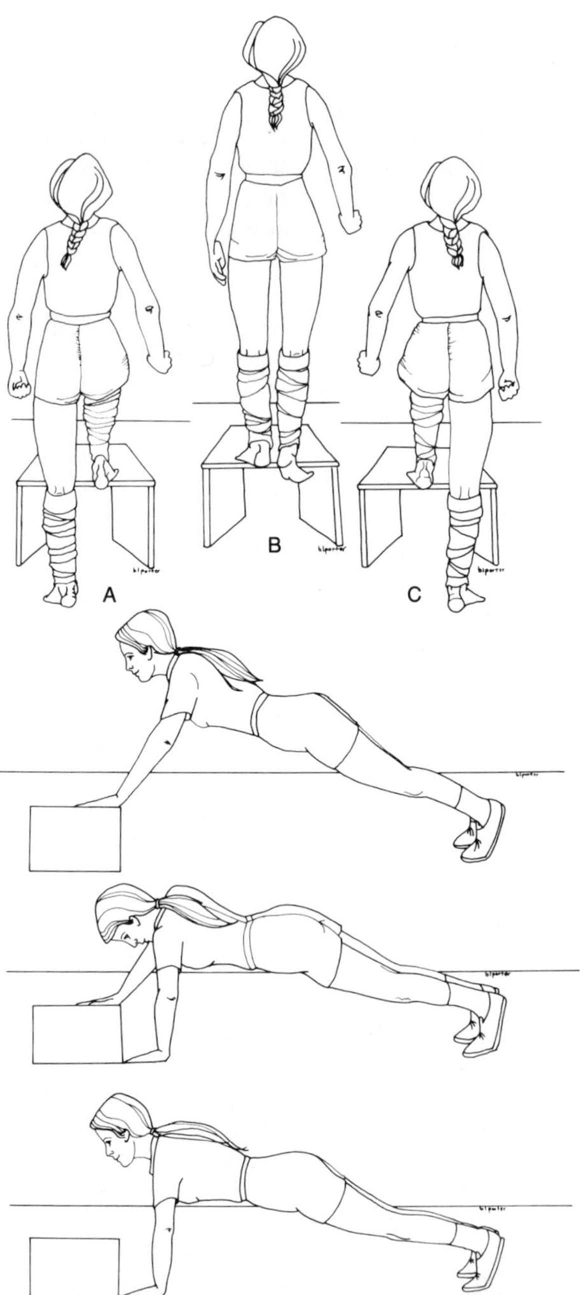

Figure 7.1 Bench Blasts and Arm Sprints. The Whitney bench blast can be used for developing leg power. After placing one foot on the bench and the other on the floor, the exerciser jumps (blasts) upward; the feet are "switched" in the air so that the opposite feet are now on the bench and the floor. The Arm Sprints can be used for developing arm and shoulder girdle strength; they are similar to bench stepping except the hands are used instead of the feet. Adapted from Fox and Mathews (1974). ***Interval Training.***

skills. However, free-weight PRE programs require much more in the way of coaching and supervision because incorrect lifting techniques can cause injuries.

All of the aforementioned PREs require minimal to extensive equipment. Items such as books, sandbags, or concrete weights could be substituted for barbells or dumbbells. A facsimile of accommodating resistance exercises can be contrived by having partner-type activities wherein each partner provides the accommodating resistance. Strength development programs can also include activities that use an individual's body weight as the primary resistance. Examples of these types of exercises include sit-ups, push-ups, dips, and pull-ups. Fox and Mathews (1974) discuss *arm sprints* and *bench blasts*, related to push-ups and step tests respectively. (See Figure 7.1). However, their designs make them very strenuous and challenging.

Plyometric-type exercises are often used as adjuncts to the more typical PREs in many athletic training programs; their equipment requirements are also negligible. In plyometric exercise a muscle group is typically put on stretch prior to its contraction (e.g., jumping to the floor from a bench and then immediately jumping for height).

PRE programs have commonalities regardless of the type of training followed. The terms *load, repetitions maximum,* and *sets* are fundamental to most PRE programs. *Load* refers to the total number of pounds or kilograms of resistance lifted. *Repetitions maximum* (RM) refers to the number of consecutive times an exercise can be done without interruption or rest. *Set* refers to the number of times an exercise regimen (e.g., all different exercises in a workout) is repeated. An example of a workout regimen is depicted in Figure 7.2.

Each exercise description in Figure 7.2 includes a means of estimating beginning load based on the participant's body weight. For optimal strength gains, a training regimen typically follows a 4-8 RM protocol; three sets are usually done and the workout is done every other day (or three times per week). To appreciate maximum strength gains, following the overload principle by increasing the resistance whenever RM exceeds 6-8 is important. Overload can also be reached with a lighter load

Figure 7.2a-f Weight Training Program for Developing Strength

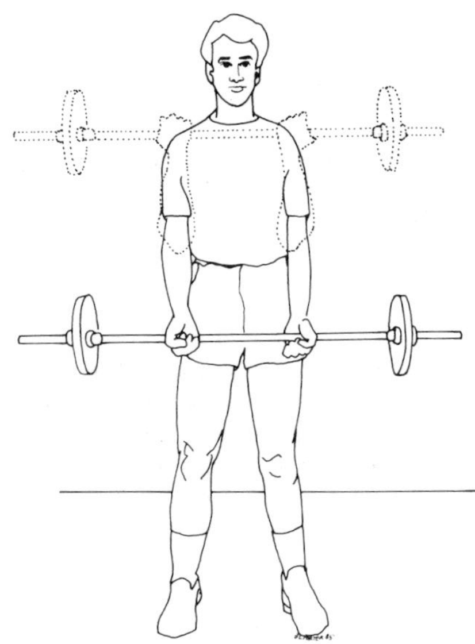

Figure 7.2a ***Arm Curl.*** **With arms extended, hold the barbell with an underhand grip. While keeping the elbows close to the sides, flex the forearms and raise the barbell to the chest; lower to the starting position. Suggested beginning load: 1/4 to 1/3 of body weight.**

Figure 7.2b ***Overhead Press.*** **Hold the barbell at chest level with an overhand grip. Push the bar straight up to full extension and then lower to the starting position. Do not hyperextend the back. Suggested beginning load: 1/4 to 1/3 of body weight.**

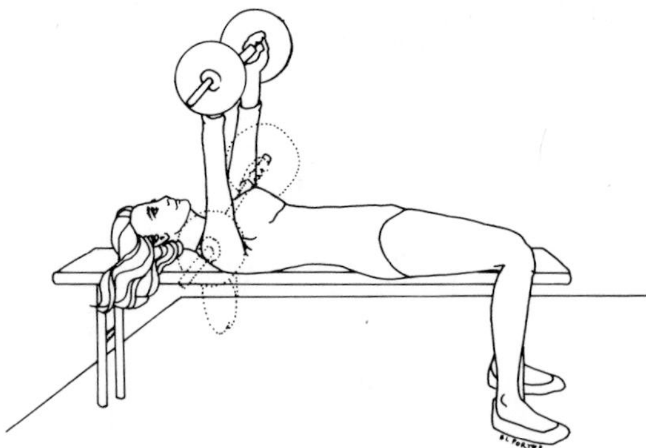

Figure 7.2c ***Bench Press.*** **Hold barbell above chest with hands slightly wider than shoulder width. Lower barbell to chest and push back to starting position. Suggested starting load: 1/4 to 1/3 of body weight.**

Figure 7.2d ***Upright rowing.*** **Hold barbell with an overhand grip with hands one to two inches apart. Keep elbows above the bar while raising it to shoulder position. Suggested beginning load: 1/4 to 1/3 of body weight.**

Figure 7.2e ***Heel Lifts.*** **With barbell behind shoulder at the back of the neck, raise upward on toes and then slowly return the heels to the floor. Suggested beginning load: 1/2 to 2/3 of body weight.**

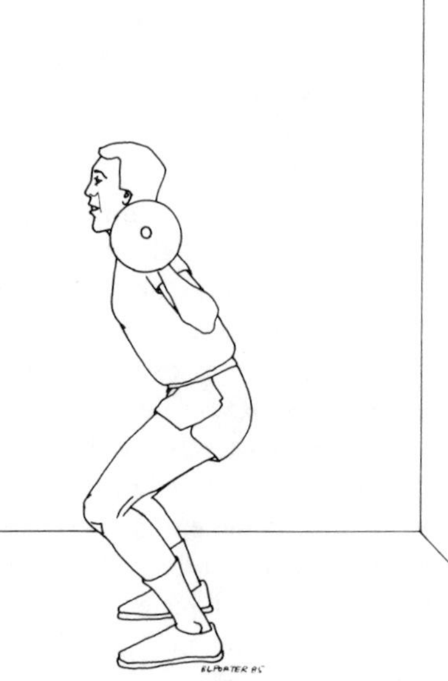

Figure 7.2f ***Half Squats.*** **With barbell behind shoulders at the back of the neck, gradually lower body to a semi-squat position. Keep back straight. Suggested beginning load: 1/2 to 2/3 of body weight.**

and a greater RM number (e.g., 10-25 RM); such a workout places a greater emphasis on muscle endurance development, whereas a 6-8 RM places more emphasis on strength development.

Assessing Muscular Strength

Many tests can be used to assess muscular strength and endurance. Dynamometers and cable tensiometers can be used to measure strength at most specific joint angles or positions. For the ingenious and budget conscious, the mass-produced torque wrench can be an effective strength-measurement instrument (Liemohn & Kovatch, 1979). Although the aforementioned devices provide a fairly accurate measurement of strength, they are limited because only static strength assessment is permitted.

A popular test that involves movement is the one-repetition maximum test. This test utilizes a trial-and-error process to determine the greatest amount of weight an individual can lift. Isokinetic testing devices are available to provide information about strength throughout the range of movement; some of these, such as the Cybex II, are very accurate but expensive.

Because abdominal strength plays an important role in the prevention of low-back pain, a modified sit-up test is presented in this chapter; a low score on this test may be indicative of a high risk for future low-back problems. (The relationship between abdominal strength and low-back problems is described in more detail in a later section of this chapter.) In this test, the exerciser assumes a hook-lying position (i.e., on back with knees bent) with the arms crossed and the hands placed on the opposite shoulders. The exerciser curls the neck and back until the scapulae are lifted from the exercise surface; he or she then returns to the starting position. This test and normative data are depicted in Figure 7.3 and Table 7.1.

Figure 7.3 The Head and Shoulder Raise test for abdominal strength. Subject "curls" the neck and upper back until the trunk reaches a 30°-40° angle with the exercise surface; then returns to the starting position.

Table 7.1 Standards for 1-Min Sit-Up Test

Rating	Number of Sit-Ups
Good	>35
Acceptable	20-30
Needs work	<15

Flexibility

Flexibility is the capacity to move a joint throughout its ROM. Maintaining a reasonable degree of flexibility is necessary for efficient body movement; being flexible and lithe may also decrease the chances of sustaining (a) muscle injury and/or soreness and (b) low-back pain. In order to move body segments, the muscles opposite those performing the movement (antagonistic muscles) must lengthen sufficiently. Tight muscles, tendons, and ligaments limit lengthening of the antagonistic muscles and thus reduce the range of movement of body segments. Soreness or injury may result when tight muscles are subjected to strenuous physical activity. Lack of flexibility in the hamstrings and low-back area may increase an individual's susceptibility to low-back pain. (This relationship is discussed in greater detail in a later section of this chapter.)

Improving Flexibility

Hartley-O'Brien (1980) discusses two approaches to improve flexibility. One is to decrease the resistance of the target (tight) muscles; a second technique is to increase the strength of the antagonistic muscles. Decreasing the resistance of the target muscles can be accomplished by either (a) increasing connective tissue length or (b) attaining a greater degree of relaxation in the target muscle. Many flexibility regimens employ a prolonged static stretch technique to address both of these factors. Static stretching typically involves slowly lengthening the muscle(s) to a point of slight discomfort; when this point is reached, the position is held for several seconds. If an attempt to progressively increase range of motion exists (somewhat analogous to the overloading of skeletal muscle to increase strength), flexibility improves.

Athletic trainers often utilize the static stretching procedure; furthermore, they often employ an additional step once the elongated or stretched position is established. After the latter point is reached, the trainer applies resistance while the athlete concurrently contracts the target muscle group. Although several variations of this technique exist, they all essentially fit under the rubric of proprioceptive neuromuscular facilitation (PNF). PNF might hold as great a promise as any technique in improving flexibility. However, a major limitation exists in its employment—it requires two individuals to work together. If PNF is done as a partner exercise and the partners are not adequately instructed in the technique, injury can result (Surburg, 1983).

Hartley-O'Brien's other approach to increase flexibility (i.e., increasing the strength of the muscle group antagonistic to the target or tight muscles) might be effective; however, research regarding its efficacy is lacking. A third approach, dynamic stretching, often involves bouncy or jerky movements; because momentum is involved, this type of stretching is also referred to as a ballistic method. When a muscle on one side of a joint rapidly contracts, the muscles opposite the contracting muscle often must quickly relax to permit lengthening. However, as a protective mechanism against overstretching in fast jerky movements, the antagonist muscles resist lengthening by contracting. This phenomenon, which actually opposes the desired stretch in dynamic flexibility exercises, is called the myotatic or stretch reflex. This reflex-type contraction may result from the dynamic stretching; this can be a drawback to its effectiveness.

DeVries (1980), who did some of the pioneer research in the area of flexibility, concludes that both static and dynamic methods are equally effective. However, deVries suggests that the use of static methods might be preferred because (a) there is less chance of stretching beyond the limits of the muscle tissue, (b) the energy requirements are lower, and (c) static stretching may result in less muscle soreness. For best results, stretching exercises should be performed on a regular basis. Stretching during the warm-up phase of an exercise bout is particularly important. Stretching exercises at the conclusion of the workout may be helpful in decreasing muscle soreness. Several flexibility exercises are depicted in Figure 7.4.

Assessing Flexibility

Because flexibility is joint-specific, determining the ROM of a few joints does not necessarily provide an indicator of flexibility in other joints. Some tests can be used to estimate flexibility of certain body joints; these indicators of joint flexibility range from simple tests to the more complex tests that require specific measuring equipment.

A test commonly used by fitness instructors is the Sit-and-Reach Test. Results of this test serve as an estimate of an individual's flexibility in the posterior thigh (i.e., hamstrings) and low-back area (i.e., lumbar erector spinae). In this test the individual being evaluated sits on the floor with

Figure 7.4a-f Common stretching exercises.

Figure 7.3a *Side Stretch.* **With the feet shoulder width apart, bend trunk to one side, return to upright position and repeat to opposite side.***

Figure 7.4b *Trunk Rotation.* **With heels flat on floor and arms extended laterally, twist trunk SLOWLY as far as you can go to each side.**

Figure 7.4c *Stride Stretch.* **Flex one leg under chest (knee over ankle and foot) and extend opposite one. Lean forward while pushing your hips downward; repeat on opposite side.**

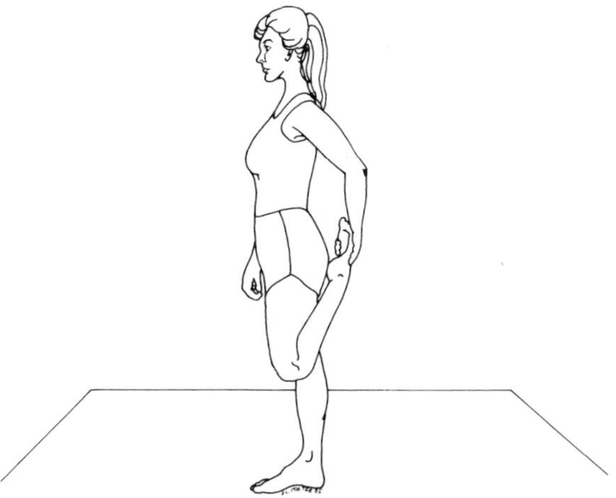

Figure 7.4d *Anterior Thigh Stretch.* **Pull one foot with the opposite hand until slight discomfort is felt in the anterior thigh; repeat on opposite side.**

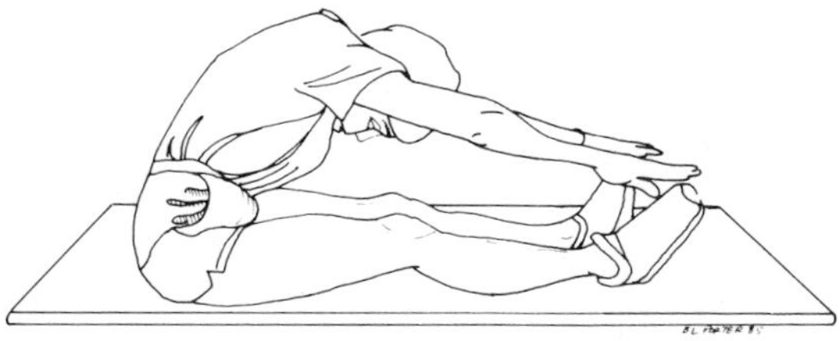

Figure 7.4e *Posterior Thigh/Low Back Stretch.* **Curl your back and reach forward and hold.**

Figure 7.4f *Calf Stretch.* **Stand 3-4 feet from wall with feet parallel and heels flat on floor. Lean forward while keeping body straight.**

***Static stretches are typically held for 15-30 seconds.**

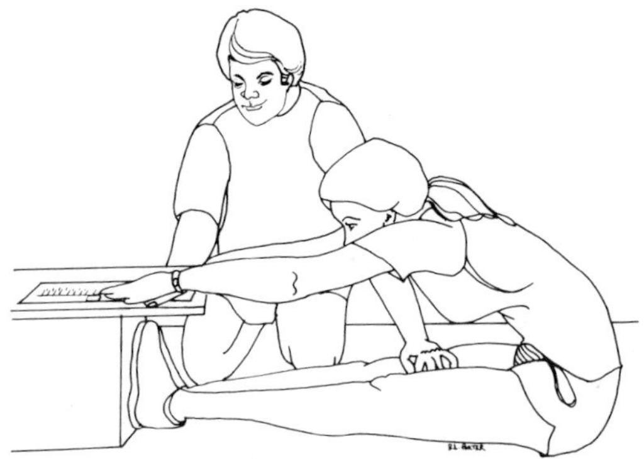

Figure 7.5 Sit and Reach Test of flexibility. Subject's feet (without shoes) are flat against the box; observer holds knees down while subject reaches forward as far as possible with one hand on top of the other.

his or her legs extended and feet flat against a box. A meter stick is attached to the top of the box with the 23 cm mark located above the junction of the feet with the box. The individual being evaluated is instructed to slowly reach forward as far as possible; the distance reached can be entered in Table 7.2 for interpretation.

Table 7.2 Standards for Sit-and-Reach Test

Rating	Sit-and-Reach (cm)
Good	>35
Acceptable	20-30
Needs work	<20

Although the Sit-and-Reach Test is very reliable, it is not without limitations. For example, hyperflexibility in one area may mask inflexibility in another area. Furthermore, this field test cannot be used to determine if any significant differences exist between flexibility of the right and left limbs of the body. Lastly, low scores in obese populations may be caused by the amount of fatty tissue rather than a lack of flexibility. The Leighton Flexometer and the goniometer have been used to assess actual ROM; the latter can be purchased for a nominal price at most medical supply sources. In the hands of the experienced tester, both devices can provide an accurate estimate of joint ROM. This equipment can also be used to determine if there is balance between right and left limb flexibility measurements. A drawback is that little normative data exist and much that does is based on clinical populations (Boone & Azen, 1979).

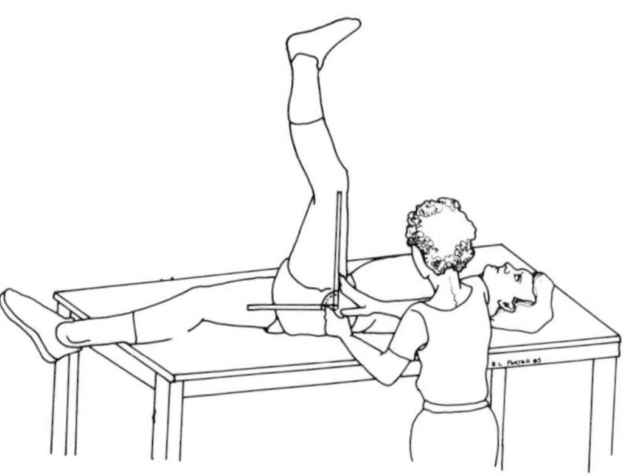

Figure 7.6 Measuring flexibility with a Goniometer.

Low-Back Problems

Low-back pain is one of the most common complaints among adults in the U.S. Low-back problems (a) account for more lost work-hours than any other type of occupational injury and (b) are the most frequent cause of activity limitation in individuals under 45 years old in the U.S. Muscular deficiencies, including lack of abdominal strength, have been recognized as important considerations in physical medicine regimens for some time. The abdominal muscles play a major role in preventing excessive anterior or forward tilt of the pelvis, and strong abdominal musculature appears to play a very important role in supporting the trunk in postures often considered compromising to the low back. In forward leaning postures, strong abdominal muscle contraction can appreciably increase intraabdominal pressure; this appears to create a splinting-type effect on the trunk, which in turn decreases the stress placed on intervertebral discs.

Two groups of antagonistic muscles (the hip flexors and the hip extensors) are also associated with low-back pain; the former tilts the pelvis anteriorly and the latter tilts the pelvis posteriorly. Here the concern is lack of extensibility or too much tightness in the pelvis rather than lack of strength. Extreme shortening of either group can have a deleterious effect on the functioning of the lower back.

Exercises for the Back

Many who suffer from low-back pain can alleviate the problem by doing exercises that strengthen and stretch the supportive muscles of the back. Williams (1974), an orthopedic surgeon, suggests a series of exercises aimed at preventing or remediating low-back problems. Williams believes that while standing erect, as well as standing in other typically assumed postures, an excessive lordotic curve tends to occur (e.g., swayback); he contends that these postures may aggravate or be responsible for low-back pain and/or ruptured disks. With this reasoning, Williams recommends flexion-type exercises that emphasize reduction of the lumbar lordotic curve; his exercises include abdominal curls, pelvic tilts, and stretching the lumbar erector spinae, hip extensors, and hip flexors. Many medical exercise prescription regimens have been based on Williams' flexion exercises. (See Figure 7.7).

In addition to his exercise recommendations, Williams also discusses exercises that he believes are potentially harmful to the back. Exercises in Figure 7.8 appear to be particularly contraindicated if they are done ballistically. Regardless of how the toe-touch exercise is done, returning to the upright position can increase intradiscal pressures markedly (Andersson, Ortengren, & Nachemson, 1977); this is further discussed in a later section. The deleterious effects of the double-leg-lift exercise can be decreased by increasing the thigh/floor angle (i.e., the higher the feet are held, the easier it is to avoid a lordotic curve and stress to the low back).

In contradistinction to Williams' exercise recommendations, some programs suggest that maintaining the lordotic curve and doing back extension exercises are important in preventing back

Figure 7.7a-c Low Back Exercises (Williams, 1974)

Figure 7.7a Supine with knees bent, slowly curl upward and gradually lower trunk to starting position.

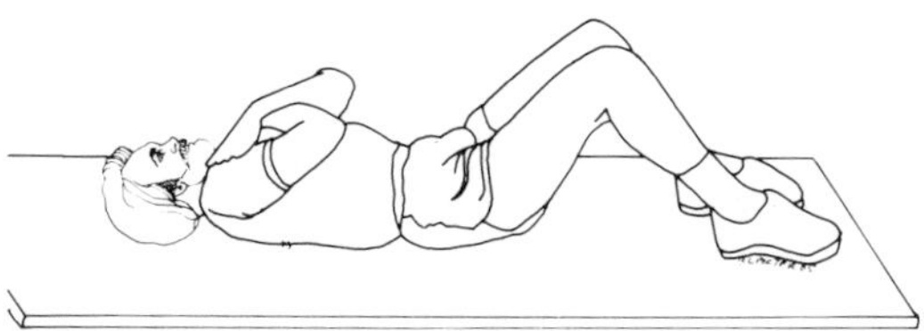

Figure 7.7b Supine with knees bent, raise buttocks and hold for a few seconds; slowly lower the buttocks to the starting position.

Figure 7.7c Supine with knees bent, grasp knees, and gradually pull knees to chest, lifting buttocks off floor as far as possible.

trouble (McKenzie, 1981). McKenzie contends that postural stresses cause adaptive shortening that can alter the relationship of the two structural components of the intervertebral discs (i.e., the nucleus and its fibrous periphery). He believes that loss of back extensibility is an important factor and one of the major causes of low-back problems; therefore he recommends participating in exercises that restore or maintain the lumbar lordotic curve and maintain ROM. One of the activities that he

Figure 7.8a-b EXERCISES TO AVOID.

Figure 7.8a ***Standing Toe-Touch.***

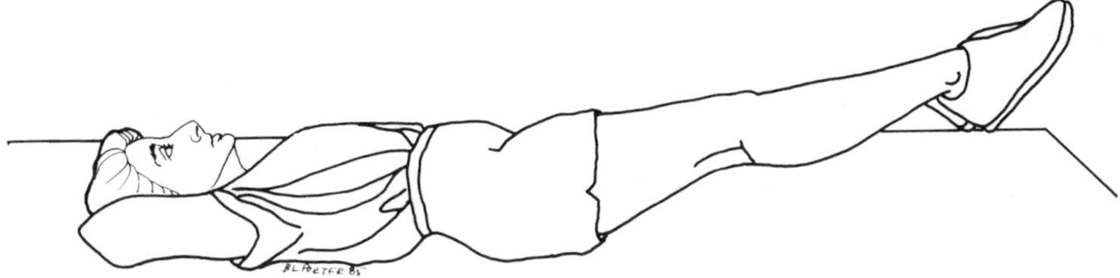

Figure 7.8b ***Double-Leg Lift.***

recommends is a push-up-type exercise wherein the individual keeps the pelvis in contact with the floor as he or she slowly pushes the torso up; this of course results in a hyperextension in the low-back area. (See Figure 7.9). This type of exercise activity, according to McKenzie, moves the nucleus anteriorly rather than toward the weaker posterior aspect of the disc. McKenzie also includes lumbar flexion exercises in later stages of his exercise protocol; full range of spinal flexion as well as extension are goals of his program.

Because little substantive research has been completed which compares the efficacy of Williams' and Mckenzie's protocols (Ponte, Jensen, & Kent, 1984), an individual with back problems may be best advised to consult with a physician and physical therapist before engaging in any type of an exercise program. The fact that discordant views with respect to exercises for back functioning (a) exist and (b) appear to be beneficial may explain why regimens developed by physical therapists often take an eclectic approach and draw from both the Williams and the McKenzie recommendations, dependent upon individual patient needs. For example, Williams' flexion exercises appear to be beneficial for most individuals with

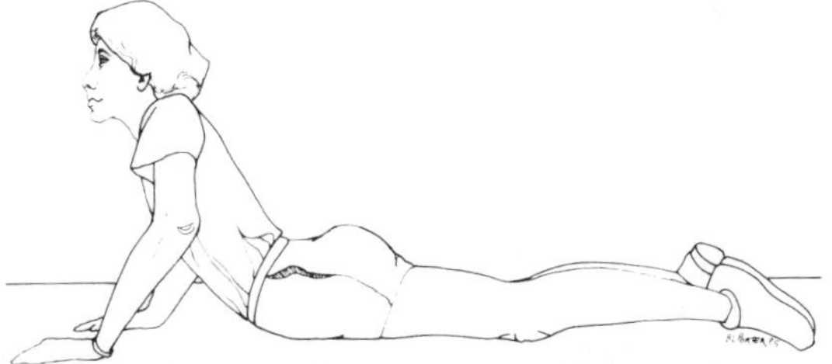

Figure 7.9 McKenzie's back hyperextension exercise.

low-back pain; however, instead of trying to stay in the continued-flexed postures recommended by him, it seems that the periodic assumption of lordotic postures and maintenance of ROM are also important considerations. A nonexercise technique recommended by McKenzie for facilitating a good lordotic posture is using a cylindrical lumbar pillow while sitting for prolonged periods. This, plus inclusion of the aforementioned exercises, is often the recommendation made by physical therapists who have extensive experience in working with patients with low-back pain.

Most acute low-back pain symptoms disappear with time, even if an exercise regimen is not implemented, only to occur again and again. Moreover, these episodes diminish with age; a physiological explanation would be the concomitant increase in the viscosity of the nucleus of the intervertebral disk. This may suggest that good body mechanics and other preventive measures such as maintaining at least adequate flexibility are important considerations that should be addressed by exercise leaders. Low-back pain may be related to poor posture; the following hints are often recommended for those with low-back pain symptomatology. Because poor sleeping postures can increase tension in the low-back area, sleeping posture can be an important consideration. For example, lying on the stomach or the back with the legs straight tends to increase the lordotic curve in the lower back; thus these two recumbent postures, possibly because of changes in intradisc and/or nerve root pressure, may be a cause of low-back pain or discomfort in some individuals. Sleeping on the side or the back with the hips and knees bent appears to be comfortable and appropriate for most individuals. (The type of mattress can also be a factor; for example, a posture that results in discomfort after sleeping on a firm mattress might not have caused a problem if it had been used on a water bed.)

Standing for long periods of time may cause fatigue in the supporting muscles of the trunk. Whenever possible, an individual should avoid prolonged standing; however, variance in standing postures may be helpful to some who must remain on their feet for extended periods. Changes in posture might include (a) altering the placement of the feet and/or (b) periodically increasing and decreasing pelvic tilt. Controversy exists concerning which sitting postures are most appropriate for relieving back pain symptomatology. Although Williams' flexion postures are often comfortable for many, these same postures are uncomfortable for others. A lumbar pillow, as recommended by McKenzie, ensures a lordotic curve and concurrently takes pressure off the area of discomfort.

Exercise/Activity Contraindications

Improper lifting techniques can be detrimental to low-back functioning. The lifter should not keep the legs straight when bending forward to lift an object (regardless of the object's weight) because the large turning moment (i.e., torque) of the head and trunk (plus the object) must be balanced by the force of contraction of the lumbar erector spinae musculature. Because these muscles have little leverage (i.e., a very short force arm compared to the long resistance arm of the trunk and head), the magnitude with which they must contract to perform the movement can result in alarmingly high intradisc pressures (Andersson et al., 1977). Therefore, in lifting, the individual should bend at the knees, keep the feet staggered and the trunk straight, and then use the strong musculature of the hips and thighs to lift the object; concurrently, the object should be held as close as possible to the lifter's center of gravity. (See Figure 7.10).

The toe-touching exercise has been criticized as being a potentially damaging exercise to low-back functioning (Williams, 1974); the mathematical model devised by Strait, Inman, and Ralston (1947) and the intradisc pressure transducer technique employed by Andersson, et al. (1977) provide research evidence that condemns the toe-touching exercise's inclusion in exercise protocols. Particularly to be avoided is the bouncing toe touch wherein intradisc pressures could even be higher. Kraus and Raab (1961), however, include toe-touching in both their test and their exercise protocols; because the YMCA's low-back exercise protocol follows their ideas, toe-touching is also incorporated in their exercise activities (Melleby, 1982). Ostensibly they recommend toe-touching to improve flexibility; however, because this ex-

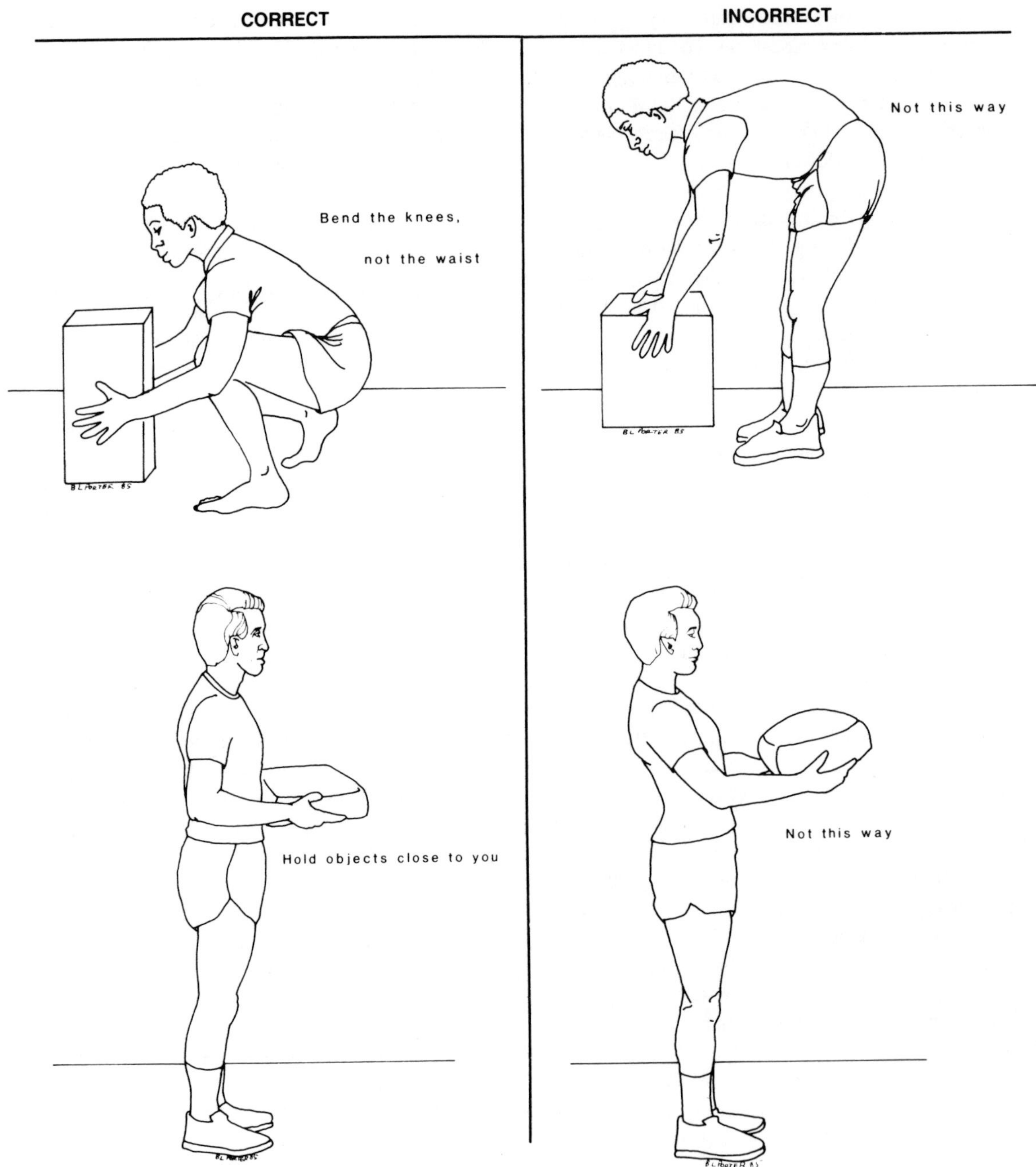

Figure 7.10 Lifting and carrying postures.

ercise is typically prescribed for stretching the hamstrings, a sitting toe-touch should accomplish the same goal with fewer drawbacks (e.g., less intradisc pressures).

The drawbacks to straight-leg situps and double-leg raises have been known for some time; perhaps the greatest indictment against the former was LeVeau's (1977) radiographic study that showed anterior displacement of lumbar vertebra while the exercise was performed. Bent-leg sit-ups are much preferred; however, the head/shoulder raise may be the exercise of choice because it appears to accomplish the same results with few if any contraindications. (See Figure 7.11).

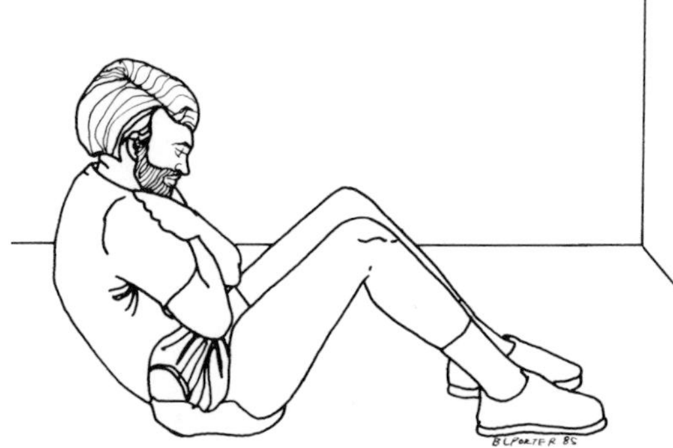

Figure 7.11 Head and shoulder raise.

Summary

Muscular strength, muscular endurance, and flexibility exercises should be parts of the total fitness program; each component plays an important role in the positive health concept. Maintaining a reasonable degree of strength and flexibility may (a) increase efficiency in performing daily tasks, (b) increase resistance to muscle injuries, and (c) aid in preventing low-back pain.

Isometric, isotonic, and isokinetic strength training regimens each have advantages and disadvantages. Several strength-measuring tools are also available.

Two basic types of flexibility development programs are described (i.e., static and dynamic) and a third type is mentioned. Static stretching appears to have advantages, and flexibility exercises should be performed during the warm-up and cool-down phases of an exercise bout. Flexibility assessment methods are also discussed.

Strength and flexibility have pertinent roles in preventing low-back pain. Several exercises that may be helpful in preventing and/or alleviating low-back pain are included in the chapter. In addition, exercises that may be harmful to the back are mentioned.

Suggested Reading for Chapter 7

Andersson, Ortengren, and Nachemson (1977)

Boone and Azen (1979)

deVries (1980)

Fox and Mathews (1974)

Gracovetsky, Farfan, and Lamy (1977)

Hartley-O'Brien (1980)

Kraus and Raab (1961)

LeVeau (1977)

Liemohn and Kovatch (1979)

McKenzie (1981)

Melleby (1982)

Ponte, Jensen, and Kent (1984)

Smith (1982)

Strait, Inman, and Ralston (1947)

Surburg (1983)

Williams (1974)

Wilmore (1982b)

See reference list at the end of the book for a complete source listing.

Chapter 8
Relaxation and Arousal

- The components
- Relation to health
- Effects of personality
- Stress
- How to cope with stress

Cardiovascular function, relative leanness, and low-back function have been accepted as physical fitness components. Physical fitness also assumes minimum levels of balance, flexibility, and muscular strength and endurance to be able to do daily tasks efficiently.

Although acknowledging our inability to separate mental, physical, psychological, social, and spiritual aspects of life, this book has emphasized *physical* fitness. This chapter deals with one of those areas that bridges the psychological and physiological aspects of fitness. The topics included can assist the HFI in dealing effectively with fitness participants.

The healthy life involves the ability to relax and disregard irrelevant stimuli during quiet times. The fit person can also work and play with vigor and enthusiasm. This relaxation (parasympathetic nervous system dominance, and vitality (sympathetic nervous system dominance) are both enhanced by physical conditioning. One of the keys to a healthy life is a balance between arousal and relaxation. People who are always relaxed and easygoing do not accomplish very much. On the other hand, people who have the "get-up-and-go" attitude toward all aspects of life at all times exhibit "coronary-prone" behavior.

This chapter deals with this fitness component by describing the relationships among personality, physical activity, stress, and health. Dealing extensively with all psychological aspects of fitness is beyond the scope of this chapter. Pathological traits or behaviors should be referred to psychological professionals. We are dealing with different levels of "normal" personality and stress and their implications for fitness programs.

Personality and Physical Activity

Providing definitive comments about the psychophysiological effects of a specific external stimulus is impossible because individuals perceive and react to the same situation differently. The same movie may evoke anger, laughter, or no emotion from three different people. A series of the same stimuli in a game environment might cause best and worst performances in different people.

Part of the different perception of and reaction to the same situation is related to personality. Although completely characterizing someone's personality or predicting exactly how that personality will interact with physical activity or other stimuli is not possible, some generalizations aid the HFI in dealing with individuals in fitness programs. The Health Status Questionnaire (*HSQ*) in Appendix B has several questions dealing with the individual's personality and perception of health and illness. Relevant questions on the HSQ are indicated in appropriate sections of this chapter.

Type A-B

There is general agreement that one's personality and ability to cope with stress are related to CHD. However, the exact characteristics that cause the higher risk are difficult to enumerate or measure. One attempt to do this separates people's behaviors into Type A and Type B. Type A behavior (i.e., the go-getter, hard driving, time conscious, impatient person—see question 82 on HSQ) describes coronary-prone behavior. A Type A person has a greater stress response to psychological stressors. Therefore this person should learn to relax, should be cautious about overdoing exercise, and should be engaged in more relatively noncompetitive activities. The Type B person, on the other hand, may need more stimulation and motivation to begin and continue in the exercise program.

Anger

Some evidence suggests that a relationship exists between anger and CHD. People who keep their anger "bottled-up" inside rather than expressing it (e.g., talking to a close friend about it) have increased risk of CHD (see question 69 on HSQ). Three recommendations can be made to help people with anger: (a) try to develop positive attitudes toward self, others, and the world in general so that anger is less frequent; (b) express emotions, such as anger, rather than denying the emotions or keeping them inside; (c) develop the kind of relationship with others so that emotions can be shared (see question 68 on HSQ). The HFI can help people acknowledge their emotions by being open about his or her own feelings (e.g., "that . . . really made me angry yesterday") and by being sensitive about the fitness participants' moods (e.g., "you seem upset today").

Aggression, Assertiveness, Hostility, and Denial

All of these characteristics may, for different reasons, cause a person to do too much. Aggressive or hostile individuals may try to do too much exercise because they get so involved in the activity that they don't pay attention to signs of discomfort or danger. Some people try to deny that they have pain and thus tend to do too much. One of the distinctions between assertiveness and aggression or hostility is that the assertive person is sensitive to others, whereas the aggressive or hostile person tends to be less concerned with others' feelings. The HFI needs to protect other members of the group from aggressive or hostile behavior.

Anxiety, Depression, and Fear

Postcardiac patients have high levels of anxiety, fear, and depression. Others with low fitness levels may also be bothered by one or more of these conditions (see questions 29, 77-79 on HSQ). People who are unduly worried or afraid need support. They must be able to ease into activity and to see that positive results can occur with minimum risks; gradually they can be introduced to higher levels of activity. Another aspect of a person becoming physically active and adopting other healthy behaviors is the increased perception of control over his or her own life. The feeling of lack of control is often a part of the anxiety, fear, or depression.

Rationalization

One of the difficult skills in dealing with people is to be able to differentiate between real reasons for behavior and rationalizations that are given which sound better than the real reasons. It will not be possible to help a person deal with exercise or other health behaviors until the real reasons for the current behaviors are known. The HFI hears many excuses for why someone can't develop healthy activities or discontinue unhealthy behaviors. One technique to help the person deal with the underlying reasons for his or her inactivity is to keep asking questions aimed at uncovering the real reasons. Chapter 13 provides assistance for helping people modify behavior.

Rejection

Rejection is relevant in two ways for the HFI. Some people in the fitness program have rejected exercise in the past or feel that active people have rejected them (e.g., last chosen to play games). The HFI must be sensitive to this feeling and help the person feel included and welcome. On the other hand, the HFI should realize that he or she will not be 100% successful in helping people become active. Some potential fitness participants will reject fitness programs; it is important for the HFI not to take that rejection personally.

Catharsis

Some people use exercise as a cleansing agent for the mind and emotions. The fitness activities are used to erase the cluttered state and to be able to start fresh following the exercise. After a minimum level of fitness is reached, a place in the fitness program is available for activities that allow individuals to "let go." Chapter 11 describes a variety of activities that might be utilized in this type of atmosphere.

Euphoria

Numerous reports show that some people experience a special emotional state (e.g., "runner's high") while exercising. This state resembles a deep religious experience or some of the emotional states achieved by drugs. It cannot be planned, nor can it serve as the basis for motivation, because all people will not experience it. However, a positive addiction to exercise can take place as people achieve the almost universal good feeling as a result of appropriate physical activities. One of the main purposes of the HFI is to help people progress to the fitness level where they become "addicted" to exercise by looking forward to their regular workouts. As with all healthy behaviors, it is possible to go to the extreme, so that instead of a healthy addiction to exercise as one part of life, some may become obsessed and overemphasize its importance, spending exercising time that should be spent on other parts of their lives (e.g., working, or with family). The HFI assists at both extremes, helping inactive people become active and discouraging exercise fanatics from spending excessive amounts of time in physical fitness activities.

Motivation

The HFI is concerned with motives for exercise at two levels. The first level is How can we get people to *begin* a fitness program? What kind of contact can be made with people in our communities to encourage them to begin fitness programs? The public has been educated to realize, in general, what healthy behaviors are (e.g., most people agree that they should exercise on a regular basis). However, convenient programs that provide personal contact and concern by exercise professionals are needed to complement information about the healthy life. The second level deals with the things that can be done to get people to continue exercise as a part of their lifestyles. Individual attention, realistic goals that are periodically tested, option for group participation, involvement of spouse and/or important others, contracts, and programs that minimize injury all seem to help adherence to fitness programs. Chapter 13 deals with characteristics of people who tend to drop out of fitness programs and suggests ways to enhance regular exercise behavior. Whether the HFI is motivating a participant to begin or to continue activity, fitness has to achieve priority status (like eating and sleeping) in a person's life. Efforts at increasing motivation must have that end in sight at all times. Thus external (extrinsic) rewards must be viewed as a temporary means to change behavior, but the behavior can only be maintained over the long haul with internal (intrinsic) motivation.

Empathy

One of the most difficult attributes for the HFI is to really understand the feelings of many people who join fitness programs. The HFI must try to understand and appreciate how it feels to have a low self-esteem in terms of a person's body, to be unable to perform well on many physical tasks, and to be slow at learning new physical skills. For example, the HFI should pay attention to emotional feelings in situations that are uncomfortable. Many potential fitness participants have similar feelings when involved in fitness tests and activities. An HFI's empathic sensitivity to all emotional feelings of participants is part of the individual attention and concern that is important for motivation.

Play and Goal Orientation

One of the key elements in achieving an arousal/relaxation balance and in defusing the Type A or Type B personality is to help people appreciate a balance of work and play. The Type A individual has difficulty taking time just to play and enjoy an activity (that is not directly related to productivity); the Type B person has a problem in getting down to a task and getting it done. People who try to pattern fitness programs after military or athletic models often have the goal orientation without the play. Others who are not discriminating about the selection of activities, as long as everyone is happy, may achieve the playfulness without fitness gains. The good fitness program achieves this balance by including activities designed to improve all fitness components (goal orientation) and a playful atmosphere where participating is fun for its own sake.

State/Trait

A distinction between the usual (*trait*) personality characteristics and the specific situational (*state*) personality characteristics is helpful in dealing with people. For example, a person may normally be very quiet and introverted but may become an extrovert during competitive games. A person may be normally very relaxed, but may get anxious about exercise. Generally the personality traits do not change very much, or quickly. An HFI should use an understanding of the traits to work with individuals on a long-term basis. The personality and emotional states vary with situations and are more susceptible to change. For example, people afraid or anxious about physical activity can be introduced to activity in such a way to have them become relaxed and unafraid when exercising.

Stress Continuums

Personality is related to stress in that a person's perception of a stimulus or situation determines to a large extent how stressful the situation is (see questions 70-74 on HSQ). No uniform agreement exists on definitions of stress terms. For our purposes, a *stressor* is defined as any stimulus or condition that causes physiological arousal beyond what is necessary to accomplish the activity. This excessive arousal is called *stress*.

Stress has three major components. A complete description of a stressful event includes the amount by which the stress response exceeds the functional demand, how pleasant it is to the individual, and whether it causes development or deterioration.

Functional—Severe Stress

The physiological response at any one time lies on a continuum from what is essential to provide the energy for that task on one end of the continuum to extreme physiological response beyond what is needed. Table 8.1 illustrates how typical resting and submaximal HRs include not only the HR needed to provide energy for the body, but also the increased HR (stress) from chronic stressors (e.g., excess fat) and acute stressors (e.g., emotional state).

Table 8.1 Model of Functional and Stress Components of Heart Rate

Component	Sitting	Heart Rate, b/min[a] Climbing Stairs	Running
Functional			
Energy	30	50	100
Chronic stressors			
Poor CRF	+15	+20	+40
Excess fat	+ 5	+15	+20
Acute Stressors			
Not relaxed	+10	+ 5	0
Emotional state	+15	+10	0
Total heart rate	75	100	160

[a]This HR model illustrates the contribution of functional and stress responses to HR at rest and during submaximal exercise. The actual HR components vary with the individual depending on body size and type and severity of stressors.

Enjoyable—Unpleasant Stressors

Another aspect of stress is how the stressor is perceived by the individual. A person might have a similar stress response to an exciting concert and to taking the Health Fitness Instructor Certification examination; however, the concert is perceived as more enjoyable.

Results in Development—Deterioration

The third aspect of stress is what happens to the person as a result of the stressful experience. This is, of course, the main criterion for determining whether the stressful event was positive or negative. The positive stressor results in a healthier, stronger person. The negative stressor leads to a weaker individual. The end result of stress is somewhat independent of the other two aspects of stress. For example, a very stressful event (i.e., causing a large stress response beyond what is essential physically) could result in a person being inspired to achieve great things or it might destroy a person's initiative. On the other hand, conditions that cause little stress response might lead to steady development or could gradually wear down a person's desire to excel. In addition, a person might grow and develop from stressors that are both pleasant (e.g., positive reinforcement) and unpleasant (e.g., deadline to have a project done). Either pleasant or unpleasant stressors might tempt a person to escape from dealing with important areas of life. Thus the HFI should be cautious in identifying a specific stressor as being healthy or unhealthy based on the degree of physiological and psychological stress response or how much the individual liked the situation. A better criterion is to determine whether the experience led the person toward higher levels of mental, social, and/or physical health.

Physical Activity and Stress

One of the advantages of separating functional stimuli from stressors is that they interact with physical activity differently. Separating the effects of immediate and long-term physical activity on stress responses is also helpful.

Response to Acute Physical Activity and Other Functional Stimuli

The physiological response to acute physical activity and other functional stimuli is additive. Numerous stimuli such as exercise, heat, altitude, and pollution cause a functional increased physiological response. If more than one of these is present, the physiological response is greater than if only one stimulus were present. Thus when people exercise in hot, humid, or polluted conditions, or at high altitude, they should do less exercise for the same physiological response (e.g., THR). The one exception is exercising in the cold because the heat by-product of exercise helps deal with the cold.

Response to Acute Exercise and Psychological Stressors

The physiological response to acute exercise and psychological stressors varies with the intensity of exercise, but generally it is not additive. Nonfunctional stimuli appear to affect the physiological response at rest and during light exercise but have little effect on the response to moderate or hard exercise. Nonfunctional stimuli also affect a person's decision about when to stop during a maximal task. Thus if a person is very angry or happy, the HR and BP at rest and during light exercise may be elevated, and the person may decide to continue exercising longer or quit early. If the person is sad or relaxed, the HR and BP during light work may be depressed, and the decision to stop exercising may come earlier or later than usual.

Physical Activity May Reduce Stress

Many writers have justified exercise programs partly on the basis of stress reduction. Although the claims have often exceeded the evidence, some basis exists for the relationship between stress reduction and acute (immediate) and chronic (long-range) exercise.

Acute activity. Three primary bases cause single bouts of exercise to reduce stress.

Distraction. Exercise (as many other activities) can serve as a temporary distraction from stressors. Stepping away from a problem then coming back to it at a later time is often helpful. This technique is healthy as long as exercise does not become an escape from the problem. The ultimate reduction of stress must come from coping with the stressor. However, one part of the coping strategy can be the distraction of physical activity.

Control of the situation. One of the primary concepts in a person's ability to cope with stressors is the perception of personal control (see questions 76 and 81 on HSQ). In some cases, exercise enhances this feeling of control. Increased practice and skill acquisition causes less stress in playing a game in the presence of others. One of the benefits of a postcardiac program is that it reduces the fear that any exertion will cause another heart attack (thus exercise increases feelings of control).

Interaction with others. A third way that acute exercise may influence stress is by providing a time to be alone for people where one of the daily stressors is in constant contact with other people (e.g., the working parent who has almost every waking moment filled in the presence of others, such as children, spouse, employees, employer, and colleagues, demanding time and attention).

That person can use a walk/jog program as a time to be alone with his or her own thoughts. At the other extreme is the person who has little contact with other people during the typical day and has loneliness as a potential stressor. Doing activities with other people in an exercise program can aid that person. The HFI needs to be aware of the needs of individuals in terms of the exercise sessions.

Chronic activity. The long-term effects of a regular exercise program also provide bases for stress reduction.

Reduction of chronic stressors. Increased CRF and decreased body fat cause the person to be less stressed throughout the day.

Physical activity becoming less of a stressor. With increased fitness levels, physical activity itself becomes less of a stressor. For example, numerous studies have shown that a fit person can do the same amount of external work with lower HR, BP, catecholamines, and so forth. Thus the functional response to the work (energy necessary to accomplish the task) remains the same, but the stress response is reduced.

Cross adaptation. Some people believe, with inconsistent support, that increased adaptation to physical activity provides a basis for better adaptation to other stressors. Others believe, with some support, that increased adaptation is specific to different stimuli and stressors. This question needs additional research before definitive claims can be made.

Stress and Health

Stress is important for both positive and negative aspects of health. No discussion of the highest quality of life possible or of serious health problems would be complete without including the relevance of stress.

Positive Attributes

People often think of stress as primarily a negative influence on their lives, but many positive features exist.

Variety. Involvement with many stimuli and stressors provides interesting aspects to a full life. A person would live a bland existence without stress.

Development and growth. Try to imagine people developing, learning, growing, and striving for their optimal potential without encountering stress.

Special high moments. One feature of "the good life" is the involvement in those special emotional experiences that are remembered forever. These peak moments likely are stressful.

Negative Aspects

Stress is also included whenever a person deals with the health problems of society.

Secondary risk factor for major health problems. Stress is listed as a risk factor for many major health problems (e.g., CHD, hypertension, cancer, ulcers, low-back pain, and headaches). Although inability to cope with stress probably is not sufficient to cause any of these problems if no predispositions exist in that direction, stress seems to manifest itself wherever the "weak link" is found. So for some people, stress results in a myocardial infarction (MI); for others, it results in hypertension, ulcers, low-back pain, or headaches.

Transfer of inability to cope with a stressor. Many people find themselves getting upset (stressed) over something that normally would not bother them because of stressors in another area of their lives. Two aspects of the inability to cope are perception of and reaction to illness (see questions 67, 70-74 on HSQ). Although the positive transfer of adaptation of one stressor to other stressors is an open question, little doubt exists that a negative transfer results from an inability to cope in one area leading to coping problems in other areas of life.

Aging

Separating the effects of chronological age from other things that typically happen as a person gets older is difficult. Certain experiences are more likely to have happened more often as a person becomes older. The positive aspects related to aging include the increased opportunities to deal with a variety of stressors that a person has as he or she gets older. Many people develop a repertoire of coping behaviors.

On the negative side, a person is more likely to develop a serious health problem the longer he or she lives (although not living longer does not appear to be an attractive alternative). Another aspect of aging is the number of special life events (see question 28 on HSQ) that appear to cause stress. Obviously some of these events (e.g., death of a loved one) become more frequent with increasing age. Another factor is the often dramatic change for parents when all of the children leave home and for people when they retire. Lifestyle patterns developed over decades undergo major modifications, sometimes with additional financial difficulties. Evidence shows that people are more likely to have a number of health problems following a series of stressful life events.

Older people often become less active, causing more deterioration in fitness and performance than would occur simply because of increased age. Careful warmup, safety precautions, taper-down, and gradual progression in activity become even more important in older populations because of the higher risk of health problems and injury and decreased fitness and performance skills.

Recommendations

People can do many things to maximize the positive aspects of stress while minimizing stress's negative side.

Exposure to Many Stimuli and Stressors

Simply being exposed to a wide range of experiences helps a person become better educated and less stressed by new situations. A good fitness program provides a variety of different types of experiences, including cooperative, problem solving, competitive, individual, partner, and team activities. This variety enriches the participant by improving fitness and improving the ability to cope with different movement experiences.

Developing Range of Coping Abilities

People should observe the different strategies that seem to enhance coping with a potentially stressful situation. Facing the problem, looking at alternatives, talking about the problem with close friends, seeking professional or technical advice when needed, stepping back or away from it for a brief time, and so forth are all behaviors that people use to cope with stress. Which ones are better suited for particular situations? Do some help but feel uncomfortable to the individual? The HFI might encourage people to practice coping behaviors in "easy" settings. In terms of fitness, the variety of activities in a good program require different coping strategies. In addition, the HFI should be sensitive to participants who need help just coping with physical activity itself. After easing these people into exercise, the HFI can use a variety of fitness activities found in chapter 11 to develop coping abilities.

Developing Optimal Fitness

Developing physical, mental, and social fitness characteristics cause potential stressors to be less threatening. If a person can do hard work, then physical stressors are not dreaded. If people are used to the mental processes that lead to problem solving, then having a difficult problem is not as stressful. Aspects of social fitness, such as establishment of meaningful relationships to other people, provide a support group that assists a person in having positive responses to stressful situations.

Gain Control of as Much of Life as Possible

Perception of control repeatedly looms as a major element in coping with stress. Therefore, whatever a person can do to help gain control of his or her life diminishes potentially stressful conditions.

Healthy behaviors. One of the by-products of exercising, eating nutritious foods, and refraining from use of harmful drugs is the feeling that people are taking responsibility for their own lives. Not only do the healthy behaviors reduce stress, but also the fact that the person has "taken charge'' reduces stress levels. Chapter 13 includes recommendations concerning ways to increase healthy behaviors.

Competence in important areas. Attention should be given to whatever things, tasks, and relationships are important to the person so that increased skill can be achieved in those areas. Thus when a person is asked to do something important, an enhanced self-confidence in being successful occurs. In the fitness program, the HFI helps people to improve skills in the activities in which they are interested.

Be assertive concerning unreasonable demands. People must recognize unreasonable demands whether imposed by themselves or by someone else. A person must be able to point out the ''problem'' and to work with others (e.g., boss, spouse) to try to accomplish common goals in a reasonable way within an appropriate time frame; this is essential to good health. The HFI must be careful not to place unrealistic goals or demands for future activities and fitness gains on that person. The HFI can also help the individual set goals that will not be a source of stress.

Learn to relax. Techniques can be learned to help people relax. Benson (1975) and others have demonstrated the benefits of the ''relaxation response.'' The HFI should include these as part of the program. One easily used technique, introduced by Jacobsen (1938) is aimed at having people recognize the feelings produced by tension. When using this technique, the HFI should have participants sit in a comfortable position with their eyes closed. We recommend that the technique be done with the participants lying on mats, but it can be done sitting. The procedure is to have people tense a specific area of the body, hold for about 20 sec, then relax; then tense a larger segment, hold, relax, and so forth. The HFI talks in a calm voice asking the people to feel the tension during the hold period and to feel the tension leave the area during the relax period. The following sequence can be used:

Right toes

Left toes

Right foot

Left foot

Right leg below knee

Left leg below knee

Right leg below hip

Left leg below hip

Both legs below hips

Abdomen and buttocks

Right fingers

Left fingers

Right arm below elbow

Left arm below elbow

Right arm below shoulder

Left arm below shoulder

Both arms below shoulders

Chest

Neck

Jaw

Forehead

Entire head

Entire body

Extend this last relaxation period, have people feel tension leaving their bodies, feel their breathing, then be silent for several minutes.

Summary

One aspect of a healthy lifestyle is a balance between arousal and relaxation. Personality characteristics can influence a person's response to a situation. Type A individuals may have an excessive response and need relaxation activities to achieve a better balance. Those who tend to hold in anger have a higher incidence of CHD. The HFI can aid such individuals by expressing emotions and being sensitive to the moods of participants. People who display aggression, hostility, or who deny pain may do too much in an exercise session. The HFI should protect others from aggressive or hostile participants. Anxious or fearful participants may need to be eased into activities through special attention by the HFI. People who have experienced rejection need additional support to feel welcome and wanted in the program. Some people use exercise as a catharsis, while others seek a special euphoria that keeps them coming back for more. The HFI must be concerned with motivating people to begin the exercise program and continue in it. If the exercise takes on a special value, it is more likely to become a regular part of a person's lifestyle.

A *stressor* can be defined as a stimulus or condition that causes physiological arousal beyond what is necessary to accomplish an activity. The response of the individual to the stressor (Was it a pleasant experience?) and whether or not the stressor caused development or deterioration are important questions when evaluating a stressful event. The physiological response to physical activity and additional environmental stimuli (e.g., altitude) are additive. Psychological stressors may influence a person's physiological responses at rest and during light work, but they have little influence during heavy work. Physical activity itself may reduce stress by being a distraction, giving the person a sense of control over the situation and encouraging interaction with others. Chronic physical activity causes a reduction in body fatness and an increase in CRF, which can cause a person to be less stressed throughout the day.

Stress can provide the variety and excitement in a person's life or can be a secondary risk factor for CHD. The inability to cope with one stressor affects a person's ability to cope with others. Ways to emphasize the positive aspects of stress and minimize the negative aspects include increasing the number of stressors that a person is exposed to, developing a range of coping abilities, developing optimal fitness, gaining control of as much of a person's life as possible, developing healthy behaviors, becoming competent in important areas, being assertive to unreasonable demands, and learning to relax.

Suggested Reading for Chapter 8

American Heart Association Committee on Stress, Strain, and Heart Disease (1977)

Averill (1982)

Benson (1975)

Burchfield (1979)

Eliot (1977)

Franks (1983)

Franks (1984a)

Franks (1984b)

Haynes et al. (1980)

Jacobsen (1938)

Jenkins (1979)

Maddox and Douglass (1974)

Mason (1975a)

Mason 1975b)

Mihevic (1981)

Morgan (1985)

Murphy (1984)

Noble, Borg, Cafarelli, Robertson, and Pandolf (1982)

Rose et al. (1979)

Schwartz, Weinberger, and Singer (1981)

Selye (1956)

Selye (1975)

Selye (1976)

Sonstroem (1978)

Spielberger, Gorsuch, and Lushene (1970)

Thaxton (1982)

See reference list at the end of the book for a complete source listing.

Part IV

Activity Recommendations

- What the HFI needs to know to be able to make recommendations for fitness activities

The first three sections have defined physical fitness, reviewed the exercise sciences, and described the fitness components and how they can be evaluated. The effects of physical conditioning have been listed, but the means of obtaining fitness improvements have been referred to only generally. This section of the book deals directly with that major responsibility of HFIs; namely, what should be done to enhance physical fitness for specific individuals. Chapter 9 includes both general recommendations that can be made for the normal masses as well as suggestions for increasing cardiorespiratory fitness in people with specific characteristics and test values. Chapter 11 includes suggestions for a wide variety of different types of fitness activities that can enrich a fitness program. Chapters 10 and 12 include information that is needed to determine energy costs of activities and to become familiar with basic ECG and medication information. The final chapter in this section (chapter 13) is extremely important for anyone dealing with voluntary human behavior. All of the technical information and abilities, the fitness testing skills, and the fitness activities available go for naught unless HFIs are able to help individuals develop an intrinsic motivation to begin and continue physical activity as an ongoing part of their lifestyles.

Chapter 9

Exercise Programming for Aerobic Activity

- General guidelines
- Phases of progression
- Workout components
- Effects of health status
- Basis for modification

What should I do to be fit? This question is one that the HFI hears not only from participants registered in a fitness program, but from many people at parties, on the bus, at family reunions, . . . whenever and wherever an HFI is recognized.

General Basis for Physiological Changes

Two major principles are basic for improvement of any physiological function.

Overload

The first principle is a dynamic characteristic of living creatures. That is, *use increases functional capacity*. Thus if some physiological system is caused to work over and over again, instead of wearing out and becoming weaker, the system becomes stronger. The slang is "use it or lose it." Whether a person is trying to increase the strength of the abdominal muscles or the heart muscles, the first principle is to overload it for enhanced function.

Specificity

The next principle is that people improve functions very specifically. For example, if the arms are overloaded, the legs benefit little; or large increases in flexibility have little effect on speed. In general, training is quite specific.

Basis for Improvement in Cardiorespiratory Function

To apply these two principles to CRF, activities that overload the heart and vascular and respiratory systems need to be done. Large muscle groups contracting in a rhythmic manner and on a continuous basis are essential to specifically overload the CR systems. Small-muscle activities or resistive exercise (e.g., weight-training) are less appropriate because they tend to generate very high cardiovascular loads relative to energy expenditure. Activities that improve CRF are high in caloric cost and therefore also help achieve a relative leanness goal.

Format for Fitness Workout

The main body of the fitness workout consists of dynamic large-muscle activities at an intensity high enough and a duration long enough to accomplish enough total work to specifically overload the cardiorespiratory systems. Stretching and light endurance activities are included prior to (warm-up) and following (taper-down) for safety and to improve or maintain low-back function.

Exercise Recommendations for the Untested Masses

Certain general recommendations can be made for any person wanting to begin a fitness program. Although the HFI might wish to have each individual go through a complete testing protocol before beginning exercise, that simply is not realistic. In addition, people without known health problems who follow these general guidelines can begin to exercise at low risk. In fact, continuing *not* to exercise places a person at a higher risk for CHD than if he or she begins a modest exercise program.

Screening

Chapter 2 provides guidelines for who should and who should not seek medical clearance before exercising. This section deals with those people for whom beginning an exercise program is a low risk (apparently healthy).

Regular Participation

Exercise must become a valuable part of a person's lifestyle. It is not something that can be done sporadically nor can it be done for a few months or years in order to build up a fitness reserve. Dramatic gains accomplished through fitness activities are quickly lost with inactivity. Studies show that former athletes who are now sedentary have no higher fitness levels than do people who have never been active. Only those people who continue activity as a way of life receive its benefits.

Start Slowly

Most of the problems associated with fitness programs result from people doing too much too soon. The HFI must counteract many influences to help people start slowly. For example, past experience with conditioning for athletics or the military (''no pain—no gain''), instant cures offered in ads, and certain people who are accustomed to competing against others rather than against themselves tempt people to do too much too soon. The HFI should teach people to listen to their bodies—instead of expecting to be stiff, sore, and fatigued later in the day after exercise, participants should realize that those characteristics indicate that they should reduce their activities the next day. The HFI needs to help people realize that when they do not feel good, it's okay to take it easy rather than ''gut'' it out.

Warm-Up and Taper-Down

Physiological, psychological, and safety bases exist for warm-up and taper-down. In general the warm-up and taper-down consist of (a) activities similar to the activities done in the main body of the workout, but done at a lower intensity (e.g., walking, jogging, or cycling below THR); (b) stretching, especially in the midtrunk area; and (c) muscular endurance especially for the muscles in the abdominal region. These activities help the participants ease into and out of a workout and provide activities for a healthy low-back. If a workout is going to be shorter than usual, the reduction in time should take place in the main body of the workout while maintaining the warm-up and taper-down.

Periodic Testing

Testing to determine progress can be motivational and may help alter programs that are not achieving desired results. The HFI can help this process by setting realistic goals for the next testing session when discussing test results. A rule of thumb would be a 10% increase in 3 months in those test scores that need improvement. Once the person has reached a desirable level, then the goal is to maintain that level.

Frequency

People who start a fitness program should plan to exercise three or four times per week. The work-a-day rest-a-day routine long recommended by fitness experts has been validated in several research studies. Exercising for fewer than 3 days per week can cause some CRF improvements, but it seems to be ineffective in the body composition area. Exercising for more than 4 days per week for previously sedentary people seems to be too much and results in more dropouts, injuries, and less psychological adjustment to the exercise.

Total Work

Although determining exactly how much total work is needed for fitness changes is difficult, evidence shows that about 300 kcal per workout can provide significant fitness improvements over a relatively short period of time. Chapter 10 includes methods for determining caloric costs.

Progression

The importance of beginning at work levels that can be easily completed has to be continually emphasized. People should be encouraged to gradually increase the amount of work they can do during a workout. Participants should begin walking a distance that they can go without feeling fatigued or sore. They will be able to walk a greater distance at a faster pace without discomfort each week. After a person can walk 4 or 5 mi briskly without stopping, then he or she can gradually work up to jogging 3 mi continuously per workout. For the participant who is ready to begin jogging, introduce the interval-type workout with walking-jogging-walking-jogging. As individuals adapt to the interval workouts, they will be able to gradually increase the amount of jogging while decreasing the distance walked (see the walking-jogging program in chapter 11).

Intensity

The intensity question is How hard does a person have to work to provide sufficient overload for the cardiac, respiratory, and vascular systems to increase their functional capacities? Most agree that a threshold exists in the intensity of exercise that must be reached in order to develop or maintain a CRF training effect. Three methods are used to determine the intensity threshold.

Metabolic load. Cardiorespiratory improvements are based on the amount and intensity of metabolic work done. The most direct way to determine the appropriate intensity is to use a percentage of the measured maximal oxygen consumption. The ACSM recommends 50-85% of maximal oxygen consumption as the range of exercise intensities needed to bring about or maintain a training effect in people ranging from very sedentary to very active, respectively. The advantage of using this method for determining exercise intensity is that the method is based on the criterion test for CRF—maximal oxygen consumption. The major disadvantages are the expense and difficulty of measuring oxygen consumption for each individual and trying to suit specific fitness activities to meet the specific metabolic demand for each person.

Because the HR response to work is linearly related to the metabolic load, the concept of a THR has been used to determine exercise intensity. One direct and two indirect methods have been developed to determine the THR.

Direct method. In the direct method, the HR is monitored at each stage of a maximal GXT. The HR is then plotted on a graph against the $\dot{V}O_2$ (or MET) equivalents of each stage of the test. The HFI determines the THR range by taking appropriate percentages of the maximal $\dot{V}O_2$ at which the person should train and finds what the HR response was at those points. Figure 9.1 shows this method being used for a subject with a functional capacity of 10.5 METs. Work rates of 60-80% of max MET demanded HR responses of 132-156 b/min, respectively. The HR values become the intensity guide for the subject and represent the THR range.

Indirect methods. Two indirect methods have been developed to estimate an appropriate THR.

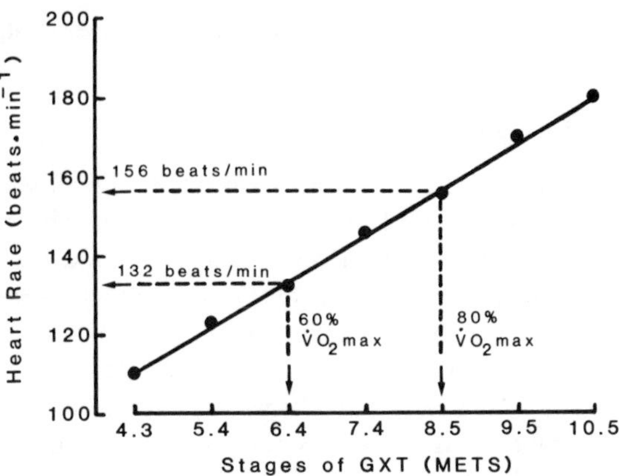

Figure 9.1 Direct method of determining the target heart rate zone when maximal aerobic power (functional capacity) is measured during a graded exercise test. Adapted from the American College of Sports Medicine (1980). *Guidelines for Graded Exercise Testing and Exercise Prescription*. *Reprinted with permission.*

Heart rate reserve. This method, made popular by Karvonen, requires a few simple calculations to estimate the THR range:

1. Subtract resting HR from maximal HR to obtain HR reserve.
2. Take 60% and 80% of the HR reserve.
3. Add each value to resting HR to obtain the THR range.

The advantage of this procedure for determining exercise intensity is that the recommended THR is always between the person's resting and maximal HR. A disadvantage is that resting HR is relatively unreliable and is often elevated by factors other than CRF. Fortunately, this disadvantage does not introduce a serious error into the calculation of the THR.

Percentage of maximal HR. Another method of determining THR is to take a percentage of the maximal HR. The advantage of this method is its simplicity. The disadvantage is that, in some extreme cases, the THR may be inappropriate (e.g., fall below the resting HR).

Relationship of percentages of maximal oxygen consumption and HR. One area of potential confusion about the calculation of exercise intensity by the two indirect methods is that the percentage value used in the HR reserve method is about 10-15% lower than the values used in the percent of maximal HR procedure for the same work level. Table 9.1 presents values for both of these methods versus work rates expressed as a percentage of maximal oxygen consumption. If the HFI wishes the participant to exercise at 60-80% of $\dot{V}O_2$max, the THR will be 60-80% of HR reserve, or about 70-85% (72-87%) of max HR.

Maximal HR. The indirect methods for determining exercise intensity utilize maximal HR. It is recommended that the maximal HR be measured directly (GXT) when possible. If it cannot be measured, then any estimation must consider the effect of age on maximal HR. Maximal HR can be estimated by the formula

Max HR = 220 − age

That estimate is a potential source of error for both the HR reserve and the percent of max HR methods. For example, a 45-year-old person's true max HR may be anywhere between 145 and 205 rather than the estimated 175 (two/thirds of the population would be between 165 and 185).

Table 9.1 Relationship of Percent of Max HR, HRR[a], and % $\dot{V}O_2$max

% Max $\dot{V}O_2$	% HRR	% Max HR
50	50	65
55	55	68
60	60	72
65	65	76
70	70	79
75	75	83
80	80	87
85	85	91
90	90	94

[a]HRR is the difference between max HR and resting HR.

Threshold. The intensity of exercise that provides an adequate stimulus for cardiorespiratory improvement varies with activity level and age. For *most* of the population, the intensity threshold ranges from

60-80% of $\dot{V}O_2$max

60-80% of HR reserve

70-85% of max HR

The threshold is toward the lower part of the range for older sedentary populations. The threshold is toward the upper part of the range for younger healthy populations. The threshold may be lower (i.e., < 60% max$\dot{V}O_2$) or higher (i.e., > 80% max$\dot{V}O_2$) than this range for diseased and extremely deconditioned or for very active people, respectively. The middle of the range (70% max$\dot{V}O_2$, 70% HHR, or 80% max HR) is appropriate for the typical apparently healthy person who is not engaging in a regular fitness program. Participating in activities in this intensity range places a reasonable load on the cardiorespiratory system to constitute an overload, resulting in an adaptation over time.

Balke (ACSM, 1980) developed a sliding scale method to estimate the *average conditioning intensity*. This method is quite consistent with the previous discussion. An exercise intensity equal to 60% of max METs is taken as the baseline in this calculation. The HFI adds to this a value equal to the subject's maximal METs (e.g., for a person with a functional capacity of 5 METs, the calculation is 60% + 5 = 65%. The 65% value is then multiplied by either the subject's maximal METs or the HR reserve to obtain the average conditioning intensity). In the previous example the person would exercise at an average intensity of 3.3 METs (65% of 5 METs). Given that the vast majority of apparently healthy individuals have functional capacities between 7 and 10 METs, the sliding scale method would yield a value similar to 70% max METs.

Calculations. The threshold range is determined by taking a direct percent from the max$\dot{V}O_2$ when that value is available. Activities that fall into that metabolic range are then prescribed:

Max $\dot{V}O_2$ = 3 ℓ/min

Prescribed activities = 1.8–2.4 ℓ/min (3 ℓ/min × 60% and 80%)

Max $\dot{V}O_2$ = 3 ℓ/min or 15 kcal/min (3 ℓ/min × 5 kcal/ℓ)

Prescribed activities = 9-12 kcal/min (15 × 60% and 80%)

Max $\dot{V}O_2$ = 50 ml(kg•min)$^{-1}$ (3 ℓ/min divided by weight in kilograms)

Prescribed activities = 30-40 ml(kg•min)$^{-1}$ (50 × 60% and 80%)

Max METs = 14.3 (50 ml(kg•min)$^{-1}$ divided by 3.5)

Prescribed activities = 8.6-11.4 METs (14.3 METs × 60% and 80%)

Using the direct THR method, the HFI plots the HR response against the stages of the GXT and identifies the HR responses associated with 60-80% of max $\dot{V}O_2$ (see Figure 9.1).

When the $\dot{V}O_2$ is not available, then either of the indirect HR methods can be used. Examples using the indirect HR methods are the following:

Max HR = 180 b/min, Resting HR = 70 b/min

HR reserve = 110 b/min (180 − 70)

THR range = 136-156 b/min (110 × 60% = 66; 66 + 70 = 136; 110 × 80% = 88; 88 + 70 = 156)

The easiest way to determine THR is to take a percent of max HR. Using the same example, as with HR reserve (HRR) determine it this way:

Max HR = 180 b/min

THR range = 126-153 b/min (180 × 70% and 85%)

If the max HR is known (e.g., from a GXT), then it should be used to determine THR. Using the percentage of max HR, the HFI simply multiplies the max HR by the desired percentage (70-85%). People who are less active and have more risk factors should use the lower part of the THR range. More active people with fewer risk factors should use the upper part of the THR range. The THR can be divided by six to provide the desired 10-sec THR. If the person's max HR is unknown, then the estimated THR for 10 sec, by age and activity level, can be found in Table 9.2. People can learn to exercise at their THRs by walking or jogging for several minutes and then stopping and *immediately* taking a 10-sec HR. If the person's HR is not within the target range, then an adjustment is made in intensity (by going slower or faster to try to get within the THR range) for a few minutes and again taking a 10-sec count. Using the THR to set exercise intensity has many advantages: (a) It has a built-in individualized progression (i.e., as a person increases fitness, harder work has to be done to achieve the HR); (b) It takes into account environmental conditions (e.g., a person decreases the intensity while working in very high temperatures); and (c) It is easily determined, learned, and monitored.

Use of THR. This concept of an intensity threshold provides the basis for the importance of regular fitness workouts. Low-intensity activity around the house, yard, and office are to be encouraged, but specific workouts above the intensity threshold are necessary to achieve optimum CRF results. At the other extreme, a person who pushes himself or herself near maximum does not have a fitness advantage because the same results can be obtained at a moderate intensity that is above the threshold.

The THR can be used for large muscle, continuous, whole body types of activities such as walking, running, and dancing. However, the same training results may not occur from activities using small muscle groups or resistive exercises because these exercises elevate the HR much higher for the same metabolic load.

These recommendations are appropriate for the majority of people, but individuals differ in terms of threshold, maximal levels, and other factors that influence exercise intensity. The HFI must use

Table 9.2 Estimated 10-Sec THR[a]

Population	Intensity % $\dot{V}O_2$max	20	30	40	50	60	70	80
		Age (Years)						
Inactive with several risk factors	50	22	21	20	18	17	16	15
	55	23	22	21	19	18	17	16
	60	24	23	22	20	19	18	17
Normal activity with few risk factors	65	25	24	23	21	20	19	18
	70	26	25	24	22	21	20	18
	75	28	26	25	24	22	21	19
	80	29	28	26	25	23	22	20
Very active with low risk	85	30	29	27	26	24	23	21
	90	31	30	28	27	25	24	22

[a]To be used only for people whose max HR is unknown.

subjective judgment based on observation of the person exercising to determine whether the intensity should be higher or lower. If the work is so easy that the person experiences little or no increase in ventilation and is able to do the work without effort, then the intensity should be increased (e.g., in some extreme cases, the lower part of the THR range might be prescribed below the person's resting HR). At the other extreme, if a person shows signs of maximal work and is still unable to reach THR, then a lower intensity should be chosen (in extreme cases, the THR top part of the THR range might be above the person's true max HR). The HFI should not rely on the THR as the only method of judging whether or not the participant is exercising at the correct intensity. Attention should be paid to other signs and symptoms of overexertion.

Types of Activities

A fitness program starts with easily quantified activities, such as walking or cycling, so that the THR can be achieved. After a minimum level of fitness is achieved, then a variety of activities are included in the program. Chapter 11 outlines three phases of activities: (a) work up to walking briskly for 4-5 mi per workout; (b) gradually begin jogging and work up to jogging continuously for 3 mi; and (c) introduce a variety of activities.

Exercise Programming for the Fit Population

Exercise recommendations written for people who possess a reasonably high level of fitness tend to be associated with less risk, and the participant requires less supervision. In fact, people in this group may focus on performance, in contrast to health maintenance, as the primary goal. A wide variety of programs, activities, races, and competitions are available to address the needs of this group.

The THR range will be calculated as described above, but these people will function at the top part of the range (75-85% $\dot{V}O_2max$ or 83-91% HRmax). As was mentioned earlier, a less fit person can be started at the low end of the range and experience a training effect. The more fit individual needs to work at the top end of the range to maintain a high level of fitness.

Training for competition demands more than the training intensity needed for CRF. Individuals who do interval-type training programs have peak HRs close to maximum during the intervals. The recovery period between the intervals should include some work at a lower intensity (near 40-50% functional capacity) to help metabolize the lactate produced during the interval and to reduce the chance of cardiovascular complications that can occur when a person comes to a complete rest at the end of a strenuous exercise bout.

For those people who participate in sports that are intermittent in nature but that still require a high level of aerobic fitness for success, a running/jogging program is a good way to maintain general conditioning when not playing the activity. However, given the specificity of training, no substitute for the real activity exists when conditioning for a sport.

People in this category who work at the top end of the THR range, exercise 4-6 times per week, and exercise for longer than 30 min each exercise session tend to experience more musculoskeletal injuries than the 3-day-a-week participant. When this is coupled with the inherent musculoskeletal risks associated with competitive activities, a need exists to build-in alternative activities that can be done when participation in the primary activity is not possible. This reduces the chance of becoming detrained when injuries do occur.

Exercise Recommendations With Knowledge of Functional Capacity and Cardiovascular Responses to Exercise

In the previous section, the exercise recommendation was made on the basis of little or no specific information about the person involved. In many adult fitness programs, potential participants have had a general medical exam and/or a GXT with appropriate monitoring of the HR, BP, and possibly ECG responses. Unfortunately, this information is sometimes not used in designing the exercise program; instead, the measured maximal HR is used in the THR formulas and the rest of the data is ignored. This section outlines the steps that should be followed when making the exercise recommendation based on information about the person's functional capacity and the cardiovascular responses to graded exercise. While the HFI is not directly involved in the clinical evaluation of a GXT, an understanding of the steps and the procedures used to make clinical judgments clearly enhances communication between the HFI and the Program Director, Exercise Specialist, and medical doctor. The following section was written with this intent. A series of case studies follows, representing submaximal and maximal GXT responses of individuals ranging from the apparently healthy to those people with identified disease.

Steps to Follow in GXT Analysis

1. Analyze the person's history and list the known risk factors of CHD; also, identify those factors that might have a direct bearing on the exercise program, such as orthopedic problems, previous physical activity, current interests, and so forth.

2. Determine if the functional capacity is a true maximum or if it is sign- or symptom-limited. Express the functional capacity in METs, and record the highest HR and RPE reached.

3. If monitored, itemize the person's ECG changes indicated by the physician.

4. Examine the HR and BP responses to see if they are normal.

5. List the symptoms reported at each stage.

6. List the reasons why the test was stopped (e.g., ECG changes, falling systolic pressure, dizziness, etc.).

Steps to Follow in Designing an Exercise Program

1. Based on the overall response to the GXT, make a decision to either refer for additional medical care or initiate an exercise program.
2. Identify the THR range and approximate MET intensities of selected activities needed to be within that THR range.
3. Specify the frequency and duration of activity needed to meet the goals of increased cardiorespiratory fitness and weight loss.
4. Recommend that the person participate in either a supervised or unsupervised program, be monitored or unmonitored, do group or individual activities, and so forth.
5. Select a variety of activities at the appropriate MET level that allows the person to achieve THR. Consider environmental factors, medication, and any physical limitations of the participant when making this recommendation.

The following section includes a variety of case studies on individuals varying in age, fitness, disease, and orthopedic limitations. They have been selected to give the HFI an idea of the variety of responses to a GXT and how the exercise recommendations would be made.

Case Study 9.1

The subject is a white male, 46 years of age, 88 kg, 178 cm tall, and 28% body fat. Blood chemistry values indicate that total cholesterol = 270 ml/dl and HDL cholesterol = 38 mg/dl. His mother died of a heart attack at the age of 63 and his father had a heart attack at the age of 78. He is sedentary and has engaged in no endurance training program since college. The following are the results of maximal GXT conducted by his physician.

Test: Balke, 3 mph; 2.5% per 2 min

Grade (%)	METs	Systolic	Diastolic	HR	ECG	Symptoms
	Rest	126	88	70	—	—
2.5	4.3	142	86	142	—	—
5	5.4	148	88	150	—	—
7.5	6.4	162	86	160	—	—
10	7.4	174	84	168	—	—
12.5	8.5	186	84	176	—	—
15	9.5	194	84	190	—	calf tight
17.5	10.5	198	84	198	—	fatigue

If a person has a normal response to a GXT, the heart rate and systolic blood pressure increase with each stage of the test while the diastolic pressure remains the same or decreases slightly. In addition, the ECG response shows no significant ST-segment depression or elevation, and no significant arrhythmias occur. In these cases it can be assumed that the last load achieved on the test represents the true functional capacity (max METs). The above GXT is representative of such a test.

This individual has normal resting blood pressure and a negative family history for CHD. Risk factors include a relatively high percent body fat (indicating borderline obesity), sedentary lifestyle, and a poor blood lipid profile. Based on these findings, a THR range of 139-168 b/min was calculated (70-85% HRmax). This range of heart rates corresponds to work rates equal to 4-7.5 METs. Initially, he will work at the low end of this THR range, with the emphasis on the duration of activity. As he becomes more active he will work at the upper end of the THR range, depending, of course, on his interests. He was referred for nutritional counseling to improve his blood lipid profile. The subject in Case Study 1 has an estimated maximal heart rate of 174 b/min; his measured heart rate was 24 b/min higher. Given the inherent biological variation in the estimated maximal heart rate, use the measured values when they are available.

Case Study 9.2

In some instances a physician may confirm the existence of an old "functional" ECG abnormality on a resting ECG tracing and feel the need for a more complete picture of how the individual's ECG would respond with the heart under stress. Case Study 2 is such an example. The subject is a 44-year-old white male who has been active in sports most of his life but has not recently engaged in any regular endurance training program. Blood chemistry values indicate the following: glucose = 100 mg/dl, cholesterol = 220 mg/dl, HDL cholesterol = 53 mg/dl, and triglycerides = 87 mg/dl. His resting ECG shows that he has Left Bundle Branch Block (LBBB) and his physician thinks the man should have a maximal GXT prior to increasing his activity level.

Test: Balke, 3 mph; 2% per minute

Grade (%)	METs	Systolic	Diastolic	HR	ECG	Symptoms
	Rest	128	90	76	LBBB	—
0	3.3	146	90	95	LBBB	—
2.5	4.3	152	90	100	LBBB	—
5	5.4	154	90	107	LBBB	—
7.5	6.4	154	90	113	LBBB	—
10	7.4	164	90	125	LBBB	—
12.5	8.5	172	90	144	LBBB	—
15	9.5	184	90	156	LBBB	—
17.5	10.5	180	90	164	LBBB	fatigue

The results show that he has a normal heart rate and blood pressure response to the GXT. Further, the test was judged to be a true maximal test. His blood chemistry values are considered normal. A THR range was calculated to be 114-140 b/min (70-85% HRmax), representing activities in the 6-8 MET range. The beginning of his exercise program will emphasize an exercise intensity at the low end of his THR range, progressing toward the upper end to facilitate his participation in a variety of sports.

The next three case studies use a submaximal GXT to evaluate fitness. Recommendations include modifications in smoking behavior, diet, stress, and physical activity.

Case Study 9.3

The subject is a 38-year-old white female, 170 cm tall, 61.4 kg, and 30% body fat. Blood chemistry values indicate a total cholesterol of 188 mg/dl and a HDL cholesterol of 59 mg/dl. Her resting blood pressure is 124/80. Family history indicates that her father suffered a nonfatal heart attack at the age of 67. She has smoked a pack-a-day of cigarettes for the past 13 years. The following is the result of her submaximal cycle ergometer test.

Test: Y Way of Fitness

Pedal Rate: 50 rpm
Predicted HRmax: 182 b/min

Seat Height: 6
85% HRmax: 155 b/min

Work Rate	HR	HR
kgm/min	Minute 2	Minute 3
150	118	120
300	134	136
450	152	156

The maximal aerobic power was estimated to be 1.65 l/min by extrapolating the HR/work rate relationship to the predicted maximal heart rate (see chapter 6). This is equivalent to a $\dot{V}O_2max$ of 27 $ml(kg \cdot min)^{-1}$, or 7.7 METs.

Her blood chemistry values and blood pressure are normal. Her family history is negative for CHD. Her heart rate response to the test is normal and indicates poor cardiorespiratory fitness. The low maximal aerobic power is related to the sedentary lifestyle, the cigarette smoking (carbon monoxide) and the 30% body fatness. She was encouraged to participate in a smoking cessation program and was given the names of two local professional groups.

The recommended exercise program emphasized the low end of the THR zone (70% HRmax: 127 b/min) with long duration. She preferred a walking program to begin with because of the freedom it gave her schedule. She was given the walking program in chapter 11 and was asked to record her heart rate response to each of the exercise sessions.

A body fatness goal of 22% resulted in a target body weight of 121 lb (55 kg). She did not feel the need for dietary counseling at this time, but she agreed to record her food intake for 10 days to determine the patterns of eating behavior that would be beneficial to change (see chapter 5). She made an appointment for a meeting with the HFI in 2 weeks to discuss the progress with her program.

Case Study 9.4

The subject is a white female, 49 years of age, 164 cm tall, 93 kg, and 40% body fat. Serum total cholesterol is 190 mg/dl, serum triglycerides are 100 mg/dl, blood glucose is 92 mg/dl, and resting blood pressure is 130/84. She had been active in swimming and tennis in college but had led a relatively sedentary lifestyle since that time. Her goal is to lose weight and become active again. The following are the results of a submaximal GXT taken to 85% of predicted maximal heart rate:

Test: Balke, 3 mph; 2.5% per 2 min

	Predicted HRmax: 171 b/min		85% HRmax: 145 b/min		
Grade (%)	METs	Systolic mmHg	Diastolic mmHg	HR	RPE
2.5	4.3	134	90	122	11
5	5.4	140	90	132	13
7.5	6.4	162	80	143	14

The subject has normal heart rate, blood pressure, and RPE responses to the GXT. The HR/MET relationship was extrapolated to predicted maximal heart rate and her functional capacity is estimated to be 9.3 METs.

Her blood chemistry values and resting blood pressure are normal. The major problem is the 40% body fat. Given this fatness, a $\dot{V}O_2$max of 9.3 METs is surprisingly high. A gradual reduction in body fatness would increase her functional capacity and increase the variety of physical activities in which she could participate.

A weight reduction plan was designed to result in a weight loss of about 1-2 lb per week. In spite of her reasonably high functional capacity, activities were selected to keep her at the low end of the THR zone (70% HR max: 120 b/min) and to put only a small load on the weight-bearing joints. She was given a walking program to do at home (see chapter 11) and a swimming program to do at the fitness club. The emphasis was on a level of work that would not cause fatigue.

She was given a dietary recall form (see chapter 5) to record her daily food intake for 1 week. She was instructed to not make changes in her diet during that week, but to simply record the information. At the end of the week she discussed the results with the HFI to see what major "junk food" items could be eliminated from her diet. In addition, she was given the name of three weight control programs in the community to contact for additional advice.

Case Study 9.5

The subject is a 38-year-old male, 71 inches tall (180 cm), 212 lb (96.2 kg), and 24% body fat. Two years ago he shifted jobs and now works for a well-known brokerage house. He is also finishing up the last year of a 6-year evening law school program. He got married 1.5 years ago and his wife is 5 months pregnant. He played most American sports in high school and was involved in long-distance bicycle rides (> 50 mi) as recently as 2 years ago. His weight has fluctuated from 185 to the present value over the past few years. He desires to get back to a regular program of activity. The following are the results of a submaximal GXT:

Test: Y Way of Fitness

Pedal Rate: 50 rpm Predicted HRmax: 182 b/min	Seat Height: 8 85% HRmax: 155
Work Rate	**Minute 3 Heart Rate**
kgm/min	beats/min
300	116
600	127
750	skipped
900	141

The heart rate/work rate line was extrapolated to the predicted maximal heart rate, and functional capacity was estimated to be 4.0 l/min, which is 41.6 $ml(kg \cdot min)^{-1}$, or 11.9 METs.

In the interview with this person it became clear that the last 2 years were full of stressful life events that were not yet under control. It was recommended that he talk with the stress management counselor at his place of employment. Further, his schedule of travel to work and the evening law school program left little time in the day to add one more thing. He agreed to exercise on his own with a walk/jog program until the law school program ended. At that time he would join a structured exercise program aimed at increasing his ability to participate in vigorous activities and sports at a health club. His calculated THR range is 127-155 beats/min (70-85% HRmax). He was given the walk/jog program and asked to record his heart rate and comments following each run (see chapter 11).

The following four cases represent a sample of the types of people who are tested prior to entry into an in-hospital cardiac rehabilitation program. The severity of their diseases varies, and the recommendations that follow each GXT is consistent with the subject's response to the GXT.

Sometimes the subject demonstrates inappropriate signs (ECG change or an inappropriate blood pressure response) or experiences symptoms (angina or claudication pain) during the course of a GXT. It is very important to consider these when writing the exercise prescription. The ''end'' point used in such a test may be quite different from the last measurements made on a test. Case Study 9.6 demonstrates this point.

Case Study 9.6

Subject: Male Age: 50

Test: Balke 3 mph (80 m/min); 2.5% per 2 min

Grade (%)	METs	Systolic	Diastolic	HR	ECG	Symptoms
	Rest	140	86	83	—	—
0	3.3	150	84	96	—	—
2.5	4.3	156	84	108	—	—
5	5.4	166	92	120	—	—
7.5	6.4	160	96	130	—	Chest pain
10	7.4	154	96	135	—	Chest pain/ dizziness

Calculating a THR range for this 50-year-old using the 220 minus age formula gives the values of 119-145 beats/min (70% and 85% maxHR). This presents some problems because the subject did not achieve a heart rate of 145! The second choice might be to use the subject's measured maximal heart rate, and a THR range of 95-115 would be calculated. On the surface this might appear to be appropriate, but the 5% grade is the last stage in which the subject did not experience chest pain and where the blood pressure response might still be considered normal. After that, the systolic pressure fell and the diastolic pressure increased. By checking the blood pressure responses and the symptoms experienced by the subject, the true "functional" limit was achieved at the 5% grade. The THR calculated would be based on the heart rate measured at the 5.4 METs stage. A THR range of 96-108 beats/min (60-80% functional capacity) includes work rates in which the person was sign- and symptom-free. The emphasis would be on light work of long duration. The THR could be adjusted upward on subsequent retesting if the response merited a change.

If the %HR max method were used to calculate a THR (70-85% HR max) in this test, the bottom part of the THR zone would equal resting HR. In GXT where the heart rate response is blunted, the direct THR method (60-80% functional capacity) is the method of choice.

Case Study 9.7

The subject is a 56-year-old black male who had unstable angina for several weeks. He had paroxysmal atrial fibrillation which was converted to a normal sinus rhythm by Digitalis. His physician recommended an 8-week in-hospital rehabilitation program. His GXT follows:

2 mph; 3.5% per 2 min

Grade (%)	METs	Systolic	Diastolic	HR	ECG
	Rest	112	74	77	—
0	2.5	100	78	110	1 mm ST seg depress
3.5	3.5	114	80	112	3 mm ST seg depress

Note. ST seg depress = ST segment depression

Based on the results of this treadmill test he was referred for coronary angiography and subsequently had 3-vessel bypass surgery.

Case Study 9.8

The subject is a 59-year-old white male who is 75 kg and 178 cm tall. He had been a 1.5-pack-a-day cigarette smoker for 38 years prior to experiencing chest pain and then a myocardial infarction. After being discharged from the hospital, he experienced angina from mild exertion. Coronary angiography was carried out and triple bypass surgery followed. An in-hospital cardiac rehabilitation program was recommended; the GXT that follows represents his status as he entered the program. He was not taking any medication at the time of the GXT.

Test: 2 mph; 3.5% per 2 min

Grade (%)	METs	Systolic	Diastolic	HR	ECG	Symptoms
	Rest	120	68	83		—
0	2.5	154	80	119	*	—
3.5	3.5	170	86	122	*	—
7	4.5	184	84	132	*	—
10.5	5.5	196	100	135	*	Mild fatigue

Note. * = no changes from the resting ECG

The symptom of fatigue and the elevation of the diastolic pressure in the last stage suggest that 5.5 METs is this subject's functional capacity. Work rates equal to 60% and 80% of this value are approximately the 3.5% and 7% grades, corresponding to a THR range of 122-132 b/min. Calculation of the THR by the usual procedure (70-85% HRmax) yields a THR range of 95-115 beats/min. The reason for the discrepancy in the THR range between the methods is a somewhat nonlinear HR response in addition to a contracted HR response, which is a change of only 16 b/min across a 3-MET work rate change. The change is typically 25-30 b/min. The upper limit of the THR, calculated by taking 80% of the highest work rate, yielded a heart rate of 132 b/min, or 98% of the highest heart rate measured. Clearly one must examine the reasonableness of the THR independent of the method of calculation.

Case Study 9.9

The subject is a 56-year-old white male who is 80 kg and 180 cm tall. His mother died at age 72 of a heart attack and his father died at age 92 of congestive heart failure. All other family members are healthy. Prior to his myocardial infarction, he was a 2-pack-a-day cigarette smoker; he has had none since the MI. The following stress test was administered prior to an in-hospital exercise program. He was taking Lanoxin, Isordil, and nitroglycerine at the time of the test.

Test: 2 mph; 3.5% per 2 min

Grade (%)	METs	Systolic	Diastolic	HR	ECG
	Rest	116	84	51	PVC
0	2.5	140	84	83	—
3.5	3.5	152	96	96	—
7	4.5	162	88	109	PVC
10.5	5.5	172	100	116	1 mm ST seg depress
14	6.5	168	110	126	2 mm ST seg depress

Note. PVC = preventricular contraction; ST seg depress = ST segment depression

The heart rate response was normal but the blood pressure and the ECG responses were not. These abnormal changes must be used in choosing the real end point for the test. The heart rate, blood pressure, and ECG could be considered normal at 7% grade. A THR range of 83-96 beats/min (60-80% functional capacity) was calculated for this subject. This THR range is achieved at MET values of 2.5-3.5. A supervised, in-hospital program was recommended to allow close monitoring of progress. Beginning exercises included walking on a treadmill at 2 mph, 0% grade; pedaling a cycle ergometer 150 kgm/min; and stepping at a rate of 12 steps/min on a 6-in. step. The work was done intermittently at first (1 min work, 1 min rest) until he could sustain 3-5 minutes of work comfortably and within the THR range.

Special Considerations in Making Exercise Recommendations

A variety of conditions demand additional attention when exercise recommendations are made.

Orthopedic

Orthopedic limitations (e.g., ankle, knee, or hip pain when walking or jogging) must be considered on a case-by-case basis when designing an exercise program. The exercise recommendation still indicates the THR range, but the participant should be advised to stay at the low end of the THR range while the problem exists. The emphasis should be on light work interspersed with rest periods. The type of activity recommended is somewhat dependent on the interests and abilities of the participant; however, weight-supported activities (cycle ergometer, rowing) and aquatic activities tend to reduce the chance of aggravating the problem. Chapter 14 outlines procedures to follow in caring for chronic injuries. The participant should be informed of proper procedures for warm-up, cool-down, and immediate care of the affected part following an activity session.

Diabetic

Blood glucose is the primary fuel for the brain, and the concentration of blood glucose is maintained within close limits to assure a constant supply. If the concentration of blood glucose is falling, the liver releases glucose to bring the blood level back to normal. If the concentration is too high (following a meal), the pancreas releases insulin to allow glucose to be taken up into the tissues at a faster rate; the blood glucose concentration then returns to normal.

An insulin-dependent diabetic cannot produce enough insulin to regulate or control the blood glucose concentration, so insulin is injected to help the process along. In general, by carefully balancing food intake with insulin injections, the glucose concentration can be maintained within reasonable limits. Exercise can complement and complicate this balancing act, and the HFI needs to be aware of some general facts about the diabetic and exercise.

An interaction exists between exercise and insulin. When a diabetic's blood glucose level is normal or slightly elevated, exercise lowers the glucose level. This response is greater when the exercise takes place at the time of the peak effect of the insulin. In this way, exercise is helpful in regulating the blood glucose and reducing the need for insulin. However, if exercise takes place when there is insufficient insulin, the rate at which glucose is mobilized from the liver exceeds the rate at which the tissues take it up, and the diabetic becomes more hyperglycemic (high blood glucose condition).

Based on these observations, the diabetic needs to be informed of proper procedures to follow prior to an activity session. The information includes details on site of injection of the insulin, food consumption immediately prior to exercise, and the possible need for carbohydrates during the exercise. The physician and nurse-educator are the primary sources of information and guidance for the diabetic.

Exercise increases blood flow to the active muscle mass. If a diabetic injects insulin into one of the active limbs prior to exercise, an enhanced movement of the injected insulin into the blood and a greater chance for a hypoglycemic (low blood glucose) condition occur. It is generally recommended that the insulin be injected into a nonexercising area prior to exercise to reduce the chance of hypoglycemia.

The diabetic is also instructed to be consistent in his or her dietary and insulin habits prior to each exercise session. The exercise program can then be adjusted for intensity and total calorie expenditure to match these dietary and insulin habits. This procedure allows the diabetic and physician to make a judgment about the reasonableness of the insulin and dietary habits relative to the regular exercise session. Knowing that a diabetic is in the exercise class, the HFI should anticipate any problem by having fruit juices, candy, and sugar available at each exercise session. In addition, the HFI needs to be aware of the emergency procedures to follow in the event of insulin shock or a diabetic coma. These procedures are outlined in chapter 14.

Asthmatic

Exercising at the typical THR equal to 60-80% $\dot{V}O_2max$ has been associated with bronchospasms, usually following the exercise bout, in susceptible people. Breathing cold dry air, coupled with the exercise, increases the chance of an attack. The problem tends to be more commonly associated with running, in contrast to walking, cycling, or swimming. However, recent information suggests that when the pulmonary ventilation is identical from one type of activity to another, no difference exists in the exercise-induced asthma. Consequently, asthmatics, especially children, are encouraged to participate in a wide variety of activities at moderate intensities.

Three steps are recommended to minimize the likelihood of the problem: (a) pretreatment with special medication prior to the activity, (b) a long warm-up period, and (c) breathing warm, moist air. The medication that the physician might prescribe can vary greatly; however, the *inhalation* of a drug (a beta-2 agonist) seems to be very effective in preventing the problem. The asthmatic can inhale the drug prior to or during the activity. Asthmatics are encouraged to have the aerosol with them when they are exercising.

The warm-up period should include the regular stretching and lead-up activities prior to the main body of the activity session. Swimming is highly recommended because the high ventilation rates needed to trigger the attack may not be reached. In addition, the air close to the water is warm and moist. Runners, walkers, and cyclists are encouraged to prevent the drying of the respiratory passages by wearing a scarf or mask in front of the mouth.

Obese

Exercise programs are used with dietary programs to increase the rate of weight loss in the obese individual (see chapter 5). The activity should couple low-intensity and the low end of the THR range with long duration. In addition, the activities should not put unnecessary loads on weight-bearing joints. Three excellent choices are walking, riding a bicycle or cycle ergometer, and aquatic activities. The latter activities could include walking and jogging across the pool as well as swimming laps (see chapter 11).

Hypertensive

Finding participants who are borderline hypertensive (about 140/90) or who are taking medication to control blood pressure within normal limits is not uncommon for an HFI. A generally accepted view is to treat the borderline participant the same as the normotensive participant because the former's blood pressure response to exercise may not be excessive.

Hypertensives who are "controlled" need to be reminded to take their medication at the same time of the day. The HFI needs to be aware that hypertension can be controlled by a variety of drugs, some of which affect the THR calculation. If a hypertensive individual receives a drug that blocks the beta adrenergic receptors (e.g., Inderal), the subject's heart rate is affected. Therefore, the 220 minus age formula *cannot* be used to estimate the maximal HR. Individuals who take diuretics to control hypertension can calculate the THR in the usual manner. In either case, attention should be paid to these individuals, especially when they exercise in a hot and humid environment. Excess fluid loss could lead a controlled hypertensive toward a hypotensive response and/or cause changes in serum electrolyte balance. As with any participant, emphasize the importance of adequate fluid and electrolyte replacement.

Seizure-Prone

Individuals with a *controlled* seizure disorder (e.g., epilepsy) are able and encouraged to lead normally active lives. In many cases, the individual is aware of the unique circumstances that might trigger a seizure, and he or she can avoid the situation. The HFI should be aware of any member of an exercise group that has a seizure disorder. Recommendations include participation in a variety of activities with little or no restriction. Suggestions for safety include exercising with another person who can physically support and aid the individual in case of a seizure in potentially dangerous situations, such as jogging on a road or swimming.

Elderly

In the elderly population, maintaining bone mineral content and flexibility in the limbs is increasingly important, along with maintaining a reasonable level of CRF. Fortunately, activities that affect one factor enhance the others in this population. Studies have shown that light activities (2-4 METs) can favorably influence the bone mineral content, flexibility, and CRF in elderly people. The emphasis is on controlled activities that are rhythmical in nature and can be done indoors or outdoors.

Program Selection

The nature of the information given fitness participants by the HFI depends on whether the individual is in a supervised or unsupervised program.

Supervised Program

The risk factors, the response to the GXT, the health and activity history, and personal preference influence the type of program in which an individual should participate. Generally, the higher the risk the more important it is that the person participate in a supervised program. People at high risk for CHD or those who have some overt form of CHD should be encouraged to participate under supervision, at least at the beginning of the exercise program. The personnel in the supervised program are trained to provide the necessary instruction in the appropriate activities, to help monitor the participant's response to the activity, and to administer appropriate first aid/emergency care. Supervised programs run the continuum from those conducted within a hospital for CHD patients or for people at high risk for CHD, to those programs conducted in fitness clubs for people at low risk for CHD. In general, as a person moves along the continuum from "in" hospital to "out" hospital, less formal monitoring is required. In addition, the background and training of the personnel tend to vary. The exercise programs aimed at maintaining the fitness level of the CHD patients who went through a hospital-based program have medical personnel and appropriate emergency equipment consistent with the population being served. Supervised fitness programs for the apparently healthy have an HFI who can focus more on the appropriate exercise, diet, and other lifestyle behaviors needed to increase positive health.

The supervised program offers a socially supportive environment for individuals to become and stay active. This is important given the difficulty of changing life-style behaviors. The group programs allow for more variety in the types of activities to be used (games) and reduce the chance of boredom. To be effective in the long run, the program should try to wean the participant from the group so that the participant's activity pattern will remain, even if the individual is no longer in the program.

Unsupervised Program

In spite of what was just presented, the vast majority of people at risk from and possessing CHD participate in unsupervised exercise programs. Reasons for this include the limited number of supervised programs, the level of interest of the participant and physician in such programs, and the financial resources required to bring them about.

Participation in an unsupervised exercise program requires clear communication of correct information from the HFI or physician about how to begin and maintain the exercise program. The emphasis in the unsupervised exercise program is on low intensity, at or below 60% functional capacity (70% max HR), because the threshold for a training effect is lower in deconditioned people. The emphasis is on increasing the duration of the activity with exercise frequency approaching every day. This reduces the chance of muscular, skeletal, or cardiovascular problems caused by the intensity and increases the conditioning of the muscles with the expenditure of a relatively large number of calories. Quite importantly, the regularity of the exercise program encourages a habit. The outcome of such programs results in the individual being able to conduct his or her daily affairs with more comfort and sets the stage for those people who would like to exercise at higher levels.

In an unsupervised exercise program, the person needs to be provided with explicit information about the intensity (THR), duration, and frequency of exercise so that no doubt remains about what should be done. For example, the exercise recommendation might read, "Walk 1 mi in 30 min each day for 2 weeks. Monitor and record your heart rate." The person has to receive information about how to take the pulse rate and be encouraged to follow through on the recording.

Updating the Exercise Program

As an individual participates in an endurance training program, his or her capacity for work increases. The best sign of this is that the "regular" exercise is no longer enough of a stimulus to reach THR. This is clear evidence that the person is adapting to the exercise. Taking the HR during a regular activity session thus provides a sound basis for upgrading the intensity or duration of the exercise session.

However, the exercise program, including the THR, should be periodically updated. The need to update is greater the lower the initial level of fitness and the higher the number of risk factors. An individual who has a low functional capacity because of heart disease, orthopedic limitations, or chronic inactivity that might include prolonged bed rest has difficulty reaching a true maximum on a first treadmill test, and he or she experiences the greatest improvements in the shortest period of time in a fitness program. This individual benefits from frequent retesting because the test allows progress (or the lack of) to be monitored, and it may give new information that influences the exercise prescription. If the person has had a change in medication that influences the HR response to exercise, a special need exists for a reevaluation of the exercise program.

For those people who reach a true maximum in the first test, little change occurs in the actual THR caused by a fitness program because the maximal heart rate is affected very little by regular endurance exercise. However, the person may still benefit from an evaluation of the overall exercise program on a regular basis. A need may exist to modify the type of activity caused by a change in interest or the presence of an orthopedic problem that did not exist before. The reevaluation allows the HFI to probe for information that may be useful in making a decision to refer the person for treatment at a time when treatment will do the most good. Lastly, such contact increases the chance that the person will stay involved in an activity program—the most important factor in maintaining aerobic fitness.

Environmental Concerns

The GXT is used to evaluate the individual's cardiovascular and metabolic responses to progressive increments in the work rate. The functional capacity and the maximal HR are used in the exercise prescription to calculate the THR. The assumption underlying the THR is that the HR is proportional to the metabolic load. Exercises of a certain MET load to achieve THR are then prescribed. Unfortunately, this assumption has a problem. Several factors independent of metabolic load can influence the HR response. These include emotion (see chapter 8), medication, meals, humidity, heat, pollution, and altitude.

The Influence of Heat and Humidity

While the metabolic load is clearly the primary determinant of the HR response, the heat load provides an important secondary influence. The total heat load experienced by the subject is determined by the degree of water balance, the environmental temperature and humidity, the clothing the person is wearing, and the metabolic load itself. The core temperature increases with metabolic load, stabilizing at a temperature proportional to the metabolic load. However, at the same metabolic load, the HR increases with increasing environmental temperature.

The effect of an increase in the relative humidity is just as clear. As the relative humidity increases, the sweat rate and the HR for a fixed submaximal task also increase. Understandably, a person in these environments must cut back on the work rate (MET load) to stay within the THR zone.

A special need exists for increased water intake during times of high temperature and humidity. Because of the increased sweat rate, more water is lost from the body and the individual becomes more prone to heat illness if the water is not replaced. Water should be replaced as it is lost. An inadequate water intake can lead to a high core temperature (and HR) response for the same work rate.

Clothing has a direct effect on the core temperature response to a fixed exercise load. In general, the more clothing an individual wears the greater is the core temperature and HR response to a work task. The clothing reduces the chance for evaporation of sweat and the result is an elevation in these measures. The use of impermeable materials to encourage weight loss presents a real risk for some individuals because the HR response is higher during the exercise session and the person becomes progressively dehydrated from one exercise session to the next. This results in a greater chance of heat injury. The general recommendation is to wear as little clothing as possible when exercising in the heat.

Based on these concerns, should a person continue a regular exercise program in hot weather? We believe the answer to that is "yes," but the HFI should take special precautions to reduce the chance of heat injury. If the individual is going to do recreational activities in the heat and humidity, then participation in regular exercise in a hot and humid environment helps him or her adapt to the heat. The educational information provided by the HFI about how to deal with high heat/humidity reduces the risk of heat injury when the participant exercises on his or her own. The THR acts as the best guide to offer safe, enjoyable, and appropriate activities in these adverse environments. The effects of acclimatization are quickly obtained (7-10 days) and result in many benefits: When exercising at a fixed work rate there is (a) an increased sweat rate, (b) a decreased salt loss, (c) a decreased HR and body temperature, and (d) a decreased risk of heat injury.

Precautions for exercise in hot/humid conditions include (a) using the THR as a guide, (b) gradually introducing the participants to the conditions to achieve acclimatization, (c) educating about water and salt replacement, (d) watching for signs of trouble, especially for people on medication, (e) educating about clothing, (f) having indoor activities planned when environmental conditions cannot be tolerated, and (g) having emergency measures set up for heat injury (Sharkey, 1984; Fox & Mathews, 1981).

Exercising in the Cold

Cold air can cause an increase in peripheral vasoconstriction, which can lead to frostbite and, through the increase in peripheral resistance, angina. In addition, the cold air can irritate the respiratory passages because cold air is dry.

When the air temperature is −20 °F there is cause for concern. Air at this temperature cannot be adequately warmed as it moves through the respiratory passages and thus it can lead to respiratory tract damage. This temperature is also regarded as a frostbite alert, and special attention should be paid to this possibility. Educating participants about the selection of proper clothing and offering modified activities to be done at home should help prevent frostbite. If frostbite does occur, immersion of the body part in warm water (45 °C or 113 °F) without massaging is the recommended approach.

Hypothermia is a condition in which heat production is less than heat loss. In most cases hypothermia occurs at temperatures warmer than 30 °F. Factors that predispose an individual to hypothermia are cold water or rain associated with the cold temperature, the wind, and the state of fatigue of the individual. Heat is lost at a much faster rate in cold water compared to cold air (about 20 times faster) (Sharkey, 1984).

The windchill is a major factor. The effective temperature that is felt on the skin is a function of the air temperature and the velocity at which the wind is blowing. This is shown in Table 9.3. This combination is sometimes overlooked, and injury or death is the result. The signs and symptoms of hypothermia include violent shivering; impaired neuromuscular function; a decrease in higher brain function, as seen in slurred speech and poor coordination; and a feeling that you must lie down and rest which could eventually lead to

Table 9.3 Wind Chill Index

Wind Speed in MPH	Actual Thermometer Reading (°F) 50	40	30	20	10	0	−10	−20	−30	−40	−50	−60
	Equivalent Temperature (°F)											
Calm	50	40	30	20	10	0	−10	−20	−30	−40	−50	−60
5	48	37	27	16	6	−5	−15	−26	−36	−47	−57	−68
10	40	28	16	4	−9	−21	−33	−46	−58	−70	−83	−95
15	36	22	9	−5	−18	−36	−45	−58	−72	−85	−99	−112
20	32	18	4	−10	−25	−39	−53	−67	−82	−96	−110	−124
25	30	16	0	−15	−29	−44	−59	−74	−88	−104	−118	−133
30	28	13	−2	−18	−33	−48	−63	−79	−94	−109	−125	−140
35	27	11	−4	−20	−35	−49	−67	−82	−98	−113	−129	−145
40	26	10	−6	−21	−37	−53	−69	−85	−100	−116	−132	−148
(Wind speeds greater than 40 MPH have little additional effect	LITTLE DANGER (for properly clothed person)				INCREASING DANGER			GREAT DANGER				
					Danger from freezing of exposed flesh							

Note. From *Physiology of fitness* (p. 191) by B.J. Sharkey, 1984, Champaign, IL: Human Kinetics. Reprinted with permission.

death. The state of fatigue of the individual influences this latter response very much. The energy required to balance heat loss cannot be produced when fatigued, resulting in a fall of body temperature.

Hypothermia can be prevented in several ways: (a) do not exercise in the extreme cold/wind, (b) wear appropriate clothing in layers, (c) remove layers as you warm up to reduce sweating, and (d) stay as dry as possible. The treatment for hypothermia might include getting the person out of the cold, wind, or rain; removing all wet clothing; providing dry clothing, warm drinks, and a warm sleeping bag; and if the person is semiconscious, put another person into the sleeping bag with the person who is hypothermic (Sharkey, 1984).

Effect of Altitude

An increase in altitude decreases the partial pressure of oxygen and reduces the amount of oxygen bound to hemoglobin. As a result, the volume of oxygen carried in each liter of blood decreases. This effect of altitude influences both the functional capacity (maximal aerobic power), and the HR and ventilation responses to submaximal work.

Figure 9.2 shows the effect of altitude on maximal aerobic power. Maximal aerobic power steadily decreases with increasing altitude so that by 2,300 m (7,500 ft) the value is only 88% of that measured at sea level. This means that an activity that demanded 88% of $\dot{V}O_2max$ at sea level now requires 100% of the "new" $\dot{V}O_2max$.

More than maximal aerobic power is affected

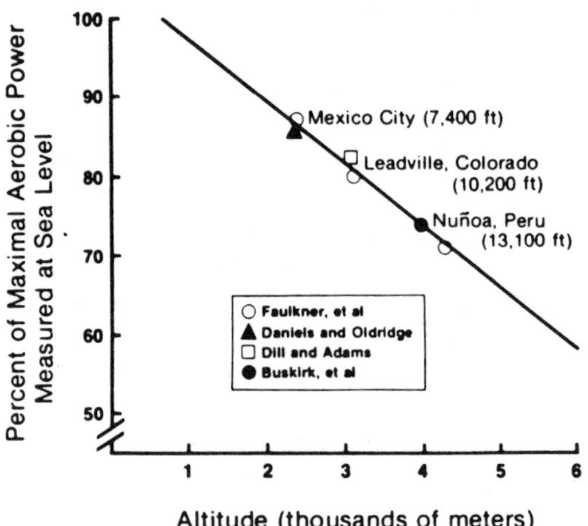

Figure 9.2 Effect of altitude on maximal aerobic power. From Howley, E.T. (1980). *Encyclopedia of Physical Education, Fitness, and Sports.* Reprinted with permission of AAHPERD.

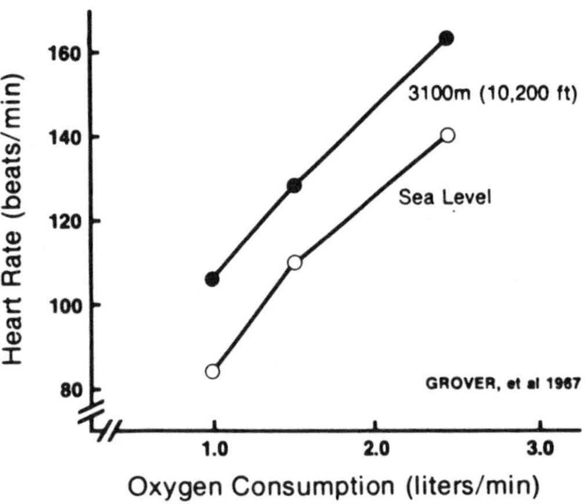

Figure 9.3 Effect of altitude on the heart rate response to submaximal work rates. From Howley, E.T. (1980). *Encyclopedia of Physical Education, Fitness, and Sports.* Reprinted with permission of AAHPERD.

by altitude exposure. Any submaximal work rate is going to demand a higher HR at altitude compared to sea level (shown in Figure 9.3). The reason is quite simple; because each liter of blood has less oxygen, more blood is required to deliver the same quantity of oxygen to the tissues. Consequently, the HR response is elevated at any given submaximal work rate. To stay within the THR range, a person must cut back on the intensity of the exercise when at altitude. Just like exercise in high heat and humidity, the THR allows the modification of the intensity of the activity relative to any additional environmental demand (Howley, 1980).

Pollution

Carbon monoxide (CO) is produced from a variety of sources (incomplete combustion of gasoline, coal, oil) and has the potential for significantly influencing performance. Carbon monoxide binds to hemoglobin (COHb) about 200 times more readily than does oxygen, and carbon monoxide can therefore decrease the volume of oxygen carried in arterial blood (similar to the effect of altitude). The normal COHb level is 1% in nonsmokers, but it may be as high as 5% in people who live in urban areas where the carbon monoxide level is high. Smokers may have blood levels of COHb above 10%. Performance has been shown to be affected when the blood level of COHb is near 3%, but $\dot{V}O_2$max is unaffected until COHb levels exceed 4.3%.

Sulfur dioxide and ozone increase airway resistance (bronchoconstriction). In the case of ozone, long-term exposure to 0.37 parts per million (ppm) decreases lung function, and exposure to 0.75 ppm during intermittent exercise decreases $\dot{V}O_2$max. The latter effect is enhanced by high heat and humidity.

In some communities, special attention clearly must be paid to a "pollution index" when recommending exercise. In fact, on certain days the environmental conditions are dangerous enough to cancel outdoor physical activity. An HFI must be aware of this problem in his or her community and provide specific guidelines to follow, especially for the individual who is exercising alone. Generally, most pollutants are at their lowest levels in the early morning, before the rush hour (Raven, 1980).

Summary

Two major principles of training related to the improvement of cardiovascular function are *overload* and *specificity*. The apparently healthy but sedentary participant should start out slowly with a goal to become a regular exerciser. Each exercise session should start with a warm-up and finish with a taper-down. Exercise sessions should be scheduled three to four times per week, and each workout should be long enough to expend about 300 kcal. The intensity of the exercise session should be 60-80% of functional capacity. The exercise intensity is usually set by identifying HR values equivalent to these work loads. The THR can be obtained directly by seeing what HRs were equivalent to 60% and 80% of the functional capacity measured on a GXT. Two indirect methods of estimating the THR are the Karvonen method and the simple percent of maximal HR method. In the Karvonen method, the HFI takes 60-80% of the HR reserve (HRR = maximal HR − resting HR) and adds the result to resting HR. In the other method, the HFI takes 70-85% of maximal HR. Maximal HR is determined from a GXT, or it can be estimated to be equal to 220 − age. However, considerable variability exists in the estimated compared with the measured value. The average person experiences a training effect at the above intensities of exercise. Extremely deconditioned individuals experience some training effect at relatively low intensities. Very fit people, on the other hand, have to train at the upper end (80-90% of maximal aerobic power) to improve their CRF.

A series of case studies are presented to show how to write exercise recommendations. These recommendations should give special consideration to the elderly and those with orthopedic problems, diabetes, or asthma. Participation in a supervised program is appropriate for many of these people, at least at the beginning of an exercise program.

The HR response to exercise is influenced by more than the exercise intensity. Heat, humidity, altitude, and pollution can all cause a higher-than-expected HR response. Under these circumstances, the HFI should recommend a decrease in the intensity of exercise to keep the person within the THR zone. The participant should be educated about needed precautions for exercising in extreme hot, humid, or cold conditions to prevent heat illness, hypothermia, or frostbite.

Suggested Reading for Chapter 9

ACSM (1978)

ACSM (1980)

Bundgaard, A. (1985)

Fox and Mathews (1981)

Franks (1983)

Hage (1983)

Hooper and Noland (1984)

Howley (1980)

Jette and Cureton (1976)

Koivisto and Sherwin (1979)

Noble, Borg, Cafarelli, Robertson, and Pandolf (1982)

Pollock, Wilmore, and Fox (1984)

Raven (1980)

Sager (1984)

Sharkey (1984)

Williams (1983a)

See reference list at the end of the book for a complete source listing.

Chapter 10

Energy Costs of Activity

- Determining energy expenditure
- Expressing energy expenditure
- Activity values

Health and fitness instructors are usually concerned about the following two questions when they recommend specific physical activities to participants: (a) Are the activities appropriate in terms of exercise intensity to achieve THR? and (b) Is the combination of intensity and duration appropriate for achieving an energy expenditure goal to balance or exceed caloric intake? (see chapter 5). To deal with these questions, an exercise leader should become familiar with the energy costs of various activities. The purpose of this chapter is to offer some basic information about how to estimate the energy requirement of various physical activities and to summarize the values associated with common recreational activities.

Ways to Measure Energy Expenditure

Energy expenditure can be measured by *direct* and *indirect calorimetry*. Direct calorimetry requires that the person perform an activity of interest within a specially constructed chamber that is insulated and has water flowing through its walls. The water is warmed by the heat given off by the subject, and heat production can be calculated by knowing the volume of water flowing through the chamber per minute and the change in the temperature of the water from the time of entry to the time of exit. Additional heat is lost from the subject by evaporation of water from the skin and respiratory passages. This heat loss can be measured and added to that picked up by the water to yield the rate of energy produced by the subject for that task.

Indirect calorimetry estimates energy production by measuring oxygen consumption. This technique relies on certain constants to convert the liters of oxygen consumption to kilocalories expended. Some of the constants are derived from measurements made in a *bomb calorimeter*, a heavy metal chamber into which carbohydrate, fat, or protein can be placed with 100% oxygen under pressure. The chamber is immersed in a water bath and the food stuff is oxidized to CO_2 and H_2O when an electric spark sets the process in motion. The heat given off warms the water; it has been determined that carbohydrates, fats, and proteins give off 4, 9, and 5.6 kcal of heat per gram. Knowing how much oxygen is required to oxidize 1 g of substrate makes it possible to calculate the number of kilocalories derived from 1 ℓ of oxygen. Values for carbohydrate, fat, and protein are listed in Table 10.1. The table shows that carbohydrates give more energy per liter of oxygen while fats give more energy per gram of substrate. The ratio of the carbon dioxide produced to the oxygen consumed is the *Respiratory Quotient* (RQ).

Table 10.1 The Caloric Density, Caloric Equivalent, and the Respiratory Quotient Associated With the Oxidation of Carbohydrate, Fat, and Protein

Measurement	Carbohydrate	Fat	Protein[a]
Caloric density (kcal/gm)	4.0	9.0	5.6
Caloric equivalent of 1 ℓ of O_2 (kcal/ℓ)	5.0	4.7	4.5
Respiratory quotient	1.0	0.7	0.8

[a]Does not include the energy derived from the oxidation of nitrogen in the amino acids because the body excretes this as urea.

Note. From "Energy metabolism" by L.K. Knoebel, 1984, in *Physiology* (5th edition), E. Selkurt (Ed.). Boston: Little Brown & Co.

Indirect calorimetry employs two techniques to measure oxygen consumption: closed circuit and open circuit. In the closed circuit technique the subject usually breathes 100% oxygen from a spirometer and the subject's exhaled air passes through a chemical to absorb the carbon dioxide produced. The decrease in the volume of oxygen contained in the spirometer is a measure of the oxygen consumption. The fact that the carbon dioxide is absorbed does *not* allow one to calculate a respiratory quotient, so a caloric equivalent of 4.82 kcals/liter oxygen is used to indicate that a mixture of carbohydrates, fats, and protein is used. This closed-circuit technique has been used extensively to measure the basal metabolic rate.

The open-circuit technique for measuring oxygen consumption and carbon dioxide production is the most common indirect calorimetry technique. In this procedure oxygen consumption is calculated by simply subtracting the volume of oxygen exhaled from the volume of oxygen inhaled. The difference is taken as the oxygen uptake or oxygen consumption (see chapter 3 for details). Carbon dioxide production is calculated in the same manner. This makes it possible to calculate the RQ (also called the Respiratory Exchange Ratio or R). One can then determine which substrate, fat, or carbohydrate, provided the most energy during work and also determine what value for the caloric equivalent of 1 ℓ of oxygen to use in the calculation of energy expenditure.

Ways to Express Energy Expenditure

The energy requirement for an activity is calculated on the basis of a subject's *steady state* oxygen uptake ($\dot{V}O_2$) measured during an activity. Once the steady state (leveling off) oxygen uptake is reached, the energy (ATP) supplied to the muscles is derived from the aerobic metabolism of the various substrates. The measured oxygen uptake can then be used to express energy expenditure in different ways. The most common expressions follow:

1. $\dot{V}O_2$ (liters/min). The calculation of oxygen uptake (Appendix E) yields a value expressed in liters of oxygen used per minute.
2. $\dot{V}O_2$ ml(kg•min)$^{-1}$. If the measured oxygen uptake, expressed in liters/min, is multiplied by 1,000 to yield ml•min^{-1} and then divided by the subject's body weight in kilograms, the value is expressed in ml O_2 per kilogram body weight per minute, or ml(kg•min)$^{-1}$.
3. METs. The resting metabolic rate (oxygen uptake) is approximately 3.5 ml(kg•min)$^{-1}$. This is called 1 MET. Activities are expressed in terms of multiples of the MET unit. An 8-MET activity is 8 times the resting metabolic rate, or 28 ml(kg•min)$^{-1}$.
4. Kcal/min. The oxygen uptake can be expressed in kilocalories used per minute. The caloric equivalent of 1 ℓ of oxygen ranges from 4.7 kcal when fat is used as the sole fuel to 5.0 kcal when carbohydrate is used as the only fuel. For practical reasons, and with little loss in precision, 5 kcal/ℓ O_2 is used to convert the oxygen uptake to kcal/min. A person working at a $\dot{V}O_2$ of 2 ℓ/min expends about 10 kcal/min. The total kilocalorie expenditure is calculated by multiplying the kilocalories expended per minute (kcals/min) by the duration of the activity in minutes.
5. Kcal(kg•hr)$^{-1}$. The resulting value of expressing energy expenditure in kcal/kg body weight per hour is the same as the MET expression, with one advantage: calculating how many kilocalories a person uses in an exercise session is easier. If a person is working at 8 METs, the $\dot{V}O_2$ is estimated to be 28 ml(kg•min)$^{-1}$. If this value is multiplied by 60 min/hr, then it equals 1,680 ml(kg•hr)$^{-1}$, or 1.68 ℓ(kg•hr)$^{-1}$. If the person is using a mixture of carbohydrates and fats as the fuel, then this oxygen consumption is multiplied by 4.85 kcal/ℓ O_2 to give 8.1 kcal (kg•hr)$^{-1}$. So 8 METs is approximately equal to 8 kcal(kg•hr)$^{-1}$.

Problem: If an 80-kg person works for 30 min at an average of 8 METs, how many kilocalories are expended?

Answer: 8 METs = 8 kcal(kg•hr)$^{-1}$ times 0.5 hr times 80 kg = 320 kcal.

Formulas for Estimating the Energy Cost of Activities

In the mid-1970s the ACSM identified some simple formulas to estimate the *steady state* energy requirement associated with common modes of activities used in graded exercise stress tests: walking, stepping, running, and cycle ergometry. The oxygen uptake calculated from these formulas is an estimate, and a typical standard deviation around these estimates is 7-8% of the value.

The ACSM formulas have been applied to graded exercise stress tests to estimate functional capacity or maximal aerobic power. This application has been shown to give reasonable estimates when the subjects are healthy and the rate at which the GXT progresses is slow enough to allow a steady state oxygen uptake to be achieved at each stage (Nagle, Balke, Baptista, Alleyia, & Howley, 1971; Montoye, 1975). In situations where the increments in the stages of the GXT are large and/or the subject being tested is somewhat unfit, the subject's oxygen uptake will not keep pace with each stage of the test. In these cases the formulas overestimate the actual measured oxygen uptake. The fact that this overestimation is more likely to happen in diseased populations (COPD, cardiac, etc.) suggests that the GXTs used may be too aggressive. A test that progresses at a slower rate and allows the subject to reach the steady state $\dot{V}O_2$ at each stage reduces the chance of an overestimation of functional capacity and still requires the subject to work at an appropriate metabolic rate to overload the system (see chapter 6). The previous information is presented to clarify the usefulness of the following equations. They estimate the steady state energy requirements for activities.

In the development of the ACSM equations, an attempt was made to use a true physiological oxygen cost for each type of work. Each activity is broken down into the energy components (i.e., in estimating the total oxygen cost of grade walking, add the net oxygen cost of the horizontal walk to the net oxygen cost of the vertical (grade) walk to the resting metabolic rate, which is taken to be 1 MET (3.5 $ml(kg{\bullet}min)^{-1}$).

Total O_2 Cost = Net Oxygen Cost of Activity + 3.5 $ml(kg{\bullet}min)^{-1}$

Note that the subject cannot hold onto the treadmill railing during any test if the estimated $\dot{V}O_2$ is going to be of any use. In addition, if the treadmill speed/grade settings and the cycle ergometer are not calibrated or the subject does not step up completely during a step test, then the calculations are of little use.

Energy Requirements of Common Activities

The following sections provide formulas to estimate the energy cost of walking, running, cycle ergometry and stepping. These activities are common to cardiac rehabilitation, as well as, adult fitness programs. Examples are provided to show how the formulas are used in designing exercise programs.

Walking

On a horizontal surface. One of the most common activities used in an exercise program and in GXTs is walking. The following formula can be used to estimate the energy requirement between the walking speeds of 50 and 100 m/min. Dill (1965) showed that the net cost of walking 1 m/min on a horizontal surface is 0.100-0.106 $ml(kg{\bullet}min)^{-1}$. A value of 0.1 $ml(kg{\bullet}min)^{-1}$ is used in the ACSM equations to simplify calculations without too much loss in precision.

$\dot{V}O_2$ = 0.1 $ml(kg{\bullet}min)^{-1}$ (horizontal velocity) + 3.5 $ml(kg{\bullet}min)^{-1}$

Question: What is the estimated steady state $\dot{V}O_2$ and METs for a walking speed of 90 m/min (3.4 mph)?

Answer: $\dot{V}O_2$ = 90 m/min × 0.1 $ml(kg{\bullet}min)^{-1}$ per m/min + 3.5 $ml(kg{\bullet}min)^{-1}$.

$\dot{V}O_2 = 9.0 + 3.5 = 12.5$ $ml(kg{\bullet}min)^{-1}$

METs = 12.5 $ml(kg{\bullet}min)^{-1}$/3.5 $ml(kg{\bullet}min)^{-1}$ = 3.6

Question: An unfit participant is told to exercise at 11.5 $ml(kg{\bullet}min)^{-1}$ to achieve THR. What walking speed should be recommended to the participant?

Answer: 11.5 $ml(kg{\bullet}min)^{-1}$ = ? m/min × 0.1 $ml(kg{\bullet}min)^{-1}$ per m/min + 3.5 $ml(kg{\bullet}min)^{-1}$. Subtract 3.5 from 11.5 to get the net O_2 cost of the activity [8.0 ml(kg•min)$^{-1}$]. The net cost is divided by 0.1 ml(kg•min)$^{-1}$ per m/min to yield 80 m/min (3 mph).

Up a grade. The oxygen cost of grade-walking is the sum of the oxygen cost of horizontal walking, the oxygen cost of the vertical component, and 3.5 ml(kg•min)$^{-1}$ for rest. Work by Balke and Ware (1959) and Nagle, Balke, and Naughton (1965) has shown that the oxygen cost of moving (walking or stepping) 1 m/min vertically is 1.8 ml(kg•min)$^{-1}$. The vertical velocity is calculated by multiplying the grade (expressed as a fraction) times the speed in meters per minute. A person walking at 80 m/min on a 10% grade is walking 8 m/min vertically.

$\dot{V}O_2$ = 0.1 ml(kg•min)$^{-1}$ (horizontal velocity) + 1.8 ml(kg•min)$^{-1}$ (vertical velocity) + 3.5 ml(kg•min)$^{-1}$

Question: What is the total oxygen cost of walking 90 m/min up a 12% grade?

Horizontal component: Calculated as above and equals 9 ml(kg•min)$^{-1}$.

Vertical component: $\dot{V}O_2$ = 0.12 (grade) × 90 m/min × 1.8 ml/kg•min per m/min = 19.4 ml(kg•min)$^{-1}$.

$\dot{V}O_2$ = 9.0 (horizontal) + 19.4 (vertical) + 3.5

Answer: = 31.9 ml(kg•min)$^{-1}$ or 9.1 METs.

Question: Set the treadmill grade to achieve an energy requirement of 6 METs [21.0 ml(kg•min)$^{-1}$] when walking at 60 m/min.

Answer: The net O_2 cost of the activity is 21 − 3.5 ml(kg•min)$^{-1}$, or 17.5 ml(kg•min)$^{-1}$.

Horizontal component = 60 m/min × 0.1 ml(kg•min)$^{-1}$ per m/min, or 6.0 ml(kg•min)$^{-1}$.

Vertical component = 17.5 − 6 = 11.5 ml(kg•min)$^{-1}$.

11.5 ml/kg/min = fractional grade × 60 m/min × 1.8 ml(kg•min)$^{-1}$ per m/min

11.5 ml(kg•min)$^{-1}$ = 108 ml(kg•min)$^{-1}$ × grade

Fractional Grade = .106, or 10.6%

At different speeds. The above formulas are useful within the range of walking speeds of 50-100 m/min; beyond that, the oxygen requirement for walking increases in a curvilinear manner. Because many people choose to walk at a fast speed rather than jog, knowledge of the energy requirements for walking at these higher speeds is useful in prescribing exercise. Based on a recent study, values for the energy requirement for walking at these faster speeds (4.0-5.0 mph) are included in Table 10.2. Walking at a fast pace clearly can provide an effective metabolic demand to achieve THR.

Jogging and Running

Jogging and running are common activities used in fitness programs for apparently healthy individuals. Using ACSM equations it is possible to estimate the oxygen cost of these activities for a broad range of speeds, generally, from 130 to 350 m/min. However, the equations are also useful at speeds below 130 m/min, as long as the person is really jogging. The fact that a person can walk or jog at speeds below 130 m/min complicates the issue. The O_2 cost of walking is less than that of jogging at slow speeds; however, at approximately 130 m/min, the oxygen cost of jogging and walking are about the same. Above this speed the oxygen cost of walking exceeds that of jogging.

On a horizontal surface. The net oxygen cost of jogging or running 1 m/min on a horizontal surface is about twice that of walking, 0.2 ml(kg•min)$^{-1}$ per m/min (Balke, 1963; Margaria, Cerretelli, Aghemo & Sassi, 1963; Bransford & Howley, 1977).

$\dot{V}O_2$ = 0.2 ml(kg•min)$^{-1}$ (horizontal velocity) + 3.5 ml(kg•min)$^{-1}$

Question: What is the oxygen requirement for running a 10,000-m race on a track in 60 min?

Answer: 10,000 m/60 min = 167 m/min.

Table 10.2 Energy Requirement, in METs, for Walking at Various Speeds/Grades

mph	2.0	2.5	3.0	3.5	4.0	4.5	5.0
m/min	54	67	80	94	107	121	134
% Grade							
0	2.5	2.9	3.3	3.7	4.9	6.2	7.9
2	3.1	3.6	4.1	4.7	5.9	7.4	9.3
4	3.6	4.3	4.9	5.6	7.1	8.7	10.6
6	4.2	5.0	5.8	6.6	8.1	9.9	12.0
8	4.7	5.7	6.6	7.5	9.3	11.1	13.4
10	5.3	6.3	7.4	8.5	10.4	12.4	14.8
12	5.8	7.1	8.3	9.5	11.4	13.6	16.6
14	6.4	7.7	9.1	10.4	12.6	14.9	17.5
16	6.9	8.4	9.9	11.4	13.6	16.1	18.9
18	7.5	9.1	10.7	12.4	14.8	17.4	20.3
20	8.1	9.8	11.6	13.3	15.9	18.6	21.7
22	8.6	10.3	12.4	14.3	17.0	19.9	23.1
24	9.1	11.1	13.2	15.3	18.1	21.1	
26	9.7	11.9	14.0	16.2	19.2	22.3	
28	10.3	12.5	14.9	17.2	20.3	23.6	
30	10.8	13.2	15.7	18.2	21.4		

Adapted from *Guidelines for Exercise Stress Testing and Prescription* (3rd edition, 1986) and Bubb, W.J., A.D. Martin, and E.T. Howley (1985).

$\dot{V}O_2$ = 167 m/min × .2 ml(kg•min)$^{-1}$ per m/min + 3.5 ml(kg•min)$^{-1}$.

$\dot{V}O_2$ = 36.9 ml(kg•min)$^{-1}$, or 10.5 METs.

Question: A person with a $\dot{V}O_2$max of 50 ml(kg•min)$^{-1}$ wants to run intervals at 90% of $\dot{V}O_2$max. At what speed should he or she run on a track?

Answer: 90% of 50 = 45 ml(kg•min)$^{-1}$

45 ml(kg•min)$^{-1}$ = .2 ml(kg•min)$^{-1}$ per m/min + 3.5 ml(kg•min)$^{-1}$

41.5 ml(kg•min)$^{-1}$ = .2 ml(kg•min)$^{-1}$ per m/min

He or she should run at 207 m/min (41.5/.2), or 7:45 min/mile pace.

Up a grade. There is not as much information about the oxygen cost of grade running as there is about the previous activities. But one thing is clear—the oxygen cost of running up a grade is about one-half that of walking up a grade (Margaria, Cerretelli, Aghemo & Sassi, 1963). Some of the vertical lift associated with running on a flat surface is used to accomplish some grade work during inclined running, lowering the net oxygen requirement for the vertical work. The oxygen cost of running 1 m/min vertically is about 0.9 ml(kg•min)$^{-1}$. As in grade walking, the vertical velocity is calculated by multiplying the fractional grade times the horizontal velocity.

$\dot{V}O_2$ = 0.2 ml(kg•min)$^{-1}$ (horizontal velocity) + 0.9 ml(kg•min)$^{-1}$ (vertical velocity) + 3.5 ml(kg•min)$^{-1}$

Question: What is the oxygen cost of running 150 m/min up a 10% grade?

Answer: Horizontal component:

$\dot{V}O_2$ = 150 m/min × .2 ml(kg•min)$^{-1}$ per m/min = 30 ml(kg•min)$^{-1}$.

Vertical component:

$\dot{V}O_2$ = 0.10 (fractional grade) × 150 m/min × 0.9 ml(kg•min)$^{-1}$ per m/min = 13.5 ml(kg•min)$^{-1}$.

$\dot{V}O_2$ = 30.0 + 13.5 + 3.5 = 47 ml(kg•min)$^{-1}$.

Question: The oxygen cost of running 350 m/min on the flat is about 73.5 ml(kg•min)$^{-1}$. What grade should be set on a treadmill for a speed of 300 m/min to achieve the same $\dot{V}O_2$?

Answer: Horizontal component:

$\dot{V}O_2$ = 300 m/min × .2 ml(kg•min)$^{-1}$ per m/min = 60 ml(kg•min)$^{-1}$

Vertical component:

Net $\dot{V}O_2$ = 73.5 − 60 − 3.5 = 10.0 ml(kg•min)$^{-1}$.

10 ml(kg•min)$^{-1}$ = fractional grade × 300 m/min × 0.9 ml(kg•min)$^{-1}$ per m/min.

10 ml(kg•min)$^{-1}$ = 270 ml(kg•min)$^{-1}$ = .037, or 3.7% grade.

Caloric Cost of Walking and Running 1 Mile

The formulas for estimating the energy cost of walking and running can be used to estimate the caloric cost of walking and running 1 mile, a piece of information that is useful in achieving energy expenditure goals.

Walking

If a person walks at 3 mph (80 m/min), 1 mile will be completed in 20 min. The caloric cost for walking 1 mile for a 70-kg person is

$\dot{V}O_2$ = 80 m/min × 0.1 ml(kg•min)$^{-1}$ + 3.5 ml(kg•min)$^{-1}$

$\dot{V}O_2$ = 11.5 ml(kg•min)$^{-1}$

Table 10.3 Energy Requirement, in METs, for Jogging/Running at Various Speeds and Grades

mph	3	4	5	6	7	8	9	10
m/min	80	107	134	161	188	215	241	268
% Grade								
0	5.6	7.1	8.7	10.2	11.7	13.3	14.8	16.3
1	5.8	7.4	9.0	10.6	12.2	13.8	15.4	17.0
2	6.0	7.7	9.3	11.0	12.7	14.4	16.0	17.7
3	6.2	7.9	9.7	11.4	13.2	14.9	16.6	18.4
4	6.4	8.2	10.0	11.9	13.7	15.5	17.3	19.1
5	6.6	8.5	10.4	12.3	14.2	16.1	17.9	19.8
6	6.8	8.8	10.7	12.7	14.6	16.6	18.5	20.4
7	7.0	9.0	11.0	13.1	15.1	17.1	19.1	21.1
8	7.2	9.3	11.4	13.5	15.6	17.7	19.7	21.8
9	7.4	9.6	11.7	13.9	16.1	18.3	20.3	22.5
10	7.6	9.9	12.1	14.3	16.6	18.8	21.0	23.2

Adapted from *Guidelines for Exercise Stress Testing and Prescription*, ACSM, 1986, Philadelphia: Lea & Febiger. Reprinted with permission.

VO_2 (liters/mile) = 11.5 ml(kg•min)$^{-1}$ × 70 kg × 20 min/mile

$\dot{V}O_2$ = 16.1 ℓ/mile

At about 5.0 kcal/ℓ O_2, the gross caloric cost per mile of walking is 80.5 kcal.

Running

If the same 70-kg individual ran the mile at 6 mph (161 m/min), the cost could be calculated by the following method:

$\dot{V}O_2$ = 161 m/min × 0.2 ml(kg•min)$^{-1}$ + 3.5 ml(kg•min)$^{-1}$

$\dot{V}O_2$ = 35.5 ml(kg•min)$^{-1}$

$\dot{V}O_2$ (liters/mile) = 35.5 ml(kg•min)$^{-1}$ × 70 kg × 10 min/mile

$\dot{V}O_2$ = 24.8 ℓ/mile.

At about 5 kcal/ℓ 0_2, 124 kcal are used to jog or run 1 mile. The gross caloric cost per mile is about 50% higher for jogging than for walking. The net caloric cost of jogging or running 1 mile (kilocalories used above resting) is relatively independent of speed and is about twice that of walking. Table 10.4 lists values for the caloric cost of walking and running 1 mile.

Cycle Ergometry

Cycle ergometry exercise is common to a sport club, home, or rehabilitation program. Generally, energy expenditure is accomplished with less trauma to ankle, knee and hip joints compared to jogging. Cycle ergometers are used for conventional leg exercise programs, but are also adapted for arm exercise (by placing the ergometer on a table). The following sections describe how to estimate the energy costs of doing leg and arm cycle ergometry.

Legs. In the previous activities the individual was carrying his or her body weight and the oxygen requirement was therefore proportional to body weight (ml(kg•min)$^{-1}$). This is not the case in cycle ergometry in which an individual's body weight is supported by the cycle seat, and the work rate is determined by the pedal rate and the resistance on the wheel. The oxygen requirement for the same work rate is approximately the same for people of different sizes. Thus when a light person has the same work rate as a heavy person, the relative $\dot{V}O_2$ [ml(kg•min)$^{-1}$], or MET level, is higher for the lighter person.

The work rate is set on the simple, mechanically braked cycle ergometers by varying the force (weight or load) on the wheel and the number of pedal revolutions per minute. On the Monark cycle ergometer the wheel travels 6 m per pedal

Table 10.4 Gross and Net Caloric Cost Per Mile for Walking, Jogging, and Running

	Walking						
mph	2	2.5	3	3.5	4	4.5	5
m/min	54	67	80	94	107	121	134
Gross cost kcal/kg•mile	1.27	1.16	1.09	1.05	1.21	1.37	1.58
Net cost kcal/kg•mile	.77	.77	.77	.77	.96	1.15	1.38

	Jogging/Running							
mph	3	4	5	6	7	8	9	10
m/min	80	107	134	160	188	215	241	268
Gross cost kcal/kg•mile	1.86	1.78	1.73	1.69	1.68	1.66	1.64	1.63
Net cost kcal/kg•mile	1.53	1.53	1.53	1.53	1.53	1.53	1.53	1.53

Note. Multiply by body weight in kilograms to obtain the number of kilocalories used per mile.

revolution, while on the Tunturi ergometer the wheel travels only 3 m per revolution. Using the Monark ergometer as an example, a pedal rate of 50 rpm causes the wheel to travel a distance of 300 m (6 m per pedal revolution times 50 rpm). If a 1-kp force (1-kg weight) were applied to the wheel, the work rate would be 300 kpm/min. The work rate could be doubled by changing the force from 1 kp to 2 kp or by changing the pedal rate from 50 rpm to 100 rpm. Some cycle ergometers are electrically controlled to deliver a specific work rate somewhat independent of pedal rate; as the pedal rate falls, the load on the wheel is proportionally increased.

The oxygen cost of doing 1 kpm work is approximately 1.8 ml. During cycle ergometer exercise, some unmeasured "friction" work occurs in addition to the work rate that is set on the basis of pedal rate and force. This additional work requires about 10% of the oxygen required to do the measured work, so 0.2 ml/kpm is added to the 1.8 ml/kpm to get the net cost per kpm of work on a cycle ergometer (2 ml/kpm). The oxygen cost of sitting on the cycle ergometer is approximately 300 ml/min. The estimates from the following equation are reasonable for work rates between 150 and 1,200 kpm/min (see Table 10.5).

$\dot{V}O_2$ (ml/min) = work rate (kpm/min) (2 ml 0_2/kpm) + 300 ml/min

Question: What is the oxygen cost of doing 600 kpm/min (about 100 watts) on a cycle ergometer for 50-kg and 100-kg subjects?

Answer: $\dot{V}O_2$ = 600 kpm/min × 2 ml O_2/kpm + 300 ml/min

$\dot{V}O_2$ = 1,500 ml/min, or 1.5 ℓ/min.

For the 50-kg subject: 1,500 ml/min ÷ 50 kg = 30 ml(kg•min)$^{-1}$, or 8.6 METs.

For the 100-kg subject: 1,500 ml/min ÷ 100 kg = 15 ml(kg•min)$^{-1}$, or 4.3 METs.

Question: A 70-kg participant must work at 6 METs to achieve THR. What force (load) should be set on a Monark cycle ergometer at a pedal rate of 50 rpm?

Answer: 6 METs = 6(3.5 ml[kg•min]$^{-1}$) × 70 kg = 1,470 ml/min

Table 10.5 Energy Expenditure, in METs, for Cycle Ergometry for Legs and Arms

Body Weight		Work Rate (kpm/min and watts)						
		300	450	600	750	900	1050	1200 kpm/min
kg	lb	50	75	100	125	150	175	200 watts
50	110	5.1 (6.9)	6.9 (9.4)	8.6 (12.0)	10.3 (—)	12.0 (—)	13.7 (—)	15.4 (—)
60	132	4.3 (5.7)	5.7 (7.8)	7.1 (10.0)	8.6 (12.1)	10.0 (—)	11.4 (—)	12.9 (—)
70	154	3.7 (4.9)	4.9 (6.7)	6.1 (8.6)	7.3 (10.4)	8.6 (12.2)	9.8 (—)	11.0 (—)
80	176	3.2 (4.3)	4.3 (5.9)	5.4 (7.5)	6.4 (9.1)	7.5 (10.7)	8.6 (12.3)	9.6 (—)
90	198	2.9 (3.8)	3.8 (5.2)	4.8 (6.7)	5.7 (8.1)	6.7 (9.5)	7.6 (10.9)	8.6 (12.3)
100	220	2.6 (3.4)	3.4 (4.7)	4.3 (6.0)	5.1 (7.3)	6.0 (8.6)	6.9 (9.9)	7.7 (11.1)

Values in ( ) are for arm work. Adapted from *Guidelines for Exercise Stress Testing and Prescription*, ACSM 1986, and Franklin, Vanders, Wrisley and Rubenfire (1983). Reprinted with permission.

$\dot{V}O_2$ = kpm/min × 2 ml O_2/kpm + 300 ml/min

Net cost of cycling = 1,470 − 300 = 1,170 ml/min

1,170 ml/min = ? kpm/min × 2 ml/kpm

1,170/2 = 585 kpm/min

585 kpm/min = (50 rpm × 6 m/rev) × force

585 kpm/min = 300 m/min × force

Force = 1.95 kp.

Arms. A cycle ergometer can be used to exercise the arm/shoulder girdle muscles by modifying the pedals and placing the cycle on a table. Arm ergometry is used on a limited basis as a GXT to evaluate cardiovascular function. It is used more generally as a routine exercise in rehabilitation programs.

Remember several factors when considering this type of exercise: (a) functional capacity ($\dot{V}O_2$ peak) for the arms is only 70% of that measured with the legs in a normal healthy population and less in an unfit, elderly, or diseased population; (b) the natural endurance of the muscles used in this work is less than that of the legs; (c) the HR and BP responses are higher for arm work compared to leg work at the same $\dot{V}O_2$; and (d) the oxygen cost of doing 1 kpm of work is about 50% higher (3 ml O_2/kgm) for arm work because of the action's inefficiency (Franklin, Vanders, Wrisley & Rubenfire, 1983).

$\dot{V}O_2$ (ml/min) = work rate (kpm/min) (3 ml O_2/kpm) + 300 ml/min

Question: What is the oxygen requirement of doing 150 kpm/min on an arm ergometer?

Answer: $\dot{V}O_2$ = 150 kpm/min × 3 ml/kpm + 300 ml/min = 750 ml/min

Stepping

One of the most useful and inexpensive forms of exercise is bench stepping. The activity is easily done at home and requires little or no equipment. The work rate is easily adjusted by simply increasing step height or cadence (number of lifts per minute).

The total oxygen cost of this exercise is the sum of the costs of (a) stepping up, (b) stepping down, and (c) moving back and forth on a level surface

Table 10.6 Energy Expenditure in METs During Stepping at Different Rates on Steps of Different Heights

Step Height		Steps/min			
cm	in.	12	18	24	30
0	0	1.2	1.8	2.4	3.0
4	1.6	1.5	2.3	3.1	3.8
8	3.2	1.9	2.8	3.7	4.6
12	4.7	2.2	3.3	4.4	5.5
16	6.3	2.5	3.8	5.0	6.3
20	7.9	2.8	4.3	5.7	7.1
24	9.4	3.2	4.8	6.3	7.9
28	11.0	3.5	5.2	7.0	8.7
32	12.6	3.8	5.7	7.7	9.6
36	14.2	4.1	6.2	8.3	10.4
40	15.8	4.5	6.7	9.0	11.2

Note. From *Guidelines for Graded Exercise Testing and Exercise Prescription,* ACSM 1980, Philadelphia: Lea & Febiger. Reprinted with permission.

at the specified cadence. The oxygen cost of stepping up is 1.8 ml(kg•min)$^{-1}$ per m/min, as in walking (Nagle, Balke, & Naughton, 1965). The oxygen cost of stepping down is a third of the cost of stepping up, therefore the oxygen cost of stepping up and down is 1.33 times the cost of stepping up. The number of meters moved up or down per minute is calculated by multiplying the number of lifts per minute by the height of the step (e.g., if the step height is .2 m (20 cm) and the cadence is 27 lifts/min then the total lift or descent per minute is 27 times 0.2 m, or 5.4 m/min).

The oxygen cost of stepping back and forth on a flat surface is proportional to the cadence. If the cadence is 15, then the energy cost of moving back and forth at that rate is about 1.5 METs; if the cadence is 27, then the energy requirement for moving back and forth on a flat surface is 2.7 METs. In essence the oxygen cost of stepping back and forth on a flat surface can be estimated in METs by dividing the cadence by 10.

$\dot{V}O_2$ = (step height in meters) (cadence in lifts/min) (1.33) (1.8 ml[kg.min]$^{-1}$) + cost of stepping back and forth.

Question: What is the oxygen requirement for stepping at a rate of 20 lifts/min on a 20-cm bench?

Answer: $\dot{V}O_2$ = (.2 m/lift) (20 lifts/min) (1.33) (1.8 ml[kg•min]$^{-1}$) + 2 METs (7 ml[kg•min]$^{-1}$) = 16.6 ml(kg•min)$^{-1}$, or 4.7 METs.

Caloric Costs of Other Activities

When designing a fitness program, many activities are available (see chapter 11). These include exercise to music, rope skipping, swimming, and games. Unfortunately, the energy expenditure associated with these activities is difficult to predict when compared to walking or running. In the latter activities the energy cost between people is similar because of the natural movements associated with those activities. In contrast, many activities have a variable energy cost dependent on the skill level of the participant and the motivation that he or she brings to the activity. With that in mind, the following attempts to estimate the energy requirements of some common aerobic activities.

Exercise to Music

Exercising to music is a good alternative to walking and running. The energy requirement is dependent not only on the beat of the music and the exercise leader's choice of movements, but also on the initiative that the participant brings to class. A person who is starting out might simply walk through the movements, while an experienced person might go through the full range of motion with each step. Thus the energy cost of this activity varies considerably, depending on the person. Values might range from as low as 4 METs for someone walking through the routine to 10 METs for the experienced dancer. Remember that this activity often involves small-muscle groups and includes some static (stabilizing) muscle contractions; as a result, the heart rate response is higher for the same oxygen uptake measured in walking and running.

Rope Skipping

In walking and running, the energy requirement is proportional to the rate at which the person moves. But the energy requirement for rope skipping at only 60-80 turns/min (about as slow as the rope can be turned) is about 9 METs. At 120 turns/min the energy cost increases to only 11 METs. Consequently, rope skipping is not a graded activity as is walking and running. Secondly, the HR response is higher than expected from the oxygen cost of the activity. This, again, may be because a small muscle mass (lower leg) is the primary muscle group involved in the activity. In spite of this, rope skipping can be included as an effective part of a fitness program when done in an intermittent manner, using the THR as the guide. However, rope skipping should not be used in the early part of a fitness program.

Swimming

Swimming is a preferred activity for many people because of the dynamic, large-muscle nature of the task and because little joint trauma is associated with it. The limitation is in finding a convenient facility that allows lap swimming and, of course, having enough skill to do the activity. The energy requirement is dependent on the velocity of movement and the stroke being used, but it is also influenced by the skill of the swimmer. A skilled swimmer requires less energy to move through the water, so that person has to swim a greater distance than an unskilled person to achieve the same caloric expenditure.

The energy cost of simply treading water can be as high as 1.5 ℓ/min (7.5 kcal/min). Elite swimmers use this same number of kcal/min to swim at 36 m/min, while an unskilled swimmer might require twice that energy expenditure to maintain the same velocity. For elite swimmers the front and back crawl are the most efficient, and butterfly is the least efficient. The net caloric cost per mile of swimming has been estimated to be more than 400 kcal, or about 4 times that of running 1 mile and about 8 times that of walking 1 mile. However, the actual caloric cost per mile of swimming varies greatly, depending on skill and gender. The following table is a summary of the values presented by Holmer (1979) for men and women.

Table 10.7 Caloric Cost Per Mile of Swimming the Front Crawl for Men and Women by Skill Level

Skill Level	Women (kcal/mi)	Men (kcal/mi)
Competitive	180	280
Skilled	260	360
Average	300	440
Unskilled	360	560
Poor	440	720

Note. From "Physiology of Swimming Man" by I. Holmer, 1979, in *Exercise and Sport Sciences Review*, **7**, R.S. Hutton and D.I. Miller (Eds.).

Table10.8 Summary of Measured Energy Cost of Various Physical Activities

Activity	METs	kcal(kg•min)	kcal/hour 50 kg	kcal/hour 70 kg	kcal/hour 90 kg
Archery	3-4	.050-.066	150-200	210-280	270-360
Back packing	5-11	.083-.183	250-550	350-770	450-990
Badminton	4-9	.066-.150	200-450	280-630	360-810
Basketball	3-12	.050-.200	150-600	210-840	270-1080
Billiards	2.5	.042	125	175	225
Bowling	2-4	.033-.066	100-200	140-280	180-360
Boxing	8-13	.133-.216	400-650	560-910	720-1170
Canoeing, rowing, and kayaking	3-8	.050-.133	150-400	210-560	270-720
Cricket	4-7	.066-.117	200-350	280-490	360-630
Croquet	3.5	.058	175	245	315
Cycling	3-8+	.050-.133+	150-400+	210-560+	270-720+
Dancing—social/tap	3-7	.050-.117	150-350	210-490	270-630
aerobic	4-10	.066-.167	200-500	280-700	360-900

(Cont.)

Table 10.8 Cont.

Fencing	6-10	.100-.167	300-500	420-700	540-900
Field hockey	8	.133	400	560	720
Fishing—from bank	2-4	.033-.066	100-200	140-280	180-360
wading	5-6	.083-.100	250-300	350-420	450-540
Football (touch)	6-10	.100-.167	300-500	420-700	540-900
Golf—power cart	2-3	.033-.050	100-150	140-210	180-270
pull/carry clubs	4-7	.066-.117	200-350	280-490	360-630
Handball	8-12	.133-.200	400-600	560-840	720-1080
Hiking	3-7	.050-.117	150-350	210-490	270-630
Horseback riding	3-8	.050-.133	150-400	210-560	270-720
Horseshoe pitching	2-3	.033-.050	100-150	140-210	180-270
Hunting (bow/gun)	3-7	.050-.117	150-350	210-490	270-630
small game					
Jogging (see Table 10.3)					
Mountain climbing	5-10	.083-.167	250-500	350-700	450-900
Paddleball/racquetball	8-12	.133-.200	400-600	560-840	720-1080
Rope jumping	9-12	.15-.20	450-600	630-840	810-1080
Running (see Table 10.3)					
Sailing	2-5	.033-.083	100-250	140-350	180-450
Scuba diving	5-10	.083-.167	250-500	350-700	450-900
Shuffleboard	2-3	.033-.050	100-150	140-210	180-270
Skating (ice and roller)	5-8	.083-.133	250-400	350-560	450-720
Skiing (snow)					
downhill	5-8	.083-.133	250-400	350-560	450-720
cross-country	6-12	.100-.200	300-600	420-840	540-1080
Skiing (water)	5-7	.083-.117	250-350	350-490	450-630
Sledding, tobogganing	4-8	.066-.113	200-400	280-560	360-720
Snowshoeing	7-14	.117-.233	350-700	490-980	630-1260
Squash	8-12	.133-.200	400-600	560-840	720-1080
Soccer	5-12	.083-.200	250-600	350-840	450-1080
Swimming (see Table 10.7)					
Table tennis	3-5	.050-.083	150-250	210-350	702-450
Tennis	4-9	.066-.150	200-450	280-630	360-810
Volleyball (recreational)	3-6	.050-.100	150-300	210-420	270-540

Note. From *Guidelines for Graded Exercise Testing and Exercise Prescription* (p. 42-45) by American College of Sports Medicine, 1980, Philadelphia: Lea & Febiger. And from *Exercise Physiology* (p. 486-493) by W.D. McArdle, F.I. Katch, and V.L. Katch, 1981, Philadelphia: Lea & Febiger.

The HR response measured during swimming at a specific $\dot{V}O_2$ is lower than that measured during running at the same $\dot{V}O_2$. In fact, the maximal HR response is about 13 b/min lower for swimming. With this in mind, the THR range should be decreased when prescribing swimming activities.

Table 10.8 contains a summary of the measured energy requirements for a variety of physical activities. Please keep in mind that a range of values is presented for most activities and that in some cases the values are based on a small sample size.

Estimation of the Energy Expenditure Without Formulas

An exercise prescription includes activities that cause the individual to operate within the THR range that demands about 60-80% $\dot{V}O_2$max. It should therefore be possible to estimate the energy expenditure for each individual on the basis of the subject's $\dot{V}O_2$max and the portion of the THR range at which the person is working. If a person has a functional capacity of 10 METs, energy expenditure can be estimated in the following way. Ten METs are equal to about 10 kcal/kg per hour. If a person is working at the bottom portion of the THR range, about 60% $\dot{V}O_2$max, then the energy expenditure should be about 6 METs. If the person weighs 70 kg, then 420 kcal are expended per hour. A 30-min workout would require 210 kcal. These simple calculations assume that the person is performing a large-muscle activity and that the environmental factors do not have a major influence on the HR response. Table 10.9 shows the estimated kilocalorie expenditure for a 30-min workout at 70% $\dot{V}O_2$max for a variety of fitness levels and body weights (Sharkey, 1984).

Environmental Concerns

In chapter 3 the effect of high temperature/humidity and altitude on the THR were discussed. Remember that THR is the crucial factor to consider in the exercise prescription. The participants must be instructed to cut back on the intensity of the activity when environmental factors drive the HR response. The duration of the activity can be increased to accommodate any energy expenditure goal.

Summary

The HFI should be able to make recommendations in the selection of activities to meet THR and

Table 10.9 Estimated Energy Expenditure for 30 Min of Exercise at 70% Functional Capacity ($\dot{V}O_2$max)

$\dot{V}O_2$max (METs) kcal$(kg \cdot hr)^{-1}$	70% Max METs kcal$(kg \cdot hr)^{-1}$	Body Weight 50 kg	70 kg	90 kg
20	14.0	350	490	630
18	12.6	315	441	567
16	11.2	280	392	504
14	9.8	245	343	441
12	8.4	210	294	378
10	7.0	175	245	315
8	5.6	140	196	252
6	4.2	105	147	189

Note. Adapted from *Physiology of Fitness* (p. 310) by B.J. Sharkey, 1984, Champaign, IL: Human Kinetics Publishers. Reprinted with permission.

energy expenditure goals. Energy expenditure is measured by direct and indirect calorimetry. Indirect calorimetry estimates energy expenditure by measuring oxygen consumption, knowing that 1 ℓ of oxygen equals 4.7-5.0 kcal. Indirect calorimetry uses either a closed system in which the subject breathes 100% oxygen from a spirometer, or an open system in which the subject breathes room air. The latter method is the most common. Energy expenditure is expressed in liters O_2/min, ml $O_2(kg \cdot min)^{-1}$, METs, kcal/min, and kcal$(kg \cdot hr)^{-1}$. The ACSM has developed formulas for estimating the steady state energy requirements of a variety of activities—walking, running, stepping, and cycle ergometry exercise. These estimates are helpful in identifying the functional capacity and in selecting activities for the participant. Comments are offered on the energy requirements for exercise to music, rope skipping, and swimming. A table on the energy cost of common activities is presented along with a method of estimating the energy cost on the basis of knowing functional capacity and working at 70% of functional capacity.

Suggested Reading for Chapter 10

Balke (1963)

Balke and Ware (1959)

Bransford and Howley (1977)

Bubb, Martin, and Howley (1985)

Dill (1965)

Fox and Mathews (1981)

Franklin, Vanders, Wrisley, and Rubenfire (1983)

Guber, Montoye, Cunningham, and Dinks (1972)

Holmer (1979)

Howley and Glover (1974)

Howley and Martin (1978)

Knoebel (1984)

Margaria, Cerretelli, Aghemo, and Sassi (1963)

Montoye (1975)

Nagle, Balke, Baptista, Alleyia, and Howley (1971)

Nagle, Balke, and Naughton (1965)

Sharkey (1984)

See reference list at the end of the book for a complete source listing.

Chapter 11
Exercise Programs

- Tips for exercise leaders
- Walking/jogging/running
- Cycling/swimming
- Fitness games
- Exercise to music

The purpose of a fitness program must be kept uppermost in the HFI's mind. The HFI is trying to help people include appropriate physical activity as a vital part of their lifestyles. This assumes that the participants understand what is appropriate, have sufficient skills to achieve satisfaction from the activities, have the abilities to evaluate their fitness progress, and have the intrinsic motivation to continue to be active for the rest of their lives. Thus HFIs try to help people increase their physical fitness levels in ways that are psychologically, mentally, and socially relevant and appealing.

Phases of Activities

Sedentary people who want to begin a fitness program should follow a logical sequence of fitness activities.

Phase 1—Regular Walking

The first phase is to get these people in the habit of including exercise as a part of their weekly patterns. The major fitness gain is to be able to increase the exercise that can be done comfortably, so no emphasis on intensity is necessary at this point. The person starts with the distance that can be walked easily without pain or fatigue, then gradually increases the distance and pace until 4-5 mi can be walked briskly every other day.

Phase 2—Recommended Work Levels for Fitness Base

Once Phase 1 is accomplished, then the person is taught about recommended levels of work for fitness changes (see chapter 9). A work/relief interval training program is introduced—jogging is the work, and walking is the relief. So the person walks, jogs a few steps, then walks, and so forth. Gradually, jogging covers more distance than walking, until the person can jog continuously for 3 mi at THR.

Phase 3—Variety of Fitness Activities

The first two phases are generally recommended for everyone (with alternative activities for people who cannot jog, e.g., cycling, running in water). However, Phase 3 is quite individualized, based on the person's interests. The purpose is to promote the continued activity habit. Some people prefer to continue to stretch, walk, and jog, some prefer to workout alone, and others (the majority) enjoy working out with others. Some people like cooperative and relatively low-level competitive activities, while others like the thrill of competition. Some enjoy a variety of different movement forms, while others enjoy repeating the same activity. The HFI must provide an atmosphere where people feel free to try new things without embarrassment and allow individuals to choose from among a variety of options for their fitness activities.

Exercise Leadership

On the basis of the exercise programs offered on television and found on the "best sellers" list it might be concluded that little or no formal training is required to be a fitness instructor. This is unfortunate, given the real need of the HFI to be informed about exercise, nutrition, emergency first aid, and so forth. The traditional training of an exercise leader was accomplished in undergraduate physical education programs that were aimed at the public schools. This person may have had the necessary physical skills to work with adults, but the type of course work and practical experiences did not deal with sedentary adults or people with disease. Nurses, physical therapists, and physicians who had the necessary backgrounds to deal with the high risk individual had little or no formal training in exercise and nutrition. There was a need to develop some systematic guidelines outlining the information and skills that an exercise leader needed in order to work with healthy and nonhealthy adults.

The ACSM took a leadership role in this area by developing a variety of certification programs for individuals who used exercise in preventive and rehabilitative programs. Qualification in these certification areas requires the applicant to have a specific knowledge base and demonstrate specific behaviors. The current certification programs include:

- Health/Fitness Instructor—qualified in exercise prescription and leadership in preventive programs.
- Health/Fitness Director—qualified as HFI and responsible for administration in preventive programs.
- Exercise Technologist—qualified in exercise testing in preventive and rehabilitative programs
- Exercise Specialist—qualified in exercise testing, prescription, and leadership for all populations
- Program Director—qualified as an exercise specialist and responsible for administration, community education programs, research and development, and so forth in preventive and rehabilitative programs

These certifications are considered the "standard" by many in the fitness and cardiac rehabilitation areas.

Role Model

The authors of this book clearly support the notion of a role model as an appropriate way to view the HFI. The idea of an overfat, out-of-shape exercise leader is one whose time has passed. A leader must plan appropriate activities, evaluate the progress of the participants, provide incentives, and so forth. However, the leadership associated with many exercise programs is in the form of quite subtle value statements that do not require words. The HFI's presence and behaviors, consistent with a healthy lifestyle, add much meaning and value to his or her words and programs.

Day-To-Day Planning

All activity programs must have daily, weekly, and monthly plans to provide appropriate activities, meet the needs of the participants, and reduce the chance of boredom. This planning allows the HFI to judge the usefulness of the activity and encourage systematic modification from one month to the next. If the HFI is working with individuals who exercise on their own, then the reasonableness of detailed activities becomes obvious. The value of the feedback received from these individuals is dependent upon the information provided them on the front end. The following comments address various aspects of an exercise program, be it conducted within a group structure or planned around an individual's schedule.

Variety. A program needs to have variety built in as a cornerstone. Some elements are a part of each exercise session: warm-up/stretching, stimulus phase, and cool-down. The variety comes in the form of different exercises used in each part of a session, short educational messages presented to the class while they are stretching or cooling down, or the use of games to add spice to routine exercises. The most important thing is to plan the activity sessions far enough in advance so that repetition is maintained at a low level and variety is maintained at a high level.

Control. The exercise leader must have control over the exercise session. This is especially true in the use of games, where the intensity is not as easily controlled as in jogging. Control implies an ability to modify the session as needed to meet the THR and total work goals of each individual. Some people will have to slow down, and others may need more encouragement. The element of control (at a distance) for people who exercise on their own can be provided by using written guidelines about what to do and when to move from one stage to the next. In addition, specific information should be provided about symptoms that indicate an inappropriate response to exercise.

Monitoring and record keeping. The ability to keep track of the participant's response to the exercise session will give clues about that individual's adaptation to that particular session and about overall day-to-day changes. This information is important for updating exercise prescriptions and answering specific questions that the participant may raise. Each exercise class should have regular pauses to check the HR and determine whether or not individuals are close to their THRs. Rather than keeping track of a large number of 10-sec THRs, ask each participant to indicate the number of beats over or under the 10-sec goal. This increases the participant's awareness of the THR and indicates how the intensity of the exercise should be adjusted to stay on target.

While each person's HR response is probably the best and most objective indicator of his or her adjustment to an exercise session, do not stop at that. Elicit information about how the participant feels in general; ask about any new pains, aches, or strange sensations. Record keeping should include a daily attendance check, a weekly weigh-in, a regular BP check (if appropriate), and a column asking for comments (e.g., THR, perceived intensity, symptoms). An example of such a form is the Daily Activity Form. This information allows the HFI to make better recommendations about the participant's exercise programs or to refer him or her to an appropriate professional if needed.

Walk/Jog/Run Programs

During walking, at least one foot is in contact with the ground at all times. In jogging and running, more muscular force is exerted to propel the body completely off the ground, causing a non-support phase. The distinction between jogging and running is not as clearly defined. Some people view the speed as being the difference, but no commonly accepted speed for running exists, although 6 mph is often mentioned. Others distinguish between the two by the intent of the participant—a runner is a person who trains for and enters road races regardless of his or her speed.

Footwear

Any comfortable pair of good, well-supported shoes can be worn for walking. The serious walker and all joggers should invest in good jogging shoes, which should have well-padded heels that are higher than the soles, and a fitted heel cup. The shoes should be flexible enough to bend easily. The same kind of socks that will be worn while exercising should be worn during the fitting to ensure a comfortable and proper fit. Only the serious competitive runner needs racing shoes, which are a lighter weight and offer less cushioning.

Clothing

The weather conditions and vigorousness of the activity determine the amount and type of clothing to be worn. Warm weather dictates light, preferably cotton, loose-fitting clothing. Nothing should be worn that prevents perspiration from reaching the outside air. A brimmed hat should cover the head on hot, sunny days. For the jogger, long pants are probably not needed until the temperature (wind chill factor considered) drops below 40 °F.

During cold weather, the jogger should dress in layers so he or she has the flexibility of removing/adding clothing when necessary. Wool and the new polypropylene fabrics are good choices to deal with the extreme cold, but most joggers have a tendency to overdress. A hat, preferably a wool stocking cap, that can be pulled down over the forehead and ears also should be worn. Gloves and/or mittens are also a necessity. Cotton socks worn as mittens are useful not only to keep hands warm but also to act as "wipers" for the sniffling nose that often accompanies cold weather jogging.

Surface

The surface for walkers is not as crucial as it is for joggers, although some walkers need a soft surface, such as grass or a running track with a shock-absorbant surface. While many people prefer exercising off of the track, regular jogging on hard surfaces such as concrete or blacktop can lead to stress problems in the ankle, knee, and hip joints and in the lower back. Joggers need to observe special precautions when running on the road: jog facing traffic; assume cars at crossroads do not see joggers; beware of cracks and curbs. Running cross-country usually means a softer surface is available, but joggers must be aware of the uneven terrain and the increased potential for ankle injuries.

Walking

The advantages of walking include its convenience, practicality, and naturalness. Walking is an excellent activity, especially for people who are overfat, poorly conditioned, and whose joints cannot handle the stresses of jogging.

Daily Activity Form

Name: ______________________ Target Weight: ________ Target Heart Rate Zone: ________

Week	Day	Weight	Resting BP	Resting HR	Exercise HR	Comments
1	Mon					
	Wed					
	Fri					
2	Mon					
	Wed					
	Fri					
3	Mon					
	Wed					
	Fri					
4	Mon					
	Wed					
	Fri					

Walking Program

Rules:

1. Start at beginning.
2. Be aware of new aches or pains.
3. Don't progress to next level if not comfortable.
4. Monitor heart rate and record it.
5. It would be healthful to walk each day.

Day	Duration	Heart Rate	Comments
1	15 min	______	______
2	20 min	______	______
3	25 min	______	______
4	30 min	______	______
5	30 min	______	______
6	30 min	______	______
7	35 min	______	______
8	40 min	______	______
9	45 min	______	______
10	45 min	______	______
11	45 min	______	______
12	50 min	______	______
13	55 min	______	______
14	60 min	______	______
15	60 min	______	______
16	60 min	______	______
17	60 min	______	______
18	60 min	______	______
19	60 min	______	______
20	60 min	______	______

As with all exercise programs, begin with static stretching and warm-up activities before the actual walk. Begin the walk at a slow speed, gradually increasing the speed to elicit the THR. While walking, the arms should swing freely and the trunk should be kept erect with a slight backward pelvic tilt. The feet should be pointing forward at all times.

Walking programs can progress by increasing either the distance and/or the speed. Participants should gradually increase their distances until they can easily walk 4 mi at a brisk pace. Thinking about jogging or achieving the THR is not necessary until the walking goal (i.e., 4 mi at a brisk pace) can be reached. The preceding walking program is graduated and leads to an activity level needed for those who wish to start a jogging program.

Jogging

No single factor determines when an individual can begin jogging. A person who can walk 4-5 mi briskly but is unable to reach the THR range by walking should consider a jogging program if he or she wants to make additional improvements in CRF. A slow to moderate walker whose HR is within the THR zone should increase the distance and/or speed of walking rather than begin jogging. Also, the ability of the individual's joints to withstand the additional stresses of jogging should be considered.

The techniques of jogging are basically the same as walking. In jogging, there is a greater flexion of the knee of the recovery leg, and the arms are bent more at the elbows. The arm swing is exaggerated slightly but should still be in the forward/backward direction. The heel makes the first contact with the ground; then the foot immediately rolls forward to the ball of the foot and then to the toes. As speed increases, the landing foot may contact the ground closer to a flat-footed position. Breathing is done through both the nose and mouth. Common faults of the beginning jogger include breathing with the mouth closed, insufficiently bending the knee during the recovery phase, and swinging the arms across the body.

Many people begin jogging at too high a speed which results in an inability to continue for a sufficient length of time to accomplish the desired amount of total work and often causes a dislike of the activity. This problem can be prevented by jogging at a speed slow enough to allow conversation, and using work/relief intervals, which for beginners is slow jogging for a few seconds, then walking, then slow jogging, and so forth. Participants should be reassured that they will be walking less and/or jogging more as they become more fit. An example of such a jogging program is on page 176.

After a person has progressed to the point where 3 mi can be jogged continuously within the THR zone, several approaches to a jogging program are available. A person can just go out and jog four or five times a week with the only plan being to exercise at an intensity that will elevate the HR to the training zone for a predetermined minimum length of time (or distance), with the option to go longer (further) on days when so desired. Other people do better with a specific program to follow which gives progressive speed and distance goals, even if they do not have plans for competition.

The HFI should include variety in a jogging program by having the participants move backward or laterally, moving all parts of the arms, or by having them occasionally change the speed. Several runners can run together, one behind the other, with the last jogger running up to become the new head of the line. Established exercise or fitness trails, found in many communities, combine walking/jogging with specific exercises for all parts of the body. Temporary exercise trails for the track, road, or countryside can be designed easily, or the jogger can interrupt jogging occasionally to perform exercises (e.g., especially those exercises for the back, found in chapter 7). "Fun runs" are often held; the goal is to finish the distance, and a small prize is usually the reward.

Joggers who are not fast enough to compete successfully in road races may enjoy other types of competition in which speed does not determine the winner. The purpose of a prediction run is to see which jogger comes closest to his or her predicted

Jogging Program

Rules:

1. Complete the Walking Program before starting this program.
2. Begin each session with stretching and walking.
3. Be aware of new aches and pains.
4. Don't progress to next level if not comfortable.
5. Stay at low end of THR zone; record heart rate for each session.
6. Do program on a work-a-day, rest-a-day basis.

Level 1 Jog 10 steps, walk 10 steps. Repeat five times and take your heart rate. Stay within THR zone by increasing or decreasing walking phase. Do 20-30 min of activity.

Level 2 Jog 20 steps, walk 10 steps. Repeat five times and take your heart rate. Stay within THR zone by increasing or decreasing walking phase. Do 20-30 min of activity.

Level 3 Jog 30 steps, walk 10 steps. Repeat five times and take your heart rate. Stay within THR zone by increasing or decreasing walking phase. Do 20-30 min of activity.

Level 4 Jog 1 min, walk 10 steps. Repeat three times and take your heart rate. Stay within THR zone by increasing or decreasing walking phase. Do 20-30 min of activity.

Level 5 Jog 2 min, walk 10 steps. Repeat two times and take your heart rate. Stay within THR zone by increasing or decreasing walking phase. Do 30 min of activity.

Level 6 Jog 1 lap (400 m, or 440 yd) and check heart rate. Adjust pace during run to stay within the THR zone. If heart rate is still too high, go back to the Level 5 schedule. Do 6 laps with a brief walk between each.

Level 7 Jog 2 laps and check heart rate. Adjust pace during run to stay within the THR zone. If heart rate is still too high, go back to Level 6 activity. Do 6 laps with a brief walk between each.

Level 8 Jog 1 mi and check heart rate. Adjust pace during the run to stay within THR zone. Do 2 mi.

Level 9 Jog 2-3 mi continuously. Check heart rate at the end to ensure that you were within THR zone.

time of finishing, which is declared before the race. A handicap run does require joggers to know and declare their previous fastest times for the distance. A percentage (80-100%) of the time difference between the fastest runner's declared time and each other runner's time is subtracted from each runner's actual finish time. For example, runner A has the fastest previous time of 18 min for 3 mi; runner B, 19 min; and runner C, 20 min. Forty eight seconds (.8 × 60-sec difference between A & B) is subtracted from B's finish time, and 96 sec (.8 × 120-sec difference) is subtracted from runner C's. Say runner A completes the race in 17:50, runner B in 18:30, and C in 20:10. The adjusted finish times would be runner A – 17:50 (actual time); runner B – 17:42 (18:30 – 48); and C – 18:34 (20:10 – 96). Runner B is the winner. Another method of handicapping a race is to stagger the start according to each jogger's previous best time, with the slowest runner starting first, the fastest last. The first one over the finish line is the winner. Teams can be formed in which each four-member team, for example, could have one runner from each quadrant of times.

Competitive Running

The last few years have seen an increase in the number of road races sponsored by track clubs and service organizations as a means of raising funds, many for worthy purposes. Each entrant pays a registration fee for entering. Most of the races have gender and age divisions, and prizes are awarded to the top finishers, both overall and in each division. Usually every finisher receives an award, such as a certificate or t-shirt. The race distances range between 1 mi (often considered a "fun run") and 100 mi, but the most common are the 5K (3.1 miles) and 10K (6.2 miles).

The training methods for competitive running depend in part on the race distance, but runners train at the top part of the THR range 6-7 times per week and for durations longer than 30 min per exercise session. Performance goals, in contrast to CRF goals, are more difficult to achieve.

Cycling

Riding a bicycle or stationary exercise cycle is another good fitness activity. Some people who have problems walking, jogging, or playing sports may be able to cycle without difficulty. Table 11.1 presents a progressive cycling program. It follows the guidelines (chapter 9) for making CRF improvements. Although the type of bicycle and terrain vary widely, checking the THR allows the

Table 11.1 Suggested Cycling Program[a]

Stage[b]	Distance (mi)	THR[c] (% of max HR)	Time (min)	Frequency (days/week)
1	1-2	—[d]	—[d]	3
2	1-2	60	8-12	3
3	3-5	60	15-25	3
4	6-8	70	25-35	3
5	6-8	70	25-35	4
6	10-15	70	40-60	4
7	10-15	80	35-50	4-5

[a]Program can be used for riding a regular bicycle or a stationary exercise cycle.
[b]The individual begins at whatever stage can be accomplished without becoming fatigued or sore and progresses to the next stage when it can be done without fatigue or soreness.
[c]THR = target heart rate (see chapter 9).
[d]In Stage 1, the person simply gets used to riding for 1-2 mi without being concerned about time or THR.

cyclist to adjust the speed so that he or she is working at the appropriate intensity. Generally, a person covers three to five times the distance cycling compared to jogging (e.g., a person works up to 3 mi jogging or 10-15 mi cycling per workout). The seat should be comfortable and its height should be adjusted so that the knee is slightly bent at the bottom of the pedaling stroke.

Games

One of the characteristics of children that is often lost in adulthood is a sense of playfulness. A child does not feel a need to justify spending time playing a game just for the fun of it. One of the attributes that seems to be present in coronary-prone behavior is the inability to appreciate play for its own sake. Perhaps one of the things that a good fitness program can do for people is to provide them with activities that increase both fitness and playfulness. The *New Games Book* (New Games Foundation, 1976) provides a number of specific games for different numbers of people with varying intensity. More importantly, the book has a playful, fun, and inclusive approach to games.

Use of Games for Fitness Enhancement

Games that meet fitness standards are used to achieve or maintain fitness levels. Many fitness participants enjoy a variety of activities, including games and sports.

Fun. The first component of games is the element of enjoyment. This requires a balance of cooperation and competition, continued participation by everyone, and the chance for everyone to be a winner.

Inclusive. A key ingredient for a fitness game is that everyone is included. This may mean modifying the rules. For example, in a tag game, if someone is tagged by the person who is "it," then the tagged player also becomes "it" and continues to play (rather than sit down until the game is over).

Vigorous. Many good games are inclusive and fun, but are relatively inactive. These can be used as part of a warm-up and taper-down or can be interspersed between vigorous games. But the main body of the workout should include games where all people are continuously active in the THR range. Once again, rules may have to be altered to ensure this continued vigorous activity. For example, in games like kickball, where most players are normally inactive, a new rule might require all players to shift positions each time another player comes to the plate to kick. In games like soccer, basketball, or ultimate frisbee, where a few people may tend to dominate the action, playing with two or three balls (or frisbees) at the same time increases participation by everyone.

Cooperative/competitive balance. Having small groups solve problems together, or cooperate to accomplish fitness tasks can be enjoyable and healthy. Some games can be both at the same time. For example, have each volleyball team see which one can keep their ball in the air for the longest time (using one ball on each side). Competitive games can be changed to cooperative events by simple rule changes. Once again, using volleyball as an example, the usual rules can be used, but the score is changed to show the number of times the ball is hit across the net (or the total number of hits counting both sides) before hitting the ground. Competition is not to be avoided, but little emphasis should be put on winning, and the game should not be used to exclude people from participating.

Games of Skill

Most games can become fitness games when they are played vigorously. Some require certain minimum levels of skill that can be taught as part of the fitness program.

Racquet sports. Games like badminton, racquetball or paddleball, squash, and tennis all require a certain amount of skill in hitting a ball (or bird) with a racquet. Some general guidelines that enhance the fitness qualities of these games include singles play and matching players with similar abilities. The energy expenditure is often a little less than the same amount of time running, but these types of games can be used as a part of the fitness program.

Low-organized games and activities. Some activities and games require a minimum of special skills, equipment, or facilities. Normal fitness activities can be done in ways to accomplish other purposes. For example, creativity can be enhanced with groups of 3-4 playing "follow the leader" for warm-up, aerobic, or taper-down activities, changing the leader often so that each person has a chance to lead the group. Trust can be developed by having one person lead a partner (with eyes closed) in warm-up or taper-down activities, communicating solely through the hands.

Tag is another example of low-organized activity. Some variations of tag include having people hold the spot on their bodies where they were tagged as they try to tag others; making the rule that people cannot be tagged while they're hugging someone (with a time limit for hugs); or requiring people to be enclosed (rather than tagged) by the two people holding hands who are "it," then the tagged person joins hands with those people who are "it" until everyone has been enclosed by the "its."

A good example of modifications of a low-organization game to make it a physical fitness game is changing musical chairs (people walk around chairs—one less than the number of players—until the music stops, and then each person sits in a chair except for the last one who is "out"). Two changes can make this a good fitness game. First of all, the people jog, rather than walk, around the chairs which are put in a big circle. Second, as soon as two people are "out," they begin a second circle. As the first circle gets smaller, the second one gets larger (i.e., each person who is "out" in the first circle continues to participate in the second circle—each time the music stops, a chair is deleted from circle 1 and one added to circle 2). Thus everyone continues to play in one of the circles. Another modification changes musical chairs from a competitive to a cooperative game—instead of people who cannot find a chair being put out of the circle or going to another circle, they have to sit or stand on a part of a chair or on a person on a chair; the game continues by taking one more chair out each time the music stops (or whistle blows), until everyone has to be supported by one chair.

Special Considerations

The warm-up and taper-down activities can be done for people at any fitness level. However, the more vigorous games usually involve high-intensity bursts, stopping, starting, and quickly changing directions. They are not recommended for the early stages of a fitness program. Some additional stretching and easy movements in different directions should be included as part of the warm-up. Obviously the space, number of people, equipment, and so forth have to be considered in the selection of activities. The leader must emphasize safety and should change the rules immediately when something is not working. For example, if the person who is "it" is not able to tag anyone, the space can be made smaller, or a second "it" can be named. If a few people are dominating a team game, then a new rule can be introduced—everyone on the team has to touch the ball before a goal can be attempted. One modification of a team game, such as basketball, soccer, or volleyball, is to award the number of points based on how many people touched the ball by the team as part of the scoring play—one point if only one person made contact with the ball, two points for contact by two players, and so forth.

Different activities may go on simultaneously. For example, if there are only two handball courts, then most of the fitness participants will be engaged in some activity other than racquetball, but four people could play each period. A variety of games should be offered so that people with different skill levels can participate. When large groups are involved in activities, the activities should be changed frequently to maintain interest.

Finally, in addition to warm-up and taper-down activities, higher- and lower-intensity activities should be alternated to prevent undue fatigue. People should be encouraged to go at their own paces. THR should be checked periodically to ensure that people are within their ranges.

Aquatic Activities

Aquatic activities can be a major part of a person's exercise program or can be the needed relief from other forms of exercise, especially when a person is injured. The intensity of the activity can be graded to suit the needs of the least and the most fit, from the recent postmyocardial infarction patient to the endurance athlete. The HR can be checked at regular intervals to see if THR has been reached, and a caloric expenditure goal can be achieved given the high energy requirement associated with aquatic activities. Individuals with orthopedic problems who cannot run or dance or play in games can exercise in water. The water supports the person's body weight, and problems associated with weight-bearing joints are minimized. The following sections address specific points related to these introductory comments.

THR

One consistent finding is that the maximal HR response to a swimming test is about 13 b/min lower than that found in a maximal treadmill test. This suggests that for swimming the THR should be shifted downward to achieve the 60-80% $\dot{V}O_2max$ goal associated with an endurance training effect.

Progression

Swimming activities can be graded not only by varying the speed of the swim, but also by varying the activity that is done. A postmyocardial infarction patient with an extremely low functional capacity benefits from simply walking through the water. Those people with recent bypass surgery benefit from moving the arms as they walk across the pool. The following are examples of the types of activities that can be used in aquatic exercise programs.

Side of pool activities. A wide variety of activities can be done while holding on to the side of the pool. These range from simple movements of the legs to side, front, or back while holding on to the side of the pool with one hand to practicing a variety of kicks that can ultimately be used while swimming. The range-of-motion-type movements are a good way to warm up before undertaking the more vigorous activities of walking or jogging across the pool.

Walking and jogging across the pool. A person with a low functional capacity can begin an aquatic program by simply walking across the shallow end of the pool. The water offers resistance to the movement while supporting the body weight, resulting in a reduced load on the ankles, knees, and hips. The arms can be involved in the activity to simulate a swimming motion; this increases the range of motion of the arms and shoulder girdle. The speed and/or the form of the walk can be changed as the person becomes accustomed to the activity. The person can walk with long strides with the head just above the water or do a side step across the pool. Lastly, the person can practice jogging across the pool with the water at chest height. Remember to check to see if THR has been achieved.

Using floatation devices. People with limited skill can use floatation devices (e.g., water ski jacket or a kick board) to move side to side or up and down the pool. The extra resistance offered by the jacket compensates for the extra buoyancy provided. The participant can stop periodically to determine if THR has been reached.

Lap swimming. The participant must be skilled if he or she wants to use swimming as a substitute activity for running or cycling. An unskilled swimmer operates at a very high energy cost, even when moving slowly, and he or she may not be able to achieve the duration of the workout because of fatigue. This observation is usually used to eliminate swimming as a possibility in a personal fitness program. That should not be the case. A person can learn to swim over a period of several months. During that time the person is gradually adjusting to the exercise and is able to use swimming as the primary activity, even if elementary strokes are used. Increasing the number of activities that a person can do increases the chance that the person will remain active when something interferes with a primary activity.

Lap swimming should be approached the same way as lap running. Warm-up with stretching activities, start slowly, take frequent breaks to check the pulse rate, and gradually build up the distance.

Remember, the caloric cost of swimming to running is about a 4:1 ratio. If jogging a total distance of 1 mi is a reasonable goal in someone's physical activity program, then swimming 400 m is equivalent in terms of energy expenditure. The following describes a series of steps that could be included in an endurance swimming program, beginning with walking across the pool. All steps assume that a warm-up has preceded the activity and that a cool-down follows.

Step 1—Standing chest deep in water, walk across the width of the pool. Do 4 widths at a time and evaluate THR. Gradually increase the duration of the walk until two 10-min walks can be done at THR. Total time per session is 30 min.

Step 2—Standing chest deep in water, walk across the width of the pool and jog back. Do a walk, jog, walk, jog cycle and evaluate THR. Continue with another cycle if THR range has been achieved. Gradually increase the duration of the jogging until four 5-min jogs can be completed at THR. Total time per session is 30 min.

Step 3—Standing chest deep in water, walk across the width of the pool and swim back (any stroke); repeat and check THR. Complete enough walk/swim combinations to achieve 20-30 min of activity per session.

Step 4—Standing chest deep in water, jog across the width of the pool and swim back (any stroke); repeat and check THR. Gradually decrease the jogging and increase the duration of the swim until 4 widths of swimming can be completed before THR is checked. Repeat 4-width routine to achieve 20-30 min of jogging and swimming per session.

Step 5—Slowly swim 25 yd, rest 30 sec, slowly swim 25 yd, and check THR. Repeat to achieve 20-30 min of swimming. Vary the speed of the swim and the duration of the rest period to achieve THR. Gradually reduce the resting period so that 2 lengths can be completed without rest, then 3 lengths, and so forth.

Step 6—Gradually increase the duration of the swim to accomplish 20-30 continuous minutes of swimming at THR.

The HFI should not view these as discrete steps that must be followed in a particular order. He or she may wish to mix the contents of one step with another or introduce games to make the walk and jog and width swims more enjoyable. The major point to keep in mind is to gradually increase the intensity and duration of the aquatic activities.

Exercise to Music

Music is popular in fitness programs. Exercising and moving to the rhythm of music is enjoyable as a private or group activity.

Advantages

Exercise to music provides an enjoyable fitness activity for many participants.

Motivation. Music provides motivation to continue exercising. The variety of tempos and rhythms of the different songs keeps the workout exciting and challenges participants to keep up with the beat. Music makes routine exercises fun.

THR. Movement to music programs can develop all the fitness components. The recommended frequency, intensity, and total work (see chapter 9) can be achieved in exercise to music programs. THR can be easily monitored following a music segment. Beginners need to be cautioned about doing too much too soon, because exceeding the THR in this type of activity is easy.

Skill level. Movement to music can be adapted to any skill level because no competition is involved. The only rule is to keep moving at a pace needed to achieve THR. The routines can be adapted for all ages and skill levels. Gradual progression within each session, as well as from one workout to the next, is needed to enhance enjoyment.

Disadvantages

Injury is always a potential risk in fitness programs. There are alarming reports of injuries in exercise to music programs. People should participate in movement to music programs only after they achieve a minimum level of fitness (i.e., can jog 3 mi continuously at THR without discomfort).

Other ways to minimize the risk of injury include the following:

1. Warm-up and cool-down with walking and static stretching
2. Include calf stretching throughout exercising
3. Avoid hyperextension of the back
4. Bend at least one knee in front hip flexion exercises
5. Concentrate on correct standing posture (i.e., pelvis forward, buttocks tight, head/chin up with shoulders back)
6. Avoid deep knee bends
7. Keep the knees aligned directly over the feet
8. Wear shoes with good cushion and support
9. Come all the way down on the heels when jumping

Music Selection

Selection of music for different phases of the exercise session sets the tone for the appropriate intensity of warm-up, aerobic phase, and cool-down.

Warm-up/stimulus/cool-down. The music used can vary depending on choice from "top 40 hits" to instrumental "Muzak." Typically, the program consists of a warm-up, stimulus phase, and cool-down. The warm-up starts slowly with the music tempo about 100 b/min. The stimulus phase includes an increasing intensity of floor and aerobic exercises at a faster pace (about 140 b/min). As the intensity decreases into the cool-down, the music tempo and volume decrease to invoke a relaxing conclusion.

Variety to work muscle groups. An easy way to keep variety of movement within the program is by using one particular music selection for a specific area of the body. Exercises for a specific area of the body can be kept in mind while choosing an appropriate song. For example, the first selection might be used for upper-body flexibility, while the second song is used for lower-body flexibility exercises. As the program progresses in duration or difficulty, two or more music selections can be used for one area of the body. Music selections should be periodically changed for more variety.

Routines. There are no set routines; the program can be individualized by the instructor. Suggested components of an exercise session include the following:

1. Full-body flexibility (static, then dynamic)
2. Muscular endurance/strength for the arms, legs/thighs, and abdominal region
3. Cardiorespiratory endurance

An easy progression for beginners would include 25-30 min of mostly flexibility activities, with light muscular and cardiorespiratory endurance activities (see Table 11.2). A more advanced program would include 45-60 min with longer duration for all of the fitness components (see Table 11.3).

Warm-up. For a gradual progression, static stretches for the whole body should be first on the program before dynamic flexibility exercises are performed. Examples of static stretches include neck, arm across the chest, arm to side, crossed leg hamstring, and achilles/calf (see chapter 7 for additional low-back stretches). Dynamic flexibility includes exercises such as arm circles, side bends, and half-knee bends. The warm-up should continue for 5-10 min.

Muscular endurance. Once the warm-up activities are completed, the muscular endurance exercises can be performed for 10-20 min. These include variations of side lying leg lifts, situps, and push-ups.

Cardiorespiratory endurance. To continue increasing the intensity of the exercise session, the cardiorespiratory endurance portion follows. This section of movement is done while on the feet, using large muscles (legs) and movements with the

Table 11.2 Exercise to Music Outline for Beginners

Duration (min)	Song (no.)	Exercises
2-3	1	Sitting/standing static flexibility (lower body)
2-3	2	Sitting/standing static flexibility (upper body)
2-3	3	Standing dynamic flexibility
5-6	4	Side lying flexibility and muscular endurance
	5	Hands and knees flexibility
12	6	Aerobic—stationary
	7	Aerobic—moving
	8	Aerobic—stationary and moving
2-3	9	Cool-down—dynamic
2-3	10	Cool-down—static

Table 11.3 Exercise to Music Advanced Outline

Duration (min)	Song (no.)	Exercises
2-3	1	Sitting/standing static flexibility (lower body)
2-3	2	Sitting/standing static flexibility (upper body)
4-5	3	Standing dynamic flexibility
3-4	4	Side lying muscular endurance
3-4	5	Hands and knees muscular endurance
3-4	6	Sit-ups & push-ups
20-30	7	Aerobic—stationary
	8	Aerobic—crossing
	9	Aerobic—jogging
	10	Peel off
	11	Stationary walk
2-3	12	Cool-down—dynamic
2-3	13	Cool-down—static

arms. Hops, strides, skips, kicks, and jogging variations are used in addition to moving hands and arms to get the HR within the THR zone. Variety in this section can be accomplished by using stationary exercises on the spot or in a circle, crossing the floor in a line together, or introducing variations with a couple going down the center of parallel lines or with jogging variations around the room. Other exercises include jumping jacks, step hops, cross-over steps, toe-heel kicks, and so forth. The duration of this section is 15-30 min, with THR taken after every couple of songs. The intensity of this section can be increased by using more vigorous arm movements or higher hops. Intensity can be decreased by using fewer body parts, slowing the pace, and walking rather than jogging through the movement.

Cool-down. The cool-down should be the last portion on the program. It should start with a lower-intensity activity, such as walking to get the HR back below THR. Dynamic flexibility exercises should be included, with the session ending with static stretching.

Summary

Exercise programs should begin with regular walking, progress to rhythmical activities needed to achieve the THR, and finally, include games and sport activities to provide enjoyment and variety. Exercise leaders should be role models for the participants, should plan classes to reduce boredom, maintain a high level of control to ensure safety, and monitor and keep records of the participants' responses to each session. Walking programs should be structured enough to provide clear guidelines to the participant about knowing how much to do, being aware of signs of over exertion, and recording the HR achieved. Sample walking and cycling programs are provided. The jogging program follows the walking program, beginning with short jog/walk intervals and slowly, over weeks, building up to continuous jogging. The HFI should learn to use games as a part of a regular exercise session. They provide variety and are a good distraction from the exercise. Games at appropriate intensities must include, not exclude, participants; so care must be taken in the selection of games. Exercise sessions can be conducted in a pool, even if swimming will not be used as a primary activity. Participants can progress from pool side activities to walking and jogging across the pool, to lap swimming. A series of steps in such a program is provided. Exercise to music has become a popular fitness activity. The music seems to provide motivation to keep up with the activity, and exercise can be adapted to any skill level. Participants must be alert for lower-leg problems and must keep track of their THRs. Music selection should be consistent with the warm-up/stimulus/cool-down phases of the session. Programs for different levels are presented.

Suggested Reading for Chapter 11

Anderson (1980)

Bucher and Prentice (1985)

Dintiman, Stone, Pennington, and Davis (1984)

Fox (1983)

Getchell (1983)

Goodrick and Iammarino (1982)

Heyward (1984)

Hockey (1985)

Kisselle and Mazzeo (1983)

Krasevec and Grimes (1984)

Mazzeo (1984)

New Games Foundation (1976)

See reference list at the end of the book for a complete source listing.

Chapter 12
ECG and Medications

A. Daniel Martin

- A normal ECG
- Determining HR
- Common ECG changes
- Common medications
- Medications' effects on exercise

This chapter is not intended to be a complete guide to ECG interpretation and cardiovascular medications; several excellent texts on these topics are listed in the reference section. The purposes of this chapter are to provide the HFI with background information on the heart, the basics of ECG analysis, cardiovascular medications, and how these factors affect exercise testing and prescription.

The heart is a muscular organ, composed of four chambers. The flow of blood through the heart is directed by pressure differences and valves between the chambers. Venous blood from the body enters the right atrium via the inferior and superior vena cava. From the right atrium, blood passes through the tricuspid valve into the right ventricle. The right ventricle pumps blood through the pulmonary valve into the pulmonary arteries to the lungs. In the lungs, blood gives up carbon dioxide and picks up oxygen. The oxygen-rich blood is returned to the heart via the pulmonary veins emptying into the left atrium. From the left atrium, blood passes through the mitral valve into the left ventricle. The left ventricle pumps oxygenated blood past the aortic valve and into the aorta, coronary arteries, and to the rest of the body. The left ventricle, which generates more pressure than the right ventricle, is thicker and requires a greater blood supply.

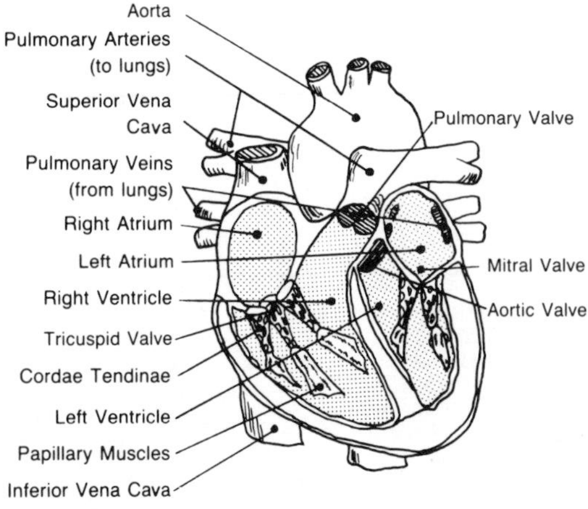

Figure 12.1 The chambers and valves of the heart. ***Note.*** **From *Living anatomy* by J.E. Donnelly, 1982, Champaign, IL: Human Kinetics. Reprinted with permission.**

Coronary Arteries

The heart muscle, or myocardium, does not receive a significant amount of oxygen directly from blood in the atria or ventricles. Oxygenated blood is supplied to the myocardium via the coronary arteries, which branch off the aorta at the aortic root. The two coronary artery systems are the right and left coronary arteries. The left main coronary artery follows a course between the left atria and pulmonary artery and branches into the left anterior descending and left circumflex arteries. The left anterior descending artery follows a path along the anterior surface of the heart and lies over the interventricular septum, which separates the right and left ventricles. The left circumflex artery follows the groove between the left

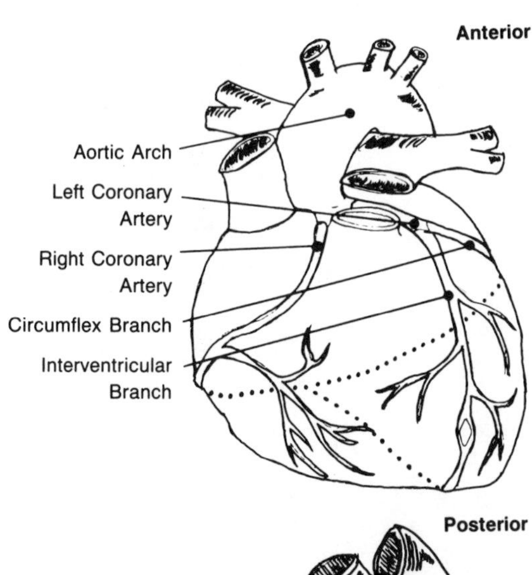

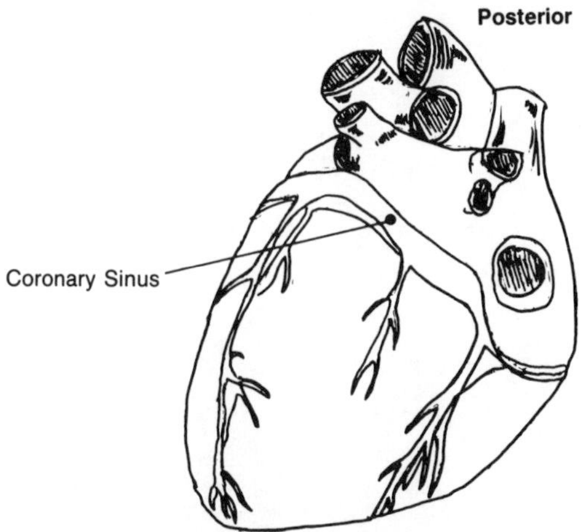

Figure 12.2 Coronary arteries of the heart. ***Note.*** **From *Living anatomy* by J.E. Donnelly, 1982, Champaign, IL: Human Kinetics. Reprinted with permission.**

atrium and left ventricle on the anterior and lateral surfaces of the heart. The right coronary artery follows the groove that separates the atria and ventricles around the posterior surface of the heart, and forms the posterior descending artery or posterior interventricular artery. Numerous smaller arteries branch off each of the major arteries and form smaller and smaller arteries, finally forming the capillaries in the muscle cells where gas exchange occurs. A major obstruction in any of these coronary arteries results in a reduced blood flow to the myocardium (myocardial ischemia) and decreases the ability of the heart to pump blood. If the coronary arteries become blocked and the heart muscle does not receive oxygen, then a portion of the heart muscle might die, which is known as a *myocardial infarction* or *heart attack*.

Venous drainage of the right ventricle is supplied via the anterior cardiac veins, which normally have two or three major branches and eventually empty into the right atrium. The venous drainage of the left ventricle is primarily provided by the anterior interventricular vein, which roughly follows the same path as the left anterior descending artery, and eventually forms the coronary sinus and empties into the right atrium.

Oxygen Use of the Heart

The myocardium is the most aerobic muscle in the body. Approximately 40% of the volume of a heart muscle cell is composed of mitochondria, the cellular organelle responsible for producing ATP with oxygen. The oxygen consumption of the heart in a resting person is about 8-10 ml of oxygen/min/100 g of myocardium, while the resting oxygen consumption for the body is about 0.35 ml of oxygen/min/100 g of body mass (Berne & Levy, 1977). Myocardial oxygen consumption can increase six- to sevenfold during heavy exercise, while the total body oxygen consumption can easily increase 12-15 times in young people. The myocardium has a limited capacity to produce energy via anaerobic pathways; it depends on the delivery of oxygen to the mitochondria to produce ATP. At rest, the whole body extracts only about 25% of the oxygen present in each 100 ml of arterial blood, and the body can meet its need for oxygen by simply extracting more from the blood. In contrast, the heart extracts about 75% of the oxygen available in arterial blood. The heart muscle's oxygen needs must be met by increasing the delivery of blood via the coronary arteries. An adequate oxygen supply to the heart is needed not only to allow the heart to pump blood, but to help maintain normal electrical activity, which is covered in the next section.

Electrophysiology of the Heart

At rest, the inside of myocardial cells are negatively charged and the exterior of the cells are positively charged. When the cells are depolarized, the inside of the cells are positively charged and the exterior of the cells are negatively charged. If a recording electrode is placed so the wave of stimulation spreads toward the electrode, the ECG records a positive deflection. If the wave of depolarization spreads away from the recording electrode, a negative deflection occurs. When the myocardial muscle cell is completely at rest, or completely stimulated, the electrocardiogram records a flat line, known as the *isoelectric line*. These steps leading from rest to complete stimulation to repolarization are shown in Figures 12.3-12.7.

The Conduction System of the Heart

The *sinoatrial node* is the normal pacemaker of the heart and is located in the right atrium near the vena cava. Depolarization spreads from the sinoatrial node across the atria and results in the P wave. There are also three intra-atrial conduction tracts within the atria that conduct depolarization to the atrioventricular node. Impulses travel from the sinoatrial node through the atrial muscle and intra-atrial tracts and enter the *atrioventricular node* where the speed of conduction is slowed to allow the atrial contraction to empty blood into the ventricles before the start of ventricular contraction. The *Bundle of His* is the conduction pathway that connects the atrioventricular node with bundle branches in the ventricles. The right *bundle*

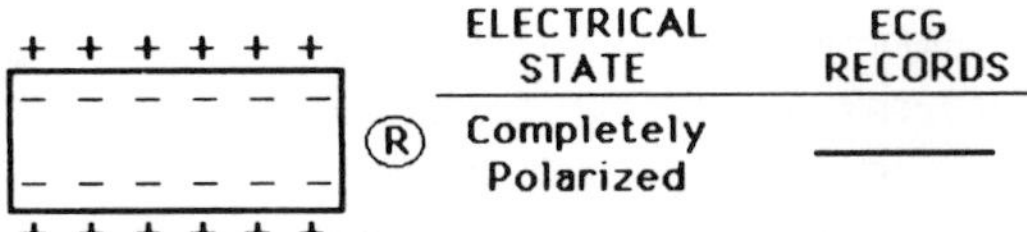

Figure 12.3 The myocardial cell is at rest and is completely polarized. The electrocardiogram records the isoelectric line.

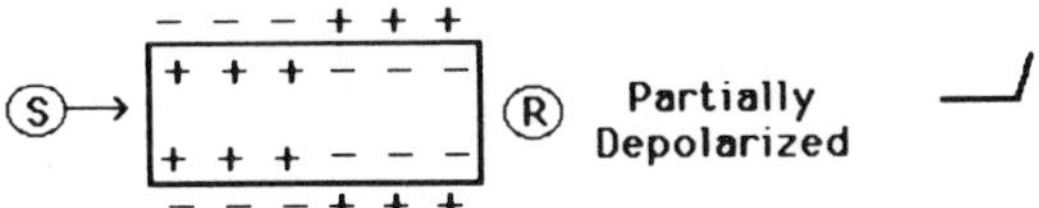

Figure 12.4 The heart muscle cell has been stimulated on the left end, and the wave of depolarization (depolarization equals negative charges extracellularly) spreads from the left to the recording electrode on the right. The depolarization moves from the interior of the myocardium to the surface of the heart muscle, and the ECG records a positive deflection. The amplitude of the deflection is proportional to the mass of the myocardium undergoing depolarization.

Figure 12.5 Depolarization is now complete. The ECG has recorded a positive deflection corresponding to depolarization and is now recording no electrical activity, or the isoelectric potential.

Figure 12.6 Repolarization has started from the right and moves to the left. The recording electrode senses a wave of positivity moving away from it, and a positive deflection results. Repolarization is thought to occur in the opposite direction (surface to interior) from depolarization in the human heart and is the reason the ECG complexes for depolarization and repolarization are both normally positive. If repolarization had started on the left and moved to the right, the ECG deflection would have been negative.

Figure 12.7 The myocardial cell is now completely repolarized, or in the resting state, and the ECG records the isoelectric line. The myocardial cell is now ready to depolarize again.

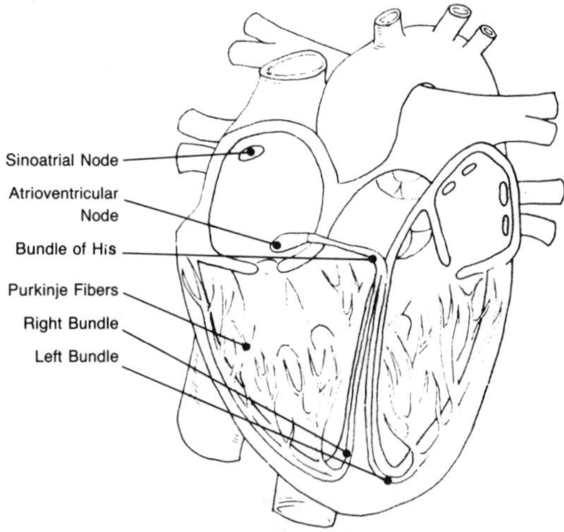

Figure 12.8 The electrical conduction system of the heart. These are the normal pathways used to ensure the rhythmical contraction and relaxation of the chambers of the heart.

branch splits off the Bundle of His and forms ever-smaller branches that serve the right ventricle. The left bundle splits into two major branches that serve the thicker left ventricle. *Purkinje fibers* are the terminal branches of the bundle branches and form the link between the specialized conductive tissue and the muscle fibers.

Electrocardiogram

This section on the analysis of the ECG may appear to be beyond what an HFI should know about the topic. In fact, the physician is the person to make judgments about whether or not an ECG response is normal. However, the HFI must be aware of the basic information related to ECG interpretation to facilitate communication with the physician, program director, and exercise specialist.

A systematic approach to ECG evaluation allows the examiner to determine the heart rate, rhythm, and conduction pathways and to search for signs of ischemia or infarction. Physicians normally evaluate a 12-lead ECG, but for our purposes a single ECG lead is adequate. The most commonly used single ECG lead for exercise testing is the CM5, which looks very similar to lead V5 on a 12-lead ECG.

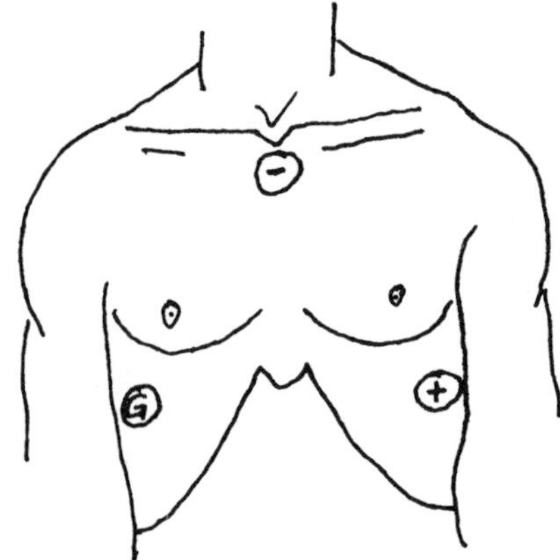

Figure 12.9 **Lead placement for CM5: (−) negative electrode, (+) positive electrode, (G) ground. Adapted from Figure 8-1, *Stress testing: Principles and Practice*, M.H. Ellestad (2nd edition). Reprinted with permission.**

Time and Voltage

ECG paper is marked in a standard manner to allow measurement of time intervals and voltages. Time is measured on the horizontal axis, and the paper normally moves at 25 mm (millimeters) per second. Most ECG machines can be set to run at 50 or 25 mm. It is important to know the paper speed when measuring ECG complexes. ECG paper is marked with a repeating grid. Major grid lines are 5 mm apart and at a paper speed of 25 mm per second, 5 mm corresponds to 0.20 sec. Minor lines are 1 mm apart, and at a paper speed of 25 mm per second, 1 mm equals 0.04 sec. Voltage is measured on the vertical axis, and the calibration of the machine must be known to evaluate the ECG. The standard calibration factor is normally 0.1 mv (millivolt) per mm of deflection. Most ECG machines can be adjusted to reduce this factor by 50% or double it. Like paper speed, the voltage calibration should be known before evaluating an ECG. All ECG measurements in this book refer to a paper speed of 25 mm per second and a voltage calibration of 0.1 mv per mm.

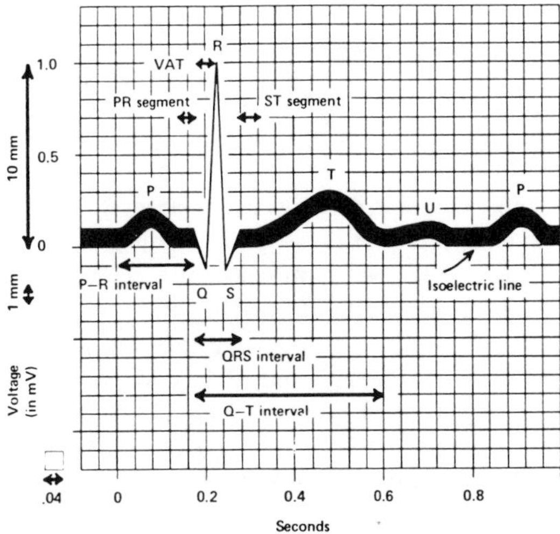

Figure 12.10 **ECG Complex with time and voltage scales. *Note*. From M.J. Goldman: *Principles of Clinical Electrocardiography, 11 Edition*. Copyright 1982 by Lange Medical Publications, Los Altos, CA. Adapted with permission.**

The Basic Electrocardiographic Complexes

The P wave is the graphical representation of atrial depolarization. The normal P wave is less than 0.12 sec in duration and has an amplitude of 0.25 mv or less.

The Ta wave is the result of atrial repolarization. It is not normally seen because it occurs during ventricular depolarization, and the larger electrical forces generated by the ventricles "hide" the Ta wave.

The Q wave is the first downward deflection after the P wave; the Q wave signals the start of ventricular depolarization.

The R wave is a positive deflection after the Q wave and is the result of ventricular depolarization. If more than one R wave occurs in a single complex, then the second occurrence is called R' (R prime).

The S wave is a negative deflection preceded by Q or R waves and is also the result of ventricular depolarization.

The T wave follows the QRS complex and represents ventricular repolarization.

A U wave is occasionally seen but is unlikely to be a factor in ECG interpretation for exercise prescription. The origin of the U wave is unclear.

Electrocardiograph Intervals

The R-R interval is the time between successive R waves. An approximate HR can be determined by dividing 1,500 (60 sec × 25 mm/sec) by the number of millimeters between adjacent R waves, provided the heart is in normal rhythm.

The P-P interval represents the time between two successive atrial depolarizations.

The P-R interval is measured from the start of the P wave to the beginning of the QRS complex. The interval is called P-R even if the first deflection following the P wave is a Q wave. The P-R interval represents the time from the start of atrial depolarization, delay through the AV node and to the start of ventricular depolarization. The upper limit for the P-R interval is 0.20 sec or 5 small blocks.

The QRS interval represents the time for depolarization of the ventricles. A normal QRS complex lasts less than 0.10 sec, or 2.5 small blocks on the ECG paper.

The Q-T interval is measured from the start of the QRS complex to the end of the T wave and corresponds to the duration of ventricular systole.

Segments and Junctions

The P-R segment is measured from the end of the P wave to the beginning of the QRS complex. This segment forms the isoelectric line, or baseline, that ST-segment deviations are measured from.

The RS-T segment, or J point, is the point at which the S wave ends and the ST segment begins.

The ST segment is formed by the isoelectric line between the QRS complex and the T wave. This segment is closely examined during an exercise test for depression, which may indicate the development of myocardial ischemia. ST-segment depression is usually measured 60 or 80 ms after the J point.

Atrioventricular Conduction Disturbances

There are three categories of atrioventricular conduction defects: first, second and third degree blocks. Atrioventricular conduction defects are present when electrical impulses are slowed or completely blocked while passing through the atrioventricular node.

First-degree atrioventricular block. When the P-R interval exceeds 0.20 sec and all P waves result in ventricular depolarization, a first-degree atrioventricular block exists. Causes of a first-degree atrioventricular block can include medications, such as digitalis and quinidine; infections; or vagal stimulation.

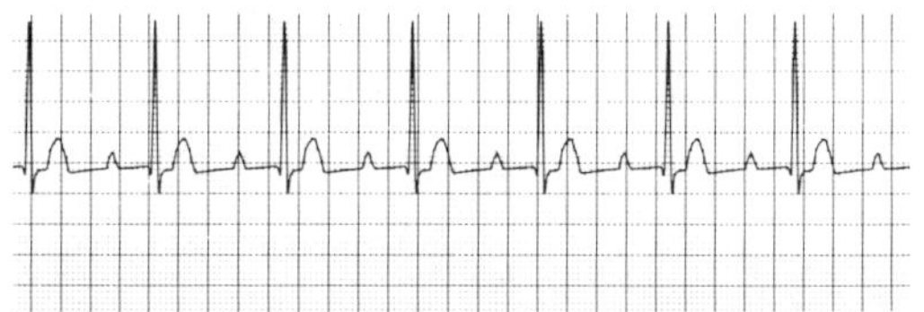

Figure 12.11 First degree atrioventricular block

Second-degree atrioventricular block. The main distinguishing factor of the second degree atrioventricular block is that some, but not all, P waves result in ventricular depolarization. There are two types of second-degree atrioventricular blocks: Mobitiz Type I or Wenchebach and Mobitiz Type II. Mobitiz Type I, or Wenchebach, atrioventricular block is a form of second-degree atrioventricular block characterized by a progressively lengthening P-R interval until an atrial depolarization fails to initiate a ventricular depolarization. This type of conduction disturbance is most commonly seen after a myocardial infarction. The site of the block is within the atrioventricular node and is probably the result of reversible ischemia.

Mobitiz Type II atrioventricular block is the more serious of the second-degree atrioventricular blocks and is characterized by atrial depolarization, occasionally not resulting in ventricular depolarization with constant P-R intervals. The site of the block is beyond the Bundle of His and is usually the result of irreversible ischemia of the interventricular conduction system.

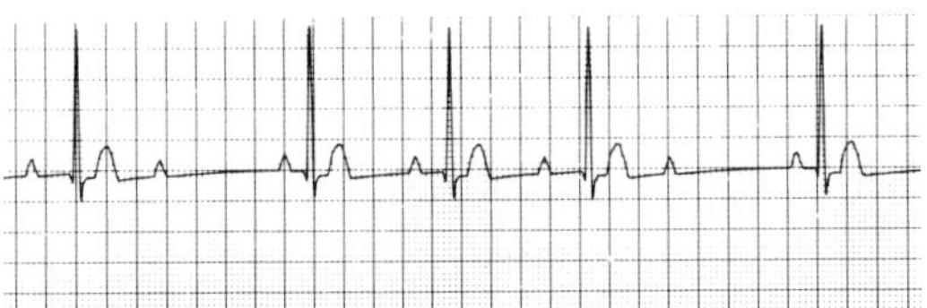

Figure 12.12 Mobitiz Type I Atrioventricular Block

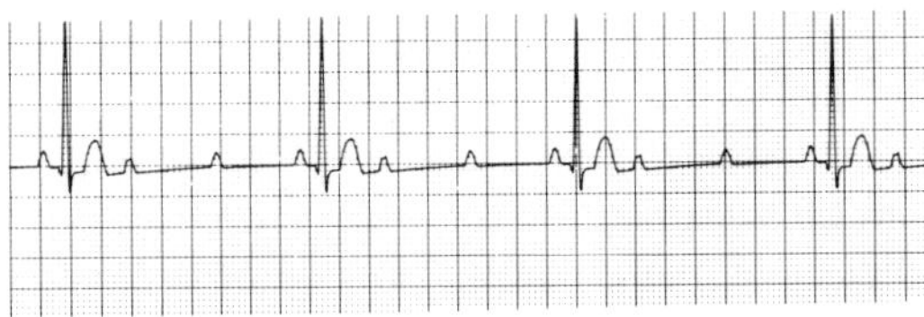

Figure 12.13 Mobitiz Type II Atrioventricular Block

Third-degree atrioventricular block. This type of atrioventricular block is present when the ventricles contract independently of the atria. The P-R interval varies and follows no regular pattern. The ventricular pacemaker may be either the atrioventricular node, Bundle of His, Purkinje fibers, or the ventricular muscle and almost always results in a slow ventricular rate of less than 50 b/min.

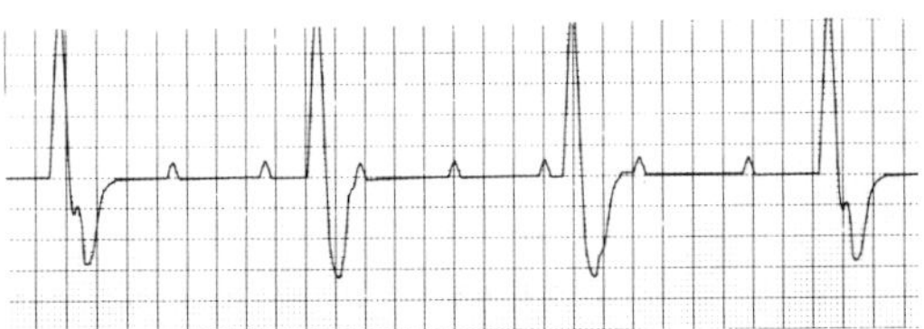

Figure 12.14 Third Degree Atrioventricular Block

Rhythms and Arrhythmias

The HFI needs a general understanding of the various rhythms and arrhythmias in order to communicate effectively with the health care team members. The following section contains examples of normal rhythms, the more common arrhythmias and explanations of their significance.

Sinus rhythm. This is the normal rhythm of the heart. The rate is 60-100, and the pacemaker is the sinoatrial node.

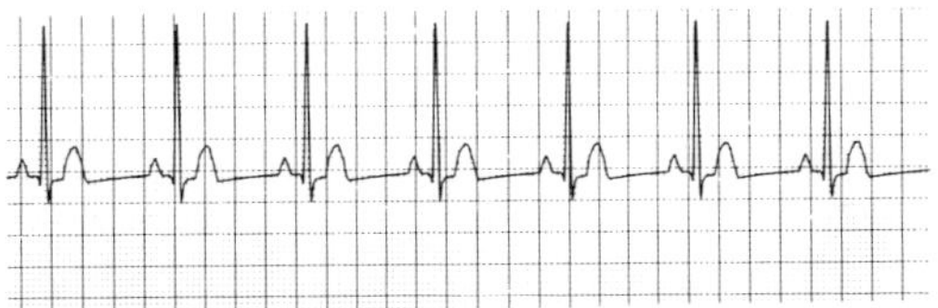

Figure 12.15 Normal Sinus Rhythm

Sinus arrhythmia. This is a normal variant and is defined as a sinus rhythm in which the R-R interval varies by more than 10% beat to beat. Sinus arrhythmia is often seen in highly trained subjects and occasionally in patients taking Beta-adrenergic receptor-blocking medications, such as Inderal®. The rhythm may be associated with respiration because the HR increases with inspiration and decreases with expiration.

Sinus bradycardia. The pacemaker is the sinoatrial node, and the rate is 60 or less. This is

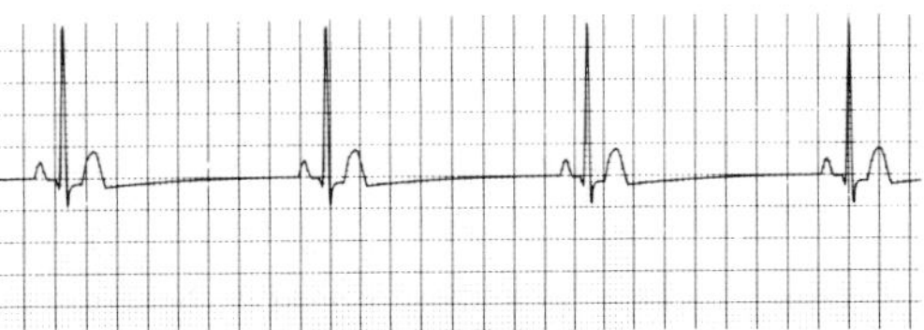

Figure 12.16 Sinus Bradycardia

a normal rhythm and is often seen in trained subjects and patients taking Beta-adrenergic receptor-blocking medications.

Sinus tachycardia. This is the normal rhythm during moderate and heavy exercise. The rate is greater than 100 and may approach 200 in young people during very hard exercise. HRs of 100 or more may be seen at rest in deconditioned people or in apprehensive individuals prior to exercise testing.

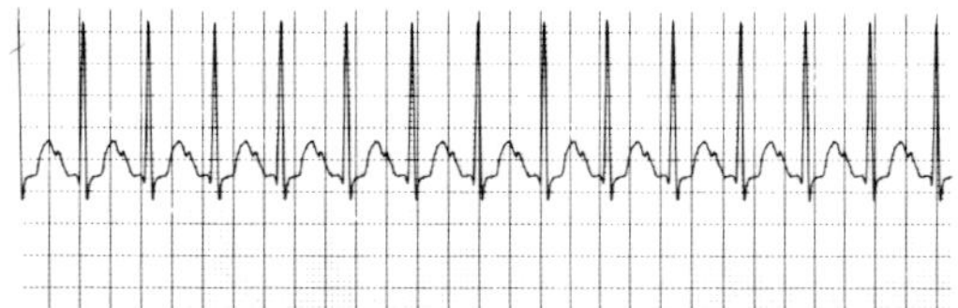

Figure 12.17 Sinus Tachycardia

Premature atrial contraction. The rhythm is irregular and the R-R interval is short between a normal sinus beat and the premature beat. The origin of the premature beat is somewhere other than the sinoatrial node and is known as an ectopic focus. Premature atrial contractions may be caused by stimulants such as coffee or tea and may be seen prior to exercise testing in apprehensive subjects.

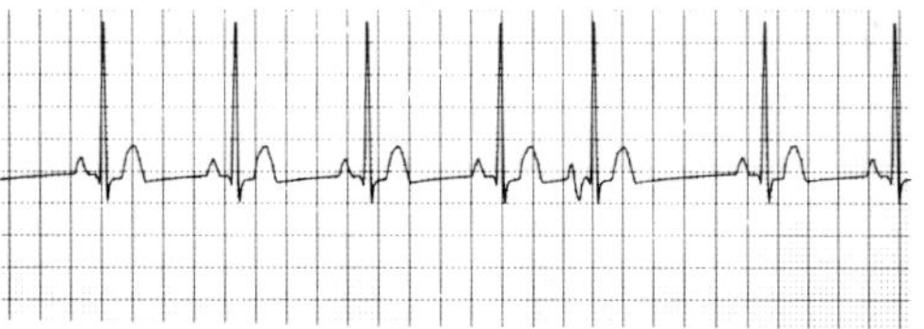

Figure 12.18 Premature Atrial Contraction

Atrial flutter. The atrial rate may be 200-350 with a ventricular response of 60-160 b/min. The atrial rhythm is usually irregular while the ventricular rhythm is either regular or irregular. The pacemaker site during atrial flutter is not the sinoatrial node, and as a result normal P waves are not present. F waves, resembling a sawtooth pattern, may be seen. The causes of atrial flutter include increased sympathetic drive, hypoxia, and congestive heart failure.

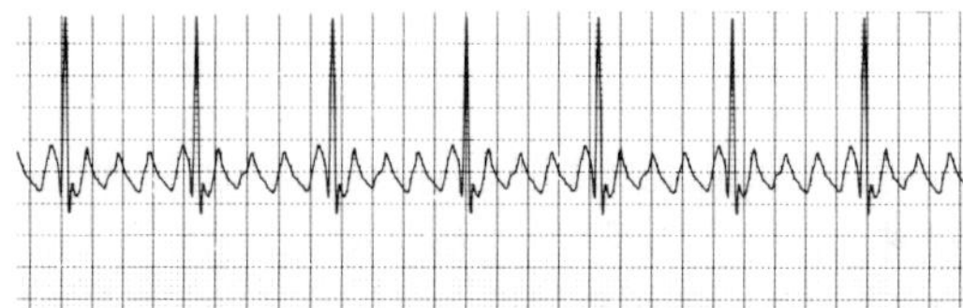

Figure 12.19 Atrial Flutter

Atrial fibrillation. The atrial rate is 400-700, and the ventricular rate is usually 60-160 and is irregular. Multiple pacemaker sites are present in the atria and P waves cannot be discerned. The significance of atrial fibrillation in an exercise testing and training setting lies in its effect on ventricular function. During atrial fibrillation, the atria and ventricles do not work together in a coordinated fashion, and the ability of the left ventricle to maintain an adequate cardiac output may be impaired. The causes of atrial fibrillation are essentially the same as those for atrial flutter.

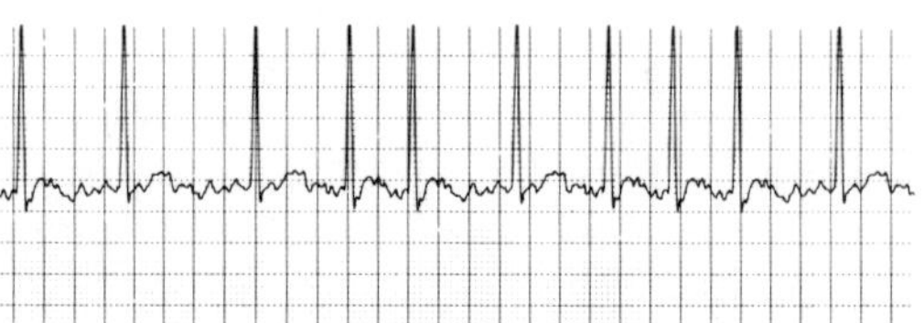

Figure 12.20 Atrial Fibrillation

Premature junctional contraction. A premature junctional contraction results when an ectopic pacemaker in the atrioventricular junctional area depolarizes the ventricles. Inverted P waves are frequently seen with premature junctional contractions as the atrial depolarization proceeds in an abnormal direction. If the atrioventricular nodal tissue is still in the refractory phase after a premature junctional contraction, then normally conducted waves of depolarization initiated from the sinoatrial node are not conducted into the ventricles and a compensatory pause develops. Premature junctional contractions usually result in a QRS complex of normal duration, or they may slightly prolong the QRS complex. The causes of premature junctional contractions include catecholamine-type medications, increased parasympathetic tone, or damage to the atrioventricular node. Premature junctional contractions are of little consequence unless they occur very frequently (more than 4-6 premature junctional contractions per minute) or compromise ventricular function.

While arrhythmias originating in the atria (supraventricular) may cause concern among exercise leaders and patients, Ellestad (1980) has found that the long-term survival of CAD patients with exercise-induced supraventricular arrhythmias does not seem to be compromised. The significance of the supraventricular arrhythmias lies in the uncoupling of coordination between the atria and ventricles and the resulting effect on the ability of the ventricles to maintain an adequate cardiac output. Recurrent atrial fibrillation may have little effect on the exercise response of an individual with good left ventricular function, but may cause significant symptoms in another person with poor ventricular function.

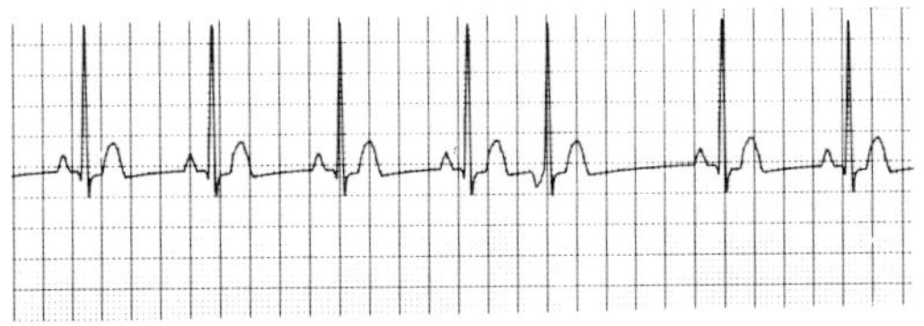

Figure 12.21 Premature Junctional Contraction

Premature ventricular contractions. Premature ventricular contractions are the result of an abnormal impulse arising (ectopic focus) in the His-Purkinje system, initiating a ventricular contraction. Premature ventricular contractions last more than 0.12 sec, and the T wave is usually oriented in the opposite direction from the QRS complex. Premature ventricular contractions often result in the ventricles being in the refractory phase of depolarization when the normal sinus depolarization wave reaches the ventricles, and a compensatory pause develops. Premature ventricular contractions are among the most common arrhythmias seen with exercise testing and training in CAD patients. If premature ventricular contractions have the same shape, they originate from the same site and are called *unifocal*. Multiple-shape premature ventricular contractions originate from multiple sites in the ventricles are called *multifocal* and are much more serious than unifocal contractions. Normal contractions alternating with premature ventricular contractions are called *bigeminy*, and three or more consecutive premature ventricular contractions are known as *ventricular tachycardia*. If a single premature ventricular contraction falls on the descending portion of the T wave, the "vulnerable time," then the ventricles may be thrown into fibrillation. Premature ventricular contractions have an adverse effect on the survival of CAD patients; generally, the more complex the premature ventricular contractions, the more serious the problem. Ellestad (1980) and coworkers have shown that the combination of ST-segment depression and premature ventricular contractions increase the incidence of future cardiac events.

If premature ventricular contractions occur during pulse counting, then the person may report that the heart "skipped a beat" and may undercount his or her HR. Participants in an exercise program should be instructed not to increase the exercise intensity in an attempt to keep the HR in the target zone as a result of the skipped beats. They should immediately reduce the exercise intensity and report the appearance or increase in the number of skipped beats to the exercise leader and physician.

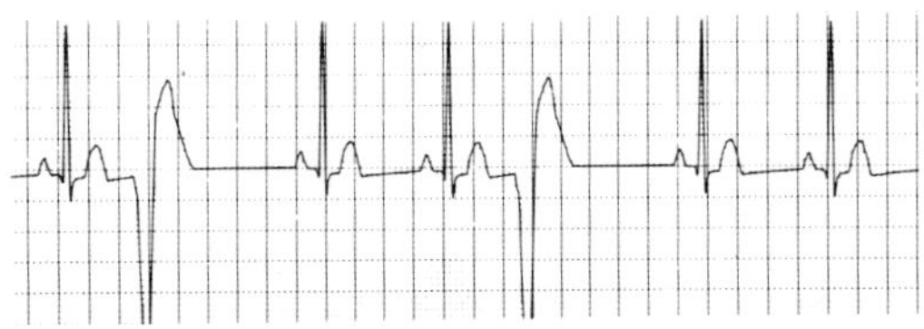

Figure 12.22 Premature Ventricular Contractions

Ventricular tachycardia. Ventricular tachycardia is present whenever three or more consecutive premature ventricular contractions occur. This is an extremely dangerous arrhythmia that may degenerate into ventricular fibrillation. The ventricular rate is usually 100-220, and the heart may be unable to maintain adequate cardiac output during ventricular tachycardia. Ventricular tachycardia may be caused by the same factors that initiate premature ventricular contractions; it *requires immediate medical attention*.

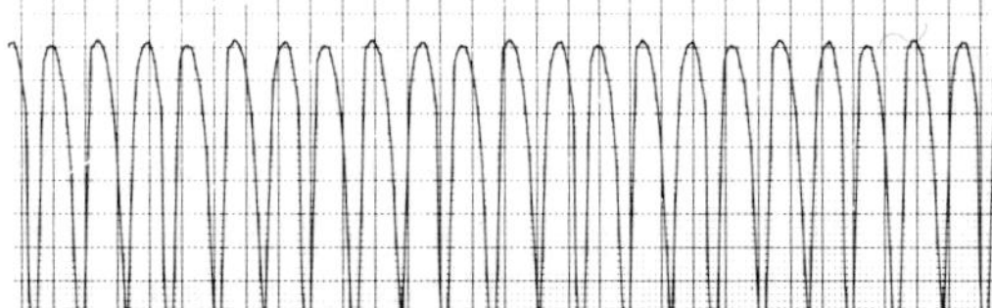

Figure 12.23 Ventricular Tachycardia

Ventricular fibrillation. This is a *life-threatening rhythm and requires immediate cardiopulmonary resuscitation* (CPR) until a defibrillator can be used to restore a coordinated ventricular contraction; otherwise, death will result. A fibrillating heart contracts in an unorganized, quivering manner and is unable to maintain significant cardiac output. P waves and QRS complexes are not discernable; instead, the electrical pattern is a fibrillatory wave.

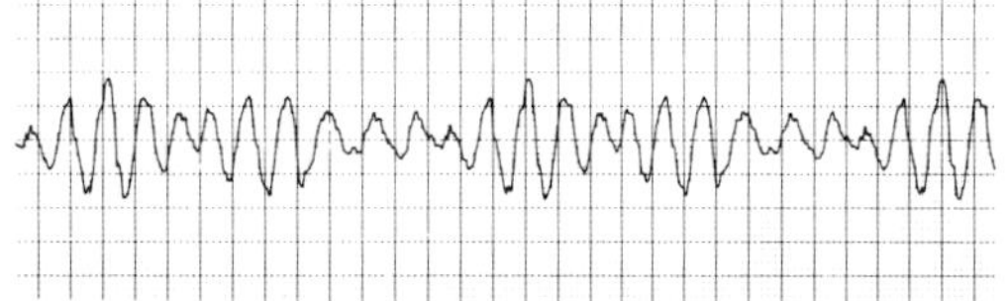

Figure 12.24 Ventricular Fibrillation

Myocardial Ischemia

Myocardial ischemia is defined as a lack of oxygen in the myocardium caused by inadequate blood flow. Obstruction of the coronary arteries is the most common cause of myocardial ischemia. A coronary artery is significantly obstructed if more than 50% of the opening is blocked (Hurst, 1978). A 50% reduction in diameter is equal to a loss of

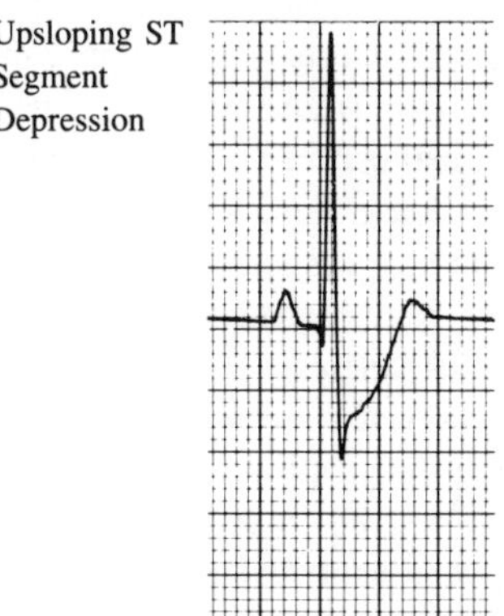

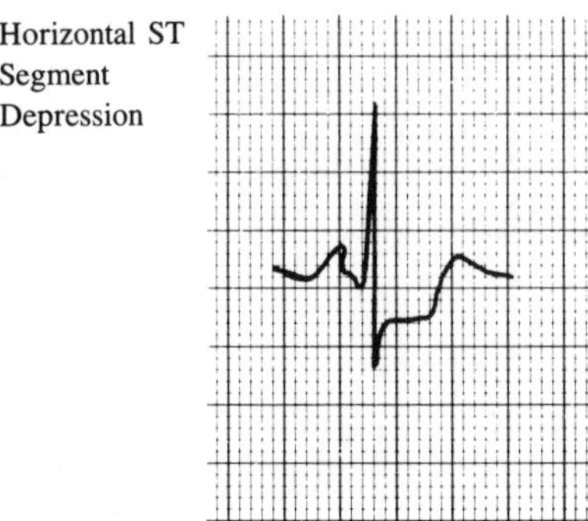

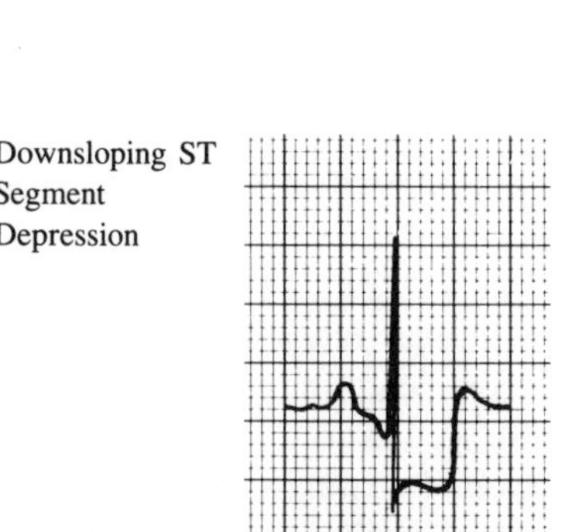

Figure 12.25 ST Segment Depression

75% of the arterial lumen. An obstructed coronary artery may be able to supply an adequate blood supply at rest, but may be unable to provide enough blood and oxygen during periods of increased demand, such as exercise. Ischemia often, but not always, results in angina pectoris.

Angina pectoris is defined as pain/discomfort caused by temporary, reversible ischemia of the myocardium that does not result in death or infarction of the heart muscle. The pain is often located in the center of the chest, but may occur in the neck, jaw, shoulders, or radiate into the arm(s) and hand(s). Angina pectoris tends to be reproducible, often appearing at roughly the same level of exertion. During exercise, an individual experiencing anginal discomfort may deny pain, but upon further questioning will admit to the sensation of burning, tightness, pressure, or heaviness in the chest or arms. Anginal pain is frequently confused with musculoskeletal pain. Anginal pain generally is not altered by movements of the trunk or arms, while musculoskeletal pain may be increased or decreased by trunk or arm movement. Discomfort is probably not angina if the pain is changed in quality or intensity by pressing on the affected area.

Myocardial ischemia may cause ST-segment depression on the ECG during an exercise test. ST-segment depression usually occurs at a relatively constant double product. The double product equals the HR times systolic BP and is a good estimate of the amount of work the heart is doing. Three types of ST-segment depression are recognized: upsloping, horizontal, and downsloping. (see Figure 12.25). Ellestad (1980) and coworkers have shown that individuals with upsloping and horizontal ST-segment depression have roughly similar life expectancies, while downsloping ST-segment depression has a more adverse impact on survival.

ST-segment elevation may also occur during exercise testing. ST-segment elevation during an exercise test usually indicates the development of an aneurysm, or an area of noncontracting myocardium and/or scar tissue.

Myocardial Infarction

If the myocardium is deprived of oxygen for a sufficient length of time, a portion of the myocardium dies; this is known as a *myocardial infarction*. Pain is the hallmark symptom of a myocardial infarction. It is often very similar to anginal pain, only more severe, and may be described as a heavy feeling, squeezing in the chest, or a burning sensation. Other symptoms that may accompany a myocardial infarction are nausea, sweating, and shortness of breath.

Recent information from the Framingham project indicates that up to 25% of myocardial infarctions may be *silent infarctions*, meaning that the infarction does not cause sufficient symptoms for the victim to seek medical attention (Kannel & Abbot, 1984). These silent infarctions may be recognized during routine ECG examinations.

Cardiovascular Medications

A wide variety of medications are used to treat people with heart disease. Some medications control BP, others control the heart rate or rhythm, while still others affect the force of contraction of the ventricles. While the HFI will not be dealing on a day-to-day basis with cardiac patients taking these medications, he or she will eventually encounter participants taking some of these medications. The purpose of this section is to summarize the major classes of drugs, describe how they affect the exercise HR response, and indicate possible side effects.

Beta-Adrenergic Blockers

This class of medications includes Inderal®, Tenormin®, Lopressor®, and Corgard®. All of these medications compete with the endogenous stimulators of the Beta-adrenergic receptors. Beta-adrenergic blocking medications are commonly prescribed for individuals with coronary artery disease; because these medications lower the HR, they have a profound impact on the exercise prescription. Individuals should be tested on Beta-adrenergic blocking medications if they will be training on these medications. All of the beta-adrenergic receptor blockers lower HR at rest and particularly during exercise, as seen in Figure 12.26.

Beta blockers are prescribed for hypertension, angina pectoris, and supraventricular arrhythmias.

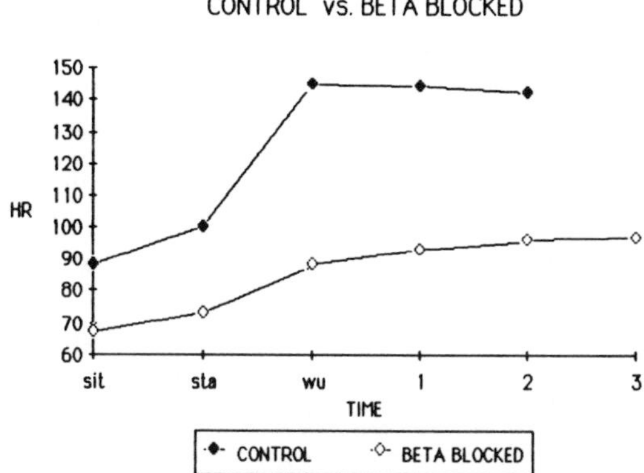

Figure 12.26 The heart rate before and after beta blockade (2 days of 40 mg of Inderal® per day) in a very apprehensive patient during treadmill testing (sit = sitting, sta = standing, wu = warmup @ 1.0 mph, 0% grade. Minutes 1 and 2 are 2.0 mph, 0% grade. Minute 3 was at 2.0 mph and 3.5% grade).

In addition, Inderal® is sometimes used to treat migraine headaches. The use of Beta-blocking medications for such diverse conditions increases the chance that an HFI will encounter "healthy" individuals who take these medications. When the HFI encounters a participant taking beta blockers, he or she should ask why the beta blockers were prescribed, if the participant has been cleared by his or her physician to participate in an exercise program for healthy subjects, and if the THR has been calculated from the results of an exercise test conducted while taking the current dosage of beta blockers.

The use of Inderal® does not invalidate the target heart rate method of prescribing exercise intensity. Hossack, Bruce, and Clark (1980) have shown that the relationship between percent maximal heart rate and percent maximal oxygen consumption are similar in beta blocked and non-blocked CAD patients. There has been little work in the area, but it is assumed that the heart rate method of exercise prescription is valid with the other beta blocking medications. Because beta blocking medications lower maximal heart rate, the use of these medications invalidates estimating target heart rate based on taking 70-85% of age-adjusted, predicted maximal heart rate (predicted maximal heart rate = 220 − age). For example, a 40-year-old individual has a predicted maximal heart rate of about 180, with an estimated 70-85% target heart rate of 126-153 beats per minute. If this individual were given a Beta blocking medication, maximal heart rate could easily be reduced to 150 beats per minute. If the estimated target heart rate of 126-153 b/min was used for training, this individual would be training at maximal heart rate. Measurement of maximal heart rate is required to calculate an appropriate target heart rate for anyone taking beta blocking medications and should be repeated following any change in beta blocking medication dosage.

A question that has been raised is whether the use of beta blocking medicines reduces or blocks the effectiveness of endurance training. Sable et al. (1982) has reported that chronic use of Inderal® diminishes the effects of endurance training in healthy, young subjects. Pratt and coworkers (1981), using patients with CAD have found that chronic use of Beta-blocking medications do not prevent the typical endurance training effects.

Nitrates

This class of drugs exists in several forms including patches and ointment applied to the skin, long-acting tablets, and sublingual tablets. Nitroglycerin is used to prevent or stop attacks of angina pectoris. The physiological mechanism of action is via relaxation of vascular smooth muscle, which reduces venous return and the quantity of blood the heart has to pump. Arterial smooth muscle is also relaxed, although to a lesser degree than venous smooth muscle, and this reduces the resistance against which the heart has to pump. Both of these actions help reduce the work and resulting oxygen requirement of the heart. Many patients use nitroglycerin on a 24-hr basis with ointment or patches. Longer-acting tablet forms of nitroglycerin (Cardilate,® Sorbitrate,® and Isordil®) may be taken prior to activities that are likely to provoke anginal attacks, while sublingual tablets (Nitrostat®) are used to treat acute anginal episodes. Headaches, dizziness, and hypotension are the main side effects of nitroglycerin use. Beta-blocking medications may potentiate the hypotensive actions of nitroglycerin.

Calcium Antagonists

This class of drugs is a relative newcomer to the medical treatment of coronary artery disease in the U.S. and currently has three members: Verapamil (Isoptin®), Nifedipine (Procardia®), and Diltiazem (Cardizem®). These drugs interfere with the slow calcium currents during depolarization in cardiac and vascular smooth muscle. Isoptin® is used primarily to treat atrial and ventricular arrhythmias, while Procardia® and Cardizem® are used in the treatment of exertional angina and angina pectoris attacks that occur at rest.

The effects of these medications on exercise prescription and training have received little attention. Chang and Hossack (1982) have shown that the regression equations relating percent maximal HR and percent maximal oxygen consumption are the same in patients who take Diltiazem and nonmedicated patients. Isoptin® and Procardia® are assumed to not alter the relationship between percent maximal HR and percent maximal oxygen consumption. The effects of calcium antagonists on endurance training in CAD patients have not been determined. Duffey, Horwitz, and Brammell (1984) have shown that Nifedipine does not diminish training responses in healthy, young subjects.

Anti-Arrhythmic Medications

Some of the more commonly used members of this class include Procainamide (Pronestyl®), Disopyramide phosphate (Norpace®), Quinidine (Quinidine Sulphate®), and the digitalis preparations. The beta-blocking medications are also used to treat some types of arrhythmias. With the exception of the beta blockers, these medications have little influence on the HR response to exercise, but the reduction in arrhythmias may improve work capacity.

Digitalis Preparations

The digitalis medications are used to increase the vigor of myocardial contractions and treat atrial flutter and fibrillation. The increased vigor of contraction resulting from digitalis medications may increase work capacity in individuals with poor ventricular function. Cardiac side effects of the digitalis group include premature ventricular contractions, Wenchebach AV block, and atrial tachycardia.

Anti-Hypertensives

This class of medications can be broken down into four groups according to the mechanism of action. The first group, diuretics, works by increasing the excretion of electrolytes and water. Drugs in this group include furosemide (Lasix®), hydrochlorothiazide (HydroDIURIL®), and others. This group is often used as the first treatment for hypertension. Potential side effects of these medications include *hypokalemia*, or low blood levels of potassium. Hypokalemia can induce arrhythmias and is a potentially serious problem.

The second group of antihypertensive medications is the vasodilators. These medications decrease BP by relaxing vascular smooth muscle. Members of this group are hydralazine (Apersoline®) and others. Potential side effects associated with these medications include hypotension, dizziness, and tachycardia.

The third group of antihypertensive medications works through the alpha and beta receptors of the autonomic nervous system. This group includes the beta blockers discussed earlier and alpha stimulators such as methyldopa (Aldomet®), prazosin (Minipres®), and clonidine (Catapres®).

The fourth group of antihypertensive medications works through the renin-angiotensin system and has one member—Captopril (Capoten®). Capoten® works by inhibiting the conversion of angiotensin I to angiotensin II and is usually reserved for patients who are unresponsive to the other antihypertensive treatment options.

Summary

The heart is a muscular organ composed of four chambers—the right atrium and ventricle and the left atrium and ventricle. The coronary arteries supply the heart muscle (myocardium) with blood, and the heart meets the increasing oxygen demands by increasing blood flow. Any restriction in the blood flow to the myocardium could result in a change in electrical activity across the heart or in damage to the myocardium itself. The pattern of electrical activity across the heart is called the electrocardiogram (ECG). The ECG is recorded with an electrocardiograph and provides information about the rhythm of the heart. The ECG can indicate the presence of inadequate blood flow (ischemia), and it can indicate if a portion of the heart muscle has died (myocardial infarction). Various common ECG abnormalities and their significance are presented.

Medications are prescribed for a variety of reasons: high blood pressure, abnormal heart rhythms, and so forth. The HFI must be aware of the most common medications because they may directly affect the THR or indirectly affect the participant's overall response to exercise training. This chapter summarizes the major classes of cardiovascular medications and indicates what effect they may have on the cardiovascular response to exercise.

Suggested Reading for Chapter 12

Ellestad (1980)

Froelicher (1983)

Goldman (1982)

See reference list at the end of the book for a complete source listing.

Chapter 13

Behavior Modification

Mark A. Hector

■ How to develop and maintain healthy habits:
- Exercise
- Smoking, alcohol, and drugs
- Diet
- Stress

Everyone has times in his or her life when there is a desire to change some behavior. People are continually facing problems that necessitate increasing or decreasing the frequency of a particular behavior. This chapter focuses on five behaviors that are directly related to positive health. The healthy life includes one or more of the following for many people: a reduction in smoking, alcoholic drinking, weight, stress, and an increase in exercise. The initial portion of the chapter includes general points that the HFI should consider in trying to help individuals modify any behavior. The subsequent sections deal with some of the reasons for and ways to help people deal with inactivity, smoking, alcoholism, overfatness, and stress. Specific procedures for resolving these problems are recommended.

Table 13.1 General Model for Changing Behavior

Step	Activity
1	Desire to change
2	Analyze history of problem
3	Record current behavior
4	Analyze current status
5	Set long-term goal
6	Set short-term goals
7	Sign contract with friend(s)
8	List many possible strategies that could be used
9	Select one or two strategies to be used
10	Learn new coping skills
11	Contact helper regularly
12	Outline potential maintenance problems after goal is reached
13	Learn new coping skills
14	Contact helper periodically

General Points to Consider in Modifying Behavior

Some general steps can be recommended for helping individuals adopt healthy behaviors. This general plan includes several components; it is not intended that the HFI should use all of these components with all of the individuals who seek help. A single set of procedures would not work for all people and the variety of problems that they face. The HFI needs to be familiar with different strategies and combinations of strategies. Effectively helping an individual requires the helper to be knowledgeable, creative, and flexible. The steps found in Table 13.1 provide a general plan from which steps can be eliminated, added, or modified depending on the individual case. The general plan also provides a preview of the procedures discussed in terms of modifying specific behaviors in later portions of this chapter.

The HFI needs to do whatever can reasonably be done to help an individual adopt healthy behaviors by being a facilitator, consultant, advocate, and encourager. However, it must be realized that the change of behavior is basically the responsibility of the person whose behavior is being changed.

Initially, the HFI helps the individual analyze the problem. The analysis includes dealing with such questions as When did the behavior start, What were the conditions, Why does it continue, and When did it last happen under what conditions. Both the helper and helpee need to reach a mutual understanding of the problem. This analysis is often aided with the collection of some base-line data concerning the extent of the behavior over a period of several days. After the initial analysis, the participant should be able to clearly describe the current status of the problem.

The past and present having been analyzed; the future is addressed by a discussion of goals. Goal statements are about future conditions and they often include time constraints. The participant suggests the desired goal, and the HFI assists in making the goal realistic and clear. In the case where a large amount of behavior change is desired, subgoals are advisable. Success with single days may lead to 2 days, 3 days, a week, and so forth. In order to increase the chances of achieving the goal, a reward can be made contingent on the successful accomplishment of the goal. The reward is obtained only if the goal is reached. Another procedure that has helped individuals achieve goals is the signing of a contract. The written agreement specifying conditions to be met and the rewards or consequences if it is or is not met is more successful if made between the individual desiring to change and a close friend. In some cases, contracts are made with groups of individuals, forming a support group that can provide encouragement and increase the commitment level of the participants.

Once a problem has been analyzed and a goal has been agreed upon, the next step is to determine a plan for reaching the goal. The first step in developing a plan is for the HFI and participant to list as many different plans as possible without taking time to evaluate each one as it is mentioned (brainstorming). From this list, the participant can pick the one or two strategies that seem to have the best chance of success.

Depending on the strategy selected, the participant might need to learn new coping behaviors, such as new social skills, increasing professional competence, learning how to relax, and/or learning how to be assertive. The coping behaviors focused upon depend upon what goals and strategies are selected.

Individuals who have had difficulty in changing their behaviors in the past often have feelings such as fear and helplessness when they try to change again. Throughout the process, the HFI has the potential for being an effective facilitator by modeling desired behaviors. Becoming a respected and effective model depends in large part on the HFI being accepting, friendly, and aware of the feelings of the participants.

After an individual has reached a goal of change, a very difficult stage is entered; namely, How can long-term results be maintained? Participants need practice in recognizing the environmental conditions under which old behaviors are likely to occur. Being able to recognize the onset of these potentially dangerous conditions increases the likelihood that steps will be taken to avoid them. Long-term contacts (becoming less frequent) between the HFI and the participant also help to maintain change over time.

Exercise Adherence

Exercise is good for people. The 1990 health objectives for the USA include a three-fold increase (from 20% to 60%) in appropriate aerobic exercise in the adult population. The HFI is in a position to help that goal become a reality. Exercise seems to be good both physiologically (see chapter 3) and psychologically (see chapter 8). Chapter 9 deals with specific factors (e.g., intensity) needed for improvement in health-related fitness. Chapter 11 presents a variety of activities that can be used for fitness.

The current emphasis on and interest in fitness assists fitness programs in attracting participants, even though new ways must be found to motivate many sedentary people in society to begin participating in fitness programs. A major problem for the HFI is to keep up the involvement (adherence) of those who do start, because up to 50% have quit within 6 months in many programs. Characteristics of people who are more likely to drop out include smoking, low self-motivation, lack of social reinforcement, and the belief that additional exercise is not needed. Reasons often given for quitting exercise are inconvenience and lack of time. Several strategies have been suggested to increase adherence to exercise.

1. *Available program.* Change is facilitated by accessible programs. The time and location of the programs need to be convenient for the targeted population.
2. *Social support.* The fitness program should deal with the family and "significant others" (i.e., people who are important to the individual such as a spouse, work colleagues, or friends) so that others can encourage and support participation in the fitness program.
3. *Emphasize enjoyable and positive aspects.* Learning new behaviors must be pleasurable if old behaviors are to be discarded. Physical fitness programs need to recognize the fitness changes that are made and need to happen in an enjoyable atmosphere. The performance models (e.g., military or athletic) aimed only at producing results regardless of the enjoyment of the participant will not work in a lifelong fitness program. Education for a new behavior should direct attention to potential gains more than losses. A contract between the individual and a program leader which

focuses on these gains is an effective method of behavior change in this area.

4. *Program characteristics*. Qualified and enthusiastic personnel, regular assessment of important fitness components, relevant personal and general communication, participant choice of a variety of group/individual exercises, games, and sports are all qualities of a good fitness program. Physical exercise and socialization make a profitable combination, as evidenced by the success of many dance/physical fitness groups. Many enjoy the social interaction with others, and a support group develops to help continue the exercise.
5. *Role models*. People learn from each other and from others they admire. The importance of an HFI who displays healthy behaviors cannot be overemphasized.

Smoking Behaviors

There is little disagreement outside cigarette-producing circles that smoking is bad for health. Data are ample to show that smoking is the largest avoidable cause of death in the United States. Through warning labels on packages and in advertisements, virtually everyone has been made aware of the dangers. Millions have quit smoking. However, the overall number of smokers has remained almost constant since the late 1960s because of the increases in the number of new smokers, especially young females.

Why People Smoke

Three models have been proposed to explain smoking behavior: (a) social learning; (b) nicotine addiction; and (c) opponent process.

The social learning theory indicates that smokers often acquire the habit with social reinforcement, usually with peer pressure. The "rewards" of smoking include the nicotine reaching the brain in a few seconds after inhaling, giving the smoker a series of "highs." This positive reinforcement of smoking and the decreased aversion to the smoke itself produce a habit difficult to break.

The second model holds that the smoker becomes addicted to smoking in ways similar to addiction to other drugs. Thus smokers crave for a cigarette, and withdrawal symptoms make it a habit resistant to change.

The opponent process model proposes that two opposing processes (one pleasurable and one aversive) interact to continue the smoking habit. For example, the social reinforcement and the nicotine highs cause a pleasant emotion, whereas attempts to quit smoking cause unpleasant withdrawal symptoms that can be eliminated by having a smoke. Thus the positive effects of smoking and negative effects of not smoking combine to encourage a continuation of the habit.

A Plan for Smoking Cessation

The following plan for stopping smoking includes (a) preparation, (b) cessation, and (c) maintenance.

Stage 1—preparation. Smokers need to gain confidence that they can be successful in quitting smoking. Confident, organized, sensitive, nonsmoking leaders can foster smokers' self-confidence through clear presentation of goals, procedures, and rationale for the program. During this stage, participants self-monitor their current frequency of smoking. This self-observation often temporarily helps to reduce the smoking behavior.

Stage 2—cessation. An abrupt end to the smoking behavior has been found to be more effective than gradually cutting down. An effective method to stop smoking is to have a contract to quit on a specific date. The behavioral contract involves a specific agreement between the smoker and some other person. The goal is specified in precise behavioral terms. For example, no cigarette will be smoked by Robert Jones between the dates of December 31, 1986 and January 1, 1988. The behavior, or lack of behavior, should be specifically described and linked to a time constraint. The contract also specifies what contingency comes into effect if the contract is broken. For example, if Robert Jones is a liberal democrat, it might be included in his contract that for each cigarette smoked during 1987, he will send a $100 political contribution to Senator Jesse Helms of North Carolina (who is a political figure he particularly dislikes). The contract is individually tailored to the capabilities and needs of the individual who is to abide by the contract. How long does Robert Jones feel that he has to refrain from smoking for him to feel that he has quit? To whom should the donation be sent to make the penalty especially aversive? What is the maximum amount of money he can send and still be able to abide by the conditions of the contract? Robert Jones will most likely feel committed and motivated if he is involved in the development of the contract. He knows best what contingencies will help him abide by the conditions of the contract. Frequent contact between the abstaining smoker and the leader of the program during the early part of the contract is needed for encouragement and discussion of unanticipated problems.

Another smoking cessation strategy that has a good record of success is rapid smoking. This strategy is based on the principle of satiation whereby an individual is encouraged to smoke as rapidly and continuously as possible until he or she becomes sick and has to quit. Because of the possibility of nicotine poisoning along with physiological abnormalities, this method should include careful screening and supervision.

Stage 3—maintenance. Contact with the leader and the development of new behavioral skills are essential ingredients of maintaining the behavioral change. Communication with the leader should include learning the advantages of a smokeless life (e.g., lower risk of major health problems, less stress in daily activities). The nonsmoker should be helped to learn new skills for dealing with old stimuli that were associated with cigarette smoking. If drinking coffee at the end of a meal was an old cue to light up, then avoid coffee. If cigarette smoke in the lobby of a basketball arena provided a cue for lighting up, then either remain seated in the arena or chew gum in the lobby as new behaviors. Once again, it needs to be emphasized that the determination of what new behaviors are needed and what will be effective involves both the participant and the leader. It is unlikely that leaders who rigidly prescribe what *must* be done will be as effective as those who mutually work out the strategies with the new nonsmoker.

Alcoholic Drinking Habits

Alcoholism is one of our nation's leading public health problems. There are an estimated 5-15 million alcoholics in the USA. The problems of family disruption, lost time at work, bodily injury, and death that are directly and indirectly caused by excessive drinking are not disputed even by the producers of these beverages. The drinking problem exacts a heavy toll on the health and financial well-being of the people of our nation.

While there is no debate on the reality of the alcoholism problem, there is heated debate on the appropriate goals for treatment of the problem. Should the alcoholic person strive for controlled moderate drinking or complete abstinence? Those who feel that abstinence is the correct goal tend to conceptualize the problem as a disease. Alcoholics Anonymous (AA) is a successful treatment group with an approach based on the disease concept. One fundamental precept of AA is that once a person has the disease of alcoholism, he or she will always have it—there is no cure. As a means of combating the disease, total abstinence is required. Individuals are helped to achieve this goal by the support of other alcoholics in person-to-person contacts and regular group meetings.

Others contend that alcoholism is not a disease, rather it is believed that no crucial difference distinguishes the social drinker from the problem drinker other than the amount of alcohol consumed. Four factors that determine the probability of excessive drinking have been proposed: (a) the degree to which the individual feels controlled; (b) the availability of an adequate coping response; (c) expectations about the results of the drinking; and (d) the availability of alcohol and situational constraints. For example, at a New Year's Eve party, the individual may feel strong pressure to drink (Factor a), may not have an adequate coping response (e.g., "I'd like a ginger ale on the rocks'') (Factor b), may have pleasant memories of previous New Year's Eve parties that included excessive drinking (Factor c), and plenty of alcohol is available for party-goers to consume (Factor d).

Social Skills Training

Social skills training to reduce excessive drinking normally includes instruction in assertive responding, refusing alcohol, preventing a relapse, and obtaining reinforcement other than drinking. In assertiveness training an individual learns how to communicate feelings in a productive and caring manner. This type of training is helpful to some problem drinkers because the excessive drinking behavior is related to an inability to communicate feelings to intimates and other associates. Helping individuals learn how to refuse alcoholic drinks is important. Some alcoholics simply lack the cognitive awareness of verbalized sentences or words that can be used to refuse a drink. Role playing is a widely used technique to learn and practice ways of refusing a drink.

Relapse prevention is probably the most important component of the social skills training plan. Many techniques can enable a person to abstain or drink less for a given period of time. However, maintaining these improvements over a long period of time is difficult. One of the key elements in maintaining the desired behavior is to be able to anticipate problem situations. Prior planning of ways to avoid problems can lead to discovering that there are behaviors other than excessive drinking that can provide positive reinforcement from peers and important others. For example, improving a person's conversation or storytelling skills can substitute for his or her excessive drinking habits in some situations. Once again, role playing can be used to avoid relapses. The leader works with the person to discuss feelings and coping behaviors in potential problem situations.

Choice Between Abstinence and Controlled Drinking

The choice of an appropriate goal for problem drinkers must involve the individual working with the leader. In general, people who have longstanding chronic problems with alcohol abuse and who have developed serious life problems associated with their drinking may be more suited to the complete abstinence approach. But younger people who are open to learning new social skills may respond well to the controlled drinking approach.

Weight Reduction

Obesity seems to be more difficult to overcome than smoking or problem drinking. Less than 5% of obese individuals successfully maintain a lower weight, whereas, 20-25% report success at quitting smoking or alcohol abuse. One problem seems to be an emphasis on ''negative change'' goals, rather than developing healthy substitute behaviors. For example, instead of concentrating on eating less cheese, why not encourage a plan to promote eating fruit at snack time. Another problem is the disregard for either energy intake or expenditure. Both decreased caloric intake and increased exercise (caloric expenditure) are normally essential for maintaining desired weight. Either one by itself is doomed to failure for most people. Another problem is the direct attack on the behavior rather than the indirect reasons for the behavior. Thus if a particular cue results in poor eating behavior, then either avoid the cue or learn to react to it differently. The ready access of food and drink and the mass media message of the relationship between happiness and what is consumed contribute to the problem for those people trying to change their eating behaviors.

Chapter 5 deals with methods for determining percent fat and estimating ideal weight. The participant should be counseled to work toward the goal gradually in ways that can be accepted physiologically and psychologically.

No one weight-loss program can be recommended for all people. However, the following eight components appear to be common ingredients for successful programs. Much of the success depends on the leader working with the participant to decide what steps to take and deciding what is likely to work for that person, then working with the person to make it happen.

1. *Self-monitoring*. Before any specific steps are implemented, the participant keeps a daily diary. The 2-week diary should describe food quantity and the eating environment (see chapter 5 for a form that can be used).

2. *Treatment goals*. The participant, in consultation with the leader, determines the ultimate goal of ideal weight, then sets weekly goals (from 1/2 to 2 lb). Extremely obese people should be referred for medical supervision.

3. *Diet selection*. A dietary plan that specifies food type, portions, and calorie amounts needs to be agreed upon. Several sound diets are available (see chapter 5).

4. *Stimulus control*. Certain situations or cues often are strongly related to eating patterns (e.g., watching a movie or TV). The participant needs to agree to eat only at certain places (e.g., dining room table) at certain times (e.g., breakfast, lunch, supper, and one snack time).

5. *Self-reward*. Some people are helped by providing small rewards for progress toward their goals (a new audio tape for each 3-lb loss), and a larger reward (e.g., a Broadway show) when the final goal is reached. The rewards should be consistent with healthy behaviors, something desired by the person, and things for which there are no acceptable alternatives.

6. *Exercise*. The first section of this chapter dealt with ways to begin and continue regular exercise. Although everyone who begins an exercise program does not necessarily need to begin a diet reduction program, most people who need to lose fat need to begin a diet and exercise program simultaneously.

7. *Family support*. The awareness and support of a spouse or other important person greatly assists the participant in adhering to the program. Involvement of friends or family members early in the program enhances its possibility of success.

Reducing Stress

Attempts to understand human stress (see chapter 8) and to develop plans to alleviate it are relatively recent. Three approaches have been used. Some emphasize the stress response itself, using Selye's (1956) stages of alarm, resistance, and exhaustion. A second approach focuses on the stimulus (stressor) that deals primarily with changes in the environment. Life crises such as the death of a loved one, the loss of a job, serious injury, or even holidays or vacations can be stress-producing events. The third approach deals with the interaction of the person and the environment. The studies showing stress reactions of people with various personality traits (e.g., Type A) to psychological stressors (e.g., work deadline) are examples of the interaction approach.

Three stages in the stress inoculation model are cognitive preparation, skill acquisition, and application training. In cognitive preparation, the stressed individual is prepared mentally for the coming stressful situation. The leader provides a manual that deals with a particular stressor. The participant keeps a diary of the frequency and conditions surrounding the stressor.

In the skill acquisition stage, the main emphasis is on learning basic cognitive and behavioral coping skills. One of the skills is *private speech*, where individuals learn sentences to say to themselves prior to, during, and following the stressor (e.g., prior to a major test, "It's going to be hard, but I have prepared for it"; during the event, "If I stay calm I will be less likely to block on a question"; and/or "I'm getting tense—relax and take it easy"; and following, "I did as well as I could because I stayed calm").

A second component of the skill acquisition stage is relaxation training. Chapter 8 includes an example of tensing and relaxing specific muscle groups. With practice, a relaxed state can be achieved rapidly in a potentially stressful situation.

In the application training, or final stage of the stress inoculation training program, the stressed individual is guided through a series of practice situations that help him or her learn to apply the previously taught skills. The sequence of situations progresses from relatively mild to more severe so that the participant can experience success and gain confidence in using the skills.

Summary

One of the primary responsibilities of the HFI is to help participants modify lifestyle behaviors. While the focus of attention is on increasing exercise, it should be clear that other unhealthy behaviors need to be decreased. These behaviors include smoking, alcohol consumption, obesity, and stress. Each of these behaviors is discussed in terms of what causes them to occur, and methods that can be used to change the specific behavior. Some commonalities exist among the behavior change techniques; the following is a set of guidelines to follow in helping people change behavior. If the person has a desire to change a behavior, then analyze the history of the problem and record the current status of the behavior. Set a long-term goal and several short-term goals, and sign a contract with a friend. List as many strategies as possible, selecting one or two that will be effective. The individual should learn new coping skills and have regular meetings with the HFI. Once the goal is reached, a maintenance schedule is outlined, including periodic contacts with the HFI.

Suggested Reading for Chapter 13

Allen and Iwata (1980)

Andrew et al. (1981)

Bandura (1969)

Ben-Sira (1982)

Bernacki and Baun (1984)

Brownell, Stunkard, and Albaum (1980)

Cormier and Cormier (1979)

Danaher (1977)

Davidson and Davidson (1980)

Dishman and Gettman (1980)

Dishman, Ickes, and Morgan (1980)

Epstein, Wing, Thompson, and Griffen (1980)

Flaxman (1978)

Franklin (1978)

Franks, Wilson, Kendal, and Brownell (1982)

Gettman, Pollock, and Ward (1983)

Goodrick and Iammarino (1982)

Gormally and Rardin (1981)

Hage (1983)

Hall (1978)

Hau and Fischer (1974)

Horan, Linberg, and Hackett (1977)

Hussina and Lawrence (1978)

Jarvik, Cullen, Gritz, Vogt, and West (1977)

Jellinek (1960)

Johnson (1981)

Keefe and Blumenthal (1980)

Kendall and Hollon (1979)

Kincey (1983)

Krumboltz and Thoresen (1976)

Martin (1982)

Martin and Dubbert (1982)

Miller (1980)

Montgomery (1983)

Murphy et al. (1982)

National Institute on Alcohol Abuse and Alcoholism (1971, 1974, & 1978)

Oldridge (1979)

Oldridge and Streiner (1985)

Oldridge et al. (1983)

Pattison, Sobell, and Sobell (1977)

Polly, Turner, and Sherman (1976)

Riddle (1980)
Rimm and Masters (1974)
Roskies (1980)
Sachs (1982)
Selye (1956)
Selye (1974)
Serfass and Gerberich (1984)
Shephard (1985)
Sobell and Sobell (1978)
Sonstroem (1978)
Spielberger and Sarason (1975)
Stalonas, Johnson, and Christ (1978)
Thompson and Wankel (1980)
Watson and Tharp (1977)
Williams and Long (1983)
Wysocki, Hall, Iwata, and Riordan (1979)

See reference list at the end of the book for a complete source listing.

Part V
Special Concerns

- Safe and effective operation of a fitness program

This section of the book deals with two aspects of a fitness program that could distinguish a good program from a great one. HFIs often become so enthralled with the benefits of fitness that basic injury prevention and treatment is neglected. Yet increasing evidence suggests that people who engage in fitness activities have higher risks of certain types of injuries. What can be done to minimize injuries in the programs? When injuries do occur, how can the HFI work with the participant to aid recovery? Finally, personnel selection and evaluation, budget priorities, and maximal use of facilities and equipment in a safe and appropriate environment all depend on careful planning. Good administration allows time and energy to be spent on providing the best possible fitness program to the maximum number of people. Lack of good administration results in wasted time and money and a reduced level of service.

Chapter 14

Injury Prevention and Treatment

Sue Carver

- Preventing injuries
- Treating injuries
- Exercise modifications for acute and chronic problems

Certain inherent risks are associated with participation in physical activity. The HFI should be aware of those risks and take steps to control factors that contribute to an increased injury potential. Advanced planning, adequate equipment and facilities, and counseling in the selection of the activities all help to reduce the possibility of injury. The following is a brief discussion of the factors contributing to injury occurrence and steps that can be taken to reduce injury risk.

Activity implies movement, and with increased movement comes a corresponding increase in the risk of injury. In fitness programs, the frequency of injuries increases when the frequency of the exercise sessions increases and when the intensity of the exercise is maintained at the high end of the THR zone. Increased speed of movement, as found in competitive activities, further increases the possibility of trauma. In addition, environmental conditions such as extreme heat or cold can increase the risk associated with physical activity. Lack of proper adaptation to the environment, as well as lack of education in the prevention, recognition, and methods of dealing with problems associated with these extreme environments can lead to devastating results (see chapter 9).

The age, gender, and body structure of the participant influences the risk of injury. In general, very young and very old people are at the greatest risk. However, if an injury is sustained, the older individual usually requires a longer period of time for recovery. Because of body structure and strength differences, females are often more susceptible to injury in particular activities than males. For either gender, a lack and/or an imbalance of muscle strength, a lack of joint flexibility, and poor CRF increase the chance that an injury will occur. The obese individual not only has a low CRF, but the excess weight places additional stress on the weight-bearing joints.

The dictum that the rate and risk of injury are lower for those people who follow the rules of the game is usually applied to athletic contests. However, in exercise programs where games are used as a part of the aerobic activities, the HFI must instruct the participants to follow whatever rules exist. Games with few rules and in which the HFI controls the tempo help to reduce the chance of an injury.

Finally, the HFI should encourage participants to seek professional advice regarding the selection and fitting of proper equipment. The most common equipment used, and most widely abused, is footwear. Inadequate protection of the foot is a major contributor to a variety of leg and low-back problems. Improperly maintained exercise equipment and facilities also contribute to a higher overall injury risk.

Minimizing Injury Risk

The first thing to do to reduce the chance of a minor or major problem is to require the screening of participants prior to entry into a physical activity program. The screening should highlight the major areas contributing to increased health risk (see chapter 2 for additional details). Proper screening assists the participant in recognizing problems and alerts the HFI to potential problems that could occur in an exercise session (i.e., asthma attack, diabetic shock). If the latter problems do occur, proper planning to deal with emergency situations contributes to a low overall risk while participating in an exercise program. Individuals who cannot be properly supervised or given adequate care as a result of their physical problems should be referred to a program or facility that can provide the needed services. Policies to handle such referrals and all major emergency situations should be written and communicated to all HFIs involved in a fitness center (see chapter 15 for additional details).

A major factor involved in reducing the risk associated with physical activity is in the design and implementation of an individual's exercise program. The program can focus attention on problems encountered in the preliminary tests, which might include the following:

1. Flexibility measures (chapter 7)
2. Body-fatness determination (chapter 5)
3. Muscular strength, power, and endurance evaluation (chapter 7)

4. Posture assessment
5. Cardiovascular fitness evaluation (chapter 6)

The manner in which the HFI conducts the exercise program has a major bearing on the risk of injury to the participant. The contrast of the "no pain, no gain" school of thought with the recommendation of warm-up, stretching, and cool-down makes this point. Educating the participants about the proper intensity of the exercise session (stay in THR zone) and about the recognition of the signs and symptoms of overuse is important in minimizing injury risk. The HFI should emphasize the graduated nature of the entire program and each session to avoid doing too much too soon. This is especially true for individuals who have not been involved in a regular exercise program and have a tendency to overestimate their abilities. Failure to do so leads to chronic overuse injuries, extreme muscle soreness, and undue fatigue.

In educating the participants about the signs and symptoms of overuse, attention should be focused on their abilities to distinguish between simple muscle soreness and an injury. Muscle soreness tends to peak 24-48 hr postexercise and dissipate with use and time. The signs and symptoms of injury include the following:

1. Exquisite point tenderness
2. Pain that persists even when the body part is at rest
3. Joint pain
4. Pain that does not go away after warming up
5. Swelling and/or discoloration
6. Increased pain on weight-bearing or active movement
7. Changes in normal bodily functions

Treatment of Common Injuries

Sprains (stretching of ligamentous tissue) and strains (stretching of muscle or tendon) are common injuries associated with adult fitness programs. Most significant injuries to joint structures or to soft tissue require *rest* and the immediate application of *ice, compression* and *elevation* (RICE). Usually, a wet wrap is applied first to give compression. Start distal to the injury and wrap toward the heart. Compression should be firm but not tight. If a joint structure is involved, surround the entire area with ice and secure with another elastic wrap. If the injury involves a contusion or strain to a muscle belly, put the muscle on mild stretch before applying ice, and secure in that position if feasible to do so. If possible, elevate the injured part above heart level to minimize the effect of gravity and to reduce bleeding into tissues. With any injury, the person can go into shock. The HFI should be prepared to handle this situation, should it occur.

In most cases, the participant needs to be informed that the application of ice should be continued anywhere from 24 to 72 hr, depending on the severity of the injury. Ice causes vasoconstriction of the blood vessels, thus helping to control bleeding into tissues. It also reduces the sensation of pain. Standard treatment times are 20-30 min with reapplication of ice occurring hourly or when pain is experienced. In the acute phase, when ice is not being used, the compression bandage should be in place to minimize swelling. Using ice or compression at bedtime is not necessary unless pain interferes with sleeping. If this occurs, frequent application of ice may help to control the pain. Physician referral is recommended in moderate to severe cases.

An injured participant may want to apply heat sooner than warranted. He or she needs to be informed that heat is usually applied in the later stages of an acute injury, when the risk of bleeding into tissues is minimal. The application of heat is a common treatment for chronic inflammatory conditions as well as generalized muscle soreness. Heat causes a vasodilation of the blood vessels and reduces muscle spasm. Standard treatment times for a moist heat pack is 20-30 min. When in doubt about which mode of treatment to use, ice is the safer choice.

Another group of common injuries associated with activity programs is wounds. The major concern with an open wound is bleeding. Once bleeding is controlled, steps can be taken to give further care. This may consist of treating for shock or immediate referral to a physician for suturing. In minor cases, a thorough cleaning and application of a sterile dressing may be all that is needed. Internal bleeding is a very serious condition. The HFI should treat for shock and obtain medical assistance immediately.

Table 14.1 outlines some of the most common injuries encountered in fitness programs, lists the signs and symptoms, and provides guidelines for immediate care.

Table 14.1 Common Injuries

Injury	Signs and Symptoms	Immediate Care
Sprain—stretching or tearing of ligamentous tissue. *Strain*—overstretching or tearing of a muscle or tendon. *Contusion*—impact force which results in bleeding into the underlying tissues.	1st Degree—Mild injury resulting in stretching or minor tearing of tissue. Range of motion is not limited. Point tenderness is minimal. No swelling. 2nd Degree—Moderate injury resulting in partial tearing of tissue. Function is limited. There is point tenderness and probable muscle spasm. Range of motion is painful. Swelling and/or discoloration is probable if immediate first aid care is not given. 3rd Degree—Severe tearing or complete rupture of tissue. Exquisite point tenderness. Immediate loss of function. Swelling and muscle spasm likely to be present with discoloration appearing later. Possible palpable deformity.	Rest Ice Compression Elevation Support Usual treatment time: Initially—30-60 min—ice bag Later—20-30 min—ice bag 5-7 min—ice cup or ice slush How often: Moderate and severe—every hour or when pain is experienced Less severe—as symptoms necessitate Continue with ice treatments at least 24 to 72 hours depending on the severity of the injury Refer to a physician if function is impaired Mild to moderate strains—gradual stretching to the point of pain is recommended
Heel Bruise (stone bruise)—sudden abnormal force to heel area which results in trauma to underlying tissues.	Severe pain Immediate disability May develop into a chronic inflammatory condition of the periosteum	Rest Ice Compression Elevation Support Pad for comfort when weight bearing resumed

(Cont.)

Table 14.1 Cont.

Injury	Signs and Symptoms	Immediate Care
Fractures—disruption of bone continuity ranging from periosteal irritation to complete separation of bony parts. Simple—bone fracture without external exposure. Compound—bone fracture with external exposure.	*Acute:* Direct trauma to bone resulting in disruption of continuity and immediate disability. Deformity or bony deviation Swelling Pain Palpable tenderness Referred pain or indirect point tenderness Crepitation False joint Discoloration—will usually become apparent later	*Acute:* Control bleeding—elevation, pressure points, direct pressure Treat for shock If an open fracture, control bleeding and apply a sterile dressing; DO NOT MOVE BONES BACK INTO PLACE Control swelling with pressure and ice if wound is closed Splint above and below the joint and apply traction if necessary Protect body part from further injury Refer to physician
	Chronic: Low-grade inflammatory process causing proliferation of fibroblasts and generalized connective tissue scarring. Pain progressively worsens until present all of the time Direct point tenderness	*Chronic:* Rest Heat Refer to physician
Laceration—tearing of skin resulting in an open wound with jagged edges and exposure of underlying tissues.	Redness Swelling Increase in skin temperature Tender, swollen, and painful lymph glands Mild fever Headache	Soak in antiseptic solution such as hydrogen peroxide to loosen foreign material. Clean with antiseptic soap and water, moving away from injury site. Apply a sterile dressing. Instruct to seek medical attention if signs of infection are recognized. Usually refer to a physician—a tetanus shot may be needed. If injury is extensive, control bleeding, cover with thick sterile bandages, and treat for shock. Refer to physician.
Incision—cutting of skin resulting in an open wound with cleanly cut edges and exposure of underlying tissue.		Clean wound with soap and water, moving away from the injury site. Minor cuts can be closed with a butterfly or steri-strip closure. Apply a sterile dressing. Refer to physician if wound may require suturing (i.e., facial cuts and large or deep wounds).

(Cont.)

Table 14.1 Cont.

Injury	Signs and Symptoms	Immediate Care
Puncture—direct penetration of tissues by a pointed object.	Redness Swelling Increase in skin temperature Tender, swollen, and painful lymph glands Mild fever Headache	If object is imbedded deeply, protect body part and refer to physician for removal and care. Treat for shock. Clean around wound and away from injury site. Allow wound to bleed freely to minimize risk of infection. Apply a sterile dressing. Puncture wounds are usually referred to a physician. A tetanus shot may be needed. Instruct to seek medical attention if signs of infection are recognized.
Abrasion—scraping of tissues resulting in removal of the outermost layers of skin and resulting in the exposure of numerous capillaries.		Debride and flush with antiseptic solution such as hydrogen peroxide. Follow with soap and water cleansing. Apply a petroleum-based antiseptic agent to keep the wound moist. This allows healing to take place from the deeper layers. Cover with nonadherent gauze. Instruct to seek medical help if signs of infection are recognized.
Excessive Bleeding	External Hemorrhage 1. Arterial Color: bright red Flow: spurts, bleeding is usually profuse 2. Venous Color: dark red Flow: steady 3. Capillary Flow: oozing	Elevate part above heart level Put direct pressure over the wound using a sterile compress if possible Apply a pressure dressing Use pressure points Treat for shock Refer to a physician
Internal Bleeding	Internal Hemorrhage—Bleeding into chest, abdominal, or pelvic cavity and bleeding of any of the organs contained within these cavities. Generally, there are no external signs. However, anytime an individual coughs up blood or finds blood in the urine or feces, internal hemorrhage must be suspected. The following signs are also indicative of internal bleeding: Restlessness Thirst Faintness Anxiety	Treat for shock Refer to hospital immediately

(Cont.)

Table 14.1 Cont.

Injury	Signs and Symptoms	Immediate Care
	Skin temperature—cold, clammy Dizziness Pulse—rapid, weak and irregular Blood pressure—significant fall	
Shock Caused by Bleeding	Restlessness	Maintain an open airway
	Anxiety	Control bleeding
	Pulse—weak, rapid	Elevate lower extremities approximately 12 in. (Exceptions: heart problems, head injury or breathing difficulty—place in comfortable position—usually semireclining unless spinal injury is suspected in which case DO NOT MOVE)
	Skin Temperature—cold, clammy, profuse sweating	
	Skin Color—pale, later cyanotic	Splint any fractures
	Respiration—shallow, labored	Maintain normal body temperature
		Avoid further trauma
	Eyes—dull	Monitor vital signs and record at regular intervals—every 5 min or so
	Pupils—dilated	
	Thirsty	DO NOT feed or give any liquids
	Nausea and possible vomiting	
	Blood pressure—marked fall	

Heat Illness

Heat illness can strike anyone. Poor physical condition, although a contributing factor, is not the primary cause. Even the most highly conditioned person can suffer a heat-related disorder. The exercise load and/or the environment can place a large heat load on an individual. When this occurs, sweat is produced at a high rate because evaporation of sweat is the major mechanism for heat loss. As a result, large amounts of water may be lost during physical activity. If too much water is lost, circulatory collapse and death can occur. The following information outlines methods of recognizing dehydration and presents measures that can be used to prevent heat illness.

Water Loss

A water loss equal to 3% of body weight is considered safe. A 5% loss is considered borderline, and an 8% loss is considered dangerous. Water loss can be monitored by weighing participants before and after activity. Individuals who are outside the allowable 3% range from one workout to the next should be monitored carefully if allowed to participate.

Symptoms of Overexertion

Participants should be educated to recognize symptoms of overexertion: nausea or vomiting, extreme breathlessness, dizziness, unusual fatigue, and headache.

Symptoms of Heat Illness

Participants should be educated to recognize when they are experiencing symptoms related to heat illness: hair standing on end at chest or upper arms, chilling, headache or throbbing pressure, vomiting or nausea, labored breathing, dry lips or extreme cotton mouth, faintness or muscle cramping, and cessation of sweating. If these symptoms are present, the risk for developing heat exhaustion or heat stroke rises dramatically. The participant should stop the activity and get into the shade. In addition, the participant should be instructed to ask for help if he or she is disoriented or the symptoms are severe. The HFI should provide fluids and encourage the individual to drink.

Individuals Highly Susceptible to Heat Illness

Individuals who have previously suffered from heat stroke may have sustained permanent damage to their thermoregulatory systems. Because their systems are no longer effective in controlling body temperature, these people are highly susceptible to heat injury. Individuals who use medications such as antihistamines or diuretics, use high quantities of salt in their diet or who use salt tablets, and/or use alcohol in large quantities (particularly, prior to activity) will have a higher risk of heat injury. Finally, those people who participate in physical activity while experiencing fever could elevate their body temperatures to dangerous levels.

Prevention of Heat Injury

Be aware of environmental factors such as humidity and temperature. The relative humidity can be calculated by measuring dry bulb and wet bulb atmospheric temperatures using a sling psychrometer. Use Table 14.2 as a guideline for participation.

Table 14.2 Guidelines for Exercising in Hot Weather

Wet Bulb Temperature	Action of HFI
Under 60° F	No precaution necessary.
61-65° F	Alert observation of all participants, especially if any are overfat.
66-70° F	Insist on frequent hydration.
71-75° F	In addition to the above, schedule frequent rest periods.
76° F or above	Light or no participation; take great caution.

Guidelines for Preventing Heat Injury

The practical experience of the military, and athletic teams to work in the heat and humidity has led to the development of guidelines to prevent heat injury. The HFI's application of these guidelines to adult fitness programs will enhance the enjoyment and safety of the participants.

1. Acclimatize to heat and humidity by training over a period of 7-10 days.
2. Hydrate prior to activity and frequently during activity.
3. Decrease the intensity of exercise if the temperature or humidity is high; use THR as a guide.
4. Monitor weight loss by weighing before and after workouts. Force fluids if more than 3% of body weight is lost during an activity. Minimize participation until weight is within the 3% range.
5. Avoid a high intake of protein because it requires a large amount of water for digestion; a diet high in carbohydrates contains a high water content and helps to maintain fluid balance.
6. Wear appropriate clothing for hot or humid weather conditions. Expose as much skin surface as possible. Light-colored clothing does not absorb as much heat as darker clothing. Cotton materials absorb sweat and allow evaporation to occur. Certain synthetic materials and/or clothing with paint screens do not absorb sweat and should be avoided.

Use of sauna suits prevents the evaporation of sweat and should be avoided.

Guidelines for Salt and Water Replacement

As mentioned earlier, the evaporation of sweat is a primary means to lose heat during exercise. This fluid loss must be replaced to minimize health risk, and maximize safe and enjoyable participation in an exercise program. The following discussion deals with topics related to fluid replacement.

When to drink. For most individuals who participate in CRF programs, thirst is an adequate indicator of when to hydrate. Generally, replacing fluids as they are used is the best way to meet the demands of the body. However, when extreme sweating or dry atmospheric conditions are present, the thirst mechanism may not be able to keep up with the need for fluid intake.

Normal daily intake of fluid for the sedentary individual is between 60 and 80 oz. The actual fluid requirement is dependent on too many factors to establish a single recommendation for maintaining hydration. However, drinking 8-10 oz of fluid prior to heavy exercise, in addition to frequent hydration during activity, helps to prevent heat illness.

The use of salt tablets. Loss of salt and other minerals may occur during prolonged exercise, particularly during hot and humid weather. Even so, the use of salt tablets is not recommended unless accompanied by a large intake of water. Water with a .1-.2% salt solution may be given to individuals with high water loss. However, just increasing the use of table salt along with high intake of water meets the body's need for sodium and fluid replacement.

Plain water versus special electrolyte drinks. Most electrolyte drinks are diluted solutions of glucose, salt, and other minerals with added artificial flavoring. Some brands also contain as much as 200-300 calories per quart of solution. Other than sodium, the minerals provided by an electrolyte solution do not provide much benefit. When sweating is profuse, large amounts of electrolyte solution may help to serve the same function as a diluted salt solution. In cases of mild to moderate sweating, the normal intake of salt in food provides adequate sodium replacement.

The main advantage of using a flavored solution is that the participant might drink more than if ingesting plain water or a salt solution. However, when considering the price of a commercially prepared electrolyte solution, plain water or homemade solutions are much more economical.

Homemade Electrolyte Solution

1 qt water

1/2 t salt

Add some sugar for flavoring

Fluid temperature. Fluids at a temperature of 5-15° C (41-59° F) are absorbed faster than fluids at other temperatures.

Table 14.3 outlines the various stages of heat illness, the signs and symptoms associated with each, and guidelines for immediate care.

Handling the Diabetic

The HFI should be familiar with the signs and symptoms of two conditions associated with the diabetic participant: diabetic coma and insulin shock (see Table 14.4). If an emergency situation arises with a diabetic and if the individual is conscious, he or she is usually able to indicate what the problem is. If he or she cannot, then ask when food was last eaten and if insulin was taken that day. If the diabetic has eaten but has not taken insulin, the person is probably going into a diabetic coma, a condition in which there is too little insulin to fully metabolize the carbohydrates. If the individual has taken insulin but has not eaten, then he or she is probably suffering from insulin shock, a condition in which there is too much insulin or not enough carbohydrate to balance the insulin intake.

In some instances, the individual may lapse into unconsciousness. If this occurs, check for a medic alert identification tag. This may help to identify the present problem. If undecided as to

Table 14.3 Heat-Related Problems

Heat Illness	Signs and Symptoms	Immediate Care
Heat Syncope	Headache	Normal intake of fluids
	Nausea	
Heat Cramps	Muscle cramping (calf is very common)	Isolated Cramps:
		Direct pressure to cramp and release, stretch muscle slowly and gently, gentle massage, ice
	Multiple cramping (very serious)	Multiple Cramps:
		Danger of heat stroke, *treat as heat exhaustion*
Heat Exhaustion	Profuse sweating	Move individual out of sun to a well-ventilated area
	Cold, clammy skin	Place in shock position (feet elevated 12-18 in.); prevent heat loss or gain
	Normal temperature or slightly elevated	Gentle massage of extremities
	Pale	Gentle range of motion of the extremities
	Dizzy	Force fluids
	Weak, rapid pulse	Reassure
	Shallow breathing	Monitor body temperature and other vital signs
	Nausea	Refer to physician
	Headache	
	Loss of consciousness	
Heat Stroke	Generally, no perspiration	This is an *extreme medical emergency*
	Dry skin	Transport to hospital quickly
	Very hot	Remove as much clothing as possible without exposing the individual
	Temperature as high as 106° F	Cool quickly starting at the head and continuing down the body; use any means possible (fan, hose down, pack in ice)
	Skin color bright red or flushed (blacks—ashen)	Wrap in cold, wet sheets for transport
	Rapid and strong pulse	Treat for shock; if breathing is labored, place in a semi-reclining position
	Labored breathing—semi-reclining position	

Table 14.4 Diabetic Reactions

Diabetes	Signs and Symptoms	Immediate Care
Diabetic Coma—too little insulin to fully metabolize carbohydrates. Because foods are only partially broken down, they form various acid compounds. This is referred to as *acidosis*.	May complain of a headache Confused Disoriented Stuporous Nauseated Coma Skin color—flushed Lips—cherry red Body temperature—decreased; skin—dry Breath odor—sweet, fruity Intense thirst Vomiting common Abdominal pain is frequently present	Call for medical assistance. Little can be done unless insulin is at hand. If medical assistance is not quickly available 1. Treat as shock 2. Administer fluids in large amounts by mouth if conscious 3. Maintain an open airway 4. If nauseated, turn the head to the side to prevent aspirating vomitus 5. Do not give sugar, carbohydrates, or fats in any form Recovery—gradual improvement over 6-12 hr. Fluid and insulin therapy should be directed by a physician.
Insulin Shock—too much insulin or not enough carbohydrates to balance insulin intake.	Skin color—pale; (blacks—ashen color) Skin temperature—moist and clammy; cold sweat Pulse—normal or rapid Breathing—normal or shallow and slow No odor of acetone on breath Intense hunger Double vision may be present	Administer sugar as quickly as possible (orange juice, candy, etc.) If unconscious, place sugar granules under tongue If individual is unconscious or recovery is slow, call for medical assistance Recovery—generally quick; 1 or 2 min. Refer to physician if unconscious or slow recovery.

whether the individual is suffering from diabetic coma or insulin shock, give sugar. Brain damage or death can occur quickly if insulin shock is left untreated; it is a far more criticial state than diabetic coma. If the problem is insulin shock, the individual should respond quickly—within 1-2 min. Transport him or her to a hospital as quickly as possible. If the individual is in a diabetic coma, there is little chance of seriously worsening the condition by giving sugar. Several hours of fluid and insulin therapy will be needed and this is directed by a physician. Table 14.4 outlines the diabetic reactions, signs, symptoms, and immediate care of each.

Common Orthopedic Problems

Many injuries that are commonly referred to an orthopedic physician for diagnosis and treatment result from overuse or irritation of a chronic musculoskeletal problem. In most instances, the injuries do not incapacitate the participant immediately. It may be weeks or months after the onset of pain before the participant deems the injury significant enough to warrant medical consultation. By this time, the inflammation is severe and generally prevents normal function of the part involved. In many cases, a severe injury can be avoided if proper care is initiated early enough. Table 14.5 outlines common orthopedic problems, their causes, signs, symptoms, and general treatment guidelines. Shin splint syndrome is a common orthopedic problem; information is presented in a separate section and in greater detail.

Shin Splints

Shin splints is a catch-all expression used to describe a variety of conditions of the lower leg. It is often used to define any pain located between the knee and the ankle. A diagnosis of shin splints should be limited to conditions that involve an inflammation of the musculotendinous unit caused by overexertion of muscles during weight-bearing activity. A more specific diagnosis is preferred over the term *shin splints*. In any event, the physician needs to rule out the following conditions: stress fracture, metabolic or vascular disorder, compartment syndrome, and muscular strain. The physical complaints often accompanying shin splints pain include the following:

1. A dull ache in the lower leg region following workouts.
2. Performance and work output decrease because of pain.
3. Soft tissue pain.
4. Mild swelling along the area of inflammation.
5. Slight temperature elevation at the site of inflammation.
6. Pain on moving the foot up and down.

The individual usually has no history of trauma. Usually the symptoms start gradually and progress if activity is not reduced. The usual symptomatic treatment consists of the following:

1. Rest in the acute stage and reduction of weight-bearing activity.
2. In mild cases brought about by overuse, reduced participation and/or modification of activity for a few days (e.g., swimming or cycle ergometer workout instead of running).
3. Heat or ice before activity; ice after activity. Heat treatments may consist of moist heat packs for 20 min or whirlpool treatments. The temperature of the water for whirlpool treatment should be approximately 104-106° F. Treatment time is usually 20 min. Ice applications may consist of ice bag treatments for 20 min or ice massage/ice slush treatments for 5-7 min.

Treatment should begin at the first sign of pain. If pain is extreme, a medical consultation should be obtained. Determination and treatment of the cause, in addition to symptomatic treatment is necessary to prevent a recurrence of the problem. Table 14.6 cites the major causes for shin splints as well as the signs and symptoms accompanying those causes and steps that can be taken to help prevent the onset or recurrence of lower-leg pain.

Table 14.5 Common Orthopaedic Problems

Injury	Common Causes	Signs and Symptoms	Treatment
Inflammatory Reactions— Bursitis—inflammation of bursa (sac between a muscle and bone which is filled with fluid; facilitates motion, pads, and helps to prevent abnormal function) Tendinitis—inflammation of a tendon (a band of tough inelastic fibrous tissue that connects muscle to bone) Myositis—inflammation of voluntary muscle Synovitis—inflammation of the synovial membrane (a highly vascularized tissue that lines articular surfaces) Epicondylitis—inflammation of muscles or tendons attaching to the epicondyles of the humerus Tenosynovitis—inflammation of a tendon sheath Plantar Fasciitis—inflammation of connective tissue that spans the bottom of the foot Capsulitis—inflammation of the joint capsule	Overuse Improper joint mechanics Improper technique Pathology Trauma Infection	Redness Swelling Pain Increased skin temperature over the area of inflammation Tenderness Involuntary muscle guarding	Ice and rest in the acute stages Chronic—generally heat is used before exercise or activity, followed by ice after activity Massage Muscle strengthening and stretching exercises Correct cause of problem If correction of cause and symptomatic treatment does not relieve symptoms, referral to a physician is recommended; antiinflammatory medication is usually prescribed If disease process or infection is suspected, refer to a physician immediately
Tennis Elbow—inflammation of the musculotendinous unit of the elbow extensors where they attach on the outer aspect of the elbow (lateral epicondylitis)	Faulty backhand mechanics—faults may include leading with the elbow, using an improper grip, dropping the racket head, or using a topspin backhand with a whipping motion Improper grip size—usually too small Racket strung too tightly Improper hitting—hitting off center, particularly if using wet, heavy balls	Pain directly over the outer aspect of the elbow in the region of the common extensor origin Swelling Increased skin temperature over the area of inflammation Pain on extension of the middle finger against resistance with the elbow extended Pain on racket gripping and extension of the wrist	Ice and rest in the acute stages Chronic—generally heat is used before exercise or activity, followed by ice after activity Deep friction massage at the elbow Strengthening and stretching exercises for the wrist extensors Correct cause of problem: 1. Use proper techniques

(Cont.)

Table 14.5 Cont.

Injury	Common Causes	Signs and Symptoms	Treatment
(Tennis Elbow cont.)			2. Use proper grip size (when racket is gripped, there should be room for one finger to fit in the gap between the thumb and fingers) 3. Racquet should be strung at the proper tension (usually between 50 and 55 lb) 4. Avoid stiff racquets that vibrate easily Keep elbow warm, particularly in cold weather Use of a counterforce brace, a circular band that is placed just below the elbow (serves to reduce the stress at the origin of the extensors) If correction of cause and symptomatic treatment does not relieve symptoms, referral to a physician is recommended; antiinflammatory medication is usually prescribed
Stress Fracture—a defect in bone occurs because of accelerated rate of remodeling which occurs to accommodate the stress to weight-bearing bones. This results in a loss of continuity in the bone and periosteal irritation. Tibial stress fractures are more common in individuals with high-arched feet. Fibula stress fractures are more common in pronators.	Overuse or abrupt change in training program Change in running surface Change in running gait	Referred pain to the fracture site when a percussion test is used. (Example: hitting the heel may cause pain at the site of a tibial stress fracture) Pain is usually localized to one spot and is exquisitely tender to palpation Pain is generally present all of the time but increases with weight-bearing activity. Pain does not subside after warm-up	Referral to physician. X-ray films should be obtained. Usually no crack is detected in bone. A cloudy area becomes visible when the callus begins to form. Often this does not show up until 2-6 weeks after onset of pain. Early detection can usually be made through a bone scan or thermogram. If a stress fracture is suspected but not diagnosed, treat as a stress fracture. Running and other high-stress weight-bearing activities should not be allowed until the fracture has healed and bone is no longer

(Cont.)

Table 14.5 Cont.

Injury	Common Causes	Signs and Symptoms	Treatment
(*Stress Fracture* cont.)			tender to palpation. Tibial stress fractures usually take 8-10 weeks to heal; fibular stress fractures take approximately 6 weeks. When acute symptoms have subsided, bicycling and swimming activities can usually be initiated to maintain cardiovascular levels. This should be cleared with the supervising physician. If a specific cause is attributed to the development of a stress fracture, steps should be taken to correct the cause. (See common causes for shin splints and their prevention.)
Mechanical Low-Back Pain—Low-back pain which results from poor body mechanics, inflexibility of certain muscle groups or muscular weakness.	Tight lower-back musculature Tight hamstrings Poor posture or habits Weak trunk musculature, particularly abdominals Differences in leg length because of a structural or functional problem Structural abnormality	Generalized low-back pain usually aggravated by activity that accentuates the curve in the low back (Example: hill running) Muscle spasm Palpable tenderness that is limited to musculature and not located directly over the spine May see a difference in pelvic height or other signs that would indicate a possible leg length discrepancy Muscle tightness, particularly of the hamstrings, hip flexors and low back	Acute case of low-back pain or any individual who displays signs of nerve impingement should be referred to a physician for evaluation and x-ray. It is necessary to rule out structural abnormalities such as spondylolisthesis, ruptured disc, fractures, neoplasms, or possible segmental instability prior to instituting a general exercise program. Further diagnostic procedures may be warranted. Symptomatic treatment consists of ice application and referral to physician in acute cases. Chronic cases are generally treated with moist heat to reduce muscle spasm and ice after activity. Correct the causes of low-back pain. 1. Stretch tight muscles 2. Strengthen weak muscles

(Cont.)

Table 14.5 Cont.

Injury	Common Causes	Signs and Symptoms	Treatment
(*Low Back Pain* cont.)			3. Proper warm-up prior to activity and proper cool-down following activity 4. Correct leg-length differences 5. Emphasize correct postural positions 6. If possible, correct or compensate for structural abnormalities (Example: orthotics for a biomechanical problem)

Table 14.6 Shin Splint Syndrome

Injury	Common Causes	Signs and Symptoms	Prevention
Shin Splints—inflammatory reaction of the musculotendinous unit caused by overexertion of muscles during weight-bearing activity. The following conditions must be ruled out: Stress fracture, metabolic or vascular disorder, compartment syndrome, and muscular strain	Prominent callus in metatarsal region	Keep callus filed down Metatarsal arch pad	
	Weak longitudinal arch	Lower longitudinal arch on one side in comparison to the opposite side	Strengthening exercises Longitudinal arch tape support
		Tenderness in arch area	Arch supports
	Muscular imbalance		Strengthening exercises; generally weakness of the dorsiflexors and invertors
	Poor leg, ankle, and foot flexibility		Exercise to increase range of motion
	Improper running surface		Avoidance of hard surfaces Decrease in hill-running Avoidance of running on uneven terrain

(Cont.)

Table 14.6 Cont.

Injury	Common Causes	Signs and Symptoms	Prevention
(*Shin Splints* cont.)			Minimization of changing from one surface to another
	Improper running shoes		Selection of shoe with good shock absorbency qualities
			Properly fitted shoes
	Overuse		Gradual increase in workouts
			Flexibility in changing training program if signs of too much physical stress is occurring
			Encourage year-round conditioning
			Proper warm-up
			Rest when indicated
	Biomechanical problems or structural abnormalities	Abnormal wear pattern of shoes	Refer to podiatrist or professional specializing in foot care; orthotics may be indicated
			Design a special training program to allow for individual differences (Example: increase intensity of workouts, reduce duration)
	Improper running or skills technique		Correct technique
			Specific stretching or strengthening exercises as well as technique-work
	Training in poor weather conditions		Use common sense when training in cold or foul weather
			Dress properly to maintain warmth
			Warm-up and cool-down properly

Exercise Modification

Most orthopedic-related problems can be grouped into mild, moderate, or severe in terms of denoting the significance of an injury. When in doubt, conservative treatment is recommended. Any injury resulting in acute pain or affecting performance, and any injury in which the individual hears or feels a pop at the time of injury should be referred to a physician. Any time conservative measures fail to result in improvement of the condition within a reasonable period of time (2-4 weeks), physician consultation is again recommended.

Other conditions may call for a modification of an exercise program. The participant may be obese, arthritic, or possess a history of musculoskeletal problems. Pool work is often employed with these individuals. Warm water is very therapeutic, body weight is supported, and the water generally allows for a greater range of movement. In any case, the activity should be suited to the condition. Any individual who requires exercise modification should be monitored closely. Table 14.7 summarizes the general guidelines used to classify injuries and offers suggestions for modifying activity.

Table 14.7 Injury Classification and Exercise Modification

Classification of Injury	Modifications
Mild	
1. Performance not affected	1. Reduce activity level
2. Pain experienced only after athletic activity	2. Modify activity to take stress off of the injured part
3. Generally, no tenderness on palpation	3. Symptomatic treatment
4. No or minimal swelling	4. Gradual return to full activity
5. No discoloration	
Moderate	
1. Performance mildly affected or not affected at all	1. Rest the injured part
2. Pain experienced before and after athletic activity	2. Modify activity to take stress off of the injured part
3. Mild tenderness on palpation	3. Symptomatic treatment
4. Mild swelling may be present	4. Gradual return to full activity
5. Some discoloration may be present	
Severe	
1. Pain experienced before, during, and after activity	1. Complete rest
2. Performance definitely affected because of pain	2. Referral to a physician
3. Normal daily function affected because of pain	
4. Movement limited because of pain	
5. Moderate to severe point tenderness on palpation	
6. Swelling most likely present	
7. Discoloration may be present	

CPR and Emergency Procedures

All HFIs should be well-versed in CPR techniques. (Courses are generally available through the local Heart Association or Red Cross.) In an emergency situation, there is little time to think. Most reactions occur automatically. Having a plan of action and running through practice drills on a routine basis help to ensure that proper procedures are followed in an emergency situation.

Be Prepared

Make sure a phone is available for use during the exercise class, and know where the phone is located. If a phone is not available, have an alternative emergency plan in mind. The HFI should identify the medical services that are to be used (ambulance, hospital, doctor, etc.), and have a phone list located in a convenient place. Decide who is to phone for medical help in an emergency situation, and make sure that he or she knows how to direct help to the location of the injured (see chapter 15). All necessary medical information (release forms, medical history forms, etc.) should be readily available, and all emergency equipment and supplies should be easily accessible (stretcher, emergency kit and supplies, splints, ice, money for phone call, blanket, spine board, etc.). The equipment should be checked periodically to ensure that it is in proper working order, and the supplies should be up-to-date. Finally, know where the fire alarms and fire exits are located.

Remain Calm

Remaining calm reassures the injured person and helps prevent the onset of shock. Clear thinking allows for sound judgment and proper execution of rehearsed plans. In most instances, speed is not necessary. Cases of extreme breathing difficulty, stoppage of breathing and/or circulation, choking, severe bleeding, shock, head and/or neck injury, heat illness, and internal injury are exceptions to this and require urgent action. Otherwise, careful evaluation and a deliberate plan of action is desirable. The HFI should have a system for evaluating and dealing with a life-threatening situation. All procedures should be conducted in a calm, professional manner.

Determine How the Injury Occurred

The history of the injury can be surmised from observation of what happened, the injured person's response as to what happened, or by witness response to the injury. If the injured is unconscious or semiconscious and no cause is determined, check for a medical alert identification tag.

Check Vital Signs

The HFI should determine the seriousness of the situation by checking vital signs: HR, breathing, BP, bleeding, and so on. The outcome of this evaluation will identify a course of action. The following describes a list of vital signs, how to monitor each, and a planned course of action to follow.

Level of consciousness. Is the individual conscious? If not, there may be a possible head, neck, or back injury. If unsure as to why the individual is unconscious, check for a medical alert identification tag. Assess airway, breathing, and circulation. DO NOT USE AMMONIA CAPSULES TO AROUSE.

If breathing has stopped and the individual is in a prone position, he or she should be log-rolled as carefully as possible, keeping the head, neck, and spine in the same relative position, to begin CPR techniques.

If the individual is unconscious but breathing, protect from further injury. Do not move unless the individual's life is in danger. Wait for medical assistance to arrive. Make a systematic evaluation of the entire body and perform necessary first aid procedures.

Respiration. Is the individual breathing? If not, establish an airway and administer artificial respiration. Summon medical help. The following will aid in determining the problem:

- Normal—12-20 breaths per minute
- Well-Trained Individuals—6-8 times per minute
- Shock—rapid, shallow respiration
- Airway Obstruction, Heart Disease, Pulmonary Disease—deep, gasping, labored breathing
- Lung Damage—frothy sputum with blood at the nose and mouth accompanied by coughing
- Diabetic Acidosis—alcohol or sweet, fruity odor
- Cessation of Breathing—note movement of abdomen and chest as well as airflow at nose and mouth

Pulse. Check pulse by using light finger pressure over an artery. The most common sites are the carotid, brachial, radial, and femoral pulses. If there is no pulse and the individual is unconscious, begin CPR.

Bleeding. Is the individual bleeding profusely? If so, control bleeding by elevating the body part, putting direct pressure over the wound, pressure points, and as a last resort, putting on a tourniquet. A TOURNIQUET SHOULD ONLY BE USED IN LIFE-THREATENING SITUATIONS IN WHICH CHOOSING TO RISK A LIMB IS A REASONABLE ACTION IN ORDER TO SAVE A LIFE. Treat for shock.

Blood pressure. BP is usually taken at the brachial artery with a blood pressure cuff and a sphygmomanometer. The following will aid in determining the problem:

- Normal—In men, systolic pressure, the pressure during the contraction phase of the heart, is equal to 100 plus the age of the individual up to 140-150 mm/hg; diastolic pressure, the pressure during the relaxation phase of the heart, is equal to 65-90 mm/hg. In females, both readings are generally 8-10 mm/hg lower.
- Severe Hemorrhage, Heart Attack—marked fall in blood pressure.
- Damage or Rupture of Vessels in the Arterial Circuit—abnormally high BP.
- Brain Damage—rise in systolic pressure with a stable or falling diastolic pressure.
- Heart Ailment—fall in systolic pressure with a rise in diastolic pressure.

Eye pupil size and response. Is there evidence of a head injury? This can be determined through a history of a blow to the head or a fall onto the head, deformity of the skull, loss of consciousness, clear or straw-colored fluid coming from the nose and/or ears, unequal pupil size, dizziness, loss of memory, and nausea. Prevent any unnecessary movement. If necessary to move, remove on a stretcher with the head elevated. If the individual is unconscious, assume that there is also a neck injury. Summon medical help immediately. The following will aid in determining the problem:

- Drug Addict or Nervous System Disorder—constricted
- Unconscious, Cardiac Arrest—dilated
- Head Injury—unequal size
- Disease, Poisoning, Drug Overdose, Injury—failure to react to light
- Death—widely dilated and failure to respond to light

Pain reaction. Is there evidence of a neck or back injury? The history of the injury may give a clue. Other indications of a possible neck or back injury include pain directly over the spine, burning or tingling in the extremities, and loss of muscle function or strength in the extremities. WHEN IN DOUBT, ASSUME THERE IS A NECK OR BACK INJURY. The following will aid in determining the problem:

- Probable Injury of Spinal Cord—numbness or tingling in the extremities
- Occlusion of a Main Artery—severe pain in the extremity with loss of cutaneous sensation; pulse is absent in the extremity
- Hysteria, Violent Shock, Excessive Drug or Alcohol Use—no pain

Although the following information lists the steps for artificial respiration and cardiopulmonary techniques for an adult only, the HFI should review current recommended techniques for all age categories: adults, children, and infants.

Artificial Respiration

If the HFI believes the person has stopped breathing, artificial respiration should be initiated. The following is a list of steps to use in the mouth-to-mouth resuscitation.

1. Determine responsiveness by shaking and shouting, "Are you okay?"
2. Call for help.
3. Open the airway by using a jaw thrust, head tilt, or chin lift.
4. Determine whether the victim is breathing. Listen and feel for air exchange. Look for chest movement.
5. If there is no breathing, give four quick, full ventilations using mouth-to-mouth or mouth-to-nose technique.
6. Determine if there is a pulse by checking the carotid artery.
7. Implement the emergency medical system—911.
8. If there is a pulse, ventilate once every 5 sec for an adult.
9. Assess the victim's condition after 1 min and approximately every 2-3 min thereafter.

One-Person CPR

If the HFI finds that breathing has stopped and there is no pulse, he or she should initiate CPR. The following outlines the steps for one-person CPR.

1. Determine responsiveness by shaking or shouting, "Are you okay?"
2. Call for help.
3. Open the airway by using a jaw thrust, head tilt, or chin lift.
4. Determine whether the victim is breathing. Listen and feel for air exchange. Look for chest movement.
5. Give four ventilations using mouth-to-mouth or mouth-to-nose technique.
6. Determine if there is a pulse by checking the carotid artery.
7. Implement the emergency medical system—911.
8. If there is no breathing and no pulse, give 15 compressions followed by 2 ventilations at a rate of 80 compressions per minute for an adult.
9. Assess the victim's condition after 1 min and every 2-3 min thereafter.

Two-Person CPR

If the HFI is doing one-person CPR and another CPR-trained individual appears, two-person CPR can be initiated. The following outlines the steps in two-person CPR.

1. Second rescuer states that he or she knows CPR and asks to assist. The second rescuer then takes a position at the head when the first rescuer moves down to give chest compressions.
2. Second rescuer checks for pulse while compressions are being given. This determines the effectiveness of compressions. The second rescuer then tells the first rescuer to stop compressions and checks again for a pulse.
3. If a pulse is found, respiration should be checked. If there is no respiration, continue ventilation only, once every 5 sec.
4. If there is no pulse, the second rescuer tells the first rescuer to continue CPR and then gives 1 ventilation.
5. The first rescuer follows the ventilation with 5 chest compressions at a rate of 60 per minute for an adult.
6. The second rescuer gives 1 ventilation after the last compression.
7. Assess the victim's condition after 1 min and every 2-3 min thereafter.

Summary

Certain inherent risks are associated with physical activity. The HFI should be aware of these risks and take steps to minimize them. Advanced planning, proper equipment and facilities, and appropriate exercise recommendations for the participant help to reduce the possibility of injury. These recommendations include participant evaluation, a graduated program of exercises with clear guidelines to follow, and an education program about signs and symptoms of injuries.

When injuries occur, there are clear steps to take to reduce the possibility of more trauma and to aid in the healing process. Rest, ice, compression, and elevation (RICE) are the four important steps associated with the immediate treatment of most skeletal/muscle/joint injuries. Heat is used in the later stages of acute injury and as a treatment for muscle soreness and chronic inflammatory conditions. A list of steps for the most common orthopedic injuries is provided.

Heat illness is potentially deadly, and the HFI must be aware of the steps to prevent its occurrence, and simultaneously, be able to recognize the signs of heat illness and act on them. Proper hydration, evaluated through a weight chart, is a good first step in prevention. Gradually acclimatizing the participants to the heat/humidity and reducing exposure in extreme heat/humidity are reasonable guidelines to follow to reduce the possibility of a problem.

The HFI should be able to deal with heart attacks and other emergencies by having a series of steps outlined that will be followed if an emergency occurs. Be prepared, remain calm, determine how the injury occurred, check vital signs, and if appropriate, administer artificial respiration or CPR. HFIs are cautioned to work within the limits of their qualifications to provide assistance and to not hesitate to refer a problem to appropriate professional health care services.

Suggested Reading for Chapter 14

American Academy of Orthopaedic Surgeons (1977)

American College of Sports Medicine (1975)

American Heart Association (1981)

American Red Cross (1981)

Anderson (1980)

D'Ambrosia and Drez (1982)

Darden (1976)

Fox and Mathews (1981)

Henderson (1973)

Klafs and Arnheim (1977)

Kuland (1982)

O'Donoghue (1984)

Williams (1980)

See reference list at the end of the book for a complete source listing.

Chapter 15

Administrative Concerns

- Responsibilities
- Issues
- Process that can be used
- Person and program protection

In small fitness programs the HFI may be in charge of administering the program, but in most cases a fitness or program director has the major administrative responsibilities. However, all staff personnel should have an understanding of the types of decisions that have to be made and the processes that are used by the program executive.

The key concept to administration is planning. Many different programs and management styles can be successful when carefully planned. On the other hand, almost nothing works well over the long-term without prior thought. This chapter deals with the items that need to be considered in establishing a long-range plan for a fitness center. The chapter is divided into two major sections. The first section deals with responsibilities that administrators normally have in any type of program and provides suggestions for how these can be handled. The second section deals with controversial issues that administrators face. Guidelines are presented that deal more with how the controversial questions are processed than with what the final outcome is.

Responsibilities

The program director is normally responsible for long-range planning; decisions about what specific classes will be offered, when, where, and for whom; the hiring and evaluation of personnel; budget; communications; and quality control.

Long-Range Goals

Any organization—private, public, for profit, or nonprofit—needs to clearly indicate what it wants to accomplish. The long-range plan includes what goals should be accomplished, what is needed to accomplish these goals, how the organization will move from where it is to where it wants to be, and what processes should be followed to implement the program. The Board of Directors (governing body) must approve the long-range plan. However, advisory committee(s) (key people in the community and in related groups), staff, and participants (consumers) should all have input concerning the long-range goals. The administrator facilitates the establishment of the long-range plan by working with the governing body to define the areas that should be addressed, seeking input by all related people and groups, and providing working drafts for reactions and revisions. The program director also helps the governing body set realistic time lines for the draft plan, get reactions, make modifications, and obtain final approval. The administrator implements the plan, including periodic evaluation. The HFI's role is to provide details concerning possible fitness programs that are consistent with the aims of the fitness center and will be popular with current and potential participants. The HFI works with the fitness director in determining appropriate equipment, facilities, scheduling, personnel, and supplies.

Personnel

The most important aspect of any program is the quality of the staff. The recruitment, hiring, support for, and evaluation of personnel to help achieve the organization's goals is extremely important, time consuming, and often sensitive.

Who is needed. The first question is what types of people are needed to carry out the program that has been planned. In fitness programs, staff personnel are needed who can present and supervise the fitness activities. A typical fitness center needs the following personnel:

Full time:

- Program Director
- HFI
- Educational Coordinator
- Secretary

Part time:

- Medical Advisor
- Fitness Leaders
- Nutritionist

Sample Job Description

GENERIC FITNESS PROGRAM

Health/Fitness Instructor

Qualifications

B.S. in Physical Education or related field (M.S. preferred)
ACSM Health/Fitness Instructor Certification
Experience in testing and leading exercise in adult fitness setting
Ability to relate to people with diverse backgrounds

Responsibilities

Administer physical fitness tests
Lead physical fitness exercise sessions
Work with Program Director in
  Scheduling fitness programs and staff
  Adding variety to fitness classes
  Training new staff members

Application Process

Send a letter of application, vita, and the names, addresses, and phone numbers of three references to

Dr. Drawde Yelwoh, Director
Generic Fitness Program
Yarbrogh, MI 22222

To ensure consideration for position, applications should be received by March 1, 1923.

Title and Starting Date

The Health/Fitness Instructor will begin September 1, 1923. The 12-month position includes 2 weeks of vacation and an excellent fringe benefit package. The salary will be within the range $17,500-$25,000, depending on qualifications.

Affirmative Action

The Generic Fitness Program encourages minority, female, and physically challenged candidates to apply for this position.

- Psychologist
- Physical Therapist
- Equipment Technician

Qualifications. A related question is What characteristics are desired for the staff? The qualifications include education, personal qualities, and professional competence. Include a realistic list of required and preferred qualifications (see Sample Job Description). For example, how much education is needed for each position. Requiring more than is needed or failing to require enough causes problems. For fitness programs, the appropriate ACSM cerfification can be useful in establishing minimum qualifications. Use the certification that matches the position. For example, the original certifications were aimed at postcardiac programs: people working with apparently healthy individuals do not need all of the competencies required for those working with postcardiac patients.

Working environment. Provide a good working environment and accurately describe the working conditions to prospective staff members. The physical environment should be safe, clean, cheerful, with functioning equipment, available supplies, and quick repairs when needed. The professional environment is one in which the expectations for each staff member are clearly described, and supervision is ample enough to assist professional growth and ensure quality performance. The psychological environment ensures that employees are valued, their input is solicited and welcomed, they are communicated with openly and honestly, and they have support for any problems that might arise.

Evaluation. A clear job description that is mutually understood provides the basis for periodic evaluations. The main purpose of the evaluation is to assist the staff member in improving himself or herself. However, the evaluation is also used to determine whether or not employees are retained in the position, and if so, what merit raises should be awarded. Evaluation of the HFI includes the content of the fitness program; the manner in which the program is conducted; rapport with fitness participants, other staff, and the fitness director; response to emergency and unusual situations; accurate collection and recording of test data; and prompt and professional manner of carrying out other assigned responsibilites. The Evaluation Checklist includes questions to be asked in an annual evaluation conference.

Program

Although the general types of experiences offered by the organization are determined prior to staff selection, the staff can assist in fine tuning the specific classes that will be offered to take advantage of the strengths of each staff member and provide the activities needed by the participants. Chapter 11 includes suggestions and examples of activities to be included in the fitness program.

Scheduling

Scheduling of personnel and facilities requires attention to the types of programs being offered, the desires of consumers for specific times, and the optimal work performance from staff. Priorities are established to ensure that the more important objectives receive the needed staff and facilities. Public relations is enhanced by making the facilities available to other groups (see Sample Form), although that is usually a lower priority. Guidelines have to be established to ensure that the top priority activities have adequate time.

Testing Procedures

Fitness participants should be tested to decide whether or not they should be excluded, can enter the program only with medical clearance, or can begin immediately (see chapter 2). For those people in the program, testing is important to determine the extent to which their individual objectives are being met. The test results can motivate participants to continue and provide the basis for activity modification. Fitness testing procedures are included in chapters 2, 5, 6, and 7.

Sample Evaluation Checklist

GENERIC FITNESS PROGRAM

Evaluation of a Health/Fitness Instructor

Attainment of Current Goals

Did the HFI

Adhere to Center procedures?

Make proper screening decisions?

Administer tests efficiently with accurate results and good records?

Provide appropriate content for the exercise sessions?

Conduct the sessions with enthusiasm?

Provide a variety of fitness activities?

Relate well with the clients?

Relate well with the staff?

Provide comprehensive training and supervision of new staff members?

Understand and carry out emergency procedures?

Make suggestions for improvement in all aspects of the Center's activities and procedures?

Make efforts to improve in identified areas of weakness?

Accomplish things not listed as specific goals for this year?

Evaluation of Past Activities

What responsibilities were carried out (be specific)

Very well?

Adequately, but could be improved?

Below expectations that must be corrected?

Future Goals

What responsibilities should be

Continued?

Added?

Deleted or handled by someone else?

What additional knowledge, skills, and so forth are needed? How will they be obtained?

How can the evaluation process be improved?

Sample Form for Use of Facility by Outside Group

GENERIC FITNESS CENTER

Use of Facility

Name of Group:

Person responsible for the group:

Name:

Phone:

Purpose for use of building:

Estimated number of participants:

Age range of participants:

Room(s) desired:

Date(s) & Time(s):	Date	Time
First choice:		
Second choice:		
Third choice:		

On behalf of the group desiring to lease a part of the Fitness Center, I have read and agree to follow the regulations for the building. Our group understands that the security deposit may be used for any damage that occurs as a result of our group's activities. In addition, we will reimburse the Generic Fitness Center for any damages that exceed the deposit.

____
Signed

____
Witness

____
Date

Criteria for Entry Into Program

All participants must be screened before they can be placed in appropriate fitness programs. Chapter 2 deals with criteria for admission to various programs. For example, people with known or suspected health problems are not allowed in fitness programs aimed to increase the positive health of apparently healthy people. The administrator ensures that the testing criteria for exclusion or referral is consistently applied and that the staff personnel leading activities are able to recognize signs and symptoms indicative of problems requiring special attention.

Informed Consent

Any fitness program should follow the informed consent procedures established to protect participants. Informed consent has several elements.

Clear description of program and procedures. The first component of informed consent is to clearly describe the fitness program and all of the procedures that will be used. This description should be in writing, and each individual should receive and read a copy. In addition, each person should be given an opportunity to have any questions answered.

Potential benefits and risks. The second element of this procedure, included in the written description of the program, is a list of the possible benefits and risks of such a program. The fitness benefits are extensive; however, the risk of certain kinds of injuries is increased (e.g., ankle, knee), and heart attacks do occasionally happen during or after exercise.

Voluntary participation with right to withdraw at any time. After reading the description of the program with the potential benefits and risks, the person signs the form indicating that he or she is participating voluntarily, with the provision that a test or any activity can be stopped at any time without penalty or coercion to continue.

Information is confidential. Finally, each individual's data is confidential unless permission is given to release it. People normally agree to have their test scores used in fitness reports and research, but these reports should be presented in such a manner that an individual's test score remains confidential. An exception to this guideline is using test scores to recognize people in newsletters or news releases—in these cases, permission should be obtained (and usually is granted) from the person before publishing the individual scores.

Sample form. A sample contest form that might be used in a fitness program is shown on the next page. Specific procedures need to be modified to fit the particular fitness testing and program.

Safety and Legal Concerns

The main concern for the fitness program is that it be conducted safely for everyone permitted to participate in the program. Fortunately, the same kinds of things done to make the program safe also help protect the program legally. Chapter 14 includes detailed procedures to prevent and deal with injuries and emergencies, including CPR procedures that are essential for all staff members who will be in contact with fitness participants.

Liability. The program and its staff have a responsibility to perform the procedures as described in a professional manner, watch for any danger signs that might indicate a problem, and take appropriate actions to stop the activity before problems occur. If problems do occur, take the appropriate actions to deal with minor problems and get immediate help for major problems. Professional organizations (e.g., AAHPERD, ACSM) have liability insurance available for individuals—staff members should be encouraged to have this type of insurance. In addition, the organization should include liability for the program and facilities in its insurance coverage.

Negligence. No amount of informed consent procedures can justify negligence. Participants and areas need supervision. Staff personnel need training in appropriate emergency procedures. This supervision and these emergency procedures need to be followed. Failure to do so, or failure to act in a manner fitting a fitness professional, constitutes negligence. If injury or death occurs as a result

Sample Consent Form

GENERIC FITNESS PROGRAM

Informed Consent for Physical Fitness Test

In order to more safely carry on an exercise program, I hereby consent, voluntarily, to exercise tests. I shall perform a graded exercise test by riding a cycle ergometer or walking/running on a treadmill. Exercise will begin at a low level and be advanced in stages. The test may be stopped at any time because of signs of fatigue. I understand that I may stop the test at any time because of my feelings of fatigue or discomfort or for any other personal reason.

I understand that the risks of this testing procedure may include disorders of heart beats, abnormal blood pressure response, and, very rarely, a heart attack. I further understand that selection and supervision of my test is a matter of professional judgment.

I also understand that skinfold measurements will be taken at (number) sites to determine percentage of body fat and that I will complete a sit and reach test and a 60-sec sit-up test to evaluate factors related to low-back function.

I desire such testing so that better advice regarding my proposed exercise program may be given to me, but I understand that the testing does not entirely eliminate risk in the proposed exercise program.

I understand that information from my tests may be used for reports and research publications. I understand that my identity will not be revealed.

I understand that I can withdraw my consent or discontinue participation in any aspect of the fitness testing or program at any time without penalty or prejudice toward me.

I have read the statement above and have had all of my questions answered to my satisfaction.

____
Signed

____
Witness

____
Date

(Copy for participant and for program records.)

of the negligence, then the leader and program are legally liable.

Consent. Although getting the participant's consent does not prevent legal actions or protect against negligence, it does indicate that the program is concerned with the participant and has acted in good faith.

Safety procedures. These procedures include regular checks of the equipment and facilities and periodic reviews of the procedures used by the staff both in testing and in the classes. Records showing when the review, training, and practice were carried out should be kept in the central office.

Emergency procedures. A written emergency procedure is established and staff members are trained to carry out the procedure. Local emergency services to be used are contacted to help establish the procedure and comprehend and agree with the procedure that is to be followed. The sample form can be modified for a specific situation.

Budget

The budget is one aspect of long-range planning. The Sample Budget Process includes the steps in setting the budget.

Third-party payments. Insurance companies have always been interested in health by providing health education, supporting research, and providing payment for treatment of health problems (e.g., postcardiac rehabilitation programs). More recently, they have offered incentives for healthy behaviors such as lower premiums for nonsmokers and cash paybacks for people who did not use the medical for a set period of time. Unfortunately, the insurance companies, for the most part, still do not provide payment for preventive programs. With increasing evidence of the health benefits of fitness programs emphasizing a variety of healthy behaviors, the program director should approach insurance companies with proposals for third-party payment for some of the services and for premium incentives for people engaging in healthy behaviors.

Personnel. The biggest part of the budget involves salary and benefits for the staff. Relatively high base salaries and benefits, with regular increments based on evaluations, can assist the program in employing people with better qualifications. An attractive salary and benefit package results in higher job satisfaction, higher quality performance, and a lower turnover rate. Administrators attempting to economize in terms of staff salaries, benefits, and raises often find out that it is false economy.

Facilities. There is a regular and ongoing expense in terms of insurance, maintenance, and repair of facilities. People are often tempted to ignore regular maintenance and repair, but keeping the facilities in good shape is more economical than incurring major expenses as a result of not having done so. New or expanded facilties are usually handled in a separate fund-raising campaign and are not part of the normal budget process.

Equipment. Equipment should be available so participants may accomplish their goals; this equipment should be kept in good repair. However, programs often go beyond what is needed in terms of equipment. For a beginning program, exercise tests can be done without the most expensive treadmill. Gas analysis equipment, necessary for many research projects, is a luxury for a beginning fitness program. Much of the muscular strength and endurance needed for fitness can be gained with strength exercises with minimal weights, thus expensive resistive exercise machines are not needed. Many program administrators use nice-looking equipment to sell their programs, when the fitness benefits might be accomplished better with activities requiring very little equipment supervised by qualified personnel. Some testing equipment is needed, but once again, inexpensive items are often satisfactory for the essential fitness tests.

Supplies. The supplies for the testing equipment and for the participant's use of the facilities must be kept in stock, with a procedure for identifying what is needed. Normally, one person is designated to be in charge of checking supplies on a regular basis. Other staff members report

Sample Emergency Procedures

GENERIC FITNESS CENTER

Cardiac Emergency

1. Do NOT move the victim, except to try to get him or her into a lying position
2. Check for breathing and pulse; if absent, begin CPR immediately
3. Call, or have someone call the Emergency Room at (name) Hospital, (phone number) , ext. (number) .
4. Read the statement above the phone to the person:

(Statement to be posted by all phones:)
This is (name) at the (name) Fitness Center. We have a cardiac emergency, please send an ambulance to the (name) Street entrance of the (name) building, at (address) .

5. Send someone to get Dr. (name) , whose schedule is posted by the phone (this is for the Centers that have medical personnel on the site).
6. Continue CPR until medical personnel arrive, then follow their instructions.

Other Serious Accidents or Injuries

For any of the following:

Airway problems of any type
Unconsciousness
Head injury
Bleeding from ear, nose, or mouth
Neck or back injuries
Limb injury with obvious deformity
Severe chest pains

1. Do NOT move the person, except to try to get him or her into a lying position, with feet elevated (unless you suspect back injuries).
2. Contact ambulance and medical personnel—same as cardiac emergencies.
3. Treat for shock
4. Control bleeding

Other Injuries or Accidents

1. Do not allow a sick or injured person to sit, stand, or walk until you are sure that his or her condition warrants it.
2. Do not encourage a person who is "feeling bad" to begin or continue working-out.
3. Check on people who have questionable symptoms in the locker room.
4. For less serious injuries, a first aid kit is available at (place) .

As soon as the situation is under control, inform (person) about the accident, complete accident report, and turn into (name or place) within 24 hr.

Your suggestions for improving these instructions and the emergency procedures are welcome—talk to (name) .

Sample Budget Process

GENERIC FITNESS CENTER

---

1. What are the purposes of your program?
2. Describe the current program.
3. What are your current expenditures:
   - A. Personnel
   - B. Facilities
     - (1) Loan repayment
     - (2) Insurance
     - (3) Maintenance and repairs
     - (4) Utilities
     - (5) Taxes
   - C. Supplies
   - D. Other
4. What is your current income:
   - A. Membership
   - B. Insurance
   - C. Gifts
   - D. Investments
   - E. Other
5. A. What changes should be made in your program (e.g., classes, workshops, personnel, facilities, equipment, renovation, repair) over the next 5 years?
   - B. For each of these changes, indicate the change in cost and potential income.
   - C. Can the changes be phased in logical steps?
6. A. What are potential sources of increased revenue?
   - B. What is needed to achieve this increased revenue?
   - C. How much will it cost to secure the additional funding?
   - D. What will be the net increase for each potential source of money?
7. What is a reasonable estimate for income for each year over the next 5 years?
8. What aspects of the program can be supported with this income for each year?
9. If the income exceeds expectations, what additional aspects of the program should be added?
10. If the income falls short of expectations, what aspects of the program can be reduced or eliminated?

potential shortages to this one person. Guidelines for ordering equipment and supplies are found in Table 15.1.

Financial management. Careful inventory, assessment of needs, and a balance among personnel, equipment, facilities, and other expenses provide the maximum service for the minimum costs.

Communication

One of the traits of the successful administrator is the quality of communication at all levels.

Staff. Open and honest communication is essential so that staff personnel know what is expected and how they are evaluated. The staff personnel need to feel appreciated and encouraged to try to find better ways of accomplishing the goals. Many advances in organizations come from staff personnel who are encouraged to help find better ways to improve the content and procedures of the program.

Participants. The consumers need basic information concerning what the fitness program can (and cannot) do for them; with periodic progress reports and educational information to enhance their positive health knowledge and status. Mini lectures during warm-up, bulletin boards, and newsletters all have been used to help educate participants. Make the information accurate, brief, and to the point.

Public. Fitness programs have a responsibility to help educate the public concerning positive health—its definition, components, and recommendations for its achievement. Share the effects of fitness programs on health, with corresponding benefits for the family, community, and work performance, via the mass media and with interested groups such as local industry.

Records

Careful, systematic collection of personal and testing information, properly recorded and filed provides the basis for much of the communication with the board, staff, and participants. In addition, this information can be used to evaluate the effectiveness of various programs and the extent that the long-range goals are being met. Keep records of staff training, including a demonstration of competence in emergency and safety procedures.

Data entry, storage, and retrieval. What information is needed? How is it obtained? What forms are used? Where is the information stored? How is it retrieved? When is it used? Who evaluates particular programs? Address these questions prior to the beginning of the program. After a reasonable amount of time working with the procedure, reevaluate it to determine if modifications would make it better.

Accident/injury reports. A sample form is provided here that can be used to keep a record of all accidents and injuries. Be sure to follow up

Table 15.1 Guidelines for Ordering Equipment and Supplies

Generic Fitness Center
1. Follow established purchasing procedures
2. Order early
3. Order on the basis of accurate inventory and estimate of needs. Include replacement of old equipment, new equipment, and supplies for all programs.
4. Buy from suppliers who have a record of good service.
5. Each year, ask all involved personnel in the process to make suggestions to improve the system.

Sample Accident/Injury Form

1. ________________________________ ________________
   Name of victim Date

2. Describe, in detail, the nature of the injury or health problem:

3. Describe, in detail, how the accident occurred:

4. List, in order, the things you or other staff members did in response to the incident:

5. Describe any problems encountered in dealing with the situation:

6. List the names of people who witnessed the accident or emergency procedures being performed:

Turn in this form, within 24 hr of accident, to (name or place) .

Your suggestions concerning safety, emergency procedures, and/or this form are welcome; please talk to (name) .

to be sure that the individual is recovering. The completed form provides a check on whether staff personnel used appropriate emergency procedures; it is essential in case there are questions raised about a particular incident.

Evaluation

Evaluation has been mentioned throughout this chapter. A value judgment should be based on the best data available concerning the extent to which the program objectives are being reached. How many people are included in the fitness program? What kind of body composition, CRF, and low-back function changes have been made? Do the participants enjoy the activities? How many drop-outs were there? Why? How many injuries? Why? What can be done to help more people make better fitness gains, and decrease the number of drop-outs and injuries? Are some staff members better than others in some of these areas? What can be done to help staff personnel maintain their strengths and improve in their weak areas?

Quality

The most important element of a program is setting up procedures to try to ensure a high standard of quality in all information, personal contact, and activities that are conducted in the name of the fitness program. One aspect of establishing high standards is to ensure the inclusiveness of the program. All people should feel welcome in the program regardless of gender, ethnic background, or social class. The administrator can do several things to achieve this atmosphere: (a) have a staff with varied backgrounds; (b) train the staff to be sensitive to people from different backgrounds; (c) schedule programs at convenient times and places; (d) contact various groups within the community; (e) provide ways for people with low income to participate; and (f) make it clear that inappropriate (e.g., sexist or racist) comments or actions by staff members or participants will not be tolerated.

Issues

The first part of this chapter has dealt with typical administrative responsibilities. Although there will be slight variations in the way these responsibilities are carried out, there is wide agreement concerning both the importance of the responsibilities and the manner by which they are discharged. The second part of the chapter deals with more controversial questions and issues that must be resolved in organizations. There are valid differences of opinion concerning what should be done, and how it should be accomplished. Increasing attention is being paid to these questions in the literature both in terms of administrative theory and managerial practice. Each administrator is encouraged to consider these issues and work with appropriate people to establish consistent behavior—the basis for which is clearly communicated with people related to and affected by the program. The HFI in larger fitness centers is in a middle-management-type position under the program director and is the administrator to some of the staff members working in the fitness programs.

Administrative Behavior

Many early administration textbooks characterized the way an administrator dealt with problems as authoritarian, democratic, or laissez-faire. Recent writings in administrative theory deal with different styles of management (e.g., theory X, Y, or Z). In both cases, the inference is that an administrator adopts one basic style of behavior and employs it in all situations. One of the insights that Mosston (1966) provided about teaching—that the good teacher is one who has the ability to use many different teaching styles, depending on the situation—can be applied to administrative behaviors. Table 15.2 illustrates some of the issues that any kind of organization faces, with suggestions concerning the appropriate roles and behaviors for the governing board, administrator, staff, and participants (consumers). It would, for example, be very inefficient to use indirect behavior to help staff and participants "discover" the safety and emergency procedures. Although suggestions concerning ways to improve the procedures are welcomed and encouraged, the basic procedures are communicated directly with all concerned. On the other hand, it would not be effective to announce what each person's fitness interests are and to force everyone into the same

Table 15.2 Administrative Behaviors

Responsible Group/ Person	Basic Values	Routine Procedure	Fitness Activity	Performance
Policy board	Set	Approve	Set guidelines	Set guidelines
Administrator	Implement	Recommend	Set general program	Provide general opportunities
Staff	Know/ implement	Suggest changes	Implement and suggest changes	Work with participants to set up
Participant	Understand	Know	Follow/suggest changes	Help set up activities

type of program. In that case, the more time-consuming, indirect process of working with individuals to outline the basic goals of their individual fitness and performance programs is appropriate.

Staff Behavior

The HFI usually works directly under a particular administrator. Thus the staff behavior in Table 15.2 applies to the relationship between the HFI and the administrator above and directly with the fitness participants. In general, as a staff member, the HFI tries to understand the general aims, policies, and procedures so he or she can make suggestions for possible improvements; help make decisions about specific fitness personnel and programs; work with fitness participants to provide the services; and evaluate the program's effectiveness.

Responsibility to Individuals, Profession, and Society

These responsibilities do not seem to be issues, at first glance. However, the needs of the individual, profession, and society are different, and attempting to meet these needs can sometimes lead to conflict. One of the most important needs for society in general is to have results of carefully controlled research projects that prove the best ways to test and improve components of fitness. If that were the only concern, all kinds of individuals would be tested on a variety of tests to determine exactly how much risk there is for various types of people on different tests, rather than automatically screening out people at high risk. The fitness programs would be strictly regimented; some people would be assigned to no-exercise control groups so the effects of specific fitness activities could be more precisely determined.

In terms of responsibility to the profession, programs would not be offered until all staff personnel were properly educated and had appropriate certifications. People interested in the field would be screened, so that only the number that were needed in the market would receive the training, and there would not be duplication of efforts with more fitness programs than needed in any area. The fitness programs would charge enough to pay professional wages and provide recommended facilities and equipment.

It should be obvious from the preceding description of what could be done for society and the profession, that a primary concern for individuals would provide some conflicts. With the individual put first, the programs are tailor-made and varied for all who want to become fit, making it impossible to determine exactly what aspect of the program produced what result. Presently, programs are made available to people at minimum costs and in convenient locations, sometimes causing less than ideal conditions for the program and the staff.

Balance Among Goals

It might appear that this is an impossible situation that causes the fitness program to choose one important goal while ignoring other goals equally deserving. Yet each center wants to be responsible to society, the profession, and individuals. The aim is to provide a balance among these goals.

Describing this balance exactly is not possible because each center has to define its own relative contribution to society, the profession, and individuals. One aspect of the balance is that different centers have relatively more emphasis in some areas and less in others. Another implied necessity is communication and cooperation within a fitness profession. Many centers cannot provide basic research with extensive testing and random assignment of diverse subjects to a variety of fitness programs; however, each center can keep careful records of what activities are done via self-report of outside activities and health behaviors and periodic test results. Analysis of these data can help set up hypotheses to be tested at the more research-oriented centers. The research results can be used to suggest modifications in the more individual-oriented centers. All centers can strive to upgrade the professional competence of the staff and provide the highest quality program possible, with a reasonable fee schedule.

Another responsibility is to individuals in the society who cannot pay the going rate or cannot take off the required time in the middle of the day. Centers need to find ways to secure funds to provide part of the fees for people with low income and to schedule classes at places and times convenient for all people within a community.

Fitness and Performance

The most important goal is to help every individual in our society obtain a high level of physical fitness. Many individuals who do achieve a reasonable fitness level want a variety of performance opportunities. Other aspects of the book have cautioned against including performance-type activities too early in a program. It has also been pointed out that individuals have unique interests—some want to concentrate on one activity, while others like a variety. The HFI must be careful to provide an atmosphere where individual choices are available without undue pressure toward one type of preference. For example, perhaps a person wants to extend his or her running to more than 15 mi per week and wants to participate in various sorts of road races with distances ranging from 3 to 100 mi. That interest has taken the fitness activity of running (10-15 mi per week) into running performance, which is fine for interested individuals, but should *not* be held up as some sort of ultimate fitness activity, nor should everyone in the program feel pressured into moving up to those levels. Others enjoy various sports, such as soccer or racquetball. Once again, fitness levels can be maintained using some vigorous sports, but these are not right for everyone. To reiterate, the main purpose is to have people work slowly up to the energy equivalent of jogging 3 mi at THR four times per week and practice stretching and strengthening activities for the midtrunk. Once this fitness level is obtained, then work with individuals to set up activities that will ensure their continuation of an active lifestyle.

Summary

The key to administration is planning. Long-range goals need to be established with input from staff, participants, and the community. The most important aspect of any program is the quality of the staff. Qualified individuals should be selected to do the expected tasks, and they should be evaluated on a regular basis. Scheduling of personnel and facilities revolves around the type of program being offered. Testing procedures need to be established, and the criteria for entry into the program must be followed. Participants should sign an informed consent form prior to entry into the program. The HFI needs to understand liability and the concept of negligence.

The budget should include realistic estimates of income and expected expenditures for personnel, facilities, equipment, and supplies. Records of testing procedures, activity schedules of the participants, informed consent forms, and so forth need to be filed for later reference. Accidents and injuries should be recorded on a special form and reported. The form should be filed for any follow-up. Administrators must also deal with issues related to administrative style and the responsibility of the program to the individual, profession, and society.

Suggested Reading for Chapter 15

Baun and Baun (1984)

Bayless and Adams (1985)

Ben-Sira (1982)

Bowers (1976)

Chenoweth (1983)

Cooper and Collingwood (1984)

D'Aprix (1982)

Donoghue (1977)

Drucker (1980)

Fielding (1982)

Filley (1975)

Gibbins, Cooper, Meyer, and Ellison (1980)

Goodman et al. (1982)

Haskell (1978)

Marcotte and Price (1983)

Mosston (1966)

Peters and Waterman (1982)

Pigors and Myers (1977)

Reinertsen (1983)

Roszak (1978)

Shephard, Corey, and Cox (1982)

Shephard, Cox, and Corey (1981)

Shephard, Corey, Renzland, and Cox (1982)

Sheppard and Carroll (1980)

Thompson, Stern, Williams, Duncan, Haskell, and Wood (1979)

Vuori, Makarainen, and Jaaselainen (1978)

Waller and Robert (1980)

Wright (1982)

See reference list at the end of the book for a complete source listing.

Appendix A

ACSM Preventive Tract: Core Behavioral Objectives

Exercise Physiology

Define aerobic and anaerobic metabolism in terms of energy expenditure. (chp. 10)

Describe the role of carbohydrates, fats, and protein as fuels for anaerobic and aerobic performance. (chp. 5)

Describe the normal cardiorespiratory responses to an exercise bout in terms of heart rate, blood pressure, and oxygen consumption. Describe how these responses change with adaptation to chronic exercise training and how men and women may differ in response. (chp. 3)

Define and explain the relationship of METs and Kilocalories to physical activity. (chp. 10)

Describe the heart rate and blood pressure responses to static (isometric), dynamic (isotonic), and isokinetic exercise. (chp. 3)

Define and explain the concept of specificity of exercise conditioning. (chp. 9)

Describe how heart rate is determined by pulse palpation. List precautions in the application of these techniques. (chp. 6)

Calculate predicted maximal heart rate for various ages. (chp. 9)

Define the following terms: ischemia (chp. 12), angina pectoris (chp. 12), premature ventricular contraction (chp. 12), premature atrial contraction (chp. 12), tachycardia (chp. 12), bradycardia (chp. 12), myocardial infarction (chp. 12), Valsalva maneuver (chp. 7), hyperventilation (chp. 3), oxygen consumption (chp. 3), cardiac output (chp. 3), stroke volume (chp. 3), lactic acid (chp. 3), hypertension (chp. 2), high density lipoprotein cholesterol (HDL-C) (chp. 5), total cholesterol/high density lipoprotein cholesterol ratio (chp. 5), anemia (chp. 5), bulimia (chp. 5), and anorexia nervosa (chp. 5).

Describe blood pressure responses associated with changes in different body positions. (chp. 3)

Describe the purpose and function of an electrocardiogram. (chp. 12)

Identify the physiological principles related to warm-up and cool-down. (chp. 9)

Identify the physiological principles related to muscular endurance and strength training: define overload, specificity, use-disuse, progressive resistance. (chp. 7)

Define muscular atrophy, hypertrophy, hyperplasia, concentric and eccentric contractions, sets, and repetition. (chp. 7)

Describe the common theories of muscle fatigue and delayed muscle soreness. (chp. 7)

Describe the muscle stretch reflex. (chp. 7)

Nutrition and Weight Management

Give the recommended ranges for percent body fat (male and female). (chp. 5)

Contrast the effectiveness of diet plus exercise, diet alone, or exercise alone for fat loss or body composition changes. (chp. 5)

Define the following terms: obesity, overweight, underweight, percent fat, and lean body mass. (chp. 5)

Describe the procedures for maintaining normal hydration at times of heavy sweating; contrast plain water replacement with the use of special electrolyte drinks. (chp. 14)

Explain the concept of energy balance as it relates to weight control. (chp. 5)

Explain the difference between fat and water soluble vitamins and the potential risk of toxicity with oversupplementation. (chp. 5)

Discuss the inappropriate use of salt tablets, diet pills, protein powders, liquid protein diets, and nutritional supplements. (chp. 5)

Discuss the misconceptions of spot reduction and rapid weight loss. (chp. 5)

Be familiar with the Dietary Goals recommended by the Senate Select Committee on Nutrition and Human Needs and the exchange lists of the American Dietetic Association. (chp. 5)

Identify the basic four food groups and give examples of each. (chp. 5)

Describe the interaction of diet and/or exercise as they relate to the blood lipid profile. (chp. 5)

Exercise Programming

Given a case study containing the following information: health history, risk factors, medical information, and results of a fitness evaluation, the candidate will be able to:

A. Use these data for recommending appropriate exercise based on proper intensity (training heart rate), duration, frequency, progression, type of physical activity, and whether exercise is to be performed in a supervised or unsupervised program. (chp. 9)

B. Modify an exercise program (i.e., intensity and duration) under such environmental conditions as cold, heat, humidity, and altitude. (chp. 9)

C. Describe the importance of flexibility and recommend proper exercises for improving range of motion of all major joints. Describe the difference between static and dynamic (ballistic) stretching. (chp. 7)

D. Describe and demonstrate appropriate exercise used in warm-up and cool-down. (chps. 9, 11)

E. Describe and demonstrate exercises for the improvement of muscular strength and endurance. (chp. 7)

F. Describe the difference between interval and continuous training. (chp. 9)

G. Describe the relationship of the heart rate response to physical activity and perceived exertion. Demonstrate various methods for monitoring physical effort such as heart rate, blood pressure, and perceived exertion. (chp. 6)

H. Describe the signs and symptoms of overexercising that would indicate the need to decrease the intensity, duration, or frequency of an exercise session. (chp. 14)

Explain the effects of the following categories of substances on exercise responses: beta blockers, nitroglycerin, diuretics, antihypertensives, antihistamines, tranquilizers, alcohol, diet pills, cold tablets, illicit drugs, and caffeine. (chp. 12)

Explain appropriate modifications in exercise programs due to acute illness (such as colds), and controlled conditions (such as diabetes, chronic obstructive pulmonary diseases, allergies, hypertension, and cardiovascular disease) that a physician might recommend for your exercising client. (chp. 9)

Emergency Procedures

Possess current cardiopulmonary (CPR) certification or equivalent credentials. (chp. 14)

Demonstrate an understanding of appropriate emergency procedures (i.e., telephone procedures, preconceived written emergency plan, and personnel responsibilities). (chps. 14, 15)

Understand basic first aid procedures for heat cramps, heat exhaustion, heat stroke, lacerations, incisions, puncture wound, abrasion, contusion, simple-compound fractures, bleeding/shock, hypoglycemia/hyperglycemia, sprains/strains, and fainting. (chp. 14)

Health Appraisal and Fitness Evaluation Techniques

Demonstrate knowledge of health history appraisal to obtain information on past and present medical history, prescribed medication, activity patterns, nutritional habits, stress and anxiety levels, family history of heart disease, smoking history, and alcohol and illicit drug use. (chp. 2)

Demonstrate the ability to interview individuals on health hazards such as positive family history, chest pain/chest discomfort, orthopedic limitations, and present activity levels. (chp. 2)

Demonstrate the ability to measure pulse rate accurately both at rest and during exercise. (chp. 6)

Describe appropriate tests for assessment of cardiovascular fitness. (chp. 6)

Identify the difference between maximal and submaximal cardiovascular evaluations. (chp. 6)

Describe appropriate tests for assessment of muscular strength, muscular endurance, and flexibility assessment. (chp. 7)

Identify appropriate criteria for discontinuing a fitness evaluation. (chp. 6)

Identify techniques used to determine body composition. (chp. 5)

Identify the needs for retest evaluations for participants in exercise programs and the appropriate time intervals for reevaluation. (chp. 9)

Exercise Leadership

A. Describe an organizational plan for facilities equipment, and consumable supplies for an exercise program. (chp. 15)

B. Describe considerations involved in scheduling events and staff. (chp. 15)

C. Identify factors related to efficient data entry, storage, retrieval, and feedback to participants, physicians, and other involved persons. (chp. 15)

D. Implement evaluation procedures of testing, exercise, and patient education programs. (chp. 15)

Explain appropriate modifications in the exercise program due to musculoskeletal problems (e.g., arthritis, overweight, chondromalacia, and lower back discomfort). (chps. 7, 11, 14)

Describe the components of an exercise class or session from the time the participant enters until the end of the class. (chps. 9, 11)

Describe appropriate exercise apparel for a variety of activities and environmental conditions. (chp. 11)

Describe methods to establish appropriate exercise intensity. (chp 9)

Identify inappropriate exercise responses that would indicate termination of the exercise session. (chp. 9)

Describe the myths and dangers pertaining to body composition changes and/or improved fitness in relation to the following: saunas, vibrating belts, body wraps, electric muscle stimulators (legal implications), and sweat suits. (chp. 5)

Describe the dangers and precautions of the following exercises: straight leg sit ups, double leg raises, full squats, hurdlers stretch exercise, plough exercise, back hyperextension, and standing straight leg toe touch. (chp. 7)

Human Behavior/Psychology

Given a series of hypothetical situations involving exercise program participants, the candidate will:

A. Describe the appropriate motivational counseling, behavioral techniques, and teaching techniques used in conducting exercise and promoting lifestyle changes. (chp. 13)

B. Describe how to manage the group facilitator, comedian, chronic complainer, and disruptor.

C. Define each of the following terms: behavior modification, reinforcement, goal setting, motivation, social support, and peer group pressure. (chp. 13)

D. Describe factors affecting the learning process by use of part-whole and progressive learning theories. (chp. 13)

Demonstrate and describe an understanding of counseling skills to motivate an individual to begin an exercise program, enhance exercise adherence, and return to regular exercise. (chp. 13)

Human Development/Aging

Describe the natural changes that occur from childhood through adolescence and aging in the following: skeletal muscle, bone structure, maximal oxygen uptake, grip strength, flexibility, heart rate, and body composition. (chps. 3, 4, 5, 7, 9)

Identify common orthopedic problems of the adolescent and older participant and explain how an exercise program could be modified to avoid aggravation of these problems. (chps. 7, 9, 14)

Identify the predominant psychological factors involved in the aging process. (chp. 8)

Describe the physiological effects of the following factors across the age range: smoking, hypertension, obesity, stress, substance abuse, and chronic and acute exercise. (chps. 3, 5, 8)

Functional Anatomy and Kinesiology

Explain the properties and function of bone muscle and connective tissue. (chp. 4)

Describe the basic anatomy of the heart, cardiovascular system, and respiratory system. (chp. 12)

Identify major bones and muscle groups. (chp. 4)

Describe the action of major muscle groups (e.g., trapezius, pectoralis major, latissimus dorsi, biceps, triceps, abdominals, erector spinae, gluteus maximus, quadriceps, hamstrings, gastrocnemius, and tibialis anterior). (chp. 4)

Define the following terms: shin splints, tennis elbow, stress fracture, bursitis and tendonitis, supination, pronation, flexion, extension, adduction, abduction, and hyperextension. (chps. 4, 14)

Explain the use of rest, cold, compression, and elevation in the initial treating of athletic injuries. (chp. 14)

Discuss the application of heat in the long-term treatment of athletic injuries. (chp. 14)

Explain low back syndrome and describe exercises used to prevent this problem. (chp. 7)

Risk Factor Identification

Identify primary and secondary risk factors for coronary heart disease that may be favorably modified by regular and appropriate physical activity habits. (chp. 1)

Identify major risk factors that may require further consideration prior to participation in physical activity habits. (chps. 1, 2)

Be familiar with the plasma cholesterol levels for various ages as recommended by the National Institutes of Health Consensus Statement.

Identify the following cardiovascular risk factors or conditions that may require consultation with medical or allied health professionals prior to participation in physical activity or prior to a major increase in physical activity intensities and habits: inappropriate resting, exercise, and recover HR and BPs; new discomfort or changes in the pattern of discomfort in the chest area, neck, shoulder, or arm with exercise or at rest; heart murmurs; myocardial infarction; fainting or dizzy spells, claudication, and ischemia. (chp. 2)

Identify the following respiratory risk factors that may require consultation with medical or allied health professionals prior to participation in physical activity or prior to major increases in physical activity intensities and habits: extreme breathlessness after mild exertion or during sleep; asthma; exercise-induced asthma; bronchitis; and emphysema. (chps, 2, 9)

Identify the following metabolic risk factor that may require consultation with medical or allied health professionals prior to participation in physical activity or prior to major increases in physical activity intensities and habits; body weight more than 20% above optimal; thyroid diseases; and diabetes. (chps. 2, 5, 9)

Identify the following musculoskeletal risk factors that may require consultation with medical or allied health professionals prior to physical activity or prior to major increases in physical activity intensities and habits: osteoarthritis, rheumatoid arthritis; low back pain, and prosthesis-artificial joints. (chps. 2, 7)

Health/Fitness Instructor: Behavioral Objectives

Exercise Physiology

Describe the primary difference between aerobic and anaerobic metabolism and their relative importance in exercise programs. (chp 3)

Define the properties of cardiac muscle, the generation of the action potential, and normal pathways of conduction. (chp. 12)

Identify and describe the relationship between resting values and the normal response to increasing work intensity (i.e., heart rate [HR], stroke volume [SV], cardiac output [Q], arteriovenous O_2 difference [a-v O_2 diff], O_2 uptake [$\dot{V}O_2$], systolic and diastolic blood pressure [SBP, DBP], minute ventilation [V_E], tidal volume [TV], and breathing frequency [f]). (chp. 3)

Define and explain the concept of the Metabolic Equivalent Unit (MET) and Kcal. Calculate the energy cost in METs and Kcal for given exercise intensities in stepping exercise, bicycle ergometry, and during horizontal and grade walking and running. (chp. 10)

Identify MET equivalents for various sport, recreational, and work tasks. (chp. 10)

Explain the difference in the cardiorespiratory responses to static (isometric) exercise compared with dynamic (isotonic) exercise; include possible hazards of isometric exercise for sedentary or asymptomatic adults. (chps. 3, 7)

Explain the specificity of conditioning and the physiological differences among cardiorespiratory, endurance, and muscular strength conditioning. (chps. 3, 6, 7, 9)

Describe and demonstrate acceptable laboratory and field exercise test protocols from which functional capacity or $\dot{V}O_2$max determinations or estimations may be obtained. (chps. 3, 6)

Define the following terms: apnea, dyspnea, hyperemia, respiratory alkalosis and acidosis, hypoxia, orthostatic hypotension, arterial pressures, calorimetry, hyperpnea, and hypoventilation. (chps. 3, 10)

Describe the physiological implications of active and passive warm-up and cool-down. (chp. 9)

Describe the energy continuum with reference to aerobic and anaerobic metabolism during various intensities of work. (chps. 3, 10)

Describe the implications of anaerobic threshold in physical conditioning programs.

Define and demonstrate reciprocal innervation and its relationship to proprioceptive neuromuscular facilitation (PNF). (chp. 7)

Discuss the physical and psychological signs of overtraining.

Define the properties of skeletal muscle. (chp. 4)

Nutrition and Weight Control

Identify guidelines for caloric intake for an individual desiring to lose or gain weight. (chp. 5)

Calculate ideal body weight based upon body composition evaluation of lean body weight and fat weight. (chp. 5)

Exercise Programming

Describe and discuss the advantages/disadvantages and the implementation of interval and continuous conditioning programs. (chp. 9)

Describe the most effective methods for accurate monitoring of exercise heart rate and physical effort and demonstrate specific functional evaluations. (chps. 6, 9, 10)

Describe the precautions taken before exposure to or in preparation for altitude, different ambient temperatures, and humidities. (chp. 9)

Describe and demonstrate specific flexibility exercises for inclusion in a warm-up program. (chps. 7, 11)

Describe and design the use and implementation of circuit training program in a health enhancement program.

Describe special precautions and modifications of exercise programming for special populations (i.e., diabetics and arthritics). (chp. 9)

Emergency Procedures

Teach the principles and techniques used in cardiopulmonary resuscitation. (chp. 14)

Demonstrate the emergency procedures, equipment, and materials needed during exercise testing, fitness evaluations, and exercise sessions. (chps. 14, 15)

Discuss the individual responsibility and legal implications related to emergency care. (chp. 15)

Design and update emergency procedures for a preventive exercise program. (chp. 15)

Identify emergency drugs that should be available during exercise testing and demonstrate ability to assist a physician during an emergency situation.

Exercise Leadership

Identify and describe possible causes and intervention techniques regarding common orthopedic problems associated with physical activity and adaptations required in exercise prescription: Include myositis ossificans, shin splints, tennis elbow, bursitis, stress fracture, lordosis, tendonitis, contusion, and osteoporosis. (chp. 14)

Human Behavior/Psychology

Describe psychological and physiological responses to stressful situations. Discuss stress management techniques to elicit relaxation. (chps. 8, 13)

Define or describe each of the following terms in relation to the management of an exercise program: aggression, hostility, denial, identification, operant conditioning, rapport, anxiety, empathy, fear, rationalization, relaxation, euphoria, depression, and rejection. (chp. 8)

Human Development/Aging

List the differences in conditioning older versus younger participants. (chp. 9)

Describe leadership techniques that might need to be adjusted because of vision or hearing impairments of participants.

Describe the modification of exercise programming as it relates to the aging process (childhood through the older adult). (chp. 9)

Functional Anatomy and Kinesiology

Given anatomic models or diagrams the fitness instructor will:

A. Identify the major bones, muscle groups, and diarthradial joints of the human body; describe how each affects the joint range of motion. (chp. 4)

B. Identify the cardiovascular anatomy; specifically, chambers, valves, vessels, and the conduction system. (chp. 12)

Describe differences in the mechanics of human locomotion in walking, jogging, running, lifting weights, and carrying or moving objects. (chp. 4)

Define and describe the practical application of the following: center of gravity, base of support, heel strike, dissipation of force, and rebound. (chp. 4)

Describe and demonstrate exercises for specific muscle groups. (chp. 7)

Note. From American College of Sports Medicine: *Guidelines for Exercise Testing and Prescription,* 3rd ed. (1985). Lea & Febiger, Philadelphia. Reprinted with permission.

Appendix B

Health Status Questionnaire—Long Form

Health Status Questionnaire—Long Form

The following code will assist you in using the information on this form.

EI = Emergency Information—must be readily available

MS = Medical Supervision needed (*SEP* assumed)

MC = Medical Clearance needed (*SEP* assumed)

SEP = Special Emergency Procedures needed (may also need *SLA*)

PRF = Primary Risk Factor for CHD (*ED* also needed)

SRF = Secondary Risk Factor for CHD (*ED* needed)

SLA = Special or Limited Activities may be needed

ED = Provide Educational Material and/or Workshop in this area

OTHER (not marked) = Personal Information that may be helpful for files, or research

Instructions

Complete each question accurately. All information provided is confidential. In most cases, please CIRCLE the correct answers. Fill in the spaces provided.

Part 1. Information About the Individual

1. ________ - ______ - __________   ____________________
   Social Sec. No.   Date

2. ____   ____________________
   Legal Name   Nickname

3. ____   ____________________
   Mailing Address   Home Phone

   ____   ____________________
   Bus. Phone

4. *EI* ____   ____________________
   Personal Physician   Phone

   ____
   Address

5. *EI* ____   ____________________
   Person to contact in emergency   Phone

6. *SRF* Gender (circle one): Female Male (*SRF*)

7. *SRF* Date of Birth: ____________ ____ ______
Month Day Year

8. Citizenship: USA Other: ____________

9. Grew up in what environment: Rural Small Town Suburb Urban

10. Marital status: Single Married Widowed Divorced Separated

    Remarried Other:____________

11. *SRF* Race: American Indian Black (*SRF*) Caucasian Hispanic Oriental

    Other ____________

12. Number of children you have: 0 1 2 3 4 5+

13. Number of brothers, sisters: 0 1 2 3 4 5 6 7 8+

14. Years of education (circle highest):

    Elem 0 1 2 3 4 5 6 7 8 High Sch 9 10 11 12

    College 13 14 15 16 Grad/Prof 17 18 19 20+

15. Occupation:

Artist	Manager, administrator	White collar (sales, clerical, secretarial)
Designer	Professional	Writer
Businessperson	Student	Other ____________
Farmer	Technician, skilled worker	Retired (also circle former occupation above)
Homemaker		

16. Number of hours worked per week:

    Less than 20 20-40 41-60 Over 60

17. *SLA* More than 25% of time spent on job (circle all that apply):

Sitting at desk   Lifting or carrying loads   Standing   Walking   Driving

18. Total family income:
Less than $15,000 $15-24,999 $25-39,999 $40-60,000   Over $60,000

Part 2. Medical History

19. Family medical history—please circle all items that apply to blood relatives—natural children, brothers, sisters, parents, and grandparents:

Alcoholism	Emphysema	Obesity
Allergies	Epilepsy	Rheumatoid arthritis
Anemia—sickle cell	Gout	Stroke
Anemia—other	Heart disease (*SRF*)	Suicide
Asthma	High blood pressure	Thyroid problem
Bleeding trait	Hyperlipidemia (high blood fats)	Tuberculosis
Cancer	Kidney problems	Ulcer
Diabetes (sugar)	Mental illness	Other: ________

SRF Circle any who died of heart attack before age 60:

Father   Mother   Brother   Sister   Grandparent

20. Date of

Last medical physical exam: ________ Year

Last dental check-up: ________ Year

Last physical fitness test: ________ Year

21. Circle all reasons you have been hospitalized:

Check-up	Injury	Operation	Other ______
Illness	Mental illness	Pregnancy	

22. Circle operations you have had:

Appendix	D and C	Joint *SLA*	Stomach
Back *SLA*	Ears	Kidney	Testicle
Bone	Eyes *SLA*	Lung *SLA*	Thyroid
Brain	Gallbladder	Neck *SLA*	Tonsils
Breast	Heart *MS*	Nose	Tubal ligation
Colon	Hemorrhoids	Ovary	Vasectomy
C-section	Hernia *SLA*	Prostate	Other ______
Cystoscopy	Hysterectomy	Spleen	

23. Please circle any of the following for which you have been diagnosed or treated by a physician or health professional:

Acne *ED*	Bladder infection, cystitis
Alcoholism *SEP*	Bleeding trait *SEP*
Anemia, sickle cell *SEP*	Bronchitis, chronic *SEP*
Anemia, other *SEP*	Cancer *SEP (MC?)*
Appendicitis	Breast
Asthma *SEP*	Cervix
Back strain *SLA*	Colon

- Hodgkins disease or lymphosarcoma
- Leukemia
- Lung
- Ovary
- Prostate
- Rectum
- Stomach, esophagus
- Uterus
- Other cancer

Cirrhosis—liver *MC*

Colitis, spastic

Colitis, ulcerative *SEP*

Concussion *MC*

Congenital defect *SEP*

- Heart rhythm problem *MC*
- Heart valve problem *MC*
- Rheumatic heart disease *MC*
- Other heart problem *MC*

Constipation *ED*

Depression *ED*

Diabetes, controlled *SEP*

Diabetes, uncontrolled *SEP*

Diarrhea *ED*

Emphysema *SEP*

Epilepsy *SEP*

Eye problems *SLA*

- Amblyopia (lazy eye)
- Astigmatism
- Blind eye
- Farsighted
- Glasses, contacts
- Glaucoma
- Nearsighted
- Retinal detachment
- Visual problem not correctable

Fibrocystic breast

Gallbladder problem

Gonorrhea

Gout *SLA*

Hay fever

Hearing loss *SLA*

Heart problems

- Coronary disease *MS*
- Enlarged heart *MC*
- Heart attack *MS*
- Heart murmur *MC*

Hemorrhoids

Hepatitis

Herpes, genital

Hiatal hernia *SLA*

High blood pressure, controlled *PRF*

High blood pressure, uncontrolled *PRF*

Hypoglycemia (low blood sugar) *SEP*

Hyperlipidemia (high blood fat) *PRF*

Infectious mononucleosis

Kidney infection

Other kidney problem

Mental illness *SEP*

Migraine headache *ED*

Neck strain *SLA*

Nervous stomach *ED*

Obesity *PRF*

Ovarian cyst

Pelvic infection

Peptic ulcer *SEP*

Phlebitis *MC*

Pneumonia

Polyps in colon

Prostate infection

Regional ileitis

Rheumatic fever

Rheumatoid arthritis *SLA*

Sinus trouble, chronic

Serious injury, permanent impairment *SLA*

Stroke *MC*

Suicide attempt *SEP*

Syphilis

Thyroid, overactive *SEP*

Thyroid, underactive *SEP*

Tension headaches *ED*

Tuberculosis

Vaginitis, chronic

Other, specify: ______________________

24. *ED* for all. Circle all medicine taken in last six months:

Amphetamines	Cough med.	Nasal spray
Antacid	Diabetic pill *SEP*	Nitroglycerin *MS*
Antibiotic	Diet pill *ED*	Nerve med.
Antidepressant	Digitalis *MS*	Pain med., prescription *SLA*
Antihistamines	Diuretic *MC*	Pain med., not prescribed *SLA*
Allergy shots *SEP*	Epilepsy med. *SEP*	Penicillin
Arthritis med. *SLA*	Estrogen (hormone)	Rheumatic heart med. *MC*
Aspirin	Headache med.	Sleeping pill
Asthma med.	Heart rhythm med. *MC*	Stomach med.
Barbiturate	High blood pressure med. *MC*	Sulfa
Blood thinner *MC*	Insulin *MC*	Tetracycline
Birth control *SRF*	Iron	Thyroid hormone *SEP*
Coronary med. *MS*	Laxative	Tranquilizer
Cortisone (steroid)	Muscle relaxant	Other, specify: ____________

25. *SLA* Circle all fractures (broken bones) you have had:

Ankle	Hand (wrist to fingers)	Pelvis
Arm (shoulder to elbow)	Hip	Ribs
Back	Jaw	Shoulder
Collarbone	Kneecap	Skull
Facial bones	Leg (knee to ankle)	Tailbone
Fingers	Neck	Thigh (hip to knee)
Forearm (elbow to wrist)	Nose	Wrist
Foot		

26. *SEP* Circle all allergies:

Animal(s)	Eggs	Penicillin	Tetanus toxoid
Aspirin	Food(s)	Poison ivy	X-ray media
Bee stings	Grasses	Pollens, ragweed	Drug not listed
Dust	Molds, fungi	Sulfa	Other, specify: ____________

27. *ED* Circle each of following you have had (infection or immunization):

DPT (baby shots)	German measles	Mumps	Smallpox
Diptheria	Measles	Polio	Tetanus

28. *SRF* (Increased number of stressful situations—positive and negative—is associated with numerous minor and major health problems.) Circle all of the following that have happened to you during the PAST YEAR:

Death of a spouse or lover

Death of a loved one (relative, friend)

Divorce, separation, or breakup with lover

Getting engaged, married, or moving in with a lover

Loss of job, being fired, or being demoted

Starting a new job, being promoted, entering a new school, or graduating

Change of residence

Serious financial difficulties

Birth of a child

Serious illness or injury

Serious illness or injury to loved one

Victim of a crime

Failure to achieve expectation (not hired, promoted, or accepted into a program)

29. (Any of these health symptoms that occur frequently is the basis for medical attention.) Circle the number indicating how often you have each of the following:

5 = VERY OFTEN
4 = Fairly Often
3 = Sometimes
2 = Infrequently
1 = PRACTICALLY NEVER

a. Fatigue

1 2 3 4 5

b. Cough

1 2 3 4 5

c. Cough up blood *MC*

1 2 3 4 5

d. Colds

1 2 3 4 5

e. Sore throat

1 2 3 4 5

f. Nasal trouble

1 2 3 4 5

g. Digestive upsets *ED*

1 2 3 4 5

h. Constipation *ED*

1 2 3 4 5

i. Abdominal pain *MC*

1 2 3 4 5

j. Low back pain *SLA*

1 2 3 4 5

k. Leg pain *PRF MC*

1 2 3 4 5

l. Arm or shoulder pain *PRF MC*

1 2 3 4 5

m. Chest pain *PRF MC*

1 2 3 4 5

n. Knee discomfort *SLA*

1 2 3 4 5

o. Ankle or foot discomfort *SLA*

1 2 3 4 5

p. Swollen joints *MC*

1 2 3 4 5

q. Pain when moving joint *SLA*

1 2 3 4 5

r. Headaches *ED*

1 2 3 4 5

s. Nervousness *ED*

1 2 3 4 5

t. Feel faint *MC*

1 2 3 4 5

u. Dizziness *PRF MC*

1 2 3 4 5

v. Breathless with slight exertion *PRF MC*

1 2 3 4 5

For Women Only

ED (All of these areas of health for women provide the basis for education and/or workshops.)

30. Has your mother or sister had breast cancer? Yes No

31. Do you examine your breasts each month to detect cancer? Yes No

32. Do you go to the doctor for a breast examination at least once each year? Yes No

33. Has your uterus (womb) been removed? Yes No

    If yes, was it because of cancer? Yes No

34. Has your cervix (neck of womb) been removed? Yes No

    If yes, was it because of cancer? Yes No

35. Have both of your ovaries (sex glands) been removed? Yes No

    If yes, at what age? ________ years old

36. At what times do you have vaginal (birth canal) bleeding?

    a. Between menstrual periods Yes No

    b. During or after sexual intercourse Yes No

    c. My periods have stopped, but I still have bleeding once in a while. Yes No

    d. I am taking female hormones (estrogens) and I only bleed when I am off these hormones. Yes No

    e. None of these Yes No

37. Have you ever had sexual intercourse? Yes No

If so, at what age:

Before 20 years old Between 20 and 25 years of age After 25 years old

38. Are you now taking birth control pills? Yes No

39. Circle the appropriate answer concerning how often you have had pap smears.

Annually Once in last five years None in last five years Never

Part 3. Health-Related Behavior

40. *SLA* How many total miles do you travel in a car or truck, either driver or passenger, PER YEAR: ________ miles

41. About how many of these miles traveled are on a freeway, expressway, divided highway, or other limited access highway? ________ miles

42. *ED* What percent (%) of the time do you fasten your seat belt?

Less than 10% 10-24% 25-74% More than 75%

43. *ED* On the average, how many alcoholic beverages do you drink EACH WEEK? (One drink = 1-1/2 ounces of liquor OR 12 ounces of beer OR 6 ounces of wine. If your drinks are larger, multiply as needed).

41 or more	7-15	Ex-drinker
25-40	3-6	Nondrinker
16-24	1-2 (or occasionally)	

44. *PRF* Do you now smoke? Yes No

45. Have you ever smoked? Yes No

46. If yes for either 44 or 45, indicate number smoked PER DAY:

Cigarettes: 40 or more 20-39 10-19 1-9

Cigars or pipes ONLY: 5 or more or any inhaled Less than 5, none inhaled

47. If you are a former smoker—how many years since you stopped smoking?

    0 1 2 3 4 5 6 7 8 9 10+ years

48. *SEP* Have you ever been arrested for a crime involving violence or threat of violence on your part? Yes No

49. *SEP* Do you carry a gun or knife (other than a pocket knife) at work or during leisure?

    Yes No

50. *PRF* Do you exercise regularly? Yes No

51. Can you walk one mile without stopping? Yes No

52. Can you walk 4 miles briskly without fatigue? Yes No

53. Can you jog 3 miles continuously at a moderate pace without discomfort? Yes No

54. Indicate the total time spent in EACH CATEGORY EACH WEEK for an AVERAGE WEEK:

    Light activities, such as slow walking (3 mph), golf (walking), cycling (7 mph), doubles tennis, easy swimming, active gardening:

    0 1 2 3 4 5 6 7 8 9 10+ PER WEEK

    Moderate activities, such as moderate walking (4.5 mph), cycling (10 mph), singles tennis, moderate swimming, weight lifting

    0 1 2 3 4 5 6 7 8 9 10+ PER WEEK

    Vigorous activities, such as walking/jogging (5-6 mph), cycling (12 mph), court sports (average pace), fast jumping rope, fast swimming

    0 1 2 3 4 5 6 7 8 9 10+ PER WEEK

    Strenuous activities, such as running (7+ mph), competitive court sports, cycling (15+ mph), competitive swimming

    0 1 2 3 4 5 6 7 8 9 10+ PER WEEK

55. About how many hours do you spend in an AVERAGE WEEK:

    Work, or studying: 0 10 20 30 40 50 60 70 80+

    Asleep 10 20 30 40 50 60 70 80+

56. *ED* In terms of VITAMIN supplements, circle the most accurate statement for you:

    Never Occasionally One multivitamin daily Several vitamins daily

    Five or more vitamin supplements daily

57. What do you consider a good weight for yourself? ________ lbs.

58. What is the most you ever weighed? ________ lbs. At what age? ________ yrs

59. Weight now: ________ lbs. One year ago: ________ lbs. Age 21: ________ lbs

60. Number of meals you usually eat PER DAY: ________

61. *ED* Number of eggs you usually eat PER WEEK (do NOT count those used in cooking and baking): ________

62. *ED* Number of times PER WEEK you eat:

    Beef ________ Fish ________ Desserts ________

    Pork ________ Fowl ________ Fried foods ________

63. *ED* Number of servings PER WEEK:

    Whole milk ________ Buttermilk ________

    Two % milk ________ Tea (iced or hot) ________

    Skim (nonfat milk) ________ Coffee ________

    Soft drinks ________ Decaffeinated coffee ________

    Diet soft drinks ________

64. Do you brush your teeth daily? Yes No

65. Do you use dental floss daily? Yes No

66. How often do you visit a dentist?

    Every 6 months   Year   2 Years   5 Years   Less often

Part 4. Health-Related Attitudes

67. *ED* What was your ONE MAIN reaction the last time you stayed home with a MINOR illness:

    Relief. I needed a rest.

    Happiness. I sometimes enjoy being sick.

    Anger. I take care of myself too well to get sick.

    Irritation. I was too busy to get sick.

    Sadness. I felt my body had betrayed me.

    Frustration. There was nothing I could do about it.

    Guilt. I felt that I hadn't taken care of myself.

    Other: ______________________________

68. *ED* (One important element of stress management is being able to share feelings with another person.) Do you have a close friend or family member in whom you can confide?

    Definitely yes   Probably   Not sure   Definitely not

69. *ED* (There is a relationship between keeping anger in, items f-h, and CHD. Extreme frequency, item m, of anger and physiological reactions to anger, items a-e, are not healthy.) When you get extremely ANGRY or ANNOYED, circle the number indicating how often you respond:

    5 = VERY OFTEN
    4 = Fairly Often
    3 = Sometimes
    2 = Infrequently
    1 = PRACTICALLY NEVER

    a. Get tense or worried

       1   2   3   4   5

b. Get a headache

1 2 3 4 5

c. Feel weak

1 2 3 4 5

d. Feel depressed

1 2 3 4 5

e. Get nervous or shaky

1 2 3 4 5

f. Try to act as though nothing much happened

1 2 3 4 5

g. Keep it to myself

1 2 3 4 5

h. Apologize even though I am right

1 2 3 4 5

i. Take it out on others

1 2 3 4 5

j. Blame someone else

1 2 3 4 5

k. Get it off my chest

1 2 3 4 5

l. Talk to a friend or relative

1 2 3 4 5

m. In a typical WEEK I get extremely angry or annoyed

1 2 3 4 5

70. *ED* How does your health this year compare with other years?

Improved a great deal   Stayed about the same   Worsened a great deal

Improved somewhat   Worsened somewhat

71. *ED* Compared with other people your age, how would you rate your PHYSICAL health?

Excellent   Good   Fair   Poor

72. *ED* Compared with other people your age, how would you rate your MENTAL health?

Excellent   Good   Fair   Poor

73. *ED* How old do you feel physically? __________

74. *ED* How old do you feel mentally? __________

75. Until what age do you hope to live? __________

76. *ED* (The perceived control one has over one's life is a key ingredient in dealing with stress.) Do you find yourself saying YES to a request when you really want to say NO?

Consistently   Often   Sometimes   Rarely   Never

77. *ED* Circle the appropriate number for each part of the question:

5 = VERY OFTEN
4 = Fairly Often
3 = Sometimes
2 = Infrequently
1 = PRACTICALLY NEVER

a. How often do you have the feeling that there is nothing you can do well?

1 2 3 4 5

b. How often do you feel you have handled yourself well at a social gathering?

1 2 3 4 5

c. How often do you have the feeling that you can do everything well?

1 2 3 4 5

d. When you have to talk in front of a group of people your own age, are you often afraid or worried?

1 2 3 4 5

e. How often do you worry about whether other people like to be with you?

1 2 3 4 5

f. How often do you feel self-conscious?

1 2 3 4 5

g. When you talk in front of a group of people your own age, how frequently are you pleased with your performance?

1 2 3 4 5

h. How often are you troubled with shyness?

1 2 3 4 5

i. Are you comfortable when starting a conversation with people you don't know?

1 2 3 4 5

j. How often do you feel inferior to most of the people you know?

1 2 3 4 5

k. How often do you feel that you are a successful person?

1 2 3 4 5

l. How frequently do you feel confident that your eventual success is assured?

1 2 3 4 5

m. When you speak in a group discussion, how often do you feel sure of yourself?

1 2 3 4 5

n. Do you ever think that you are a worthless individual?

1 2 3 4 5

o. How often do you feel sure of yourself when among strangers?

1 2 3 4 5

p. How often do you worry about how well you get along with other people?

1 2 3 4 5

q. How frequently do you feel confident that some day the people you know will look up to and respect you?

1 2 3 4 5

r. How often do you feel that you dislike yourself?

1 2 3 4 5

s. Do you ever feel so discouraged with yourself that you wonder whether anything is worthwhile?

1 2 3 4 5

t. In general, do you often feel confident about your abilities?

1 2 3 4 5

78. *ED* In general, how satisfying do you find the way you're spending your life these days?

Very satisfying　　Neither satisfying nor dissatisfying　　Very dissatisfying

Somewhat satisfying　　Somewhat dissatisfying

79. *ED* How have you been feeling RECENTLY?

a. Have you felt depressed, blue, down, or sad much of the time? Yes No

b. Have you had trouble with waking up too early or being unable to stay asleep?

Yes No

c. Have you lost your appetite or have you had very much less desire to eat?

Yes No

d. Has there been any significant change in your weight? Yes No

e. Have you often felt alone and lonely even when there were others around you?

Yes No

f. Have you seriously considered killing yourself? Yes No

g. Have you had physical symptoms that seem to have no explanation? Yes No

80. *ED* Circle the degree of satisfaction (1-6). Circle YES if you plan to change, and NO if you do not plan to change:

6 = Completely SATISFIED
5 = Largely satisfied
4 = Somewhat satisfied
3 = Somewhat dissatisfied
2 = Largely dissatisfied
1 = Completely DISSATISFIED

							Plan to Change	
My weight	1	2	3	4	5	6	Yes	No
My use of alcohol	1	2	3	4	5	6	Yes	No
My use of over-the-counter drugs	1	2	3	4	5	6	Yes	No
My level of exercise	1	2	3	4	5	6	Yes	No
My pattern of sleeping	1	2	3	4	5	6	Yes	No
My pattern of eating	1	2	3	4	5	6	Yes	No
My use of cigarettes	1	2	3	4	5	6	Yes	No
My blood pressure	1	2	3	4	5	6	Yes	No

My overall physical fitness	1	2	3	4	5	6	Yes	No
My handling of tension/stress	1	2	3	4	5	6	Yes	No
My use of seat belts	1	2	3	4	5	6	Yes	No

81. *ED* Circle the number that corresponds to how you feel:

6 = Strongly AGREE
5 = Moderately agree
4 = Slightly agree
3 = Slightly disagree
2 = Moderately disagree
1 = Strongly DISAGREE

a. If I get sick, it is my own behavior which determines how soon I will get well again.

1 2 3 4 5 6

b. No matter what I do, if I am going to get sick, I will get sick.

1 2 3 4 5 6

c. Having regular contact with my physician is the best way for me to avoid illness.

1 2 3 4 5 6

d. Most things that affect my health happen to me by accident.

1 2 3 4 5 6

e. Whenever I don't feel well, I should consult a medically trained professional.

1 2 3 4 5 6

f. I am in control of my health.

1 2 3 4 5 6

g. My family has a lot to do with my becoming sick or staying healthy.

1 2 3 4 5 6

h. When I get sick, I am to blame.

1 2 3 4 5 6

i. Luck plays a big part in determining how soon I will recover from an illness.

1 2 3 4 5 6

j. Health professionals control my health.

1 2 3 4 5 6

k. My good health is largely a matter of good fortune.

1 2 3 4 5 6

l. The main thing which affects my health is what I myself do.

1 2 3 4 5 6

m. If I take care of myself, I can avoid illness.

1 2 3 4 5 6

n. When I recover from an illness, it's usually because other people (for example, doctors, nurses, family, friends) have been taking good care of me.

1 2 3 4 5 6

o. No matter what I do, I'm likely to get sick.

1 2 3 4 5 6

p. If it's meant to be, I will stay healthy.

1 2 3 4 5 6

q. If I take the right actions, I can stay healthy.

1 2 3 4 5 6

r. Regarding my health, I can only do what my doctor tells me to do.

1 2 3 4 5 6

82. *SRF* (These are traits that have been associated with coronary-prone behavior.) Circle the number that corresponds to how you feel:

6 = Strongly AGREE
5 = Moderately agree
4 = Slightly agree
3 = Slightly disagree
2 = Moderately disagree
1 = Strongly DISAGREE

I am an impatient, time-conscious, hard-driving individual.

1 2 3 4 5 6

83. List everything not already included on this questionnaire that might cause you problems in a fitness test or fitness program:

Appendix C
Percent Fat Estimates for Men and Women

Percent Fat Estimate for Men: Sum of Triceps, Chest, and Subscapular Skinfolds

Sum of Skinfolds (mm)	Age to Last Year: Under 22	23-27	28-32	33-37	38-42	43-47	48-52	53-57	Over 57
8-10	1.5	2.0	2.5	3.1	3.6	4.1	4.6	5.1	5.6
11-13	3.0	3.5	4.0	4.5	5.1	5.6	6.1	6.6	7.1
14-16	4.5	5.0	5.5	6.0	6.5	7.0	7.6	8.1	8.6
17-19	5.9	6.4	6.9	7.4	8.0	8.5	9.0	9.5	10.0
20-22	7.3	7.8	8.3	8.8	9.4	9.9	10.4	10.9	11.4
23-25	8.6	9.2	9.7	10.2	10.7	11.2	11.8	12.3	12.8
26-28	10.0	10.5	11.0	11.5	12.1	12.6	13.1	13.6	14.2
29-31	11.2	11.8	12.3	12.8	13.4	13.9	14.4	14.9	15.5
32-34	12.5	13.0	13.5	14.1	14.6	15.1	15.7	16.2	16.7
35-37	13.7	14.2	14.8	15.3	15.8	16.4	16.9	17.4	18.0
38-40	14.9	15.4	15.9	16.5	17.0	17.6	18.1	18.6	19.2
41-43	16.0	16.6	17.1	17.6	18.2	18.7	19.3	19.8	20.3
44-46	17.1	17.7	18.2	18.7	19.3	19.8	20.4	20.9	21.5
47-49	18.2	18.7	19.3	19.8	20.4	20.9	21.4	22.0	22.5
50-52	19.2	19.7	20.3	20.8	21.4	21.9	22.5	23.0	23.6
53-55	20.2	20.7	21.3	21.8	22.4	22.9	23.5	24.0	24.6
56-58	21.1	21.7	22.2	22.8	23.3	23.9	24.4	25.0	25.5
59-61	22.0	22.6	23.1	23.7	24.2	24.8	25.3	25.9	26.5
62-64	22.9	23.4	24.0	24.5	25.1	25.7	26.2	26.8	27.3
65-67	23.7	24.3	24.8	25.4	25.9	26.5	27.1	27.6	28.2
68-70	24.5	25.0	25.6	26.2	26.7	27.3	27.8	28.4	29.0
71-73	25.2	25.8	26.3	26.9	27.5	28.0	28.6	29.1	29.7
74-76	25.9	26.5	27.0	27.6	28.2	28.7	29.3	29.9	30.4
77-79	26.6	27.1	27.7	28.2	28.8	29.4	29.9	30.5	31.1
80-82	27.2	27.7	28.3	28.9	29.4	30.0	30.6	31.1	31.7
83-85	27.7	28.3	28.8	29.4	30.0	30.5	31.1	31.7	32.3
86-88	28.2	28.8	29.4	29.9	30.5	31.1	31.6	32.2	32.8
89-91	28.7	29.3	29.8	30.4	31.0	31.5	32.1	32.7	33.3
92-94	29.1	29.7	30.3	30.8	31.4	32.0	32.6	33.1	33.4
95-97	29.5	30.1	30.6	31.2	31.8	32.4	32.9	33.5	34.1
98-100	29.8	30.4	31.0	31.6	32.1	32.7	33.3	33.9	34.4
101-103	30.1	30.7	31.3	31.8	32.4	33.0	33.6	34.1	34.7
104-106	30.4	30.9	31.5	32.1	32.7	33.2	33.8	34.4	35.0
107-109	30.6	31.1	31.7	32.3	32.9	33.4	34.0	34.6	35.2
110-112	30.7	31.3	31.9	32.4	33.0	33.6	34.2	34.7	35.3
113-115	30.8	31.4	32.0	32.5	33.1	33.7	34.3	34.9	35.4
116-118	30.9	31.5	32.0	32.6	33.2	33.8	34.3	34.9	35.5

Note. From "Practical assessment of body composition" by A.S. Jackson and M.L. Pollock, 1985, *The Physician and Sportsmedicine*, **13**, pp. 76-90, Minneapolis: McGraw-Hill. Reprinted with permission.

Percent Fat Estimate for Women: Sum of Triceps, Abdomen, and Suprailium Skinfolds

Sum of Skinfolds (mm)	Age to Last Year								
	18-22	23-27	28-32	33-37	38-42	43-47	48-52	53-57	Over 57
8-12	8.8	9.0	9.2	9.4	9.5	9.7	9.9	10.1	10.3
13-17	10.8	10.9	11.1	11.3	11.5	11.7	11.8	12.0	12.2
18-22	12.6	12.8	13.0	13.2	13.4	13.5	13.7	13.9	14.1
23-27	14.5	14.6	14.8	15.0	15.2	15.4	15.6	15.7	15.9
28-32	16.2	16.4	16.6	16.8	17.0	17.1	17.3	17.5	17.7
33-37	17.9	18.1	18.3	18.5	18.7	18.9	19.0	19.2	19.4
38-42	19.6	19.8	20.0	20.2	20.3	20.5	20.7	20.9	21.1
43-47	21.2	21.4	21.6	21.8	21.9	22.1	22.3	22.5	22.7
48-52	22.8	22.9	23.1	23.3	23.5	23.7	23.8	24.0	24.2
53-57	24.2	24.4	24.6	24.8	25.0	25.2	25.3	25.5	25.7
58-62	25.7	25.9	26.0	26.2	26.4	26.6	26.8	27.0	27.1
63-67	27.1	27.2	27.4	27.6	27.8	28.0	28.2	28.3	28.5
68-72	28.4	28.6	28.7	28.9	29.1	29.3	29.5	29.7	29.8
73-77	29.6	29.8	30.0	30.2	30.4	30.6	30.7	30.9	31.1
78-82	30.9	31.0	31.2	31.4	31.6	31.8	31.9	32.1	32.3
83-87	32.0	32.2	32.4	32.6	32.7	32.9	33.1	33.3	33.5
88-92	33.1	33.3	33.5	33.7	33.8	34.0	34.2	34.4	34.6
93-97	34.1	34.3	34.5	34.7	34.9	35.1	35.2	35.4	35.6
98-102	35.1	35.3	35.5	35.7	35.9	36.0	36.2	36.4	36.6
103-107	36.1	36.2	36.4	36.6	36.8	37.0	37.2	37.3	37.5
108-112	36.9	37.1	37.3	37.5	37.7	37.9	38.0	38.2	38.4
113-117	37.8	37.9	38.1	38.3	39.2	39.4	39.6	39.8	39.2
118-122	38.5	38.7	38.9	39.1	39.4	39.6	39.8	40.0	40.0
123-127	39.2	39.4	39.6	39.8	40.0	40.1	40.3	40.5	40.7
128-132	39.9	40.1	40.2	40.4	40.6	40.8	41.0	41.2	41.3
133-137	40.5	40.7	40.8	41.0	41.2	41.4	41.6	41.7	41.9
138-142	41.0	41.2	41.4	41.6	41.7	41.9	42.1	42.3	42.5
143-147	41.5	41.7	41.9	42.0	42.2	42.4	42.6	42.8	43.0
148-152	41.9	42.1	42.3	42.4	42.6	42.8	43.0	43.2	43.4
153-157	42.3	42.5	42.6	42.8	43.0	43.2	43.4	43.6	43.7
158-162	42.6	42.8	43.0	43.1	43.3	43.5	43.7	43.9	44.1
163-167	42.9	43.0	43.2	43.4	43.6	43.8	44.0	44.1	44.3
168-172	43.1	43.2	43.4	43.6	43.8	44.0	44.2	44.3	44.5
173-177	43.2	43.4	43.6	43.8	43.9	44.1	44.3	44.5	44.7
178-182	43.3	43.5	43.7	43.8	44.0	44.2	44.4	44.6	44.8

Note. From "Practical assessment of body composition" by A.S. Jackson and M.L. Pollock, 1985, *The Physician and Sportsmedicine,* **13**, pp. 76-90, Minneapolis: McGraw-Hill. Reprinted with permission.

Appendix D

Nutritive Value of Commonly Used Foods

Note. From *Coaches Guide to Nutrition and Weight Control* (pp. 189-224) by P. Eisenman and D.A. Johnson, 1982, Champaign, IL: Human Kinetics.

Food, Approximate Measure, and Weight (in Grams)			Water (%)	Food Energy (kcal)	Protein (g)	Fat (g)	Fatty Acids: Saturated (total) (g)	Fatty Acids: Unsaturated Oleic (g)	Fatty Acids: Unsaturated Linoleic (g)	Carbohydrate (g)	Calcium (mg)	Iron (mg)	Vitamin A value (I.U.)	Thiamin (mg)	Riboflavin (mg)	Niacin (mg)	Ascorbic acid (mg)
MILK, CHEESE, CREAM, IMITATION CREAM; RELATED PRODUCTS																	
Milk:																	
Fluid:																	
Whole, 3.5% fat	1 cup	244	87	160	9	9	5	3	Trace	12	288	0.1	350	0.07	0.41	0.2	2
Nonfat (skim)	1 cup	245	90	90	9	Trace	—	—	—	12	296	.1	10	.09	.44	.2	2
Partly skimmed, 2% nonfat milk solids added	1 cup	246	87	145	10	5	3	2	Trace	15	352	.1	200	.10	.52	.2	2
Canned, concentrated, undiluted:																	
Evaporated, unsweetened	1 cup	252	74	345	18	20	11	7	1	24	635	.3	810	.10	.86	.5	3
Condensed, sweetened	1 cup	306	27	980	25	27	15	9	1	166	802	.3	1100	.24	1.16	.6	3
Dry, nonfat instant:																	
Low-density (1⅓ cups needed for reconstitution to 1 qt)	1 cup	68	4	245	24	Trace	—	—	—	35	879	.4	20[a]	.24	1.21	.6	5
High-density (7/8 cup needed for reconstitution to 1 qt)	1 cup	104	4	375	37	1	—	—	—	54	1345	.6	30[a]	.36	1.85	.9	7
Buttermilk:																	
Fluid, cultured, made from skim milk	1 cup	245	90	90	9	Trace	—	—	—	12	296	.1	10	.10	.44	.2	2
Dried, packaged	1 cup	120	3	465	41	6	3	2	Trace	60	1498	.7	260	.31	2.06	1.1	—
Cheese																	
Natural:																	
Blue or Roquefort type:																	
Ounce	1 oz.	28	40	105	6	9	5	3	Trace	1	89	.1	350	.01	.17	.3	0
Cubic inch	1 cu in	17	40	65	4	5	3	2	Trace	Trace	54	.1	210	.01	.11	.2	0
Camembert, packaged in 4-oz pkg with 3 wedges per pkg	1 wedge	38	52	115	7	9	5	3	Trace	1	40	.2	380	.02	.29	.3	0

[a]Value applies to unfortified product; value for fortified low-density product would be 1500 I.U. and the fortified high-density product would be 2290 I.U.

Data are from the Home and Garden Bulletin No. 72, USDA, Washington, DC. Revised 1971.

Food, Approximate Measure, and Weight (in Grams)			Water (%)	Food Energy (kcal)	Protein (g)	Fat (g)	Fatty Acids: Saturated (total) (g)	Fatty Acids: Unsaturated: Oleic (g)	Fatty Acids: Unsaturated: Linoleic (g)	Carbohydrate (g)	Calcium (mg)	Iron (mg)	Vitamin A value (I.U.)	Thiamin (mg)	Riboflavin (mg)	Niacin (mg)	Ascorbic acid (mg)
MILK, CHEESE, CREAM, IMITATION CREAM; RELATED PRODUCTS—Con.																	
Cheese—Continued																	
Cheddar:																	
Ounce	1 oz	28	37	115	7	9	5	3	Trace	1	213	0.3	370	0.01	0.13	Trace	0
Cubic inch	1 cu in	17	37	70	4	6	3	2	Trace	Trace	129	.2	230	.01	.08	Trace	0
Cottage, large or small curd:																	
Creamed:																	
Package of 12-oz net wt	1 pkg	340	78	360	46	14	8	5	Trace	10	320	1.0	580	.10	.85	0.3	0
Cup, curd pressed down	1 cup	245	78	260	33	10	6	3	Trace	7	230	.7	420	.07	.61	.2	0
Uncreamed:																	
Package of 12-oz net wt	1 pkg	340	79	290	58	1	1	Trace	Trace	9	306	1.4	30	.10	.95	.3	0
Cup, curd pressed down	1 cup	200	79	170	34	1	Trace	Trace	Trace	5	180	.8	20	.06	.56	.2	0
Cream:																	
Package of 8-oz net wt	1 pkg	227	51	850	18	86	48	28	3	5	141	.5	3500	.05	.54	.2	0
Package of 3-oz net wt	1 pkg	85	51	320	7	32	18	11	1	2	53	.2	1310	.02	.20	.1	0
Cubic inch	1 cu in	16	51	60	1	6	3	2	Trace	Trace	10	Trace	250	Trace	.04	Trace	0
Parmesan, grated:																	
Cup, pressed down	1 cup	140	17	655	60	43	24	14	1	5	1893	.7	1760	.03	1.22	.3	0
Tablespoon	1 tbsp	5	17	25	2	2	1	Trace	Trace	Trace	68	Trace	60	Trace	.04	Trace	0
Ounce	1 oz	28	17	130	12	9	5	3	Trace	1	383	.1	360	.01	.25	.1	0
Swiss:																	
Ounce	1 oz	28	39	105	8	8	4	3	Trace	1	262	.3	320	Trace	.11	Trace	0
Cubic inch	1 cu in	15	39	55	4	4	2	1	Trace	Trace	139	.1	170	Trace	.06	Trace	0
Pasteurized processed cheese:																	
American:																	
Ounce	1 oz	28	40	105	7	9	5	3	Trace	1	198	.3	350	.01	.12	Trace	0
Cubic inch	1 cu in	18	40	65	4	5	3	2	Trace	Trace	122	.2	210	Trace	.07	Trace	0

Swiss:																	
Ounce	1 oz	28	40	100	8	8	4	3	Trace	1	251	.3	310	Trace	.11	Trace	0
Cubic inch	1 cu in	18	40	65	5	5	3	2	Trace	Trace	159	.2	200	Trace	.07	Trace	0
Pasteurized process cheese food:																	
American:																	
Tablespoon	1 tbsp	14	43	45	3	3	2	1	Trace	1	80	.1	140	Trace	.08	Trace	0
Cubic inch	1 cu in	18	43	60	4	4	2	1	Trace	1	100	.1	170	Trace	.10	Trace	0
Pasteurized process cheese spread, American	1 oz	28	49	80	5	6	3	2	Trace	2	• 160	.2	250	Trace	.15	Trace	0
Cream:																	
Half-and-half (cream and milk)	1 cup	242	80	325	8	28	15	9	1	11	261	.1	1160	.07	.39	.1	2
	1 tbsp	15	80	20	1	2	1	1	Trace	1	16	Trace	70	Trace	.02	Trace	Trace
Light, coffee or table	1 cup	240	72	505	7	49	27	16	1	10	245	.1	2020	.07	.36	.1	2
	1 tbsp	15	72	30	1	3	2	1	Trace	1	15	Trace	130	Trace	.02	Trace	Trace
Sour	1 cup	230	72	485	7	47	26	16	1	10	235	.1	1930	.07	.35	.1	2
	1 tbsp	12	72	25	Trace	2	1	1	Trace	1	12	Trace	100	Trace	.02	Trace	Trace
Whipped topping (pressurized)	1 cup	60	62	155	2	14	8	5	Trace	6	67	—	570	—	.04	—	—
	1 tbsp	3	62	10	Trace	1	Trace	Trace	Trace	Trace	3	—	30	—	Trace	—	—
Whipping, unwhipped (volume about double when whipped):																	
Light	1 cup	239	62	715	6	75	41	25	2	9	203	.1	3060	.05	.29	.1	2
	1 tbsp	15	62	45	Trace	5	3	2	Trace	1	13	Trace	190	Trace	.02	Trace	Trace
Heavy	1 cup	238	57	840	5	90	50	30	3	7	179	.1	3670	.05	.26	.1	2
	1 tbsp	15	57	55	Trace	6	3	2	Trace	1	11	Trace	230	Trace	.02	Trace	Trace
Imitation cream products (made with vegetable fat):																	
Creamers:																	
Powdered	1 cup	94	2	505	4	33	31	1	0	52	21	.6	200[b]	—	—	Trace	—
	1 tsp	2	2	10	Trace	1	Trace	Trace	0	1	1	Trace	Trace[b]	—	—	—	—
Liquid (frozen)	1 cup	245	77	345	3	27	25	1	0	25	29	—	100[b]	0	0	—	—
	1 tbsp	15	77	20	Trace	2	1	Trace	0	2	2	—	10[b]	0	0	—	—

[b]Contributed largely from beta-carotene used for coloring.

Food, Approximate Measure, and Weight (in Grams)			Water (%)	Food Energy (kcal)	Protein (g)	Fat (g)	Fatty Acids: Saturated (total) (g)	Fatty Acids: Unsaturated Oleic (g)	Fatty Acids: Unsaturated Linoleic (g)	Carbohydrate (g)	Calcium (mg)	Iron (mg)	Vitamin A value (I.U.)	Thiamin (mg)	Riboflavin (mg)	Niacin (mg)	Ascorbic acid (mg)
MILK, CHEESE, CREAM, IMITATION CREAM; RELATED PRODUCTS—Con.																	
Imitation cream products (made with vegetable fat):—Con.																	
Sour dressing (imitation sour cream) made with nonfat dry milk	1 cup	235	72	440	9	38	35	1	Trace	17	277	.1	10	.07	.38	.2	1
	1 tbsp	12	72	20	Trace	2	2	Trace	Trace	1	14	Trace	Trace	Trace	Trace	Trace	Trace
Whipped topping:																	
Pressurized	1 cup	70	61	190	1	17	15	1	0	9	5	—	340[b]	—	0	—	—
	1 tbsp	4	61	10	Trace	1	1	Trace	0	Trace	Trace	—	20[b]	—	0	—	—
Frozen	1 cup	75	52	230	1	20	18	Trace	0	15	5	—	560[b]	—	0	—	—
	1 tbsp	4	52	10	Trace	1	1	Trace	0	1	Trace	—	30[b]	—	0	—	—
Powdered, made with whole milk	1 cup	75	58	175	3	12	10	1	Trace	15	62	Trace	330[b]	.02	.08	.1	Trace
	1 tbsp	4	58	10	Trace	1	1	Trace	Trace	1	3	Trace	20	Trace	Trace	Trace	Trace
Milk beverages:																	
Cocoa, homemade	1 cup	250	79	245	10	12	7	4	Trace	27	295	1.0	400	.10	.45	.5	3
Chocolate-flavored drink made with skim milk and 2% added butterfat	1 cup	250	83	190	8	6	3	2	Trace	27	270	.5	210	.10	.40	.3	3
Malted milk:																	
Dry powder, approx. 3 heaping teaspoons/oz	1 oz.	28	3	115	4	2	—	—	—	20	82	.6	290	.09	.15	.1	0
Beverage	1 cup	235	78	245	11	10	—	—	—	28	317	.7	590	.14	.49	.2	2
Milk desserts:																	
Custard, baked	1 cup	265	77	305	14	15	7	5	1	29	297	1.1	930	.11	.50	.3	1
Ice cream:																	
Regular (approx. 10% fat)	½ gal	1064	63	2055	48	113	62	37	3	221	1553	.5	4680	.43	2.23	1.1	11
	1 cup	133	63	255	6	14	8	5	Trace	28	194	.1	590	.05	.28	.1	1
	3 fl oz	50	63	95	2	5	3	2	Trace	10	73	Trace	220	.02	.11	.1	1
Rich (approx. 16% fat)	½ gal	1188	63	2635	31	191	105	63	6	214	927	.2	7840	.24	1.31	1.2	12
	1 cup	148	63	330	4	24	13	8	1	27	115	Trace	980	.03	.16	.1	1

Ice milk:																	
Hardened	½ gal	1048	67	1595	50	53	29	17	2	235	1635	1.0	2200	.52	2.31	1.0	10
	1 cup	131	67	200	6	7	4	2	Trace	29	204	.1	280	.07	.29	.1	1
Soft-serve	1 cup	175	67	265	8	9	5	3	Trace	39	273	.2	370	.09	.39	.2	2
Yogurt																	
Made from partially skimmed milk	1 cup	245	89	125	8	4	2	1	Trace	13	294	.1	170	.10	.44	.2	2
Made from whole milk	1 cup	245	88	150	7	8	5	3	Trace	12	272	.1	340	.07	.39	.2	2
EGGS																	
Eggs, large, 24 ounces per dozen:																	
Raw or cooked in shell or with nothing added:																	
Whole, without shell	1 egg	50	74	80	6	6	2	3	Trace	Trace	27	1.1	590	.05	.15	Trace	0
White of egg	1 white	33	88	15	4	Trace	—	—	—	Trace	3	Trace	0	Trace	.09	Trace	0
Yolk of egg	1 yolk	17	51	60	3	5	2	2	Trace	Trace	24	.9	580	.04	.07	Trace	0
Scrambled with milk and fat	1 egg	64	72	110	7	8	3	3	Trace	1	51	1.1	690	.05	.18	Trace	0
MEAT, POULTRY, FISH, SHELLFISH; RELATED PRODUCTS																	
Bacon, (20 slices per lb raw) broiled or fried, crisp	2 slices	15	8	90	5	8	3	4	1	1	2	.5	0	.08	.05	.8	—
Beef,[c] cooked:																	
Cuts braised, simmered, or pot roasted:																	
Lean and fat	3 oz	85	53	245	23	16	8	7	Trace	0	10	2.9	30	.04	.18	3.5	—
Lean only	2.5 oz	72	62	140	22	5	2	2	Trace	0	10	2.7	10	.04	.16	3.3	—
Hamburger (ground beef), broiled:																	
Lean	3 oz	85	60	185	23	10	5	4	Trace	0	10	3.0	20	.08	.20	5.1	—
Regular	3 oz	85	54	245	21	17	8	8	Trace	0	9	2.7	30	.07	.18	4.6	—
Roast, overcooked, no liquid added:																	
Relatively fat, such as rib:																	
Lean and fat	3 oz	85	40	375	17	34	16	15	1	0	8	2.2	70	.05	.13	3.1	—
Lean only	1.8 oz	51	57	125	14	7	3	3	Trace	0	6	1.8	10	.04	.11	2.6	—
Relatively lean, such as heel of round:																	
Lean and fat	3 oz	85	62	165	25	7	3	3	Trace	0	11	3.2	10	.06	.19	4.5	—
Lean only	2.7 oz	78	65	125	24	3	1	1	Trace	0	10	3.0	Trace	.06	.18	4.3	—

[b]Contributed largely from beta-carotene used for coloring.

[c]Outer layer of fat on the cut was removed to within approximately ½-in. of the lean. Deposits of fat within the cut were not removed.

Food, Approximate Measure, and Weight (in Grams)			Water (%)	Food Energy (kcal)	Protein (g)	Fat (g)	Fatty Acids: Saturated (total) (g)	Fatty Acids: Unsaturated: Oleic (g)	Fatty Acids: Unsaturated: Linoleic (g)	Carbohydrate (g)	Calcium (mg)	Iron (mg)	Vitamin A value (I.U.)	Thiamin (mg)	Riboflavin (mg)	Niacin (mg)	Ascorbic acid (mg)
MEAT, POULTRY, FISH, SHELLFISH; RELATED PRODUCTS—Con.																	
Steak, broiled:																	
Relatively fat, such as sirloin:																	
Lean and fat	3 oz	85	44	330	20	27	13	12	1	0	9	2.5	50	.05	.16	4.0	—
Lean only	2 oz	56	59	115	18	4	2	2	Trace	0	7	2.2	10	.05	.14	3.6	—
Relatively lean, such as round:																	
Lean and fat	3 oz	85	55	220	24	13	6	6	Trace	0	10	3.0	20	.07	.19	4.8	—
Lean only	2.4 oz	68	61	130	21	4	2	2	Trace	0	9	2.5	10	.06	.16	4.1	—
Beef, Canned:																	
Corned beef	3 oz	85	59	185	22	10	5	4	Trace	0	17	3.7	20	.01	.20	2.9	—
Corned beef hash	3 oz	85	67	155	7	10	5	4	Trace	9	11	1.7	—	.01	.08	1.8	—
Beef, dried or chipped	2 oz	57	48	115	19	4	2	2	Trace	0	11	2.9	—	.04	.18	2.2	—
Beef and vegetable stew	1 cup	235	82	210	15	10	5	4	Trace	15	28	2.8	2310	.13	.17	4.4	15
Beef pot pie, baked, 4¼-in. diam., weight before baking about 8 oz	1 pie	227	55	560	23	33	9	20	2	43	32	4.1	1860	.25	.27	4.5	7
Chicken, cooked:																	
Flesh only, broiled	3 oz	85	71	115	20	3	1	1	1	0	8	1.4	80	.05	.16	7.4	—
Breast, fried, ½ breast:																	
With bone	3.3 oz	94	58	155	25	5	1	2	1	1	9	1.3	70	.04	.17	11.2	—
Flesh and skin only	2.7 oz	76	58	155	25	5	1	2	1	1	9	1.3	70	.04	.17	11.2	—
Drumstick, fried:																	
With bone	2.1 oz	59	55	90	12	4	1	2	1	Trace	6	.9	50	.03	.15	2.7	—
Flesh and skin only	1.3 oz	38	55	90	12	4	1	2	1	Trace	6	.9	50	.03	.15	2.7	—
Chicken, canned, boneless	3 oz	85	65	170	18	10	3	4	2	0	18	1.3	200	.03	.11	3.7	3
Chicken pot pie, baked, 4¼-in. diam., weight before baking about 8 oz	1 pie	227	57	535	23	31	10	15	3	42	68	3.0	3020	.25	.26	4.1	5

Chili con carne, canned:																
With beans	1 cup	250	72	335	19	15	7	7	Trace	30	80	4.2	150	.08	.18	3.2	—
Without beans	1 cup	255	67	510	26	38	18	17	1	15	97	3.6	380	.05	.31	5.6	—
Heart, beef, lean, braised	3 oz	85	61	160	27	5	—	—	—	1	5	5.0	20	.21	1.04	6.5	1
Lamb,[c] cooked																	
Chop, thick, with bone, 1 chop, broiled	4.8 oz	137	47	400	25	33	18	12	1	0	10	1.5	—	.14	.25	5.6	—
Lean and fat	4 oz	112	47	400	25	33	18	12	1	0	10	1.5	—	.14	.25	5.6	—
Lean only	2.6 oz	74	62	140	21	6	3	2	Trace	0	9	1.5	—	.11	.20	4.5	—
Leg roasted:																	
Lean and fat	3 oz	85	54	235	22	16	9	6	Trace	0	9	1.4	—	.13	.23	4.7	—
Lean only	2.5 oz	71	62	130	20	5	3	2	Trace	0	9	1.4	—	.12	.21	4.4	—
Shoulder, roasted:																	
Lean and fat	3 oz	85	50	285	18	23	13	8	1	0	9	1.0	—	.11	.20	4.0	—
Lean only	2.3 oz	64	61	130	17	6	3	2	Trace	0	8	1.0	—	.10	.18	3.7	—
Liver, beef, fried	2 oz	57	57	130	15	6	—	—	—	3	6	5.0	30,280	.15	2.37	9.4	15
Pork, cured, cooked:																	
Ham, light cure, lean and fat, roasted	3 oz	85	54	245	18	19	7	8	2	0	8	2.2	0	.40	.16	3.1	—
Luncheon meat:																	
Boiled ham, sliced	2 oz	57	59	135	11	10	4	4	1	0	6	1.6	0	.25	.09	1.5	—
Canned, spiced or unspiced	2 oz	57	55	165	8	14	5	6	1	1	5	1.2	0	.18	.12	1.6	—
Pork, fresk,[c] cooked:																	
Chop, thick, with bone 1 chop	3.5 oz	98	42	260	16	21	8	9	2	0	8	2.2	0	.63	.18	3.8	—
Lean and fat	2.3 oz	66	42	260	16	21	8	9	2	0	8	2.2	0	.63	.18	3.8	—
Lean only	1.7 oz	48	53	130	15	7	2	3	1	0	7	1.9	0	.54	.16	3.3	—
Roast, oven-cooked, no liquid added:																	
Lean and fat	3 oz	85	46	310	21	24	9	10	2	0	9	2.7	0	.78	.22	4.7	—
Lean only	2.4 oz	68	55	175	20	10	3	4	1	0	9	2.6	0	.73	.21	4.4	—
Cuts, simmered:																	
Lean and fat	3 oz	85	46	320	20	26	9	11	2	0	8	2.5	0	.46	.21	4.1	—
Lean only	2.2 oz	63	60	135	18	6	2	3	1	0	8	2.3	0	.42	.19	3.7	—
Sausage:																	
Bologna, slice, 3-in. diam. by 1/8 in.	2 slices	26	56	80	3	7	—	—	—	Trace	2	.5	—	.04	.06	.7	—

[c]Outer layer of fat on the cut was removed to within approximately ½-in. of the lean. Deposits of fat within the cut were not removed.

Food, Approximate Measure, and Weight (in Grams)			Water (%)	Food Energy (kcal)	Protein (g)	Fat (g)	Fatty Acids: Saturated (total) (g)	Fatty Acids: Unsaturated Oleic (g)	Fatty Acids: Unsaturated Linoleic (g)	Carbohydrate (g)	Calcium (mg)	Iron (mg)	Vitamin A value (I.U.)	Thiamin (mg)	Riboflavin (mg)	Niacin (mg)	Ascorbic acid (mg)
MEAT, POULTRY, FISH, SHELLFISH; RELATED PRODUCTS—Con.																	
Sausage:—Con.																	
Braunschweiger, slice 2-in. diam. by ¼ in.	2 slices	20	53	65	3	5	—	—	—	Trace	2	1.2	1310	.03	.29	1.6	—
Deviled ham, canned	1 tbsp	13	51	45	2	4	2	2	Trace	0	1	.3	—	.02	.01	.2	—
Frankfurter, heated (8 per lb. purchased pkg)	1 frank	56	57	170	7	15	—	—	—	1	3	.8	—	.08	.11	1.4	—
Pork links, cooked (16 links per lb. raw)	2 links	26	35	125	5	11	4	5	1	Trace	2	.6	0	.21	.09	1.0	—
Salami, dry type	1 oz	28	30	130	7	11	—	—	—	Trace	4	1.0	—	.10	.07	1.5	—
Salami, cooked	1 oz	28	51	90	5	7	—	—	—	Trace	3	.7	—	.07	.07	1.2	—
Vienna, canned (7 sausages per 5-oz can)	1 sausage	16	63	40	2	3	—	—	—	Trace	1	.3	—	.01	.02	.4	—
Veal, medium fat, cooked, bone removed:																	
Cutlet	3 oz	85	60	185	23	9	5	4	Trace	—	9	2.7	—	.06	.21	4.6	—
Roast	3 oz	85	55	230	23	14	7	6	Trace	0	10	2.9	—	.11	.26	6.6	—
Fish and shellfish:																	
Bluefish, baked with table fat	3 oz	85	68	135	22	4	—	—	—	0	25	.6	40	.09	.08	1.6	—
Clams:																	
Raw, meat only	3 oz	85	82	65	11	1	—	—	—	2	59	5.2	90	.08	.15	1.1	8
Canned, solids and liquid	3 oz	85	86	45	7	1	—	—	—	2	47	3.5	—	.01	.09	.9	—
Crabmeat, canned	3 oz	85	77	85	15	2	—	—	—	1	38	.7	—	.07	.07	1.6	—
Fish sticks, breaded, cooked, frozen; stick 3¾ by 1 by ½ in	10 sticks or 8 oz pkg	227	66	400	38	20	5	4	10	15	25	0.9	—	.09	.16	3.6	—
Haddock, breaded, fried	3 oz	85	66	140	17	5	1	3	Trace	5	34	1.0	—	.03	.06	2.7	2
Ocean perch, breaded, fried	3 oz	85	59	195	16	11	—	—	—	6	28	1.1	—	.08	.09	1.5	—
Oysters, raw, meat only (13-19 med. selects)	1 cup	240	85	160	20	4	—	—	—	8	226	13.2	740	.33	.43	6.0	—

Salmon, pink, canned	3 oz	85	71	120	17	5	1	1	Trace	0	167[d]	.7	60	.03	.16	6.8	—
Sardines, Atlantic, canned in oil, drained solid	3 oz	85	62	175	20	9	—	—	—	0	372	2.5	190	.02	.17	4.6	—
Shad, baked with table fat and bacon	3 oz	85	64	170	20	10	—	—	—	0	20	.5	20	.11	.22	7.3	—
Shrimp, canned, meat	3 oz	85	70	100	21	1	—	—	—	1	98	2.6	50	.01	.03	1.5	—
Swordfish, broiled with butter or margarine	3 oz	85	65	150	24	5	—	—	—	0	23	1.1	1750	.03	.04	9.3	—
Tuna, canned in oil, drained solids	3 oz	85	61	170	24	7	2	1	1	0	7	1.6	70	.04	.10	10.1	—
MATURE DRY BEANS AND PEAS, NUTS, PEANUTS; RELATED PRODUCTS																	
Almonds, Shelled whole kernels	1 cup	142	5	850	26	77	6	52	15	28	332	6.7	0	.34	1.31	5.0	Trace
Beans, dry:																	
Common varieties as Great Northern, navy, and others:																	
Cooked, drained:																	
Great Northern	1 cup	180	69	210	14	1	—	—	—	38	90	4.9	0	.25	.13	1.3	0
Navy (pea)	1 cup	190	69	225	15	1	—	—	—	40	95	5.1	0	.27	.13	1.3	0
Canned, solids and liquid:																	
White with —																	
Frankfurters (sliced)	1 cup	255	71	365	19	18	—	—	—	32	94	4.8	330	.18	.15	3.3	Trace
Pork and tomato sauce	1 cup	255	71	310	16	7	2	3	1	49	138	4.6	330	.20	.08	1.5	5
Pork and sweet sauce	1 cup	255	66	385	16	12	4	5	1	54	161	5.9	—	.15	.10	1.3	—
Red kidney	1 cup	255	76	230	15	1	—	—	—	42	74	4.6	10	.13	.10	1.5	—
Lima, cooked, drained	1 cup	190	64	260	16	1	—	—	—	49	55	5.9	—	.25	.11	1.3	—
Cashew nuts, roasted	1 cup	140	5	785	24	64	11	45	4	41	53	5.3	140	.60	.35	2.5	—
Coconut, fresh, meat only:																	
Pieces, approx. 2 by 2 by ½ in	1 piece	45	51	155	2	16	14	1	Trace	4	6	.8	0	.02	.01	.2	1
Shredded or grated, firmly packed	1 cup	130	51	450	5	46	39	3	Trace	12	17	2.2	0	.07	.03	.7	4
Cowpeas or blackeye peas, dry, cooked	1 cup	248	80	190	13	1	—	—	—	34	42	3.2	20	.41	.11	1.1	Trace
Peanuts, roasted, salted, halves	1 cup	144	2	840	37	72	16	31	21	27	107	3.0	—	.46	.19	24.7	0

[d] If bones are discarded, value will be greatly reduced.

Food, Approximate Measure, and Weight (in Grams)			Water (%)	Food Energy (kcal)	Protein (g)	Fat (g)	Fatty Acids: Saturated (total) (g)	Fatty Acids: Unsaturated Oleic (g)	Fatty Acids: Unsaturated Linoleic (g)	Carbohydrate (g)	Calcium (mg)	Iron (mg)	Vitamin A value (I.U.)	Thiamin (mg)	Riboflavin (mg)	Niacin (mg)	Ascorbic acid (mg)
MATURE DRY BEANS AND PEAS, NUTS, PEANUTS; RELATED PRODUCTS—Con.																	
Peanut butter	1 tbsp	16	2	95	4	8	2	4	2	3	9	.3	—	.02	.02	2.4	0
Peas, split, dry, cooked	1 cup	250	70	290	20	1	—	—	—	52	28	4.2	100	.37	.22	2.2	—
Pecans, halves	1 cup	108	3	740	10	77	5	48	15	16	79	2.6	140	.93	.14	1.0	2
Walnuts, black or native	1 cup	126	3	790	26	75	4	26	36	19	Trace	7.6	380	.28	.14	.9	—
VEGETABLES AND VEGETABLE PRODUCTS																	
Asparagus, green:																	
Cooked, drained:																	
Spears, ½-in diam. at base	4 spears	60	94	10	1	Trace	—	—	—	2	13	.4	540	.10	.11	.8	16
Pieces, 1½ - 2-in lengths	1 cup	145	94	30	3	Trace	—	—	—	5	30	.9	1310	.23	.26	2.0	38
Canned, solids and liquid	1 cup	244	94	45	5	1	—	—	—	7	44	4.1	1240	.15	.22	2.0	37
Beans:																	
Lima, immature seeds, cooked, drained	1 cup	170	71	190	13	1	—	—	—	34	80	4.3	480	.31	.17	2.2	29
Snap:																	
Green:																	
Cooked, drained	1 cup	125	92	30	2	Trace	—	—	—	7	63	.8	680	.09	.11	.6	15
Canned, solids and liquid	1 cup	239	94	45	2	Trace	—	—	—	10	81	2.9	690	.07	.10	.7	10
Yellow or Wax:																	
Cooked, drained	1 cup	125	93	30	2	Trace	—	—	—	6	63	0.8	290	.09	.11	.6	16
Canned, solids and liquid	1 cup	239	94	45	2	1	—	—	—	10	81	2.9	140	.07	.10	.7	12
Sprouted mung beans, cooked, drained	1 cup	125	91	35	4	Trace	—	—	—	7	21	1.1	30	.11	.13	.9	8

Beets																	
Cooked, drained, peeled:																	
Whole beets, 2-in diam.	2 beets	100	91	30	1	Trace	—	—	—	7	14	.5	20	.03	.04	.3	6
Diced or sliced	1 cup	170	91	55	2	Trace	—	—	—	12	24	.9	30	.05	.07	.5	10
Canned, solids and liquid	1 cup	246	90	85	2	Trace	—	—	—	19	34	1.5	20	.02	.05	.2	7
Beet greens, leaves and stems, cooked, drained	1 cup	145	94	25	3	Trace	—	—	—	5	144	2.8	7,400	.10	.22	.4	22
Blackeye peas. See Cowpeas.																	
Broccoli, cooked, drained:																	
Whole stalks, medium size	1 stalk	180	91	45	6	1	—	—	—	8	158	1.4	4,500	.16	.36	1.4	162
Stalks cut into ½-in pieces	1 cup	155	91	40	5	1	—	—	—	7	136	1.2	3,880	.14	.31	1.2	140
Chopped, yield from 10-oz frozen pkg	1-3/8 cups	250	92	65	7	1	—	—	—	12	135	1.8	6,500	.15	.30	1.3	143
Brussels sprouts, 7-8 sprouts (1¼ - 1½-in diam) per cup, cooked	1 cup	155	88	55	7	1	—	—	—	10	50	1.7	810	.12	.22	1.2	135
Cabbage:																	
Common varieties:																	
Raw:																	
Coarsely shredded or sliced	1 cup	70	92	15	1	Trace	—	—	—	4	34	.3	90	.04	.04	.2	33
Finely shredded or chopped	1 cup	90	92	20	1	Trace	—	—	—	5	44	.4	120	.05	.05	.3	42
Cooked	1 cup	145	94	30	2	Trace	—	—	—	6	64	.4	190	.06	.06	.4	48
Red, raw, coarsely shredded	1 cup	70	90	20	1	Trace	—	—	—	5	29	.6	30	.06	.04	.3	43
Savoy, raw, coarsely shredded	1 cup	70	92	15	2	Trace	—	—	—	3	47	.6	140	.04	.06	.2	39
Cabbage, celery or Chinese, raw, cut in 1-in pieces	1 cup	75	95	10	1	Trace	—	—	—	2	32	.5	110	.04	.03	.5	19
Cabbage, spoon (or pakchoy), cooked	1 cup	170	95	25	2	Trace	—	—	—	4	252	1.0	5,270	.07	.14	1.2	26
Carrots:																	
Raw:																	
Whole, 5½ by 1 in (25 thin strips)	1 carrot	50	88	20	1	Trace	—	—	—	5	18	.4	5,500	.03	.03	.3	4
Grated	1 cup	110	88	45	1	Trace	—	—	—	11	41	.8	12,100	.06	.06	.7	9

Food, Approximate Measure, and Weight (in Grams)			Water (%)	Food Energy (kcal)	Protein (g)	Fat (g)	Fatty Acids: Saturated (total) (g)	Fatty Acids: Unsaturated: Oleic (g)	Fatty Acids: Unsaturated: Linoleic (g)	Carbohydrate (g)	Calcium (mg)	Iron (mg)	Vitamin A value (I.U.)	Thiamin (mg)	Riboflavin (mg)	Niacin (mg)	Ascorbic acid (mg)
VEGETABLES AND VEGETABLE PRODUCTS—Con.																	
Cooked, diced	1 cup	145	91	45	1	Trace	—	—	—	10	48	.9	15,220	.08	.07	.7	9
Canned, strained or chopped (baby food)	1 oz	28	92	10	Trace	Trace	—	—	—	2	7	.1	3,690	.01	.01	.1	1
Cauliflower, cooked, flowerbuds	1 cup	120	93	25	3	Trace	—	—	—	5	25	.8	70	.11	.10	.7	66
Celery, raw:																	
Stalk, large outer, 8 by about 1½ in, at root end	1 stalk	40	94	5	Trace	Trace	—	—	—	2	16	.1	100	.01	.01	.1	4
Pieces, diced	1 cup	100	94	15	1	Trace	—	—	—	4	39	.3	240	.03	.03	.3	0
Collards, cooked	1 cup	190	91	55	5	1	—	—	—	9	289	1.1	10,260	.27	.37	2.4	87
Corn, sweet:																	
Cooked, ear 5 by 1¾ in[e]	1 ear	140	74	70	3	1	—	—	—	16	2	.5	310[f]	.09	.08	1.0	7
Canned, solids and liquid	1 cup	256	81	170	5	2	—	—	—	40	10	1.0	690[f]	.07	.12	2.3	13
Cowpeas, cooked, immature seeds	1 cup	160	72	175	13	1	—	—	—	29	38	3.4	560	.49	.18	2.3	28
Cucumbers, 10 oz; 7½ by about 2 in:																	
Raw, pared	1 cucumber	207	96	30	1	Trace	—	—	—	7	35	.6	Trace	.07	.09	.4	23
Raw, pared, center slice 1/8-in thick	6 slices	50	96	5	Trace	Trace	—	—	—	2	8	.2	Trace	.02	.02	.1	6
Dandelion greens, cooked	1 cup	180	90	60	4	1	—	—	—	12	252	3.2	21,060	.24	.29	—	32
Endive, curly (including escarole)	2 oz	57	93	10	1	Trace	—	—	—	2	46	1.0	1,870	.04	.08	.3	6
Kale, leaves including stems, cooked	1 cup	110	91	30	4	1	—	—	—	4	147	1.3	8,140	—	—	—	68
Lettuce, raw:																	
Butterhead, as Boston types; head, 4-in diam.	1 head	220	95	30	3	Trace	—	—	—	6	77	4.4	2,130	.14	.13	.6	18
Crisphead, as Iceberg; head, 4¾-in diam.	1 head	454	96	60	4	Trace	—	—	—	13	91	2.3	1,500	.29	.27	1.3	29

Looseleaf, or bunching varieties, leaves	2 large	50	94	10	1	Trace	—	—	—	2	34	.7	950	.03	.04	.2	9
Mushrooms, canned, solids and liquid	1 cup	244	93	40	5	Trace	—	—	—	6	15	1.2	Trace	.04	.60	4.8	4
Mustard greens, cooked	1 cup	140	93	35	3	1	—	—	—	6	193	2.5	8,120	.11	.19	.9	68
Okra, cooked, pod, 3 by 5/8 in	8 pods	85	91	25	2	Trace	—	—	—	5	78	.4	420	.11	.15	.8	17
Onions:																	
Mature:																	
Raw, onion 2½-in diam.	1 onion	110	89	40	2	Trace	—	—	—	10	30	.6	40	.04	.04	.2	11
Cooked	1 cup	210	92	60	3	Trace	—	—	—	14	50	.8	80	.06	.06	.4	14
Young green, small, without tops	6 onions	50	88	20	1	Trace	—	—	—	5	20	.3	Trace	.02	.02	.2	12
Parsley, raw, chopped	1 tbsp	4	85	Trace	Trace	Trace	—	—	—	Trace	8	.2	340	Trace	.01	Trace	7
Parsnips, cooked	1 cup	155	82	100	2	1	—	—	—	23	70	.9	50	.11	.12	.2	16
Peas, green:																	
Cooked	1 cup	160	82	115	9	1	—	—	—	19	37	2.9	860	.44	.17	3.7	33
Canned, solids and liquid	1 cup	249	83	165	9	1	—	—	—	31	50	4.2	1,120	.23	.13	2.2	22
Canned, strained (baby food)	1 oz	28	86	15	1	Trace	—	—	—	3	3	.4	140	.02	.02	.4	3
Peppers, hot, red, without seeds, dried (ground chili powder), added seasonings	1 tbsp	15	8	50	2	2	—	—	—	8	40	2.3	9,750	.03	.17	1.3	2
Peppers, sweet:																	
Raw, about 5 per pound:																	
Green pod without stem and seeds	1 pod	74	93	15	1	Trace	—	—	—	4	7	.5	310	.06	.06	.4	94
Cooked, boiled, drained	1 pod	73	95	15	1	Trace	—	—	—	3	7	.4	310	.05	.05	.4	70
Potatoes, medium (about 3 per pound raw):																	
Baked, peeled after baking	1 potato	99	75	90	3	Trace	—	—	—	21	9	.7	Trace	.10	.04	1.7	20
Boiled:																	
Peeled after boiling	1 potato	136	80	105	3	Trace	—	—	—	23	10	.8	Trace	.13	.05	2.0	22
Peeled before boiling	1 potato	122	83	80	2	Trace	—	—	—	18	7	.6	Trace	.11	.04	1.4	20

[e]Measure and weight apply to entire vegetable or fruit including parts not usually eaten.

[f]Based on yellow varieties, white varieties contain only a trace of cryptoxanthin and carotenes, the pigments in corn that have biological activity.

Food, Approximate Measure, and Weight (in Grams)			Water (%)	Food Energy (kcal)	Protein (g)	Fat (g)	Fatty Acids: Saturated (total) (g)	Unsaturated: Oleic (g)	Unsaturated: Linoleic (g)	Carbohydrate (g)	Calcium (mg)	Iron (mg)	Vitamin A value (I.U.)	Thiamin (mg)	Riboflavin (mg)	Niacin (mg)	Ascorbic acid (mg)
VEGETABLES AND VEGETABLE PRODUCTS—Con.																	
Potatoes—Con.																	
French-fried, piece 2 by ½ by ½ in:																	
Cooked in deep fat	10 pieces	57	45	155	2	7	2	2	4	20	9	.7	Trace	.07	.04	1.8	12
Frozen, heated	10 pieces	57	53	125	2	5	1	1	2	19	5	1.0	Trace	.08	.01	1.5	12
Mashed:																	
Milk added	1 cup	195	83	125	4	1	—	—	—	25	47	.8	50	.16	.10	2.0	19
Milk and butter added	1 cup	195	80	185	4	8	4	3	Trace	24	47	.8	330	.16	.10	1.9	18
Potato chips, medium, 2-in diam.	10 chips	20	2	115	1	8	2	2	4	10	8	.4	Trace	.04	.01	1.0	3
Pumpkin, canned	1 cup	228	90	75	2	1	—	—	—	18	57	.9	14,590	.07	.12	1.3	12
Radishes, raw, small, without tops	4 radishes	40	94	5	Trace	Trace	—	—	—	1	12	.4	Trace	.01	.01	.1	10
Sauerkraut, canned, solids and liquid	1 cup	235	93	45	2	Trace	—	—	—	9	85	1.2	120	.07	.09	.4	33
Spinach:																	
Cooked	1 cup	180	92	40	5	1	—	—	—	6	167	4.0	14,580	.13	.25	1.0	50
Canned, drained solids	1 cup	180	91	45	5	1	—	—	—	6	212	4.7	14,400	.03	.21	.6	24
Squash:																	
Cooked:																	
Summer, diced	1 cup	210	96	30	2	Trace	—	—	—	7	52	.8	820	.10	.16	1.6	21
Winter, baked, mashed	1 cup	205	81	130	4	1	—	—	—	32	57	1.6	8,610	.10	.27	1.4	27
Sweet potatoes:																	
Cooked, medium, 5 by 2 in, weight raw about 6 oz																	
Baked, peeled after baking	1 sweet-potato	110	64	155	2	1	—	—	—	36	44	1.0	8,910	.10	.07	.7	24
Boiled, peeled after boiling	1 sweet-potato	147	71	170	2	1	—	—	—	39	47	1.0	11,610	.13	.09	.9	25
Candied, 3½ by 2¼-in	1 sweet-potato	175	60	295	2	6	2	3	1	60	65	1.6	11,030	.10	.08	.8	17

Canned, vacuum or solid pack	1 cup	218	72	235	4	Trace	—	—	—	54	54	1.7	17,000	.10	.10	1.4	30
Tomatoes:																	
Raw, approx. 3-in diam. 2-1/8-in high; wt 7 oz	1 tomato	200	90	40	2	Trace	—	—	—	9	24	.9	1,640	.11	.07	1.3	42[g]
Canned, solids and liquid	1 cup	241	94	50	2	1	—	—	—	10	14	1.2	2,170	.12	.07	1.7	41
Tomato catsup:																	
Cup	1 cup	273	69	290	6	1	—	—	—	69	60	2.2	3,820	.25	.19	4.4	41
Tablespoon	1 tbsp	15	69	15	Trace	Trace	—	—	—	4	3	.1	210	.01	.01	.2	2
Tomato juice, canned:																	
Cup	1 cup	243	94	45	2	Trace	—	—	—	10	17	2.2	1,940	.12	.07	1.9	39
Glass (6 fl oz)	1 glass	182	94	35	2	Trace	—	—	—	8	13	1.6	1,460	.09	.05	1.5	29
Turnips, cooked, diced	1 cup	155	94	35	1	Trace	—	—	—	8	54	.6	Trace	.06	.08	.5	34
Turnip greens, cooked	1 cup	145	94	30	3	Trace	—	—	—	5	252	1.5	8,270	.15	.33	.7	68
FRUITS AND FRUIT PRODUCTS																	
Apples, raw (about 3 per lb)[e]	1 apple	150	85	70	Trace	Trace	—	—	—	18	8	.4	50	.04	.02	.1	3
Apple juice, bottled or canned	1 cup	248	88	120	Trace	Trace	—	—	—	30	15	1.5	—	.02	.05	.2	2
Applesauce, canned:																	
Sweetened	1 cup	255	76	230	1	Trace	—	—	—	61	10	1.3	100	.05	.03	.1	3[h]
Unsweetened or artificially sweetened	1 cup	244	88	100	1	Trace	—	—	—	26	10	1.2	100	.05	.02	.1	2[h]
Apricots:																	
Raw (about 12 per lb)[e]	3 apricots	114	85	55	1	Trace	—	—	—	14	18	.5	2,890	.03	.04	.7	10
Canned in heavy syrup	1 cup	259	77	220	2	Trace	—	—	—	57	28	.8	4,510	.05	.06	.9	10
Dried, uncooked (40 halves per cup)	1 cup	150	25	390	8	1	—	—	—	100	100	8.2	16,350	.02	.23	4.9	19
Cooked, unsweetened, fruit and liquid	1 cup	285	76	240	5	1	—	—	—	62	63	5.1	8,550	.01	.13	2.8	8
Apricot nectar, canned	1 cup	251	85	140	1	Trace	—	—	—	37	23	.5	2,380	.03	.03	.5	8[h]

[e]Measure and weight apply to entire vegetable or fruit including parts not usually eaten.

[g]Year-round average. Samples marketed from November through May, average 20 milligrams per 200-gram tomato; from June through October, around 52 milligrams.

[h]This is the amount from the fruit. Additional ascorbic acid may be added by the manufacturer. Refer to the label for this information.

Food, Approximate Measure, and Weight (in Grams)			Water (%)	Food Energy (kcal)	Protein (g)	Fat (g)	Fatty Acids: Saturated (total) (g)	Fatty Acids: Unsaturated: Oleic (g)	Fatty Acids: Unsaturated: Linoleic (g)	Carbohydrate (g)	Calcium (mg)	Iron (mg)	Vitamin A value (I.U.)	Thiamin (mg)	Riboflavin (mg)	Niacin (mg)	Ascorbic acid (mg)
FRUITS AND FRUIT PRODUCTS—Con.																	
Avocados, whole fruit, raw[e]																	
California (mid- and late-winter; diam. 3-1/8-in	1 avocado	284	74	370	5	37	7	17	5	13	22	1.3	630	.24	.43	3.5	30
Florida (late summer, fall; diam. 3-5/8-in	1 avocado	454	78	390	4	33	7	15	4	27	30	1.8	880	.33	.61	4.9	43
Bananas, raw, medium size[e]	1 banana	175	76	100	1	Trace	—	—	—	26	10	.8	230	.06	.07	.8	12
Banana flakes	1 cup	100	3	340	4	1	—	—	—	89	32	2.8	760	.18	.24	2.8	7
Blackberries, raw	1 cup	144	84	85	2	1	—	—	—	19	46	1.3	290	.05	.06	.5	30
Blueberries, raw	1 cup	140	83	85	1	1	—	—	—	21	21	1.4	140	.04	.08	.6	20
Cantaloupes, raw; medium, 5-in diam., about 1⅔ lbs[e]	½ melon	385	91	60	1	Trace	—	—	—	14	27	.8	6.540[i]	.08	.06	1.2	63
Cherries, canned, red, sour, pitted, water pack	1 cup	244	88	105	2	Trace	—	—	—	26	37	.7	1.660	.07	.05	.5	12
Cranberry juice cocktail, canned	1 cup	250	83	165	Trace	Trace	—	—	—	42	13	.3	Trace	.03	.03	.1	40[j]
Cranberry sauce, sweetened, canned, strained	1 cup	277	62	405	Trace	1	—	—	—	104	17	.6	60	.03	.03	.1	6
Dates, pitted, cut	1 cup	178	22	490	4	1	—	—	—	130	105	5.3	90	.16	.17	3.9	0
Figs, dried, large, 2 by 1 in	1 fig	21	23	60	1	Trace	—	—	—	15	26	.6	20	.02	.02	.1	0
Fruit cocktail, canned, in heavy syrup	1 cup	256	80	195	1	Trace	—	—	—	50	23	1.0	360	.05	.03	1.3	5
Grapefruit:																	
Raw, medium, 3¾-in diam[e]																	
White	½ grapefruit	241	89	45	1	Trace	—	—	—	12	19	.5	10	.05	.02	.2	44
Pink or red	½ grapefruit	241	89	50	1	Trace	—	—	—	13	20	.5	540	.05	.02	.2	44
Canned, syrup pack	1 cup	254	81	180	2	Trace	—	—	—	45	33	.8	30	.08	.05	.5	76

Grapefruit juice:																	
Fresh	1 cup	246	90	95	1	Trace	—	—	—	23	22	.5	[k]	.09	.04	.4	92
Canned, white:																	
Unsweetened	1 cup	247	89	100	1	Trace	—	—	—	24	20	1.0	20	.07	.04	.4	84
Sweetened	1 cup	250	86	130	1	Trace	—	—	—	32	20	1.0	20	.07	.04	.4	78
Frozen, concentrate, unsweetened:																	
Undiluted, can, 6 fl oz	1 can	207	62	300	4	1	—	—	—	72	70	.8	60	.29	.12	1.4	286
Diluted with 3 parts water, by volume	1 cup	247	89	100	1	Trace	—	—	—	24	25	.2	20	.10	.04	.5	96
Dehydrated crystals	4 oz	113	1	410	6	1	—	—	—	102	100	1.2	80	.40	.20	2.0	396
Prepared with water (1 lb yields about 1 gal)	1 cup	247	90	100	1	Trace	—	—	—	24	22	.2	20	.10	.05	.5	91
Grapes, raw:[e]																	
American type (slip skin)	1 cup	153	82	65	1	1	—	—	—	15	15	.4	100	.05	.03	.2	3
European type (adherent skin)	1 cup	160	81	95	1	Trace	—	—	—	25	17	.6	140	.07	.04	.4	6
Grapejuice:																	
Canned or bottled	1 cup	253	83	165	1	Trace	—	—	—	42	28	.8	—	.10	.05	.5	Trace
Frozen concentrate, sweetened:																	
Undiluted, can, 6 fl oz	1 can	216	53	395	1	Trace	—	—	—	100	22	.9	40	.13	.22	1.5	12
Diluted with 3 parts water, by volume	1 cup	250	86	135	1	Trace	—	—	—	33	8	.3	10	.05	.08	.5	[l]
Grapejuice drink, canned	1 cup	250	86	135	Trace	Trace	—	—	—	35	8	.3	—	.03	.03	.3	[l]
Lemons, raw, 2-1/8 in. diam. size 165.[e] Used for juice	1 lemon	110	90	20	1	Trace	—	—	—	6	19	.4	10	.03	.01	.1	39
Lemon juice, raw	1 cup	244	91	60	1	Trace	—	—	—	20	17	.5	50	.07	.02	.2	112
Lemonade concentrate:																	
Frozen, 6 fl oz per can	1 can	219	48	430	Trace	Trace	—	—	—	112	9	.4	40	.04	.07	.7	66
Diluted with 4⅓ parts water, by volume	1 cup	248	88	110	Trace	Trace	—	—	—	28	2	Trace	Trace	Trace	.02	.2	17

[e]Measure and weight apply to entire vegetable or fruit including parts not usually eaten.

[i]Value for varieties with orange-colored flesh; value for varieties with green flesh would be about 540 I.U.

[j]Value listed is based on product with label stating 30 milligrams per 6 fl oz serving.

[k]For white-fleshed varieties value is about 20 I.U. per cup; for red-fleshed varieties, 1,080 I.U. per cup.

[l]Present only if added by the manufacturer. Refer to the label for this information.

Food, Approximate Measure, and Weight (in Grams)			Water (%)	Food Energy (kcal)	Protein (g)	Fat (g)	Fatty Acids: Saturated (total) (g)	Fatty Acids: Unsaturated: Oleic (g)	Fatty Acids: Unsaturated: Linoleic (g)	Carbohydrate (g)	Calcium (mg)	Iron (mg)	Vitamin A value (I.U.)	Thiamin (mg)	Riboflavin (mg)	Niacin (mg)	Ascorbic acid (mg)
FRUITS AND FRUIT PRODUCTS—Con.																	
Lime juice:																	
Fresh	1 cup	246	90	65	1	Trace	—	—	—	22	22	.5	20	.05	.02	.2	79
Canned, unsweetened	1 cup	246	90	65	1	Trace	—	—	—	22	22	.5	20	.05	.02	.2	52
Limeade concentrate, frozen:																	
Undiluted, can, 6 fl oz	1 can	218	50	410	Trace	Trace	—	—	—	108	11	.2	Trace	.02	.02	.2	26
Diluted with 4⅓ parts water by volume	1 cup	247	90	100	Trace	Trace	—	—	—	27	2	Trace	Trace	Trace	Trace	Trace	5
Oranges, raw 2-5/8 in diam., all commercial varieties[e]	1 orange	180	86	65	1	Trace	—	—	—	16	54	.5	260	.13	.05	.5	66
Orange juice, fresh, all varieties	1 cup	248	88	110	2	1	—	—	—	26	27	.5	500	.22	.07	1.0	124
Canned, unsweetened	1 cup	249	87	120	2	Trace	—	—	—	28	25	1.0	500	.17	.05	.7	100
Frozen concentrate:																	
Undiluted, can, 6 fl oz	1 can	213	55	360	5	Trace	—	—	—	87	75	.9	1620	.68	.11	2.8	360
Diluted with 3 parts water by volume	1 cup	249	87	120	2	Trace	—	—	—	29	25	.2	550	.22	.02	1.0	120
Dehydrated crystals	4 oz	113	1	430	6	2	—	—	—	100	95	1.9	1900	.76	.24	3.3	408
Prepared with water (1 lb yields about 1 gal)	1 cup	248	88	115	2	1	—	—	—	27	25	.5	500	.20	.07	1.0	109
Orange-apricot juice drink	1 cup	249	87	125	1	Trace	—	—	—	32	12	.2	1440	.05	.02	.5	40[j]
Orange and grapefruit juice:																	
Frozen concentrate:																	
Undiluted, can, 6 fl oz	1 can	210	59	330	4	1	—	—	—	78	61	.8	800	.48	.06	2.3	302
Diluted with 3 parts water by volume	1 cup	248	88	110	1	Trace	—	—	—	26	20	.2	270	.16	.02	.8	102
Papayas, raw, ½-in cubes	1 cup	182	89	70	1	Trace	—	—	—	18	36	.5	3190	.07	.08	.5	102
Peaches:																	
Raw:																	
Whole, medium, 2-in diam., about 4 per lb[e]	1 peach	114	89	35	1	Trace	—	—	—	10	9	.5	1320[m]	.02	.05	1.0	7
Sliced	1 cup	168	89	65	1	Trace	—	—	—	16	15	.8	2230[m]	.03	.08	1.6	12

Canned, yellow-fleshed, solids and liquid:																	
Syrup pack, heavy:																	
Halves or slices	1 cup	257	79	200	1	Trace	—	—	—	52	10	.8	1100	.02	.06	1.4	7
Water pack	1 cup	245	91	75	1	Trace	—	—	—	20	10	.7	1100	.02	.06	1.4	7
Dried, uncooked	1 cup	160	25	420	5	1	—	—	—	109	77	9.6	6240	.02	.31	8.5	28
Cooked, unsweetened, 10-12 halves and juice	1 cup	270	77	220	3	1	—	—	—	58	41	5.1	3290	.01	.15	4.2	6
Frozen:																	
Carton, 12 oz, not thawed	1 carton	340	76	300	1	Trace	—	—	—	77	14	.7	2210	.03	.14	2.4	135[n]
Pears:																	
Raw, 3 by 2½-in diam.[e]	1 pear	182	83	100	1	1	—	—	—	25	13	.5	30	.04	.07	.2	7
Canned, solids and liquid:																	
Syrup pack, heavy:																	
Halves or slices	1 cup	255	80	195	1	1	—	—	—	50	13	.5	Trace	.03	.05	.3	4
Pineapple:																	
Raw, diced	1 cup	140	85	75	1	Trace	—	—	—	19	24	.7	100	.12	.04	.3	24
Canned, heavy syrup pack, solids and liquid:																	
Crushed	1 cup	260	80	195	1	Trace	—	—	—	50	29	.8	120	.20	.06	.5	17
Sliced, slices and juice	2 small or 1 large	122	80	90	Trace	Trace	—	—	—	24	13	.4	50	.09	.03	.2	8
Pineapple juice, canned	1 cup	249	86	135	1	Trace	—	—	—	34	37	.7	120	.12	.04	.5	22[h]
Plums, all except prunes:																	
Raw, 2-in diam., about 2 oz[e]	1 plum	60	87	25	Trace	Trace	—	—	—	7	7	.3	140	.02	.02	.3	3
Canned, syrup pack (Italian prunes):																	
Plums (with pits) and juice[e]	1 cup	256	77	205	1	Trace	—	—	—	53	22	2.2	2970	.05	.05	.9	4
Prunes, dried, "softenized," medium:																	
Uncooked[e]	4 prunes	32	28	70	1	Trace	—	—	—	18	14	1.1	440	.02	.04	.4	1
Cooked, unsweetened, 17-18 prunes and ⅓ cup liquid[e]	1 cup	270	66	295	2	1	—	—	—	78	60	4.5	1860	.08	.18	1.7	2

[e]Measure and weight apply to entire vegetable or fruit including parts not usually eaten.

[h]This is the amount from the fruit. Additional ascorbic acid may be added by the manufacturer. Refer to the label for this information.

[j]Value listed is based on product with label stating 30 milligrams per 6 fl oz serving.

[m]Based on yellow-fleshed varieties; for white-fleshed varieties value is about 50 I.U. per 114 gram peach and 80 I.U. per cup of sliced peaches.

[n]This value includes ascorbic acid added by manufacturer.

Biscuits, baking powder from home recipe with enriched flour, 2-in diam.	1 biscuit	28	27	105	2	5	1	2	1	13	34	.4	Trace	.06	.06	.1	Trace
Biscuits, baking powder from mix, 2-in diam.	1 biscuit	28	28	90	2	3	1	1	1	15	19	.6	Trace	.08	.07	.6	Trace
Bran flakes (40% bran), added thiamin and iron	1 cup	35	3	105	4	1	—	—	—	28	25	12.3	0	.14	.06	2.2	0
Bran flakes with raisins, added thiamin and iron	1 cup	50	7	145	4	1	—	—	—	40	28	13.5	Trace	.16	.07	2.7	0
Breads:																	
Boston brown bread, slice 3 by ¾-in	1 slice	48	45	100	3	1	—	—		22	43	.9	0	.05	.03	.6	0
Cracked-wheat bread:																	
Loaf, 1 lb	1 loaf	454	35	1190	40	10	2	5	2	236	399	5.0	Trace	.53	.41	5.9	Trace
Slice, 18 slices per loaf	1 slice	25	35	65	2	1	—	—	—	13	22	.3	Trace	.03	.02	.3	Trace
French or Vienna bread:																	
Enriched, 1 lb loaf	1 loaf	454	31	1315	41	14	3	8	2	251	195	10.0	Trace	1.27	1.00	11.3	Trace
Unenriched, 1 lb loaf	1 loaf	454	31	1315	41	14	3	8	2	251	195	3.2	Trace	.36	.36	3.6	Trace
Italian bread:																	
Enriched, 1 lb loaf	1 loaf	454	32	1250	41	4	Trace	1	2	256	77	10.0	0	1.32	.91	11.8	0
Unenriched, 1 lb loaf	1 loaf	454	32	1250	41	4	Trace	1	2	256	77	3.2	0	.41	.27	3.6	0
Raisin bread:																	
Loaf, 1 lb	1 loaf	454	35	1190	30	13	3	8	2	243	322	5.9	Trace	.23	.41	3.2	Trace
Slice, 18 slices per loaf	1 slice	25	35	65	2	1	—	—	—	13	18	.3	Trace	.01	.02	.2	Trace
Rye bread:																	
American, light (⅓ rye, ⅔ wheat):																	
Loaf, 1 lb	1 loaf	454	36	1100	41	5	—	—	—	236	340	7.3	0	.82	.32	6.4	0
Slice, 18 slices per loaf	1 slice	25	36	60	2	Trace	—	—	—	13	19	.4	0	.05	.02	.4	0
Pumpernickel, loaf, 1 lb	1 loaf	454	34	1115	41	5	—	—	—	241	381	10.9	0	1.04	.64	5.4	0
White bread, enriched:[o]																	
Soft-crumb type:																	
Loaf, 1 lb	1 loaf	454	36	1225	39	15	3	8	2	229	381	11.3	Trace	1.13	.95	10.9	Trace
Slice, 18 slices per loaf	1 slice	25	36	70	2	1	—	—	—	13	21	.6	Trace	.06	.05	.6	Trace
Slice, toasted	1 slice	22	25	70	2	1	—	—	—	13	21	.6	Trace	.06	.05	.6	Trace

[e]Measure and weight apply to entire vegetable or fruit including parts not usually eaten.

[h]This is the amount from the fruit. Additional ascorbic acid may be added by the manufacturer. Refer to the label for this information.

[o]Values for iron, thiamin, riboflavin, and niacin per pound of unenriched white bread would be as follows: soft crumb—Iron · 3.2 mg, Thiamin · .31 mg, Riboflavin · .39 mg, Niacin · 5.0 mg.

Food, Approximate Measure, and Weight (in Grams)			Water (%)	Food Energy (kcal)	Protein (g)	Fat (g)	Fatty Acids: Saturated (total) (g)	Fatty Acids: Unsaturated: Oleic (g)	Fatty Acids: Unsaturated: Linoleic (g)	Carbohydrate (g)	Calcium (mg)	Iron (mg)	Vitamin A value (I.U.)	Thiamin (mg)	Riboflavin (mg)	Niacin (mg)	Ascorbic acid (mg)
FRUITS AND FRUIT PRODUCTS—Con.																	
Prune juice, canned or bottled	1 cup	256	80	200	1	Trace	—	—	—	49	36	10.5	—	.03	.03	1.0	5[h]
Raisins, seedless:																	
Packaged, ½ oz or 1½ tbsp per pkg	1 pkg	14	18	40	Trace	Trace	—	—	—	11	9	.5	Trace	.02	.01	.1	Trace
Cup, pressed down	1 cup	165	18	480	4	Trace	—	—	—	128	102	5.8	30	.18	.13	.8	2
Raspberries, red:																	
Raw	1 cup	123	84	70	1	1	—	—	—	17	27	1.1	160	.04	.11	1.1	31
Frozen, 10-oz carton, not thawed	1 carton	284	74	275	2	1	—	—	—	70	37	1.7	200	.06	.17	1.7	59
Rhubarb, cooked, sugar added	1 cup	272	63	385	1	Trace	—	—	—	98	212	1.6	220	.06	.15	.7	17
Strawberries:																	
Raw, capped	1 cup	149	90	55	1	1	—	—	—	13	31	1.5	90	.04	.10	1.0	88
Frozen, 10-oz carton, not thawed	1 carton	284	71	310	1	1	—	—	—	79	40	2.0	90	.06	.17	1.5	150
Tangerines, raw, medium, 2-3/8-in diam., size 176[e]	1 tangerine	116	87	40	1	Trace	—	—	—	10	34	.3	360	.05	.02	.1	27
Tangerine juice, canned, sweetened	1 cup	249	87	125	1	1	—	—	—	30	45	.5	1050	.15	.05	.2	55
Watermelon, raw, wedge, 4 by 8 in (1/16 of 10 by 16-in melon, about 2 lbs with rind)[e]	1 wedge	925	93	115	2	1	—	—	—	27	30	2.1	2510	.13	.13	.7	30
GRAIN PRODUCTS																	
Bagel, 3-in diam.:																	
Egg	1 bagel	55	32	165	6	2	—	—	—	28	9	1.2	30	.14	.10	1.2	0
Water	1 bagel	55	29	165	6	2	—	—	—	30	8	1.2	0	.15	.11	1.4	0
Barley, pearled, light, uncooked	1 cup	200	11	700	16	2	Trace	1	1	158	32	4.0	0	.24	.10	6.2	0

Food, Approximate Measure, and Weight (in Grams)			Water (%)	Food Energy (kcal)	Protein (g)	Fat (g)	Fatty Acids: Saturated (total) (g)	Fatty Acids: Unsaturated Oleic (g)	Fatty Acids: Unsaturated Linoleic (g)	Carbohydrate (g)	Calcium (mg)	Iron (mg)	Vitamin A value (I.U.)	Thiamin (mg)	Riboflavin (mg)	Niacin (mg)	Ascorbic acid (mg)
GRAIN PRODUCTS—Con.																	
White bread, enriched,[O] soft-crumb type:																	
Slice, 22 slices per loaf	1 slice	20	36	55	2	1	—	—	—	10	17	.5	Trace	.05	.04	.5	Trace
Slice, toasted	1 slice	17	25	55	2	1	—	—	—	10	17	.5	Trace	.05	.04	.5	Trace
Loaf, 1½ lb	1 loaf	680	36	1835	59	22	5	12	3	343	571	17.0	Trace	1.70	1.43	16.3	Trace
Slice, 24 slices per loaf	1 slice	28	36	75	2	1	—	—	—	14	24	.7	Trace	.07	.06	.7	Trace
Slice, toasted	1 slice	24	25	75	2	1	—	—	—	14	24	.7	Trace	.07	.06	.7	Trace
Slice, 28 slices per loaf	1 slice	24	36	65	2	1	—	—	—	12	20	.6	Trace	.06	.05	.6	Trace
Slice, toasted	1 slice	21	25	65	2	1	—	—	—	12	20	.6	Trace	.06	.05	.6	Trace
White bread, enriched,[O] firm-crumb type:																	
Loaf, 1 lb	1 loaf	454	35	1245	41	17	4	10	2	228	435	11.3	Trace	1.22	.91	10.9	Trace
Slice, 20 slices per loaf	1 slice	23	35	65	2	1	—	—	—	12	22	.6	Trace	.06	.05	.6	Trace
Slice, toasted	1 slice	20	24	65	2	1	—	—	—	12	22	.6	Trace	.06	.05	.6	Trace
Loaf, 2 lb	1 loaf	907	35	2495	82	34	8	20	4	455	871	22.7	Trace	2.45	1.81	21.8	Trace
Slice, 34 slices per loaf	1 slice	27	35	75	2	1	—	—	—	14	26	.7	Trace	.07	.05	.6	Trace
Slice, toasted	1 slice	23	35	75	2	1	—	—	—	14	26	.7	Trace	.07	.05	.6	Trace
Whole-wheat bread, soft-crumb type:																	
Loaf, 1 lb	1 loaf	454	36	1095	41	12	2	6	2	224	381	13.6	Trace	1.36	.45	12.7	Trace
Slice, 16 slices per loaf	1 slice	28	36	65	3	1	—	—	—	14	24	.8	Trace	.09	.03	.8	Trace
Slice, toasted	1 slice	24	24	65	3	1	—	—	—	14	24	.8	Trace	.09	.03	.8	Trace
Whole-wheat bread, firm-crumb type:																	
Loaf, 1 lb	1 loaf	454	36	1100	48	14	3	6	3	216	449	13.6	Trace	1.18	.54	12.7	Trace
Slice, 18 slices per loaf	1 slice	25	36	60	3	1	—	—	—	12	25	.8	Trace	.06	.03	.7	Trace
Slice, toasted	1 slice	21	24	60	3	1	—	—	—	12	25	.8	Trace	.06	.03	.7	Trace
Breadcrumbs, dry, grated	1 cup	100	6	390	13	5	1	2	1	73	122	3.6	Trace	.22	.30	3.5	Trace
Buckwheat flour, light, sifted	1 cup	98	12	340	6	1	—	—	—	78	11	1.0	0	.08	.04	.4	0
Bulgur, canned, seasoned	1 cup	135	56	245	8	4	—	—	—	44	27	1.9	0	.08	.05	4.1	0
Cakes made from cake mixes:																	
Angelfood:																	
Whole cake	1 cake	635	34	1645	36	1	—	—	—	377	603	1.9	0	.03	.70	.6	0
Piece, 1/12 of 10-in diam. cake	1 piece	53	34	135	3	Trace	—	—	—	32	50	.2	0	Trace	.06	.1	0

Cupcakes, small, 2½-in diam.:																	
Without icing	1 cupcake	25	26	90	1	3	1	1	1	14	40	.1	40	.01	.03	.1	Trace
With chocolate icing	1 cupcake	36	22	130	2	5	2	2	1	21	47	.3	60	.01	.04	.1	Trace
Devil's food, 2-layer, with chocolate icing:																	
Whole cake	1 cake	1107	24	3755	49	136	54	58	16	645	653	8.9	1660	.33	.89	3.3	1
Piece, 1/16 of 9-in diam. cake	1 piece	69	24	235	3	9	3	4	1	40	41	.6	100	.02	.06	.2	Trace
Cupcake, small, 2½-in diam.	1 cupcake	35	24	120	2	4	1	2	Trace	20	21	.3	50	.01	.03	.1	Trace
Gingerbread:																	
Whole cake	1 cake	570	37	1575	18	39	10	19	9	291	513	9.1	Trace	.17	.51	4.6	2
Piece, 1/9 of 8-in square cake	1 piece	63	37	175	2	4	1	2	1	32	57	1.0	Trace	.02	.06	.5	Trace
White, 2-layer, with chocolate icing:																	
Whole cake	1 cake	1140	21	4000	45	122	45	54	17	716	1129	5.7	680	.23	.91	2.3	2
Piece, 1/16 of 9-in diam. cake	1 piece	71	21	250	3	8	3	3	1	45	70	.4	40	.01	.06	.1	Trace
Cakes made from home recipes:[p]																	
Boston cream pie; piece 1/12 of 8-in diam.	1 piece	69	35	210	4	6	2	3	1	34	46	.3	140	.02	.08	.1	Trace
Fruitcake, dark, made with enriched flour:																	
Loaf, 1-lb	1 loaf	454	18	1720	22	69	15	37	13	271	327	11.8	540	.59	.64	3.6	2
Slice, 1/30 of 8-in loaf	1 slice	15	18	55	1	2	Trace	1	Trace	9	11	.4	20	.02	.1	Trace	
Plain sheet cake:																	
Without icing:																	
Whole cake	1 cake	777	25	2830	35	108	30	52	21	434	497	3.1	1320	.16	.70	1.6	2
Piece, 1/9 of 9-in square cake	1 piece	86	25	315	4	12	3	6	2	48	55	.3	150	.02	.08	.2	Trace
With boiled white icing, piece, 1/9 of 9-in square cake	1 piece	114	23	400	4	12	3	6	2	71	56	.3	150	.02	.08	.2	Trace

[o]Values for iron, thiamin, riboflavin, and niacin per pound of unenriched white bread would be as follows:

	Iron (mg)	Thiamin (mg)	Riboflavin (mg)	Niacin (mg)
Soft crumb	3.2	.31	.39	5.0
Firm crumb	3.2	.32	.59	4.1

[p]Unenriched cake flour used unless otherwise specified.

Food, Approximate Measure, and Weight (in Grams)			Water (%)	Food Energy (kcal)	Protein (g)	Fat (g)	Fatty Acids: Saturated (total) (g)	Fatty Acids: Unsaturated: Oleic (g)	Fatty Acids: Unsaturated: Linoleic (g)	Carbohydrate (g)	Calcium (mg)	Iron (mg)	Vitamin A value (I.U.)	Thiamin (mg)	Riboflavin (mg)	Niacin (mg)	Ascorbic acid (mg)
GRAIN PRODUCTS—Con.																	
Cakes made from home recipes:[p]																	
Pound:																	
Loaf, 8½ by 3½ by 3 in	1 loaf	514	17	2430	29	152	34	68	17	242	108	4.1	1440	.15	.46	1.0	0
Slice, ½-in thick	1 slice	30	17	140	2	9	2	4	1	14	6	.2	80	.01	.03	.1	0
Sponge:																	
Whole cake	1 cake	790	32	2345	60	45	14	20	4	427	237	9.5	3560	.40	1.11	1.6	Trace
Piece, 1/12 of 10-in diam. cake	1 piece	66	32	195	5	4	1	2	Trace	36	20	.8	300	.03	09	.1	Trace
Yellow, 2-layer, without icing:																	
Whole cake	1 cake	870	24	3160	39	111	31	53	22	506	618	3.5	1310	.17	.70	1.7	2
Piece, 1/16 of 9-in diam. cake	1 piece	54	24	200	2	7	2	3	1	32	39	.2	80	.01	.04	.1	Trace
Yellow, 2-layer, with chocolate icing:																	
Whole cake	1 cake	1203	21	4390	51	156	55	69	23	727	818	7.2	1920	.24	.96	2.4	Trace
Piece, 1/16 of 9-in diam. cake	1 piece	75	21	275	3	10	3	4	1	45	51	.5	120	.02	.06	.2	Trace
Cake icings. See Sugars, Sweets.																	
Cookies:																	
Brownies with nuts:																	
Made from home recipe with enriched flour	1 brownie	20	10	95	1	6	1	3	1	10	8	.4	40	.04	.02	.1	Trace
Made from mix	1 brownie	20	11	85	1	4	1	2	1	13	9	.4	20	.03	.02	.1	Trace
Chocolate chip:																	
Made from home recipe with enriched flour	1 cookie	10	3	50	1	3	1	1	1	6	4	.2	10	.01	.01	.1	Trace
Commercial	1 cookie	10	3	50	1	2	1	1	Trace	7	4	.2	10	Trace	Trace	Trace	Trace
Fig bars, commercial	1 cookie	14	14	50	1	1	—	—	—	11	11	.2	20	Trace	.01	.1	Trace
Sandwich, chocolate or vanilla, commercial	1 cookie	10	2	50	1	2	1	1	Trace	7	2	.1	0	Trace	Trace	.1	0

Corn flakes, added nutrients:																	
Plain	1 cup	25	4	100	2	Trace	—	—	—	21	4	.4	0	.11	.02	.5	0
Sugar-covered	1 cup	40	2	155	2	Trace	—	—	—	36	5	.4	0	.16	.02	.8	0
Corn (hominy) grits, degermed, cooked:																	
Enriched	1 cup	245	87	125	3	Trace	—	—	—	27	2	.7	150[q]	.10	.07	1.0	0
Unenriched	1 cup	245	87	125	3	Trace	—	—	—	27	2	.2	150[q]	.05	.02	.5	0
Cornmeal:																	
Whole-ground, unbolted, dry	1 cup	122	12	435	11	5	1	2	2	90	24	2.9	620[q]	.46	.13	2.4	0
Bolted (nearly whole-grain) dry	1 cup	122	12	440	11	4	Trace	1	2	91	21	2.2	590[q]	.37	.10	2.3	0
Degermed, enriched:																	
Dry form	1 cup	138	12	550	11	2	—	—	—	108	8	4.0	610[q]	.61	.36	4.8	0
Cooked	1 cup	240	88	120	3	1	—	—	—	26	2	1.0	140[q]	.14	.10	1.2	0
Degermed, unenriched:																	
Dry form	1 cup	138	12	500	11	2	—	—	—	108	8	1.5	610[q]	.19	.07	1.4	0
Cooked	1 cup	240	88	120	3	1	—	—	—	26	2	.5	140[q]	.05	.02	.2	0
Corn muffins, made with enriched degermed cornmeal and enriched flour; muffin 2-3/8-in diam.	1 muffin	40	33	125	3	4	2	2	Trace	19	42	.7	120[q]	.08	.09	.6	Trace
Corn muffins, made with mix, egg, and milk; muffin 2-3/8-in diam.	1 muffin	40	30	130	3	4	1	2	1	20	96	.6	100	.07	.08	.6	Trace
Corn, puffed, presweetened, added nutrients	1 cup	30	2	115	1	Trace	—	—	—	27	3	.5	0	.13	.05	.6	0
Corn, shredded, added nutrients	1 cup	25	3	100	2	Trace	—	—	—	22	1	.6	0	.11	.05	.5	0
Crackers:																	
Graham, 2½-in square	4 crackers	28	6	110	2	3	—	—	—	21	11	.4	0	.01	.06	.4	0
Saltines	4 crackers	11	4	50	1	1	—	1	—	8	2	.1	0	Trace	Trace	.1	0
Danish pastry, plain (without fruit or nuts):																	
Packaged ring, 12 oz	1 ring	340	22	1435	25	80	24	37	15	155	170	3.1	1050	.24	.51	2.7	Trace
Round piece, approx. 4¼-in diam. by 1 in	1 pastry	65	22	275	5	15	5	7	3	30	33	.6	200	.05	.10	.5	Trace
Ounce	1 oz	28	22	120	2	7	2	3	1	13	14	.3	90	.02	.04	.2	Trace

[p]Unenriched cake flour used unless otherwise specified.

[q]This value is based on product made from yellow varieties of corn; white varieties contain only a trace.

Food, Approximate Measure, and Weight (in Grams)			Water (%)	Food Energy (kcal)	Protein (g)	Fat (g)	Fatty Acids: Saturated (total) (g)	Fatty Acids: Unsaturated: Oleic (g)	Fatty Acids: Unsaturated: Linoleic (g)	Carbohydrate (g)	Calcium (mg)	Iron (mg)	Vitamin A value (I.U.)	Thiamin (mg)	Riboflavin (mg)	Niacin (mg)	Ascorbic acid (mg)
GRAIN PRODUCTS—Con.																	
Doughnuts, cake type	1 doughnut	32	24	125	1	6	1	4	Trace	16	13	.4[r]	30	.05[r]	.05[r]	.4[r]	Trace
Farina, quick-cooking, enriched, cooked	1 cup	245	89	105	3	Trace	—	—	—	22	147	.7[S]	0	.12[S]	.07[S]	1.0[S]	0
Macaroni, cooked:																	
Enriched:																	
Cooked, firm stage (undergoes additional cooking in a food mixture)	1 cup	130	64	190	6	1	—	—	—	39	14	1.4[S]	0	.23[S]	.14[S]	1.8[S]	0
Cooked until tender	1 cup	140	72	155	5	1	—	—	—	32	8	1.3[S]	0	.20[S]	.11[S]	1.5[S]	0
Unenriched:																	
Cooked, firm stage (undergoes additional cooking in a food mixture)	1 cup	130	64	190	6	1	—	—	—	39	14	.7	0	.03	.03	.5	0
Cooked until tender	1 cup	140	72	155	5	1	—	—	—	32	11	.6	0	.01	.01	.4	0
Macaroni (enriched) and cheese, baked	1 cup	200	58	430	17	22	10	9	2	40	362	1.8	860	.20	.40	1.8	Trace
Canned	1 cup	240	80	230	9	10	4	3	1	26	199	1.0	260	.12	.24	1.0	Trace
Muffins, with enriched white flour; muffin, 3-in diam.	1 muffin	40	38	120	3	4	1	2	1	17	42	.6	40	.07	.09	.6	Trace
Noodles (egg noodles), cooked:																	
Enriched	1 cup	160	70	200	7	2	1	1	Trace	37	16	1.4[S]	110	.22[S]	.13[S]	1.9[S]	0
Unenriched	1 cup	160	70	200	7	2	1	1	Trace	37	16	1.0	110	.05	.03	.6	0
Oats (with or without corn) puffed, added nutrients	1 cup	25	3	100	3	1	—	—	—	19	44	1.2	0	.24	.04	.5	0
Oatmeal or rolled oats, cooked	1 cup	240	87	130	5	2	—	—	1	23	22	1.4	0	.19	.05	.2	0
Pancakes, 4-in diam.:																	
Wheat, enriched flour (home recipe)	1 cake	27	50	60	2	2	Trace	1	Trace	9	27	.4	30	.05	.06	.4	Trace

Buckwheat (made from mix with egg and milk)	1 cake	27	58	55	2	2	1	1	Trace	6	59	.4	60	.03	.04	.2	Trace
Plain or buttermilk (made from mix with egg and milk)	1 cake	27	51	60	2	2	1	1	Trace	9	58	.3	70	.04	.06	.2	Trace
Pie (piecrust made with unenriched flour):																	
Sector, 4-in, 1/7 of 9-in diam. pie:																	
Apple (2-crust)	1 sector	135	48	350	3	15	4	7	3	51	11	.4	40	.03	.03	.5	1
Butterscotch (1-crust)	1 sector	130	45	350	6	14	5	6	2	50	98	1.2	340	.04	.13	.3	Trace
Cherry (2-crust)	1 sector	135	47	350	4	15	4	7	3	52	19	.4	590	.03	.03	.7	Trace
Custard (1-crust)	1 sector	130	58	285	8	14	5	6	2	30	125	.8	300	.07	.21	.4	0
Lemon meringue (1-crust)	1 sector	120	47	305	4	12	4	6	2	45	17	.6	200	.04	.10	.2	4
Mince (2-crust)	1 sector	135	43	365	3	16	4	8	3	56	38	1.4	Trace	.09	.05	.5	1
Pecan (1-crust)	1 sector	118	20	490	6	27	4	16	5	60	55	3.3	190	.19	.08	.4	Trace
Pineapple chiffon (1-crust)	1 sector	93	41	265	6	11	3	5	2	36	22	.8	320	.04	.08	.4	1
Pumpkin (1-crust)	1 sector	130	59	275	5	15	5	6	2	32	66	.7	3210	.04	.13	.7	Trace
Piecrust, baked shell for pie made with:																	
Enriched flour	1 shell	180	15	900	11	60	16	28	12	79	25	3.1	0	.36	.25	3.2	0
Unenriched flour	1 shell	180	15	900	11	60	16	28	12	79	25	.9	0	.05	.05	.9	0
Piecrust mix including stick form:																	
Package, 10-oz, for double crust	1 pkg	284	9	1480	20	93	23	46	21	141	131	1.4	0	.11	.11	2.0	0
Pizza (cheese) 5½-in sector;	1 sector	75	45	185	7	6	2	3	Trace	27	107	.7	290	.04	.12	.7	4
Popcorn, popped:																	
Plain, large kernel	1 cup	6	4	25	1	Trace	—	—	—	5	1	.2	—	—	.01	.1	0
With oil and salt	1 cup	9	3	40	1	2	1	Trace	Trace	5	1	.2	—	—	.01	.2	0
Sugar coated	1 cup	35	4	135	2	1	—	—	—	30	2	.5	—	—	.02	.4	0
Pretzels:																	
Dutch, twisted	1 pretzel	16	5	60	2	1	—	—	—	12	4	.2	0	Trace	Trace	.1	0
Thin, twisted	1 pretzel	6	5	25	1	Trace	—	—	—	5	1	.1	0	Trace	Trace	Trace	0
Stick, small, 2¼-in	10 sticks	3	5	10	Trace	Trace	—	—	—	2	1	Trace	0	Trace	Trace	Trace	0
Stick, regular, 3-1/8-in	5 sticks	3	5	10	Trace	Trace	—	—	—	2	1	Trace	0	Trace	Trace	Trace	0

[r]Based on product made with enriched flour. With unenriched flour, approximate values per doughnut are: Iron, 0.2 milligram; thiamin, 0.01 milligram; riboflavin, 0.03 milligram; niacin, 0.2 milligram.

[s]Iron, thiamin, riboflavin, and niacin are based on the minimum levels of enrichment specified in standards of identity promulgated under the Federal Food, Drug, and Cosmetic Act.

Food, Approximate Measure, and Weight (in Grams)			Water (%)	Food Energy (kcal)	Protein (g)	Fat (g)	Fatty Acids: Saturated (total) (g)	Fatty Acids: Unsaturated: Oleic (g)	Fatty Acids: Unsaturated: Linoleic (g)	Carbohydrate (g)	Calcium (mg)	Iron (mg)	Vitamin A value (I.U.)	Thiamin (mg)	Riboflavin (mg)	Niacin (mg)	Ascorbic acid (mg)
GRAIN PRODUCTS—Con.																	
Rice, white:																	
Enriched:																	
Raw	1 cup	185	12	670	12	1	—	—	—	149	44	5.4[t]	0	.81[t]	.06[t]	6.5[t]	0
Cooked	1 cup	205	73	225	4	Trace	—	—	—	50	21	1.8[t]	0	.23[t]	.02[t]	2.1[t]	0
Instant, ready-to-serve	1 cup	165	73	180	4	Trace	—	—	—	40	5	1.3[t]	0	.21[t]	—[t]	1.7[t]	0
Unenriched, cooked	1 cup	205	73	225	4	Trace	—	—	—	50	21	.4	0	.04	.02	.8	0
Parboiled, cooked	1 cup	175	73	185	4	Trace	—	—	—	41	33	1.4[t]	0	.19[t]	—[t]	2.1[t]	0
Rice, puffed, added nutrients	1 cup	15	4	60	1	Trace	—	—	—	13	3	.3	0	.07	.01	.7	0
Rolls, enriched:																	
Cloverleaf or pan:																	
Home recipe	1 roll	35	26	120	3	3	1	1	1	20	16	.7	30	.09	.09	.8	Trace
Commercial	1 roll	28	31	85	2	2	Trace	1	Trace	15	21	.5	Trace	.08	.05	.6	Trace
Frankfurter or hamburger	1 roll	40	31	120	3	2	1	1	1	21	30	.8	Trace	.11	.07	.9	Trace
Hard, round or rectangular	1 roll	50	25	155	5	2	Trace	1	Trace	30	24	1.2	Trace	.13	.12	1.4	Trace
Rye wafers, whole-grain, 1-7/8 by 3½-in	2 wafers	13	6	45	2	Trace	—	—	—	10	7	.5	0	.04	.03	.2	0
Spaghetti, cooked, tender stage, enriched	1 cup	140	72	155	5	1	—	—	—	32	11	1.3[S]	0	.20[S]	.11[S]	1.5[S]	0
Spaghetti with meat balls, and tomato sauce:																	
Home recipe	1 cup	248	70	330	19	12	4	6	1	39	124	3.7	1590	.25	.30	4.0	22
Canned	1 cup	250	78	260	12	10	2	3	4	28	53	3.3	1000	.15	.18	2.3	5
Spaghetti in tomato sauce with cheese:																	
Home recipe	1 cup	250	77	260	9	9	2	5	1	37	80	2.3	1080	.25	.18	2.3	13
Canned	1 cup	250	80	190	6	2	1	1	1	38	40	2.8	930	.35	.28	4.5	10
Waffles, with enriched flour, 7-in diam.	1 waffle	75	41	210	7	7	2	4	1	28	85	1.3	250	.13	.19	1.0	Trace

[S]Iron, thiamin, riboflavin, and niacin are based on the minimum levels of enrichment specified in standards of identity promulgated under the Federal Food, Drug, and Cosmetic Act.

[t]Iron, thiamin, and niacin are based on the minimum levels of enrichment specified in standards of identity promulgated under the Federal Food, Drug, and Cosmetic Act. Riboflavin is based on unenriched rice. When the minimum level of enrichment for riboflavin specified in the standards of identity becomes effective the value will be 0.12 milligram per cup of parboiled rice and of white rice.

Waffles, made from mix, enriched, egg and milk added, 7-in diam.	1 waffle	75	42	205	7	8	3	3	1	27	179	1.0	170	.11	.17	.7	Trace
Wheat, puffed, added nutrients	1 cup	15	3	55	2	Trace	—	—	—	12	4	.6	0	.08	.03	1.2	0
Wheat, shredded, plain	1 biscuit	25	7	90	2	1	—	—	—	20	11	.9	0	.06	.03	1.1	0
Wheat flakes, added nutrients	1 cup	30	4	105	3	Trace	—	—	—	24	12	1.3	0	.19	.04	1.5	0
Wheat flours:																	
Whole-wheat, from hard wheats, stirred	1 cup	120	12	400	16	2	Trace	1	1	85	49	4.0	0	.66	.14	5.2	0
All-purpose or family flour, enriched:																	
Sifted	1 cup	115	12	420	12	1	—	—	—	88	18	3.3[S]	0	.51[S]	.30[S]	4.0[S]	0
Unsifted	1 cup	125	12	455	13	1	—	—	—	95	20	3.6[S]	0	.55[S]	.33[S]	4.4[S]	0
Self-rising, enriched	1 cup	125	12	440	12	1	—	—	—	93	331	3.6[S]	0	.55[S]	.33[S]	4.4[S]	0
Cake or pastry flour, sifted	1 cup	96	12	350	7	1	—	—	—	76	16	.5	0	.03	.03	.7	0
FATS, OILS																	
Butter:																	
Regular, 4 sticks per lb:																	
Stick	½ cup	113	16	810	1	92	51	30	3	1	23	0	3750[U]	—	—	—	0
Tablespoon (approx. 1/8 stick)	1 tbsp	14	16	100	Trace	12	6	4	Trace	Trace	3	0	470[U]	—	—	—	0
Pat (1-in sq, ⅓-in high; 90 per lb)	1 pat	5	16	35	Trace	4	2	1	Trace	Trace	1	0	170[U]	—	—	—	0
Whipped, 6 sticks or 2 8-oz containers per lb																	
Stick	½ cup	76	16	540	1	61	34	20	2	Trace	15	0	2500[U]	—	—	—	0
Tablespoon (approx. 1/8 stick)	1 tbsp	9	16	65	Trace	8	4	3	Trace	Trace	2	0	310[U]	—	—	—	0
Pat (1¼-in sq ⅓-in high; 120 per lb)	1 pat	4	16	25	Trace	3	2	1	Trace	Trace	1	0	130[U]	—	—	—	0

[S]Iron, thiamin, riboflavin, and niacin are based on the minimum levels of enrichment specified in standards of identity promulgated under the Federal Food, Drug, and Cosmetic Act.

[t]Iron, thiamin, and niacin are based on the minimum levels of enrichment specified in standards of identity promulgated under the Federal Food, Drug, and Cosmetic Act. Riboflavin is based on unenriched rice. When the minimum level of enrichment for riboflavin specified in the standards of identity becomes effective the value will be 0.12 milligram per cup of parboiled rice and of white rice.

[U]Year-round average.

Food, Approximate Measure, and Weight (in Grams)			Water (%)	Food Energy (kcal)	Protein (g)	Fat (g)	Fatty Acids: Saturated (total) (g)	Fatty Acids: Unsaturated Oleic (g)	Fatty Acids: Unsaturated Linoleic (g)	Carbohydrate (g)	Calcium (mg)	Iron (mg)	Vitamin A value (I.U.)	Thiamin (mg)	Riboflavin (mg)	Niacin (mg)	Ascorbic acid (mg)
FATS, OILS—Con.																	
Fats, cooking:																	
Lard	1 cup	205	0	1850	0	205	78	94	20	0	0	0	0	0	0	0	0
	1 tbsp	13	0	115	0	13	5	6	1	0	0	0	0	0	0	0	0
Vegetable fats	1 cup	200	0	1770	0	200	50	100	44	0	0	0	—	0	0	0	0
	1 tbsp	13	0	110	0	13	3	6	3	0	0	0	—	0	0	0	0
Margarine:																	
Regular, 4 sticks per lb:																	
Stick	½ cup	113	16	815	1	92	17	46	25	1	23	0	3750[V]	—	—	—	0
Tablespoon (approx. 1/8 stick)	1 tbsp	14	16	100	Trace	12	2	6	3	Trace	3	0	470[V]	—	—	—	0
Pat (1-in sq 1/3-in high; 90 per lb)	1 pat	5	16	35	Trace	4	1	2	1	Trace	1	0	170[V]	—	—	—	0
Whipped, 6 sticks per lb:																	
Stick	½ cup	76	16	545	1	61	11	31	17	Trace	15	0	2500[V]	—	—	—	0
Soft, 2 - 8-oz tubs per lb:																	
Tub	1 tub	227	16	1635	1	184	34	68	68	1	45	0	7500[V]	—	—	—	0
Tablespoon	1 tbsp	14	16	100	Trace	11	2	4	4	Trace	3	0	470[V]	—	—	—	0
Oil, salad or cooking:																	
Corn	1 cup	220	0	1945	0	220	22	62	117	0	0	0	—	0	0	0	0
	1 tbsp	14	0	125	0	14	1	4	7	0	0	0	—	0	0	0	0
Cottonseed	1 cup	220	0	1945	0	220	55	46	110	0	0	0	—	0	0	0	0
	1 tbsp	14	0	125	0	14	4	3	7	0	0	0	—	0	0	0	0
Olive	1 cup	220	0	1945	0	220	24	167	15	0	0	0	—	0	0	0	0
	1 tbsp	14	0	125	0	14	2	11	1	0	0	0	—	0	0	0	0
Peanut	1 cup	220	0	1945	0	220	40	103	64	0	0	0	—	0	0	0	0
	1 tbsp	14	0	125	0	14	3	7	4	0	0	0	—	0	0	0	0
Safflower	1 cup	220	0	1945	0	220	18	37	165	0	0	0	—	0	0	0	0
	1 tbsp	14	0	125	0	14	1	2	10	0	0	0	—	0	0	0	0
Soybean	1 cup	220	0	1945	0	220	33	44	114	0	0	0	—	0	0	0	0
	1 tbsp	14	0	125	0	14	2	3	7	0	0	0	—	0	0	0	0

FATS, OILS—Con.																	
Salad dressings:																	
Blue cheese	1 tbsp	15	32	75	1	8	2	2	4	1	12	Trace	30	Trace	.02	Trace	Trace
Commercial, mayonnaise type:																	
Regular	1 tbsp	15	41	65	Trace	6	1	1	3	2	2	Trace	30	Trace	Trace	Trace	—
Special dietary, low-calorie	1 tbsp	16	81	20	Trace	2	Trace	Trace	1	1	3	Trace	40	Trace	Trace	Trace	—
French:																	
Regular	1 tbsp	16	39	65	Trace	6	1	1	3	3	2	.1	—	—	—	—	—
Special dietary, lowfat with artifical sweeteners	1 tbsp	15	95	Trace	Trace	Trace	—	—	—	Trace	2	.1	—	—	—	—	—
Home cooked, boiled	1 tbsp	16	68	25	1	2	1	1	Trace	2	14	.1	80	.01	.03	Trace	Trace
Mayonnaise	1 tbsp	14	15	100	Trace	11	2	2	6	Trace	3	.1	40	Trace	.01	Trace	—
Thousand island	1 tbsp	16	32	80	Trace	8	1	2	4	3	2	.1	50	Trace	Trace	Trace	Trace
SUGARS, SWEETS																	
Cake icings:																	
Chocolate made with milk and table fat	1 cup	275	14	1035	9	38	21	14	1	185	165	3.3	580	.06	.28	.6	1
Coconut (with boiled icing)	1 cup	166	15	605	3	13	11	1	Trace	124	10	.8	0	.02	.07	.3	0
Creamy fudge from mix with water only	1 cup	245	15	830	7	16	5	8	3	183	96	2.7	Trace	.05	.20	.7	Trace
White, boiled	1 cup	94	18	300	1	0	—	—	—	76	2	Trace	0	Trace	.03	Trace	0
Candy:																	
Caramels, plain or chocolate	1 oz	28	8	115	1	3	2	1	Trace	22	42	.4	Trace	.01	.05	.1	Trace
Chocolate, milk, plain	1 oz	28	1	145	2	9	5	3	Trace	16	65	.3	80	.02	.10	.1	Trace
Chocolate-coated peanuts	1 oz	28	1	160	5	12	3	6	2	11	33	.4	Trace	.10	.05	2.1	Trace
Fondant; mints, uncoated; candy corn	1 oz	28	8	105	Trace	1	—	—	—	25	4	.3	0	Trace	Trace	Trace	0
Fudge, plain	1 oz	28	8	115	1	4	2	1	Trace	21	22	.3	Trace	.01	.03	.1	Trace
Gum drops	1 oz	28	12	100	Trace	Trace	—	—	—	25	2	.1	0	0	Trace	Trace	0
Hard	1 oz	28	1	110	0	Trace	—	—	—	28	6	.5	0	0	0	0	0
Marshmallows	1 oz	28	17	90	1	Trace	—	—	—	23	5	.5	0	0	Trace	Trace	0
Chocolate-flavored syrup or topping:																	
Thin type	1 fl oz	38	32	90	1	1	Trace	Trace	Trace	24	6	.6	Trace	.01	.03	.2	0
Fudge type	1 fl oz	38	25	125	2	5	3	2	Trace	20	48	.5	60	.02	.08	.2	Trace

[V]Based on the average vitamin A content of fortified margarine. Federal specifications for fortified margarine require a minimum of 15,000 I.U. of vitamin A per pound.

Food, Approximate Measure, and Weight (in Grams)			Water (%)	Food Energy (kcal)	Protein (g)	Fat (g)	Fatty Acids: Saturated (total) (g)	Fatty Acids: Unsaturated Oleic (g)	Fatty Acids: Unsaturated Linoleic (g)	Carbohydrate (g)	Calcium (mg)	Iron (mg)	Vitamin A value (I.U.)	Thiamin (mg)	Riboflavin (mg)	Niacin (mg)	Ascorbic acid (mg)
SUGARS, SWEETS—Con.																	
Chocolate-flavored beverage powder (approx. 4 heaping tsp per oz):																	
With nonfat dry milk	1 oz	28	2	100	5	1	Trace	Trace	Trace	20	167	.5	10	.04	.21	.2	1
Without nonfat dry milk	1 oz	28	1	100	1	1	Trace	Trace	Trace	25	9	.6	—	.01	.03	.1	0
Honey, strained or extracted	1 tbsp	21	17	65	Trace	0	—	—	—	17	1	.1	Trace	Trace	.01	.1	Trace
Jams and preserves	1 tbsp	20	29	55	Trace	Trace	—	—	—	14	4	.2	Trace	Trace	.01	Trace	Trace
Jellies	1 tbsp	18	29	50	Trace	Trace	—	—	—	13	4	.3	Trace	Trace	.01	Trace	1
Molasses, cane:																	
Light (first extraction)	1 tbsp	20	24	50	—	—	—	—	—	13	33	.9	—	.01	.01	Trace	—
Blackstrap (third extraction)	1 tbsp	20	24	45	—	—	—	—	—	11	137	3.2	—	.02	.04	.4	—
Syrups:																	
Sorghum	1 tbsp	21	23	55	—	—	—	—	—	14	35	2.6	—	—	.02	Trace	—
Table blends, chiefly corn, light and dark	1 tbsp	21	24	60	0	0	—	—	—	15	9	.8	0	0	0	0	0
Sugars:																	
Brown, firm packed	1 cup	220	2	820	0	0	—	—	—	212	187	7.5	0	.02	.07	.4	0
White:																	
Granulated	1 cup	200	Trace	770	0	0	—	—	—	199	0	.2	0	0	0	0	0
	1 tbsp	11	Trace	40	0	0	—	—	—	11	0	Trace	0	0	0	0	0
Powdered, stirred before measuring	1 cup	120	Trace	460	0	0	—	—	—	119	0	.1	0	0	0	0	0
MISCELLANEOUS ITEMS																	
Barbecue sauce	1 cup	250	81	230	4	17	2	5	9	20	53	2.0	900	.03	.03	.8	13
Beverages, alcoholic:																	
Beer	12 fl oz	360	92	150	1	0	—	—	—	14	18	Trace	—	.01	.11	2.2	—
Gin, rum, vodka, whiskey:																	
80-proof	1½ fl oz jigger	42	67	100	—	—	—	—	—	Trace	—	—	—	—	—	—	—

86-proof	1½ fl oz jigger	42	64	105	—	—	—	—	—	Trace	—	—	—	—	—	—	—
90-proof	1½ fl oz jigger	42	62	110	—	—	—	—	—	Trace	—	—	—	—	—	—	—
94-proof	1½ fl oz jigger	42	60	115	—	—	—	—	—	Trace	—	—	—	—	—	—	—
100-proof	1½ fl oz jigger	42	58	125	—	—	—	—	—	Trace	—	—	—	—	—	—	—
Wines:																	
Dessert	3½ fl oz glass	103	77	140	Trace	0	—	—	—	8	8	—	—	.01	.02	.2	—
Table	3½ fl oz glass	102	86	85	Trace	0	—	—	—	4	9	.4	—	Trace	.01	.1	—
Beverages, carbonated, sweetened, nonalcoholic:																	
Carbonated water	12 fl oz	366	92	115	0	0	—	—	—	29	—	—	0	0	0	0	0
Cola type	12 fl oz	369	90	145	0	0	—	—	—	37	—	—	0	0	0	0	0
Fruit-flavored sodas and Tom Collins mixes	12 fl oz	372	88	170	0	0	—	—	—	45	—	—	0	0	0	0	0
Ginger ale	12 fl oz	366	92	115	0	0	—	—	—	29	—	—	0	0	0	0	0
Root beer	12 fl oz	370	90	150	0	0	—	—	—	39	—	—	0	0	0	0	0
Bouillon cubes, approx. ½-in	1 cube	4	4	5	1	Trace	—	—	—	Trace	—	—	—	—	—	—	—
Chocolate:																	
Bitter or baking	1 oz	28	2	145	3	15	8	6	Trace	8	22	1.9	20	.01	.07	.4	0
Semisweet, small pieces	1 cup	170	1	860	7	61	34	22	1	97	51	4.4	30	.02	.14	.9	0
Gelatin:																	
Plain, dry powder in envelope	1 envelope	7	13	25	6	Trace	—	—	—	0	—	—	—	—	—	—	—
Dessert Powder, 3-oz package	1 pkg	85	2	315	8	0	—	—	—	75	—	—	—	—	—	—	—
Gelatin dessert, prepared with water	1 cup	240	84	140	4	0	—	—	—	34	—	—	—	—	—	—	—
Olives, pickled:																	
Green	4 medium or 3 extra large or 2 giant	16	78	15	Trace	2	Trace	2	Trace	Trace	8	.2	40	—	—	—	—
Ripe: Mission	3 small or 2 large	10	73	15	Trace	2	Trace	2	Trace	Trace	9	.1	10	Trace	Trace	—	—

Food, Approximate Measure, and Weight (in Grams)			Water (%)	Food Energy (kcal)	Protein (g)	Fat (g)	Fatty Acids Saturated (total) (g)	Unsaturated Oleic (g)	Linoleic (g)	Carbohydrate (g)	Calcium (mg)	Iron (mg)	Vitamin A value (I.U.)	Thiamin (mg)	Riboflavin (mg)	Niacin (mg)	Ascorbic acid (mg)
MISCELLANEOUS ITEMS—Con.																	
Pickles, cucumber:																	
Dill, medium, whole, 3¾-in long, 1¼-in diam.	1 pickle	65	93	10	1	Trace	—	—	—	1	17	.7	70	Trace	.01	Trace	4
Fresh, sliced, 1½-in diam., ¼-in thick	2 slices	15	79	10	Trace	Trace	—	—	—	3	5	.3	20	Trace	Trace	Trace	1
Sweet, gherkin, small, whole, approx. 2½-in long, ¾-in diam.	1 pickle	15	61	20	Trace	Trace	—	—	—	6	2	.2	10	Trace	Trace	Trace	1
Relish, finely chopped, sweet	1 tbsp	15	63	20	Trace	Trace	—	—	—	5	3	.1	—	—	—	—	—
Popcorn. See Grain Products.																	
Popsicle, 3 fl oz size	1 popsicle	95	80	70	0	0	0	0	0	18	0	Trace	0	0	0	0	0
Pudding, home recipe with starch base:																	
Chocolate	1 cup	260	66	385	8	12	7	4	Trace	67	250	1.3	390	.05	.36	.3	1
Vanilla (blanc mange)	1 cup	255	76	285	9	10	5	3	Trace	41	298	Trace	410	.08	.41	.3	2
Pudding mix, dry form, 4 oz package	1 pkg	113	2	410	3	2	1	1	Trace	103	23	1.8	Trace	.02	.08	.5	0
Sherbet	1 cup	193	67	260	2	2	—	—	—	59	31	Trace	120	.02	.06	Trace	4
Soups:																	
Canned, condensed, ready-to-serve:																	
Prepared with an equal volume of milk:																	
Cream of chicken	1 cup	245	85	180	7	10	3	3	3	15	172	.5	610	.05	.27	.7	2
Cream of mushroom	1 cup	245	83	215	7	14	4	4	5	16	191	.5	250	.05	.34	.7	1
Tomato	1 cup	250	84	175	7	7	3	2	1	23	168	.8	1200	.10	.25	1.3	15
Prepared with an equal volume of water:																	
Bean with pork	1 cup	250	84	170	8	6	1	2	2	22	63	2.3	650	.13	.08	1.0	3
Beef broth, bouillon consomme	1 cup	240	96	30	5	0	—	—	—	3	Trace	.5	Trace	Trace	.02	1.2	—
Beef noodle	1 cup	240	93	70	4	3	1	1	1	7	7	1.0	50	.05	.07	1.0	Trace

Clam chowder, Manhattan type (with tomatoes, without milk)	1 cup	245	92	80	2	3	—	—	—	12	34	1.0	880	.02	.02	1.0	—
Cream of chicken	1 cup	240	92	95	3	6	1	2	3	8	24	.5	410	.02	.05	.5	Trace
Cream of mushroom	1 cup	240	90	135	2	10	1	3	5	10	41	.5	70	.02	.12	.7	Trace
Minestrone	1 cup	245	90	105	5	3	—	—	—	14	37	1.0	2350	.07	.05	1.0	—
Split pea	1 cup	245	85	145	9	3	1	2	Trace	21	29	1.5	440	.25	.15	1.5	1
Tomato	1 cup	245	90	90	2	3	Trace	1	1	16	15	.7	1000	.05	.05	1.2	12
Vegetable beef	1 cup	245	92	80	5	2	—	—	—	10	12	.7	2700	.05	.05	1.0	—
Vegetarian	1 cup	245	92	80	2	2	—	—	—	13	20	1.0	2940	.05	.05	1.0	—
Dehydrated, dry form:																	
Chicken noodle (2-oz package)	1 pkg	57	6	220	8	6	2	3	1	33	34	1.4	190	.30	.15	2.4	3
Onion mix (1½-oz package)	1 pkg	43	3	150	6	5	1	2	1	23	42	.6	30	.05	.03	.3	6
Tomato vegetable with noodles (2½-oz pkg)	1 pkg	71	4	245	6	6	2	3	1	45	33	1.4	1700	.21	.13	1.8	18
Frozen, condensed:																	
Clam chowder, New England type (with milk, without tomatoes):																	
Prepared with equal volume of milk	1 cup	245	83	210	9	12	—	—	—	16	240	1.0	250	.07	.29	.5	Trace
Prepared with equal volume of water	1 cup	240	89	130	4	8	—	—	—	11	91	1.0	50	.05	.10	.5	—
Cream of potato:																	
Prepared with equal volume of milk	1 cup	245	83	185	8	10	5	3	Trace	18	208	1.0	590	.10	.27	.5	Trace
Prepared with equal volume of water	1 cup	240	90	105	3	5	3	2	Trace	12	58	1.0	410	.05	.05	.5	—
Cream of shrimp:																	
Prepared with equal volume of milk	1 cup	245	82	245	9	16	—	—	—	15	189	.5	290	.07	.27	.5	Trace
Prepared with equal volume of water	1 cup	240	88	160	5	12	—	—	—	8	38	.5	120	.05	.05	.5	—
Oyster stew:																	
Prepared with equal volume of milk	1 cup	240	83	200	10	12	—	—	—	14	305	1.4	410	.12	.41	.5	Trace
Prepared with equal volume of water	1 cup	240	90	120	6	8	—	—	—	8	158	1.4	240	.07	.19	.5	—

Food, Approximate Measure, and Weight (in Grams)			Water (%)	Food Energy (kcal)	Protein (g)	Fat (g)	Fatty Acids: Saturated (total) (g)	Fatty Acids: Unsaturated Oleic (g)	Fatty Acids: Unsaturated Linoleic (g)	Carbohydrate (g)	Calcium (mg)	Iron (mg)	Vitamin A value (I.U.)	Thiamin (mg)	Riboflavin (mg)	Niacin (mg)	Ascorbic acid (mg)
MISCELLANEOUS ITEMS—Con.																	
Tapioca, dry quick-cooking	1 cup	152	13	535	1	Trace	—	—	—	131	15	.6	0	0	0	0	0
Tapioca desserts:																	
Apple	1 cup	250	70	295	1	Trace	—	—	—	74	8	.5	30	Trace	Trace	Trace	Trace
Cream pudding	1 cup	165	72	220	8	8	4	3	Trace	28	173	.7	480	.07	.30	.2	2
Tartar sauce	1 tbsp	14	34	75	Trace	8	1	1	4	1	3	.1	30	Trace	Trace	Trace	Trace
Vinegar	1 tbsp	15	94	Trace	Trace	0	—	—	—	1	1	.1	—	—	—	—	—
White sauce, medium	1 cup	250	73	405	10	31	16	10	1	22	288	.5	1150	.10	.43	.5	2
Yeast:																	
Baker's, dry, active	1 pkg	7	5	20	3	Trace	—	—	—	3	3	1.1	Trace	.16	.38	2.6	Trace
Brewer's, dry	1 tbsp	8	5	25	3	Trace	—	—	—	3	17	1.4	Trace	1.25	.34	3.0	Trace
Yogurt. See Milk, Cheese, Cream, Imitation Cream.																	

Appendix E

Calculation of Oxygen Uptake and Carbon Dioxide Production

Calculation of Oxygen Consumption ($\dot{V}O_2$)

The air we breathe is composed of 20.93% oxygen (O_2), 0.03% carbon dioxide (CO_2), and the balance, 79.04%, nitrogen. When we exhale, the fraction of the air represented by O_2 is decreased and the fraction represented by CO_2 is increased. To calculate the volume of O_2 used by the body ($\dot{V}O_2$), we simply subtract the number of liters of O_2 exhaled from the number of liters of O_2 inhaled. Equation (1) summarizes these words.

(1) Oxygen consumption =

[Volume of O_2 inhaled]

− [Volume of O_2 exhaled]

Now, using $\dot{V}O_2$ to mean volume of *oxygen* used, V_I to mean volume of *air* inhaled, V_E to mean volume of *air* exhaled, F_{IO_2} to mean fraction of oxygen in inhaled air, and F_{EO_2} to mean fraction of oxygen in exhaled air, equation (1) can be written:

(2) $\dot{V}O_2 = [V_I \cdot F_{IO_2}] - [V_E \cdot F_{EO_2}]$

You know that $F_{IO_2} = 0.2093$ and F_{EO_2} will be determined on an oxygen analyzer. Consequently, you are left with only two unknowns, the volume of air (liters) inhaled (V_I) and the volume of air (liters) exhaled (V_E). It appears that you must measure both volumes, but fortunately, this is not necessary. It was determined years ago that N_2 is neither used nor produced by the body. Consequently, the number of liters of N_2 inhaled must equal the number of liters of N_2 exhaled. Equation (3) states this equality using the symbols mentioned earlier.

(3) $V_I \times F_{IN_2} = V_E \times F_{EN_2}$

This is a very important relationship because it permits you to calculate V_E when V_I is known or vice versa. Using equation (3) here are two formulas, one to give V_E when V_I is known, and one to give V_I when V_E is known.

$$V_I = \frac{V_E \bullet F_{EN_2}}{F_{IN_2}} \qquad V_E = \frac{V_I \bullet F_{IN_2}}{F_{EN_2}}$$

Now that you know how to do this, there is only one other piece to the puzzle needed to permit you to calculate $\dot{V}O_2$. The value for F_{IN_2} is constant (0.7904) so we must determine F_{EN_2}. When the expired gas sample is analyzed you will obtain a value for F_{EO_2} and F_{ECO_2}, but not F_{EN_2}. However, since all the gas fractions must add up to 1.0000, you can calculate F_{EN_2}. (In the same way, we calculated F_{IN_2}: 1.0000 − .0003 (CO_2) − .2093 (O_2) = .7904).

Problem: Calculate F_{EN_2} when F_{EO_2} = .1600 and F_{ECO_2} = .0450

Answer: F_{EN_2} = 1.0000 − .1600 − .0450 = .7950

The following problem shows how these equations are used. Given that V_I equals 100 liters, F_{EO_2} = .1600, and F_{ECO_2} = .0450, calculate V_E.

$$V_E \bullet F_{EN_2} = V_I \bullet F_{IN_2}, \text{ so } V_E = \frac{V_I \bullet F_{IN_2}}{F_{EN_2}}$$

F_{IN_2} = .7904 and

F_{EN_2} = 1.0000 − .1600 − .0450 = .7950

$$V_E = 100 \text{ liters} \times \frac{.7904}{.7950} = 99.4 \text{ liters}$$

At this point, the equation for $\dot{V}O_2$ can be rewritten, using V_I, V_E, F_{IO_2}, and F_{EO_2}.

$$\dot{V}O_2 = V_I \bullet F_{IO_2} - V_E \bullet F_{EO_2}$$

Assuming that you measure only V_I this formula is rewritten:

$$\dot{V}O_2 = V_I \bullet F_{IO_2} - \frac{V_I \bullet F_{IN_2}}{F_{EN_2}} \bullet F_{EO_2}$$

V_I can be factored out of this equation, so:

$$\dot{V}O_2 = V_I[F_{IO_2} - \frac{F_{IN_2}}{F_{EN_2}} \bullet F_{EO_2}]$$

We will repeat the last two steps assuming that V_E is the volume that is measured and then factor out V_E.

$$\dot{V}O_2 = \frac{V_E \bullet F_{EN_2}}{F_{IN_2}} \bullet F_{IO_2} - V_E \bullet F_{EO_2}$$

$$= V_E[\frac{F_{EN_2}}{F_{IN_2}} \bullet F_{IO_2} - F_{EO_2}]$$

At this point you know how to calculate $\dot{V}O_2$. If you ever get stuck, always go back to the formula: $\dot{V}O_2 = V_I \bullet F_{IO_2} - V_E \bullet F_{EO_2}$ and simply substitute for V_E or V_I, depending on what was measured.

Some comments:

1. You must always match the volume measurement with the F_{EO_2} and F_{ECO_2} values measured in that expired volume. If you measure V_I for two minutes, you must have a single two-minute bag of expired gas to get F_{EO_2} and F_{ECO_2} values. If you measure a 30-second volume your expired bag must be collected over those 30 seconds.
2. $\dot{V}O_2$ and $\dot{V}CO_2$ are usually expressed in liters/min: The *rate* at which O_2 is used or

CO_2 is produced per minute. To signify this *rate*, we write $\dot{V}O_2$ (read Vee dot). You would convert 30-second or 2-minute volumes to one-minute values before making calculations of $\dot{V}O_2$.

Sample problem:

$\dot{V}_I = 100\ \ell/\text{min}$, $F_{EO_2} = .1600$, $F_{ECO_2} = .0450$

Calculate $\dot{V}O_2$:

$$\dot{V}O_2 = \dot{V}_I \cdot F_{IO_2} - \dot{V}_E \cdot F_{EO_2}$$

$$\dot{V}_E = \frac{\dot{V}_I\, F_{IN_2}}{F_{EN_2}}$$

$$\dot{V}O_2 = \dot{V}_I \cdot F_{IO_2} - \frac{\dot{V}_I\, F_{IN_2}}{F_{EN_2}} \cdot F_{EO_2}$$

$$= \dot{V}_I\, [F_{IO_2} - \frac{F_{IN_2}}{F_{EN_2}} \cdot F_{EO_2}]$$

$$F_{EN_2} = 1.0000 - .1600 - .0405 = .7950$$

$$\dot{V}O_2 = 100\ \ell/\text{min}\ [.2093 - \frac{.7904}{.7950} \cdot .1600]$$

$$= 5.02\ \ell/\text{min}$$

The volume (let's assume that $\dot{V}_E$ was measured) used in the above equations was measured at room temperature (23 °C) and at the barometric pressure of that moment (740 mm Hg). The environmental conditions under which the volume was measured are called ambient conditions. If this volume of gas were transported to 10,000 feet above sea level, where the barometric pressure is lower, the volume would increase because of the reduced pressure. The volume of a gas varies inversely with pressure (at a constant temperature). Another factor influencing the volume of a gas is the temperature. If that volume, measured at 23 °C, were placed in a refrigerator at 0 °C, the volume of gas would decrease. The volume of gas varies directly with the temperature (at constant pressure).

Since the volume ($\dot{V}_E$) is influenced by both pressure and temperature, the value measured as O_2 used ($\dot{V}O_2$) might reflect changes in pressure or temperature, rather than a change in workload, training, and so on. Consequently, it would be convenient to express $\dot{V}_E$ in such a way as to make measurements comparable when they are obtained under different environmental conditions. This is done by standardizing the temperature, barometric pressure, and water vapor pressure at which the volume is expressed. By convention, volumes are expressed at Standard Temperature and Pressure, Dry (STPD): 273 °K (equals 0 °C), 760 mm Hg pressure (sea level), and with no water vapor pressure. When VO_2 is expressed STPD you can calculate the number of molecules of oxygen actually used by the body because *at STPD one mole of oxygen equals 22.4 liters*.

Let's make the correction to STPD one step at a time. Let's assume that a volume ($\dot{V}_E$) was measured at 740 mm Hg, 23 °C and equalled 100 ℓ/min. This *expired* volume is *always* saturated with water vapor.

To correct for temperature you use 273 °K as the standard (0 °C).

$$\text{Volume} \times \frac{273\ °K}{273\ °K + x\ °C} = \frac{273\ °K}{273 + 23}$$

$$100\ \ell/\text{min} \times \frac{273\ °K}{296\ °K} = 92.23\ \ell/\text{min}$$

When we make corrections for pressure we must remove the effect of water vapor pressure because the gas volume is adjusted on the basis of the standard pressure (760 mm Hg) which is a dry pressure.

To correct the volume to the standard 760 mm Hg pressure (dry) use:

$$\text{Volume} \times \frac{\text{barometric pressure} - \text{water vapor pressure}}{760\ \text{mm Hg (dry)}}$$

Water vapor pressure is dependent on two things: the temperature and the relative humidity. In expired gas the gas volume is saturated (100% relative humidity). Consequently, you can obtain a value for water vapor pressure directly from a table:

Temperature (°C)	Saturation Water Vapor Pressure (mm Hg)
18	15.5
19	16.5
20	17.5
21	18.7
22	19.8
23	21.1
24	22.4
25	23.8
26	25.2
27	26.7

Going back to our pressure correction:

$$92.23\ \ell/\text{min} \times \frac{740 - 21.1}{760}$$

$$= 87.24\ \ell/\text{min (STPD)}$$

To combine the temperature and pressure correction:

$$100\ \ell/\text{min} \times \frac{273\ °K}{273\ °K + 23} \times \frac{740 - 21.1}{760}$$

$$= 87.24\ \ell/\text{min (STPD)}$$

A special note must be made here. If you are using an inspired (inhaled) volume measure ($\dot{V}_I$), you are rarely dealing with a gas saturated with water vapor. Consequently, when you correct for pressure you must find what the water vapor is in the inspired air. You do this by finding the relative humidity of the air. You then multiply this value by the water vapor pressure value for saturated air at whatever the temperature is. To clarify, if our volume in the above example was $\dot{V}_I$ and had a relative humidity of 50%, the pressure correction would have been:

$$\text{Volume} \times \frac{740 - (.50 \times 21.1\ \text{mm Hg})}{760\ \text{mm Hg}}$$

While this may seem like a minor point, it is critical to the accurate measurement of $\dot{V}O_2$ that the proper water vapor correction be used. When you do calculations for $\dot{V}O_2$ you usually find the STPD factor first since you will be multiplying this factor by each volume measured.

Problem: Given $V_I = 100\ \ell/\text{min}$, $F_{EO_2} = .1700$, $F_{ECO_2} = .0385$. The temperature = 20 °C, barometric pressure = 740 mm Hg, and the relative humidity = 30%.

Answer:

$$\text{STPD factor} = \frac{740\ \text{mm Hg} - (.30)17.5\ \text{mm Hg}}{760}$$

$$\times \frac{273\ °K}{273\ °K + 20\ °C} = .900$$

$$100\ \ell/\text{min} \times .900 = 90\ \ell/\text{min STPD}$$

$$\dot{V}O_2 = V_{I_{STPD}}\ [F_{IO_2} - \frac{F_{IN_2}}{F_{EN_2}} \bullet F_{EO_2}]$$

$$\dot{V}O_2 = 90\ \ell/\text{min}\ [.2093 - \frac{.7904}{.7915} \bullet .1700]$$

$$\dot{V}O_2 = 3.56\ \ell/\text{min}$$

Carbon Dioxide Production ($\dot{V}CO_2$)

When O_2 is used, CO_2 is produced. The ratio of CO_2 production ($\dot{V}CO_2$) to O_2 consumption ($\dot{V}O_2$) is an important measurement in metabolism. This ratio ($\dot{V}CO_2 \div \dot{V}O_2$) is called the respiratory exchange ratio and is abbreviated as "R."

How do we measure $\dot{V}CO_2$? We start at the same step as for $\dot{V}O_2$:

$$\dot{V}CO_2 = \text{liters of } CO_2 \text{ expired} - \text{liters of } CO_2 \text{ inspired} = V_E \bullet F_{ECO_2} - V_I\ F_{ICO_2}$$

The steps to follow are the same as for measuring $\dot{V}O_2$. Always use an STPD volume in your calculations. The following is the equation to use when V_I is measured:

$$V_{CO_2} = V_{I_{STPD}}\ [\frac{F_{IN_2}}{F_{EN_2}} \bullet F_{ECO_2} - F_{ICO_2}]$$

The following steps summarize the calculations for VCO_2 and R for the previous problem.

$$VCO_2 = 90\ \ell/\text{min}\ [\frac{.7904}{.7915} \bullet .0385 - .0003]$$

$$= 3.43\ \ell/\text{min}$$

$$R = VCO_2 \div \dot{V}O_2 = 3.43\ \ell/\text{min} \div 3.56\ \ell/\text{min}$$

$$R = .96$$

Definitions

- Words the HFI needs to be able to define

The following list of words are terms with which the HFI will come into contact. The meanings are related to physical fitness. Many of these words have more general and/or alternative meanings. The health and fitness implications of appropriate terms are noted. The chapter(s) in which the terms are used is indicated (with the exception of standard weight measurements).

Abdominal muscular endurance, chapter 7—the ability of the muscles in the abdominal area to continue to contract without fatigue. Abdominal muscular endurance appears to be an important element in the prevention of low-back pain.

Abdominal pain, chapter 2—a distressful feeling in the area of the abdomen. A person suffering abdominal pain should be referred for medical attention.

Abnormal, chapter 6—not typical. Abnormal is often defined as one, two, or three standard deviations above or below the mean for a test score, which would include about 68% (+ and − one standard deviation above and below the mean), 96%, and 99% of the population, respectively. An abnormal score may be related to positive (e.g., low-resting heart due to a high level of physical condition) or negative (e.g., S-T segment depression on the ECG) health.

Abrasion, chapter 14—a superficial injury to skin, usually from scraping a surface.

Acclimatization, chapter 9—a physiological adaptation to a new environment. For example, a person can do the same work with less effort and can do more total work after becoming acclimatized to a higher altitude (or temperature).

Acidosis, chapter 3—a disturbance in the acid-base balance of the body tissues in which the tissues become more acid (pH is lowered).

Acromion, chapter 4—a bony process on the superior lateral aspect of the scapula (shoulder blade).

Action potential, chapter 12—a change in electrical potential at the surface of a nerve or muscle cell, occurring at the moment of its excitation.

Active, chapters 1, 6—communicating motion, as opposed to being passive. Active people include regular physical activity as a part of their lifestyles.

Activity revision, chapter 6—recommending changes in the level (e.g., frequency, intensity, duration) and/or type of physical activity for better fitness results.

Acute stressor, chapter 8—a situation or condition that causes an immediate and temporary physiological reaction in excess of what is needed to carry out the task.

Adaptation, chapter 8—the ability to adjust mentally and physically to circumstances or a changing situation. Acclimatization is one example of adaptation.

Additive, chapter 8—two or more conditions that result in a greater physiological response than would have been caused by any one by itself. For example, there is greater risk of CHD with two risk factors than with one.

Adenosine diphosphate (ADP), chapter 3—one of the chemical products of the breakdown of ATP for energy during muscle contraction.

Adenosine triphosphate (ATP), chapter 3—a high-energy compound from which the body derives energy.

Adherence, chapter 8—state of continuing. Often used to describe people who continue to participate in a physical fitness program.

Adipose tissue, chapter 5—a connective tissue in which fat is stored.

Adrenal glands, chapter 3—endocrine glands directly above each kidney, composed of the medulla (which secretes the hormones epinephrine and norepinephrine) and the cortex (which secretes cortical hormones).

Adrenalin, chapter 3—see ***epinephrine***.

Aerobic activities, chapter 9—the activities of moderate intensity that use large muscle groups with energy supplied aerobically.

Aerobic metabolism, chapter 3—the energy supplied when oxygen is utilized while a person is working.

Aerobic power, chapter 6—the maximal oxygen uptake, or the amount of oxygen that can be utilized during maximal physical work.

Aggression, chapter 8—high levels of animosity or hostility, often unprovoked, which sometimes result from frustration or a feeling of inferiority.

Aging, chapters 1, 6, 8—the process of becoming older. Changes associated with aging are caused by various factors, including the lapse of time. These factors include decreased physical activity and an increased number and severity of health problems.

Agonist, chapter 4—a muscle directly engaged in contraction.

Alcoholism, chapter 2—alcoholic poisoning. In its chronic form it causes severe disturbances of the nervous and digestive systems.

Alkalosis, chapter 3—an increase of pH of the body caused by excessive alkaline substances such as bicarbonate or by a removal of acids or chlorides from the blood.

Allergy, chapter 2—an altered or exaggerated response to various substances or physical agents that are harmless to the majority of individuals. It is important to know of any allergies to medication in case of an emergency.

Altitude, chapters 4, 9, 10—the height above sea level for a given point. A person has lower maximal aerobic power with increasing altitudes because of the decreased partial pressure of oxygen in the air.

Alveolus (plural, ***alveoli***), chapter 4—a tiny air sac of the lungs where carbon dioxide and oxygen are exchanged with the surrounding pulmonary capillaries.

American Alliance of Health, Physical Education, Recreation, and Dance, chapter 11—an organization of professionals interested in these fields.

American College of Sports Medicine, chapter 11—an organization of professionals interested in the relationship of sport (and other physical activity) to medicine (and health and performance).

Amino acid, chapter 3—a compound present in proteins from which the body builds tissue. Amino acids can be used for energy.

Amphetamine, chapter 2—a drug that is a powerful stimulant to the central nervous system, used for nasal congestion, to "lift" a person's mood, or to control appetite. In children, an amphetamine is sometimes used to control hyperactive behavior. A danger of addiction and psychosis exists.

Amphiarthrodial joint, chapter 4—a type of joint that allows slight movement.

Anaerobic activities, chapters 3, 10—high-intensity activities during which energy demands exceed the ability to work aerobically with energy that is supplied anaerobically.

Anaerobic metabolism, chapter 3—energy supplied without oxygen, causing an oxygen debt.

Anaerobic threshold, chapter 3—the point where the metabolic demands of exercise cannot be met aerobically.

Anatomy, chapter 4—the science that deals with the structure of the human body.

Anemia, chapter 2—a disorder caused by a deficiency in the number of red blood cells, or of their hemoglobin content, or both. Symptoms include pallor, easy fatigue, breathlessness after exertion, giddiness, palpitation, and loss of appetite.

Aneurysm, chapter 2—a spindle-shaped or saclike bulging of the wall of a blood-filled vein, artery, or ventricle.

Anger, chapters 2, 8—a strong emotion of displeasure or antagonism, which is often excited by a sense of injury or insult and frequently paired with a desire to retaliate.

Angina, angina pectoris, chapters 2, 6, 12—severe cardiac pain which may radiate to the jaws, arms, or legs. Angina is caused by myocardial ischemia, which is often induced by exercise. Exercise should be stopped and the person should be referred for medical attention.

Angular momentum, chapter 4—the quantity of rotation. Angular momentum is the product of the rotational inertia and angular velocity.

Anorexia, chapter 2—an abnormal lack of appetite.

Antagonist, chapter 4—a muscle that causes movement at a joint located opposite its agonist.

Anthropometry, chapter 5—the measurement of the body and its parts.

Antibiotic, chapter 2—an antibacterial substance, such as penicillin or tetracycline.

Anticoagulant, chapter 12—a drug that delays the clotting of the blood.

Antidepressant, chapter 2—a drug used to decrease depression.

Antihistamine, chapter 2—a drug that inhibits the effect of histamine, which is used chiefly in the treatment of allergies and colds.

Anxiety, chapters 2, 8—a feeling of fear, apprehension, and dread, often without apparent cause.

Aorta, chapter 12—the main artery coming out of the left ventricle.

Apoplexy, stroke, chapter 3—the loss of consciousness, and paralysis caused by an inadequate blood supply to a portion of the brain.

Apparently healthy, chapter 6—a term used to describe people without a known disease or illness. These people may vary widely in terms of levels of physical fitness (or positive health).

Aquatics, chapter 11—physical activities performed on or in water.

Arousal, chapter 8—the act of becoming excited, causing a stress response (i.e., a greater physiological response than is needed to perform the task). Arousal often occurs in competitive situations.

Arrhythmia, chapter 12—any deviation from the normal rhythm of the heart. A person with arrhythmia should be referred for medical clearance before increasing his or her activity.

Arteriosclerosis, chapter 2—an arterial disease characterized by the hardening and thickening of vessel walls.

***Arteriovenenous oxygen difference, A-V O_2* difference,** chapter 3—the difference between the oxygen contents of arterial blood and venous blood.

Artery, chapters 6, 12—a blood vessel carrying blood from the heart to the various tissues.

Arthritis, chapter 2—the inflammation of a joint.

Articular cartilage, chapter 4—hyaline cartilage over bone surfaces that articulate with other bone surfaces.

Aspirin, chapter 2—acetylsalicyclic acid used to relieve pain, inflammation, and fever. People need not be referred for medical clearance before taking aspirin unless they take excessive quantities.

Assertiveness, chapter 8—the positive and firm statement of a position or feeling, done without aggression or hostility.

Asthma, chapter 2—the obstruction of airways caused by the generalized narrowing of the bronchi, and characterized by wheezing and constriction in the chest.

Astigmatism, chapter 2—defective vision caused by the inequality of one or more refractive surfaces, usually the corneal, so that light rays do not converge to a point on the retina. As astigmatism may be congenital or acquired.

Atherosclerosis, chapter 5—a disease in which the inner layer of the artery wall becomes thick and irregular with deposits of fatty substances.

Athlete's foot, chapter 14—a foot fungus often accompanied by a bacterial infection that causes itching, redness, and a rash on the soles, toes, or between toes.

Atrioventricular, chapter 6—pertaining to the atria and the ventricles of the heart, such as a node, a tract, and a valve.

Atrioventricular node, chapter 12—the origin of the bundle of His in the right atrium of the heart. Normal electrical activity of the heart passes through the AV node prior to depolarization of the ventricles.

Atrium, also called ***auricle*** (plural is ***atria***, adjective is ***atrial***), chapter 12—one of the two (i.e., left and right) upper cavities of the heart.

Atrophy, chapter 7—a reduction in the size of a muscle or other body part. Atrophy is often caused by disuse.

Attitude, chapter 2—a set mode of thinking.

Autonomic nervous system, chapter 3—the nerves that innervate the heart, viscera, and glands and control their involuntary functions. The autonomic nervous system consists of sympathetic and parasympathetic divisions.

AV block, chapter 6—obstruction of the nerve impulse at the AV node.

Background information, chapter 6—health problems, characteristics, lifestyle, habits, signs, and symptoms of a person (and family) that are related to positive health and/or risks of health problems.

Ballistic movement, chapter 4—a rapid movement with three phases: An initial concentric muscle contraction by agonists to begin movement, a coasting phase, and a deceleration by the eccentric contraction of the antagonist muscles.

Barbiturates, chapter 2—a group of sedative drugs derived from barbituric acid. Continual use may result in addiction. A person does not need medical clearance prior to exercise while taking barbiturates, unless the drugs were taken in extreme amounts.

Basal metabolic rate, chapter 5—the minimum energy expenditure required for life in the resting, postabsorptive state.

Behavior, chapters 2, 8, 13—the manner of conducting oneself, often in relation to others or in a particular environment. Behavior usually refers to a person's activities (rather than his or her thoughts or intentions).

Bench, chapter 6—a step used to test cardiorespiratory function. The height of the bench and the number of steps per minute determine the intensity of the effort.

Beta-adrenergic, chapter 12—receptors in the heart and lungs that respond to catecholamines.

Bigeminy, chapters 6, 12—on ECG, alternating normal and premature ventricular contractions.

Birth control, chapter 2—regulation of the number of a person's children through the restriction of ovulation or conception. Some oral birth control pills may increase the risk of hypertension.

Bleeding trait, chapter 2—see ***hemophilia***.

Blood, chapter 2—the red fluid that fills the heart and blood vessels. Blood consists of plasma with red (erythrocytes) and white (leukocytes) cells, as well as blood platelets (thrombocytes).

Blood chemistry, chapter 6—the analysis of the content of the blood, used to determine the levels of substances related to health (e.g., cholesterol) or performance (e.g., lactic acid).

Blood pressure, chapters 1, 2, 6, 9—the pressure exerted by the blood on the vessel walls, measured in millimeters of mercury by the sphygmomanometer. The systolic pressure (SBP, when the left ventricle is in maximal contraction) is the first sound, followed by the diastolic pressure (DBP, when the left ventricle is at rest) which is recorded when there is a change of tone of the sound.

Blood pressure cuff, chapter 6—the cuff that is wrapped around the arm and pumped up to block off the artery. The pressure in the cuff is then slowly released to determine SBP and DBP. It is important to have the right size cuff for the arm, because improper sized cuffs may result in inaccurate readings (e.g., too small a cuff will provide an artificially elevated blood pressure).

Blood vessels, chapter 6—any vessel (i.e., artery, vein, or capillary) through which blood circulates.

Body composition, chapters 5, 6—the relative amounts of muscle, bone, and fat in the body. Body composition is usually divided into fatness (% body fat) and lean body mass (% lean body mass).

Body density, chapter 5—the relative weight of the body compared to an equal volume of water, or weight of the body per unit volume. Body density can be used to estimate percent fat.

Bone, chapters 2, 4—the hard tissue forming the skeleton.

Bradycardia, chapter 12—slow heart rate, below 60 b/min at rest. Bradycardia is healthy if it is the result of physical conditioning.

Breast, chapter 2—the anterior upper part of the thorax; the mammary gland. Regular breast examinations are recommended for women to detect breast cancer early.

Breathing, ventilation, chapter 11—the inhalation and exhalation of air.

Breathless, chapter 2—the inability to breathe without difficulty. Breathlessness may indicate a pulmonary disorder or a risk of CHD if it occurs with mild exertion; a person with this should be referred to medical personnel.

Bronchiole, chapter 4—a small branch of the airway. A bronchiole sometimes undergoes a spasm and makes breathing difficult, such as in exercise-induced asthma.

Bronchitis, chapter 2—the inflammation of the bronchi. Symptoms are a productive cough, wheezy breathing, and varying degrees of breathlessness.

Budget, chapter 15—an estimate of income and expenditure which is often itemized.

Buffer, chapter 3—a substance in blood that soaks up hydrogen ions to minimize changes in the acid-base balance.

Bundle branch block, chapter 6, 12—a heart block caused by a lesion in one of the bundle branches.

Bundle of His, chapter 12—the bundle of nerve fibers between atria and ventricles that conducts impulses into both ventricles.

Bursa, chapter 4—a fibrous sac lined with synovial membrane that contains a small quantity of synovial fluid. Bursae are found between tendon and bone, skin and bone, and between muscle and muscle. Their function is to facilitate movement without friction between these surfaces.

Bursitis, chapter 14—the inflammation of a bursa.

Caffeine, chapter 12—a stimulant drug used in coffee, tea, cola drinks, and some other sodas.

Calibrate, chapter 6—to determine the accuracy of an instrument, by measurement of its variation from a standard.

Calisthenics, chapter 7—exercise without equipment performed for flexibility or muscular development.

Caloric cost, chapters 9, 10, 11—the number of calories used for a specific task, normally reported in C or kcal/min.

Calorie, chapter 5—calorie = kilocalories = amount of heat required to raise the temperature of 1 g of water 1 °C.

Calorimetry, chapter 10—the method used to measure the number of calories in something.

Cancer, chapter 2—a general term that covers many malignant growths in various parts of the body. The growth is apparently purposeless, parasitic, and flourishes at the expense of the human host. Characteristics of cancer are the tendencies to cause local destruction within the body, spread by metastasis, recur after removal, and cause toxemia.

Capillary, chapter 3—the smallest blood vessel; the link between the end of the arteries and the beginning of the veins.

Capsular ligament, chapter 4—the ligament lined with synovial membrane surrounding the diarthrodial or synovial joints.

Capsulitis, chapter 14—the inflammation of a capsule.

Carbohydrate, chapter 5—a group of chemical compounds containing only carbon, hydrogen, and oxygen; sugars, cellulose, and starches are carbohydrates.

Carbon dioxide, chapter 12—a gas; a waste product of many forms of combustion and metabolism, excreted via the lungs.

Cardiac cycle, chapter 3—one total heart beat with one complete contraction (systole) and relaxation (diastole) of the heart.

Cardiac output, chapter 3—the amount of blood circulated by the heart each minute; cardiac output = heart rate × stroke volume.

Cardiac rehabilitation, chapter 11—a program designed to help cardiac patients return to normal lives with reduced risk of additional health problems.

Cardiopulmonary resuscitation (CPR), chapter 14—a method to restore normal pulse and breathing by mouth-to-mouth respiration and rhythmical compression on the chest. People working in fitness programs should be certified in CPR.

Cardiorespiratory function, chapters 1, 6, 9—pertaining to the heart and respiration.

Cardiovascular, chapters 1, 6—pertaining to the heart and blood vessels.

Carotid artery, chapter 6—the principal artery in each side of the neck.

Catecholamines, chapter 3—epinephrine and norepinephrine.

Catharsis, chapter 8—purification of the emotions through action.

Cellulite, chapter 5—a label given to lumpy deposits of fat commonly appearing on the back and front of the legs and buttocks in overweight individuals.

Center of gravity, chapter 4—the theoretical point about which the entire weight of the body (or body part) can be considered to be acting.

Cerebral vascular disease, chapter 2—a disease of the blood vessels of the brain.

Certification, chapter 11—a document that serves as evidence of a certain status or qualification. For example, several groups certify that people are qualified to conduct specific aspects of a fitness program.

Chest pain, chapter 2—a tightness, compression, or sharp sensation in the chest, which may be caused by myocardial ischemia. People with chest (arm, shoulder, or jaw) pain should be referred for medical attention.

Cholesterol, chapters 2, 5—a fat-like substance found in animal tissues. The normal plasma level is considered to be between 180 and 230 milligrams per 100 ml. Higher levels are associated with increased risk of atherosclerosis.

Chronic obstructive pulmonary disease (COPD), chapters 1, 9—is a term used to describe a number of specific diseases which cause a chronic unremitting obstruction to flow of air in the airways of the lungs.

Chronic stressors, chapter 8—a continuing condition or situation that causes physiological responses in excess of those needed to complete a task. For example, excess fat causes chronic stress responses at rest and during exertion.

Chronotropic, chapter 3—affects time or rate, especially of the heart beat.

Circuit training, chapter 11—a sequence of exercises done one after the other in the same workout.

Circulation, chapters 3, 12—the continuous movement of blood through the heart and blood vessels.

Cirrhosis, chapter 2—the hardening of an organ. Cirrhosis is applied almost exclusively to degenerative changes in the liver with resulting fibrosis. Damage to liver cells can be by virus, microbes, toxic substances, and/or dietary deficiencies interfering with the nutrition of the cells—often the result of alcoholism.

Claudication, chapter 6—limping due to interference with the blood supply to the legs.

Clothing, chapters 9, 11—apparel for the body. Proper clothing is an important aspect of exercising in extreme weather conditions.

Coagulation, blood clotting, chapter 3—the formation of fibrin, a threadlike clot or clump of solid material in the blood.

Colitis, chapter 2—inflammation of the colon.

Collateral circulation, chapter 3—additional, supplementary, or substitute vessels that increase circulation to a part of the tissue, such as in the heart.

Collection bag, chapter 6—an air-tight container used to store expired air during exercise tolerance test. Samples from air in bags are analyzed for percent of oxygen and carbon dioxide.

Colon, chapter 2—the large bowel extending from the cecum to the rectum.

Competent, chapter 8—having suitable skill for some purpose.

Competitive running, chapter 11—running in a race with the main object of trying to win the race.

Concentric contraction, chapter 4—a shortening of the muscle as a result of the contraction of that muscle.

Concussion, chapter 2—a condition resulting from a violent jar or shock. A concussion is associated with the brain and may result in loss of consciousness, pallor, coldness, and an increase in heart rate.

Condition, chapter 8—a particular state or situation.

Conditioning, chapter 9—chronic physical training.

Conduction, chapters 6, 12—the transmission of energy, heat, electricity, or sound. For example, conduction is the passage of electrical currents and nerve impulses through body tissues.

Confidentiality, chapter 15—the act of keeping information about an individual private. One of the elements of "informed consent" of fitness participants is that the information and data will be kept in a secure place and not shared with anyone without the individual's permission.

Congenital defect, chapter 2—existing from birth or before.

Congestive heart failure, chapter 2—failure of the heart caused by its inability to pump a sufficient proportion of the blood it contains, with subsequent congestion.

Constipation, chapter 2—infrequent and often difficult evacuation of feces.

Contractility, chapter 4—the property of shortening (e.g., a muscle) in response to a stimulus.

Contraindications, chapter 9—a sign or symptom suggesting that a certain activity should be avoided.

Control, chapter 8—the power to influence the outcome. The perception of control of a situation is one of the key elements in coping with potentially stressful conditions. In an experimental sense, control refers to the extent to which related variables are accounted for so that the result is the effect of the experimental treatment. Often the experimental control is in the form of one or more control groups.

Contusion, chapter 14—a bruise; slight bleeding into tissues while the skin remains unbroken.

Convulsions, chapter 2—a series of involuntary muscular contractions of a very generalized nature.

Cool down, taper off, chapters 11, 14—a period of light activity following moderate to heavy exercise. The cool-down period is important because the leg muscles continue to pump blood back to the heart, whereas stopping immediately after exercise causes pooling of the blood in the legs and a lack of venous return.

Cope, chapter 8—to struggle or strive to deal with a difficult situation with some degree of success.

Core temperature, chapter 9—the temperature of the central portion of the body, usually estimated by a rectal probe.

Coronary arteries, chapter 12—blood vessels that supply the heart muscle.

Coronary artery thrombosis, chapter 12—occlusion of a coronary vessel by a clot of blood.

Coronary heart disease (CHD), chapter 2—coronary atherosclerosis, an irregular thickening of the inner layer of the coronary arteries.

Coronary occlusion, chapter 2—the blockage of a coronary artery.

Coronary-prone personality, chapters 1, 8—a person with "Type A" behavior (e.g., hard-driving, impatient, time-conscious). Someone with a coronary-prone personality may have a higher risk of CHD.

Coronary thrombosis, chapter 2—blockage of a coronary artery by a blood clot.

Coronary sinus, chapter 12—the channel receiving most cardiac veins and opening into the right atrium.

Cortisone, chapter 2—one of the principal hormones of the adrenal gland, converted into cortisol before use by the body. It has powerful antiinflammatory properties and the side effects of salt and water retention.

Criteria for entry into program, chapter 15—standards for deciding which people should be referred for medical attention and which should be allowed to participate in fitness testing and activities.

Cross adaptation, chapter 8—the transfer of increased adaptation from one stimulus (or stressor) to another stimulus. For example, some have claimed that increased adaptation to physical work from physical conditioning carries over to better adaptation to mental or emotional stressors. The evidence is not clear.

Cyanosis, chapter 6—a bluish tinge frequently observed under the nails, lips, and skin, caused by lack of oxygen. If found, exercise test or activity should be stopped.

Cycle ergometer, chapter 6—a one-wheeled stationary cycle with adjustable resistance used as a work task for exercise testing or conditioning.

Defibrillator, chapter 12—any agent or measure, such as an electric shock, that stops an uncoordinated contraction of the heart muscle and restores a normal heartbeat.

Degenerative disease, chapter 2—a disease involving gradual deterioration and impairment of a tissue or organ.

Dehydration, chapter 3—the excessive loss of body fluids.

Denial, chapter 8—refusal to acknowledge a truth. In fitness programs, people sometimes deny pain and discomfort—they need to be cautioned about doing too much.

Depolarization, chapter 12—the change of polarity, specifically the electrical stimulus changing the atrium or ventricle from the resting to the working state.

Depression, chapters 2, 8—emotional dejection greater than that warranted by any objective reasons, often with symptoms such as insomnia, headaches, exhaustion, anorexia, irritability, loss of interest, impaired concentration, feelings that life is not worth living, and suicidal thoughts.

Deterioration, chapters 1, 8—becoming worse in quality or value.

Detrained, chapter 9—the results of becoming sedentary after a physical conditioning program. The effects (e.g., increased fat, decreased CRF) are opposite those of conditioning.

Development, Part 1, chapter 8—growing or advancing to a higher level.

Development . . . Deterioration, chapter 8—a continuum describing the effects of stress. Positive stress results are found toward the development end, and negative stress results are near the deterioration end of the continuum.

Diabetes, chapters 1, 2, 5, 9, 14—a metabolic disorder characterized by an inability to oxidize carbohydrates because of the disturbance of the normal insulin mechanism.

Diabetic coma, chapter 14—a lack of consciousness caused by lack of insulin.

Diagnosed medical problems, chapter 2—any health problem that has been recognized by a person in the medical profession.

Diaphysis, chapter 4—the shaft of a long bone.

Diarrhea, chapter 2—frequent and usually loose, watery defecation.

Diarthrodial joint or ***synovial joint,*** chapter 4—a freely moving joint characterized by its synovial membrane and capsular ligament.

Diastolic blood pressure (DBP), chapters 2, 6—the pressure exerted by the blood on the vessel walls, measured in millimeters of mercury by a sphygmomanometer, when the left ventricle is at rest. DBP is recorded when the tapping tone becomes muffled.

Diet, chapter 1—the food eaten by an individual. Diet sometimes refers to a special selection of food.

Digestive upsets, chapter 2—problems with digestion.

Digitalis, chapter 2—a drug that augments the contraction of the heart muscle and slows the rate of conduction of cardiac impulses through the AV node.

Dimethyl sulfoxide (DMSO), chapter 12—a controversial drug originally used by veterinarians to reduce joint inflammation in animals and presently used by some athletes for joint and soft tissue injuries.

Diphtheria, chapter 2—an acute, specific, infectious, notifiable disease characterized by a false membrane growing on a mucous surface, usually that of the upper respiratory tract. Locally there is pain, swelling, and may be suffocation. Systemically the toxins attack the heart muscle and nerves.

Disease, Part 1—a sickness or illness.

Diuretic, chapter 2—an agent that increases the flow of urine.

Diurnal variation, chapter 3—a daily variation or change.

Dizziness, chapter 2—unsteadiness with the tendency to stagger or fall.

Drugs, chapter 2—a substance (other than food) that, when taken into the body, produces a change in it. If the change helps the body, the drug is a medicine. If the change is harmful, the drug is a poison. Drugs are often addictive.

Duration, chapter 6—length of time for a fitness workout. Guidelines often include 15-30 min of aerobic work at a target heart rate; however, more importantly, the total work accomplished (e.g., distance covered) should be emphasized.

Dysmenorrhea, chapter 2—difficult or painful menstruation.

Dyspnea, chapter 6—difficult or labored breathing beyond what is expected for the intensity of work. An exercise test or activity should be stopped.

Eccentric contraction, chapter 4—a lengthening of the muscle during its contraction.

Ectopic ventricular complex, chaper 6—a ventricular contraction originating at some point other than the sinoatrial node.

Edema, chapter 2—the excessive retention of fluid in the tissue spaces which causes a swelling.

Efficiency, chapter 3—the ratio of energy expenditure to work output.

Ejection fraction, chapter 12—the difference between left ventricular end diastolic volume and end systolic volume.

Electrocardiogram (ECG), chapter 9—a tracing of the electrical activity of the heart during a complete contraction/relaxation cycle, including the depolarization of the atrium (P-wave) and the depolarization (QRS) and repolarization (T-wave) of the ventricle.

Electrode, chapter 12—a conductor of electrical activity, specifically a plate attached to various parts of the body to receive and transmit the heart's electrical activity to a recorder.

Electrophysiology, chapter 12—the study of electrical activity in the body as it relates to functional aspects of health.

Embolism, chapter 2—the obstruction of a blood vessel by a foreign object, such as a loose blood clot.

Emergency information, chapters 2, 14—information about a person (fitness participant) concerning what should be done in case of an accident or injury, including allergies, medical problems, the person's physician, and a family member or friend to be contacted.

Emergency procedure, chapters 2, 14, 15—the process to be followed to deal effectively and efficiently with any accident or injury.

Emotion, chapters 8, 9—a strong feeling, often accomplished by stress reactions and behaviors.

Empathy, chapter 8—identification with thoughts or feelings of another person.

Emphysema, chapter 2—gaseous distension of the tissues, often accompanying chronic bronchitis.

End point, chapters 6, 9—the point at which an exercise test is changed to the taper down or stopped.

Endocardium, chapter 12—the membrane lining that covers the valves in the heart.

Endorphins, chapter 8—a group of hormones that are similar in composition to morphine and normally produced and released by the pituitary gland to help reduce great pain, anxiety, and stress.

Endurance run, chapter 6—a race of a set distance (for time) or set time (for distance). Normally used to determine a person's cardiorespiratory endurance. Runs of at least 1 mile or 6 min should be used.

Energy, chapter 6—the capacity for performing work, often measured in terms of oxygen consumption.

Enjoyable . . . Unpleasant, chapter 8—one of the continuums used to describe a stressful condition.

Enlarged heart, chapter 2—a heart bigger than average size. If an enlarged heart is the result of pathological conditions, then it is weaker and unhealthy. If it results from physical conditioning, then it is stronger and healthy.

Environmental factors, Part 1, chapter 9—aspects of the surroundings (e.g., heat, altitude, pollution) that influence the response to exercise.

Enzyme, chapter 3—an organic catalyst that aids many body processes, such as digestion and oxidation.

Epicardium, chapter 12—the layer of the pericardium attached to the heart.

Epicondylitis, chapter 14—inflammation of muscles or tendons attaching to the epicondyles of the humerus.

Epidemiological studies, chapter 1—long-term studies of the distribution of diseases in whole populations. Those characteristics, signs, and symptoms that are related to major health problems based on epidemiological studies are called *risk factors*.

Epilepsy, chapter 2—a nervous disorder resulting from disordered electrical activity of the brain, often resulting in a seizure.

Epimysium, chapter 4—the connective tissue sheath surrounding a muscle.

Epinephrine, adrenaline, chapter 3—a chemical liberated from the adrenal medulla and from sympathetic nerve endings. Effects include cardiac stimulation and constriction of blood vessels.

Epiphyseal plates, chapter 4—the sites of ossification in long bones.

Epiphyses, chapter 4—the ends of long bones.

Equipment, chapters 6, 15—appartus used for exercise testing and/or conditioning.

Erythrocytes, chapter 3—the red blood cells.

Escape, chapter 8—to get away, often from a problem. Exercise is used to temporarily escape from a stressful situation.

Estrogen, chapter 2—a generic term referring to ovarian hormones.

Etiology, chapter 2—the study of the causes of disease.

Euphoria, chapter 8—an exaggerated sense of well-being.

Evaluation, chapters 6, 15—the determination or judgment of the value or worth of something or someone. In a fitness setting, an evaluation determines the health or fitness status of an individual based on his or her characteristics, signs, symptoms, behaviors, and test results.

Evaporation, chapter 9—conversion from the liquid to the gaseous state by means of heat, as in evaporation of sweat.

Exercise, Part 1, chapters 2, 8—physical activity, normally of large muscle groups, in a continuous manner, at a certain intensity and frequency, resulting in enough total work so that desirable fitness changes are made and maintained.

Exercise components, chapter 14—warmup, main body of exercise, and taper down.

Exercise modification, chapters 11, 14—adjustment to a person's exercise program in terms of type of activity, intensity, frequency, and/or total work accomplished to more nearly achieve the fitness goals.

Exercise prescription, chapter 6—a recommendation for a fitness program in terms of type of activities, intensity, frequency, and total amount of work aimed at producing or maintaining desirable fitness objectives.

Exercise progression, chapter 14—the increase in total work and/or intensity as a person gradually goes from a sedentary lifestyle to the recommended levels of physical activity.

Exercise Specialist, chapter 11—a person certified by the American College of Sports Medicine to work in exercise rehabilitation settings with high risk or diseased populations.

Exercise Technologist, chapter 11—a person certified by the American College of Sports Medicine to conduct graded exercise stress tests for a variety of populations.

Expiration, chapter 6—breathing out air from the lungs.

Expired gas, chapter 6—the air that is exhaled from the lungs, often analyzed to determine oxygen and carbon dioxide changes from the inspired air.

Extension, chapter 7—increasing the angle at a joint, such as straightening the elbow.

Extensor, chapter 4—a muscle that extends a joint.

Extrinsic, chapter 8—external, as in extrinsic motivation (e.g., reward) to begin or continue exercise.

Extrovert, chapter 8—a person who regulates self-behavior in response to others.

Facilitate, chapter 15—to make easier, less difficult, as in process.

Facility, chapter 15—something designed, built, and/or installed to serve a specific function, such as the facilities for a fitness program.

Faint, chapter 2—a state of temporary unconsciousness. A person who faints should be referred for medical attention.

Family history, chapters 1, 2—referes to the major health problems that have been found in a person's grandparents, parents, uncles/aunts, and siblings. Heart disease in a person's family is a secondary risk factor for CHD.

Farsighted, chapter 2—hyperopia; light rays are focused beyond, instead of on, the retina, resulting in a person being able to see better at a distance than up close.

Fartlek, chapter 11—a form of physical conditioning, also known as *speed play*, which alternates fast and slow running over varied terrain for 3-4 mi.

Fasciculus, chapter 4—a bundle of muscle fibers surrounded by perimysium.

Fast-twitch fiber, chapter 4—a muscle fiber characterized by its fast speed of contraction.

Fat, chapters 1, 5—a compound containing glycerol and fatty acids which is used as a source of energy and can be stored in the body.

Fat-free weight, also ***lean body weight***, chapter 5—the amount of total body weight that is free of fat, calculated by total body weight minus fat weight.

Fat weight, chapter 5—the absolute amount of total body weight that is body fat, calculated by total body weight times percent fat.

Fatigue, chapters 2, 6—weariness, a diminished reaction to stimulus, or the inability to continue without decrement in performance.

Fatty acid, chapter 5—a component of fats, composed of glycerine and an acid, such as stearic, palmitic, or oleic. Circulating fatty acids can be used for energy.

Fear, chapter 8—distressing emotion aroused by impending pain, danger, and so forth.

Field tests, chapter 6—tests that can be used in mass testing situations.

Financial management, chapter 15—an organized plan to handle budgetary income and expenditures.

First-degree AV block, chapter 12—the delayed transmission of impulse from atria to ventricles (in excess of .21 sec).

Fitness, Part 1, chapter 15—a state of health characteristics, symptoms, and behaviors enabling a person to have the highest quality of life. Increases in fitness components are related to positive health, whereas decreases in fitness components increase the risk of major health problems.

Fitness activities, chapter 11—actions that lead to increased fitness.

Fitness center, chapter 15—an organization that provides fitness tests, activities and evaluations.

Fitness continuum, Part 1—extends from death to severe disease, to lack of disease, to optimal capacity to accomplish a person's goals.

Fitness instructor, chapter 11—a person who assists people in evaluating and improving fitness. Certification is offered by the American College of Sports Medicine for those HFIs who work with apparently healthy populations.

Fitness program, chapters 2, 6—an organized series of activities aimed at promoting increased fitness.

Fitness testing, chapters 2, 6—the measurement and evaluation of status of all fitness components.

Fitness workout, chapter 9—a specific fitness session.

Fixator muscle, chapter 4—the muscle that stabilizes a joint to prevent undesirable joint movement.

Flat-footed, chapter 11—a congenital or acquired deformity marked by depression of the longitudinal arch of the feet.

Flexibility, chapters 1, 7—the ability to move a joint through the full range of motion without discomfort or pain.

Flexion, chapter 11—movement of a limb caused by concentric muscular contraction.

Flow meter, chapter 6—an instrument that measures the rate of air movement (e.g., liters of air moved per minute) in a graded exercise test.

Fracture, chapters 2, 14—a break in a bone.

Frequency, chapter 9—how often a person has a fitness workout (usually days per week).

Frostbite, chapter 9—freezing of the skin and superficial tissues resulting from exposure to extreme cold.

Fun run, chapter 11—a race with an emphasis on participation (as opposed to winning).

Functional, chapter 8—Pertaining to function. The response to a stimulus can be subdivided into the functional response needed to do the task and the stress response beyond what is essential for that task.

Functional capacity, chapters 6, 9—maximal oxygen uptake, expressed in milliliters of oxygen per kilogram of body weight per minute, or in METs.

Functional . . . Severe stress, chapter 8—a continuum describing the response to a stimulus.

Gallbladder, chapter 2—a pear-shaped bag on the undersurface of the liver which concentrates and stores bile.

Games, chapters 6, 11—a form of playing for amusement. Games may be cooperative or competitive, involving a few or many people. Games can also be used to achieve fitness improvements.

Gas analyzer, chapter 6—an instrument that measures components of air. In the case of maximal oxygen uptake, a gas analyzer is used to measure oxygen and carbon dioxide in inspired and expired air.

Gender, chapters 1, 2—the grouping of nouns into masculine, feminine, and neuter. Gender refers to classification into female and male.

Genetic potential, Part 1—the possibilities and limits imposed by a person's inherited genes.

German measles, chapter 2—rubella, an acute, infectious, eruptive fever caused by a virus and spread by droplet infection.

Glaucoma, chapter 2—a disease of the eye caused by increased pressure within the eyeball and progressive loss of vision.

Glucose, chapters 2, 5—a carbohydrate that is transported in the blood stream and metabolized by the cell as a primary energy source.

Glycogen, chapter 5—the form in which glucose is stored in the body.

Goal, chapter 15—the result toward which effort is directed.

Goal orientation, chapter 8—the tendency of a person to behave on the basis of his or her goals.

Gonorrhea, chapter 2—an infectious disease of venereal origin in adults.

Gout, chapter 2—a form of metabolic disorder in which sodium biurate is deposited in the cartilages of the joints, ears, and elsewhere.

Governing body, chapter 15—the group empowered to set policy for an organization.

Graded Exercise Test (GXT), chapters 6, 9—a multistage test that determines a person's physiological response to different intensities of exercise and/or the person's peak aerobic capacity.

Gram (g)—a basic unit of mass in the metric system. 1,000 g = 1 kg.

Habit, chapter 11—an acquired behavior pattern regularly followed until it has become almost involuntary.

Hamstring, chapter 1—the tendon in the back of the knee. A hamstring is also a large muscle group at the back of the thigh that crosses both the knee and hip joints.

Hay fever, chapter 2—the inflammation of the mucous membranes of the eyes and respiratory tract caused by an allergic response to the pollen of certain plants.

Headache, chapters 2, 8—a pain in the head.

Health, Part 1—the absence of disease is the minimum level. Positive health includes the abilities of a person to pursue his or her goals.

Health/fitness instructor (HFI), Part 1, chapter 11—a person who is certified by the American College of Sports Medicine and is thus qualified to assist in the evaluation and improvement of health and fitness in normal populations.

Health history, chapter 6—information about a person's past health record.

Health-related behavior, chapter 2—a person's actions that are associated with positive or negative health.

Health-related attitudes, chapter 2—a manner of thinking associated with healthy behaviors.

Health-related sign, chapter 2—evidence of something with a potential health consequence.

Health-related symptom, chapter 2—a sensation that arises from or accompanies a particular disease or disorder and serves as an indicator of it.

Health status, chapter 2—the current level of disease and fitness.

Healthy life, chapter 8—a lifestyle including behaviors related to enhanced fitness and excluding harmful behaviors.

Heart, chapters 2, 6, 9—the hollow muscular organ that pumps the blood through the body. The heart lies obliquely between the two lungs, behind the sternum. The heart is composed of four chambers, left and right atria, and ventricles.

Heart attack, chapter 2—a general term used to describe an acute episode of heart disease.

Heart disease, chapter 2—a general term used to describe any of several abnormalities of the heart causing it to be unable to function properly.

Heart murmur, chapter 2—an abnormal heart sound.

Heart rate, chapters 2, 6, 9—the number of beats of the heart per minute.

Heart rate reserve, chapter 9—the difference between maximal and resting heart rates.

Heart rhythm, chapter 2—the regularity of the heart beat, or components of the cardiac cycle.

Heat cramps, chapter 14—a spasmodic contraction of a muscle or group of muscles which is caused by working in extreme heat.

Heat exhaustion, chapter 14—collapse, with or without loss of consciousness, suffered in conditions of heat and high humidity, largely resulting from the loss of fluid and salt by sweating.

Heat illness, chapters 9, 14—a general term for problems caused by activity in high temperatures.

Heat stroke, chapter 14—the final stage in heat exhaustion. When the body is unable to lose heat, hyperpyrexia occurs and death may ensue.

Heat syncope, chapter 14—fainting or sudden loss of strength because of excessive heat gain.

Heel bruise, chapter 14—an injury in which the skin is not broken but the periosteum is inflamed; often caused by foot landing on a sharp object.

Hematocrit, chapter 3—the volume of red blood cells per unit volume of blood, usually about 40-45%.

Hemoglobin, chapter 9—the respiratory pigment in the red blood corpuscles. It has the reversible function of combining with and releasing oxygen.

Hemophilia, chapter 2—a deficiency of antihemophilic globulin. Hemophilia is an inherited bleeding disease that results in prolonged bleeding from minor cuts; found only in males, transmitted by carrier females (daughters of affected males).

Hemorrhage, chapter 14—the escape of blood from a vessel.

Hemorrhoids, chapter 2—swollen veins around the anus.

Hepatitis, chapter 2—inflammation of the liver.

Heredity, Part 1—the transmission of genetic characters from parents to offspring.

Hernia, chapter 2—the protrusion of an organ or tissue through an opening in its surrounding walls, especially in the abdominal region.

Herpes, chapter 2—the inflammation of skin characterized by clusters of tiny blisters.

High blood pressure, hypertension, chapter 2—blood pressure in excess of normal values for a specific age and gender.

High-calorie diet, chapter 5—food consumption of which the caloric value exceeds the total daily energy requirement, resulting in increased adipose tissue.

High-density lipoprotein cholesterol (HDL-C), chapters 1, 5—a plasma lipid-protein complex containing relatively more protein and less cholesterol and triglycerides. Low levels of HDL-C are associated with CHD.

Hodgkins disease, Lymphadenoma, chapter 2—a progressive disease of the reticuloendothelial system, noticed by the generalized enlargement of the lymphatic glands and the spleen.

Homeostasis, chapter 8—the tendency of the body to maintain internal equilibrium of temperature, fluid content, and so forth by the regulation of its bodily processes.

Hormone, chapter 3—a chemical product which is produced by an endocrine gland and secreted into the blood and which exerts a distinct and usually powerful effect on some body function or organ.

Hostile, chapter 8—antagonistic, unfriendly.

Humidity, chapter 9—the amount of moisture in the atmosphere.

Hypercholesterolemia, chapter 5—an excess of cholesterol in the blood.

Hyperlipemia, chapter 2—excess fat in the blood.

Hyperlipoproteinemia, chapter 5—an increase in the concentration of the three fatty substances of the blood: cholesterol, phospholipid, and triglyceride.

Hyperplasia, chapter 5—new fat cell formation.

Hypertension, chapters 2, 8, 9—high blood pressure. Normally systolic blood pressure exceeds 140 mmHg or diastolic pressure exceeds 90 mmHg in someone who has hypertension.

Hypertrophy, chapter 4—an increase in the size of a muscle, organ, or other body part caused by an enlargement of its constituent cells.

Hypervitaminosis, chapter 5—a condition in which the level of a vitamin in the blood or tissues is high enough to cause undesirable effects.

Hypoglycemia, chapter 2—low blood sugar, attended by anxiety, excitement, perspiration, delirium, or coma.

Hypokinetic disease, chapter 1—a disease that relates to or is caused by the lack of regular physical activity.

Hypothermia, chapter 9—below normal body temperature.

Hysterectomy, chapter 2—the surgical removal of the uterus.

Iliac crest, chapter 5—the large bony prominence at the top of each side of the hips.

Incision, chapter 14—a cut into body tissue using a sharp instrument.

Inclusive, chapter 11—including everyone. One of the characteristics of fitness games is that participation is inclusive.

Increment, chapter 6—a degree of increase. In a graded exercise test a work increment exists between stages.

Inderal, propranolol, chapter 12—a drug-blocking beta-receptor activation in the heart and lungs, aimed at reducing cardiac arrhythmias and dysrhythmias.

Infarction, chapter 12—the death of a section of tissue because the blood supply has been cut off, as in myocardial infarction.

Infectious mononucleosis, chapter 2—the most common cause of glandular fever syndrome, characterized by a fever, a sore throat, and swollen cervical glands.

Inferior vena cava, chapter 12—the large vein that discharges blood from the lower half of the body into the right atrium of the heart.

Informed consent, chapters 6, 15—a procedure used to obtain a person's voluntary permission to participate in a program. Informed consent normally requires a description of the procedures to be used, the potential benefits and risks, and written consent.

Injury, chapters 2, 9, 14, 15—damage to a bodily part.

Inotropic, chapter 4—affecting the force or energy of muscular contraction.

Inspiration, chapter 6—the drawing of air into the lungs.

Insulin, chapter 2—a pancreatic hormone, secreted into the blood that influences the carbohydrate metabolism by stimulating the transport of glucose into cells.

Insulin shock, chapter 14—a shock-like state resulting from an overdose of insulin.

Intensity, chapters 2, 9, 11—the magnitude of energy required for a particular activity, often referred to in terms of percent of max ($\dot{V}O_2$ or HR) or METs.

Intermittent work, chapter 11—exercises performed with alternate periods of harder and lighter physical work, or work and rest, rather than continuous work.

Interval training, chapter 11—a fitness workout that alternates harder and lighter work.

Intrinsic, chapters 8, 11—belonging to a thing by its very nature (e.g., people continue to be active based on intrinsic motivation).

Introvert, chapter 8—a person concerned primarily with his or her own thoughts and feelings.

Ion, chapter 12—an electrified or charged (positive or negative) particle.

Ischemia, chapter 12—inadequate blood supply.

Isoelectric, chapter 12—baseline, as in ECG.

Isokinetic contraction, chapter 4—a muscle contraction with controlled speed, allowing maximal force to be applied throughout the range of motion.

Isometric contraction, chapter 4—a muscle contraction in which the muscle length is unchanged.

Isotonic contraction, chapter 4—a muscle contraction in which the force of the muscle is greater than the resistance resulting from joint movement, with shortening or lengthening of the muscle.

Issue, chapter 15—a debatable point or position, with valid views on opposing sides.

J joint, chapter 12—on ECG, the point at which S wave ends and ST segment begins.

Job description, chapter 15—a statement of the responsibilities of and qualifications for a specific position.

Jogging, chapters 2, 9, 11—slow running.

Joint, chapters 2, 4, 11—the articulation of two or more bones.

Joint cavity, chapter 4—the space between bones enclosed by the synovial membrane and articular cartilage.

Ketosis, chapter 5—a condition brought about by restricted carbohydrate intake resulting in excessive acetones or other ketones being secreted by the liver—stored fat becomes more available for energy.

Kidneys, chapter 2—two glands situated in the upper, posterior abdominal cavity, one on either side of the vertebral column. Their function is to maintain water and electrolyte balance and to secrete urine.

Kilocalorie (kcal) or ***Calorie (cal)***, chapters 5, 9—the amount of heat required to raise the temperature of 1 kg of water 1 °C.

Kilogram (kg)—a metric unit of mass; 1 kg = 1,000 g.

Kilopond meters per minute (kpm/min), Kilogram meters per minute (kgm/min), chapter 6—in a normal gravitational field these are identical. This is a measure of power used to describe the external work load, often on a cycle ergometer.

Krebs cycle, chapter 3—a series of chemical reactions occurring in mitochondria in which carbon dioxide is produced and hydrogen ions and electrons are removed from carbon atoms (oxidation). The Krebs cycle is also referred to as the tricarboxyclic acid cycle or citric acid cycle.

Kyphosis, chapter 7—an excessive posterior curvature of the upper (thoracic) spine.

Laceration, chapter 14—a wound with rough edges.

Lactate, chapter 9—an end product of the anaerobic metabolism of glucose; the dissociated form of lactic acid.

Laxative, chapter 2—a medication or agent for relieving constipation.

Leadership, chapter 11—the ability to influence and motivate people in a group to make decisions and act on the basis of those decisions.

Lean body weight, chapter 5—the portion of the body that is not fat tissue. Lean body weight is often used to refer to all nonfat weight.

Leg pain, chapter 2—discomfort in the leg. If no apparent reason (such as an injury) exists for leg pain, then seek medical attention.

Leukemia, chapter 2—a blood disease (malignant reticuloses) in which the white cells are abnormal in type or number. Classification of leukemia is based on the type of leukocyte found and whether the condition is acute or chronic.

Leukocytes, chapter 3—white blood cells.

Liability, chapter 15—legal responsibility.

Life events, chapter 8—situations that cause stress reactions—they may be enjoyable (e.g., a vacation), or sad (e.g., the death of a loved one).

Lifestyle, chapters 1, 2, 8, 11—a person's general pattern of living, including healthy and unhealthy behaviors.

Ligament, chapter 4—the connective tissue that attaches bone to bone.

Limiting factor, chapter 6—a physiological characteristic that establishes the upper limit of performance (e.g., muscle fiber type, maximal cardiac output, maximal oxygen uptake).

Lipid, chapter 5—a fatty substance.

Lipoprotein, chapter 5—a complex consisting of lipid and protein molecules bound together. Cholesterol and triglycerides are transported in the bloodstream in the form of lipoproteins.

Liter, chapter 1—a unit of volume in the metric system.

Liver, chapter 2—the largest organ in the body, situated in the right upper section of the abdominal cavity. It secretes bile, forms and stores glycogen, and plays an important role in the metabolism of proteins and fats.

Lordosis, chapter 7—an excessive forward curvature of the lumbar spine.

Low-back function, chapters 9, 11—the ability to carry on normal activities without back pain.

Low-back pain, chapters 2, 7, 8, 14—strong discomfort in the low-back area, often caused by lack of muscular endurance and flexibility in the mid-trunk region, or improper posture or lifting.

Low blood sugar, see ***hypoglycemia.***

Low-calorie diet, chapter 5—food intake of which the caloric value is below the total energy requirement, resulting in a loss of weight.

Low-density lipoprotein cholesterol (LDL-C), chapters 1, 5—a plasma protein containing relatively more cholesterol and trigylcerides and less protein. High levels are associated with an increased risk of CHD.

Low-organized games, chapter 11—games with simple rules not requiring high levels of skill.

Lumbar, chapter 4—pertaining to the low back; five lumbar vertebrae are located just below the thoracic vertebrae and just above the sacrum.

METs, chapters 2, 6, 9, 10—multiples of resting metabolism [MET is about 3.5 $ml(kg \cdot min)^{-1}$].

Maintenance load, chapter 6—the amount of exercise that enables an individual to maintain his or her present level of fitness.

Malnutrition, chapter 5—poor or improper nutrition, usually associated with undernutrition.

Max $\dot{V}O_2$, see ***maximal oxygen uptake***.

Maximal, chapter 6—the highest level possible, such as maximal heart rate or oxygen uptake.

Maximal heart rate, chapter 9—the highest heart rate attainable. A person's maximal heart rate can be estimated by subtracting his or her age from 220.

Maximal oxygen uptake, chapter 3—the greatest rate of oxygen utilization attainable during heavy work, expressed in $liters \cdot min^{-1}$, or $ml(kg \cdot min)^{-1}$.

Maximal tests, chapter 6—tests that continue until a person has reached a maximal level (e.g., max $\dot{V}O_2$) or voluntary exhaustion.

Maximum voluntary ventilation, chapters 2, 6—the maximal amount of air that can be moved in and out of the lungs. A person is normally tested for 10-15 sec, then the result is reported in liters per minute.

Measles, chapter 2—an acute infectious disease caused by a virus, characterized by fever, a blotchy rash, and inflammation of mucous membranes.

Medical clearance, chapters 2, 6, 9—an indication by medical personnel that an individual can safely engage in specified activities.

Medical history, chapter 2—a person's previous health problems, signs, and characteristics.

Medical physical exam, chapter 2—the systematic examination of the different parts of the body, used to determine a person's health status.

Medical referral, chapter 2—a recommendation that a person get medical attention, tests, or an opinion about a characteristic, symptom, or test result to determine if medical treatment is needed, and/or to determine whether it is safe to participate in specified activities.

Medical supervision, chapters 2, 6—the presence of qualified medical personnel during a fitness test or workout.

Medication, medicine, chapters 2, 9—a therapeutic substance.

Menstruation, chapter 2—the flow of blood from the uterus once a month in females from puberty to menopause.

Metabolic load, chapter 9—the energy required to complete a task.

Metabolism, chapters 1, 6—the process of chemical changes by which energy is provided for the maintenance of life.

Migraine headache, chapter 2—a severe, periodic throbbing pain in the head.

Millisecond—one-thousandth (.001) of a second.

Mineral, chapter 5—an inorganic metallic substance necessary for proper cell functioning (e.g., iron, calcium).

Mobitiz type 1 AV block, chapter 12—on ECG, a progressively increasing P-R interval until P wave is not followed by a QRS complex. The site of the block is the AV node.

Mobitiz type 2 AV block, chapter 12—on ECG, a constant P-R interval, some but not all P waves followed by QRS. The site of the block is the Bundle of His.

Moment arm, chapter 4—the shortest or perpendicular distance from the point of force application to the axis or joint.

Monosaccharide, chapter 5—a simple sugar with the general formula CH_2O.

Morbidity rate, chapter 2—the ratio of the number of cases of a disease to the number of well people in a given population.

Motivation, chapters 6, 8, 9, 11—the incentive(s) that prompts a person to act with a sense of purpose.

Motor unit, chapter 4—a lower motor neuron and the muscle fibers which its branches innervate.

Movement forms, chapter 11—types of physical activity, such as aquatics, dance, exercise, games, gymnastics, and sports.

Mumps, chapter 2—an acute, specific inflammation of the parotid glands, caused by a virus.

Muscle group, chapter 4—a group of specific muscles that are responsible for the same action at the same joint.

Muscle relaxant, chapter 2—a drug used to decrease the force of contraction.

Myocardial infarction (MI), chapter 12—death to a section of heart tissue in which the blood supply has been cut off.

Myocardium, chapter 12—the middle layer of the heart wall; involuntary, striated, muscle innervated by autonomic nerves.

Myositis, chapter 14—inflammation of a muscle.

Nausea, chapter 6—a feeling of sickness, without actually vomiting.

Nearsightedness, myopia, chapter 2—the ability to see close, but not far away. The light rays come to a focus in front, instead of on, the retina.

Negative energy balance, chapter 5—a condition in which less energy is consumed than is expended, resulting in a decrease in body weight.

Negative health, chapter 8—the presence of characteristics and behaviors that prevent optimal functional capacity and increase risks of serious health problems.

Negligence, chapter 15—the failure to provide reasonable care, or the care required by the circumstances. The person and/or program is legally liable for injury that results from negligence.

Nerve, chapter 2—an elongated bundle of nerve cells that transmit impulses between the periphery and the nerve centers (i.e., brain and spinal cord).

Nervousness, chapter 2—the state of being restless, excitable, jumpy, apprehensive, and/or highstrung.

Neurosis, chapter 8—a psychoneurotic disorder; a type of disorganization characterized by anxiety and nervousness.

Neutralizer, chapter 4—a muscle that counteracts an undesirable action of another muscle.

Newton N—a unit of measure of force.

Nitrates, chapter 12—a class of drugs used to prevent or stop angina pectoris; side effects include headaches, dizziness, and hypotension.

Nitroglycerin, chapters 2, 12—a vasodilator drug used to treat angina pectoris.

Nonfunctional stressor, chapter 8—a stimulus or situation that causes an arousal (stress) that exceeds the physiological response needed for the task.

Noradrenalin, see ***norepinephrine***.

Norepinephrine, chapter 3—one of the adrenal medullary hormones similar in action to epinephrine. Norepinephrine is also secreted by sympathetic nervous system nerve endings.

Nutrients, chapter 5—compounds and elements contained in foods and needed by the body.

Nutrition, chapter 5—the study of foods and their use in the body.

Obesity, chapters 1, 2, 5—the accumulation and storage of excess body fat. Obese people have an increased risk of CHD, diabetes, and hypertension.

Obsession, chapter 8—an idea or emotion that persists in an individual in spite of any conscious attempts to remove it.

One repetition maximum, 1 RM, chapter 7—the maximal force that can be exerted in a single contraction by a muscle group.

Open circuit spirometry, chapter 6—the method of measuring oxygen consumption by breathing in room air, while collecting and analyzing the expired air.

Orthopedically disabled, chapter 9—a disorder of some aspect of the locomotor system.

Ossification, chapter 4—the replacement of cartilage by bone.

Ovarian cyst, chapter 2—a tumor in the ovary.

Ovary, chapter 2—one of two small oval bodies in which eggs and female hormones are produced. Ovaries are situated on either side of the uterus on the posterior surface of the broad ligament.

Overfat, chapter 5—an accumulation of more than the desirable amount of fat.

Overload, chapter 9—to place greater than usual demands upon some part of the body (e.g., picking up more weight than normal overloads the muscles involved). Chronic overloading leads to increased strength and function.

Overweight, chapter 5—a person's weight that is greater than expected for his or her height.

Oxygen, chapter 12—a colorless, odorless, gaseous element necessary for life and combustion.

Oxygen consumption, see ***oxygen uptake***.

Oxygen cost, chapter 6—the amount of oxygen used by body tissues during an activity.

Oxygen debt, chapter 3—the amount of oxygen used during recovery from work that exceeds the amount needed for rest.

Oxygen deficit, chapter 3—the difference between the theoretical oxygen requirement of a physical activity and the oxygen cost of that activity.

Oxygen requirement, chapter 6—the rate of oxygen utilization needed for an activity.

Oxygen uptake, chapter 6—the rate at which oxygen is utilized during a specific level of an activity.

P wave, chapter 12—on ECG, a small positive deflection prior to QRS complex indicating atrial depolarization, normally less than 0.12 sec with an amplitude of .25 mV or less.

pH, chapter 3—the symbol for hydrogen ion concentration or degree of acidity; 7.0 is neutral, below 7.0 is acid, and above 7.0 is alkaline; normal is about 7.3.

P-R interval, chapter 12—the time interval between the beginning of the P wave and the QRS complex. The upper limit is .2 sec. This segment is normally used as the isoelectric baseline.

Pallor, chapter 6—unnatural paleness. Exercise should be stopped.

Palpation, chapter 6—examination by touch, as in determining HR by feeling the pulse at the wrist or neck.

Palpitation, chapter 2—a rapid forceful beating of the heart of which the person is aware.

Papillary muscles, chapter 12—cardiac muscles that originate at the walls of the heart ventricles and attach to AV valves.

Parasympathetic nervous system, chapter 8—a portion of the autonomic nervous system, derived from some of the cranial and sacral nerves belonging to the central nervous system; the system produces such involuntary responses as blood vessel dilation; increased activity of the digestive organs, reproductive organs, and glands; eye pupil contraction; decreased heart rate; and others. Effects are opposite those of the sympathetic nervous system.

Partial pressure of gas, chapter 9—pressure exerted by oxygen, carbon dioxide, nitrogen, or water. The sum of these partial pressures equals the barometric pressure.

Peak heart rate, chapter 9—the highest heart rate during a specific activity.

Penicillin, chapter 2—an antibiotic drug widely used for many infections caused by Gram-positive bacteria, some cocci, and spirochetes.

Peptic ulcer, chapter 2—a nonmalignant ulcer in the parts of the digestive tract that are exposed to the gastric secretions, usually in the stomach or duodenum.

Percent fat, chapter 2—the percentage of total body weight that is fat.

Perceived exertion, chapter 6—a subjective rating of intensity of a particular task, normally rated on one of the Borg scales for rating perceived exertion.

Perception, chapters 8, 11—a conscious impression of objects or situations. The stressfulness of a situation depends largely on the way it is perceived by the individual.

Performance, Part 1, chapter 15—the carrying out of a task that requires effort, attention, and skill. A person's success depends on his or her ability to perform a specific task.

Perimyseum, chapter 4—the connective tissue surrounding fasciculi within a muscle.

Periosteum, chapter 4—the connective tissue surrounding all bone surfaces except the articulating surfaces.

Peripheral resistance, chapter 3—the resistance offered by the arterioles and capillaries to the flow of blood from the arteries to the veins. An increase in peripheral resistance causes a rise in blood pressure.

Personnel, chapter 15—people employed by an organization.

Phases of activities, chapter 11—the sequence of exercise recommended to progress from a sedentary to an active lifestyle, including a gradual progression to walking 4 mi and jogging 3 mi, including a variety of sports and games.

Phlebitis, chapter 2—the inflammation of a vein.

Physical activity, Part 1, chapters 2, 8—movement of all or large segments of the body.

Physical conditioning, chapter 6—chronic regular exercise aimed at obtaining or maintaining high levels of components of fitness.

Physical fitness, Part 1—the physical aspects of total well-being related to optimal functional capacity and low risks of serious health problems.

Physical fitness profile, chapter 14—a description of the levels of the components of physical fitness.

Physical fitness tests, chapter 2—ways to measure and evaluate the components of physical fitness.

Physical inactivity, chapter 1—a sedentary lifestyle.

Physical stimulus, chapter 8—a situation or task, such as exercise, heat, or high altitude, that requires a physiological response greater than rest.

Physical work capacity, chapter 6—the capacity to perform physical work, usually measured in oxygen uptake or kilopond meters per minute while at a set heart rate (e.g., PWC-150).

Physiological response, chapter 6—the reaction of the physiological systems to a task, condition, or stressor.

Plantar fascitis, chapter 14—the inflammation of connective tissue that spans the bottom of the foot.

Plaque, chapter 5—strands of fibrous tissue that attach to the inside of arteries to form soft and mushy (if fat) or hard (if scar tissue) atheromatous buildup. Plaque also refers to bacteria that form on the teeth.

Plasma, chapter 3—the solvent or liquid portion of the blood.

Play, chapter 8—physical activity for amusement or recreation.

Playfulness, chapter 11—activity done with an attitude of fun.

Plyometric, chapter 7—the eccentric or lengthening contraction of a muscle, usually referring to the lengthening of a muscle before its concentric contraction.

Pneumonia, chapter 2—acute inflammation of the lungs caused by bacterial or viral infection.

Polarization, chapter 12—a changing of electrical state. ECG reflects depolarization and repolarization of atria and ventricles.

Polio, polioencephalitis, chapter 2—infantile paralysis. Polio is an epidemic virus infection that attacks the motor neurons in the anterior horns of the brain stem and spinal cord.

Pollution, chapters 8, 9—potentially toxic waste products found in water and air.

Polysaccharide, chapter 5—a complex sugar that yields three or more monosaccharides when hydrolyzed.

Polyunsaturated fats, chapter 5—fats derived from vegetables, lean poultry, fish, and cereal.

Positive energy balance, chapter 5—a condition in which more energy is consumed than is expended, resulting in an increase in body weight.

Positive health, chapters 6, 8—a move toward optimal functional capacity; more than a mere absence of disease.

Postprandial, chapter 6—occurring after a meal.

Posture, chapters 1, 7—the position or carriage of the body as a whole. Improper posture is related to low-back pain.

Potential benefits and risks, chapter 15—a description of relative gains and dangers of a procedure or program; one aspect of informed consent for fitness participants.

Predicted maximum heart rate, chapter 6—an estimate of max HR; 220 minus a person's age.

Premature atrial contraction (PAC), chapter 12—on ECG, the rhythm is irregular and the R-R interval is short; the origin of beat lies somewhere other than the SA node.

Premature junctional contraction, chapter 12—on ECG, the ectopic pacemaker in the AV junctional area that cause QRS, frequently seen with inverted P waves.

Premature ventricular contraction (PVC), chapter 12—on ECG, the QRS interval longer than 0.12 sec, and the T wave usually in the opposite direction; the origin is in the His-Purkinje system.

Preparticipation physical, chapter 14—a medical physical examination prior to an increase in physical activity.

Prescribed exercise, chapter 9—a recommendation of type, intensity, frequency, duration, and total work needed to accomplish fitness objectives.

Primary risk factor, chapters 1, 2, 6—a characteristic or behavior that is associated with a major health problem regardless of other factors. For example, smoking is a primary risk factor of CHD.

Prime mover, chapter 4—a muscle that is effective in causing a joint movement.

Program director, chapters 11, 15—the administrator of a program. Program directors are certified by the American College of Sports Medicine in postcardiac rehabilitation and health fitness programs.

Progression, chapter 11—a gradual increase from a current level to a desired level. For example, a sedentary person may gradually increase walking and jogging until he or she is able to jog 3 mi continuously without discomfort over an 8-month period of time.

Prostate, chapter 2—a small conical gland at the base of the male bladder and surrounding the first part of the urethra.

Protein, chapter 5—a compound composed of amino acids that provides the basic structural properties of cells.

Psychological stressor, chapter 8—a mental condition that causes physiological arousal beyond what is needed to accomplish a task.

Psychological test, chapters 6, 8—a measure of personality states and traits.

Psychosis, chapter 8—a profound disturbance of behavior that renders an individual unable to adjust to normal daily life.

Pulmonary, chapter 1—pertaining to the lungs.

Pulmonary artery, chapter 12—the artery that carries venous blood directly from the right ventricle of the heart to the lungs.

Pulmonary function, chapter 6—the capacity of the lungs. Pulmonary function is often tested by vital capacity, maximal expiratory force, and maximal voluntary ventilation.

Pulmonary valve, chapter 12—a set of three crescent-shaped flaps at the opening of the pulmonary artery; the semilunar valves.

Pulmonary veins, chapter 12—four veins that carry oxygenated blood directly from the lungs to the left atrium of the heart.

Purkinje fibers, chapter 12—the muscle cell fibers found beneath the endocardium of the heart; the impulse-conducting network of the heart.

Q wave, chapter 12—the initial negative deflection of the QRS complex on ECG.

QRS complex, chapter 12—the largest complex on ECG, indicating a depolarization of the left ventricle, normally less than .1 sec.

Q-T interval, chapter 12—the time interval from the beginning of the QRS complex to the end of the T wave. The Q-T interval reflects the electrical systole of the cardiac cycle.

Quadriceps, chapter 4—the large muscle group at the front of the thigh responsible for extending the knee joint.

Quality of life, Part 1—those aspects of living that are important to meaning and enjoyment.

R wave, chapter 12—the positive deflection of the QRS complex in the ECG.

R-R interval, chapter 12—the time interval from the peak of the QRS of one cardiac cycle to the peak of the QRS of the next cycle; 60/R-R interval = HR, b/min.

Radial pulse, chapter 6—a pulse taken at the wrist.

Rating of perceived exertion, chapter 6—a scale, by Borg, used to quantify the subjective feeling of physical effort. The original scale was 6-20; the revised scale is 0-10.

Rationalization, chapter 8—the process of inventing plausible explanations for acts or opinions that actually have other causes.

Recommended Dietary Allowance (RDA), chapter 5—the quantities of daily specified vitamins, minerals, and proteins needed for good nutrition.

Referral, chapter 2—a recommendation that a person consult with a professional about a particular characteristic, sign, symptom, or test result.

Regional ileitis, chapter 2—a nonspecific, chronic, recurrent inflammation of the ileum (the lower part of the small intestine), that mainly affects young adults.

Rehabilitation, chapter 6—a planned program in which disabled people progress toward, or maintain, the maximum degree of physical and psychological independence of which they are capable.

Relax, chapter 8—to loosen, make less stiff, or gain relief from work or tension.

Repetitions, chapter 7—the number of consecutive contractions performed.

Repolarization, chapter 12—in the heart, to change from a working to a resting state. The T wave on ECG reflects the repolarization of the ventricle at the end of the systole and the beginning of the diastole.

Reproducibility, chapter 6—the degree to which a person is able to replicate exactly. For example, a reproducible work task is important in order to determine the progress that a person makes as a result of a fitness program.

Residual volume, chapter 5—the volume of air remaining in the lungs at the end of maximal expiration.

Resistance, chapter 7—the amount of force applied opposite a movement.

Respiration, chapters 6, 9—the act or function of breathing.

Respiratory exchange ratio; respiratory quotient (RQ), chapters 5, 10—the ratio of the volume of carbon dioxide produced to the volume of oxygen utilized during a given period of time ($VCO_2/\dot{V}O_2$).

Retest, chapter 6—to repeat a test, usually after a planned program to determine the amount of progress.

Rheumatic fever, chapter 2—a disorder tending to recur but initially most common in childhood, classically appearing as fleeting polyarthritis of the larger joints, pyrexia, and carditis within 3 weeks following a streptococcal throat infection. Sometimes symptoms are trivial and ignored, but carditis may be severe and result in permanent cardiac damage.

Rheumatoid arthritis, chapter 2—a disease of unknown etiology, characterized by a chronic polyarthritis mainly affecting the smaller peripheral joints accompanied by general ill health, and eventually resulting in varying degrees of crippling joint deformities and associated muscle wasting.

Rhythm, chapter 12—in terms of cardiac cycle, refers to the sequence and regularity of an occurrence of events.

Risk factor, chapter 2—a characteristic, sign, symptom, or test score that is associated with increased probability of developing a health program. For example, people with hypertension have an increased risk of developing CHD.

Role model, chapter 11—someone who sets an example for similar people by behaving in accordance with the highest standards for a particular position.

Rotational inertia, chapter 4—the reluctance to rotate; proportional to the mass and distribution of the mass around the axis.

Rule, chapter 11—the regulation governing conduct or procedure. In many sports and games, the rules have to be modified to enhance fitness and inclusive participation.

Runner's high, chapter 8—a special emotional experience that transcends normal sensations; reported by some runners.

Running, chapters 2, 11—moving the whole body quickly by propelling the body off the ground during part of the movement.

Running shoes, chapter 11—special athletic shoes offering good support and cushioning in the heel area to minimize trauma at impact.

S wave, chapter 12—on ECG, the last negative portion of the QRS complex representing the final portion of the depolarization of the left ventricle.

S-T segment, chapter 12—the part of the ECG between the end of the QRS complex and beginning of the T wave. Depression below (or elevation above) the isoelectric line indicates ischemia.

ST-segment displacement, chapter 6—on ECG, the depression or elevation of the portion of the ECG between the end of the QRS complex and the beginning of the T wave; ST-segment displacement may indicate the development of myocardial ischemia.

Salt, chapter 9—a crystalline compound of sodium and chlorine, occurring as a mineral. High levels of salt intake have been associated with hypertension.

Saturated fat, chapter 5—a fat that is not capable of absorbing any more hydrogen. These fats are solid at room temperature and are usually of animal origin such as the fats in milk, butter, and meat.

Scoliosis, chapter 7—an abnormal lateral curvature of the spine.

Screening, chapters 2, 6, 9—an examination used to select or reject. In fitness programs, potential participants are screened to determine whether they should be referred for medical attention prior to engaging in exercise.

Seat belt, chapter 2—a belt used to keep a passenger safely secured in his or her seat, as in an automobile.

Second-degree AV block, chapter 12—on ECG, some but not all P waves precede QRS complex.

Second wind, chapter 3—a phenomenon characterized by a sudden transition from a feeling of distress or fatigue during the early portion of a workout to a more comfortable, less stressful feeling later in the exercise.

Secondary risk factor, chapters 1, 2, 8—a characteristic, sign, symptom, or test score that has a weak independent association with a health problem, but increases the risk when other risk factors are present.

Sedentary, chapters 6, 11—an inactive lifestyle, characterized by a lot of sitting.

Sequence of testing, chapter 6—the logical order in which tests are conducted.

Serum, chapter 1—the clear, pale yellow, watery part of the blood that separates from the clot when blood coagulates.

Set, chapter 7—a designated number of repetitions.

Shin splints, chapter 14—an inflammatory reaction of the musculotendinous unit of the anterior aspect of the lower leg caused by overexertion of muscles during weight-bearing activities.

Shock, chapter 14—a circulatory disturbance produced by severe injury or illness and largely caused by a reduction in blood volume, characterized by a fall in blood pressure, a rapid pulse, pallor, restlessness, thirst, and cold clammy skin. A discrepancy exists between the circulating blood volume and the capacity of the vascular bed. The initial cause of shock is a reduction in the circulating blood volume; continuation is caused by vasoconstriction.

Skinfold caliper, chapter 5—an instrument used to measure the thickness of folds of fat that have been pinched away from the body.

Sickle cell anemia, chapter 2—a familial, hereditary hemolytic anemia peculiar to Blacks. The red cells are crescent-shaped.

Sinus, chapters 2, 12—on ECG, refers to a regular sequence of electrical activity (i.e., SA node, atrium, AV node, ventricle).

Sinus arrhythmia, chapter 12—a normal variant with sinus rhythm in which the R-R' interval varies by more than 10% per beat.

Sinus bradycardia, chapter 12—the normal rhythm (i.e., the sinus node is the pacemaker) and sequence, with slow heart rate (below 60 b/min at rest). The occurrence of sinus bradycardia may be indicative of a high level of fitness or some mental problem such as depression.

Sinus node, chapter 12—a mass of tissue in the right atrium of the heart near the vena cava that initiates the heartbeat.

Sinus rhythm, chapter 12—the normal timing and sequence of the cardiac events, with the sinus node as a pacemaker; resting rate is between 60 b/min and 100 b/min.

Sinus tachycardia, chapter 12—the normal rhythm and sequence, with a fast heart rate (above 100 b/min at rest). The occurrence of sinus tachycardia may be indicative of illness or stress.

Slow-twitch fiber, chapter 4—a muscle fiber characterized by its slow speed of contraction.

Smallpox, chapter 2—variola. Smallpox is caused by a virus, characterized by a headache, vomiting, and a high fever, followed by a widespread rash.

Smoking, chapters 1, 2—inhaling and puffing tobacco. Smoking is a primary risk factor of CHD and lung cancer.

Spasm, chapter 14—a sudden involuntary muscular contraction.

Special populations, chapter 9—people with physical or mental characteristics requiring special attention, often needing modified activities.

Specificity, chapter 9—belonging to and characteristic of a particular thing. For example, skill is specific to a certain aspect of a sport.

Spleen, chapter 2—a lymphoid, vascular organ located immediately below the diaphragm, at the tail of the pancreas, behind the stomach.

Sport, chapter 6—a game or other form of pastime involving some amount of bodily exercise and normally competition.

Spot reducing, chapter 5—refers to an effort to reduce fat at one site by doing calisthenics at that site. No research evidence supports this concept.

Sprain, chapter 14—the stretching or tearing of ligamentous tissues surrounding a joint, resulting in discoloration, swelling, and pain.

Stage, chapter 6—in exercise testing, refers to the step in the levels of work going from light to hard.

State, chapter 8—a temporary condition. For example, a person's emotional state may change rapidly depending on the particular situation, as contrasted to a personality trait that is consistent and does not change quickly.

Steady state, chapters 6, 10—unchanging, or changing very little. For example, during submaximal exercise, a person reaches a steady state (a leveling-off of oxygen, HR, etc.) after a few minutes.

Stethoscope, chapter 6—an instrument with ear pieces attached to a device used for listening to various body sounds, such as heart rate or the sound over the brachial artery while taking blood pressure.

Stimulus, chapters 8, 11—something that causes a physiological or psychological response.

Stomach, chapter 2—the most dilated part of the digestive tube, situated between the esophagus and the beginning of the small intestine. The stomach wall is composed of four coats: serous, muscular, submucous, and mucous.

Stone bruise, chapter 14—a discoloration of the skin caused by blood in the underlying tissues, without abrasion of the skin, often located on the heel of the foot and usually caused by walking or running on a sharp object.

Strain, chapter 14—the overstretching or tearing of a muscle or tendon.

Strength, chapter 7—the amount of force that can be exerted by a muscle group against a resistance.

Stress, chapters 1, 8—a physiological or psychological response to a stressor beyond what is needed to accomplish a task.

Stress continuum, chapter 8—a characteristic extending along a continuous line from one extreme to another. Three continuums appear to help describe stress, namely, functional response . . . severe stress; enjoyment . . . unpleasantness; and development . . . deterioration.

Stress fracture, chapter 14—a defect in a bone that occurs because of an accelerated rate of remodeling to accommodate the stress of weight-bearing bones; results in a loss of continuity in the bone and periosteal irritation.

Stress management, chapter 2—the ability to cope with potential stressors so that there is a minimum stress response.

Stressful situations, chapter 2—conditions that cause a stress response.

Stressor, chapter 8—a stimulus that causes a stress response.

Stretching, chapter 11—extending the limbs through a full range of motion.

Stroke, apoplexy, chapter 2—the sudden loss of consciousness resulting from a vascular accident in the brain, usually resulting in partial paralysis.

Stroke volume, chapter 3—the amount of blood pumped from the left ventricle each time the heart contracts.

Submaximal, chapters 2, 6, 9—less than maximal (e.g., an exercise that can be performed with less than maximal effort).

Substrate, chapter 10—a foodstuff used for energy metabolism.

Superior vena cava, chapter 12—the upper main vein that discharges blood from the upper half of the body into the right atrium of the heart.

Supervised fitness program, chapter 2—a group of fitness activities with instructor present.

Support, chapter 8—to uphold and aid. An important element in changing behavior or coping with stress is to have a group that provides encouragement. In an organization, the support staff personnel provide needed technical and clerical assistance.

Sweat, perspiration, chapter 9—moisture coming through the pores of the skin from the sweat glands, usually as a result of heat, exertion, or emotion.

Sympathetic nervous system, chapter 8—part of the autonomic nervous system consisting of two groups of ganglia connected by nerve cords, one on either side of the spinal cord; it releases substances that cause a physiological arousal, such as increased heart rate and decreased activity of the digestive and reproductive organs—the opposite of the parasympathetic nervous system.

Symptom, chapters 2, 11—a noticeable change in the normal working of the body that indicates or accompanies disease or sickness.

Synovial membrane, chapter 4—the inner lining of the joint capsule.

Synovitis, chapter 14—inflammation of the synovial membrane.

Syphilis, chapter 2—a contagious venereal disease, caused by a spirochete, characterized first by a painless sore at the point of invasion, then by skin eruptions and a sore throat, and finally by severe lesions affecting the bones, brain, and spinal cord.

Systolic blood pressure, chapters 2, 6—the pressure exerted on the vessel walls during ventricular contraction, measured in millimeters of mercury by the sphygmomanometer.

T wave, chapter 12—on ECG, follows QRS complex and represents ventricular repolarization.

Ta wave, chapter 12—on ECG, the result of atrial depolarization. The Ta wave is not normally seen because it occurs during ventricular depolarization and is hidden by the larger electrical forces generated by the ventricles (QRS).

Tachycardia, chapter 12—a heart rate greater than 100 b/min at rest. Tachycardia may be seen in deconditioned people or people who are apprehensive about a situation (e.g., an exercise test).

Taper down; cool down, chapter 9—light activity after a workout, allowing a gradual return to normal, with leg muscles continuing to pump blood back to the heart thus preventing pooling of blood in the lower extremities.

Target heart rate (THR), chapter 9—the heart rate recommended for fitness workouts.

Tendonitis, chapter 14—inflammation of a tendon.

Tendon, chapter 4—a band of tough inelastic fibrous connective tissue that attaches muscle to bone.

Tennis elbow, chapter 14—inflammation of the musculotendonous unit of the elbow extensors where they attach on the outer aspect of the elbow (lateral epicondylitis).

Tenosynovitis, chapter 14—inflammation of a tendon sheath.

Tension, chapter 2—mental or emotional strain.

Testing protocol, chapters 6, 9—a particular testing scheme, often the starting level, timing, and increments for each stage of an exercise tolerance test.

Tetanus, chapter 2—an infectious, often fatal, disease caused by a bacterium that enters the body through wounds; characterized by spasms and rigidity.

Tetracycline, chapter 2—a broad spectrum antibiotic related to both aureomycin and terramycin.

Third-degree AV block, chapter 12—on ECG, QRS appears independently, P-R varies with no regular pattern, rate less than 45 b/min.

Third-party payments, chapter 15—reimbursement for services rendered by someone else. Third-party payments are usually some form of insurance payment.

Threshold, chapter 9—the minimum level needed for desired effect. Often used to refer to the minimum level of exercise intensity needed for improvement in cardiorespiratory function.

Thyroid gland, chapter 2—a ductless gland in the neck with a lobe on each side of the windpipe. The thyroid secretes a hormone that regulates the rates of metabolism and body growth.

Tidal volume (TV), chapter 3—the volume of air inspired or expired per breath.

Time to exhaustion, chapter 6—the time interval from the beginning of an exercise test until the participant is unable or unwilling to continue.

Timed vital capacity, chapters 2, 6—the amount of the vital capacity that can be expelled in a certain time, usually 1 sec.

Torque, chapter 4—the effect produced by a force causing rotation; the product of the force and force arm.

Total lung capacity (TLC), chapter 3—the sum of the vital capacity and the residual volume.

Total work, chapter 9—the amount of work accomplished during a workout.

Training, chapter 6—physical conditioning through repeated bouts of exercise.

Trait, chapter 8—a semipermanent characteristic that generally is true about a person and is resistant to change.

Tranquilizer, chapter 2—a drug that has a calming effect.

Treadmill, chapter 6—a machine with a moving belt that can be adjusted for speed and grade allowing a person to walk/run in one place. Treadmills are widely used for exercise tolerance testing.

Tricuspid valve, chapter 12—a valve located between the right atrium and ventricle of the heart.

Trigeminy, chapter 12—in ECG, every third beat is a premature ventricular contraction.

Triglyceride, chapters 1, 2, 5—a compound consisting of three molecules of fatty acid and glycerol. Triglyceride is the main type of lipid found in adipose tissue and the main dietary lipid. When hydrolyzed, triglyceride releases free fatty acids into the bloodstream. A high level of triglyceride in serum is a secondary risk factor of CHD.

Tubal ligation, chapter 2—an operation to tie off the Fallopian tubes thus making pregnancy impossible.

Tuberculosis, chapter 2—a specific, infectious disease caused by Mycobacterium tuberculosis.

12-lead ECG, chapter 6—a record of the electrical activity of the heart from different directions, with six limb leads and six chest leads.

12-minute run, chapter 6—a field test for cardiorespiratory endurance, scored by the distance run in 12 min.

2-mile run, chapter 6—a field test for cardiorespiratory endurance, scored by the time it takes to complete 2 mi.

Type A behavior, chapter 8—the characterization of a person who is hard-driving, time conscious, and impatient. Some evidence suggests that this type of behavior is a secondary risk factor of CHD. Type A is the opposite of Type B.

Type B behavior, chapter 8—the opposite of Type A behavior.

U wave, chapter 12—on ECG, the wave occassionally seen after T wave. The origin of the U wave is unclear, and it is normally not a factor in interpreting the ECG for exercise prescription.

Ulcer, chapters 2, 8—an open sore on skin or mucous surface, such as peptic ulcer in the stomach.

Unsaturated fatty acid, chapter 5—the molecules of a fat, which have one or more double bonds, and are thus capable of absorbing more hydrogen. These fats are liquid at room temperature and usually are of vegetable origin.

Unsupervised program, chapter 9—a group of fitness activities without qualified fitness personnel for people with a low risk of health problems.

Uremia, chapter 2— a disease state in which waste accumulates in the blood, usually because of kidney failure.

$\dot{V}O_2$ max, chapters 6, 9—the highest amount of oxygen that can be utilized by the body during hard work.

Vaginitis, chapter 2—the inflammation of the vagina.

Valsalva maneuver, chapter 3—increased pressure in the abdominal and thoracic cavities caused by breath holding and extreme effort.

Vasoconstriction, chapter 3—the narrowing of a blood vessel.

Vasodilation, chapter 3—the opening or widening of a blood vessel.

Vein, chapter 3—a blood vessel that returns blood to the heart.

Velocity, chapter 6—the rate of motion of a body in a certain direction.

Ventilation, chapter 6—the process of oxygenating the blood through the lungs.

Ventilatory threshold, chapter 6—the intensity of work at which the rate of ventilation sharply increases.

Ventricle, chapter 12—the two (left and right) lower muscular chambers of the heart.

Ventricular arrhythmias, chapters 6, 12—irregular waveforms on the ECG caused by contraction originating in the ventricle, rather than from the SA node.

Ventricular tachycardia, chapter 6—an extremely dangerous condition in which three or more consecutive premature ventricular contractions occur. Ventricular tachycardia may degenerate into ventricular fibrillation.

Vertigo, chapter 2—dizziness.

Vigorous, chapter 11—fitness activity of sufficient intensity to result in cardiorespiratory improvements if done on a regular basis.

Vital capacity, chapters 2, 6—the amount of air that can be expelled from the lungs after a maximal inspiration.

Vital signs, chapter 14—the measurable essential bodily functions, such as pulse rate and temperature.

Vitamins, chapters 2, 5—an organic substance that is present in small amounts of food and that is necessary for the normal functioning of the cells. Vitamins are classified as water-soluble (B complex and C) or fat-soluble (A, D, E, K).

Walking, chapters 2, 9, 11—moving the body in a set direction while maintaining contact with the ground (floor).

Warmup, chapters 9, 11, 14—physical activity of light to moderate intensity prior to a workout.

Weight, chapter 2—the heaviness of the whole body.

Wenchebach AV block, see ***Mobitiz Type I AV Block***.

Windchill, chapter 9—the coldness felt on exposed human flesh by a combination of temperature and wind velocity.

Work, chapter 6—movement of a force through a distance; measured as foot, pound, and kilogram, as in the cycle ergometer.

Workrate, chapters 6, 10—power—work done per unit of time (e.g., kilogram liters per minute; watts).

Work/relief, chapter 11—the ratio of time spent in more intense and less intense exercise in an interval type of workout.

Workout, chapters 9, 14—an exercise bout aimed at improving fitness or performance.

References

■ Additional reading helpful to the fitness professional

Allen, D.L., & Iwata, B. (1980). Reinforcing exercise maintenance using existing high-rate activities. *Behavior Modification,* **4**(3), 337-354.

American Academy of Orthopaedic Surgeons. (1977). *Emergency care and transportation of the sick and injured.* WI: George Banta.

American Alliance for Health, Physical Education, Recreation, and Dance. (1980). *Health related physical fitness test manual.* Reston: Author.

American College of Sports Medicine. (1975). Prevention of heat injuries during distance running. *Medicine and Science in Sports,* **7**, vii-viii.

American College of Sports Medicine. (1978). The recommended quantity and quality of exercise for developing and maintaining fitness in healthy adults. *Medicine and Science in Sports,* **10**, vii-x.

American College of Sports Medicine. (1980). *Guidelines for graded exercise testing and exercise prescription* (2nd ed.). Philadelphia: Lea & Febiger.

American College of Sports Medicine. (1983). Proper and improper weight loss programs. *Medicine and Science in Sports and Exercise,* **15**, ix-xiii.

American College of Sports Medicine. (1985). *Guidelines for graded exercise testing and exercise prescription* (3rd ed.). Philadelphia: Lea & Febiger.

American Heart Association. (1978). *Diet and coronary heart disease.* Dallas: Author.

American Heart Association. (1981). *Student manual for basic life support—cardiopulmonary resuscitation.* Dallas: Author.

American Heart Association Committee on Stress, Strain, and Heart Disease. (1977). Report. *Circulation,* **55**, 1-11.

American Medical Association, and American Alliance for Health, Physical Education, Recreation, and Dance. (1964). Exercise and fitness. *Journal of Physical Education, Recreation, and Dance,* **35**, 42-44.

American Red Cross. (1981). *Advanced first aid and emergency care* (2nd ed.). New York: Doubleday.

Anderson, B. (1980). *Stretching.* Bolinas, California: Shelter Publications.

Andersson, G.B.J., Ortengren, R., & Nachemson, A. (1977). Intradiskal pressure, intra-abdominal pressure and myoelectric back muscle activity related to posture and loading. *Clinical Orthopaedics and Related Research,* **129**, 156-164.

Andrew, G.M., Oldridge, N.B., Parker, J.O., Cunningham, D.A., Rechnitzer, P.A., Jones, N.L., Buck, C., Kavanagh, T., Shepard, R.J., & Sutton, J.R. (1981). Reasons for dropout from exercise programs in post-coronary patients. *Medicine and Science in Sports and Exercise,* **13**(3), 164-168.

Åstrand, P.O., & Rodahl, K. (1970, 1977). *Textbook of work physiology.* New York: McGraw-Hill.

Averill, J.R. (1982). *Anger and aggression.* New York: Springer-Verlag.

Balke, B. (1963). A simple field test for assessment of physical fitness. *Civil Aeromedical Research Institute Report*, 63-66.

Balke, B. (1970). Advanced exercise procedures for evaluation of the cardiovascular system. *Monograph*, Educational Department. Milton, WI: Burdick Corporation.

Balke, B., & Ware, R.W. (1959). An experimental study of "physical fitness" of air force personnel. *Armed Forces Medical Journal,* **10**, 675-688.

Bandura, A. (1969). *Principles of behavior modification.* New York: Holt, Rinehart, & Winston.

Barham, J. (1978). *Mechanical kinesiology.* St. Louis: C.V. Mosby.

Basmajian J.V. (1980). *Grant's method of anatomy* (10th ed.). Baltimore: Williams and Wilkins.

Basmajian, J.V., & MacConaill, M.A. (1977). *Muscles and movements—A basis for human kinesiology.* Huntington, NY: R.E. Kreiger.

Baun, W.B., & Baun, M. (1984). A corporate health and fitness program: Motivation and management by computers. *Journal of Physical Education, Recreation, and Dance,* **35**, 42-45.

Bayless, M.A., & Adams, S.H. (1985). A liability checklist. *Journal of Physical Education, Recreation, and Dance,* **36**, 49.

Ben-Sira, Z. (1982). The health promoting function of mass media and reference groups: Motivating or reinforcing of behavior change. *Social Science Medicine,* **16**, 825-834.

Benson, H. (1975). *The relaxation response.* New York: Marrow.

Bernacki, E.J., & Baun, W.B. (1984). The relationship of job performance to exercise adherence in a corporate fitness program. *Journal of Occupational Medicine,* **26**(7), 529-531.

Berne, R.M., & Levy, M.N. (1977). *Cardiovascular physiology* (3rd ed.). St. Louis: C.V. Mosby.

Blackburn, H. (1974). Progress in the epidemiology and prevention of CHD. In P.N. Yu & J.F. Goodwin (Eds.), *Progress in cardiology* (pp. 1-36). Philadelphia: Lea & Febiger.

Blair, S.N., Jacobs, D.R., & Powell, K.E. (1985). Relationships between exercise or physical activity and other health behaviors. *Public Health Reports,* **100**, 180-188.

Blomquist, C.G. (1978). Clinical exercise physiology. In N.K. Wenger & H.K. Hellerstein (Eds.), *Rehabilitation of the cardiac patient* (pp. 133-148). New York: John Wiley & Sons.

Boone, D.C., & Azen, S.P. (1979). Normal range of motion of joints in male subjects. *The Journal of Bone and Joint Surgery,* **61-A**, 756-759.

Borg, G.A.V. (1982). Psychological bases of physical exertion. *Medicine and Science in Sports and Exercise,* **14**(5), 377-381.

Bowers, D.G. (1976). *Systems of organization.* Ann Arbor: University of Michigan Press.

Bransford, D.R., & Howley, E.T. (1977). The oxygen cost of running in trained and untrained men and women. *Medicine and Science in Sports,* **9**, 41-44.

Broer, M.R., & Zernicke, R.F. (1979). *Efficiency of human movement.* Philadelphia: W.B. Saunders.

Brownell, K.D., Stunkard, A.J., & Albaum, J.M. (1980). Evaluation and modification of exercise patterns in natural environment. *American Journal of Psychiatry,* **137**, 1540-1545.

Brozek, J., Grande, F., Anderson, J.T., & Keys, A. (1963). Densitometric analysis of body composition: Revision of some quantitative assumptions. *Annals New York Academy of Science,* **110**, 113-140.

Bruce, R.A. (1972). Multi-stage treadmill test of submaximal and maximal exercise, pp. 32-34. In American Heart Association, *Exercise testing and training of apparently healthy individuals: A handbook for physicians.* New York: AHA.

Bubb, W.J., Martin, A.D., & Howley, E.T. (1985). Predicting oxygen uptake during level walking at speeds of 80 to 130 meters per minute. *Journal of Cardiac Rehabilitation,* **5**(10), 462-465.

Bucher, C.A., & Prentice, W.E. (1985). *Fitness for college and life.* St. Louis: Times Mirror/ Mosby College Publishers.

Bundgaard, A. (1985). Exercise and the asthmatic. *Sports Medicine,* **2**, 254-266.

Burchfield, S.R. (1979). The stress response: A new perspective. *Psychosomatic Medicine,* **41**, 661-672.

Byrd-Bredbenner, C., & Pelican, S. (1984). Software: How do you choose? *Journal of Nutrition Education,* **16**, 77-177.

Cantu, R.C. (1982). *Diabetes and exercise.* Ithaca, NY: Mouvement Publications.

Chang, K., & Hossack, K.F. (1982). Effect of diltiazem on heart rate responses and respiratory variables during exercise: Implications for exercise prescription and cardiac rehabilitation. *Journal of Cardiac Rehabilitation,* **2**, 326-332.

Chenoweth, D. (1983). Health promotion: Benefits vs. costs. *Occupational Health and Safety,* **52**(7), 37-41.

Chisholm, D.M., et al. (1975). Physical activity readiness. *British Columbia Medical Journal,* **17**, 375-378.

Chusid, E.L. (Ed.). (1983). *The selective and comprehensive testing of adult pulmonary function.* Mount Kisco, NY: Futura.

Cooper, J.M., & Glassow, R.B. (1982). *Kinesiology.* St. Louis: C.V. Mosby.

Cooper, K.H. (1977). *The aerobics way.* New York: Bantam Books.

Cooper, K.H., & Collingwood, T.R. (1984). Physical fitness: Programming issues for total well being. *Journal of Physical Education, Recreation, and Dance,* **35**(6), 44.

Cormier, W.H., & Cormier, L.S. (1979). *Interviewing strategies for helpers: A guide to assessment, treatment, and evaluation.* Monterey, CA: Brooks/Cole.

Cureton, T.K. (1965). *Physical fitness and dynamic health.* New York: Dial Press.

D'Ambrosia, R.D., & Drez, D. (1982). *Prevention and treatment of running injuries.* Thorofare, NJ: C.B. Slack.

Danaher, B.G. (1977). Research on rapid smoking. An interim summary and recommendations. *Addictive Behaviors,* **2**, 151-166.

D'Aprix, R. (1982). *Communicating for productivity.* New York: Harper & Row.

Darden, E. (1976). *Nutrition and athletic performance.* Pasadena: The Athletic Press.

Davidson, P.O., & Davidson, S.M. (Eds.). (1980). *Behavioral medicine: Changing health lifestyles.* New York: Brunner/Mazel.

deVries, H.A. (1980). *Physiology of exercise for physical education and athletics* (3rd ed.). Dubuque, IA: W.C. Brown.

Dill, D.B. (1965). Oxygen cost of horizontal and grade walking and running on the treadmill. *Journal of Applied Physiology,* **20**, 19-22.

Dintiman, G.B., Stone, S.E., Pennington, J.C., & Davis, R.G. (1984). *Discovering lifetime fitness.* New York: West Publishers.

Dishman, R.K., & Gettman, L.R. (1980). Psychobiologic influences on exercise adherence. *Journal of Sport Psychology,* **2**, 295-310.

Dishman, R.K., Ickes, W., & Morgan, W.P. (1980). Self-motivation and adherence to habitual physical activity. *Journal of Applied Social Psychology,* **10**(2), 115-132.

Donoghue, S. (1977). The correlation between physical fitness, absenteeism, and work performance. *Canadian Journal of Public Health,* **68**, 201-203.

Drucker, P.F. (1980). *Managing in turbulent times.* New York: Harper & Row.

Duffey, D.J., Horwitz, L.D., & Brammell, H.L. (1984). Nifedipine and the conditioning response. *American Journal of Cardiology,* **53**, 908-911.

Edington, D.W., & Edgerton, V.R. (1976). *The biology of physical activity.* Boston: Houghton Mifflin.

Ekblom, B., Åstrand, P.O., Saltin, B., Stenberg, J., & Wallstrom, B. (1968). Effect of training on circulatory response to exercise. *Journal of Applied Physiology,* **24**, 518-528.

Eliot, R.S. (1977). Stress and cardiovascular disease. *European Journal of Cardiology,* **5**, 97-104.

Ellstad, M. (1980). *Stress testing: Principles and practice.* Philadelphia: F.A. Davis.

Epstein, L.H. Masek, B.J., & Marshall, W.R. (1978). The effects of pre-lunch exercise on lunchtime caloric intake. *The Behavior Therapist,* **1**, 3-15.

Epstein, L.H., Wing, R.R., Thompson, J.K., & Griffen, W. (1980). Attendance and fitness in aerobics exercise: The effects of contract and lottery procedures. *Behavior Modification,* **4**, 465-479.

Ewy, G.A., & Bressler, R. (1982). *Current cardiovascular therapy.* New York: Raven Press.

Fielding, J.E. (1982). Effectiveness of employee health improvement programs. *Journal of Occupational Medicine,* **24**(11), 907-916.

Filley, A.C. (1975). *Interpersonal conflict resolution.* Glenview, IL: Scott, Foresman.

Flaxman, J. (1978). Quitting smoking now or later: Gradual, abrupt, immediate, and delayed quitting. *Behavior Therapy,* **9**, 260-270

Fox, E.L. (1983). *Lifetime fitness.* New York: Saunders College Publishing.

Fox, E.L., & Mathews, D.K. (1974). *Interval training: Conditioning for sports and general fitness.* Philadelphia: W.B. Saunders.

Fox, E.L., & Mathews, D.K. (1981). *The physiological basis of physical education and athletics* (3rd ed.). Philadelphia: Saunders College Publishers.

Franklin, B.A. (1978). Motivating and educating adults to exercise. *Journal of Physical Education and Recreation,* **49**, 13-17.

Franklin, B., Vanders, L., Wrisley, D., & Rubenfire, M. (1983). Aerobic requirements of arm ergometry: Implications for exercise testing and training. *The Physician and Sportsmedicine,* **11**(10), 81-90.

Franks, B.D. (1979). Methodology of the exercise ECG test: Technical aspects. In E.K. Chung (Ed.), *Exercise electrocardiography: Practical approach* (pp. 46-61). Baltimore: Williams and Wilkins.

Franks, B.D. (1983a). Stress and health. *Motor skills: Theory into practice,* 7.

Franks, B.D. (1983b). Warm-up. In M. Williams (Ed.), *Ergogenic aids in sport* (pp. 340-375). Champaign, IL: Human Kinetics.

Franks, B.D. (1984a). Physical activity and stress: Part 1. Acute effects. *International Journal of Physical Education,* **21**(4), 9-12.

Franks, B.D. (1984b). Physical activity and stress: Part 2. Chronic effects. *International Journal of Physical Education,* **21**(4), 13-16.

Franks, B.D. (1984c). Physical fitness in secondary education. *Journal of Physical Education, Recreation, and Dance,* **55**(9), 41-43.

Franks, C.M., Wilson, C.T., Kendal, P.C., & Brownell, K.D. (Eds.). (1982). *Annual review of behavior therapy: Theory and practice* (Vol. 8.). New York: Guilford.

Froelicher, V.F. (1983). *Exercise testing and training.* Chicago: Year Book Medical Publishers.

Fuchs, J.A., Price, J.H., Richards, J.E., & Marcotte, B. (1985). Worksetting health promotion—A comprehensive bibliography. *Health Education,* **16**(4), 29-34.

Gerhard, H., & Schachter, E.N. (1980). Exercise-induced asthma. *Postgraduate Medicine,* **67**(3), 91-102.

Getchell, B. (1983). *Physical fitness: A way of life* (2nd ed.). New York: John Wiley & Son.

Gettman, L.R., Pollock, M.L., & Ward, A. (1983). Adherence to unsupervised exercise. *Physician and Sportsmedicine,* **11**, 56-64.

Gibbins, L.W., Cooper, K.H., Meyer, B.M., & Ellison, C. (1980). The acute cardiac risk of strenuous exercise. *Journal of American Medical Association,* **244**, 1799.

Golding, L.A., Myers, C.R., & Sinning, W.E. (1982). *The Y's way to physical fitness.* Chicago: National Board of YMCA.

Goldman, L., & Cook, E.F. (1984). The decline in ischemic heart disease mortality rates. *Annals of Internal Medicine,* **101**, 825-836.

Goldman, M.J. (1982). *Principles of clinical electrocardiography.* Cambridge, MD: Lange Medical Publications.

Goodman, P.S., et al. (1982). *Change in organizations: New perspective on theory, research, and practice.* San Francisco: Jossey-Bass.

Goodrick, G.K., & Iammarino, N.K. (1982). Teaching aerobic lifestyles: New perspectives. *Journal of Physical Education, Recreation, and Dance,* **53**, 48-50.

Gormally, J., & Rardin, D. (1981). Weight loss and maintenance and changes in diet and exercise for behavioral counseling and nutrition education. *Journal of Counseling Psychology,* **28**(4), 295-304.

Gracovetsky, S., Farfan, H.F., & Lamy, O. (1977). A mathematical model of the lumbar spine using an optimized system to control muscles and ligaments. *Orthopedic Clinics of North America,* **8**(1), 135-153.

Gray, H. (1966). *Anatomy of the human body.* Philadelphia: Lea & Febiger.

Guber, S.H., Montoye, H.J., Cunningham, D.A., & Dinks, S. (1972). Age and physiological adjustment to continuous, graded treadmill exercise. *Research Quarterly,* **43**, 175-186.

Hage, P. (1983). Prescribing exercise: More than just a running program. *The Physician and Sportsmedicine,* **11**(5), 123-133.

Hall, D. (1978). Changing attitudes by changing behavior. *Journal of Physical Education and Recreation,* **49**, 20-21.

Hartley-O'Brien, S.J. (1980). Six mobilization exercises for active range of hip flexion. *Research Quarterly for Exercise and Sport,* **51**(4), 625-635.

Haskell, W.L. (1978). Cardiovascular complications during exercise training of cardiac patients. *Circulation,* **57**, 920.

Haskell, W.L. (1984). The influence of exercise on the concentrations of triglyceride and cholesterol in human plasma. In R.L. Terjung, *Exercise and sports sciences reviews,* **12**, 205-244.

Hau, M.L., & Fischer, J. (1974). Self-modification of exercise behavior. *Journal of Behavioral Therapy and Experimental Psychiatry,* **5**, 213-214.

Hay, J.G., & Reid, J.G. (1982). *The anatomical and mechanical bases of human motion.* Englewood Cliffs, NJ: Prentice-Hall.

Hayes, S.G., Feinleib, M., & Kannel, W.B. (1980). The relationship of psychosocial factors to coronary heart disease in the Framingham study. Part III. Eight-year incidence of coronary heart disease. *American Journal of Epidemiology,* **111**(1), 37-58.

Henderson, J. (1973). *Emergency medical guide* (3rd ed.). New York: McGraw Hill.

Heyward, V.H. (1984). *Designs for fitness.* Minneapolis: Burgess.

Hinson, M.M. (1981). *Kinesiology.* Dubuque, IA: W.C. Brown.

Hockey, R.V. (1985). *Physical fitness: The pathway to healthful living* (5th ed.). St. Louis: Times Mirror/Mosby College Publishers.

Holmer, I. (1979). Physiology of swimming man. In R.S. Hutton & D.I. Miller (Eds.), *Exercise and Sport Sciences Reviews,* **7**.

Holmes, T.H., & Rahe, H. (1967). The social readjustment rating scale. *Journal of Psychosomatic Research,* **11**, 213-218.

Holmgren, A. (1967). Cardiorespiratory determinants of cardiovascular fitness. *Canadian Medical Association Journal,* **96**, 697-702.

Hooper, P.L., & Noland, B.J. (1984). Aerobic dance program improves cardiovascular fitness in men. *The Physician and Sportsmedicine,* **12**(5), 132-135.

Horan, J.J., Linberg, S.E., & Hackett, G. (1977). Nicotine poisoning and rapid smoking. *Journal of Consulting and Clinical Psychology,* **45**, 344-347.

Hossack, K.F., Bruce, R.A., & Clark, L.J. (1980). Influence of propranolol on exercise prescription of training heart rates. *Cardiology,* **65**, 47-58.

Howley, E.T. (1980). Effect of altitude on physical performance. In *Encyclopedia of physical education: Physical fitness, training, environment and nutrition related to performance,* (Vol. 2), 177-186. Salt Lake City: Brighton.

Howley, E.T., & Glover, M.E. (1974). The caloric costs of running and walking one mile for men and women. *Medicine and Science in Sports,* **6**, 235-237.

Howley, E.T., & Martin, D. (1978). Oxygen uptake and heart rate responses measured during rope skipping. *Tennessee Journal of Health, Physical Education and Recreation,* **16**, 7-8.

Hubert, H.B., Feinleib, M.N., McNamara, P.M., & Castelli, W.P. (1983). Obesity as an independent risk factor for cardiovascular disease: A 26-year follow-up of participants in the Framingham heart study. *Circulation,* **26**, 968-977.

Huelster, L.J. (1982). Social relevance perspective for sport and physical education. In E.F. Zeigler (Ed.), *Physical education and sport: An introduction* (pp. 1-22). Philadelphia: Lea & Febiger.

Hurst, J.W. (1978). *The heart*. New York: McGraw-Hill.

Hussina, R.A., & Lawrence, P.S. (1978). The reduction test, state, and trait anxiety by test-specific and generalized stress inoculation training. *Cognitive Therapy and Research,* **2**, 25-38.

Jackson, A.S., & Pollock, M.L. (1985). Practical assessment of body composition. *The Physician and Sportsmedicine,* **13**, 76-90.

Jacobsen, E. (1938). *Progressive relaxation*. Chicago: University of Chicago Press.

Jarvik, M.E., Cullen, T.W., Gritz, E.R., Vogt, T.M., & West, L.S. (Eds.). (1977). *Research on smoking behavior* (DHHS Publication No. ADM 78-581). Washington, DC: U.S. Government Printing Office.

Jellinek, E.M. (1960). *The disease concept of alcoholism*. New Brunswick, NJ: Hillhouse Press.

Jenkins, C.D. (1979). Psychosocial modifiers of response to stress. *Journal of Human Stress,* **5**, 3-15.

Jensen, C.R., Schultz, G.W., & Bangerter, B.L. (1983). *Applied kinesiology and biomechanics*. New York: McGraw-Hill.

Jette, M., & Cureton, T.K. (1976). Anthropometric and selected motor fitness measurements of men engaged in a long-term program of physical activity. *Research Quarterly,* **47**, 666-671.

Johnson, D.W. (1981). *Reaching out: Interpersonal effectiveness and self-actualization* (2nd ed.). Englewood Cliffs, NJ: Prentice-Hall.

Kammermann, S., Doyle, K., Valois, R.F., & Stafford, G.C. (1983). *Wellness RSVP*. Menlo Park, CA: Benjamin/Cummings.

Kannel, W.B. (1979). Nutrition and atherosclerosis. In D.T. Mason & H. Guthrie (Eds.), *The medicine called nutrition* (p. 37). Englewood Cliffs, NJ: Best Foods.

Kannel, W.B., & Abbot, R.D. (1984). Incidence and prognosis of unrecognized myocardial infarction. *New England Journal of Medicine,* **311**, 1144-1147.

Kasch, F.W. (1976). The effects of exercise on the aging process. *The Physician and Sportsmedicine* **4**(6), 64-68.

Kasch, F.W., Phillips, W.H., Ross, W.D., Carter, J.E.L., & Boyer, J.L. (1966). A comparison of maximal oxygen uptake by treadmill and step-test procedures. *Journal of Applied Physiology,* **21**(4), 1387-1388.

Katch, F.I., McArdle, W.D. (1977). *Nutrition, weight control, and exercise*. Boston: Houghton Mifflin.

Keefe, F.J., & Blumenthal, J.A. (1980). The life fitness program: A behavioral approach to making exercise a habit. *Journal of Behavioral Therapy and Experimental Psychiatry,* **11**, 31-34.

Kendall, P.C., & Hollon, S.D. (Eds.). (1979). *Cognitive-behavioral interventions: Theory, research, and procedures*. New York: Academic Press.

Kincey, J. (1983). Compliance with a behavioral weight-loss programme: Target setting and locus of control. *Behavior Research Therapy,* **21**(2), 109-114.

King, J.C., Cohenour, S.H., Corruccini, C.G., & Schneeman, P. (1978). Evaluation and modification of the basic four food guide. *Journal of Nutrition Education,* **10**(1), 27-29.

Kisselle, J., & Mazzeo, K. (1983). *Aerobic dance*. Englewood, CO: Morton.

Klafs, C.E., & Arnheim, D.D. (1977). *Modern principles of athletic training*. St. Louis: C.V. Mosby.

Knoebel, L.K. (1984). Energy metabolism. In E. Selkurt (Ed.). *Physiology* (5th ed.). Boston: Little, Brown.

Koivisto, V.A., & Sherwin, R.S. (1979). Exercise in diabetes. *Postgraduate Medicine,* **66**(5), 87-96.

Krasevec, J.A., & Grimes, D.C. (1984). *Hydrorobics*. New York: Leisure Press.

Kraus, H., & Raab, W. (1961). *Hypokinetic disease*. Springfield, IL: Thomas.

Kreighbaum, E., & Barthels, K.M. (1984). *Biomechanics*. Minneapolis: Burgess.

Krumboltz, J.D., & Thoresen, C.E. (Eds.). (1976). *Counseling methods*. New York: Holt, Rinehart & Winston.

Kuland, D.N. (1982). *The injured athlete*. Philadelphia: L.B. Lippincott.

Laporte, R.E., Adams, L.L., Savage, D.D., Brenes, G., Dearwater, S., & Cook., T. (1984). The spectrum of physical activity, cardiovascular disease, and health: An epidemiologic perspective. *American Journal of Epidemiology,* **120**, 507-517.

Laslett, L.J., Paumer, L., Scott-Baier, P., & Amsterdam, E. (1983). Efficacy of exercise training in patients with coronary artery disease who are taking propranolol. *Circulation,* **68**, 1029-1034.

Leblanc, C., Bouchard, C. Godbout, P., & Mondor, J. (1981). Specificity of submaximal working capacity. *Journal of Sports Medicine,* **21**, 15-19.

LeVeau, B.F. (1977). *Williams and Lissner: Biomechanics of human motion.* Philadelphia: W.B. Saunders.

Leveille, G.A., & Dean, A. (1979). Choosing foods for health. In D.T. Mason and H. Guthrie (Eds.), *The medicine called nutrition*. Englewood Cliffs, NJ: Best Foods.

Liemohn, W.P., & Kovatch, J. (1979). A torque wrench and measurement of strength. *Perceptual and Motor Skills,* **49**, 122.

Lind, A.R., & McNicol, G.W. (1967). Muscular factors which determine the cardiovascular responses to sustained and rhythmic exercise. *Canadian Medical Association Journal,* **96**, 706-713.

Logan, G.A., & McKinney, W.C. (1982). *Anatomic kinesiology*. Dubuque, IA: W.C. Brown.

Luttgens, K., & Wells, K.F. (1982). *Kinesiology scientific basis of human motion*. Philadelphia: Saunder College.

Maddox, G.L., & Douglass, E.B. (1974). Aging and individual differences: A longitudinal analysis of social, psychological, and physiological indicators. *Journal of Gerontology,* **29**(5), 555-563.

Marcotte, B., & Price, J.H. (1983). The status of health promotion programs at the worksite—a review. *Health Education,* **14**(4), 4-9.

Margaria, R., Cerretelli, P., Aghemo, P., & Sassi, J. (1963). Energy cost of running. *Journal of Applied Physiology,* **18**, 367-370.

Martin, J.E. (1982). Exercise and health: The adherence problem. *Behavioral Medicine Update,* **14**, 16-24.

Martin, J.E., & Dubbert, P.M. (1982). Exercise applications and promotion in behavioral medicine: Current status and future directions. *Journal of Consulting and Clinical Psychology,* **50**(6), 1004-1017.

Mason, J.W. (1975a). A historical view of the stress field. Part 1. *Journal of Human Stress,* **1**(1), 6-12.

Mason, J.W. (1975b). A historical view of the stress field. Part 2. *Journal of Human Stress,* **1**(2), 22-36.

Mazzeo, K.S. (1984). *Shape up*. Englewood, CO: Morton Publishers.

McArdle, W.D., Katch, F.I., & Katch, V.L. (1981). *Exercise physiology*. Philadelphia: Lea & Febiger.

McArdle, W.D., Katch, F.I., & Pechar, G.S. (1973). Comparison of continuous and discontinuous treadmill and bicycle tests for max $\dot{V}O_2$. *Medicine and Science in Sports,* **5**(3), 156-160.

McArdle, W.D., & Magel, J.R. (1970). Physical work capacity and maximum oxygen uptake in treadmill and bicycle exercise. *Medicine and Science in Sports,* **2**(3), 118-123.

McKenzie, R.A. (1981). *The lumbar spine—mechanical diagnosis and therapy*. Upper Hutt, New Zealand: Spinal Publishers Limited.

Melleby, A. (1982). *The Y's way to a healthy back*. Pisctaway, NJ: New Century.

Mihevic, P.M. (1981). Anxiety, depression, and exercise. *Quest*, **33**, 140-153.

Miller, P.M. (1976). *Behavioral treatment of alcoholism*. New York: Pergamon.

Miller, W.R. (Ed.). (1980). *The addictive behaviors: Treatment of alcoholism, drug abuse, smoking, and obesity*. New York: Pergamon.

Montgomery, D.L. (1983). Physical fitness over a 10-year period—A longitudinal comparison of exercisers and drop-outs. *Medicine and Science in Sports and Exercise*, **15**, 109.

Montoye, H.J. (1975). *Physical activity and health: An epidemiologic study of an entire community*. Englewood Cliffs, NJ: Prentice-Hall.

Morgan, W.P. (1985). Affective beneficence of vigorous physical activity. *Medicine and Science in Sports and Exercise*, **17**(1), 94-100.

Morris, J.N., Pollard, R., Everitt, M.G., & Chave, S.P.W. (1980, December 6). Vigorous exercise in leisure-time: Protection against coronary heart disease. *Lancet*, 1207-1210.

Mosston, M. (1966). *Teaching physical education: From command to discovery*. Columbus, OH: Charles E. Merrill.

Murphy, J.K., Williamson, D.A., Buxton, A.E., Moody, S.C., Abshker, N., & Warner, M. (1982). The long-term effects of spouse involvement upon weight loss and maintenance. *Behavior Therapy*, **13**, 681-693.

Murphy, L.R. (1984). Occupational stress management: A review and appraisal. *Journal of Occupational Psychology*, **57**, 1-15.

Nagle, F.J., Balke, B., Baptista, G., Alleyia, J., & Howley, E. (1971). Compatibility of progressive treadmill, bicycle and step tests based on oxygen uptake responses. *Medicine and Science in Sport*, **3**, 149-154.

Nagle, F.J., Balke, B., & Naughton, J.P. (1965). Gradational step tests for assessing work capacity. *Journal of Applied Physiology*, **20**, 745-748.

National Institute on Alcohol Abuse and Alcoholism. (1971). *Alcohol and health*. Report to the U.S. Congress. Washington, DC: U.S. Government Printing Office.

National Institute on Alcohol Abuse and Alcoholism. (1974). *Alcohol and health*. Report to the U.S. Congress. Washington, DC: U.S. Government Printing Office.

National Institute on Alcohol Abuse and Alcoholism. (1978). *Alcohol and Health*. Report to the U.S. Congress. Washington, DC: U.S. Government Printing Office.

Naughton, J.P., & Haider, R. (1973). Methods of exercise testing. In Naughton, J.P., Hellerstein, H.R., and Mohler, L.C. (Eds.), *Exercise testing and exercise training in coronary heart disease*. New York: Academic Press.

New Games Foundation. (1976). *The new games book*. Garden City, NY: Dolphin Books.

Nieman, D.C. (1985). *Health related physical fitness*. Loma Linda, CA: School of Health, Loma Linda University.

Noble, B.J., Borg, G.A.V., Cafarelli, E., Robertson, R.J., & Pandolf, K.B. (1982). Symposium on recent advances in the study and clinical use of perceived exertion. *Medicine and Science in Sports and Exercise*, **14**, 376-411.

Northrip, J.W., Logan, G.A., & McKinney, W.C. (1979). *Biomechanical analysis of sport*. Dubuque, IA: W.C. Brown.

O'Donoghue, D.H. (1984). *Treatment of injuries to athletes* (4th ed.). Philadelphia: W.B. Saunders.

Oldridge, N.B. (1979). Compliance of post myocardial infarction patients to exercise programs. *Medicine and Science in Sport*, **11**(4), 373-375.

Oldridge, N.B., & Steiner, D.L. (1985). Health locus of control and compliance with cardiac exercise rehabilitation. *Medicine and Science in Sports and Exercise*, **17**, 181.

Oldridge, N.B., et al. (1983). Predictors of dropout from cardiac exercise rehabilitation. *American Journal of Cardiology*, **51**, 70-74.

Paffenbarger, R.S., & Hyde, R.T. (1984). Exercise in the prevention of coronary heart disease. *Preventive Medicine,* **13**, 3-22.

Paffenbarger, R.S., Wing, A.L., Hyde, R.T., & Jung, D.L. (1983). Physical activity and incidence of hypertension in college alumni. *American Journal of Epidemiology,* **117**, 245-256.

Pate, R.R. (1983). A new definition of youth fitness. *Physician and Sportsmedicine,* **11**, 77-83.

Pate, R.R., & Blair, S.N. (1978). Exercise and the prevention of atherosclerosis: Pediatric implications. In W.B. Strong (Ed.), *Atherosclerosis: Its pediatric aspects* (pp. 251-286). Orlando: Grune & Stratton.

Pattison, E.M., Sobell, M.B., & Sobell, L.C. (1977). *Emerging concepts of alcohol dependence.* New York: Springer.

Peters, T.J., & Waterman, R.H., Jr. (1982). *In search of excellence.* New York: Warner.

Pigors, P., & Myers, C.A. (1977). *Personnel administration.* New York: McGraw-Hill.

Pollock, M.L., Schmidt, D.H., & Jackson, A.S. (1980). Measurement of cardiorespiratory fitness and body composition in the clinical setting. *Comprehensive Therapy,* **6**(9), 12-27.

Pollock, M.L., Wilmore, J.H. & Fox, S.M. (1984). *Exercise in health and disease.* Philadelphia: W.B. Saunders.

Polly, S., Turner, R.D., & Sherman, A.R. (1976). A behavioral approach to individualized exercise programming, pp. 106-116. In J.D. Krumboltz & C.E. Thoreser (Eds.), *Counseling methods.* New York: Holt, Rinehart, and Winston.

Ponte, D.J., Jensen, G.J., & Kent, B.E. (1984). A preliminary report on the use of the McKenzie protocol versus Williams protocol in the treatment of low back pain. *Journal of Orthopaedic and Sports Physical Therapy,* **6**(4), 130-139.

Pooley, J.C. (1984). Physical education and sport and the quality of life. *Journal of Physical Education, Recreation, and Dance,* **55**(3), 45-48.

Powell, K.E., & Paffenbarger, R.S. (1985). Workshop on epidemiologic and public health aspects of physical activity and exercise: A summary. *Public Health Reports,* **100**, 118-126.

Pratt, C.M., Welton, D.E., Squires, W.G., Kirby, T.E., Hartung, G.H., & Miller, R.R. (1981). Demonstration of training effect during chronic *B*-adrenergic blockade in patients with coronary artery disease. *Circulation,* **64**, 1125-1129.

Rasch, P.J., & Burke, R.K. (1978). *Kinesiology and applied anatomy: The science of human movement.* Philadelphia: Lea & Febiger.

Raven, P.B. (1980). Effects of air pollution on physical performance. *Encyclopedia of physical education: Physical fitness, training, environment and nutrition related to performance* (Vol. 2), 201-216. Salt Lake City: Brighton.

Raven, P.B. (1982). Questions and answers. *Journal of Cardiac Rehabilitation,* **2**, 411-414.

Reinertsen, J. (1983). Promoting health is good business. *Occupational Health and Safety,* **52**(6), 18-22.

Riddle, P.K. (1980). Attitudes, beliefs, behavioral intentions, and behaviors of women and men toward regular jogging. *Research Quarterly for Exercise and Sport,* **51**(4), 663-674.

Rimm, D.C., & Masters, J.C. (1974). *Behavior therapy: Techniques and empirical findings.* New York: Academic Press.

Robinson, S., Dill, D.B., Ross, J.C., Robinson, R.D., Wanger, J.A., & Tzankoff, S.P. (1973). Training and physiological aging in man. *Federation Proceedings,* **32**(5), 1628-1633.

Roper, N. (1978). *Pocket medical dictionary.* New York: Charles Scribner's Sons.

Rose, R.M., Mason, J., Reiser, M., Shapiro, A., Wolf, S., & Reichlin, S. (1979). Summary and overview. *Journal of Human Stress,* **5**, 46-48.

Roskies, E. (1980). Considerations in developing a treatment program for the coronary-prone (Type A) behavior pattern. In P.O. Davidson & S.M. Davidson (Eds.), *Behavioral medicine:*

Changing health lifestyles (pp. 299-333). New York: Brunner/Mazel.

Ross, J.G., McGinnis, J.M., Gilbert, G.G., Montes, H., Errecart, M.T., Ghosh, D.N., Katz, S.J., Dotson, C.O., & Pate, R.R. (1985). Report on the National Children and Youth Fitness Study (Special Issue). *Journal of Physical Education, Recreation, and Dance,* **56**(1), 44-90.

Roszak, T. (1978). *Person/Planet: The creative disintegration of industrial society*. New York: Anchor.

Rowell, L. (1969). Circulation. *Medicine and Science in Sport,* **1**, 15-22.

Sable, D.L., Brammel, H.L., Sheehan, M.W., Nies, A.S., Gerber, J., & Horwitz, L.D. (1982). Attenuation of exercise conditioning by beta-adrenergic blockade. *Circulation,* **65**, 679-684.

Sachs, M.L. (1982). Compliance and addiction to exercise. In R.C. Cantu (Ed.), *The exercising adult*. Boston: Collamore Press.

Sager, K. (1984). Exercises to activate seniors. *The Physician and Sportsmedicine,* **12**(5), 144-151.

Schwartz, G.E., Weinberger, D.A., & Singer, J.A. (1981). Cardiovascular differentiation of happiness, sadness, anger, and fear following imagery and exercise. *Psychosomatic Medicine,* **43**, 343-364.

Selye, H. (1956). *Stress of life*. New York: McGraw-Hill.

Selye, H. (1974). *Stress without distress*. Toronto: McCelland & Stewart.

Selye, H. (1975). Confusion and controversy in the stress field. *Journal of Human Stress,* **1**(2), 37-44.

Selye, H. (1976). Stress and physical activity. *McGill Journal of Education,* **11**, 3-14.

Serfass, R.C., & Gerberich, S.G. (1984). Exercise for optimal health: Strategies and motivational considerations. *Preventive Medicine,* **13**, 79-99.

Sharkey, B.J. (1984). *Physiology of fitness* (2nd ed.). Champaign, IL: Human Kinetics.

Shephard, R.J. (1985). Motivation: The key to fitness compliance. *Physician and Sportsmedicine,* **13**, 88-101.

Shephard, R.J., Corey, P., & Cox, M. (1982). Health hazard appraisal—the influence of an employee fitness program. *Canadian Journal of Public Health,* **73**, 183-187.

Shephard, R.J., Corey, P., Renzland, P., & Cox, M. (1982). The influence of an employee fitness and lifestyle modification program upon medical care costs. *Canadian Journal of Public Health,* **73**, 259-263.

Shephard, R.J., Cox, M., Corey, P. (1981). Fitness program participation: Its effect on worker performance. *Journal of Occupational Medicine,* **24**(12), 965-968.

Sheppard, C.S., & Carroll, D.C. (1980). *Working in the twenty-first century*. New York: John Wiley & Sons.

Siri, W.E. (1956). Gross composition of the body. In J.H. Lawrence & C.A. Tobias (Eds.), *Advances in biological and medical physics* (Vol. 4). New York: Academic Press.

Siscovick, D.S., Laporte, R.E., & Newman, J.M. (1985). The disease-specific benefits and risks of physical activity and exercise. *Public Health Reports,* **100**, 180-188.

Sloan, A.W., & Wier, J.B. (1970). Nomograms for prediction of body density and total body fat from skinfold measurements. *Journal of Applied Physiology,* **28**, 221-222.

Smith, E.L. (1982). Exercise for prevention of osteoporosis: A review. *The physician and sportsmedicine,* **10**(3), 72-83.

Sobell, M.B., & Sobell, L.C. (1978). *Behavioral treatment of alcoholic problems: Individualized therapy and controlled drinking*. New York: Plenum.

Sonstroem, R.J. (1978). Physical estimation and attraction scales: Rationale and research. *Medicine and Science in Sport,* **10**(2), 97-102.

Spielberger, C.D., Gorsuch, R.L., & Lushene, R.E. (1970). *The State-Trait Anxiety Inventory*. Palo Alto, CA: Consulting Psychologists Press.

Spielberger, C., & Sarason, I. (Eds.). (1975). *Stress and anxiety* (Vol. 2). New York: Wiley.

Stalonas, P.M., Johnson, W.G., & Christ, M. (1978). Behavior modification for obesity: The evaluation of exercise, contingency management, and program adherence. *Journal of Consulting and Clinical Psychology,* **46**, 463-469.

Stein, J., & Su, P.Y. (Eds.). (1980). *The Random House Dictionary*. New York: Ballantine Books.

Strait, L.A., Inman, B.T., & Ralston, H.J. (1947). Sample illustrations of physical principles selected from physiology and medicine. *American Journal of Physics,* **15**, 375-382.

Stuart, R.B., & Davies, B. (1971). *Slim chance in a fat world: Behavioral control of obesity*. Champaign, IL: Research Press.

Surburg, P.R. (1983). Flexibility exercises reexamined. *Athletic Training,* **18**, 37-39.

Thaxton, L. (1982). Physiological and psychological effects of short-term exercise addiction on habitual runners. *Journal of Sport Psychology,* **4**, 73-80.

Thomas, G.S., Lee, P.R., Franks, P., & Paffenbarger, R.S. (1981). *Exercise and health: The evidence and the implications*. Cambridge, MA: Oelgeschlager, Gunn & Hain.

Thompson, C.E., & Wankel, L.M. (1980). The effects of perceived activity choice upon frequency of exercise behavior. *Journal of Applied Social Psychology,* **10**, 436-443.

Thompson, C.W. (1981). *Manual of structural kinesiology*. St. Louis: C.V. Mosby.

Thompson, P.D., Stern, M.P., Williams, P., Duncan, K., Haskell, W.L., & Wood, P.D. (1979). Death during jogging or running. *Journal of American Medical Association,* **242**, 1265.

U.S. Dept. Health & Human Services. (1980). *Promoting health/preventing disease: Objectives for the nation*. Washington, DC: U.S. Government Printing Office.

U.S. Dept. Health & Human Services. (1981). *Exercise and your Heart* (NIH Publication 81-1677). Washington, DC: U.S. Government Printing Office.

U.S. Dept. Health & Human Services, Public Health Service, Office on Smoking and Health. (1983). *The health consequences of smoking: Cardiovascular disease, a report of the Surgeon General* (DHEW Publication No. PHS 79-50066). Washington, DC: U.S. Government Printing Office.

U.S. Senate Select Committee on Nutrition and Human Needs. (1977). *Dietary goals for the U.S.* (2nd ed.) (XXI-XXVII, pp. 1-56). Washington, DC: U.S. Government Printing Office.

Vuori, I., Makarainen, M., Jaaselainen, A. (1978). Sudden death and physical activity. *Cardiology,* **63**, 287.

Waller, B.F., & Robert, W.C. (1980). Sudden death while running in conditioned runners aged 40 years and older. *American Journal of Cardiology,* **45**, 1292.

Watson, D.L., & Tharp, R.G. (1977). *Self-directed behavior: Self-modification for personal adjustment* (2nd ed.). Monterey, CA: Brooks/Cole.

Webster's new international dictionary (2nd ed., unabridged). (1934). New York: G & C Merriam.

WHO Expert Committee. (1982). *Prevention of coronary heart disease*. Geneva: World Health Organization.

Willerson, J.T., & Dehmer, G.J. (1981). Exercise stress laboratories in the future—what should their capabilities be? (Editorial). *Chest,* **80**(1), 1-2.

Williams, J.G.P. (1980). *A color atlas of injury in sport*. Holland: Wolfe, Medical.

Williams, M. (Ed.). (1983a). *Ergogenic aids in sport*. Champaign, IL: Human Kinetics.

Williams, M. (1983b). *Nutrition for fitness and sport*. Dubuque, IA: W.C. Brown.

Williams, P.C. (1974). *Low back and neck pain*. Springfield, IL: C.C. Thomas.

Williams, R.L., & Long, J.D. (1983). *Toward a self-managed life style*. Boston: Houghton Mifflin.

Wilmore, J.H. (1982a). Objectives for the nation—physical fitness and exercise. *Journal of Physical Education, Recreation, and Dance,* **53**(3), 41-43.

Wilmore, J.H. (1982b). *Training for sport and activity: The physiological basis of the conditioning process*. Boston: Allyn & Bacon.

Wilmore, J.H. (1982a). Objectives for the nation—physical fitness and exercise. *Journal of Physical Education, Recreation, and Dance,* **53**(3), 41-43.

Wing, R.R., & Jeffrey, R.J. (1979). Outpatient treatments of obesity: A comparison of methodology and results. *International Journal of Obesity,* **3**, 261-279.

Wright, C.C. (1982). Cost containment through health promotion programs. *Journal of Occupational Medicine,* **24**(12), 965-968.

Wysocki, T., Hall, G., Iwata, B., & Riordan, M. (1979). Behavioral management of exercise contracting for aerobic points. *Journal of Applied Behavior Analysis,* **12**(1), 55-64.

Index

A

Abdominal muscular endurance, 105, 109
Abrasion, 216
Accident, 212-231, 242, 245
Acclimatization, 148
Acromion, 39
Active, 91, 93
Activity revision, 147
Acute stressor, 119
Adaptation, 121
Additive, 120
Adenosine diphosphate, ADP, 24
Adenosine triphosphate, ATP, 24
Adherence, 201
Administration, 234-248
Administrative behavior, 247
ADP, *see* Adenosine diphosphate
Aerobic activities, 133, 170-184
Aerobic metabolism, 24-25
Aerobic power, 29, 85, 88
Aggression, 117
Aging, 6, 121, 146
Agonist, 42
Alcoholic beverage, 15, 203-204
Alcoholism, 12, 203-204
Altitude, 29, 150
American Alliance of Health, Physical Education, Recreation, and Dance, ix
American College of Sports Medicine, ix, 5, 171, 251-256
Amino acid, 63
Amphiarthrodial joint, 39
Anaerobic metabolism, 24, 27
Anaerobic threshold, 30
Anatomy, 38
Anatomy of the heart, 186
Anger, 116
Angina,
  angina pectoris, 195
Angular momentum, 47
Antagonist, 42
Anti-arrhythmic, 197
Anti-hypertensive, 197
Anxiety, 117
Aorta, 186
Apparently healthy, 128
Aquatics, 46, 163-164, 179-181
Archimedes principle, 53
Arm ergometer, 161, 162
Arousal, 116
Arrhythmia, 191
Arteriovenous oxygen difference,
  a-$\bar{v}O_2$ difference, 32
Artery, 186
Articular cartilage, 39
Assertiveness, 117, 123
Asthma, 146
Atherosclerosis, 76
ATP, *see* Adenosine triphosphate
Atrioventricular node, 187
Atrium, 186
Attitude, 14
Autonomic nervous system, 197
AV block, 190-191

B

Background information, 82
Ballistic movement, 42
Basal metabolic rate, 60
Behavior, 122

Bench, 86, 91, 162
Beta-adrenergic, 195
Beta-blocking drugs, 195
Bigeminy, 193
Biomechanical, 46
Blood pressure, 18, 33, 86
Blood vessels, coronary, 186, 187
Body composition, 52
Body density, 53
Bomb calorimeter, 154
Bone, 38-39
Breathing, 33
Breathless, 14, 18, 89
Budget, 241-244
Bundle branch block, 137, 191
Bundle of His, 188
Bursae, 39
Bursitis, 223

C

Calcium antagonist, 197
Calibration, 86, 156
Caloric cost, 154-167
Caloric deficit, 60
Calorie, 59, 154
Calorimetry, 154
Capillary, 25, 187
Capsular ligament, 39
Capsulitis, 223
Carbohydrate, 62, 154
Carbon dioxide, 64, 154
Cardiac output, 31
Cardiac rehabilitation, 143
Cardiopulmonary resuscitation, 229-231
Cardiorespiratory function, 25, 82, 128
Cardiovascular, 25, 82
Carotid artery, 230
Case studies, 136-144
Catharsis, 117
Center of gravity, 46
Certification, 5, 171
Chemical bond, 24
Chest pain, 13, 18
Cholesterol, 18, 76-78
Chronic obstructive pulmonary disease, 7
Chronic stressors, 119
Cigarette smoking, 14, 202-203
Circumference, 58
Claudication, 89
Clothing, 148, 172
Communication, 244
Competitive, 178
Competitive running, 177
Computer assisted dietary analysis, 71-72
Concentric contraction, 41, 101
Conditioning, 28-35
Confidentially, 239
Contraction, 41
Contraindications, 18, 83, 111, 228
Control, 120, 171
Contusions, 214
Cool down, 129, 182
Cooperative, 178
COPD, *see* Chronic obstructive pulmonary disease
Core temperature, 148
Coping with stress, 122-123
Coronary arteries, 186
Coronary-prone personality, 7, 15
Coronary sinus, 186
Creatine phosphate, 24
Cross-adaptation, 121
Cyanotic, 217
Cycle ergometer, 29, 86, 90-97, 161
Cycling, 45, 161, 177

D

Dehydrated, 148
Denial, 117
Depolarization, 187-189
Depression, 117
Detrained, 128
Development . . . Deterioration, 119
Diabetes, 135, 219-222
Diabetic coma, 221
Diaphysis, 38
Diarthrodial joint, 39
Diastolic blood pressure, 18, 33, 86-87
Diet, 7, 61, 66-76
Dietary exchange list, 69
Digitalis, 197
Disease, 4
Distraction, 120
Dizziness, 18, 89, 217

Double product, 33
Drugs, 195-197, 200, 203-204
Dyspnea, 89

E

Eccentric contraction, 41, 101
ECG, *see* electrocardiogram
Ectopic ventricular complexes, 193
Elderly, 6, 121, 146
Electrocardiogram, 188-195
Electrode, 189
Electrophysiology, 187
Emergency information, 11
Emergency procedure, 229-231, 242
Emotion, 116
Empathy, 118
Endurance run, 84-85
Energy, 24, 154-167
Enjoyable . . . Unpleasant, 119
Environmental factors, 148, 166
Epicondylitis, 223
Epidemiological studies, 6
Epimysium, 40
Epiphysis, 38
Equipment, 241, 244
Escape, 120
Essential fat, 57
Euphoria, 117
Evaluation, 237, 246
Evaporation, 148
Exercise, 61, 102-110, 170-184
Exercise modification, 147, 228
Exercise recommendations, 128-151
Exercise Specialist, 171
Exercise Technologist, 171
Exercise to music, 163, 181-184
Extension, 109
Extensor, 43-45
Extrinsic, 118

F

Facilities, 236, 238, 241
Family history, 6
Fasciculi, 40
Fast twitch fiber, 25, 41
Fat, 52, 57, 63, 154
Fat-free weight, 52
Fatigue, 89
Fatty acid, 63
Fear, 117
Field tests, 84
Financial management, 244
First degree AV block, 190
Fitness, 4, 248
Fitness activities, 18, 102-110, 170-184
Fitness center, 234-248
Fitness continuum, 4
Fitness Instructor, 5, 170-172, 251-255
Fitness program, 17, 128-151, 170-184
Fitness testing, 16, 52-59, 82-96, 105, 108
Fitness workout, 102-110, 170-184
Fixator muscle, 42
Flexibility, 40, 105-108
Food groups, 69
Forced expiratory volume, 16, 18
Fracture, 215
Free fatty acids, 63
Frequency, 129
Fun run, 175-177
Functional capacity, 88
Functional . . . Severe stress, 119

G

Games, 178-179
Gas analyzer, 26
Gender, 6, 34
Genetic potential, 4
Glucose, 18
Glycogen, 24, 63
Glycolysis, 24
Goal, 247
Goal Orientation, 118
Governing body, 247
Graded Exercise Test (GXT), 85, 130, 134
GXT, *see* Graded exercise test

H

Hamstring, 41
HDL-C, *see* High-density lipoprotein cholesterol
Health, 4, 10, 121
Health/Fitness Instructor, 5, 170-172, 251-255
Health history, 12
Health related behavior, 15, 122

Health status, 11-15
Heart, 186
Heart disease, 6, 18, 77
Heart rate, 18, 28, 30, 32, 86, 131, 150
Heart rate reserve, 130
Heart rhythm, 191
Heat illness, 148, 217-220
Heel bruise, 214
Hemorrhage, 216
Heredity, 6
High blood pressure, *see* Hypertension
High-density lipoprotein cholesterol, 7, 18, 76-78
Hostility, 117
Humidity, 148, 218
Hydrostatic weighing, 53-54
Hypercholesterolemia, 76-78
Hyperlipoproteinemia, 77
Hypertension, 7, 145
Hypertrophy, 100
Hypervitaminosis, 64
Hypothermia, 149

I

Iliac crest, 55
Illness, 4
Inactive, 7, 91-92
Incision, 215
Inclusive, 178
Increment, 90
Inderal, 195
Infarction, 195
Inferior vena cava, 186
Informed consent, 83, 239-240
Injury, 212-231, 242, 245
Insulin shock, 221
Intensity, 129-133
Interval training, 170
Intrinsic, 118
Ischemia, 194
Isocaloric balance, 59
Isoelectric, 189
Isokinetic contraction, 102
Isometric contraction, 42, 101
Isotonic contraction, 101
Issues, 246

J

J point, 190
Job description, 235
Jogging, 43, 157-160, 175-176
Joint, 39

K

Ketosis, 74
Kilocalorie, 59, 154
Kilopond meters per minute, 161
Kinetics, 27

L

Laceration, 215
Lactate, 24, 30
Lactate threshold, 30
Lactic acid, 24, 30
Leadership, 170-172
Lean body weight, 52
Leg pain, 14
Liable, 239
Life events, 122
Lifestyle, 7, 14, 116, 170
Ligament, 39
Lipid, 76-78
Lipoprotein, 76-78
Loneliness, 121
Long range plans, 234
Lordosis, 109
Low back function, 7, 108-113
Low back pain, 108-113, 225-226
Low blood sugar, *see* hypoglycemia
Low calorie diet, 72
Low-density lipoprotein cholesterol, 7, 76-78
Low organized games, 179
Lumbar, 109-113

M

Maintenance load, 129
Maximal aerobic power, 28-30
Maximal heart rate, 131
Maximal oxygen uptake, 26, 28, 85, 131, 150
Maximal tests, 26, 89
Maximum voluntary ventilation, 16
Max $\dot{V}O_2$, *see* Maximal oxygen uptake
Measurement, 52-59, 82-97, 105, 108, 129
Medical clearance, 17
Medical history, 12
Medical referral, 17, 18, 83
Medical supervision, 11, 17, 83
Medication, 195-197
Metabolic load, 130

Metabolism, 24-33, 60, 154-160
METs, 155
M.I., *see* Myocardial infarction
Mineral, 65
Mitochondria, 25, 101, 187
Mobitiz type I AV block, 190
Mobitiz type II AV block, 190
Moment arm, 47
Monosaccharide, 62
Motivation, 118
Motor unit, 41
Muscle, 25, 40-45
Muscle fiber type, 25, 41
Myocardial infarction, 195
Myocardial oxygen demand, 187
Myocardium, 186
Myositis, 223

N

Nausea, 89
Negative energy balance, 59
Negative health, 121
Negligence, 239
Neutralizer, 42
Nitrates, 196
Nonfunctional stressor, 119-120
Nutrient, 69
Nutrition, 7, 66

O

Obesity, 7, 145
One repetition maximum, 105
Open circuit, 26, 154-155
Orthopedic disabled, 135, 222-227
Ossification, 38
Overfat, 57-58
Overload, 100, 128
Overweight, 52-53
Oxygen consumption, *see* Oxygen uptake
Oxygen cost, 154-167
Oxygen debt, 27
Oxygen deficit, 27
Oxygen requirement, 27, 154-167
Oxygen uptake, 26, 28, 32, 155

P

P wave, 189
P-R interval, 190
Pallor, 89
Palpation, 86
Papillary muscles, 186
Parasympathetic nervous system, 116
Partial pressure of oxygen, 150
Peak heart rate, 131
Perceived exertion, 87-88
Percent fat, 52-59
Perception, 122
Performance, 4, 134, 248
Perimyseum, 40
Periosteum, 38
Personality, 7, 116-119
Personnel, 234-236
Phases of activities, 170
Phlebitis, 12, 18
Physical activity, 18, 61, 102-110, 170-184, 201-202
Physical conditioning, 102-110, 170-184
Physical fitness, 5, 49-50
Physical fitness tests, 16, 52-59, 82-97, 105, 108, 129
Physical inactivity, 7, 201-202
Physical stimulus, 120
Planning, 171
Plantar fasciitis, 223
Play, 118
Playfulness, 118
Plyometric, 103
Polarization, 187-189
Pollution, 150
Polysaccharide, 62
Polyunsaturated fats, 63
Positive energy balance, 59
Positive health, 4, 10, 121
Postabsorptive, 60
Posture, 5, 108
Predicted maximal oxygen uptake, 88-97
Predicted maximal heart rate, 131
Premature atrial contraction, 192
Premature junctional contraction, 192-193
Premature ventricular contraction, 193
Prescribing exercise, 101-112, 128-151
Primary risk factor, 7, 11
Prime mover, 42
Program, 17-18, 170-184, 236
Program Director, 234-248
Progression, 129
Protein, 63, 154
Psychological stressor, 120

Pulmonary function, 16
Pulmonary valve, 186
Pulmonary veins, 186
Pulmonary ventilation, 33
Puncture, 216
Purkinje fibers, 188

Q

Q wave, 189
QRS complex, 189
Q-T interval, 190
Quadriceps, 40
Quality, 246
Quality of life, 4

R

R wave, 189
R-R interval, 190
Race, 6
Racquet sports, 178
Range of motion, 40
Rate pressure product, 33
Rating of perceived exertion, 87-88
Rationalization, 117
Recommended Dietary Allowance, 67
Referral, 17, 18
Rejection, 117
Relaxation, 123
Repetitions, 103
Repolarization, 187-189
Reproducibility, 86
Residual volume, 54
Resistance, 100
Respiratory exchange ratio, 64, 154
Respiratory frequency, 33
Responsibility, 234, 247
Retest, 129
Rhythm, 191
Risk, 6-7, 16-19, 76-78, 83, 108-113, 121, 148-151, 212, 239
Risk factor, 6-7, 76-78, 121
Role model, 171
Rope skipping, 163
Rotational inertia, 46
Rules, 178
Runner's high, 117
Running, 43, 157-160, 175-177
Running shoes, 172

S

S wave, 189
ST segment, 190
ST-segment displacement, 190
Safety, 239-242
Salt, 65-66, 219
Saturated fat, 63
Screening, 16, 83
Second degree AV block, 190
Secondary risk factors, 7, 11, 121
Sedentary, 7
Sequence of activities, 170
Sequence of testing, 82-83
Set, 103
Shin splints, 222, 226-227
Shock, 217
Shoes, 172
Sinus arrhythmia, 191
Sinus node, 188
Sinus rhythm, 191
Sit-up, 105
Skinfold, 54
Slow twitch fiber, 25, 41
Smoking, 7, 14
Spasm, 225
Special populations, 11, 135, 145-146
Specificity, 100, 128
Spot reducing, 74
Sprain, 213-214
Stability, 46
Stage, 90-93
Starting exercise, 129
State, 118
Steady state, 25, 156
Stethoscope, 86
Stimulus, 120
Stone bruise, 214
Strain, 213-214
Strength, 100-105
Stress, 7, 119-123, 205-206
Stress continuum, 119-121
Stress fracture, 224
Stress management, 122, 205-206
Stressor, 119
Stretching, 106-112
Stroke, 18
Stroke volume, 31-32
Submaximal, 25, 89

Substrate, 154
Superior vena cava, 186
Supervised fitness program, 17, 146
Supplies, 241, 244
Surface, 172
Sweat, 148
Swimming, 46, 163-164, 179-181
Sympathetic nervous system, 116
Symptoms, 13, 89
Synovial membrane, 40
Synovitis, 223
Systolic blood pressure, 18, 33

T

T wave, 189
Ta wave, 189
Tachycardia, 192
Taper down, 129
Target heart rate, 131-133
Tendon, 39, 40
Tendonitis, 223
Tennis elbow, 223
Tenosynovitis, 223
Testing, 16, 52-59, 82-97, 105, 108, 129
Third degree AV block, 191
Third party payments, 241
THR, *see* Target heart rate
Threshold, 131
Tidal volume, 33
Time lines, 189
Time to exhaustion, 83
Timed vital capacity, 16
Torque, 47
Total lung capacity, 54
Total work, 129
Training, 28-35, 101
Trait, 118
Treadmill, 86, 90-94
Tricuspid valve, 186
Triglyceride, 7, 18, 76
12 lead ECG, 83, 189
12 minute run, 84-85
2 mile run, 84-85
Type A behavior, 15, 116
Type of activities, 133, 164-165, 170-184

U

U wave, 189
Underwater weighing, 53
Unsaturated fatty acid, 63
Unsupervised program, 147

V

Valsalva maneuver, 101
Variety, 171
Vein, 186
Velocity, 156
Ventilation, 28, 33
Ventilatory threshold, 33
Ventricle, 186
Ventricular arrhythmias, 193-194
Vital capacity, 16, 18
Vital signs, 229
Vitamin, 64
Voluntary participation, 239
$\dot{V}O_2$max, *see* Maximal oxygen uptake

W

Walking, 43, 156-160, 170-174
Warmup, 129
Weight, 52, 58-59
Wenchebach AV block, *see* Mobitiz Type I AV block
Windchill, 149
Work, 101, 129
Workout, 128
Workrate, 160-161
Work/relief, 175